THE **DYNAMICS** *of Social Welfare Policy*

THE **DYNAMICS** *of*

JOEL BLAU

with Mimi Abramovitz

Social Welfare Policy

  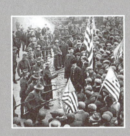  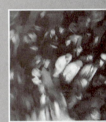

OXFORD
UNIVERSITY PRESS

2004

OXFORD
UNIVERSITY PRESS

Oxford   New York
Auckland   Bangkok   Buenos Aires   Cape Town   Chennai
Dar es Salaam   Delhi   Hong Kong   Istanbul   Karachi   Kolkata
Kuala Lumpur   Madrid   Melbourne   Mexico City   Mumbai
Nairobi   São Paulo   Shanghai   Taipei   Tokyo   Toronto

Copyright © 2004 by Joel Blau

Published by Oxford University Press, Inc.
198 Madison Avenue, New York, New York 10016

www.oup.com

Oxford is a registered trademark of Oxford University Press

Library of Congress Cataloging-in-Publication Data
Blau, Joel.
The dynamics of social welfare policy / Joel Blau; with Mimi
Abramovitz.
    p. cm.
Includes bibliographical references and index.
ISBN 0-19-510968-6
1. Public welfare—United States. , 2. United States—Social policy.
3. Social service—United States.   I. Abramovitz, Mimi.   II. Title.
HV95 .B595 2003
361.6'1'0973—dc21   2002156303

9 8 7 6 5 4 3 2 1

Printed in the United States of America
on acid-free paper

Preface

This social welfare policy text is written for students of social work and related human services. It has four underlying premises.

The first premise is that social welfare policy pervades every aspect of social welfare. This point is obviously valid for work that is plainly policy-related—lobbying, organizing, and administration—but it is also true when we counsel people. In effect, social policy pays us to have conversations with clients. Once we recognize this fact, we will have more helpful conversations and talk less angrily to ourselves.

The second premise is that knowledge about social welfare policy demands familiarity with the factors that shape it. We have woven these factors into a model of policy analysis, which is simply a tool for analyzing social welfare policy. The prospect may seem intimidating now, but when you learn how to use this tool, you will be able to analyze any social welfare policy.

The third premise is that knowledge about social welfare policy demands familiarity with some of its most prominent substantive areas. Because these subjects—income security, employment, housing, health, and food—permeate the entire field of social welfare policy, we have devoted a chapter to each of them.

The fourth and final premise of this book assumes the permanence of change in social welfare policy. What are the triggers of change in social welfare policy? What makes it evolve? And what might we do to make it evolve in a way that treats our clients better and makes our own jobs easier? We explore the answers to these questions throughout this book.

This textbook is comprehensive. Social welfare policy is a big subject, and there is much to digest. Your knowledge and confidence, however, will grow as you read. By the end, your knowledge of social welfare policy will become another essential instrument in your repertoire of helping skills. Ultimately, regardless of what particular kind of social work you do, this knowledge will empower you to function as a more effective social worker.

Acknowledgments

I want to begin by recognizing the substantial contribution of Mimi Abramovitz, who wrote three key chapters, helped to conceptualize the text's basic framework, and shared jointly in the development of an innovative policy model. Because I appreciate her time and effort, I included her name on the chapters she wrote. I am pleased that her skillful analysis of complex policy issues could be part of this book.

In the process of writing this text, I regularly sought two kinds of feedback: one from students and another from colleagues in the field. These test runs were enormously helpful. Feedback from students ensured that the text was accessible; comments from colleagues kept me on the right substantive track. Among the students at the School of Social Welfare, State University of New York at Stony Brook, I want to thank Shiela Esten, Cheryl Gabrielli, Janine Eng, Michelle Zoldak, Linda Himberger, Gail Smith, and Katie Holmes. I also want to highlight the special contribution of two other students: Allegra Baider, currently an M.S.W. student at the University of Michigan, who read several chapters and rightly demanded clarification when clarification was truly needed, and Jaimie Page, a doctoral candidate at SUNY, Stony Brook, whose comments on several chapters pointed the way to some significant revisions.

I am also indebted to a number of colleagues who gave freely of their time in their area of expertise. Among the Stony Brook faculty, I want to thank Candyce Berger for her help with chapter 11; Ruth Brandwein for her careful reading of chapter 7; Michael Lewis for his assistance with chapter 3; and Carolyn Peabody for her comments on chapter 1. In addition, Jan Poppendieck of the Hunter College Department of Sociology, whose own work on food policy has been so vital, kept me from making a number of errors of fact and emphasis in chapter 12.

Diane Johnson, a doctoral student at the School of Social Welfare, contributed significantly to the preparation of the instructor's manual. I am enormously grateful to her for all her hard work. Likewise, Amy Aronson handled the book's illustrations with her usual skill and dispatch, and my sister, Deborah Blau, provided invaluable assistance in the creation of some key graphs. A special note of thanks goes to Christopher Dykema, who not only left his imprint on how this material should be explained to social work students but also once again, made a significant editorial contribution. At Oxford University Press, Maura Roessner was very helpful in shepherding the text through editing and production. And, last, for her unmatched savvy in publishing matters, I want to express my deep appreciation to Sydelle Kramer.

Beth Baron brought her intelligence and editorial skills to the reading of the manuscript. And, as always, my wife, Sandra Baron, has been essential for her editing, her support, and her steadfastness.

Contents

I

Introducing Social Welfare Policy

1

Introduction: Social Problems,
Social Policy, Social Change

Social work students come from varied backgrounds. Some have arrived directly from school; others have worked in the human services for a while and want to refine their skills; still another group of older returning students wish to learn but are uneasy because they have not written a term paper in twenty years. Although a few of you are interested in and committed to advocacy, organizing, and political change, probably a larger number mostly think about using counseling to help people. Whatever your background, you all expect to succeed because you know your intentions are good, and you will work hard.

Then you start running into obstacles. You want to do something for a client, but your supervisor says the program will not pay for it. Or, as hard as you look, there is no apartment in the community for $400 a month. Soon you discover that day care is scarce and real job training even scarcer. And, even though you believe that your client's daughter needs more, not less, time with her mother, you have to do what the law says, and the law says the mother must find paid work. Gradually, it dawns on you: though you may be full of good intentions, good intentions alone are not enough.

That is when the frustration sets in and you start asking questions: Why won't the system let me do what I know is best for my client? Why won't it let me just do my job? Is there something lacking in my social work skills, or even with me as a social worker?

This book provides a long answer to these questions, but we can sketch a short answer in this first chapter. In brief, the answer is that although the frustration overtaking most social work students affects each of you as an individual, it has a structural cause. And this structural cause has its roots in a simple fact: every form of social work practice embodies a social policy.

Any example of social work practice will illustrate this point. Suppose you are counseling a battered woman about leaving her husband. The woman is understandably upset, and the session is intense. Because you are so emotionally involved, it is easy to imagine your relationship with her as independent and separate from the outside world. Then you think about it, and you realize it is not. You are sitting there in that room talking to that woman about leaving her husband because the women's movement organized for many years to change our view of domestic violence from a private trouble to a social problem. Eventually, the definition of domestic violence as a social problem shaped the development of a social policy that in all likelihood is paying you to sit with that client in that room. You might want to focus on only the clinical issues, but without that social policy, the relationship between you and the battered woman would probably not exist.

Social policies, then, pervade every aspect of social work practice. However much we as individuals try to help a client, our capacity to do so ultimately depends on the design of the program, benefit, or service. Students in the human services often find social policy a forbidding subject. But the truth is that the more conscious we are of its influence, the less power it has to impede our effectiveness at work.

Social policy, however, has many dimensions, and each is important and connected to all the others. For example, if we say that the purpose of social policy is to help people improve the quality of their lives, the truth of this statement cannot be separated from another proposition that social policy also contains, controls, and suppresses people. Both statements are true, but either one by itself would provide a very partial picture of how social policy functions. In the United States, at least, the evidence for this proposition is most clearly visible in public assistance policy. Public assistance gives people money; it helps them survive. At the same time, public assistance programs require work, effective parenting, and, often, acceptance of the ban against having more children. Whether these ideas are right or wrong, the point is that welfare policy makes receiving public assistance conditional on good behavior.

Why is this so? Why don't we just give money to people who are in desperate straits? Why do so many social programs come with strings attached, strings that tie people up in knots and bar them from the very help they need? The answer is that all social welfare policies have more than one objective, and all these objectives—political, social, and economic—are so intertwined that they compete and conflict with one another. We emphasize these conflicts throughout the book. By the end, you will see how these divergent objectives shape a social work practice designed at once to pursue

One example of social welfare policy's conflicting goals is reflected in the mixed messages that women receive.

the profession's highest goals and simultaneously to prevent their ultimate realization.

To understand this dynamic, we need to answer four key questions about the nature of the social issues with which we are engaged: (1) How do social problems get constructed? (2) Who gets to construct them? (3) How does the construction of a social problem help to create a social policy that shapes what social workers do? and (4) How do social policies change over time? Let's answer these questions one at a time.

How Are Social Problems Constructed?

What makes something a social, instead of a private, problem? This sounds like an easy question, but if you think about it, the answer is complicated.

To begin with, it helps to understand that social problems do not just exist but are *constructed*. This statement may surprise you. After all, from teenage pregnancy to homelessness, from drugs to AIDS, the social problems we face seem real enough. So what does it mean to say that they are constructed?

Three elements enter into constructing a social problem: (1) choosing it; (2) framing or defining it; and (3) offering an explanatory theory. Choosing a social problem means picking it out from all the other "problems" that you could choose and don't. To test this idea, consider your own situation while you read this. Maybe you are sitting at home, and it is getting hard to pay the rent. Maybe cars clog the road outside your window, and there is no cheap, reliable way to get around. Or you are trying to read this text while you worry about your children, who are playing in the next room but really need an afterschool program to care for them when you study. Now, it is true that as a profession, social workers are probably more likely than most other people to see "social problems" in daily life. But that statement does not explain why what you see and think and feel to be a social problem sometimes qualifies as one and sometimes does not.

Certainly, we can make some headway with the understanding that every social problem starts with the existence of some need. People may be aware of this need, or they may not. If they are not aware of this need, there is little likelihood it will be defined as a social problem. But even if people are aware, they may attribute the need to individual problems or choices. Nevertheless, U.S. social welfare policy is rarely so generous as to spend money on social problems where no real need exists. But why some needs and not others? What is it that draws people's attention so that just this one, of all the possible needs out there, gets recognized as genuine, truly worthy of public concern and a public policy?

Public recognition of a social need comes either from above or below. By "above," we mean that "elite" opinion—businesspeople, politicians, and the media—begins to focus on a previously hidden problem and identify it as a social need. The "Social Security crisis" belongs in this category. Most people did not know about Social Security finances; it entered public awareness only after elite opinion claimed that a problem existed.

By contrast, a social need arising from below has a very different origin. These social needs come from the direct, personal experience of ordinary people who come to realize that they feel similarly about an issue, mass their power, and organize it into a social movement. Although a small segment of elite opinion may sympathize, the common theme of social needs such as civil rights, unemployment insurance, and the eight-hour workday is that social movements pushed them onto the public agenda despite powerful opposition from most influential opinion makers. Either way, whether the identification of a social problem comes from above or from below, it is fair to say that self-interest is decisive in constructing it.

The role of self-interest becomes even clearer as this newly identified social problem is defined and people offer theories about its causes and possible solutions. Because people perceive social problems from their own distinct perspective, it is only natural for them to identify causes and remedies consistent with their own self-interest. Teenage pregnancy is a good example. From one perspective, teenage pregnancy shows the decline of the family and the spread of sexual promiscuity. This analysis suggests that we should bolster parental authority and encourage teenagers to "just say no." From another perspective, however, teenage girls get pregnant because if their choice is between flipping hamburgers at the local fast food outlet and becoming a mother, motherhood wins hands down. Of course, this analysis also comes with its own implied remedies, in this case, higher wages and social programs that would help teenage girls see postponing motherhood as actually leading to a better life.

In some sense, both of these *constructions* of teenage pregnancy as a social problem are self-interested. The first interpretation is conservative. It stresses moral issues but minimizes the effect of the job market on a teenager's behavior. Most important, because the problem is constructed in this way, it does not imply that we should raise the minimum wage, provide better job training, or help more poor students attend college. In sum, it is a view consistent with the stated self-interest of conservatives to limit taxes and restrain wages.

Although the second interpretation puts greater emphasis on the social system, it too reflects a self-interested outlook. It shifts responsibility from the young people themselves to other institutions. People holding this view may want to get a higher salary and believe that their wages will go up if the wages of people below them rise. Or they may be allies or employees of human service institutions who would benefit when their explanation of the problem produces some additional government spending. In any event, they are no more immune to charges of self-interest than those who advance the first interpretation.

Once again, we are not discussing whose interpretation is right. Instead, we simply highlight the tendency for people of a similar outlook to *construct* problems in a way that is inevitably self-interested. In our best moments, all of us may aspire to an analysis that is accurate, complete, and objective. We can certainly be fair to the views of people with whom we disagree. Nonetheless, it is true that when we identify and explain a social problem, we cannot be anyone but ourselves.

Who Gets to Define a Social Problem?

We all construct social problems, and, intentionally or unintentionally, we all do so self-interestedly. But not everyone's identification of a social problem makes it onto the public agenda. If you are reading this book in a course, you probably think that the rising cost of tuition is quite an important issue. Still, even if each of you alone believes that tuition is too high, your opinion will have little effect unless someone in a position of authority arrives at the same conclusion. The problem is not that your construction of social problems is any less valid than anyone else's. Rather, it is that some people have more political power, and this political power lets them define what is a social problem.

The power to define what constitutes a social problem is not restricted to those who hold formal political office. Other opinion makers also wield considerable influence. These include business and religious leaders, people in the media, foundations, research institutes, and lobbyists representing powerful interest groups. When they define something as a problem, that definition is more likely to circulate widely and gain acceptance. Conversely, it is always harder for people with less economic/political power and no ready access to the media to present an alternative interpretation.

The "war on drugs" is one of the most controversial examples of social problem construction. Americans ingest all sorts of chemicals that affect their bodies: they take prescription drugs for every kind of medical and emotional ailment; they consume "natural" medicines ranging from echinacea for colds to St.-John's-wort for depression; they drink large quantities of liquor, leading to a major problem with alcoholism; they smoke cigarettes, which contribute to the deaths of more than four hundred thousand people each year; and they use drugs such as Ecstasy, marijuana, crack, cocaine, and heroin, which kill a much smaller number.

How would you construct America's drug problem from this list? Are we simply seeking to medicate the feelings that people normally have? And why not define the whole drug problem as a health issue? Instead, in a classic example of social problem construction, the official definition ignores the most harmful drugs—cigarettes and alcohol—and targets substances like crack that are most commonly used in the inner city. Looking at the list of substances that Americans ingest, this construction of the problem seems quite arbitrary. But arbitrary or not, it certainly illustrates the principle that every construction of a social problem deserves careful scrutiny.

As this example also makes clear, every analysis of a problem emphasizes the features it implicitly deems most relevant. It presents a likely cause or causes, explains how these causes create the problem, and describes the problem's functioning. The social policy to remedy this problem emerges from this framework. So, too, does much of our social work practice.

Indeed, as a social work student, you may find that you often have a different conception of the problem. For most social workers, however, the difficulty is that we must live and work according to the definition of social problems as other, more powerful people construct them. That is not always easy, because the definition of a social problem shapes the social policy designed to address it. It is an unfortunate truth about social work that when a problem is badly defined, it is social workers who must cope with a flawed social policy.

Social Policy and Social Work

Social workers see clients. They counsel, advocate, organize, and administer, and they are likely to do these things even if the analysis of the social problem is misguided and the social policy badly designed. Some definitions of the problem lead to social policies that make it easier for social workers to do their jobs, while others make it harder. When it is easier for social workers to do their jobs, social policy shows respect for their professional judgment, provides enough resources, and lets them counsel, advocate, organize, and administer. But when policy makes it harder, it puts them on a tight leash and an even tighter budget, demands lots of paperwork, and insists that they thread their way among many conflicting objectives. What has happened to social work in hospitals over the past twenty years is a clear example of this contrast.

Until the early 1980s, the social problem that hospital workers addressed was straightforward: What is the best setting to which a patient should be discharged? The policy that arose from this understanding gave social workers a good deal of independence to find the right place. Because Medicare, the health care program for the elderly, reimbursed hospitals for the costs they actually incurred, budgets were more generous and social workers could take time to counsel patients and their families.

Then a new definition of the problem changed both the social policy and the social work practice that it embodied. Concerned about the rising cost of health care, the Reagan administration introduced the concept of diagnostic-related groupings (DRGs), which established a budget for hundreds of different ailments irrespective of actual costs. Now hospitals that discharged patients late would lose money, and those who pushed them out early could make a profit. In this new financial environment, the definition of the problem changed from Where should the patient be discharged? to How fast can we discharge this patient? Caught between their professional judgment of what was best for the patient and the growing insistence to do what was profitable, social workers tried to cope with a new practice model that shrank their budget, limited their independence, and increased the amount of paperwork. The construction of the problem (rising health care costs) led to a social policy (profit-driven health care) that transformed social work practice. Ever since, hospital social workers have had to discharge patients "quicker and sicker."

Medical social work is hardly the only example. Sometimes, social workers have to practice in programs where the assigned tasks range from extremely difficult to nearly impossible. Social policy obstacles to effective social work practice include lack of resources, poor program design, and conflicting objectives. Each of these obstacles is common enough to merit some further discussion.

Two different kinds of resource deficits can affect social work practice. The first kind is internal to the program and typically consists of inadequate staff, financial aid, or equipment. For example, if the original analysis of AIDS patients in a county projected five hundred cases annually, but the actual count is twice that number, then the social workers on staff are going to have a caseload that is double what it should be. Similarly, if a tuition assistance program offers financial aid that is either too little or does not last long enough, the shortage is going to affect the practice of social work. A lack of equipment, such as an insufficient number of computers in a program intended to teach computing skills, would have equally harmful effects.

A second kind of resource deficit is external. In this case, both the construction of the problem and the resulting social policy assume the existence of resources that are just not there. Jobs and housing are the most common kinds of external resource deficits. A shortage of decent jobs becomes im-

How much the government provides goes a long way toward defining the adequacy of a social welfare policy and the obstacles in a social worker's job.

portant if policy analysts construct the issue of poverty as a question of poor people's character. If they design programs on the false premise that decent jobs are readily available, they can put social workers in the uncomfortable position of insisting on work when no work is to be found. Likewise, with strict shelter regulations and a tight housing market, a social worker may have to push shelter residents to rent an apartment, knowing full well that the cost of the apartment will probably force them back to the shelter. As always, when policies have unrealistic expectations about resources, social work practice suffers.

Poor program design can also affect social work practice. Suppose you work for the foster care department of a child welfare agency. Your department gets many children adopted as well as placed in foster care. But because the agency is committed to preserving the biological family, it emphasizes foster care and has never quite reconciled itself to the need for adoption services. Because ties between foster care and adoption staff are neither supported nor encouraged, you have to scramble every time you want to find a new set of adoptive parents. In effect, bad policy and bad program design have made your job much harder.

Then there are times when our social work practice is caught between conflicting objectives. Workfare programs tell women that they are better mothers when they leave their children and go to work. To increase the placement rate, employment-training programs sometimes press participants to accept any job over a good job. What does a social worker do when a client he or she is counseling needs at least a year of therapy, but the cost-cutting managed care company that pays for the therapy insists that all major personality changes must happen within six months? Any of these conflicting objectives is going to have a substantial effect on your social work practice.

Sometimes, programs suffer from all three deficits at once: inadequate resources, poor program design, and conflicting objectives. Under these circumstances, social workers may rightly speculate whether failure was built into the program. Was the program mostly for show? Programs like these most often start up when political pressure demands that something be done, but nothing too much can be done because there is opposition to such meaningful reforms as raising wages, increasing the supply of housing, and providing national health care. Such programs represent a worst-case scenario, but they do exist and are a fact of political life. Whether it is getting homeless people off the street when there are few jobs and little housing, or youth initiatives that must cope with devastation in the inner city, the size of the problem dwarfs the size of the response. Initiatives like these often prompt observers to wonder if the purpose of the program is to provide political cover; then, if somebody complains about a difficult social problem, the responsible authority can respond, "We have a program for that."

These examples all serve to emphasize the point that social welfare policy has a significant effect on social work practice. Yet, even if you accept this point, it inevitably raises another question: What practical difference does it make to know that social work practice embodies social welfare policy? The leading professional organization, the National Association of Social Workers (NASW), offers one answer. In its *Code of Ethics*, NASW states, "A historic and defining feature of social work is the profession's focus on individual well-being in a social context and the well-being of society. Fundamental to social work is attention to the environmental forces that create, contribute to, and address problems in living. Social workers [must therefore] promote social justice and social change with and on behalf of clients."[1] The profession's own code of conduct therefore demands that, if only for purposes of effective advocacy, we must familiarize ourselves with social problems and social welfare policy issues.

There is another, equally powerful reason for knowing about social welfare policy. Because social work practice so closely reflects social welfare policy, knowledge of social welfare policy empowers you on the job. At this most practical level, sometimes you have to figure out whether what you have to do comes from the policy itself or a misinterpretation of it. Policy knowledge can clarify this issue and help you determine exactly how much freedom and autonomy you have. If you think that something you are supposed to do is bad social work practice, knowledge of social welfare policy tells you how much room you have to maneuver: it can bolster your fight to change your agency. Policy knowledge will certainly help you do well for your clients. If you use it wisely, however, it will also enable you to maintain your integrity as a social worker.

Theories of Social Change

We have established that social welfare practice comes from social welfare policy. We have also argued that by itself, this fact makes knowledge of social welfare policy an essential part of any social worker's repertoire. At the outset, however, there is at least one other fact about social welfare policy you should know: no social policy is written in stone. If you do not like a policy, if you think that it serves you and your clients poorly, then you should fight to change it. Even if you do not win at first, you may in the future, because the history of social welfare policy shows that change is one of its few constants.

How do we understand this change? Nowadays, we view social policies as just one part of the whole society. For much of the nineteenth and twentieth centuries, however, most theories of social change minimized or disregarded the individual parts of society to conceptualize society as a whole. If individual parts did exist, they were merely harmonious components of a bigger structure. Above all, in these theories, progress was thought to be inevitable, the smooth unfolding of the potential inherent in all human society.[2]

Evolutionism, cyclical theories, and historical materialism—the three classic conceptions of social change—all reflect this understanding. Evolutionists thought that society was organic. They assumed that historical change has a unique pattern and believed that it transforms everything, as a universal causal mechanism gradually propels society from primitive to more developed forms. From their perspective, progress was the rule, and stability and stagnation were exceptions. As the dominant explanation of social change for nearly one hundred years, evolutionism extends from Auguste Comte, the nineteenth-century founder of modern sociology, to famous mid-twentieth-century sociologists like Talcott Parsons.[3]

Cyclical theories present a different version of social change. Instead of proceeding from one stage to another, they contend that history repeats itself. Just as the days of the week repeat and the same seasons occur in every year, so history more closely resembles a circle rather than a straight line. Following on this premise, the classic cyclical theories have usually focused on the rise and fall of civilizations. Great theorists in this vein include Oswald Spengler, whose perspective is aptly summarized in the title of his 1922 book *The Decline of the West*, and Arnold Toynbee, whose *A Study of History* (1962) held out more hope for the prospect of renewal. Although less concerned with the rise and fall of civilizations, Pitirim Sorokin, a sociologist who identified alternating phases of materialism and idealism, and Nikolai Kondratieff, an economist who saw patterns of economic expansion and contraction lasting fifty years, also belong to the cyclical school.[4]

The third classic theory sets forth the concept of historical materialism. Most closely associated with the work of Karl Marx, historical materialism contains many elements of evolutionist theory. Like the evolutionists, Marx thought that history meant progress, and he saw this history as advancing in stages, pushed from within by the productive forces in society. Marx also noticed the evolution toward a growing complexity of society, reflected particularly in an increasing specialization of labor. Unlike many other evolutionists, however, Marx did identify workers—or more specifically, the organized working class—as a human component that could bend history to its will. In Marx, as distinguished from other evolutionists, human action is collective and purposeful and can transform the society.[5]

In recent years, sociologists have become wary about proposing such grand theories. Modern sociology sees society as heterogeneous and historical events as comparatively random. Its analysis of society is also much more finely grained. There are individual institutions that are functional, as well as individual institutions that are not. There are societies that are autonomous, as well as societies that are clustered together. Dubious about the notion that social change is a coherent phenomenon that proceeds through a series of ever more progressive stages, sociologists today insist instead on historical specificity, whereby theories of social change are partial because no grand theory can ever encompass all the infinite permutations of human history.[6]

Theories of change in social policy belong to this modern tradition. By their very nature, these theories merely seek to puzzle out what is going on in one part of a society. Most important, the theory that this text advances makes no claim to the inevitability of human progress. Instead, the direction of human society is contested. Consistent with modern sociological theory, however, it is contested by human beings, whose actions, both individual and collective, can bring about progressive social change.

Change and Social Welfare Policy: A Policy Model

Changes in social policy have their primary origins in five distinct factors: the economy, politics and the structure of government, ideology, social movements, and history. Because each, in its own unique way, shapes the evolution of social policy, they are the components of the model of policy analysis that we employ throughout this book.

A model of policy analysis is a rigorous and systematic method of analyzing social policy. Some methods of policy analysis pose specific questions. They ask about the source of revenue that pays for the program (government taxes or private contributions), who is eligible for benefits (children, adults, the aged; the poor, the nearly poor, or everybody), and what, in amount and form (cash, vouchers, or in kind), beneficiaries will receive.[7] Although these questions are important and we answer them when we analyze each policy, our model is more contextual and thematic. Drawing on this information, it seeks to identify the distinctive themes in U.S. social welfare policy that both impede and facilitate the practice of social work.

To understand and use this model, we first look within the factors to uncover the triggers of social change. After chapter 2 defines some basic terms and examines some competing functions of social welfare policy, we devote the next five chapters to explaining each part of the model. In part III, we apply this model of policy analysis to five distinct areas of social welfare policy: income supports, employment, housing, health care, and food. By the end of the book, you will know much about the programs and policies in these five areas and be able to apply the model yourself.

The Triggers of Social Change: An Overview

What precipitates change? Looking at these five factors, the actual trigger seems to be the tensions within them. These tensions involve conflicts that continue to build to the point that some resolution is necessary. Changes in social policy then constitute one important method of resolution.

The Economy

In the economy, the roots of social change lie in the marketplace. A market economy is a system for distribution and allocation of goods. Businesses produce goods for sale with the expectation that they can make a profit. Inevitably, this incentive produces a large quantity of high-quality goods for those with a lot of money to spend, but effectively rations the goods that the less affluent can purchase. Unfortunately, in the U.S. economy, the goods that the less affluent cannot purchase include many necessities, such as food, housing, and health care. When this deficiency becomes especially severe, policymakers often try to compensate for it by modifying old social policies or introducing new ones.

Just look, for example, at the effect of technology. As machines replace workers in heavy industry and computer technology sweeps through the whole economy, the change transforms the job market. Businesses need a smaller workforce to produce cars, steel, and chemicals, and the workforce they do need must be better trained. In the United States, the expectation is that workers will obtain this training themselves. Yet sometimes, if the disruption is large enough, the government may provide or partly subsidize job training.

The economy, then, has a clear and direct connection to changes in social policy. At its core, this connection stems from the dual role that people have: they are, simultaneously, workers who produce goods and services, usually for profit, and adults who care for the next generation. Sometimes, when the economy is prospering, the conflict between these two roles can be contained and no new social policy initiatives seem warranted. At other times, however, the two roles clash, and social policies are used to reconcile them. Although they never completely succeed, these policies can partly defuse the tension. Inevitably, however, over the long term, the economy changes and the conflict intensifies again.

Politics and the Structure of Government

The government is the second factor that effects change in social policy. On its face, this statement sounds patently obvious: of course the government influences social policy. Nevertheless, something beyond the dictionary definition is implied here. The government may well be "the organization, machinery, and agency through which a political unit exercises authority," but it is also, for purposes of our discussion, far more than that.

Governments enact laws and deploy police to enforce them; they raise armies and wage war; they build highways, construct sewers, and run passenger railroads. In the field of social welfare, the list of their responsibilities is even longer. Programs by age, for children, teenagers, adults, and the elderly, are all government operated. By function, government social policies encompass everything from income supports such as public assistance and Social Security to housing, health care, education, and employment training. It is a long list, and it seems initially difficult to make much sense of it.

Look carefully, however, and a pattern emerges. Any government that functions within a market economy must pay attention to the effects of its actions. Governments, after all, depend on taxes. When the economy is doing well, they collect more tax dollars; when it sags, they collect fewer. The creation of conditions for business success and the profitable accumulation of capital therefore ranks as a crucial function of the government.

The government, however, also retains another responsibility. At the same time that it seeks to make business prosper, it must also cultivate the perception of fairness, legitimacy, and social harmony. The trouble is that these tasks often conflict. The government must attend to the needs of business; it must ensure that business makes money. Nevertheless, if it does so too openly, citizens begin to criticize these policies, and if they broaden these criticisms even further, it may lead to questions about the fairness of the entire social order and, eventually, to the loss of their loyalty and support. To prevent this outcome, the government must continually reinforce perceptions about the social order's legitimacy. It must somehow find a way to justify its desire to ensure business profit as a legitimate public goal.

Naturally, when this tension escalates to an intolerable level, it frequently precipitates changes in social welfare policy. After all, social welfare policy often softens the most conspicuously negative effects of the market. For this reason, it serves as a particularly useful means of comforting those in distress and persuading them that however well other people are doing, they will not starve. Whether it is an increase in some form of cash assistance, a tax credit for college tuition, or the availability of new counseling services, a change in social welfare policies combats the perception of unfairness. By signifying that all members of the society are entitled to reap at least some of its benefits, these policies help to manage the tension between the accumulation of money in a society and perceptions of that society's legitimacy. Ultimately, it is this tension that spurs the government to bring about policy change.[8]

Ideology

An ideology is a coherent set of beliefs about ideas, institutions, and social arrangements. Ideologies function to organize the experiences of daily life into patterns with which people can cope. In this way, they help people to make better sense of their world.

In today's media-saturated society, however, people live their own lives, but few independently construct their own ideology. Suppose, for example, that you bought Enron stock in the late 1990s. What are you to make of its subsequent collapse? On your own, you might come to several different conclusions. At one extreme, you might decide that it was just one misguided company; at the other, you might conclude that because the push to deregulate has gone too far, we need stricter controls over corporations. The larger point is that nowadays, amid the proliferation of newspapers, radio, television, and the Internet, whatever the conclusion you do reach, you have not reached this conclusion alone.

This is not to suggest that people absorb every ideology around them. Sometimes, of course, people dismiss an ideological framework because it does not match their own experience: tell workers during an economic depression that people are unemployed out of choice, and few ever adopt that explanation. Nevertheless, it is true that we hear explanations of social arrangements all the time, and that even when we do not agree with them, they do influence our thinking.

When a dominant ideology clashes with an alternative explanation, conflict and tension develop. Sometimes, of course, the dominant ideology succeeds in regaining its popularity, so that after a while, there is little evidence that a conflict has even occurred. However, as with the women's movement, when alternative ideologies are more successful in explaining many people's experience, the tension builds until changes in social policy become necessary to defuse it. Once again, the ideological tension triggers a conflict that becomes embodied in a policy change.

Social Movements

Social movements fuel political tensions, which often accumulate until they bring about changes in social policy. For most social movements, the trigger is some unmet need: too little income, too little health care, or too few civil rights. Although these problems typically have political and economic origins, social movements define the issue and tell us what some think we should do about it. Sometimes, elite-driven, top-down pressures—for example, cutbacks in benefits or changes in job training—effect modifications of social policy.

Mostly, however, when the changes have significantly expanded benefits and services, broad social movements have been the trigger.

Yet social movements are themselves full of their own tensions and conflicts. They may fight about the movement's militancy (should it lobby through existing channels or should it take to the streets?); the breadth of the coalition it tries to develop (narrower, single-issue, and more committed, or broader, multi-issue, and less committed); the source of funds (should it take tobacco money for a youth center?); its public image (who constitutes the visible face of the movement?); and its willingness to cultivate new leadership.[9] The capacity of social movements to bring about policy change has often hinged on their ability to resolve these conflicts. In addition, the resolution of these conflicts involves choices that have significant implications for the specific content of the new social policies.

History

The last factor influencing change in social welfare policy is the history of social welfare itself. This history establishes precedents and thereby affects the possibilities for change. When people look at these precedents and see past victories, they are more likely to feel empowered and fight for new social reforms. Yet historical precedent, especially in the United States, does not only transmit a hopeful legacy. When the historical record highlights a pattern of obstacles and defeats, it implies that little can be done and tends to deflate political energies. It is this tension—between the hope for change and the possibility or even the likelihood of defeat—that frames social welfare's historical legacy.

U.S. social welfare history, then, speaks to all of us in a variety of ways. It can inspire confidence in the notion that changing social policies will better enable us to address some human needs. Certainly, the great social reforms of the twentieth century are there to sustain that interpretation: from workers' compensation to shelters for battered women, from public housing to Social Security, one history of social welfare is positive and uplifting. At the same time, however, there is another strain, one that contains a string of disappointments and outright failures, so that the description of the United States as a "reluctant welfare state" is well and fully earned.[10] In the tension between these two histories are some lessons to be learned about what has impelled change in social welfare policy before and what therefore might be likely to do so again.

Conclusion

Change in social policy generally arises out of conflict and tension. Whether that tension is a product of the conflict in the economy between social harmony and a favorable business environment, or the ambiguous legacy that

U.S. social welfare history hands down to us, it is clear that for each of the five factors influencing the development of the welfare state, the impetus for the change lies in the tension itself.

The model that we present here, then, is dynamic. It does not treat the five factors we have identified—the economy, politics, ideology, social movements, and history—as static and purely contextual. Instead, it seeks to explore the operation of the conflict within each factor, so that we can better understand how changes occur in both social welfare policy and social work practice. We have briefly outlined these dynamics in this chapter. After the next chapter defines our terms and discusses the various and often conflicting functions of social welfare policy, each of these factors and the dynamics within them will be treated at greater length.

2

Mimi Abramovitz

Definition and Functions of Social Welfare Policy: Setting the Stage for Social Change

Social welfare policy—the way society responds or does not respond to social need—may seem like a distant and remote subject. Yet, as chapter 1 has shown, it touches us as individuals every day. Each of us and our friends and relatives use social welfare services at various points in our lives, and we all pay taxes to support social programs so that they will be available to us when we need them. We have also seen that social welfare policy has an enormous influence on our work as professionals. The decisions that the government makes about social welfare policy shape the lives of our clients, the extent to which we can help them, and the ability of social agencies to fulfill their missions. These decisions determine who pays for and who benefits from government spending, how well or poorly people live, the nature of their relationships to each other, the overall quality of life, and the nation's commitment to social justice. It sets a tone for the way individuals in the wider society think of their obligation to people in need—either encouraging or discouraging social responsibility for others.

Although many students entering a social work program have never heard the term social welfare policy before, in fact most people have strong opinions about policy issues such as welfare for single mothers, managed health care, and affirmative action. Indeed social welfare policy is controversial because it involves political conflict over the nature and causes of and solutions to social problems such as poverty, racial discrimination, and the welfare of children. In the final analysis, social workers must understand and learn to deal with social welfare policy, given its controversial character, its importance to social work, and its impact on the wider society. However, as any social welfare policy text will tell you, no simple, clear-cut, or uniform definition of social welfare policy exists. By examining the concept from a variety of vantage points, we will develop a clearer picture of what it is all about. We begin with the broadest part of the definition and work our way toward social welfare policy itself. The chapter ends with a description of the major social welfare programs that constitute the U.S. welfare state.

What Is Social Welfare Policy?

Let's begin with the question, What is policy? Webster's dictionary defines *policy* as any governing principle, plan, or course of action that guides and governs the choices and activities of a wide variety of societal institutions. This includes the principles, guidelines, and procedures that govern the social agencies that employ social workers, but also universities, trade unions, religious organizations, government bodies, and professional associations. Virtually all societal institutions and organizations develop policies to facilitate consistent decision making. However, this book looks just at public or governmental policy and, in particular, social welfare policy.

Public Policy

Social welfare policy is one type of public policy. Public policy consists of the principles, plans, and courses of action taken by the government on behalf of society at large. But these actions fall into two large interrelated spheres: international (or foreign) and national (or domestic) policy.

International

International or foreign policy refers to activities that extend beyond a nation's borders. It addresses questions related to foreign trade, military affairs, immigration, financial aid to other nations, international finance, space exploration, cultural exchanges, and so on. The president's Cabinet includes a secretary of State, a secretary of Defense, and other posts that parallel these policy arenas.

National

National or domestic policy refers to government decisions that guide actions within a nation's borders. It includes policy related to social welfare but also to agriculture, business, the economy, the labor market, transportation systems, and taxation, to name only some of the major domestic policy arenas. Also called *social policy*, it has been defined as "a collective strategy that addresses social problems";[1] "the organized response or lack of response to a social issue or problem";[2] and the social purposes and consequences of agricultural, economic, employment, fiscal, physical development, and social welfare policies.[3] Positions within the Cabinet mirror these national concerns; they include the secretaries of Labor, Agriculture, Commerce, Health and Human Services, and the Treasury.

Of course, the line between national and international policies is not a clear one. It is well-known that government spending on war leaves less for domestic needs. Exporting the production of U.S. goods to other countries reduces the number of jobs at home and may affect wage levels in both nations. Industrial pollution contaminates the earth and water, creating health problems without heed to national boundaries. Groups persecuted by one country become another nation's refugees. With globalization—the flow of capital, labor, technology, and information across national boarders—the line between domestic and foreign policy has become even fuzzier.

Social Welfare Policy

Social welfare policy is one type of domestic or social policy. We have defined policy, but what do the terms *social* and *welfare* mean? Webster's dictionary defines *social* as "of or having to do with human beings living together as a group in a situation requiring that they have dealings with one another." The term *welfare* is confusing because it refers to both a particular program and to the condition or well-being of society. In popular discussions, people often use the term when talking about the program known as Temporary Assistance to Needy Families (TANF), formerly called Aid to Families with Dependent Children (AFDC). For this reason, many people think of social welfare policy as programs just for the poor. But, in fact, the term welfare has a much wider meaning. According to the dictionary, welfare is "the state of being or doing well; the condition of health, prosperity, happiness, and well-being." A *welfare state* exists in those societies that make the well-being of people the responsibility of the government.[4] And, as we shall see below, social welfare programs benefit the affluent as well as the poor.

Social welfare policy refers to the principles, activities, or framework for action adopted by a government to ensure a socially defined level of individual, family, and community well-being. It has been defined as "those collective interventions that contribute to the general welfare by assigning claims from one set of people who are said to produce or earn national income to another set of people who may merit compassion or charity";[5] as "a subset of social policy that regulates the provision of benefits to people to meet basic life needs";[6] and as "an organized system of laws, programs, and benefits and services which aid individuals and groups to attain satisfying standards of life, health, and relationships needed to develop their full capacities."[7] At the ground level, social welfare policy appears in the form of *social welfare programs*—benefits and services—used by people every day to address basic human needs. These needs include income security, health, education, nutrition, employment, housing, a sense of belonging, and an opportunity to participate in society.

In sum, social welfare policy can be thought of as a public response to problems that society is ready to address, a societal institution composed of government-funded programs and services targeted to some definition of basic needs, and a strategy of action that guides government intervention in the area of social welfare provision. Though not all people employed by the social welfare system are trained social workers, social work represents the largest single profession working within the social welfare system.[8]

Broadening the Definition of Social Welfare Policy

This definition of social welfare is accurate but too narrow. Ignoring the relationship between public and private provision, it does not include the social welfare system embedded in the tax code, misses the connection between social welfare and other public policies, and does not account for what some call nondecisions. These four realities complicate our definition of social welfare policy but increase our understanding of how it works in real life.

Public and Private: A Blurred Boundary

The definition of social welfare policy covers policies and programs that operate in the public sector, that is, those carried out by federal, state, and local governments. However, many social workers are employed in the private sector, which includes both not-for-profit human service agencies (voluntary agencies) and for-profit programs (proprietary agencies). The line between public and private social welfare programs has always been somewhat blurred, largely because public dollars have regularly been used to fund the delivery of human services by private sector agencies, first the nonprofits and then the for-profits. Today, many large and small private agencies rely heavily on government contracts and/or reimbursement for services provided to clients.

Unlike many Western European nations in which the government itself operates social welfare programs, the United States has preferred to fund the private sector to deliver social services. Government funding of private social welfare services dates back to the 1800s. As early as 1819, Connecticut funded the Hartford Asylum for the Deaf and Dumb. In the mid- to late 1800s, many large cities paid private institutions to care for orphans, the elderly, and the mentally ill, among others. A national survey in 1901 found that city, county, or state governments subsidized some private service agencies in almost all the states. Until the Depression of the 1930s, governments limited their private sector funding mostly to institutional care. Federal funding for noninstitutional private agencies increased during the Depression because the latter, which at this point dispensed most of the cash relief to the needy, could no longer manage the enormous demand for help. In 1933, the Roosevelt administration gave the public sector a boost by insisting that only the government's new emergency relief agencies would administer public monies. Although many social work leaders remained skeptical of the emerg-

"Three Scenes in an Almshouse."

ing federal relief, many frontline social workers left private agencies for jobs in the new public sector programs.[9]

Purchase of Services

The public and private sectors remained relatively separate until the 1960s. In 1967 new amendments to the Social Security Act permitted states to use public funds to purchase services delivered by private agencies; the Title XX Amendments (1975) made it even easier to do so. By 1976, more than 50 percent of the $2.5 billion spent on social services under Title XX involved purchase of nongovernmental service arrangements. By 1980, federal programs provided over 50 percent of the financial support that went to private nonprofit social service and community development organizations.[10]

In the 1980s and 1990s, the political climate became more pro-business and more antigovernment. As part of their downsizing, all levels of government began to fund for-profit firms as well as more nonprofit services and some faith-based agencies. The for-profits included Lockheed Martin and other companies whose Defense Department contracts had begun to dry up.

In 2002, thousands of clients received services from for-profit nursing homes, adult and child care centers, home health services, alcohol and drug treatment programs, managed care mental health systems, public schools, and welfare-to-work programs, as well as private prisons and immigrant detention centers.

Reimbursement

In addition to purchase of service contracts, the government also funds private agencies through reimbursement.[11] That is, Medicaid, Medicare, Supplemental Security Income (SSI), and other public assistance grants are used to pay private agencies for services they provide to clients who qualify for these benefits.[12] Similarly, federal rent subsidies for the poor are paid to private landlords, and food stamps pay for food bought from local grocers. In recent years, public schools have contracted with private companies to manage their systems, and conservatives favor the use of government-funded educational vouchers to offset the cost of tuition at private elementary and high schools. The Supreme Court has ruled that providing vouchers to religious schools does not violate the constitutional separation of church and state.

Although it is praised in some quarters, many social workers have concerns about the provision of social services by for-profit companies. They worry that the profit motive will undercut the quality of social services provided to clients.[13] They also point to many instances in which the need to make a profit has become an incentive for agencies to select clients based on ability to pay or severity of illness rather than on need. There is also a concern that increased provision by the private sector will weaken the public sector by draining it of funds and reducing government responsibility for social welfare.[14]

Fiscal Welfare

The standard definition of social welfare is limited as well because it does not take fiscal welfare into account. Fiscal welfare provides financial benefits to individuals and corporations through tax exemptions, deductions, and credits. These uncollected tax dollars are known in budget parlance as *tax expenditures* because the lost revenues leave the U.S. Treasury with the same dollar shortfall as does direct spending. The Joint Committee on Taxation views tax expenditures as "analogous to direct outlays." It describes the two spending streams—tax expenditures and direct government spending—as alternative ways to accomplish similar policy objectives.[15]

The tax code has been called a fiscal welfare system because tax expenditures involving billions of dollars (see below) address the same needs that are met through direct government spending. A key difference is that the fiscal welfare system extends far beyond the poor, leading some to conclude that "everyone is on welfare."[16]

The tax system serves as an important instrument of social welfare policy beyond its role as a source of revenue for government programs. The tax code deductions for child care, mortgage interest payments, certain education costs, medical expenses, retirement, and dependents mirror government spending for child care programs, rent supplements/public housing, public education, health insurance, and cash assistance programs.[17] In some cases, however, using tax expenditures, Congress allocates more money to the needs of middle- and upper-class families than to similar needs of the poor. The well-known housing differential is especially glaring. As discussed in chapter 10, on average, mortgage interest tax deductions are worth almost $13,600 a year to taxpayers earning more than $200,000, but only $859 a year to families earning between $40,000 and $50,000, and nothing to people who neither own a home nor earn enough to itemize their tax bill.[18] In 2002, middle- and upper-class housing tax deductions (i.e., mortgage interest payment, state and local property taxes, and the exclusion of capital gains tax on house sales) amounted to $102 billion. That same year the Department of Housing and Urban Development spent only $29.4 billion for low-income housing and rental subsidies for the poor, just under half of the $61.5 billion allowed for mortgage interest tax deductions.[19]

Thus, tax expenditures represent billions of dollars. The cost of tax expenditures (in lost revenues) rose from $36.6 billion in 1967 to an estimated $587 billion in 2000. The latter amount is just $379 billion less than the total $966 billion spent on entitlement benefits and $242 billion *more* than the $345 billion spent on nondefense discretionary spending, much of which goes to social welfare needs. Tax expenditures in 2000 were $352 billion *more* than the $235 billion allocated to means-tested programs for poor people; $181 billion *more* than the $406 billion for Social Security; and $292 billion *more* than the $295 billion for the military.[20]

Corporate Welfare

The claim that "everyone is on welfare" extends to business and industry. The Internal Revenue Service allows employers to deduct the cost of doing business. Some tax deductions, like that for employees' health insurance, address a basic social welfare issue, in this case the need for health care. The deduction lowers labor costs by reducing the tax bill of employers. It also subsidizes individual employees because the value of the health insurance benefit is not taxed, whereas an equivalent cash payment, provided as a wage, would be. In addition, private health insurance deductions have reduced the pressure to develop a national health system, which, among other benefits, would be more likely to cover the 41 million Americans who are currently uninsured.

Tax breaks for business increase business profits so much that critics refer to the them as "corporate welfare." In 1998, the editors of *Time* magazine estimated that the government dispenses about $125 billion a year to companies to help advertise their products, build new facilities, train their workers, and write off the cost of perks.[21] The Cato Institute, a conservative think tank in Washington, D.C., reported that every major government department is a repository for government funding of private industry.[22] The overall "aid to dependent corporations" amounted to an estimated $519 billion in uncollected taxes from 1995 to 2002.[23] Meanwhile, corporate income taxes have dropped from 21 percent of total federal revenue in 1962 to 7.5 percent in 2001.[24] Along with stopping the well-known cost overruns in government contracts, collecting these funds would go a long way toward meeting the nation's social welfare needs.

Corporations also reap indirect benefits from standard social welfare programs. Although not generally looked at in this way, as detailed later in this chapter, social welfare spending helps to create the conditions necessary for profitable business activity. The nation's income support programs put cash into people's hands, which creates a steady supply of consumers for the goods and services produced by private enterprise. By underwriting the cost of family maintenance, the dollars spent on education, public health programs, Medicaid, and cash assistance programs help to supply industry with the healthy, properly socialized, and productive workers they need. Social welfare provision also helps to mute social unrest by cushioning inequality in the wider social order. By forestalling or co-opting social movements and other political disruptions, the welfare state contributes to the social peace on which profitable economic activity also depends.

The Social Welfare Impact of Non–Social Welfare Policies

The standard definition of social welfare policy provided earlier is also too narrow because it treats social welfare policy as a discrete entity, when in fact it cannot be separated from other public policies that affect the well-being of individuals and families. A broader definition of social welfare policy would include the social purposes and consequences of fiscal, military, agricultural, economic, employment, and physical development as well as social welfare policies.

Take the well-known intersection of social welfare and military policy. Spending on military bases and armaments creates jobs for some people. However, call-ups for military service also disrupt families, most recently for the fighting in Afghanistan and the invasion of Iraq. More generally and more often, the military and human services compete for scarce federal dollars. Government spending for military purposes, especially but not only during wartime, drains funds available for social welfare (and other) purposes. For example, faced with a fiscal dividend (i.e., budget surplus) in the early 1960s, John F. Kennedy and then Lyndon B. Johnson launched a War on Poverty. But full funding for this Great Society initiative quickly gave way to military spending for the war in Vietnam, which escalated around the same time. More recently, prior to the attack on the World Trade Center and the Pentagon on September 11, 2001, for the first time in many years the nation had another federal budget surplus. Many people hoped the dollars would be used to fund long underfinanced social programs and make it unnecessary for the government to borrow from the Social Security Trust Fund. Instead, the surplus rapidly disappeared, due, in large part, to the $1.35 trillion tax cut passed by Congress in January 2001 and the post–September 11 military and security costs. In addition, the government needed to raise the debt ceiling. The added interest payments on the money borrowed means less for social spending. In recent years, the interest payments on the national debt often have been the second or third largest item in the federal budget.

Economic policy regularly affects social welfare policy because it bears directly on the nation's income maintenance programs (e.g., aid to single mothers, Social Security, Unemployment Insurance, food stamps, housing aid, Medicaid, and Medicare). The demand for cash assistance rises and falls with the government's economic policy. During economic downturns, when people lose their jobs, the demand for cash assistance inevitably rises. When the Federal Reserve Board raises the interest rates to cool off inflation, it knowingly induces a recession, believing that it is more important to control inflation than to prevent the unemployment rate from rising. In contrast, when the government raises the minimum wage or when the economy grows, the demand for welfare and Unemployment Insurance benefits falls.

Social welfare policy and transportation policy also intersect. For example, mass transit systems often compete with highway construction for government dollars. The choice between the two transportation policies has major ramifications for public well-being. Expanding or improving mass transit favors city dwellers, non–car owners, and the less well-off. In contrast, highway construction benefits car owners, the auto industry (and rubber and steel industries), surburbanites, and more affluent communities. The choice between the two ways of traveling to work also affects health care costs because highways produce more accidents, deaths, and pollution than does mass transit.

Even farm policy has social welfare implications. When the government pays farmers not to produce crops, the reduced supply increases the income of farmers, but the higher prices mean some consumers can no longer afford basic food items.

Government decisions regarding employment, especially the employment of women, also have social welfare implications, particularly for child care policy. Historically, the government has expanded child care services to meet the demand for women workers. During World War II, as men went off to battle, the government recruited women, who for years had been told that their place is in the home, to enter the workforce. To encourage them, the federal government operated a national day care program, only to shut it down at the war's end—although many mothers continued to work outside the home. The child care centers were closed in hopes that women would go back to the home (many refused) and open up jobs for returning male soldiers. Beginning in the late 1960s and early 1970s, to move women from welfare to work, the government allocated funds (never enough, however) for child care. But, when it comes to child care, the vast majority of working mothers still have to fend for themselves.

Nondecisions

The original definition of social welfare policy is too narrow for still another reason: policy includes what the government does not do as well as what it actually does. Referred to as nondecisions, these include both those issues that influential people and groups have kept off the public agenda as well as those that get on the agenda but fail to survive the political process. According to Peter Bachrach and Morton Baratz, the political scientists who coined the term:

> Non-decision making is a means by which demands for change in the existing allocation of benefits and privileges in the community can be suffocated before they are even voiced; or kept covert; or killed before they gain access to the relevant decision making arena; or failing all these things, maimed or destroyed in the decision-implementing state of the policy making process.[25]

Non–decision making occurs when those in positions of power use their influence to control the political agenda and move discussions away from issues by mobilizing bias against them. The mobilization of bias includes the manipulation of myths, dominant community values, political institutions, and procedures to prevent certain challenges from developing into calls for policies that might disrupt the status quo.[26]

More often than not, the issues that fail to get a hearing address the needs of people with limited power and lack of access to the centers of political decision making. For example, from the 1930s to the mid-1960s, health care advocates in and outside of Congress tried but failed to enact a national health insurance program covering workers and the poor. The policy fell victim to the political influence of the powerful doctors, hospitals, and insurance companies who preferred to keep health insurance for workers and their families in the private sector provided as employment-based fringe benefits.[27] In the 1960s, the welfare rights movement called for a guaranteed annual income of $5,500. This demand never made it onto the legislative table because the high amount would exert an upward pressure on private wages. In the early 1990s, heath care reform reappeared on the national agenda. But the campaign for a single-payer plan, a government-run health program like the one in Canada, failed to get press notice. This invisibility ensured that the managed care model favored by the insurance companies won the day.

Deepening the Definition of Social Welfare Policy

The definition of social welfare as government responsibility for the general welfare is too simple as well as too narrow. The standard definition of social welfare policy as meeting basic human needs implies that social welfare provision is guided by a single goal and that social welfare policy always enhances well-being. A closer look reveals a more complex reality. It shows that many social welfare policies have perpetuated oppressive agendas. The conflicting social, economic, and political functions of social welfare policy have also contributed to negative outcomes.

The positive track record of U.S. social policy is detailed throughout this book, but the negative side of the story cannot be ignored when defining social welfare policy, when working with the groups whom these policies have harmed, and when planning future policies. It is crucial to remain aware of these negatives, because awareness helps social workers to better understand why the stated goals of a policy may not materialize and, even more important, to figure out what needs to be changed.

Oppressive Goals and Outcomes

The historical record reveals that social welfare policy has not always contributed to the well-being of individuals, families, and communities, especially among groups with less power.

Native Americans

Native Americans were one of the first groups to suffer harmful social policies.[28] Some early settlers tried to convert Native Americans to Christianity, deprived them of their land, and spread new diseases (sometimes intentionally) that wiped out entire tribes. The Naturalization Act of 1790 classified American Indians as "domestic foreigners," preventing them from becoming citizens. The 1802 Indian Trade and Intercourse Act required treaties before land could be ceded to the United States, but the U.S. government often disregarded these agreements. For example, to meet the growing European demand for cotton, the United States carved several southern states out of Indian territory, forcing the tribes to relocate west of the Mississippi. When Native Americans tried to resist, the government often ignored the treaties, appropriated the lands for distribution to white settlers, and annihilated the Native Americans. To facilitate the expansion of the railroad, the 1871 Indian Appropriation Act denied the very existence of tribes as legitimate political units, eliminating the need to negotiate treaties. In the end, federal policy forcibly evicted Native Americans from their ancestral homes and placed them on reservations. Once there, the government removed tens of thousands of Indian children from their homes and placed them in government-run boarding schools in an effort to Americanize them. Although many of these laws and practices were later reversed, U.S. social policies had already done irreparable damage.

Legalized Slavery and Segregation

The legalization of slavery represents another example of social policy that harmed rather than helped people.[29] Prior to the Civil War (1861–1865),

Until the Civil Rights Act of 1964, segregation was the official policy throughout the South, and "colored only" signs appeared on many facilities.

U.S law allowed some people to own others. Slave owners, most of whom were white, could buy and sell black people, keep them from learning to read and write, punish them for any purpose, and kill them with impunity. After the Civil War, Congress created the Freedman's Bureau to assist the newly emancipated slaves (and dislocated whites) with income, education, training, and, because most of them could work the land, a promise of forty acres and a mule. This positive social welfare policy quickly gave way to strong opposition from Southern landowners who feared that it would cost them access to a cheap workforce.

To keep black people "in their place," from the late 1870s to the early 1960s, U.S. social policy regulated relations between the races. Legal segregation and racial discrimination of every kind prevailed in the nation's schools, workplaces, voting booths, restaurants, hospitals, beaches, drinking fountains, trains, buses, and movie theaters. The goal of segregation was to prevent the advance of black people and to separate the races wherever they might mingle. In 1954, the U.S. Supreme Court ruled that separate but equal schools were unconstitutional. But not until the 1960s—and then only under mounting pressure from the civil rights movement—did Congress begin to enact voting rights, antidiscrimination, and affirmative action laws to correct the history of unjust treatment of persons of color. Then, beginning in the mid-1970s, in a more conservative political climate, the government began to take back these hard-won gains.

Exclusion of Immigrants

U.S. laws regulating immigration have existed since the 1800s.[30] Prior to 1882, U.S. immigration policy allowed entry to all who applied. During the next one hundred years, immigration policy functioned to exclude groups regarded as undesirable, to admit those who served domestic economic interests, and to provide refuge for the persecuted. More often than not, the definition of undesirable was explicitly or implicitly racist.

The 1882 Chinese Exclusion Act prohibited further immigration of Chinese laborers, in part because white Americans resented the economic mobility achieved by the Chinese, who began by working in the country's mines and on the railroads. The 1924 Naturalization Act favored Western and Northern Europeans over Southern and Eastern European immigrants. Beginning in the 1950s, immigration laws included quotas for workers with needed skills, protected U.S. workers from competition from foreign workers, and otherwise advanced U.S. economic interests. The 1952 McCarren-Walter Act barred communists. Although poorly enforced, the 1986 Immigration and Control Act established sanctions for employers who hired undocumented aliens. Public policy has also restricted immigrants' access to public assistance benefits. In some localities, it supported English-only laws and standardized testing, both of which disadvantaged immigrant communities. Until 1990, immigration policy also excluded homosexuals.

Women's Rights

Throughout most of the century, U.S. social policy created barriers to women's full participation in wider society.[31] Defining women's place as the home, law, custom, and family dynamics barred women from voting, owning property, getting an education, sitting on juries, working for wages, and receiving credit in their own name and severely stigmatized women who departed from prescribed wife and mother roles. After more than eighty years of struggle, in 1919, led by the first wave of feminism, women gained the right to vote. But it took the second wave of feminism in the 1960s and 1970s to secure a fuller range of women's rights, including bans on sex discrimination and sexual harassment and the right to an abortion, to credit ratings for married women, to parental leave (still unpaid), to protection for battered women, and to stricter rape laws. The struggle persists to this day.

Antigay Policies

A long list of U.S. policies reflects hostility toward homosexuals.[32] Still on the books in one-third of the states, sodomy laws forbid physical expression of affection between persons of the same sex, even in their own home. The first sodomy law was enacted in Virginia and carried the death penalty. The federal government openly discriminated against homosexuals in the civil service system until 1975. Gays with federal jobs had to remain in the closet or lose their jobs. The first discharge of a homosexual from the military occurred in 1778. Until 1992, thousands of gay men were forced out of the armed services. Today's "Don't ask, don't tell" policy allows gay men and lesbians to serve but under severe behavioral restrictions. Other state and local laws permit employers to discriminate against homosexuals. They also tolerate hate crimes and gay bashing. Social welfare policy also prevents gay men and lesbians from marrying, securing health insurance for their partner, visiting a hospitalized partner, and having parental rights (child custody, adoption). To date, the struggle to undo these homophobic laws has had only limited success.

Single Mothers

U.S. social welfare policy has a long history of penalizing single motherhood.[33] From colonial times to the present, social welfare programs have defined women as deserving or undeserving of aid based on their marital status. Married and previously married women have always fared better with social welfare policies than separated, abandoned, or never-married women. Single mothers came under attack during the 1824 Poor Law Reform, which removed the "undeserving" from the home and placed them in institutions. In the mid-1870s, during a deep depression, many cities closed down their public aid and removed poor (mostly immigrant) children from the care of their parents. The state Mothers' Pensions laws in the early 1900s favored white widows over other husbandless women and women of color. Its successor, Aid to Dependent Children (Title IV of the 1935 Social Security Act), included no benefits for the mother until 1950. The states took longer to implement ADC than the other public assistance programs and imposed harsh moralistic work and marriage requirements on its recipients. The federal government provided less funding and lower benefits to this program. Despite some improvements after World War II, hostility toward single mothers has remained a driving force of welfare policy to this day. The 1996 federal welfare reform law known as Temporary Aid to Needy Families continued this historic tradition.

Competing Functions of Social Welfare Policy

Why, despite a stated commitment to ensuring the general welfare, has U.S. social welfare policy so often done otherwise? As foreshadowed in chapter 1, the answer to this critical but troubling question lies, in part, in the realization that any one policy performs more than one function and that these social, economic, and political functions do not always share a common agenda. Because the agendas represent the interests of different groups in society, efforts to further one set of interests often generate resistance from groups who benefit from another function of the policy. Because the economic and political functions tend to favor the haves and the social functions benefit the have-nots, social workers find that their agenda often gets lost or compromised. In addition, conservatives, liberals, and radicals often have different interpretations of the various functions.

This section sorts out the social, economic, and political functions of social welfare policy and the ideological disputes involved. The resulting discussion both expands and complicates the prevailing definition of social welfare policy. It suggests that social workers need to be clear about the various functions of any social welfare policy, to determine if the economic and political agendas override the more humanitarian social ones, and to be prepared to defend—and improve—the latter.

The Social Functions of Social Welfare Policy

The social functions of social welfare policy seek to enhance the functioning and well-being of individuals and families. To avoid chaos and disorganization, all societies need to maintain predictable patterns of behavior, to ensure that individuals comply with societal norms and rules, and to educate people to carry out their socially defined work and family roles. Prior to the Industrial Revolution, the family, the community, and religious institutions carried out these common tasks. Over time, however, the responsibility for socialization was extended from these traditional structures to governmental institutions such as schools, health care services, penal institutions—and the welfare state.

The government had to take a role in creating the conditions that promote individual development and prevent social problems for at least three reasons. First, over the years, due to geographic mobility, fewer people lived close to their family or maintained strong ties to a religious institution. Second, the process of industrialization, urbanization, and immigration created new and different types of needs that overwhelmed the caretaking and socializing capacity of individual families, communities, and religious institutions. Third, the resulting social problems had to be addressed to the extent that they impaired individual functioning and jeopardized the smooth running of wider society. If too many people became illiterate, unhealthy, criminal, unemployed, homeless, and orphaned, they could not carry out their socially defined work/breadwinning and family/caretaking responsibilities. Wider society, in turn, suffered both the loss of their productive contributions and the social problems associated with unmet needs. Therefore, local, state, and then the federal government gradually created new programs that would support family functioning, help individuals perform their roles in ways that both satisfied themselves and conformed to societal expectations, and protect society from those who did not follow the rules.

The preceding explanation describes how most liberal analysts explain the social functions of social welfare policy and reflects what is found in most social welfare histories. In contrast, conservatives think of social policy's social functions as an issue of social control, believing that punishment works better than rehabilitation. They contend that social welfare policy must regulate "deviant" behavior because failure to carry out one's socially defined work and family roles reflects personal irresponsibility and the acceptance of non-mainstream values rather than unmet needs. Contrary to their opposition to government intervention in the economy, conservatives support public policies that alter or control the behavior of delinquents, criminals, and drug addicts as well as single mothers, jobless adults, mentally ill people, homosexuals, social critics, and the poor. By subjecting these "irresponsible" and "deviant" persons to long prison sentences, mandated treatment, or minimal social welfare benefits, conservatives believe, the government will both improve individual functioning and send a message to the rest of society about what happens to those who do not conform.[34]

The radical and feminist analyses charge that in a capitalist/patriarchal society, control and discipline represent social welfare policy's *main* social function. The rules and regulations of programs and services, they argue, reward individuals and families for complying with prescribed work and family roles and penalize those who cannot or choose not to do so by reducing or denying them assistance.[35] By making benefits conditional on compliance with mainstream values and norms in this way, these more radical analyses argue, the government leaves individuals, especially poor individuals, with no choice but to conform, even when cultural mandates counter their best interests. In this view, the social functions of social welfare policy help to supply business and industry with obedient workers, male-headed households with compliant wives/mothers, and the wider society with citizens who accept mainstream norms that favor the dominant class over their own.[36] Thus, the regulatory features of the social functions of social policy enforce the very institutions that radicals and feminists believe have generated social problems in the first place.

The Economic Functions of Social Welfare Policy

The economic functions of social welfare policy regulate the relationship of the individual to the economy. Social welfare policy functions economically on several fronts: it provides a minimum level of economic security, helps to stabilize the economy during economic downturns, subsidizes the cost to business of sustaining the workforce, and underwrites family maintenance (social reproduction).

Economic Security

One economic function of social welfare policy is to ensure a minimum level of economic security to all. People need income to provide for themselves and their families. Unless we are independently wealthy, we need to be working or to be supported by an employed person in order to survive. But the labor market does not serve everyone equally, adequately, or all the time. Even in good economic times, business and industry cannot provide employment for all those people who are willing and able to work. Other people cannot work due to age, disability, illness, or other employment barriers. Still others are not in the labor force due to family responsibilities, employment discrimination, or lack of work available during economic downturns.

For these reasons, but also due to low wages, the government gradually assumed the responsibility for ensuring a minimum standard of living below which no one will have to live. To this end, the nation's cash assistance programs provide individuals and families with access to a subsistence level of income, shelter, health, education, and employment. Social welfare policies also protect people from inequalities built into the market economy by placing a floor under wages, reducing the discriminatory barriers that bar people from jobs, regulating the health and safety of the workplace, and protecting consumers against impure food, drugs, and unsafe highways.

Automatic Stabilizers

Social welfare policy functions economically as well to stimulate the economy during recessions and depressions. Economists refer to social welfare benefits as automatic stabilizers because by putting cash into people's hands, income support programs help to prime the economic pump.[37] For example, during the Depression of the 1930s, advocates of the Social Security Act won public support by arguing that cash assistance programs would turn people without dollars into active consumers and thereby keep business afloat. During subsequent recessions and depressions, the increased purchasing power provided by the nation's cash assistance programs helped to stimulate the production of goods and services, which, in turn, created jobs and reduced unemployment. Without these automatic stabilizers, when the economy sags, it would spiral even further downward, causing more businesses to lay off workers and leaving more families unable to purchase the goods and services that business and industry need to sell in order to survive.

Socializing the Cost of Production

Radicals link the economic functions of social welfare policy more directly to business profits. By asking who benefits from social welfare policy, radicals conclude that social welfare policy operates to subsidize the costs of profitable economic production for business and industry[38] in at least four different ways: by stimulating purchasing power, subsidizing wages, increasing labor productivity, and enforcing work norms.

The cash assistance provided by social welfare programs contributes directly to business profits. By *stimulating purchasing power*, as noted above, the pool of customers available to buy the goods and services produced by business and industry is enlarged. Social welfare policy improves business profits as well by *subsidizing wages*. For years, the federal government's employment and training programs have paid the wages for disadvantaged workers hired by employers for a defined period of time. This financial incentive was designed to encourage employers to hire disadvantaged workers and then to move them into an unsubsidized job. But instead of retaining the subsidized worker when the wage grant ended, employers often replaced one subsidized worker with another. Radicals argue that social welfare policy also subsidizes wages in a less direct way. To the extent that cash benefits, food stamps, housing supplements, and health insurance cover basic living costs of workers, these grants allow employers to pay workers a lower wage.

The third way that social welfare policy increases business profits is by helping to ensure the *productivity of the workforce*.[39] Public spending on health, education, and social services provides employers with the healthy and fit workforce they need at virtually no additional cost to business. The public pays the tab, but the profits stay in private hands. Further, by keeping benefits low and discouraging their use, social welfare policy *enforces both the work ethic and low wages*. The stigma attached to the receipt of public benefits conveys the message that work for any employer on any terms is better than public aid. The small grants provided to those in need encourage people to choose work over public assistance regardless of the wages paid or the safety of the working conditions. Finally, by enlarging the supply of people looking for work, the policy of deterrence makes it easier for employers to pay low wages and harder for unions to negotiate good contracts.[40]

Social Reproduction

The feminist analysis identifies social reproduction as still another economic function of social welfare policy. Social reproduction refers to a series of tasks typically assigned to the family. These include the reproduction of the species (procreation); meeting the basic survival needs of individuals (consumption); rearing and preparing the next generation for adult work and family roles, including acceptance of prevailing values and norms (socialization); and caring for those who are too old, young, ill, or disabled to care for themselves (caretaking). Women's work as consumers and caretakers not only keeps individuals fed, clothed, and sheltered, it also replenishes the energy of family members so that they can put in another day of school or work.

Families need a certain standard of living to successfully carry out their socially assigned tasks of social reproduction. However, because business profits depend on high prices, high productivity, and low labor costs, the market economy often fails to yield the jobs and income needed by the average family to reproduce and maintain itself. Low earnings, substandard housing, inadequate health care, and inferior public education undermine the family's capacity for caretaking. This unsuccessful social reproduction, in turn, harms individual well-being. It can also threaten business profits and social stability. Profits suffer because failure of social reproduction deprives business of consumers, productive workers, and contented voters/citizens. When these conditions jeopardize business interests too much or provoke large-scale social protest, the welfare state steps in with programs to support family functioning, because family maintenance is critical for both business profits and the smooth functioning of wider society.[41]

Of course, conservatives see the economic functions of social welfare policy differently. They argue that social welfare policy *increases* the costs of doing business and otherwise interferes with market functions. From this perspective, the availability of cash benefits, however meager, wrongly allows people to avoid the dirtiest and most dangerous jobs. With fewer people seeking this work, employers have to offer higher wages to recruit a workforce, which cuts into their profits. Minimum-wage laws set a floor under market wages, forcing employers to pay more. Social welfare policy also means more government spending, which conservatives say leads to budget deficits, higher interest rates on government borrowing to cover the deficit, an upward pressure on corporate income taxes, and other profit-reducing measures.

The Political Functions of Social Welfare Policy

The political functions of social welfare policy address the need to reduce social conflict. All large and diverse societies contain many groups or classes, each with distinct interests and goals. Therefore, most governments try to integrate all elements of the population into a coherent system, to win and maintain the people's loyalty, and to legitimate both themselves and the wider social order. To this end, governments hold elections that give the people the opportunity to express their will. They also offer social welfare benefits. Social welfare policy helps to reduce interest group conflict by distributing resources from those with more to those with less. Cash assistance programs, civil rights protections, and employment and training schemes also create more opportunities for those left behind by the dynamics of the market.

A more radical analysis suggests other political functions for social welfare policy. First, this analysis argues that societal conflict stems, not from interest group competition over scarce resources, but from the unequal structure of wealth and power that leaves many needs unmet. At some point, this inequality causes people to become disgruntled or more seriously aggrieved. If too many people become dissatisfied with the system, they may rise up in protest and undermine the conditions for profitable economic activity and the political stability on which it depends. The protest might take the form of not voting, abandoning one political party for another, joining a social movement, or otherwise threatening the desired political stability.

In the United States, such dissatisfaction gave rise to the demands for governmental redress from the trade union, civil rights, women's liberation, and welfare rights movements, among many others. The resulting social welfare concessions, such as greater cash assistance, a higher minimum wage, stronger protection against discrimination, and the addition of family and medical leaves for workers, help people to feel recognized, to value their membership in society, and to be willing to play by the rules rather than challenge them. To the extent that the reforms reduce popular dissatisfaction, the expansion of the welfare state helps to quell disruptive social protest and hold back demands for even wider social change.

In addition to quieting unrest, social welfare provisions help to stabilize the system in another way. By visibly demonstrating a willingness to aid those with less, social welfare provisions help to obscure the reality that governments often take the side of the haves over the have-nots. Should the state appear to be unduly captured by big business, it risks stirring up protest. For example, the recent demands for term limits for legislators and for campaign finance reform sent a loud message to elected officials that the public wanted limits placed on the ability of the rich and powerful to control the political process. In 2002, faced with seemingly endless corporate accounting scandals, President Bush chastised the business community that he typically supports. He publicly expressed "outrage" at this corporate fraud and threatened government investigations of these practices. By making it appear that the government represents the interests of all and by veiling the unequal and undemocratic features of the social structure, the welfare state also helps to legitimize the wider social order and to prevent demands for more radical change.[42]

Nations also deal with conflict and instability through repression and silencing dissent. To this end, they bypass social welfare policy for the more coercive arm of the state. The repression takes various forms, including blaming victims for their unfortunate circumstances, labeling dissenters as disloyal, jailing critics, and calling out the police/national guard to put down a protest. Although the U.S. government resorts to reform more often than repression, our history includes examples of all of the above being used to keep people in line.

Once again, conservatives take the opposite view.[43] They insist that expansive social welfare policy stimulates rather than quiets conflict. Conservatives argue that the expansion of the welfare state during the 1960s generated conflict by fostering too much democratic participation, creating a sense of entitlement to benefits, and by raising people's aspirations. Conflict erupted because social welfare policy led people to make demands on the state and to expect more than the system could provide. Therefore, to limit political conflict, conservatives called for cutting back social programs and curtailing democratic processes. The campaigns to demonize "big government," strengthen the executive branch of government, and cut back or privatize social welfare programs reflect the ongoing efforts to implement this goal.[44]

To return to our original question, social welfare policy has both positive and negative outcomes for individuals and families for at least two reasons. First, there is no agreement about the proper economic and political functions of social welfare policy. As will be discussed in greater detail in chapter 5, conservatives, liberals, radicals, and feminists consistently dispute these issues. Second, the economic and political functions of social welfare policy may undercut, override, or compromise the stated social purpose so that individuals and families get less than what they need.

Social Welfare Policy: Arena of Struggle

Perhaps the best way to define social welfare policy is as an arena of struggle. In this view, social welfare policy represents the outcome of struggles over the distribution of societal resources fueled by its often competing social, economic, and political functions. In addition, social welfare provision has the potential to strengthen the political and economic power of those with less. For example, access to income and services outside the market enables people to survive while avoiding unsafe and insecure jobs as well as unsafe or unhappy marriages.

The U.S. Capitol building, the primary site within the federal government for legislative debates about the roles and functions of social welfare.

Also, by providing an economic backup, social welfare benefits make it possible for those with less income or power to fight back. For this reason, the trade union, civil rights, gay rights, women's, and poor people's movements have struggled for years to secure welfare state protections against the abuses of living and working in a society structured by class, race, heterosexism, and gender inequality. The welfare state is an arena of social, economic, and political struggle because access to income and services outside of work and marriage provides people with the wherewithal to resist, challenge, and change power relations that shape the prevailing status quo.

Likewise for the social work profession, whose work takes place where the individual and society meet. The location of social work between the individual and society often leads practitioners to feel that they must choose between adjusting people and programs to circumstances and challenging the status quo. But, in fact, the history of the profession reveals that since its origins in the late nineteenth century, the twin pressures of containment and change have made social work, like the welfare state, an arena of struggle. Reflecting the mandates of the profession and the historic legacy of activism among social workers, this struggle regularly targeted social welfare policy and social change.[45]

Overview of Major Social Welfare Programs

Now that we have defined social welfare policy and analyzed its competing functions, we are ready to look inside the social welfare system to see, generally, what kinds of programs and services are available to people in need. What follows is a brief description of key social welfare programs in the United States, an overview of the welfare state that highlights its social functions. The chapters in part III examine five of these policy areas in greater depth. These areas—income support, employment, housing, health care, and food—are not only critical in their own right, but have been selected because they are basic to an understanding of the entire social welfare system.

The U.S. welfare state provides people with income maintenance (cash benefits), food, medical care, housing, and a wide range of social services. These programs fall into two major categories: *universal* and *selective*. The key difference between the two is that the universal programs provide benefits to individuals and families regardless of income, whereas the selective measures are designed solely for the poor. Some universal and selective programs are also referred to as *categorical* programs because they serve particular groups of people such as single mothers, veterans, the working poor, elderly individuals, or those with handicaps.[46]

Universal Programs

Universal programs reflect the idea that living and working in an industrial society entails risks over which individuals have little or no control. In the United States, most of the universal programs follow the social insurance model. Like private life, health, automobile, and homeowners insurance, social insurance programs reflect the advantages of pooled protection against known risks. When it comes to social welfare policy, this risk includes the loss of income due to unemployment, old age, illness, disability, and death of a breadwinner. The nation's three main social insurance programs provide retirement pensions, unemployment compensation, and medical care reimbursement. Some service programs for senior citizens are universal, as are some of the programs provided by the Veterans Administration to members of the armed services with service-related conditions. Although not a social welfare program per se, elementary and high school public education represents one of the nation's most universal programs for children and youth.

Many social welfare programs, both social insurance and public assistance, are also called *entitlement* programs. This label highlights the individual's right to benefits and the states' entitlement to federal funding, both of which were built into the 1935 Social Security Act, the foundation of the U.S. welfare state. As chapter 3 explains, the federal budget contains two streams of spending: entitlement and discretionary. The former refers to mandated spending that ensures the federal government will automatically provide the states with funds to cover (often with state matching) the costs of providing benefits to everyone who applies and is eligible for the benefits under state and federal rules. Because no eligible applicant can be turned away for lack of funds, individuals are said to have a *right* to benefits.

Retirement Insurance (Pensions)

The program popularly known as Social Security is technically called Old Age, Survivors, Disability and Health Insurance (OASDHI).[47] The old age, survivors, and disability components protect people against the risk of lost income due to old age, retirement, and disability regardless of income or economic status.

The Social Security Administration operates the retirement program through offices around the country. Today, upwards of 95 percent of all workers qualify for this monthly entitlement. As configured in the 1935 Social Security Act, however, the original retirement pension did not cover farm and domestic workers (the main occupations open to black people in the 1930s). Numerous religious, charitable, and educational institutions that employed many women also negotiated their way out of the program, arguing that nonprofit organizations could not absorb the cost the payroll tax imposed on employers (employers and employees each paid half the cost of the premium). State and local government workers were also exempt. Beginning in 1950, most of the excluded occupations were gradually included, so that today OASDHI is the nation's largest social welfare program.

The program is strongly tied to the labor market. Workers receive benefits based on the number of years they have worked and the level of their wages. In addition, the pension is funded by a payroll deduction. Like an insurance program, workers must purchase this income protection by paying "premiums" in the form of payroll taxes on their wages up to a specified amount. Employers contribute an equal share to the Social Security Trust Fund. By compelling people to insure themselves against the possibility of their own poverty, the Social Security Act forced workers to save for a rainy day and reduced some of problems that government might otherwise have to address.

Congress improved the benefits early on. It added monies for a retired or deceased worker's survivors and dependents in 1939, disability benefits in 1956, and health insurance as Medicare for the aged in 1965. It offered (reduced) early retirement at age 62 in 1972, added cost of living adjustments in 1975, and liberalized benefits for divorced women in 1977. These largely post–World War II expansions ended in the 1980s, when benefit reductions and a drive to privatize the old age pension began.

Although they like the idea of privatization better, conservatives supported the idea of government-sponsored social insurance because it represented a form of thrift. Liberals liked the program for its ability to redistribute income from the working population to the nonworking aged, sick, disabled, and unemployed, that is, from those who are able to pay to those who cannot.

Unemployment Insurance

Unemployment Insurance (UI) is the second entitlement program that originated in the 1935 Social Security Act.[48] This federal-state program protects workers against the temporary loss of income due to recent and involuntary joblessness. Administered by the Employment Security Administration of the U.S. Department of Labor, its target is workers with a strong tie to the labor market. Applicants, however, can qualify for this benefit regardless of their overall income status. Eligibility is based on employment in a covered occupation, work history, minimum earnings, current wage levels, reason for unemployment, availability for work, and willingness to accept a suitable job. In addition, job loss must be due to factors beyond the worker's control, meaning layoffs, not voluntary quits or firings.

Most states provide benefits of half of a worker's salary for up to six months, but not more than a specified maximum dollar amount. The program is funded by a tax on employers based on a specified percentage of each employee's wage. The size of the tax varies with a firm's use of the UI program during the previous year, so that companies with high rates of unemployment pay more than those that lay off fewer workers. Known as *experience rating*, this method was devised to reduce unemployment by giving employers an incentive to stabilize their workforce. Some emergency benefit programs were added in the 1970s for increased protection during long periods of high unemployment. Since the 1980s, both coverage and benefit levels have deteriorated.

Medicare

Medicare was added to the Social Security Act in 1965 (as Title XVIII) to cover the cost of health care for elderly persons who typically face a rising need for medical services.[49] Administered by the Centers for Medicare and Medicaid Services (CMS), of the Department of Health and Human Services, this entitlement program reimburses hospitals and doctors for medical care rendered to covered individuals. The basic payroll tax covers the hospital benefits and additional premiums must be paid to cover doctors' bills and some other outpatient services. Even so, Medicare does not cover many basic medical costs, most notably prescription drugs, long-term custodial care, and catastrophic illness. In recent years, the program has been affected by rising costs and the advent of managed care.

The Older Americans Act

The 1972 Amendments to the 1965 Older Americans Act added nutrition programs for senior citizens age 60 and over (and their spouses) regardless of income.[50] The Administration on Aging funds the states to help community agencies serve food to older Americans. The program also provides shopping assistance, nutrition education, and other supportive services. The U.S. Department of Agriculture contributes food, cash, and commodities.

Veterans' Benefits

Since the Revolutionary War, the government has recognized the service of veterans by providing them with a series of benefits.[51] Today, eligibility for this entitlement depends on discharge from active military service (Army, Navy, Air Force, Marines, Coast Guard, etc.) under other than dishonorable conditions. Administered by the Department of Veterans Affairs (VA), benefits include a veteran's compensation and pension, readjustment benefits, medical care, housing and loan guaranty programs, as well as life insurance, burial benefits, and special counseling and outreach programs. The VA is funded mostly by general revenues, along with some copayments by military personnel.

Most benefits are available regardless of income only to veterans with service-connected conditions. Veterans who fall into this group can qualify for a pension, compensation for disabilities sustained while in service, and death benefits. In 1996, about 22 million disabled veterans and 306,241 survivors received compensation payments. This group of veterans also may receive free inpatient and outpatient medical care in special VA hospitals, priority counseling for sexual trauma or exposure to Agent Orange or radiation, and access to an array of education and training programs. In the 1990s, the VA tightened eligibility rules of many of its programs and curtailed services, making it difficult for veterans to get their needs met.

Selective Programs

The 1935 Social Security Act established a dual-income maintenance system. It created universal social insurance programs administered by the federal government and selective public assistance administered through federal-state partnerships. Groups of people not covered by either of these two federally funded programs depended on state and local programs for assistance.

Selective programs reflect the idea that scarce public resources should be targeted to those most in need. Therefore, applicants for the programs must establish need, typically by proving that their income and assets fall below a specified poverty line, either the federal threshold or one established by the program itself. This process of establishing eligibility is called passing a means test or an income test. Many income maintenance and social service programs fall into the selective group. The nation's means-tested income support programs include direct cash assistance programs (TANF, SSI, and general assistance) and noncash income support programs (food stamps, public housing, and Medicaid). Selective programs tend to be funded by some combination of federal and state income tax revenues (paid by individuals and corporations).

The most well-known and most controversial selective program is widely known as welfare.[52] The original welfare program, ADC, was included in the 1935 Social Security Act (Title IV) to assist poor children deprived of financial support by the family's main breadwinner. The program's name was changed to AFDC in 1967.

ADC became increasingly controversial after World War II and subject to public hostility, in part because the composition of the caseload shifted from a predominance of white widows to young, never-married African American and Latino mothers. Originally designed to enable single mothers to stay home and care for their children, new rules began in the 1960s to mandate more work from welfare recipients and penalize poor women for having children outside of marriage.

The program's requirements were tightened many times thereafter until August 22, 1996, when Congress passed welfare reform. Officially known as the Personal Responsibility and Work Opportunity Reconciliation Act, the PRWORA stripped AFDC of its entitlement status by converting it into a state-run block grant and capping its funds at $16.5 billion for the first five years (1997–2002). Prior to welfare reform, AFDC represented a federal-state partnership with regard to funding and administration. Today, the states are largely responsible for administering TANF, although not all federal regulation has ended. Federal funding comes with a performance bonus that rewards states for moving recipients from welfare to work, state maintenance of effort requirements, and many other mandates. The states must also work within federal work, child support, and other guidelines. Nonetheless, increased state control over program decisions has led to enormous changes at the local level and even wider variation among the states than already existed in the prior AFDC program.

The main beneficiaries of TANF's cash assistance continue to be children without a father in the home and their mothers who are unable to work or who are employed but earning a very low income. The benefits, always low, rarely lift a family of three above the national poverty line in any state. They are available to low-income parents (mostly mothers) who have not reached the new five-year lifetime limit on assistance and who meet federal work participation requirements. Assistance is no longer available to individuals convicted of a drug felony, to parents under age 18 not living in an adult-supervised setting, and to many immigrants. If parents do not cooperate with child support enforcement, work requirements, and an array of other rules, benefits can be reduced. In addition to tightening the work requirement, TANF intensified the rules that regulated the marital and childbearing behavior of recipients. Since 1996, the welfare rolls have dropped sharply, although reasons for this decline are debated. More recently, changing economic conditions have caused the number of recipients to rise in thirty-seven states.

Supplemental Security Income

SSI, an entitlement program administered by the Social Security Administration, assists aged, blind, and disabled persons who do not qualify for social insurance. The 1935 Social Security Act included public assistance programs known as Old Age Assistance and Aid to the Blind. In 1956, Congress added a third program called Aid to the Permanently and Totally Disabled. In 1974, the programs were federalized and given the common name SSI. Coming under federal control, they were supported by federal funds, with the possibility of state supplementation. AFDC was the only public assistance program not federalized at this time.

SSI eligibility is based on a person's categorical status (recipients must be either aged, blind, or disabled) and strict evidence of financial need. If a person lives with a family member who provides food and shelter, the value of this support is subtracted from the benefit check. A good life insurance policy can also render someone ineligible for this assistance. With the enactment of TANF, many legal immigrants lost access to SSI (and food stamps).

Although it is not high, the average monthly SSI benefit exceeds that for TANF households. The difference reflects the widely held belief that the elderly, blind, and disabled recipients of SSI are more "deserving" of public aid than single mothers on TANF because the former are regarded as in need through no fault of their own. However, beginning in the 1980s, opponents of welfare began to accuse disabled people of faking their condition to avoid work.

General Assistance

General assistance (GA) programs are typically administered by the state or local government and cover individuals who do not qualify for federal social insurance, TANF, or SSI.[53] Most of the GA beneficiaries are men and women living on their own whose irregular work histories and lack of children in the home render them ineligible for other programs. Therefore, many cities and states provide some kind of limited GA such as cash aid for a few months, restricted access to food stamps, health benefits, and possibly burial expenses.

Food Stamps

Administered by the Food and Consumer Service of the U.S. Department of Agriculture, the current Food Stamp Program was created in 1964 to reduce the impact of agricultural price supports on low-income households and to enable the poor to secure a nutritionally balanced diet.[54] This means-tested, federally funded entitlement provides vouchers or coupons that can be used like money to buy food below regular market prices. Food stamps are available to public assistance recipients as well as other individuals and families with income below the poverty line. Since welfare reform, for a variety of reasons, national food stamp rolls have declined.

School Food Programs

Other food and nutrition programs focus exclusively on poor children.[55] This includes programs authorized by the 1946 School Lunch Act; the 1966 Child Nutrition Act, which created the smaller School Breakfast Program; the Special Milk Program (1954); the Summer Food Service Program (1968); and the Child and Adult Care Food Program.

Special Supplemental Nutrition Program for Women, Infants, and Children

Established in 1972 to improve the nutrition of women and children, the federally funded WIC program provides food assistance, nutrition risk screening, and related services to low-income pregnant and postpartum women and their infants and low-income children up to age 5.[56] Participants receive WIC coupons, which can be used to buy nutritionally organized food packages in grocery stores. Administered by the U.S. Department of Agriculture in cooperation with state health departments, Indian tribal organizations, and local agencies, the program operates at more than eight thousand sites, involves about forty-six thousand merchants, and serves more than 7 million women and children.

Medicaid

Medicaid (Title XIX) of the Social Security Act became law in 1965 (along with Medicare).[57] Unlike Medicare, which is a social insurance program for the elderly regardless of income, Medicaid is a means-tested public assistance program serving just the poor. Administered by CMS, Medicaid is an entitlement program funded by the federal government and the states. As with TANF, the states have considerable control over the parameters of the program, so benefits and rules vary widely around the country.

Medicaid provides health insurance coverage to low-income individuals and families who meet its income eligibility requirements. Most people who receive public assistance are also eligible for Medicaid, as are pregnant women and children under age 6 with income up to 133 percent of the poverty line. Almost 90 percent of the states extend coverage to people not on public assistance but whose low income renders them "medically needy," defined as groups similar to those covered by Medicaid except with slightly more income and assets. Medicaid benefits are provided in kind: instead of receiving cash to pay medical bills, patients receive services from doctors, hospitals, and other health care providers who are then reimbursed by the government. The beneficiaries do not have to pay a premium, but some states have cost-sharing rules that require small deductibles or copayments by beneficiaries. Medicaid also pays for nursing home care for older and disabled persons.

The 1996 federal welfare reform law changed some Medicaid rules. States may now end benefits to adults who do not meet TANF work requirements and deny benefits to many documented and undocumented immigrants. TANF also ended the automatic link between Medicaid and public assistance, which cost many low-income families access to Medicaid even though they remained eligible. As with TANF and food stamps, the Medicaid rolls have declined sharply since 1996.

Public Housing

One strategy for providing housing to low-income households is to build additional units.[58] In the late 1930s and early 1940s, the federal government built large apartment buildings for this purpose that came to be known as "the projects." Initially, mostly two-parent, and low-income, working-class families occupied the apartments. But by the 1960s families of color had become overrepresented in these units and federal input dwindled. During the 1960s, the U.S. Department of Housing and Urban Development (HUD) also built smaller housing units and located them in various neighborhoods. These apartments, about 1.4 million, are rented below market value at a percentage of the tenant's income, now about 30 percent. The waiting lists are very long. The U.S. Department of Agriculture's Farm Service Agency administers the housing program for rural families and domestic farm laborers.

Subsidized Rentals

The supply of low-cost housing available through private landlords and public housing has never met the country's need for affordable shelter.[59] Therefore, the federal government began to subsidize housing construction and rental payments. Section 202 of the 1959 Housing Act provides low-interest loans to nonprofit organizations interested in expanding the supply of low-cost housing for low-income elderly and disabled persons. The 1974 Housing and Community Development Act included Section 8 to provide rent subsidies for low-income families. Instead of providing an actual apartment, these programs subsidize the rent for a privately owned house or apartment. The largest and most well-known of the rent subsidy programs, Section 8 now serves more families than does public housing, providing them with a voucher to cover about 30 percent of their rent. With subsidized rent programs, the individual still must locate an affordable residence that meets housing code standards; this remains a challenge in many cities. Many low-income families benefit from rental assistance; it also helps private landlords and real estate developers.

Energy Assistance

In the 1970s and 1980s, rising fuel and weatherization costs led the federal government to provide fuel assistance.[60] In 1978, the Department of Health and Human Services established the Low-Income Home Energy Assistance Program. LHEAP provides the states with block grant funds to help the poor and very poor pay their residential heating and cooling bills.

Social Services

The welfare state also includes a wide range of social services. Many are not means-tested, and most are not entitlements. Many social workers are employed in the public and private agencies that provide these services, more than are found in the social insurance, public assistance, medical care reimbursement, housing, and food programs already described. Unlike most of the former programs, many of the social services are publicly funded but delivered by nonprofit and for-profit organizations.

Employment Services

Many programs help people with employment-related problems.[61] The largest provider is the State Employment Service, which places millions of people in jobs every year. Federally sponsored vocational rehabilitation programs provide job training as well as a range of other services to help the physically and mentally disabled become employable. Welfare recipients are often required to participate in mandatory work and training programs as a condition of receiving aid. The original mandatory employment program was the 1967 Work Incentive Program. The 1996 TANF program requires that all recipients either be employed or begin employment training within two years of entering the program. If work cannot be found, many recipients must work off their benefits in the Work Experience Program, also called workfare. The 1998 Workforce Investment Act provides a range of job search, assessment, and vocational training to youth and adults in need of work. Designed to be universal, welfare recipients and the poor in fact receive priority.

Child Welfare Services

Child welfare involves providing social services to children and youth whose parents and/or communities cannot adequately provide or care for them.[62] The 1909 White House Conference on Children, which signaled the federal government's initial concern about the welfare of children, led to the establishment of the Children's Bureau in 1912. The Bureau addressed a wide range of issues, from health and child labor to delinquency and orphaned children. Child welfare programs were also included as Title V of the 1935 Social Security Act, leading the states to develop child welfare programs. The programs were expanded beginning in the 1960s; important additions to the system included the Child Abuse Prevention and Treatment Act (1974), Title XX of the Social Security Act (1975); the Adoption Assistance and Child Welfare Act (1980), emphasizing permanency planning; and the Adoption and Safe Families Act (1997), promoting out-of-home care. In general, child welfare programs offer adoption, foster care, family preservation, permanency planning, and protective services for children at risk of neglect or abuse.

Community Maternal and Child Health Services

Many states supplement Medicaid and Medicare with other special health programs to reduce infant mortality, rehabilitate blind and disabled children, and expand prenatal health services.[63]

Mental Health Services

The federal government became involved with mental health care through the National Mental Health Act of 1946, which supported research on psychiatric disorders, training of mental health personnel, and grants to states to establish clinics and demonstration programs.[64] The Act also established the National Institute of Mental Health (1949) as a branch of the public health service. Its emphasis on community over institutional care eventually led to the Mental Retardation and Community Mental Health Center Construction Act (1963), which included $150 million for the construction of community mental health centers. Today, a variety of public and private services exist for people with mental health problems. Among others, the community mental health centers, staffed by psychiatrists, psychologists, social workers, and other specialists, offer individual and group counseling, drug and alcohol treatment, and many other mental health services. Some people receive mental health care in public and private institutions, where the care ranges from very good to just custodial. Others admit themselves for care; many others are committed involuntarily. Most recently, managed care principles designed to control costs have overhauled the delivery of mental health services.

Probation and Parole

When people are released from prison, they often are placed on parole.[65] Others convicted of a crime may be placed on probation rather than be sent to prison. In either case, to stay out of prison, the individual must submit to supervision and follow a strict set of rules. Supervision often involves regular visits and the acceptance of services from a parole or probation officer linked to the corrections system.

Legal Services

Created during the War on Poverty in the 1960s, legal services assists the poor with rent disputes, contracts, welfare rules, minor police actions, housing regulations, and more—but not criminal cases.[66] Established in 1974, the Legal Service Corporation (LSC) is financed with federal tax dollars and some private monies. Under political pressure from conservatives, congressional authorization for the LSC expired in 1980, but Congress has funded it annually since then.

In addition to helping individuals, legal service lawyers seek policy change by bringing suits against city welfare departments, housing authorities, public health agencies, and other governmental bodies. However, since the late 1970s, Congress has limited the role of legal service funds in lobbying, class action suits, political activity, cases involving nontherapeutic abortions, undocumented immigrants, and school desegregation. Due to funding cutbacks, legal services has about three hundred offices around the country, down from five hundred.

Given social welfare's increased complexity, many people need help just to find, access, and receive the help they need.[67] This need has led to the development of a wide range of information and referral services provided by the private nonprofit sector and some government-operated ombudsman programs.

Organizing Principles: Who Benefits from Universal or Selective Provision?

As noted earlier, social welfare programs fall into two main categories, universal and selective, with the key difference being that the universal programs provide benefits regardless of income, whereas selective measures are designed solely for the poor. The difference between the two types of programs also reflects different philosophies about the value of government service and who is "deserving" of government help.

Universalists argue that all people in society face similar risks and should be assisted regardless of income. At one time or another, we all face a variety of common social needs: young people need education and sick people need medical care; the elderly, disabled, and unemployed need income support. Univeralists believe that addressing these risks is a proper role for government. In sharp contrast, selectivists believe that social provision should be carefully targeted to specific beneficiaries who can demonstrate their need for government benefits. They hold that taxpayers' dollars should not be spent on benefits for people who can afford to meet their own needs, but should be restricted to groups that legitimately cannot fend for themselves.

Reflecting these divergent philosophies, the eligibility determination process, type of benefits offered, administrative auspices, and populations served by the two sets of programs vary sharply.[68]

Eligibility Process

It is much easier to qualify for universal than for selective benefits. Universal programs such as social insurance, veterans' benefits, and public education provide benefits to certain groups of people such as the retired, the disabled, the unemployed, injured workers, children under age 16, and veterans. As long as legislation includes a precise definition of the beneficiary group, membership in the group can be readily determined. Even so, it is much easier to determine age and employment status than occupational disability. The application process for universal programs tends to be short and simple, presumes need, and preserves individual dignity.

In contrast, it is much more difficult to establish eligibility for selective benefits such as those provided by the range of public assistance programs described above including TANF, SSI, and food stamps. First, poverty has to be defined, and then methods such as a means test have to be devised to separate the poor from the nonpoor. Detailed application forms demand information about income, assets, family circumstances, and a host of other topics. The application process for selective programs is long, tedious, and demeaning.

Type of Benefits

The universal and selective programs provide different kinds of benefits. Universal programs pay standardized benefits that are clearly specified in the parent legislation. Therefore, every individual who applies for the Social Security retirement benefit receives the same benefit if they have worked the same number of years, earned the same income, and retired at the same age. The benefits are standard across the nation, reasonably generous, and regarded as legitimate. Reflecting this positive assessment, the benefits are referred to as insurance and compensation.

Selective program benefits are more flexible, more complex, and less standardized. The amounts received by individuals tend to be meager, set by complicated formulas, calculated by individual caseworkers, and subject to welfare department discretion and frequently contain errors. The typically low benefit levels vary by state, family size, work effort, income, and assets. TANF introduced even greater state variation, including wide differences with regard to time limits, work requirements, family structure, and the use of sanctions. The benefits not regarded legitimate are often called a "handout" or "dole."

Administration and Financing

The universal programs tend to be federally financed and federally administered, with decisions about eligibility and benefit levels made nationally. The selective programs tend to be federally financed (at least in part) but more highly dependent on state and local funds. They are administered locally by states, counties, or cities. Local administration leaves programs subject to public debate at two or more levels of government and increases both their visibility and vulnerability to budget cuts.

Populations Served

The universal and selective programs serve different groups. The universal programs tend to serve the nonpoor as well as the poor. The beneficiaries are more likely to be middle class, white, older, and male. The selective programs serve the poor and, in some cases, the working poor. The beneficiaries tend to be younger, female, and persons of color.

Implications

In general, universal insurance programs are more popular with users, program administrators, and the general public. Because they are highly stigmatized, the selective "handouts" tend to be avoided if at all possible. By and large, the universal programs are less visible, concealed in tax laws, and clothed in protective language such as insurance and tax credits. In stark contrast, the selective programs are obvious, open, and clearly and negatively labeled as charity, relief, or assistance. The selective programs also involve considerable intervention and intrusion into personal and family life. Unlike the universal programs, which have few, if any, behavioral requirements, many of the selective programs (most notably TANF) require recipients to modify their work and family behavior as a condition of aid. In exchange for assistance, recipients have to surrender privacy, control, and autonomy.

The simplicity of the universal programs' application process, the uniformity of their benefits, and the lack of stigma and intrusion reflect a view of the recipients as worthy and deserving. Thus, the rules and regulations encourage applicants, generate solidarity, and promote social cohesion. In contrast, the complex and intrusive application process associated with the selective programs reflects a deep distrust of the poor, fear of welfare fraud, and hostility to government provision to the poor. It typically deters applicants, demeans individuals, and divides one group of people from another.

Given the different populations served by each type of program, the U.S. social welfare programs are stratified by class, gender, and race, with the more privileged groups receiving the generous, popular, nonstigmatized universal benefits and the less privileged relying on the meager, unpopular, highly stigmatized grants from selective programs.

Kinds of Benefits

The programs listed above suggest that social welfare benefits take many forms, including cash, in-kind benefits, services, opportunities, and power.

Cash Benefits

Cash benefits refer to direct grants provided to individuals and families in the nation's social insurance and public assistance programs and indirect grants such as fiscal welfare benefits. These include tax arrangements that let individuals and families keep more of their own income (see the earlier discussion of fiscal welfare). Cash benefits offer recipients considerable control over their purchasing power and place a high value on individual choice.

In-Kind Benefits

In-kind benefits help people cover basic needs through vouchers, credits, reimbursement of providers, and the direct provision of commodities. Food stamps, Section 8 rental subsidies, and child care tax credits are examples of vouchers and credits. Medicare and Medicaid offer reimbursement to health care providers. Food distribution and public housing represent the direct provision of needed commodities. In-kind benefits that ensure that public dollars are used to cover specific needs limit recipients' freedom to choose what is consumed with their government benefits. Their use places value on social control.

Social Services

Not all needs can be met by providing money. Nonmonetary types of help have a long history in the United States in mutual aid, philanthropy, and social services. Social services include counseling, supportive services, information and referral, child care, socialization, and employment and training programs that directly or indirectly increase people's ability to function fully in society. One of the advantages of social services is their individualized attention to need and the specific response to individuals in their own context. Service providers must also be alert to avoid inappropriately delving too deeply into the lives of individuals and families seeking help.[69] The provision of services places a high value on individual rehabilitation, growth, and development.

Opportunities

Government programs also create and distribute opportunities. Indeed, the federal office that administered the War on Poverty was called the Office of Economic Opportunity. The government creates opportunities in various ways by offering incentives to reach desired ends, by reducing discriminatory barriers, and by subsidizing education and training programs that help people gain new skills and attain upward mobility.

Social services to the elderly help them to maintain their dignity and independence.

Power

Some social welfare policies enhance the political power of recipients. In the 1960s and 1970s, antipoverty policy made "maximum feasible participation of the poor" a condition of funding in the decision-making centers of community programs. Community action programs hired low-income community residents as staff and increased their representation on agency boards. To the extent that government benefits redistribute income and other resources from the haves to the have-nots, they also transfer a modicum of power.

Now that you can define social welfare policy, understand its functions, and have a picture of the types of programs included in the U.S. welfare state, you are ready to examine how and why social policy changes. Chapters 3 through 6 explore the triggers of social change in the economy, the political process, ideology, social movements, and history. Chapters 7 through 12 apply this model of analysis to key welfare state programs.

II

The Policy Model

3

The Economy and Social Welfare

Economics is usually defined as "the study of how societies use scarce resources to produce valuable commodities and distribute them among different people."[1] Such a broad definition should include social welfare. Yet most people continue to think of social welfare as a separate part of the modern economy. There is the market economy, the private sector, where profit guides decisions about people's investments and work, and then somewhere off to the side there is social welfare for children, the elderly, the sick, and the disabled—those who cannot cope in this demanding environment. This formulation is misleading. Seeking to divide the indivisible, it perpetuates the idea that social welfare constitutes a charitable but not wholly essential addition to a perfectly functioning economy.

In reality, the role of social welfare in the modern U.S. economy includes three distinct tasks that go to the heart of our economic life. Without each one individually, and certainly without all of them together, the U.S. economy could not operate.

As indicated in chapter 2, the first task of social welfare is to reduce economic insecurity. Social Security for the elderly performs this function, as do unemployment benefits for the unemployed, and TANF (popularly called welfare) for poor mothers and their children. By giving their recipients a little more money to spend, these programs supplement the total amount of consumer spending in the economy and cushion the effects of poverty.

The second task of social welfare affects even more people. This task involves social regulations that aim to protect the citizenry from the harmful consequences of the market. For example, because the market does not put a price on air and water, it lacks a method of calculating the true cost of pollution. When companies claim a profit, they often can do so because the real costs do not appear on their balance sheet. That is why environmental regulations must draw on standards outside the market to preserve the quality of our air and water. Likewise, on the job, rules about occupational safety seek to limit the risks of working in dangerous conditions. These rules save lives. They also increase productivity, because it is employees' skills, and not merely their fear of unemployment, that keeps them on the job.

The third task involves government spending on many aspects of the public infrastructure. The government not only spends money to provide individuals with education and health care, it also helps to build the schools and hospitals that make these services possible. Expanding this conception of the government's role, spending on the public infrastructure can include the construction of piers, bridges, and highways to facilitate commercial activity, the development of industrial zones to subsidize business, and even the maintenance of parks to provide workers with suitable forms of recreation. Although social workers may not specifically engage in industrial development, no conception of social welfare in the modern U.S. economy would be complete without recognizing this important role.

One overriding contradiction runs through all of these tasks. When social welfare reduces economic insecurity, regulates the environment and the workplace, and spends money on the public infrastructure, it both protects people against the market *and* contributes to the market's profitability. Separate from the market, social welfare gives people money and a better quality of life. Yet, at the same time, more money, healthier and more productive workers, and a robust public infrastructure help to stimulate business. In an unavoidable contradiction, social welfare stands in opposition to the marketplace while simultaneously enhancing its functioning.

From the early 1970s through the terrorist attack of September 11, 2001, and the subsequent collapse of Enron, most U.S. policymakers tried to alter the terms of this paradox. Instead of embracing the features of social welfare that oppose the market, they tried to make social policy more market-like.[2] Pressured by business and influenced by many Americans wary of too much government intervention, they insisted on work for welfare clients, questioned the usefulness and expense of environmental regulations, and fought over which state could offer a prospective business the best public infrastructure and the largest taxpayer subsidy. The very breadth of these functions demonstrate that, contrary to popular understanding, social welfare performs a vital function in the economy. With the collapse of Enron, WorldCom, and Arthur Andersen, among others, the depth of the corporate scandals in 2002 also cast doubt on the conception of social welfare that has triumphed since the 1970s.

We will revisit these issues later in the chapter, when we understand more fully the interaction of the economy and social welfare. But first, to understand what social welfare actually does, we must familiarize ourselves with some basic economic terms. Then our work of understanding the relationship of social welfare to the economy can really begin.

The Words We Use

The words we use to describe the economy fall into three distinct categories. The first category includes words that describe the structure of the economy, especially its basic institutions. Terms like *the market* and *monopoly* belong here. Then there are the terms in the second category, which seek to measure the economy's functioning: how it is doing, as well as who in the economy is doing well. Terms like *recession* and *depression* measure how the economy is doing; phrases such as *income inequality* and *wealth distribution* measure who is doing well. Finally, in the third category, a whole cluster of terms describe the substance and tools of economic policy. Phrases such as *fiscal policy*, *monetary policy*, *entitlements*, and *social spending* belong in this group. Familiarity with the terms in these three categories will equip the student with a good basis for understanding the relationship between economics and social welfare policy.

The Structure of the Economy

Let's begin then with some definitions. The first distinction to be made is between *macroeconomics* and *microeconomics*. Macroeconomics addresses the issue of the economy as a whole. We will discuss it now and then talk about microeconomics, which deals with firms, supply, demand, and prices.

Our analysis begins with a basic question: Is the economy a *market economy?* A market is a mechanism by which buyers and sellers interact to determine the price and quantity of a good or service;[3] a market economy is one in which most products and services are commodities produced for sale, usually at a profit, on the open market. From ancient times to the present, people have bought, sold, and traded goods in many different kinds of economies. But a market economy, one that is organized around both extensive markets and a universal right to private property, is unique to capitalism.

But didn't people own things in other societies? Of course they did. Private ownership existed in medieval Europe, in ancient India, in China, and in the Islamic societies. The difference is that not everyone had this right, and there was no market system. When people did trade, the trade was mostly production and distribution following tradition or the orders of a lord, where only the leftovers made it into the market stalls. And there are other crucial distinctions. Peasants were not free to move as they wished, because without either a right of contract or a right to withhold their labor, they lacked the rights that workers would subsequently acquire and had to submit to their masters. Furthermore, because land was not for sale, economic life under feudalism was quite stable. In modern economies, it is common to talk about *factors of production*, a term that describes how land, capital, and labor are combined to produce goods. In a precapitalist economy, however, there were no factors of production, because land, capital, and labor were not for sale.[4]

This description of the feudal economy contrasts sharply with today's U.S. economy. In the modern U.S. economy, the market pervades every aspect of human life, private property is sacrosanct, and though rejecting a job may cost them dearly, employees have a legal right to work for whom they choose. In this market economy, trillions of transactions occur every day. Varying in size from the sale of a chocolate bar at the local candy store to the purchase of huge, multinational corporations, these transactions are all based on a common belief—presumably held by every buyer and every seller—that each occurred at a "fair" price. Many microeconomists praise what they perceive as the voluntary nature of this exchange, on the grounds that if the seller did not want to sell and the buyer did not want to buy, no sale would have taken place.

Of course, the setting of prices is rarely that simple. Even in the United States, where the government plays a relatively small role in the economy, the government usually establishes a legal and regulatory framework for these transactions. Indeed, when public officials moved to shrink this regulatory framework, they brought about the corporate scandals of 2002, which cost many workers their jobs and many investors their nest eggs. The scandals demonstrated once again why there are rules about what can be designated "a chocolate bar" as well as laws about how one must go about buying a corporation. These laws inevitably create a new framework for the transaction, and sometimes, they even have the effect of tilting the playing field toward the buyer or the seller.

Plainly, the most powerful exception to the notion of a voluntary exchange in a market economy is the *labor market*. The existence of a market for labor is one of the distinguishing features of a market economy: workers compete to sell their labor at the most favorable price—meaning, in practice, the highest possible wage. At the same time, however, it is clear that the market for labor is qualitatively different from the market for goods, because workers need to sell their labor to survive. By comparison, although employers may sometimes want to hire new workers, their search for additional help is hardly as pressing: even if they make less money, a labor shortage rarely jeopardizes their standard of living. In a situation where workers must work but employers may or may not need them, the difference in power is far too great to describe the wage they negotiate as a voluntary exchange.

Governments coexist with market economies at many different degrees of influence.[5] In some countries, such as the United States, market economies have broad public support and the role of the government has been limited. As a result, less than 33 percent of the economy comes from government spending—about 20 percent from the federal government and another 12 percent from states and localities. By contrast, the Western European countries spend, on average, about 50 percent more, with Sweden, the leader, circulating about 60 percent of its total economic output through the government.[6] Market economies may value markets, but the mere existence of a market economy does not dictate a particular level of government intervention. In fact, depending on the country, the government in a market economy might or might not assume responsibility for services like child care, health care, education, and housing.

In modern economies, the dominant form of business enterprise is the *corporation*. Corporations are a relatively new form of business structure; until the late nineteenth century, most businesses were small, family-owned enterprises. By themselves, each of these enterprises was too small to fix prices or influence the total quantity of goods in the marketplace.[7] Then the era of "robber barons" (1880–1900) transformed the structure of modern business. Men like John D. Rockefeller in oil and Andrew Carnegie in steel forged huge corporations, so that by the 1920s, the two hundred largest nonfinancial enterprises controlled 49 percent of all corporate wealth. Moreover, unlike the small enterprise, stockholders no longer ran these corporations. That task instead passed to management, which still tried to boost the value of the corporation for shareholders but otherwise effectively separated ownership from control.[8]

This separation of ownership and control heralded the dominance of *monopolies*. A monopoly is a corporation that effectively dominates its industry. If it is not actually the sole provider of the industry's goods or services, it is nonetheless responsible for 75 percent or more of the industry's output, a level at which it can determine prices and dictate the introduction of new products.[9] True monopolies are unusual in the United States today. Instead, *oligopolies* are far more common.

An oligopoly is an industry that is controlled by several firms. Looking at the U.S. economy today, we can identify oligopolies in many industries. For example, media ownership is tightly concentrated, with the major television and radio stations, magazines, newspapers, and publishing houses belonging to ever fewer corporations.[10] Airlines, computers, automobiles, soft drinks, household appliances—in every instance, we all can name the dominant brands. Although these brand names may not be monopolies in the strictest sense, their size and power have grown to the point where they often eclipse the economic power of whole nations. As just one index of their growing dominance, by 2000, General Motors was a bigger economic force than Denmark, IBM sales surpassed the economy of Singapore, and fifty-one of the one hundred largest economies in the world were corporations.[11]

Yet small businesses remain quite common in the United States. In fact, 58 percent of all the firms in the economy gross less than $25 million a year, and firms with fewer than twenty workers—many of the nation's druggists, dry cleaners, and local retail stores—employ 18 percent of the labor force. But although small businesses are politically influential, it is misleading to exaggerate their economic impact: the payroll of the sixteen thousand firms with more than five hundred workers exceeds that of the more than 5.5

million firms with fewer than that number. To give some sense of this difference in scale, Wal-Mart, first in the *Fortune* 500 list of 2002's biggest corporations, earned $220 billion dollars while employing 1.4 million people; ranked seventh, Citigroup earned only $112 billion, but its assets exceeded $1 trillion.[12]

Globalization is the newest and perhaps most important structural term. The term usually refers to the increasingly global nature of the world economy and, particularly, to the dominant role of the United States within it. In truth, however, globalization actually involves two distinct, though related processes. The first is the trading of goods and services; the second refers to huge shifts in financial capital and currency trading. Both of these processes have led, in turn, to the creation of a global labor market.

In the first process, goods and services move rapidly around the globe. Some of these goods—oil from Kuwait, diamonds from Africa—are raw materials that can be obtained only in their country of origin. Others—Japanese cars largely assembled in the United States, U.S. computers with parts from Malaysia, Nike sportswear made in China and Vietnam—go from one country to another, each another step in the production process of a multinational corporation. Because workers in different countries compete for new investments, this aspect of globalization always entails a risk that someone somewhere will be willing to perform the work at a lower wage. In the United States particularly, this option means that companies can play workers off against one another, using the mere threat of moving overseas to limit their wage increases.

It would be wrong to exaggerate the extent of this phenomenon. First, just 25 percent of the U.S. economy consists of imports and exports, and 70 percent of that trade occurs with other high-wage countries. Second, although it is easy to move industrial jobs overseas and the global information network makes it possible to hire cheaper technical labor in other countries, businesses cannot realistically threaten workers in service industries that rely on direct personal contact. When you buy a meal at McDonald's, the worker behind the counter must hand you the burger and fries: he or she cannot fax them to you from another country. Hence, although overall, globalization depresses wages, it affects some parts of the economy less directly.

The second dimension of globalization refers to the movement of financial capital. Currency traders play the markets, betting for or against a nation's currency. Money also speeds from one country to another as stock markets rise or fall and perceptions of political stability influence business investment. When countries in economic difficulty seek aid, they must turn to the World Bank and the International Monetary Fund. But to obtain aid from these international institutions, countries must agree to restructure their economy around the needs of external financial interests. Paring their economy's social spending, they privatize public utilities, end land reform, and reduce benefits. Because most people's living standards decline to satisfy payment of the foreign debt, they become even more willing to accept whatever private investment is offered.[13] Positioned nearer the high end of the international wage scale, U.S. workers cannot easily win this race to the bottom.

This wage pressure has significant policy implications. The principle of *less eligibility* dictates that someone on public assistance must have a lower standard of living than the worst-paid worker. A downward pressure on wages, then, usually places a downward pressure on social welfare. Although other countries have started from a higher level of spending, this consequence of globalization is one reason why, in recent years, social benefits have been cut throughout the developed world.

Altogether, some economists call the terms that we have defined in this section *a social structure of accumulation* (SSA).[14] Though it sounds imposing, the phrase is simply meant to capture the idea that different systems of production—and their accompanying socioeconomic institutions—characterize different economic periods. The South before the Civil War (1861–1865) had plantations and a slave workforce and government that rarely intervened in the economy. By comparison, in the industrial era (1930s–1970s), large corporations employed millions of workers, many of whom were unionized, and the government intervened more frequently. Most recently, we have shifted to a postindustrial service economy in which financial corporations play an ever larger role, fewer workers belong to unions, and government has cut back many social welfare benefits. In each of these eras, a distinct set of social, political, and economic institutions operated to ensure that profits could be made and the system would work smoothly. When the system did work, businesses would invest more and better economic conditions were likely to result. But when profits declined and the system became shaky, economic growth slowed, unemployment increased, and people's standard of living declined. These conditions exacerbate conflicts between classes and institutions and eventually lead to the development of a new social structure of accumulation.

Microeconomics

Beneath these large, structural, macroeconomic questions lies the entire field of microeconomics. As indicated earlier, microeconomics is concerned with the behavior of individual entities such as firms and households, most especially with the setting of prices. And fundamental to the setting of prices is the concept of *supply and demand*.[15]

The laws of supply and demand determine when markets clear, that is, when sellers can find enough buyers and buyers can find enough sellers. If the supply is greater than the demand, the price falls; if it is less, the price rises. When supply and demand balance out, they create an *equilibrium* price. Microeconomists see the existence of an equilibrium price as proof that the economy is operating efficiently. In the words of economist Robert J. Barro:

When the markets clear, it is impossible to improve on any outcomes by matching potential borrowers and lenders or by bringing together potential buyers and sellers of commodities. Cleared markets already accomplish all of these mutually advantageous trades. Thus, the assumption that markets clear is closely tied to the view that the individuals who participate in and organize markets—and who are guided by the pursuit of their own interests—end up generating efficient outcomes.[16]

In reality, the process of establishing an equilibrium price can actually be quite complicated. After all, many different factors can affect demand, including the price of the good or service; the income of the consumer (price alone may be less a factor to the affluent consumer); the price of related goods (if the original item became too expensive, is there something similar that could be substituted for it?); tastes (it is hard to sell short skirts when long skirts are in fashion); and expectations (people may not want to buy a new computer if they expect a better one to be available next month). Influences on the adequacy of the supply are equally numerous. Certainly, if the price is high, producers are likely to increase production. But other factors that might affect the supply include the cost of input prices (the price of sugar as one part of the cost of ice cream); improvements in technology (a new ice cream machine reduces the number of hours needed to produce each gallon); expectations of greater or lesser sales in the future (sales of ice cream rise in the summer); and judgments about the intentions of other sellers (too many producers making too much will reduce, rather than increase, the price).[17] Together, these factors enter into the ongoing determination of an equilibrium price, which supply and demand establish by constant readjustment to one another.

Economists, however, recognize two exceptions to this process. The first exception occurs because prices are *sticky*. A sticky price is one that fails to respond quickly to changes in demand. If wages are low, for example, workers may lack adequate incentives and reduce the quantity of work. Alternatively, prices may be fixed for a longer term because workers have successfully negotiated a multiyear contract. Last, there are *menu costs*, prices that respond slowly to changes in demand because they are listed in printed materials such as a catalogue.[18]

Pure public goods constitute the second exception to this process of supply and demand. Pure public goods have three characteristics. First, one individual's consumption of a public good does not interfere with its enjoyment by another. Unlike private goods such as the purchase of clothing or a doctor's services that cannot be used simultaneously, you and any number of other people can navigate by a lighthouse or listen to the weather service. Second, public goods cannot target their benefits at particular people: a car might benefit one person instead of another, but the benefits of a national defense system extend to everybody. Finally, there is no way that an individual, acting alone, can decide on how much of a public good should be purchased. With a public good, that decision must be made collectively.[19]

All these macro- and microeconomic terms give us a vocabulary to describe the main features of the U.S. economy. In the next section, we turn to the terms that help us measure how that economy is functioning.

Measuring the Functioning of the Economy

The *gross domestic product* (GDP) is perhaps the single most common term used to describe the economy's overall functioning. We can define the GDP as the sum of all the paid goods and services produced in the U.S. economy. In 2002, the U.S. GDP hit $10 trillion.[20]

In one sense, the GDP seems to be very straightforward and unambiguous: government statisticians simply add up the final value of all the goods and services to get the figure. Everything made for sale goes into this calculation: the cars and computers produced, as well as the estimated value of all the social services delivered. Yet it is precisely because the GDP makes no distinctions that some policy analysts have criticized it. After all, if the GDP includes everything, it reflects both the production of cigarettes and the price of the funerals for the more than four hundred thousand Americans each year whose deaths are attributable to smoking; industrial development and the cost of cancer treatments caused by environmental pollution; the amount spent building new prisons and the amount spent fighting crime. When government officials announce that the economy is growing at 3 percent per year, they are talking about the percentage of growth in the GDP. Nevertheless, when there is also a 3 percent growth in the less appealing components of the GDP, many experts have begun to question its usefulness as an accurate indicator of our nation's social health.[21]

Another frequently cited measure is the *unemployment rate*. Contrary to popular misconception, the unemployment rate has nothing to do with the number of people receiving unemployment insurance. Nor does it rise when those receiving benefits exceed the usual maximum of twenty-six weeks of being unemployed. Rather, the unemployment rate is calculated based on the size of the civilian labor force in the United States, which currently numbers about 140 million people. Using a random sample of fifty thousand interviewees, the Department of Labor figures the unemployment rate by totaling the number of those who are not working and dividing this figure by a proportionate estimate of those who are. By this method, the downturn of 2002 increased long-term joblessness by half and drove the official unemployment rate to 5.8 percent, up from its dip below 4 percent in 2000, the lowest level in the preceding thirty years.[22]

Economists recognize three distinct kinds of unemployment: *frictional*, for those between jobs; *structural*, for a mismatch between the supply of and the demand for workers; and *cyclical*, when the demand for employees is low.[23]

Together, these three terms make the unemployment rate sound like a relatively uncontroversial calculation. In recent years, however, there has been much criticism of how the government includes some workers and leaves out others.

Part of the problem lies in the Department of Labor's definition of who is either currently working or looking for work. Suppose your client loses her job. For the next three months, she wakes full of optimism each morning, gets all dressed up, and knocks on the door of every potential employer. Even if she never receives a single job offer, the Department of Labor considers her part of the labor force. Then, after three months of failure, she stops looking. The Department of Labor immediately changes her status. Reclassifying her as a "discouraged worker," it says that she is no longer unemployed. In 2002, the Department of Labor classified 337,000 workers as discouraged, and another 1.4 million as "marginally attached," meaning that they had looked for work some time in the prior year and were still available for employment.[24]

The other problematic element in the unemployment rate is the number of involuntary part-timers. If your client works just one hour a week, she is still, by the Department of Labor's standards, employed. Like the exclusion of discouraged and marginally attached workers, defining part-timers as employed drastically lowers the unemployment rate, because in 2001, there were more than 5.4 million such people.[25] Together with another 2.1 million people in prison, one of the highest per capita imprisonment rates anywhere in the world, it is estimated that the real unemployment rate in the United States is actually at least twice the official one, which in 2002 would make it something closer to 12 percent.[26]

Besides unemployment, the rate of *inflation* is another key economic indicator. Most discussions of inflation use the Consumer Price Index for all urban consumers, usually called the CPI-U. The CPI-U tracks increases in the cost of a market basket of two hundred goods that the typical urban consumer purchases, including fuel, food, and housing. If $1 buys a given amount of goods and services in one year, but the next year it requires $1.01 to buy the same amount, we say that the CPI-U and, consequently, the rate of inflation has risen 1 percent. In 2001, the actual rate of inflation in the CPI-U was 2.7 percent.[27]

Usually, economists distinguish between two kinds of inflation. *Demand-pull inflation* occurs when the total demand for goods rises more rapidly than the economy's productive potential; *cost-push inflation* occurs when costs rise despite high unemployment and a reduced use of resources.[28] Some economists have recently complained that the CPI-U overstates both kinds of inflation because it does not take into account consumers switching to cheaper products: if chicken becomes too expensive, the theory is that your client can always buy spaghetti instead. They also criticize the CPI-U for its failure to measure the savings available through technology, for example, through the introduction of the latest computers. Other economists, however, rebut these arguments. They contend that these claims are either exaggerated or that recent revisions to the CPI-U have already incorporated them. To them, it is equally likely that the CPI-U actually understates the rate of inflation. In the meantime, until this debate is fully resolved, most people seeking to measure the rate of inflation continue to use the CPI-U.[29]

Productivity is closely tied to inflation. Productivity refers to the quantity of goods and services the economy produces. Two factors enter into the rate of productivity growth. One, the human factor, relates to whether the production process is organized more efficiently and/or employees are working harder. A second, mechanical factor involves the capacity of new machines to augment what each worker produces. If workers and machines combine to produce more, they can slow the inflation rate by ensuring that there are enough goods for all the money pursuing them. Because the economy is producing more, rapid productivity growth can also have an enormous impact on budgets, corporate revenue projections, and longer-term forecasts for programs like Social Security.

From 1973 to 1990, productivity grew at 0.9 percent annually, a sharp decline from the 2.9 percent rate that it had averaged in the preceding twenty-five years. When productivity did pick up in the 1990s to 2.5 percent, technology enthusiasts claimed that computers would give productivity growth a big boost. Within a couple of years, however, it became evident that no such boost had occurred. Another, more troubling pattern did become apparent. Because wages rose at just 0.5 percent per year in the 1990s, workers clearly did not get paid for the new goods they were producing.[30]

The shift to a service economy may offer one reason why productivity growth is slowing. It does represent an increase in productivity if the same number of inputs yields more steel. But if you used to see five clients a day and now see ten, are you twice as productive? Are nurses more productive when they care for more patients? Are teachers more productive with a larger class? It is hard to quantify the production of human services. Now that they are more common, however, a service economy changes both productivity's measurement and its meaning.

The *poverty line* is another key indicator. The original line dates from the mid-1960s, when Mollie Orshansky, director of the Social Security Administration, developed it to measure poverty and determine eligibility for some of the first antipoverty programs. She used a very simple index: if the cost of a minimal food budget for four people was $1,000, and food constituted one-third of total living expenses, then the poverty line in 1965 was $3,000. In 2001, when the poverty line for a family of four rose to $18,104 and 11.7 percent of Americans were poor, all the new threshold reflected was the 1965 figure plus thirty-six years of inflation.[31]

This method is called the *absolute* method of calculating poverty. It is absolute because it measures poverty independently of what is happening with the rest of the population. By contrast, the *relative* method takes an index—typically, 50 percent of the median income ($42,228 in 2001)—that calculates poverty against broader trends in the nation, including the possibility of an increasingly skewed division of income that leaves just one segment of the population behind. Many experts prefer this method, because it comes closer to the $25,000 figure that seems, intuitively at least, to establish a minimum threshold for self-sufficiency.

The current poverty line has other problems as well. Although food was once 33 percent of the budget, it is now just 18 percent. In addition, the line does not set minimum standards for anything other than food, such as housing, medical care, child care, or transportation; it does not account for taxes; and it does not allow for regional differences in the cost of living. For these reasons, at a time when the official poverty rate was listed at 12.7 percent of the population, a National Academy of Sciences study said it should actually be set 3 percent higher. Responding to the cumulative effect of all these critiques, the federal government has introduced a number of other methods for calculating the poverty line. Nevertheless, because of the additional expense in programs like Head Start and food stamps that are tied to it, it will be years before one of these methods replaces the current one.[32]

Just as the poverty line represents an important indicator in the domestic economy, the *balance of payments* due to trade constitutes an important indicator for an economy that is increasingly global. When a company in one country purchases the goods of a company in another country, it creates a trade deficit. Unless businesses or people in the second country buy other goods from the first country that have an equivalent value, the money flowing out of the first country for imports will exceed the money flowing in for exports. Such a trade deficit is exactly what has happened to the U.S. economy in recent years.

Average annual exit rate from poverty. In addition to the problems with the official poverty rate, people in the United States leave poverty at a lower rate than citizens in other countries.

Country	Percent of the poor
Netherlands	44%
Canada	42%
Germany	37%
Sweden	36%
United Kingdom	29%
United States	29%

The U.S. *trade deficit* reflects a number of factors. When the condition of the U.S. economy improved in the 1990s, the trade deficit rose because consumers had money to buy more products from overseas. Although the ability to buy goods on the international market keeps prices down and helps consumers, it also has a downside. If you have a client who lost his or her job to a cheaper plant overseas, you have a better sense of its human cost. In 2001, the trade deficit amounted to $358 billion. The cumulative effect of such numbers is that foreigners presently hold a total of $4.1 trillion. As the U.S. economy deteriorated under a cloud of corporate scandals, foreign investors began to sell their dollar holdings, depressing the stock market and, potentially, making our economic difficulties much worse.[33]

Then there is the federal budget itself, which, after running a surplus from 1998 through 2001, is now back in deficit. A *deficit* or *surplus* simply reflects whether the federal government spent more or less money than it received in revenue. The budget bottomed out with a $290 billion deficit in 1992, but then amassed a surplus of $236 billion in 2000. Two years later, however, President Bush's tax cut, the additional money spent to combat terrorism, and the deteriorating economy drove the 2002 deficit to $159 billion.[34]

The one catch to these figures is that they include revenue from Social Security. Boosted especially by taxes on wages from the baby boomers, monies from Social Security cushion the budget. In recent years, this cushion has run between $60 and $115 billion annually. It is true that this so-called unified budget reflects all the federal government's current revenue, but because it partly disguises the deficit and there are subsequent claims on the Social Security monies, the wisdom of including it in the annual federal budget remains very much open to question.[35]

The budget deficit (or surplus) should not be confused with the *federal debt*. The federal debt is, quite simply, the sum of all prior federal deficits. If money was spent in previous years for roads, or fighter jets, or social welfare programs (after all, in a $2 trillion budget, it is impossible to determine precisely what expense pushed the federal government over the edge), the Department of the Treasury issues bonds to make up the difference. Using the borrowed money to cover the immediate deficit, it then promises to pay the bondholder regular interest on the bond plus the principle (say, $25,000, $50,000, or $100,000) some time in the future when the bond is due. This is how the federal government has accumulated its total debt, which has now reached $6 trillion. Although such a number sounds like—and indeed is—a lot of money, our annual GDP is $10 trillion and is expected to increase to more than $17 trillion by 2012. Even with an uncertain economic outlook, total debt as a percentage of our GDP should decline.[36]

In addition to words like *deficit* and *debt* that tell us something about the economic condition of the federal government, there are also a set of terms that describe how the whole economy is functioning. The most common of these terms are *business cycle, recession,* and *depression.* The business cycle describes the natural patterns of a market economy. It prospers for a while, until profits shrink, investment opportunities disappear, and growth slows; as wages stagnate and more workers are thrown out of work, the economy deteriorates, and eventually it hits bottom. The whole process then repeats itself, with the investment opportunities that some firms discern leading to more employment and a widening economic recovery. Although there is no prescription for how long the process takes, we do know that in the last half of the twentieth century, the typical cycle ranged between two and ten years.[37]

Recession and *depression* are the terms used to describe economic conditions at the bottom of the cycle. There are no official definitions that distinguish between them, although the economist's old joke—a recession is when your neighbor's unemployed, a depression is when you are—makes a nice, if informal, guideline. Technically, we say that a recession has occurred at any time when the economy (i.e., the GDP) shrinks in two consecutive quarters (six months). In recent years, recessions usually have unemployment rates in excess of 6 percent; we reached the post–World War II high of 9.7 percent in 1982. By comparison, during the Great Depression of the 1930s, unemployment hit 25 percent. It may be an arbitrary distinction, but one could probably muster a consensus among economists that an unemployment rate above 10 percent might reasonably be described as a depression.

The final indicator of economic well-being is *inequality*. In economic terminology, inequality can refer to either inequality of income or inequality of wealth. In the United States, both measures have become much less equal in recent years.

We usually describe inequality in *quintiles*—that is, in demographic units of 20 percent, or one-fifth of the population—and then specify what percentage of income or wealth each 20 percent possesses. Obviously, if income were evenly distributed, each quintile would have exactly one-fifth of the total income or wealth. That is not true in any country, but of all the modern economies, the United States is the nation with the most inequality. In 2000, for example, the bottom fifth of the population received just 3.6 percent of all after-tax income, while the top fifth got 49.6 percent. Put another way, these figures mean that the bottom 80 percent of the population—that is, the broad poor and middle classes combined (families earning less than $82,000 a year)—received just about half the nation's income.[38]

The data on *inequality of wealth* are just as skewed. The top 10 percent of the population now has 71 percent of all Americans' net worth, leaving the remaining 29 percent to the bottom 90 percent of the population. Stated even more dramatically, the richest 1 percent now possesses 38 percent of the nation's wealth.[39] Of course, one of the main factors driving this discrepancy of both wealth and income is the huge jump in chief executives' pay. CEOs currently receive 531 times the pay of the average worker; to keep pace with the soaring CEO compensation, average workers would now have to earn $120,000 annually.[40] Because they do not, and because it takes money to make money, wealth is even more unevenly distributed than income.

When economists talk about statistics like these, they often turn them into *Gini ratios*. A Gini ratio is a number between 0 and 1 that measures the

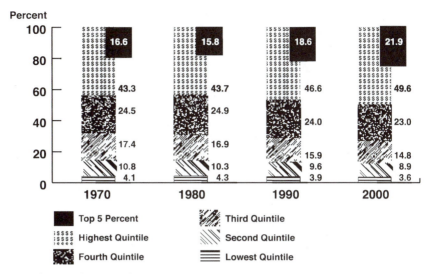

Percent

	1970	1980	1990	2000
Top 5 Percent	16.6	15.8	18.6	21.9
Highest Quintile	43.3	43.7	46.6	49.6
Fourth Quintile	24.5	24.9	24.0	23.0
Third Quintile	17.4	16.9	15.9	14.8
Second Quintile	10.8	10.3	9.6	8.9
Lowest Quintile	4.1	4.3	3.9	3.6

■ Top 5 Percent   ▨ Third Quintile

▦ Highest Quintile   ▧ Second Quintile

▩ Fourth Quintile   ≡ Lowest Quintile

Aggregate U.S. income by quintiles. Over the past thirty years, the division of income in the United States has become steadily more unequal.

extent of inequality. At 0, income and/or wealth would be evenly distributed; at 1, one person would own everything. In the United States today, the Gini ratio for income is about 0.46, up from 0.39 in 1973 and, consistent with what we said earlier, one of the highest figures in the world.[41] In a study of wealth distribution by New York University economist Edward Wolff, the top 20 percent of the population garnered 91 percent of the gain in wealth (with the top 1 percent getting 53 percent) between 1983 and 1998. Plainly, during the years leading up to the boom at the end of 1990s, many people did better, but the most affluent did best of all.[42]

The Terms and Tools of Economic Policy

The third kind of economic terminology describes the components of economic policymaking. These terms are tools that the government relies on to address problems in the market's functioning. Typically, they are both the consequence and the cause of new social change.

One set of the government's tools seeks to remedy microeconomic problems. In instances of monopoly, such as the Microsoft case, the government can file an *antitrust* suit that tries to halt a company's monopolistic practices. It can also deregulate an industry, as it did with the airlines, in the hope that new companies will spur greater competition. Both of these strategies may temporarily slow the process of concentration within an industry. Over the longer term, however, more successful businesses generally tend to drive out less successful businesses. At best, then, a half dozen closely related companies—essentially, a new oligopoly—replace the old monopoly. The classic example of this pattern is the breakup of Rockefeller's Standard Oil Company, the ancestor of most modern U.S. oil companies. Even more dramatically, in cases of significant deregulation, the new oligopoly is now free to act with less government supervision. In 2002, this policy of deregulation contributed to excess investment and the ultimate collapse of telephone companies like WorldCom that spearheaded the stock market's downward slide.

Government policy also addresses *externalities*. In economic terms, an externality is a cost or a benefit (e.g., pollution or public health) that is not normally reflected in the immediate transaction. A company that pollutes the air does not add this pollution to its cost of doing business; a mass vaccination campaign offers public health benefits that cannot be measured financially.[43] The government has enacted antipollution laws to compensate for this failure of the market. The trouble is that although these laws do have an impact on pollution, they also often involve some form of government aid—a tax abatement (reduction) or other public subsidy. Such subsidies tend to perpetuate the division between profits that are private and losses (more broadly, social costs) that are public. Under such circumstances, antipollution laws may bring about social change, but they are still an imperfect remedy.

In addition to monopolies and externalities, the third primary microeconomic flaw is a shortage of *public goods*. Markets often tend to shortchange public goods—parks, libraries, and yes, even some universal social programs such as education—because although they benefit everyone, they profit no one. In the absence of a tangible indicator like profit, it is harder to make the case for these public necessities. Nevertheless, the government does sometimes try to compensate for this oversight. Its success, however, often depends on a clear benefit accruing to some defined constituency: the neighborhood near the park or advocates for public libraries. When constituencies like these push hard, they are more likely to succeed in turning a less tangible benefit that helps everyone into a more tangible benefit that helps someone.

In addition to these microeconomic interventions, the government also has a large repertoire of macroeconomic tools. The government relies on these tools to stabilize the economy. When unemployment rises on the downside of the business cycle, the government usually tries to stimulate *aggregate demand*. This term refers to the total demand for goods and services. It includes private consumption and investment, government purchases, and net exports, that is, the difference between how much we export and how much we import. By intervening to increase demand, the government can shorten a recession.[44]

The two primary methods of increasing aggregate demand are *monetary* and *fiscal* policy. Monetary policy resides with the Federal Reserve Bank, one of our most important economic institutions. Established by act of Congress in 1913, the Federal Reserve Bank, often called the Fed, consists of member banks that monitor the condition of the economy and establish the discount rate, the interest rate the Fed sets for other banks that want to lend money.

Because this interest rate determines the cost of money throughout the economy, it can either accelerate or brake economic growth. When you go into your local bank and want to borrow money for a house, a car, or a student loan, the rate the Fed is charging your bank is the major determinant of the rate you will be charged. If the Fed's policy is tight and money is expensive, your mortgage rate might be 10 or 11 percent. But if the Fed has implemented an "easy money" policy, your bank might charge you only 7 percent for a mortgage. Faced with several hundred dollars less in monthly payments, you might then decide to buy your dream home. This kind of economic stimulus is exactly what the Fed had in mind when, in an effort to stave off recession, it reduced its prime rate eleven times in 2001, from 6.5 to 1.75 percent.

In addition to establishing the prime rate, the Fed has two other methods of increasing or decreasing the money supply. One is to change the *reserve requirements*, the amount of money your bank has to keep on hand at any time. Normally, banks loan most of their deposits, charge interest on these loans, and make a profit. When the Fed raises the reserve requirements, the bank must keep more money on hand. That means less is available for circulation throughout the economy.

The third method of affecting the money supply involves the buying and selling of government bonds. Conducted by the Fed's Open Market Committee (the seven members of its Board of Governors plus five presidents of its regional banks), this strategy buys and sells government bonds from commercial banks, which, in turn, buy and sell from other financial institutions, large corporations, and wealthy individuals. If the Fed believes that too much money is circulating, it sells government bonds and takes the money from this sale out of circulation. The reverse is also true: if the Fed thinks that too little money is circulating, it buys government bonds and puts additional money into circulation. The money supply declines or expands accordingly.[45]

From this description of all the tools at its disposal, it is easy to see the power that the Federal Reserve Bank maintains over the economy. As the institutional representative of the financial industry, the Fed is most apprehensive about inflation, which depreciates the value of money and makes every dollar that a bank loans worth less over time as it is repaid. Wages constitute about 70 percent of the cost of goods. Consequently, the Fed remains vigilant about wage increases. If the unemployment rate gets too low and corporations begin to compete for workers by raising wages, the Fed often tightens the money supply to slow the economy and prevent inflation from occurring.

Take a second look at this policy and it becomes clear why it is so controversial. In essence, when unemployment is low, wages are rising, and workers are becoming more powerful, the Federal Reserve Bank slows the economy, puncturing the upward pressure on wages, and throwing more workers out of work. Proponents of this policy in the business community contend that steps like raising the discount rate are necessary to ensure orderly, stable, long-term growth. Critics maintain, however, that in an effort to prevent the financial community's primary asset—money—from declining in value, the Fed is pulling the rug out from under workers just as they are beginning to acquire a little more power.

The second major macroeconomic instrument, *fiscal policy*, refers to the economic consequences of the federal budget. The federal government collects money from taxes and spends it on everything from grants to starving artists to the latest military hardware. This combination of revenue and expenditure then determines the surplus or deficit in the federal budget. When the government runs a deficit, it is said to be *priming the pump*. As indicated in the discussion of automatic stabilizers in chapter 2, even social spending helps to prime the pump. Derived from the work of economist John Maynard Keynes, this strategy tries to stimulate the economy through government spending: the government borrows money and then acts as if it has collected more revenue than it really has. As this borrowed money circulates through the economy, it creates a demand for new jobs, goods, services, and investment.

Taxes are the primary source of government revenues: they are the funds that keep the government running. A tax, however, can be either *regressive* or *progressive*. A regressive tax is one that taxes rich and poor at similar rates, for example, the sales tax that many states place on the purchase of consumer goods. Because some consumer goods are essential, experts often argue that it is regressive to tax poor people who have less discretionary income for these purchases. Still, because so many people need these goods, a tax on them does raise a lot of money.

Another method of raising a lot of money is the *income tax*, the best example of progressive taxation. In 2001, this tax collected $1.2 of the $2.1 trillion in government revenues. Although the income tax has gotten less progressive in recent years, it still taxes those who make more money at a higher rate than those who make less. The marginal rate—the rate paid by the most affluent taxpayers on the upper margins of their income—declined in stages from 70 to 28 percent under President Reagan. After President Clinton raised it to 39.6 percent, George W. Bush passed a tax law that will reduce it to 35 percent by 2006. This change is consistent with the overall direction of the new tax law, which, by the time it has been fully implemented in 2010, will have conferred 35 percent of its $1.35 trillion in benefits on the top 1 percent of earners.[46]

These policy reversals confirm that arguments about taxes divide along familiar political lines. Whereas conservatives believe that high tax rates punish hard work and discourage initiative, liberals assert that in any effort to fund the government, it is only reasonable to take money from those who have more of it. To judge by the changes in tax policy, conservatives have won the debate in recent years. In addition to a significant decline in the marginal rate, the capital gains tax on investment has dropped from 28 to 20 percent (18 percent if the stock is held for five years, and as low as 8 percent for those in the 15 percent tax bracket), and the proportion of federal revenues derived from corporate taxes has shrunk from 21 percent in 1962

the Welfare Line

to about 7.5 percent in 2001. Indeed, the only place where taxes have increased has been at the local level. There, the cost of basic services like police, schools, and recreation has risen at the same time that states and municipalities have assumed responsibility for programs that the federal government used to finance. The net effect of these changes is that although the overall tax burden has not changed much, some significant portion has shifted to the states and to less affluent people.[47]

The other side of fiscal policy is what the government spends. We often hear, for example, about the concept of *social spending*. This term merely refers to the total amount of money that is spent on social programs, including Social Security, Medicaid, and Medicare. In 2001, total social spending amounted to 49 percent of the federal budget. It is closely analogous to what is perhaps an even more familiar term, *military spending*. After peaking during the cold war at half of the federal budget, military spending dropped to 16 percent; it will rise again as a result of the war on terrorism.[48] Despite this reversal, the overall pattern of change in the mix of federal spending reflects an increasing diversification of the federal government's role.

In addition to the distinction between social and military, federal expenditures can also be classified as *discretionary* or *mandatory spending*. Discretionary spending involves monies that must be appropriated annually, as determined by the judgment of Congress. Accounting for about one-third of the federal budget, it includes items such as defense, education, transportation, the national parks, the space program, and foreign aid. By contrast, mandatory spending involves spending on entitlements. With mandatory spending in programs such as Social Security, Medicare, and Medicaid, Congress does not

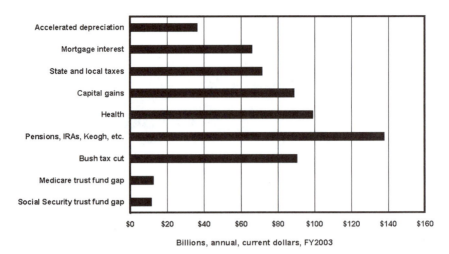

Accelerated depreciation

Mortgage interest

State and local taxes

Capital gains

Health

Pensions, IRAs, Keogh, etc.

Bush tax cut

Medicare trust fund gap

Social Security trust fund gap

$0 $20 $40 $60 $80 $100 $120 $140 $160

Billions, annual, current dollars, FY2003

Tax breaks and gaps in Social Security and Medicare. Several different kinds of tax breaks and tax reductions exceed the value of one year's (FY2003) gap in both the Social Security and Medicare trust funds.

determine the annual appropriation. Instead, after setting rules for eligibility and benefit formulas, it pays out money to everyone who meets these standards.[49]

We have now defined terms in three categories: the structure of the economy, words that measure how the economy is performing, and phrases that describe the government's economic tools, especially those relating to monetary and fiscal policy. Equipped with this vocabulary, we can now proceed to the harder question: What, exactly, is the relationship between social welfare and the economy?

Social Welfare and the Economy in Historical Context

At the beginning of this chapter, we outlined some of the basic interactions between social welfare and the economy. Social welfare, we explained, helps to reduce economic insecurity, involves the social regulation of the marketplace, and contributes to the development of the public infrastructure. Altogether, these functions make social welfare both an aid and an impediment to the private sector. The ambiguity of this role stems from social welfare's responsibility for mediating between the needs of families and individuals and the needs of the larger economic order.

What, exactly, are these needs? Obviously, to survive, families must have adequate food, clothing, housing, and health care; children have all these needs, plus they require a decent education. Referred to as social reproduction in chapter 2, some of these needs exist throughout a person's life; others are specific to a particular age, such as the need for more supportive living arrangements as we grow older.

To say that these needs exist, however, is not to prescribe how they should be met. The historical trend has increasingly been to meet these needs through some combination of the market and the state, which together are supposed to provide an adequate combination of income and services. Yet for most of human history, the responsibility for these needs lay with households and families. Indeed, this issue has hardly been resolved, because today, many conservatives again want to return responsibility for these needs to the family.

Until the late nineteenth century, the family was a plausible site to meet these needs. The economy, after all, was still rooted in the household. Instead of working for someone else and receiving a salary that could be used to purchase what they needed on the open market, many families consumed what they produced. Mothers and older sisters sewed the clothing, cared for children and the elderly, and prepared the food; fathers and sons worked the farm or operated a small, family-owned business. The typical household had highly differentiated gender roles, but it permitted most families to survive and enabled some to prosper.

There are two distinctive features about this arrangement. First, the family had relatively little to do with either the government or the marketplace. A farmer might go to town to sell his harvest, but depending on the historical period and the development of the market within a specific region, he would still have only occasional contact with the world of buying and selling. By comparison with what we experience nowadays, both the family and the economy within the family constituted a world unto itself.

The *demonetization* of services within the family constitutes the second distinctive feature of this arrangement. When a service is demonetized, no money exchanges hands. The farmer in our example does not have to pay anyone to obtain food, nor do the children in his family owe their mother any money for the day care she provides.[50] The absence of money is yet another demonstration of the boundary that existed between the family and the rest of the world. It was a boundary that the growth of a market economy would soon breach.

The growth and increasing dominance of the market economy is one of the most remarkable changes of the past one hundred years. Many factors keyed its development, including inventions such as the internal combustion engine; the availability of adequate capital for investment; revolutionary changes in production, such as the assembly line, which increased efficiency by combining human labor and new machinery; the use of advertising to create a mass consumer market; and, often, the suppression of labor militancy by corporations and the government when workers organized, demanded higher pay, or otherwise threatened disruption. The transition to a market economy transformed the social structures of society and drastically altered the way people lived. The changes that it brought about are the changes that triggered the need for new forms of social welfare: they are the changes that gave rise to the modern welfare state.

For the purpose of tracing the development of contemporary social welfare, the market economy's most significant consequence was the tendency for an ever larger percentage of the workforce to be drawn into it. To be sure, this trend did not just begin in the latter part of the nineteenth century. After all, historians have shown that people started to work for wages paid by an employer once feudalism, with its system of mutual obligations between lord and serf, first began to decline in fourteenth-century England.[51] But although this broad trend was five hundred years old, the Industrial Revolution and the accompanying rise of the market economy dramatically quickened the process. Soon, new workers were coming from everywhere: from the countryside, where the mechanization of farming made their labor superfluous; from overseas, where immigrants poured into U.S. cities and got jobs in the factories; and from the city itself, where craftspeople and families with small businesses found it steadily more difficult to make a decent living. This flood of people grew and grew, until by 2000, 93 percent worked for someone else.[52]

Americans value the work ethic. Many believe that if you work hard you will prosper, either by regular promotions throughout your career or, if you are truly lucky and resourceful, by success in your own business. Certainly, some people do succeed, rising to the top of their industry or profession, most recently, by making a fortune in computers and other information technologies. Yet just as clearly, many other hardworking and resourceful people do not do as well. They face a serious problem: although the responsibility of supporting themselves is their own, their ability to do so depends entirely on employers, who hire only when they believe that additional workers will enable them to realize a larger profit.

In these new circumstances, the economy no longer resides inside the family. This development has enormous ramifications. If workers are pulled out of the family, only to be drawn in ever larger numbers into the orbit of, first, an industrial economy and, eventually, into the production of services and information, then fewer adults are left in the home to care for children, the sick, and the elderly. Who will care for these family members? Who will cushion the effects of a downturn in the economy that prevents even the most diligent breadwinner from finding work? Shifting from a reliance on the family and the market, policymakers in the early part of the twentieth century began to add a third option. Henceforth, the government would bear some responsibility.

But responsibility for what? As we have noted, the list of human needs is always extensive, and if workers do not have money to satisfy them, the needs become acute. Food, clothing, housing, health care—how were policymakers to divvy up responsibility for these needs among the government, the family, and the market, especially as anything that the government provides for free or at below-market rates conflicts with the imperatives of a market economy?

Production for Profit versus Production for Need

A market economy thrives when everything has a market price. Ideally, from the perspective of those who benefit the most from the market and prize its operation, this "everything" includes all the essentials: the food, clothing, housing, and health care that we have previously described as basic human needs. Yet, here is the nub of the problem: from their earliest beginnings, market economies have always paid some people less than they needed to survive.

Historically, the number of these people has always varied, expanding in economic downturns and contracting in economic booms. In the United States, for example, more people had difficulty making ends meet in the Depression than they did during World War II, when unemployment sank to its twentieth-century low of just slightly over 1 percent. In addition, in any given historical period, low wages often have been associated with particular sectors of the economy, where either profit margins were thin or employers exercised disproportionate power over workers. Today, we associate low wages with sweatshop workers and employees of the fast food industry, but earlier in the twentieth century, before they were unionized, many workers in industries like coal and steel also found it hard to earn a living. Finally, low wages often have been concentrated among particular racial and ethnic groups, whom employers discriminate against in the labor market.

As chapter 2 explains, ensuring economic security is one of social welfare policy's basic functions. For generations before the establishment of a welfare state, most poor people who did not earn a living somehow managed to cope. Relying on neighbors and, if necessary, on private, local charities, they cobbled together the resources to keep a roof over their heads and prevent starvation. Nevertheless, this method of managing poverty has substantial political risks. People without money can become desperate, and when they get desperate, they may organize. Faced with demands for much greater economic and political power, the political and business elite may prefer government intervention in the form of increased social welfare spending.

This intervention can take several forms. Sometimes, the government just gives money to the members of a defined group. This is the strategy that it employs with programs such as public assistance, Social Security, and Unemployment Insurance. At other times, however, it decommodifies the consumer good; that is, members of the eligible group no longer pay the full market price, either because the government subsidizes them (food stamps is a good example), or, as in Section 8 public housing and Medicare, because it subsidizes the provider of the good or service in question.

In market economies generally, but especially in a market economy like the United States, with its tradition of laissez-faire, programs that decommodify goods and services or give money to able-bodied adults who do not work violate some basic economic principles. Workers are supposed to work, earn enough money to support themselves, and buy the goods they need. When the government gives money or otherwise subsidizes those who do not adhere to these principles, it helps them to survive, removing the absolute necessity of work and creating an alternative to the marketplace. In the purest theories about markets, government intervention is unnecessary. Yet now, in reality, we redirect some small portion of private wealth through the government toward the task of keeping people healthy, productive, and alive.

The Economy versus Social Welfare?

Because the redirection of this wealth has never won complete acceptance, three major debates continually swirl around the relationship between the economy and social welfare. The first involves the pooling or socialization of risk; the second, the presumed conflict between equality and efficiency; and the third, the question of whether the existence of the welfare state stimulates or slows the economy. The notion that government intervention might be counterproductive pervades each of these debates.

Social insurance programs such as Social Security constitute the classic example of socializing risk. Here, the risk is that of retirement without adequate means of financial support. To be sure, some people can manage without Social Security. Nevertheless, for those who cannot, guaranteeing enough money for their retirement requires putting them in a large insurance pool. Regardless of whether the pool is public or private, the larger the pool, the less is the risk to each individual member.

As a publicly funded insurance pool, Social Security is financed through a payroll tax that turns the contribution into an earned entitlement. Of course, there is no rule that socializing risk has to occur in this way. The pool could be larger—all people, not just all workers, thereby providing some kind of guaranteed minimum income—and/or the contributions could draw on general taxes rather than a defined contribution from your paycheck. Still, these details are all part of a broader question: Does participation in this pool reduce total savings, and would everyone be better off if they took care of themselves?

It is true that money channeled into Social Security is not available for private savings. But beyond this point, it is not at all clear that social insurance programs have such negative effects. First, once people know that the program provides coverage for their basic needs, those without money may try to save a little more to give themselves some additional choices. Second, unless participants are well up the income ladder, it is going to be hard for them to bank as much as they would under a voluntary plan. Many economists still believe social welfare subtracts from the private economy. Perhaps that is why they find it hard to acknowledge that social insurance programs do not diminish total saving and, indeed, may well add to it.[53]

Some critics even reject the whole premise that risk should be socialized. In the most famous version of this argument, Martin Feldstein, professor of economics at Harvard and chairman of President Reagan's Council of Economic Advisors, claimed that Social Security recipients would be better off on their own.[54] Subsequent analysis showed that he had misinterpreted his data. But his argument persists because it fits so well with the American belief in individual responsibility: each of us individually, it is said, should do better than all of us collectively. The most affluent probably would. Yet this fact inevitably raises the question of whether we are merely a group of individuals or a society with some shared responsibility for one another. In addition, quite apart from any ethical issues, do each of us separately want to bet against an economically secure old age and the certainty of disability payment for unexpected injury?

The second common criticism about the relationship between social welfare and the economy is often called "the big tradeoff," the hypothetical conflict between equality and efficiency. The idea is that if we try to introduce more equality into the economy, we can do so only at a large cost in efficiency.[55] In theory, greater equality means either that production costs more or that fewer goods are produced. To remedy inequality under these circumstances, all we can hope for are a few social programs that give some money to the poor. If we introduced stronger measures like higher taxes or stricter regulations, they would seriously damage the market system.

Because this argument assumes the existence of a well-functioning market, it is very wary of any intervention that might knock it off its track. Other economists, however, do not accept this premise. For them, measures to increase equality would not take anything away from our economy. Instead, such measures would simply make it work better:

> Ending racial and sexual discrimination . . . would eliminate the talent waste that occurs when gifted individuals end up in dead-end jobs or are underemployed because of their color or gender. Guaranteeing a top-quality education to all would have the same effect. Increasing the extent of worker ownership of their workplaces would enhance equality and reduce the extent to which resources must be allocated to maintaining work force discipline—in the form of bosses and supervisors. . . . Granting employment opportunities to all would increase equality as well as reduce the poverty and social alienation that breed drug use and criminality and, in turn, divert significant resources to the unproductive tasks of guard labor.[56]

According to this theory, social workers do not have to choose. Because equality and efficiency are complementary, not opposed, we could have both in our economic system.

The third hypothesis about the relationship between the economy and social welfare relates to its effect on economic growth. Does social welfare make the economy grow faster or slower? There are actually two forms of this question, the *levels hypothesis* and the *growth rate hypothesis*. In the levels hypothesis, a spending cut spurs a temporary rise in the growth rate, followed soon by a return to the old level. That is quite different from the growth rate hypothesis, where the increase in the growth rate is permanent.[57]

But which way does causality work? Does more welfare spending lead to higher national income, or a does a higher national income lead to a bigger welfare state? Or are both welfare spending and national income caused by a third factor? We do not know.[58] All we do know is that there is a close link between the public and private sectors, one that is not simply a matter of the public impinging on the private.

In fact, the most persuasive explanation of the relationship between the economy and social welfare is quite different. It suggests that the public sector is essential to the growth of the private sector, and that, in fact, the two grow together. The underlying premise here is that large businesses have large social costs. These costs take a variety of forms, including environmental (polluting air, water, and soil), concentration (a big office building must have roads that lead to it, cars that drive on those roads, and oil companies making gas to fuel those cars), and unemployment (what happens to the people who cannot keep up with the demand for greater technical skill?). All these costs heighten the demand for a growing, and increasingly expensive, public sector.

In addition to absorbing these costs, the public sector often directly subsidizes the private. These subsidies include tax incentives for job training, economic development through the establishment of industrial zones, and publicly funded research (through the National Institutes of Health) on drugs that private pharmaceutical companies eventually sell for a profit. Where profits are private but the losses—most dramatically, in social welfare and the environment—are public, a growing private sector of large businesses demands a growing public sector with a bigger government. You cannot have one without the other.[59]

That did not stop some people from trying. As a result, from the mid-1970s to the beginning of the twenty-first century, a powerful political movement sought to downsize government. This movement fought regulations on corporate accounting and the environment, contracted out government functions like prisons and garbage collection, relied increasingly on the private sector for health and education, and, perhaps most dramatically, cut social welfare. From the New Deal (1932–1945) to the Great Society (1964–1968), the reforms of the previous era had tried to get the government to absorb at least some of the costs of business activity. According to the principles of these market-based reforms, however, either these costs do not exist, or it is wrong for the government to try to absorb them.

These policies blended with the development of information and computer technologies to benefit more affluent people in the economy of the late 1990s. Yet their wisdom came under more severe scrutiny when Enron and WorldCom collapsed amid charges of accounting and securities fraud that turned out to be common corporate practice. Will the government intervene more forcefully now? After deregulating industries like the airlines, public utilities, the media, and securities, will it seek to reinstitute controls, or even advance some broader social welfare initiatives? The outcome depends, in part, on our assessment of these policies' role in the economic glow of the late 1990s, as well as in the less rosy aftermath of subsequent scandal.

In the 1990s, when economists and businesspeople talked about the information age and the new service economy, they usually stressed its positive features. There was all the wealth the economy created, and then there was the astonishing transformation wrought by computer technology. Surfing the Internet, consumers could purchase goods and services that just a generation ago would have been the stuff of an imaginative science fiction novel. Proponents of deregulation and a more market-based public policy contended that getting government out of the way created this prosperity by freeing the natural productivity of the U.S. economy.[60]

The stock market certainly seemed to bear them out. Between 1980 and 1999, the market value grew eightfold, while profits and assets tripled. Further into the bubble, from the end of 1995 to its peak in the spring of 2000, the stock market itself climbed 136.5 percent, a remarkable rate of 22.4 percent annually. And, of the top thirty fortunes in 1999, eight were new money, mostly first generation, in the new technology sectors.[61]

Still, these gains were not widely shared. The same five hundred corporations whose market value grew eightfold also laid off 5 million workers. While wages rose for everyone in the late 1990s, the average real after-tax income for the middle 60 percent of the population was actually lower in 1999 than it was in 1977. This outcome is hardly surprising, for from 1973 to 1997, the median worker's hourly wages dropped from \$11.61 to \$10.82, or 7.3 percent. The sharpest drop was for men—especially male high school dropouts—whose wages plummeted 30 percent between 1979 and 1997. During the same period in social welfare, the value of public assistance in the median state plunged 50 percent. Clearly, the economy did improve in the 1990s. Just as clearly, however, while nearly everyone celebrated the boom, not everyone benefited.[62]

Many trends help to explain the failure of the boom to spread its benefits. We focus here, in particular, on five: downsizing, the role of trade unions, the long-term decline in the value of the minimum wage, the proliferation of low-wage work, and the growth of part-time and temporary labor. Affecting the bottom two-thirds of the income scale, these phenomena dramatize why a deregulated economy was in fact less kind to most working people.

Downsizing

The phenomenon of mass layoffs called *downsizing* affects both blue-collar and white-collar jobs. It occurred in two distinct phases. In the first phase, during the 1980s, corporations primarily laid off factory workers, at the rate of about 2 million per year. Faced with a broad decline in manufacturing, many of these workers turned to lower-paying jobs in the service industries; in fact, one-third of them took pay cuts of at least 20 percent.

Downsizing changed during the 1990s. In this second phase, businesses turned their attention to white-collar workers, who constituted a much bigger share of the layoffs at companies like IBM (38,000 workers), Sears Roebuck (50,000), and General Motors (69,000). This trend even continued throughout the 1990s, despite an improving economy, as corporations such as AT&T and Motorola each fired 15,000 workers.

In both the 1980s and the 1990s, the justification was the same: with too many workers on the payroll in a deregulated economy, corporations could not compete. Businesses go astray, their defenders said, when they start thinking about the social consequences of their actions. Neither the remaining workers nor the nation as a whole would benefit if the corporation went bankrupt because they kept people on the payroll just to provide them with a job.

Although the stock of these businesses often rose on Wall Street when the layoffs were announced, it was frequently unclear whether these corporations realized many long-term benefits. Both quality and productivity often declined among the remaining workers, who feared that they might well be next. As a result, several studies showed that at best, half the downsizers increased profits or achieved other financial objectives. The effect on workers was much less ambiguous. As a result of downsizing, they lost income.[63]

Trade Unions

Over the past half century, the proportion of workers in trade unions has declined, from 38 percent in 1954 to 13.5 percent in 2001, including just 9 percent in the private marketplace.[64] This decline occurred for many reasons. The economy shifted from an industrial sector, where unions exercised power, to a service sector, where they did not. Unions themselves made numerous strategic errors, de-emphasizing organizing and ignoring demographic trends that brought many more women and people of color into the workforce. And, finally, after decades of accepting unions as a junior partner in the economy, the new market ethic encouraged businesses to fight back, hiring antiunion law firms, contesting organizing drives, and refusing to negotiate even when their workers had agreed to join a union.

Trade unions have always provided workers with some collective strength. Employers have more power than workers, so when workers negotiate alone, they are more likely to accept the salary and benefits that an employer offers. When workers bargain collectively, however, they can strike and deny the employer a labor force. The difference between bargaining collectively and bargaining alone is a major reason workers who are members of trade unions earn about 25 percent more.[65] The loss of this extra pay has contributed to the American labor force's stagnating income.

In 1995, the American Federation of Labor–Congress of Industrial Organizations (AFL-CIO), the umbrella group for the trade union movement that represents 13 million people, elected John Sweeney, a new president who promised to reinvigorate unions. President Sweeney committed the AFL-CIO to a long-term organizing campaign of U.S. workers. But although unions have won some notable victories, such as the 1997 United Parcel strike and the decision of ten thousand U.S. Air employees to join the Communication Workers Union, it has not yet succeeded in boosting the percentage of workers who are members of unions.

The Minimum Wage

The decline in the minimum wage is one of the primary reasons for the decline in workers' income. Although two increases in the minimum wage pushed it up from $3.35 at the beginning of the 1990s to $5.15 at the end, its value still lagged far behind the rate of inflation. In fact, to keep pace with its high point in 1968, the minimum wage would now have to be set at $8 an hour.[66]

The minimum wage establishes a floor for other wages. Sixty-two percent of the workers who receive it are women. Set above what someone is supposed to get from public assistance but below every other wage, a deflated minimum wage affects far more than the 4.2 million people who officially receive it. That is because, at least on the lower rungs of the job market, workers measure their economic position by their distance from the minimum wage. An increase in the minimum wage would therefore have a domino effect, because a worker who was once paid $1 more than the minimum would, if the minimum were raised $.50, want to reestablish the same differential. Conversely, the relative decline in the minimum wage has dropped the floor in the job

The last increase, from $4.25 to $5.15 an hour in 1996, made up for some of the decline in the minimum wage's purchasing power during the previous two decades. But unless it is raised soon, the minimum wage will once again dip below its 1996 value.

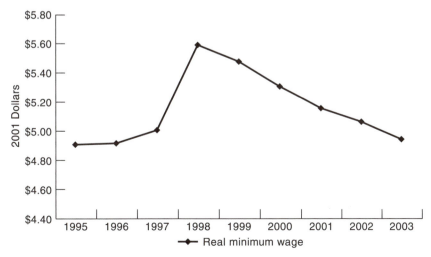

market, pushing down the social wage and enabling employers to lower and/or contain salaries.

Conservatives oppose increases in the minimum wage. For them, wages cannot reflect anything but the market's assessment of a worker's skill. They therefore believe that when the government imposes its judgment on the market, the attempt always has destructive consequences, not the least of which is large-scale layoffs of minimum wage workers who are now being paid too much. Based on the experience of the two increases in the minimum wage during the 1990s, the fears of conservatives seem unwarranted. Over the longer term, however, their concerns have consistently limited increases in the minimum wage.[67]

The Proliferation of Low-Wage Work

Although the United States has a reputation as a country with relatively high living standards, it gets that reputation from a comparatively small percentage of the workforce. In 1999, for example, about 10 percent of all workers earned more than three times poverty wage—an increase of about 2 percent from 1973. These workers were, at least in part, the true beneficiaries of the need for highly skilled white-collar workers in the technological revolution. At the same time, however, the number of workers earning an amount less than or equal to poverty wage ($8.19 an hour) increased from 23 percent in 1973 to nearly 27 percent in 1999. Hence, not only are there many more workers earning poverty-level wages, but in recent years, their numbers have increased more rapidly than the better paid.

Who are these workers? They are the people who collect your ticket when you go to the movies, wait on you at Burger King, and clean your motel room when you travel. Predominantly female, those earning poverty-level wages include 33 percent of all women with jobs, but only 20 percent of men. Their numbers are also heavily concentrated among people of color, with 29 percent of African American men, 40 percent of African American women, 40 percent of Latino men, and 52 percent of Latina women fitting this category.[68] In sum, low-wage workers do the work few people want to do at wages few people would want to be paid.

To understand their financial predicament, we only need to do some simple math. If you work 40 hours a week for 50 weeks a year, you are paid a maximum of $8.19 an hour for 2,000 hours of work, for the grand total of $16,380. That is not very much money for one person; with every additional child, survival moves one step closer to impossible. A family with this income is skating on thin ice. All it takes is a sick child or a broken car, and there may no longer be enough money for food, clothing, housing, or medical care—needs that intensify amid such economic insecurity. That more than 25 percent of all workers cope with such pressures demonstrates that even at the height of the boom, a significant percentage of American workers were left behind.

Part-Time and Temporary Workers

Between 1992 and 2000, the number of temporary workers employed in the United States more than doubled. Many people do want temporary or part-time jobs; for students who need to work and mothers who must care for their children, part-time jobs offer income and flexibility. In 1999, however, 3.3 million people qualified as involuntary part-timers, those who held part-time jobs only because they could not find full-time work. Part-time workers do not usually receive health care, vacation, and pension benefits, and the jobs themselves often come with little security, lower pay, and less chance of promotion.[69]

The proliferation of this work says much about the changing relationship between employer and employee. Although employers have always hired people for the work they do, they once assumed—through the provision of benefits—some long-term responsibility for the *person*. Now, however, 58 percent of full-time workers but just 41 percent of temporary workers get health coverage from their employer.[70] In keeping with the individualist ethic underlying the U.S. economy, those who are not in full-time jobs are increasingly responsible for their own health care.

These five indicators—downsizing, reduced trade union membership, the decline in the minimum wage, the spread of low-wage employment, and the growth of part-time and temporary work—mark the skewed distribution of benefits during the past twenty-five years of a deregulated U.S. economy. Although these facts were occasionally cited in the midst of the boom, low unemployment, rising wages, and the stock market's upward spiral muffled the critics. But then the stock market declined and $7 trillion of wealth vanished in an epidemic of corporate scandals. From Enron to WorldCom, from Merck to Xerox, the scandals cast doubt on both the reality of the earnings reported and the wisdom of the hands-off policy that had made the scandals possible.

Enron, the Corporate Scandals, and the Implications for Social Welfare

For twenty-five years, the dominant economic model preached less social welfare, less regulation, and less government intervention. Victory in these policy debates generated uneven benefits amid the flurry of economic activity in the late 1990s. When the scandals followed soon thereafter, they clearly demonstrated the consequences of unregulated markets and, for the first time in a generation, cast government intervention in a more favorable light. This new perception could have significant implications for the relationship between the economy and social welfare.

The corporate scandals began with Enron. Founded in 1985 as an energy company, by 2001 Enron had become the seventh largest corporation in the United States; *Fortune* magazine even designated it "the most innovative."

Beginning as an energy supplier, Enron gradually transformed itself into an unregulated financial institution that specialized in energy trading. In pursuit of this goal, it created thirty-five hundred subsidiaries that often were used to hide debt, boost its credit rating, and reduce the cost of borrowing for further expansion. When the debt in these subsidiaries was uncovered, Enron collapsed, taking $70 billion out of the stock market value and deflating thousands of pensions. In the year immediately before the collapse, however, Enron's top one hundred executives collected more than $300 million from the company, including $100 million to Kenneth L. Lay, its chief executive officer.[71]

The Enron saga goes to the heart of public policy in the United States. Before California deregulated energy, Enron executives asserted that deregulation would save the state some $9 billion annually. After deregulation, however, Enron played the system it had helped to create and withheld energy supplies to inflate the price. The total bill rose by 266 percent in a single year and cost consumers an additional $30 billion.[72] Similarly, in 2001, Connecticut paid Enron $220 million to buy the electricity generated from steam by the state's trash. Enron was supposed to pay off this loan by 2012 at the rate of $2.4 million a month. Enron used the loan to boost its profits, but when it collapsed, the state trash authority had to raise its dumping fee for each household in seventy towns by $50 a month.[73]

Enron pushed hard for deregulation and showered campaign donations on politicians who listened closely. It gave $100,000 to the Democrats for their help pressuring India to build a power plant, $25,000 to the Republican governor of Texas one day after he appointed the head of its Mexican subsidiary to run the Texas Public Utilities Commission, $2 million to the wife of Texas senator Phil Gramm, who chaired Enron's audit committee, and $2.5 million to George W. Bush for his 2000 presidential campaign.[74]

Yet Enron was hardly the only company to gain a freer hand. Seven years after Arthur Andersen, Enron's accounting firm, fought to shield outside accountants from liability for false corporate reporting, government prosecutors convicted it for obstruction of justice. Cable giant Adelphia Communications went bankrupt after inflating numbers and making undisclosed loans to its major shareholders. Xerox paid a $10 million fine for overstating revenues, and the investment firm Merrill Lynch settled with New York State for $100 million on charges that it misled investors.[75] These outcomes were virtually inevitable in an environment where the research departments of investment firms were always upbeat about companies they had been paid to advise, and companies consistently massaged their quarterly earnings reports to ensure that their stock rose because it had met Wall Street's estimates.[76]

The free-for-all of an unregulated market encouraged businesses to transfer resources from productive to unproductive activities, so that much of their profit soon came from simple financial speculation. Although this speculation added to some people's wealth, it did not add to the nation's productivity, infrastructure, or supply of consumer goods. Those tasks remained the responsibility of the real economy.

Ultimately, the corporate scandals may fuel the mounting perception that free market economic policy merely rigs the market in favor of those best positioned to take advantage of it. Yet it is not at all evident that a shift in favor of a more interventionist government policy will take place. The movement toward a market-based economy may have stopped. President George W. Bush did sign a law that enforces stiffer penalties for corporate fraud, but the prospects for reregulation still run counter to the preferences of most policymakers and economists, who are unlikely to budge unless they are pushed by a lot of people.[77]

This reluctance heightens the persistent tension between the economy and social welfare. Although it seems clear that the era of infatuation with the marketplace is ending, the private sector still dominates the public. Whether it is direct economic assistance, environmental regulation, or the development of the public infrastructure, social welfare initiatives have little independence from the market and must be carried out on the market's terms. The corporate scandals of 2002 may yet bring more substantial change to the economics of social welfare. But if they do, it will surely depend on political organizing. It is the possibilities for such organizing that are the subject of the next two chapters, on the politics of social welfare and the social movements of people.

4

The Politics of Social Welfare Policy

The politics of social welfare policy is the twin of the economics of social welfare policy. Together, the two go a long way to defining a policy's essential features. But what is politics? And how does it interact with social welfare? For most Americans, politics merely means elections, and the interaction with social welfare policy simply means that a piece of social welfare legislation is voted up or down.

This chapter uses a broader definition. Here, politics means the political actors, institutions, and activities involved in the process of governing. This definition is encompassing. Political actors, for example, include the 435 members of the House of Representatives plus one hundred senators, all the congressional staff people, the different levels of the judiciary, and the executive branch. The term also refers to both elected and staff positions in state, local, and county government, as well as the people who try to lobby and influence them. If you have written a letter to an elected official, sent a donation to a group that fights against domestic violence, or joined a demonstration for day care, you are part of this process, too.

Many of these political actors staff the institutions that define the U.S. political landscape. The federal, state, and most local governments have executive (president, governor, mayor), legislative (Congress, state legislatures, city councils), and judicial (Supreme Court, state court, city/county court) branches. From antitax groups to gay and lesbian activists, single-issue organizations operate at every level, as do the political parties—Republican, Democratic, and third (Green Party, Independent, Right-to-Life), whose visibility expands every presidential election and shrinks in the intervening years. There are trade unions and business groups, community development coalitions and statewide health organizations, and political foundations that range from the American Enterprise Institute and the Heritage Foundation on the right to the Institute of Policy Studies on the left. Agreeing and disagreeing on many different issues, including social welfare policies, the activities of these institutions are the lifeblood of U.S. politics.

The activities themselves are extraordinarily varied. For example, along with the general election on the first Tuesday in November, we have primary elections that determine who will be the party's candidate and elections for state and county offices. If voters do not like a candidate's performance, some states allow for recall elections to remove an official before the completion of a term. In addition, eighteen states allow voters to amend their own constitution, twenty-one permit voters to enact legislative statutes, and twenty-four permit referenda, through which the voters can pass judgment on an act of the state legislature.[1]

An African American political rally from the late nineteenth century.

The nonelectoral activities are equally diverse. Lobbying, petitions, demonstrations, strikes, and boycotts are essential parts of the political process, and all have been used to advance social welfare legislation. In this legislation, as in other political matters, the eternal question is, Who should get what? This chapter on the politics of social welfare relies on ideas from political science to help us understand how we should think about this question. It begins with discussions of decision-making theories, conceptions of democracy, and debates about majority rule. It goes on to describe the basic features of our political system, including the characteristics that make it so distinctive. Finally, after reviewing the political functions of social welfare, the chapter's concluding section draws on these characteristics to set out some guidelines for making changes in social policy.

Political Science Theories: Decision Making, Definitions of Democracy, and Majority Rule

How are political decisions made? How do we go about deciding whether to enact a social policy? These question lie at the core of one of the oldest debates in political science. For much of the twentieth century, the concept of *interest-group pluralism*, the dominant model in the United States, offered a very reassuring answer.

In its purest form, interest-group pluralism is a competitive model of power based on several essential premises: (1) that U.S. political life consists of interest groups; (2) that those interest groups have roughly equivalent power; and (3) that the U.S. government is a fundamentally neutral institution that balances these interests on a case-by-case basis, sometimes siding with one interest (logging companies over environmentalists), and sometimes siding with another (environmentalists over logging companies). The crucial link among these premises is the belief that power is noncumulative; that is, just because a businessman wins on an issue related to his business does not mean that his power is transferable to his role as a citizen in the community.[2]

Pluralists see interest groups as a means of conveying to elected officials what the people want on a day-to-day basis. They believe the interest group system is democratic because it is so easy to organize a group in the United States. Because the government is open to the influence of groups once they are formed, they reason that any interest group can have its views taken into account by some public official.[3]

Pluralism reflects the substitution of large organizational structures for the individual as the predominant force shaping government policy. Reaching its height of popularity in the twenty years after World War II, it accurately mirrored the political calm and "normality" of the 1950s. In the aftermath of Vietnam and the battle over civil rights, however, other political scientists subjected pluralism to some very sharp criticism. Pluralism, they contended, is not nearly as democratic as its proponents claim because not all groups are created equal. As political scientist E. E. Schattschneider said, "The flaw in the pluralist heaven is that the heavenly chorus sings with a strong upper-class accent."[4] Biased toward the development of the private sector, pluralism tends to de-emphasize issues such as distributive justice, equality, eradication of poverty, and unemployment. Most tellingly in this critique, pluralism takes as a given only those issues that powerful interest groups put on the public agenda as well as what they choose to ignore.[5]

The breakdown of the pluralist consensus brought about a refinement of the arguments for pluralism as well as a sharper division in political theory. In this updated pluralism, political scientists acknowledged that state agencies themselves could act as interest groups, allying with outside interests and demanding greater expenditures on an issue. Some even admitted that groups with fewer economic resources did not have as much power. Yet, because the government sometimes sided with these weaker groups, these pluralists maintained that even this admission did not fundamentally invalidate their theory.[6]

Public choice theory was the conservative response to the decline in the popularity of pluralism. Developed by political scientists James Buchanan and Gordon Tullock, public choice theory applies market principles to the study of nonmarket decision making. It studies how decisions are made in the public sector based on the notion of each person's benefiting through *mutual exchange*. Mutual exchange presumably works in the marketplace because buyer and seller each get something: if you purchase a CD player, you try to get the best CD player you can for your money, and the seller tries to make the largest possible profit. Buchanan and Tullock contend that the same principles operate in the public sector. There, it is inevitable that people will seek to maximize their gains by taxing everyone to pay for public goods used by just a few. From this reasoning, it follows that markets are a more rational system than voting because they are the only way of avoiding a constant surplus of public goods.[7]

Public choice theory rests on two key premises. First, it rejects any suggestion that the state represents the whole nation: individuals may envision a United States of America, but it does not really exist as a collective entity. Making an analogy to the market, public choice theorists instead contend that in the absence of a state, all the members of a constitutional democracy have is their own individual preferences. Second, public choice theorists insist that all policy decision making should make at least one person better off without anyone being worse off. In practice, this criterion has extremely conservative implications, because it means that no policy can help the poor if it makes a single wealthy person less affluent.[8]

Public choice theory clearly has its biases, and these biases make it vulnerable to several criticisms. To begin with, the state does exist, and people do have emotional ties to it because they do not act only out of economic motives. For example, despite low pay and less than idyllic conditions, some people even take social work jobs with the government to do something about a social problem, such as children living in poverty. And, though no one would seriously dispute the notion that we all try to use the public sector for our own benefit, most public choice theory takes this idea and applies it solely to social welfare programs. In the hands of its theorists, the notion of maximizing personal gains relates to health and education and public assistance, but not to the Department of Defense, the Department of Energy, or the Department of Commerce. By this standard, if you advocate for yourself to get a little more money in your welfare check, you are (ab)using the public sector; but if you lobby to get a large defense contract, the principle of government programs benefiting particular groups—indeed, the very notion of too much military hardware—does not apply.

Besides, it is not always quite so clear just who benefits from social welfare programs. Certainly, as this book has emphasized, recipients do, but because so much of what they get is quickly passed on to others, they are hardly the only beneficiaries. Landlords, for example, get welfare rent checks, health providers get paid for services to poor people, and business as a whole transfers to the public sector the responsibility of paying for many of the poor's most basic needs. Public choice theorists may well be right that the public sector is also a marketplace. Yet, because the poor lack money, they rarely do well in the marketplace and are hardly the group best positioned to take advantage of its existence.

Just as public choice theory criticized pluralism from the right, *elite theory* criticized it from the left. There are several varieties of elite theory, but the key difference between it and pluralism remains the permanence of the ruling minority. In pluralism, the ruling minority always changes, as one victorious interest group succeeds another—a victory for tenants following quickly on a victory for landlords. In elite theory, by contrast, although these changes may occur, a real transfer of power never takes place. Instead, regardless of what happens on any single issue, the most important people in government, business, and the military retain control. They are the group that constitutes a permanent power elite.[9]

A second variety of elite theory is more explicitly Marxist. Instead of focusing on the background or institutional affiliations of this elite, this theory contends that there is a ruling class that derives its power from its position in a capitalist economy. This ruling class may rule—that is, it may exercise direct power—but it does not have to, for the simple reason that the state in a capitalist society is a capitalist state that must, above all, remain responsive to the economically dominant class. This responsiveness does not necessarily mean that it will always side with business. Indeed, sometimes, taking a longer-range perspective, it is better for social, economic, and political stability if the government overrides business concerns and enacts some social reforms. On balance, however, a capitalist state ultimately depends on a profitable capitalist economy. If the state acts too vigorously against business interests, businesses will stop investing, the economy will slow, and the government will receive less tax revenue. As long as the state operates within these limits, it has to ensure that the ruling class remains both profitable and powerful.[10]

Most American political scientists reject the slightest suggestion that the

United States might have a ruling class. Democracies, after all, do not have ruling classes. Furthermore, the United States is supposed to be a highly mobile society, where anyone can rise to the top and no group rules, at least not permanently. Indeed, the Marxist belief that societies are organized to serve the needs of one class has never found much favor here. Instead, the vast majority of Americans see conflict as occurring between groups, not classes, and they do not believe that any group always wins.

Yet, even if we set aside these assumptions, there are still serious problems with this theory. The most pressing revolves around the issue of homeostasis, the idea that a system always tends to return to a state of balance or equilibrium. Elite theory, especially its Marxist variant, is often homeostatic: it assumes that the reproduction of capitalism is the main function of every public policy. So, according to elite theory, lower taxes on the wealthy reproduce capitalism, but so do a higher minimum wage and better housing for the poor, both of which presumably make workers more productive. In effect, by minimizing the benefits of progressive change, this theory can create a false all-or-nothing alternative: either capitalism is replaced, or every kind of intermediate social reform simply bolsters its position. Most social workers committed to social change reject the idea that these are the only two possible outcomes.

Definitions of Democracy

In addition to their disagreements about politics and government, U.S. political scientists have also had a long-standing debate about the nature of democracy. There are two different issues in this debate. The first view holds that a government is democratic if its *procedures* are democratic. The criteria for the existence of such a procedural democracy are universal participation, political equality, majority rule, and a general responsiveness to public opinion. In this view, the outcomes do not have to be particularly equal, but if most people could have participated in the decision making, then the process is democratic.

The second view sets a higher standard. Here, democracy must be evident not merely in procedures, but in the real *substance* of government policies—in freedom of religion and in the meeting of human needs. Theorists who hold this substantive definition of democracy focus on what government actually does. Some believe that the existence of civil rights alone is sufficient. For others, a genuine democracy depends on the elimination of economic insecurity, which requires the provision of social rights such as health care, employment, education, and housing.[11]

In addition to the debate about definitions, there are also two different forms of democracy. These forms are usually identified as *direct* and *indirect*. Direct democracy assumes that people act as their own representatives. Under these circumstances, there is no intermediate layer of government between the ruler and the ruled. In the United States, the mythical version of this government is the New England town meeting, where everyone gathers to debate and resolve important political issues. The modern descendents of this tradition are state referenda, which enable voters to participate directly in the making of laws.

The second form, indirect or representative democracy, involves the election of a group of people who determine state policy. Proponents of representative democracy reject the participatory variety as impractical for contemporary society. They contend that the size and complexity of modern societies prevent significant participation. In their view, because citizens possess inadequate knowledge, any demands for significant participation run counter to requirements of efficiency and leadership, which would seriously undermine modern bureaucratic, hierarchical, and industrial organizations. Following the precepts of indirect democracy, they instead prefer competition among elites for the people's votes, limited participation, and restrictions on popular control over the leaders.

In many respects, the United States today adheres to this model. State legislatures vote on amendments to the Constitution. The members of the Electoral College, not the people, elect the president. Likewise, citizens do not control who is appointed to the Supreme Court, the monetary policy of

In a representative democracy, officeholders represent the people who elected them.

the Federal Reserve Bank, or whether war will be declared. Changes in social welfare policy are not put up for a popular vote either.[12]

To be truly democratic, however, representative democracy must meet certain standards. The first of these is popular sovereignty. By popular sovereignty, advocates of representative democracy mean that government policies reflect the popular will, people participate in the political process, high-quality information and debate are available, and the majority rules. Political equality is equally important. That means one person, one vote, not "one dollar, one vote," or the old corrupt political machine slogan "Vote early, vote often." Finally, to make it all work, political liberty—freedom of speech, conscience, press, and assembly—is essential. Popular sovereignty, political equality, and political liberty: these, then, are the three fundamental prerequisites of a fair representative democracy.[13]

Majority Rule?

A democracy presumes the rule of the majority. But suppose the majority uses its position to abuse or oppress the minority? Is that democratic, too?

This is the issue that always lurks just beneath the surface of any democratic society. And it is true: a democratic majority may threaten the minority in its midst. Let us not forget, however, that no other system, whether it is a dictatorship or an oligarchy, is demonstrably less threatening. Besides, although demographic and racial minorities are fixed, the losers in the middle of the political spectrum do change. You may be in a minority on educational spending only to find that you are in a majority on the issue of gun control. In short, as long as the majority does not actually violate the civil rights of the minority, the problem of abusive majorities may be a stubborn one, but it is more amenable to reasonable solutions in a democracy than in any other system.[14]

The drafters of the Constitution, moreover, were acutely conscious of this issue. Indeed, that is why they built into the Constitution so many obstacles to majority rule. For example, Al Gore won a majority of the popular vote in the 2000 presidential election but lost the presidency to George W. Bush in the Electoral College. In Congress, it is harder to pass a law because legislators need a majority in not one, but two houses of Congress. Likewise, because all federal and many state judges are appointed rather than elected, they are always protected from direct expression of the popular will. And until the Seventeenth Amendment provided for their election in 1913, members of the state legislature—not the citizens in the state—chose its two senators.[15] Finally, in addition to these limits on each part of the government, there is also the systemwide principle of checks and balances, in which one branch of the government acts as a constraint on the other. The controversy surrounding social welfare often makes it harder to assemble a majority, but from the election process to the governing process, every one of these hurdles makes it harder for a majority to translate its political will into political action.

The United States has a federal system of government. In this system, national, state, and local authorities all share power. Indeed, at the local level, there are even quasi-governmental bodies for issues like water, power, transportation, airports, and industrial development. The officials in these bodies are usually appointed rather than elected. Americans often say they do not like government. Nevertheless, if you add up the number of governments at all levels, we actually have eighty-five thousand of them. The total bears testimony to Americans' infatuation with small local governments, an infatuation that federalism encourages and affirms.[16]

Federalism derives its authority from the Constitution, which lays out the responsibilities of different levels of government and seeks to specify the nature of the relationship among them. For example, Article 6 of the Constitution says the federal government retains supremacy in its own sphere, so that federal laws always take precedence over state legislation. But the Constitution also limits the power of national government through the Bill of Rights and confers power on the states through the reserve clause, which grants the states all those powers not specifically given to the federal government. Enacted in the aftermath of the Civil War, the Thirteen, Fourteenth, and Fifteenth Amendments to the Constitution place additional limitations on the states' powers by outlawing slavery, guaranteeing due process, and extending the vote to African Americans. At the same time, however, the Constitution provides for a state role in the national government: there are two senators from each state, and the state conducts the apportionment and election of representatives. Finally, in the relations among state governments, Article 4, section 1 of the Constitution says that each state must give the laws of other states "full faith and credit." Altogether, these provisions set out the limits and responsibilities of each level within the federal system so that the whole fabric of government is tightly interwoven.[17]

The role of federalism in U.S. history involves four distinct periods. From 1789 to 1877, the federal government put itself at the service of the states, aiding them in foreign affairs, defense, and western expansion. Then, in the second stage of U.S. federalism, from 1877 to 1913, the federal role continued to expand, but it expanded more slowly than the role of the states, often with the goal of preventing the states from regulating corporations. The era of cooperative federalism between 1913 and the early 1970s marked the third stage. This was the period when the states and the federal government pursued shared goals such as regulation of public utilities and initiated joint programs in education, highway construction, and banking regulation.

The fourth stage emerged in the final decades of the twentieth century. Originally designated by President Nixon as the New Federalism, this policy concentrated federal power at the White House but gave money to the states through block grants and revenue sharing.[18] Its premise is that although the federal government should set broad categories for programs, the states are closer to the problems and know best how to spend the money. In the most recent twist on this fourth stage, a narrow conservative majority on the Supreme Court has swung emphatically toward states' rights. In one case, it ruled that state workers could not go before a state court to sue their state employers for violations of federal labor law; in another, it declared that the states did not have to defend themselves from complaints by private citizens before federal agencies.[19]

Because it is so central to the U.S. system of government, federalism has always been the subject of intense debate. Advocates come to its defense from two different directions. Conservatives value it because their understanding of federalism—a *dual federalism*, with separate spheres for the national government and the states—requires a limited government. If the national government rules by enumerated powers alone, possesses a strictly defined list of constitutional responsibilities, and is, like the states, sovereign only within its own sphere, then, as the above Supreme Court cases suggest, the federal government is going to be hobbled. Just as conservatives desire, this is a government that will not get much done.[20]

Other political scientists, however, defend federalism because they believe it really works. Rejecting the dual sovereignty/separate spheres argument, they describe our system of government as a marble cake or *cooperative federalism*, a federalism in which all the levels of government join together to solve problems. In this vision, the FBI and local law enforcement share leads to catch criminals and terrorists, and Health and Human Services in the federal Cabinet provides information that will help state welfare departments to implement welfare reform and evaluate other new social programs.[21]

For these political scientists, federalism is simply the best system for the United States. We are a large, diverse country, with a great diversity of needs; state and local governments are closer to the people; and the states can function as laboratories of public policy. They believe federalism succeeds, at least in part, because it is the perfect vehicle for such innovation and experimentation and can foster problem solving.

Yet critics of federalism make some equally persuasive arguments. Federalism, they contend, perpetuates a lack of national standards. Today, this omission means that there are no national standards in education; for the first two-thirds of the twentieth century, it meant that blacks could not vote in the South. Likewise, on the issue of the relationship of Americans to their government, these critics claim that because the federal government gets more media attention, most people are better informed about the national government and, in some way, closer to it. There is also, on a whole host of issues like pollution, truck weights, and welfare, the problem of the lack of uniformity in rules and regulations. Only national regulations can truly address national problems such as poverty and acid rain.[22]

Inevitably, these criticisms raise some larger questions about the possibility for social change. In a decentralized federal system like the United States, advocates for social change have to coordinate the activities of their supporters across a wider range of institutions than do their opponents. That is because, though reformers need to win in every part of the government that can block change, opponents need to hold onto only one. Hence, passage of a law in Congress does little good if a reformer does not also have sufficient support from the president and the judiciary.

The same fragmentation of government makes it easier for investors to leave a jurisdiction when they do not like its laws. If a state tightens its rules about garbage disposal or pays a higher minimum wage, an investor can read-ily cross the border to a neighboring state. By encouraging each state to negotiate a separate deal, federalism accentuates the differences that promote political factionalism. In most European countries, centralized and well-run governments minimize differences. Sometimes, they can even enforce socie-tywide negotiations between opposing groups, such as those between labor and business. Decentralized structures cannot do this. Instead, they take the differences they find in a society and maximize their politically paralyzing effects. For this reason, it is much harder to bring about social change in a federal system like the one we have in the United States.[23]

Checks and Balances

Under federalism, the separation of powers assigns the law-making, law-enforcing, and law-interpreting functions of government to, respectively, the legislative, executive, and judicial branches. These branches are distinct and independent of one another. Perhaps that is why the U.S. system of govern-ment also provides a mechanism for giving each branch of government some measure of scrutiny and control over the other branches. Political scientists usually describe this control as a system of check and balances.[24]

It is quite an intricate system. The president nominates federal judges, but when they decide cases, he, as head of the executive branch, must carry out their rulings. Similarly, Congress controls the budget of the courts, can im-peach federal judges, and has the authority to change the organizational ju-risdiction of the lower courts. Yet, when it enacts laws and the president signs them, the courts can still declare them unconstitutional. The president can also propose a law, but Congress can refuse to pass it. Other powers Congress retains include the right to modify the president's budget, to withhold ap-proval of presidential administrative and judicial nominations, to reject trea-ties that the president has negotiated, and even to impeach the president. Conversely, if Congress enacts a law that the president does not like, the president can veto the legislation. Once again, however, this decision can also be overruled, but only by a two-thirds majority of Congress. In sum, the system of checks and balances works just as Thomas Jefferson envisioned it: "The powers of government should be so evenly divided and balanced among several bodies of magistracy, as that no one could transcend their legal limits, without being effectively checked and constrained by the others."[25]

The Powers of Government

The Presidency

The executive branch, the legislative branch, and the judiciary: quite apart from the system of mutual checks and balances, Jefferson wanted each branch to have its own distinct set of powers. As the U.S. government has grown in size and complexity, these powers have evolved over time. Yet they are still unique and distinctive enough to be recognizable to an original drafter of the Constitution.

The presidency is a complex job, with many roles. Sometimes, the president acts as chief of state, the world leader who represents the United States. But he is also chief executive, the person who manages the executive branch; commander in chief of the armed forces; chief diplomat; chief legislator; chief of his own political party; and occasionally, in some of his memorable moments, the voice of the people (Roosevelt's "We have nothing to fear but fear itself," or Kennedy's "Ask not what your country can do for you. Ask what you can do for your country"). Consolidating these roles, political scientists identify four subpresidencies: foreign policy, economic policy, other domestic policy functions, and symbolic/moral leadership.[26]

Opinions about these presidential roles tend to run in cycles. Often, in the aftermath of unofficial and/or unilateral military interventions, critics complain that the president has gone too far. Angry about the dangers of an imperial chief executive, they plead for a return to a more traditional conception of the president's role. At other times, however, when one party controls Congress and another occupies the White House, fears about political paralysis and ineffectuality replace concerns about an imperial presidency. In these circumstances, many commentators worry that the president is just not powerful enough to get anything done.

Certainly, over the past two hundred years, the dominant trend has been toward an expansion of presidential powers. With the exception of Jefferson, Jackson, and Lincoln, a more literal reading of the separation of powers held through much of the nineteenth century. During the past one hundred years, however, the chief executive has become much more active. Not only have the mass media turned the presidency into a more visible office with an enhanced potential for public support, but a larger number of presidents— Wilson, Franklin Roosevelt, Nixon, Reagan, and Clinton—were, by virtue of both personality and circumstances, such as a war or a depression, more inclined toward strong leadership. In Congress, the political parties frequently looked to presidential leadership on important political issues. In the nation as a whole, the chief executive's role expanded because economic and social conditions created a need for regulatory legislation that presidents could offer by virtue of their national perspective and constituency.[27]

The growth in the executive office of the president constitutes one of the most dramatic indications of the expansion of the president's job. The vice president and the Cabinet are both part of the executive office. In recent years, the president has assigned the vice president, who once held a largely ceremonial role, some policy function: President Clinton gave Vice President Gore responsibility for increasing government efficiency under his "reinventing government" initiative; President Bush assigned Vice President Cheney the task of formulating energy policy.

The role of Cabinet members is to advise the president and direct the affairs of the federal agencies under their respective departments. There are fourteen Cabinet-level departments; the five most relevant to social welfare— Health and Human Services, Housing and Urban Development, Labor, Education, and Veterans Affairs—are a big part of the reason for the expansion of the executive office. Other components of the executive office include the Office of Management and Budget, which prepares the annual budget and follows appropriations and outlays of each federal agency; the Council of Economic Advisors, which advises the president on economic policy; the National Security Council; the Environmental Protection Agency; the Office of National Drug Control Policy; and the Central Intelligence Agency.[28] Although these departments do not meet with the president as frequently as his closest advisors in the White House, they all play an important role in the development of national policy.

Congress

The U.S. Congress is a bicameral (two-house) legislature consisting of a Senate and a House of Representatives. There are one hundred senators, two from each state, elected to serve six-year terms; every two years, one-third of the seats are up for election. The House of Representatives has 435 members allocated by population among the fifty states. Unlike the Senate, every two years each member stands for election. The drafters of the Constitution developed this structure as a compromise between a vote based solely on population, which would have been biased toward the more populous states, and a vote based solely on statehood, which would have granted the smaller states disproportionate power. Politically, the structure has the effect of insulating the Senate from the direct, and possibly temporary, impulsiveness of public opinion. Although members of both the House of Representatives and the Senate average eleven years in office, the Senate is plainly the more prestigious body. It is the institution that is supposed to slow the pace of social change, the place where the passions of the House are supposed to cool.[29]

Article 1 of the Constitution entrusts Congress with "all legislative powers granted herein." Elaborating on this mandate, the Constitution specifies a detailed list of responsibilities. Among these are the power to declare war; raise and support armies; collect taxes and tariffs; ratify treaties; approve major presidential appointments, such as Supreme Court justices and ambassadors to foreign countries; borrow money; regulate commerce among the states; coin money; establish post offices; and issue patents. To fulfill these responsibilities, members of Congress introduce about eight thousand bills in each two-year session. In an average session, about 95 percent of these bills never get out of committee.[30]

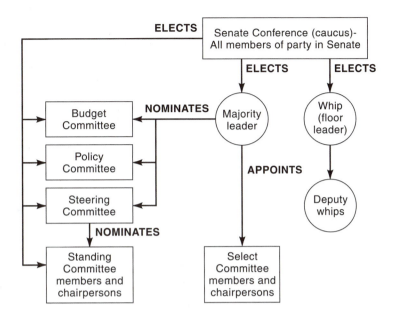

Majority party structure in the Senate.

Majority party structure in the House of Representatives.

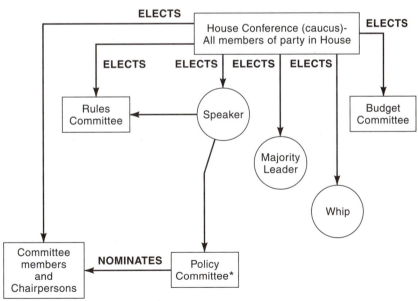

* Includes Speaker (chair), majority leader, chief and deputy whips, caucus chair, four members appointed by the Speaker, and twelve members elected by regional caucuses.

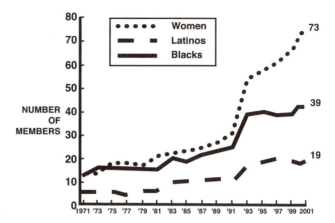

Women, African Americans, and Latinos in Congress, 1971–2002. Slowly but steadily, the U.S. Congress has become more diversified.

The House and Senate rely on different kinds of organization. In the House, the Speaker of the House is the political leader. Technically a constitutional officer, he is, in reality, the leader of the majority party. Within the majority party, the majority leader and majority whip (whose job, just as the name implies, is to count votes and keeps his fellow party members in line) follow him in the leadership hierarchy. A minority leader and minority whip provide political direction on the other side of the aisle. In the Senate, as in the House, there are majority and minority leaders and majority and minority whips, and the majority leader performs the functions of the House Speaker. It is the job of the majority leader to schedule legislation, maintain the majority coalition, and keep the peace within his or her party.[31]

The House Speaker and the Senate majority leader reign over an increasingly diverse Congress. The number of women in Congress has risen, though not as much as in the state legislatures. Between 1975 and 2002, the number of female state legislators climbed from 8 to 22.6 percent. By contrast, the number of women in Congress has now reached 13.6 percent (13 Senators and 60 Congresswomen), just below the global median of thirty countries, from Kuwait with no female representatives to Sweden with 40 percent. African Americans have made similar strides, rising from 6 percent in 1991–92 to 9 percent in 2002. During the same period, the number of Hispanic Americans more than doubled from 2 to 4 percent. In 1995, however, House Speaker Newt Gingrich cut the staff and budget support for the congressional black and Hispanic caucuses, substantially reducing the power of organized minorities in Congress.[32]

The Judiciary

The judiciary is a coequal branch of the federal government. There are ninety-four federal district courts with thirteen courts of appeals. Each judge has a lifetime appointment, and by tradition, any appointment must be acceptable to the senior senator of the state involved who belongs to the same party as the president.

The U.S. Supreme Court is perched on top of this judicial pyramid. As the final arbiter of all constitutional issues, the Supreme Court scrutinizes the interpretations of the lower courts when they apply the laws of Congress and the states to particular cases. To make these decisions, it relies on the principle of stare decisis (literally, let the decision stand), which means that unless there is a compelling reason to reverse a precedent, it is likely to decide the same issues in the same way. The senior justice on the majority side determines which judge is responsible for drafting this opinion. This is not an easy task, because if the opinion is written by someone with a more extreme view, other justices in the majority may withdraw their support, but if it is written by a more moderate justice, the decision may appear muddled and weak. The writer of the opinion must also be politically acceptable to his or her audience. For example, in 1944, Chief Justice Harlan Stone asked Justice Felix Frankfurter, whom he considered the most brilliant legal scholar on the Court, to write the majority opinion in *Smith v. Albright*, in which the majority rejected the Southern practice of preventing blacks from participating in primaries. But after he made the request, Justice Robert H. Jackson wrote to Stone noting that Frankfurter—Jewish, foreign-born, and from New England—could not win the South, regardless of his brilliance. Stone took Jackson's advice and assigned the task of opinion writing to Justice Stanley Reed, a Protestant, U.S.-born, Southern Democrat from Kentucky.[33]

In England, legal authorities believed that parliamentary laws were superimposed on purer, judge-made common law. In the United States, however, both judge-made law and legislative law get the same respect. Judges here derive some of their power from the British common law tradition. But they also benefit from a distrust of popular legislative majorities and from the ongoing need to interpret a written constitution. Nevertheless, according to the separation of powers, each branch is, in theory, the equal of the other.[34]

The power of the courts over the legislature goes back to the principle of judicial review, established by *Marbury v. Madison* in 1803, when the Supreme Court declared that it had a right to determine whether a federal law was constitutional. Sixteen years later, in *McCulloch v. Maryland* (1819), the Supreme Court extended the principle even further and applied it to state laws. For much of the Court's subsequent history, its decisions were usually intended to prevent other institutions from doing something. It was not until 1954 and the historic order to desegregate the schools in *Brown v. Board of Education* that the Court adopted a more activist role. From an insistence on due process in the termination of welfare clients (*Goldberg v. Kelly*, 1970) to the establishment of a right to abortion in *Roe v. Wade* (1973), many of the decisions that emerged from this activist role have been debated fiercely over the past thirty years.

Yet judicial activism has never been without its limits. It is true that judges are politically insulated and can therefore act more decisively than legislators on some major social problems. Judges granted legal protections to homeless people in some states—the right to vote and the right to shelter—at least partly for this reason. Nevertheless, judges do not like to make decisions that

At both the federal and local level, the courts serve as one of the key institutions in our system of checks and balances.

put themselves in the position of administering social agencies or monitoring the subsequent compliance to a ruling on desegregation or financing education. They also have a conflict between deciding a particular case and making a general policy. All these considerations incline judges to move cautiously. Before they intervene, they consider the extent to which new decisions alter judicial precedents and overturn prior legislation. They also try to determine what specific policy consequences follow from a judicial decision and how these decisions will affect future administrative discretion.[35]

Disagreement about the proper way to interpret the Constitution frames much of this debate. There are three basic positions, each of which implies a more or less activist posture toward the law. In the *original intent* theory, judges are supposed to uncover what the drafters of the Constitution intended. Because it is difficult to divine what the drafters would have thought about social and technological issues that did not exist until two centuries after ratification of the Constitution, this theory is the least interventionist. The *living Constitution* theory stands at the other end of the spectrum. Relying on the evolving history of the United States as a nation, it sees the Constitution as a document that demands new interpretations to change with the times. Between these two perspectives lies the *plain meaning of the text* theory, which contends that judges should seek to determine what the Constitution says. Relying on this theory, judges usually find sufficient latitude in the Constitution to justify a moderate degree of activism.[36] Because none of these positions has won decisive support among either legal scholars or the public at large the judiciary will continue to struggle with the issue of its role in relation to the other branches of government. In short, although the concept of separation of powers may be described in the Constitution, its practical application is the subject of a constant struggle.

The Bureaucracy

Americans frequently rail against bureaucracy, especially the bureaucracy that they associate with big government. But what is a bureaucracy? And what are distinctive features of bureaucracy in the U.S. government?

A bureaucracy is merely a large organization in which people with specialized knowledge are divided into a clearly defined hierarchy of bureaus, each with a specialized mission. There is a chain of command and a set of formal rules to guide behavior; advancement is based on merit. A bureaucracy is supposed to be able to carry out complex tasks.[37] Bureaucracies are best when the tasks are big and repetitive, but they stumble when the problem or issue they face deviates sharply from what they have been programmed to manage. There are few situations more annoying than when you are the person with one of these problems; in these circumstances, you are sure to be one of the people joining the clamor against a maddening bureaucracy.

Viewed as a whole, the federal bureaucracy is daunting. After all, the executive branch totals 181 federal agencies. These agencies vary greatly in size. In 2001, the number of people employed in the major social welfare departments included 4,581 in Education; 10,154 in Housing and Urban Development; 16,016 in Labor; and 63,323 in Health and Human Services. By contrast, the Department of Veterans Affairs employed 223,137 and the Department of Defense totaled 670,568. These numbers suggest that if the federal bureaucracy is large, it is also lopsided in its staffing, with almost 900,000 workers employed in just two departments, Veterans Affairs and Defense. This fact highlights the importance of the military during the cold war in the growth of the federal government. It also puts in perspective demands to cut the bureaucracy, for the departments that are usually targeted for these cutbacks (e.g., the Department of Education) constitute a tiny fraction of the federal government.[38]

Some of the difficulties this bureaucracy confronts are typical of bureaucracies anywhere. From teaching students to eliminating pollution, the tasks assigned to it are often difficult. There are also problems measuring performance. In the private sector, performance can easily be derived from the bottom line, but in the absence of profits, the standards for bureaucratic success are much more elusive. Also, just like anywhere else, bureaucracy in the U.S. government suffers from the problems of sluggishness and routinization as well as from frustrating red tape.

Yet some distinctive features also characterize bureaucracy in the U.S. government. Because U.S. bureaucracies lack a tradition of upper-class service to the king, we have no history of an elite civil service. Instead, many Americans consider civil servants at best consumers of their tax dollars and, at worst, potential grafters. Civil service reform in the United States did not occur until the passage of the Pendleton Act in 1883, which set up a civil service commission to establish qualifications, examinations, and procedures. This delay means that even though, by law, political patronage affects just a small percentage of the jobs in the civil service, the suspicion of patronage continues to hover over much of the federal bureaucracy.[39]

Any discussion of the federal bureaucracy must acknowledge the relationship of that bureaucracy to the private sector economy in which it functions. Valuing the private sector, the business community, together with a substantial segment of the broader American public, has either hamstrung public programs or supported them as occasional exceptions to the ideology of limited government. We discuss this problem at greater length in the policy analysis chapters, but for the moment, it is sufficient to note, for example, that on principle, public housing programs cannot be any more attractive than housing in the private sector. Similarly, as we do not recognize an ongoing role for public employment programs, we can fund 125 of them, but only on a case-by-case basis: to prevent riots by youth in the summer, or to defuse the opposition of union workers to passage of the North American Free Trade Act. A government bureaucracy that is not allowed to outdo the private sector—one that is impeded by politics, economics, and ideology from developing coherent and effective programs—is not going to succeed, and the resulting failures are going to forever taint its reputation.[40]

No wonder, then, that the federal bureaucracy is an organizational jumble. It is responsive to the president, but sometimes also to Congress. There are few unambiguous lines of authority, with some units having no clear relationship to other agencies and departments. Without a centralized authority to build it up, the federal bureaucracy is internally competitive, less cohesive, and less powerful. Situated in the midst of a sprawling federalist system, it is often responsible for overseeing the administration of federal social welfare programs in the states. Between its uncertain mandate and this unwieldy task, it is no wonder that the federal bureaucracy often gives the whole concept of bureaucracy such a bad name.[41]

U.S. Government: Its Distinctive Characteristics

Most of us have grown up in the system described above, hear regular references to it in the media, and value many of its positive features. But because we see it as "normal," we tend to underestimate how different from other countries this system is. Some of its most distinctive features include the role of political parties, the low rate of voter participation, our tendency toward divided government, the pattern of critical elections and the cycles of American social reform, and finally, the phenomenon of "American exceptionalism," a term that political scientists have coined to explain these distinctions.

A review of these features offers a guide to understanding, and changing, the politics of social welfare.

U.S. Political Parties

Republican, Democrat, Independent, or a member of one of the smaller third parties (Greens, Libertarian, Right-to-Life)? As children, we quickly discover our parents' party affiliation, an affiliation that often influences our own political choices. At the same time, we rarely learn one key piece of information: our two-party system is actually quite unusual. By comparison with other countries, for example, just a very small number of Americans have any real connection to the parties between elections, most do not pay dues to any party, and few are card-carrying members. With the chairperson and staff of the party's national and state committees handling the vast majority of ongoing political work, our parties are weak and insubstantial, a loose collection of state and local interests. As a result, our election campaigns tend to be candidate- rather than party-centered.

Why do we have such a system? Mostly, it's due to our electoral rules. The U.S. political system operates on a winner-take-all model, with single-member districts and restrictions on minor parties—for example, a large number of signatures is required to get a party on the ballot, and few states allow cross-endorsements (voting for a major party candidate on a minor party's line). Nor do we have proportional representation giving legislative power to every party above a threshold, say 5 or 10 percent of the votes cast. In this system, where simple majorities have an exaggerated effect (51 percent in every congressional district gives the victorious party 100—not 51—percent of Congress), parties appeal to the center, and voters for any minor party risk squandering their vote and electing the politician whose opinions most diverge from their own.[42]

Just look, for example, at the electoral dilemma facing those who believe in much greater social welfare spending, with sharply increased benefits and comprehensive national programs for day care, health care, and full employment—that is, something approaching what many European countries have. This model assumes "centralized and bureaucratized states with parliamentary parties dedicated to pursuing policy programs in the name of entire classes or other broad, nation-spanning collectivities."[43] We do not have these institutions. Instead, a relatively weak labor movement and electoral rules leave voters with little choice. They confront a system in which politicians make symbolic appeals or offer highly individualized benefits, but no major party advocates a redistributional welfare state or one that seriously pursues full employment. Although the two parties do occasionally expand social spending by building electoral coalitions around patronage and appeals to specific ethnic and racial groups, voters committed to more generous social policies either resign themselves to a "lesser evil" or "waste" their ballots on a minor party.[44]

The functioning of our political parties traces its roots to deep within the U.S. system. As social policy analysts Frances Fox Piven and Richard Cloward put it,

> The animus of the Founders toward parties of course reflected their fear of a populace that could be mobilized by parties. There was reason to be fearful. The protection once provided to the propertied by the armies of the British Crown was gone at a time when radical democratic currents stirred by the revolutionary war were strong, among a still-armed population. If it was unwise to simply ignore democratic aspirations, they could nevertheless be blunted and diffused by a system of 'checks and balances' which effectively divided authority for key policies between the Congress, the presidency, and the courts, and also made these decision-making centers at least partially independent of each other.

These arrangements officially restricted party influence over government, promoted shifting and flexible alliances, and made it harder to turn election victories into policy. They not only fractured the authority of the central government, but created serious obstacles to coherent party organization.[45]

Nineteenth-century American politics added its own twist to this legacy. During this period, the U.S. government was primarily a state of "courts and parties," meaning that, unlike today, it was a government without much of a bureaucratic structure. This structure did not begin to come into existence until the late nineteenth century and in fact did not reach its maturity until the New Deal.[46] The states, however, had granted voting rights to virtually all white men by the 1830s. But because mass voting preceded the establishment of a competent bureaucracy, there was little to be obtained from the state. Instead, if you wanted something from your government, you got it as patronage from your political party. From ward clerk to county commissioner, your party then relied on this patronage to nurture its organizational needs.

This development had significant implications. Because manhood suffrage and competing patronage parties existed at the very start of capitalist industrialization, workers learned to separate their politics into two parts. In one part, at their place of employment, they fought for better wages and working conditions; in another, at home, they functioned politically as citizens in ethnically defined communities. The workplace and the community: without a working-class politics that merged these two parts, American trade unions did not establish a stable relationship to working-class parties, as was done in Europe at the turn of the twentieth century.[47]

Today, political scientists divide on the issue of whether political parties are experiencing a period of decline or a period of resurgence. The argument that we have entered a period of decline usually cites the role of direct primaries, which, once they were established in the early 1970s, deprived party leaders of patronage and power. But there are surely other factors. Civil service reform means that the president controls fewer than four thousand appointments. Moreover, since the communication revolution enabled candidates to raise money without relying on parties, election campaigns can be conducted with fewer campaign workers. The result is that despite increases in fund-raising and campaign assistance, there has been a decline in party identification, confidence, popular regard, and willingness to vote a party ticket.[48]

But the picture is not completely bleak, and there is some evidence of party resurgence. As the civil rights movement pushed the suburbs to become Republican, the Democrats became a smaller, urban party: just 27 percent of all Americans now live in central cities with a population in excess of fifty thousand people.[49] This neat demographic division—Republican suburbs, Democratic cities—increased the homogeneity of the political parties and raised the confidence of office seekers that they could cede authority to party leaders without hurting their own electoral prospects. And if the party leaders can speak for everyone, perhaps the parties will return as brand names, a new, if not entirely successful method of political marketing.[50]

Today, the modern Democratic and Republican Parties agree on many fundamentals, including the role of the private sector, not too much government, and the war on terrorism. Although they do fight vigorously about some social and environmental issues, it would be wrong to mistake the ideological distance between them. Certainly, on economic matters over the past twenty-five years, the differences between the parties have diminished. Both generally accept the dominance of a market economy and the inevitability of globalization. They believe in fiscal austerity and restraints on social welfare. To be sure, the scandals about accounting and corporate fraud may yet break this apparent unanimity. But as Paul Begala, one of President Clinton's political aides, said while representing "the left" on the news program *Crossfire*, "You know, Bill Clinton saved the Democratic Party, with Al Gore, by pulling us back to the center, by disagreeing with the liberals on welfare reform and on crime and on trade. . . . If George Bush or someone would do that for the Republican Party, we would actually have a more viable and vibrant two-party system."[51] This statement reflects the conventional political wisdom of recent years. It reminds us that although the conflict between the parties sometimes gets intense, their positions within a broader spectrum are really quite close, so much so that we can reasonably say that the debates are all taking place in the same political family.

Voting

Poor voter turnout reflects a political disengagement that constitutes a second distinctive feature of the U.S. political system. Just 51 percent of the electorate voted in the 2000 presidential elections, up from 49 percent in 1996, when, for the first time since 1924, fewer than half the eligible voters participated in a presidential election. By international standards, this figure is quite low. Among other developed nations, voter participation in the most recent parliamentary elections runs from 60 percent in Japan and 61 percent in Canada, to 81 percent in Italy and 82 percent in Germany. In the United States, it has been a long, gradual decline since 72 percent of all eligible

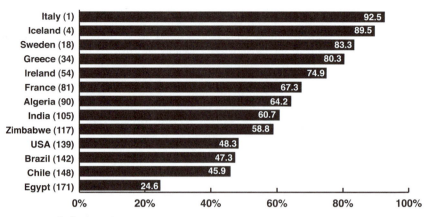

Voter turnout by country, all elections since 1945. On a list of 172 countries, the United States lags behind in average voter participation for all elections (both parliamentary and presidential) since 1945.

voters participated in the 1960 presidential campaign that elected John F. Kennedy.[52]

Why have Americans come to hate politics? Journalist E. J. Dionne attributes Americans' disinterest in politics to a series of false ideological choices. Americans, he says, want equality for women *and* a traditional family, less government interference in profoundly personal issues like abortion *and*, at same time, fewer women having abortions. Dionne claims that there is room for compromise in the middle—a provocative, not a soft compromise, one that can reengage us as citizens and help to hold the society together. [53]

Is Dionne on to something? Admittedly, it is often true that neither the policy nor the candidates offer Americans very many attractive choices. But there are still serious questions about this analysis. Like Begala, Dionne imagines a "magical midpoint" on the political spectrum that would make everyone happy. Have American politicians just been insufficiently resourceful in reaching this midpoint? Or is the very notion of this kind of middle already reflected in the convergence of our two major parties and one cause of what alienates people from politics? After all, in a 1998 Gallup poll, Americans agreed by a 70–25 margin that the government "is run by a few big interests." It is unlikely that compromises coming from this midpoint would truly satisfy them.[54]

This debate about electoral participation in the United States actually has a very long history. Although just 11 percent of all eligible voters, or one of every forty Americans, voted in the first presidential election, all states except Virginia and North Carolina had dropped property and religious requirements by 1829. Yet, though the United States was the first among the major democracies to democratize the electorate, the exclusion of blacks in the South meant that it was also the last. As the first to enfranchise all white males and the last to enfranchise everybody, the U.S. federal system from 1860 to 1960 had a mass two-party democracy in the East, North, and West, and Democratic racial oligarchy in the South.[55]

Nevertheless, some political scientists seek to reassure us about our disengagement. They maintain that just as a high turnout could indicate tension or conflict, low turnout can mean apathy or contentment. In its most elitist form, this argument even contains the suggestion that the "quality" of the electorate deteriorates as it expands. Too much participation by poor people is bad for this particular conception of democracy.

The decline in voter participation is also open to another interpretation. In this interpretation, public officials may talk about the importance of expanding the electorate, but no one makes any significant effort because it is not in their interest to do so. Until the 1960s, both the Democratic and Republican Party "machines" had a stake in mobilizing their members—the Democrats in the cities of the Northeast and Midwest, and the Republicans in the wealthier and more affluent suburbs. But now different sectors of the American upper-middle classes dominate the parties. The Republican base comes from business and professionals in the private sector, the Democrats from the upper-middle classes in sectors that are public and not-for-profit. Because each group has access to a variety of other political resources, such as money, the news media, universities, and interest groups, neither has much interest in a wider mobilization. From their perspective, poor people simply represent too great a risk: they might help a party win an election, but then they would make demands. Unwilling to meet these demands, both parties usually prefer a smaller and more affluent electorate.[56] They have gotten their wish, too. In the 2000 presidential election, about 75 percent of those earning more than $75,000 voted, compared to just 38 percent of those earning less than $10,000.[57]

Still, in recent years, two attempts have been made to reform the electoral system. The first was the so-called Motor Voter bill (1993), designed to boost participation by enabling people to register when they get a driver's license. Although the bill did make it easier to vote, one study found that 35 percent of nonvoters, but just 16 percent of voters, had moved in the prior two years.[58] Apparently, scarce locations and a long lead time continue to create obstacles. Even more critically, although registration makes it possible to vote, poor people are more likely to believe that campaigns do not focus on their issues. On election day, this belief tends to keep them at home.

The 2002 campaign finance law was the second attempt to reform the electoral system. Since the 1970s Watergate scandal, campaign finance law had always distinguished between "hard" and "soft" money. Hard money went directly to candidates; contributors sent soft money to the national and local parties. As a result, in 2000 alone, the national parties received $498 million in unregulated contributions. The new law prohibits these soft money contributions to the national parties. In exchange, however, it not only doubles from $1,000 to $2,000 the contribution that donors can make to individual candidates, but also allows contributors to donate $10,000 to each of the fifty state party committees. Although campaign finance reformers accepted this bill because they needed a win after ten years of congressional defeats, successful experiments with public financing in Maine and Arizona have already cast doubt on their basic premise that privately financed campaign systems can actually regulate the flow of big money. In the absence of such financing, the 2002 bill did little to remove the financial cloud that hangs over U.S. politics.[59]

Divided Government

A third distinctive characteristic of U.S. politics is the frequency with which we elect divided governments, with a president from one party and either or both houses of Congress from the other. Much of this chapter has emphasized the factors that lead to this arrangement, including federalism, the separation of powers between the executive and legislative branches, and the absence of disciplined national parties.[60] Yet we still have not resolved the question of whether divided government plays a positive or a negative role.

Essentially, the argument in favor of divided government is that it is carrying out the wishes of the Constitution's drafters. Concerned about tyranny and the abuse of power, they designed a structure of many parts, one that made it difficult to achieve an absolute majority. If the electorate splits its vote, electing a president and a Congress from opposing parties, it does so to frustrate the government and prevent it from acting too rashly. By impeding the formation of an absolute majority, this structure slows down the pace of social change, just as the founders intended.

Critics, however, say that divided governments occur much too frequently, and that as a consequence, the Constitution, a document written for an eighteenth-century society, fosters a political paralysis that serves us poorly in the twenty-first century. To be sure, it is important to guard against the abuse of absolute power. In the contemporary United States, however, the consequences of these protections are ever more disabling. Not only do we have checks and balances and separation of powers, but we also suffer from a decentralized and fragmented bureaucracy. From employment programs to health care, from housing to income security, this bureaucracy has difficulty managing many of the programs of the modern welfare state. For these critics, then, our ancient fear of the government's doing too much has so hamstrung the government that it cannot effectively get much done.[61] Perhaps that is why, when too much tension accumulates from this paralysis, another distinctive U.S. political phenomenon—critical elections—have consistently broken the logjam.

Critical Elections and the Cycles of American Politics

By definition, a critical election usually involves a significant shift or realignment of interests. There are three criteria for a critical election: (1) by realigning the majority and minority groupings within the parties, the election produces a new majority; (2) that realignment is sharp and lasts for a long time; (3) the political majority is decisive enough to create a new ruling coalition.[62]

Just four elections in U.S. history have met these standards. The first was in 1860, when the North elected Lincoln, the first successful Republican candidate, and brought about the Civil War. The second occurred in 1896, when Eastern Republican business interests beat back populist attacks on monopolies and the railroads, leading to a dominance that lasted for more than three decades. Franklin Roosevelt's victory in 1932 was the third, because it brought poor and working people into the Democratic Party and cemented a New Deal coalition that persisted until 1968. That is when the last, though probably somewhat more ambiguous realignment occurred. Richard Nixon, running against the civil rights reforms of the Great Society, tied blue-collar workers to the Republican Party. Although the opposing party remained in control of one house of Congress, no Democratic presidential candidate would gain a majority of white men's votes, and for the rest of the century, just two Democratic presidents, Carter and Clinton, would be elected. The high point of this realignment was the election of Ronald Reagan in 1980, which ushered in more than two decades of conservative politics.

Brown University political scientist James Morone has developed a theory about the cycle of social reform that complements this history of critical elections. His theory posits the existence of a "democratic wish," the mythic belief that Americans do not really need a government to govern themselves. In this myth, all government, even the governing of a complex technological society, should actually resemble a small New England town meeting. Because we believe in this vision, we have never adequately equipped the federal government with the authority to do its job. Hampered by states' rights, separation of powers, and the principle of checks and balances, our "big government" is not only smaller than most other similar nations, it is also much more fragmented and ineffective.[63]

Morone describes the accumulated tensions that constitute the reform cycle as played out in four stages. Political stalemate characterizes the first stage. Although ideology, institutions, and interests all block change in this stage, the pressure for reform gradually mounts. This pressure has many possible sources. It could come from a changing economy, demographic shifts as the population moves westward, or the rise of a new elite. In addition, as we shall see in chapter 6 on social movements, the poor and disenfranchised often demand inclusion and reform. The stalemate is broken when proponents of change invoke the democratic wish. Our problems, they say, would disappear if only we would listen to "the people."

The second stage occurs when this invocation provokes a wide response. Americans then follow the populist call, attack the status quo, and demand empowerment, as labor did in the 1930s and African Americans did in the 1960s. When they finally succeed in the third stage, they raise the profile of previously oppressed groups and establish new institutions to address their problems. Amid the decentralization of our political structure, however, these institutions do not have the power to translate the mythic call of "the people" into real accountability and effective governance. Caught between states and the federal government in all its branches, initiatives like the social welfare programs of the 1930s and the 1960s War on Poverty often stumble. As a result, in the fourth stage, the old political equilibrium is soon reestablished.

Morone draws an important lesson from this history. Because we have failed to institutionalize a communal spirit—an active notion of the people—within the government, "we need . . . a state that could act—more directly, with less internal contradiction. It would, most unlikely of all, have to be a more authoritative state; as a result, perhaps most unexpectedly, it could be more accountable to the citizens for what their government does."[64]

Clearly, this analysis of the social reform cycle has significant implications for the next critical election. Realigning elections have occurred every thirty-six years. If the last one occurred in 1968, it would appear we are soon due for another one. Of course, it may not happen; there is nothing necessarily magical about thirty-six-year cycles. But as the pace of social reform in the United States has consistently danced to this rhythm, the first decade of the twenty-first century may be a historically opportune time to push for the kind of changes that many in the social work profession have long desired. That is why, when they press for these changes, advocates of social reform would do well to heed Morone's warnings about what has happened before.

American Exceptionalism

Because the United States is so different from other democracies, political scientists often group these differences under the concept of *American exceptionalism*. In addition to the distinctive aspects of the political structure that we have emphasized, the concept of American exceptionalism also includes factors such as a weaker trade union movement and the absence of a significant socialist or labor party, faith in the marketplace, the lack of comprehensive social policies, and a belief in individualism and equal opportunity. Of course, to some extent, it is presumptuous to give such a label to these attributes, because every country is both different and the same. Yet there is little talk of "Canadian exceptionalism" or "Belgian exceptionalism." The reason is not only that the political scientists think the United States is different, but also because they believe its power and preeminence make these differences matter more.[65]

The explanations for American exceptionalism are many and varied. The United States, it is said, lacked a feudal tradition to develop a class-based politics. Workers, especially white workers, have experienced a long-term rise in their standard of living. A large land mass with considerable geographic mobility has also inhibited organized working-class formations. And where workers have been together in one place, ethnic, religious, and racial differences have had an equally fragmenting effect. Fed through the unique filters of U.S. politics, these social and economic factors have made the United States different from other countries.[66]

American exceptionalism defines American political culture. In particular, the complexity of the U.S. governmental structure means that every part of it must compromise to build a policy consensus. As a consequence, "because so much effort is invested in *building* the consensus, [there is] very little capacity for *moving* the consensus."[67] Admittedly, there are occasional departures from this rule: in the aftermath of the Soviet Union's launching the first space satellite, the United States turned its attention to education in the sciences and engineering; after a rash of killings in schools, Americans focused on gun control and youth violence. Nevertheless, the policies that actually emerged from all this attention tend to be modest and incremental. As political scientists have long emphasized, it is the American way.

The Political Functions of Social Welfare

The preceding portrait of the American political structure opens the way for a discussion of the role of social welfare within it. What does social welfare do, anyway? What political functions does it perform?

Although we sketched some of these answers in chapter 2, this description of U.S. politics provides an additional context. The existence of social welfare caters to the notion of an inclusive society, providing enough to mask the most conspicuous examples of poverty and suffering. Specifically, in the United States social welfare both heightens and mutes demands for social change. It heightens demands because victories empower people: win one battle, and soon you will probably think you can win another. At the same time, however, by substituting smaller conflicts about the functioning of programs and the functioning of the poor for larger conflicts about systemic inequalities, social welfare often undercuts the demand for change.

Yet social welfare is also pliable. On the one hand, if enough "worthy" people ask for help with a necessity like money, housing, or health care, social welfare has the political responsibility of attending to their needs. On the other, if attacks on the poor will help to unify the rest of the country, then social welfare can be harsh and controlling. These tensions are an integral part of the political functions of social welfare, and they are always contested. In the end, it is only by understanding these tensions that we as social workers can contest them most effectively.

The Implications for Social Welfare Policy

This chapter has described the political environment in which social workers function. As we have shown, not only is this environment often unreceptive to progressive social welfare legislation, but it is also frequently opposed to social work values. How should social workers operate in this environment? What criteria should they apply to legislative initiatives, and what should we do?

Social work has a commitment to expand choice and opportunities for all.[68] This is a difficult task in the United States, so we need to think carefully about what has been successful. By this standard, there are four criteria. First, a program must increase the capacity of the government to address human needs; that is, it must make the bureaucracy less fragmented and more efficient. Second, for legislation to be enacted, it must link this increased capacity to broad congressional support. Third, the benefits it delivers must go to a diverse group of citizens. Fourth, the program must provide these benefits without a means test. It is only programs like these, with their diverse cross-class coalitions—most spectacularly, Social Security—that American have supported and protected.[69]

The theme of this chapter is that to advance these kinds of programs, we need to pay particular attention to the distinctive features of the U.S. government structure. Called the "institutional-political" approach, this view stresses the ways that a fragmented U.S. government has interacted with urbanization and capitalist economic development, regulating its worst excesses but mostly giving it free rein. It argues that the evolution of U.S. social welfare is not simply the reflection of a conflict between workers and business, because that conflict has been so heavily influenced by the structure of the government and the organization of U.S. political parties. It further contends that no understanding can be complete without acknowledging the feedback effects of previous policies on this system: what has happened on the basis of, or in reaction to, previous policy accomplishments.[70]

These are good guidelines for social workers to consider both when they evaluate policy proposals and when they choose the kinds of advocacy and organizing that would help to make them law. We would be foolish to ignore the special features of the U.S. political system. But that does not mean changes cannot be made or, for that matter, that we as social workers cannot play an important role in making them.

5

Mimi Abramovitz

Ideological Perspectives and Conflicts

What Is Ideology?

Ideologies and ideological conflicts have persisted throughout modern times.[1] An ideology is a relatively coherent system of ideas (beliefs, traditions, principles, and myths) about human nature, institutional arrangements, and social processes held by individuals and groups in society. Deriving from many sources, including common sense, interpretations of daily experiences, and elaborate intellectual doctrines, accepted ideologies change as a society grows and develops. Ideological fervor intensifies during crises and turbulent times, when people need help to cope with confusing circumstances. Ideologies, which interpret the relationship between the individual and society, can provide this help.

When some people hear the word *ideology*, they think of rigid ideas, biased thinking, or simplistic notions. A closer look reveals ideology to be fluid, contested, and complex. First, ideologies inhabit both individual belief systems and wider social values, both of which also interact. Not only do individual beliefs affect social values and vice versa, but people regularly contest social values either individually or collectively. Second, ideology refers to more than one school of thought. One ideology or set of social values tends to prevail at any one moment in time; supporting the status quo, it tends to be regarded as the truth. In reality, other important perspectives also exist, standing by ready to be heard and to exert influence.

Ideology, both individual beliefs and social values, plays a major role in social work and social welfare policy. Indeed, scholars often depict the history of the profession and the welfare state as a series of ideological shifts over time. This chapter begins with a brief discussion of the ways in which ideology in general operates for individuals and for society. Most of the chapter, however, looks at the components of the major ideologies connected to social welfare that have shaped thinking about U.S. social policy since the birth of the nation and fueled social change.

Individuals and Ideology: A Personal Road Map

Most people possess some kind of ideology, although they may not have labeled their beliefs and values as such. Nonetheless, we use our ideology to describe and explain events in everyday life. It shapes answers to such questions as Why do we have war? Why are people out of work? What accounts for single motherhood? What causes economic depressions? Why do we have a welfare state? What explains sexism? racism? homophobia? Ideology also provides us with criteria and standards for evaluating what is right and wrong, good and bad: Should freedom of speech be honored in all instances? Is government assistance useful or harmful to individuals and families? Are affirmative action policies fair or unfair?

Our answers to such controversial questions vary with our beliefs and values, that is, with our ideology. Possessing an ideology is like having a road map or a frame of reference that organizes the tremendous complexities around us and guides individual thoughts and actions. Without such a road map, people may feel disoriented and less able to participate in society. Ideology also provides the believer with a picture of the world both as it is and as it should be. Ideology can also supply its adherents with the underpinnings of a political program—a set of social policies or a strategy for action.

We do not develop our ideologies in a vacuum. Rather, individual belief systems and social values interact with each other. Most people regularly pick up ideological messages from their family, school, peers, religion, popular culture, the mass media, and other societal institutions. For example, boys and girls learn what society expects of men and women from their parents, from grade school readers, and from watching television. Religions play a major role in defining gender roles, as do peers who ostracize nonconformists, and the mass media, which project valued role models.

These socializing institutions convey society's main or dominant ideology and cannot help but influence what we think, what we believe, and what we want. The messages received from wider society become so pervasive that people tend to take them for granted. Seemingly natural and logical, it becomes easy to miss the powerful ideological premises that lie beneath the surface. Yet these underlying premises shape our values, choices, and behavior—unless and until they are challenged by another way of thinking.

Society and Ideology: Supporting the Status Quo

The main or dominant ideology in society that influences individual thinking and behavior also tends to support the status quo. If small, homogeneous, and egalitarian societies still existed, the prevailing ideology might further the interests of almost everyone. But in today's large, internally divided, and unequal societies, the dominant ideology typically reflects the interests of the more established powers, be they white males, corporate executives, media companies, or political leaders.[2]

The ideological messages conveyed to individuals through mainstream social institutions, then, are neither accidental nor especially neutral. Instead, they encourage acceptance of the established way of life. Typically backed by the strongest power holders, the mainstream ideology defends and rationalizes a society's particular social, legal, moral, religious, political, and economic arrangements. It does so by (1) spelling out social norms and stigmatizing departures from these prescribed behaviors; (2) blaming social problems only on individuals without considering social conditions; (3) justifying social inequities instead of remedying them; and (4) otherwise suggesting that the existing status quo is natural, inevitable, beneficial, and best left unchanged.

Alternative Ideologies: Negotiating the Terrain

Despite the power of ideological messages, they do not go unchallenged or remain forever fixed. Indeed, the presence of various ideological perspectives represents a key force for social change. While many people may accommodate to the dominant view, many other individuals and groups develop alternative personal beliefs and subscribe to other social values based on their own life experiences. Some people develop other than mainstream viewpoints because they lack access to power and economic rewards. Others do so in response to intellectual ideas or participation in social groups, be it the Ku Klux Klan, the American Civil Liberties Union, the National Organization for Women, or the Democratic Socialists of America. Whatever the source, these beliefs, in turn, provide the basis for negotiating, resisting, and contesting the dominant view of social life and thus pave the way for social change. The alternative viewpoints range from the far right to the far left, with numerous stops in between.

History is filled with stories of those who resisted mainstream ideas and in the process transformed their own thinking and that of others in ways that mesh with social work values. Individuals resist the dominant ideology in various ways. Some participate in national social movements such as the trade union, civil rights, women's liberation, gay/lesbian, or disability rights movements. These local, state, and national battles implicitly indict the status quo and contest the ideology that holds it in place (see chapter 6). Others engage in social action with local community groups to fight against police brutality, drug dealers, or the location of a toxic waste site, a new highway, or a nuclear plant in their neighborhood. Still others protest individually by adopting a nontraditional lifestyle, subscribing to alternative political views, or buying nonmainstream newspapers. Even the most powerless find ways to resist the status quo. Individuals locked out of established institutions due to poverty and those for whom public action becomes too risky may take on "the system" in more individual and covert ways in language, clothing and cultural expressions.[3]

Regardless of the nature or form of the ideological challenge, officialdom may try to accommodate it by legislating change. If the challenge becomes too great, however, it may try to channel the opposition's plans into approved categories, convert them into unthreatening reforms, or simply suppress them.

Social Welfare Ideology and Social Change

Chapter 1 identified the triggers of social change as social forces, such as the economy, politics, and history, that create the need or conditions for social change; the tensions within our social system that provoke people to mobilize; and the organized force of social movements that prod the government into action. When tensions build to the point that some resolution is needed, pressure mounts for social change. The drive for changing social welfare policy also stems from ideological conflicts about the cause of social problems and strategies to address them. Chapter 2 suggested that these debates extend to interpretations of goals and functions of the welfare state. Conservatives, liberals, radicals, and feminists disagree about the best ways to serve people. These differences both fuel and complicate the process of social change as each group wants its perspective to shape the outcome of policy deliberations.

As this chapter shows, the ideological clashes over social welfare policy represent fundamental differences regarding profound questions, including (1) the character of human nature, (2) the relationship of the individual to society, (3) the determination of need, (4) the role of the government, (5) the meaning of work, (6) the nature of the family, (7) the interpretation of racial inequality, and (8) the benefits of professionalism.

It would be easier if there were just one answer to each of the above questions. But, in fact, the thinking about these broad philosophical issues has been highly contested by three long-standing opposing political traditions: conservatism, liberalism, and radicalism. Recent scholarship on women and the welfare state adds feminism to the mix. The ideological debates among these groups become heated because the beliefs arouse deeply held personal convictions. Perhaps more important, the stakes are high. The victor in any round of policy deliberations wins a lot because social welfare policy decisions touch so many people, influence the distribution of scarce resources, and, in the final analysis, determine who pays for and who benefits from government action. The contest becomes even more complicated because groups backing the various ideologies rarely have equal access to decision-making centers.

At the outset, however, this discussion demands four provisos about ideological paradigms. First, from a distance, conservatism, liberalism, radicalism, and feminism appear dramatically different. In many ways they are, but at some junctions the distinctiveness blurs. Therefore, it is important to think of these categories as frameworks and guides for understanding the issues, not as absolute pictures of real life. Second, we regularly label the nation's political parties and leaders ideologically: Republicans are conservative and Democrats are liberal. Nevertheless, it is important to realize that the words and deeds of the parties and their leaders frequently depart rather widely from the political doctrines represented by the labels. The politics of everyday life— the need to win votes, raise funds, and so on—ensure that elected officials cannot remain true to their beliefs. As a result, equating political labels with clear ideological perspectives does not work. Third, our own personal thinking may also include elements of more than one point of view. Fourth, in the United States, most social welfare policy ideology debates take place between the conservative and liberal paradigms. Although social welfare policy has not incorporated the radical or feminist standpoints, these nonmainstream perspectives have exerted considerable influence in more liberal periods, pulling policy debates and outcomes in their direction and fostering wider social change. With these provisos in mind, the remainder of this chapter explores the ideological debates that shape social welfare provision.

The Ideology of Human Nature

All four political ideologies—conservatism, liberalism, radicalism, and feminism—contain a view of human nature. These assumptions about human abilities, needs, wants, and purposes often underpin social attitudes toward government provision for individuals and families and what type of social change is necessary or possible.

Conservatism

Conservatism contains two different views of human nature, one grounded in religion (social conservatism), the other in economics (laissez-faire conservatism).[4]

Social conservatives think of human beings as creatures of God who have lost their way.[5] Because individuals are marked by original sin, driven by unlimited and often uncontrollable passions, they cannot be trusted to be the masters of their own fate. These deeply flawed, "fallen" or depraved individuals can achieve "perfection" only in the next world. Until then, society must restrain individuals by bringing them under the moral authority of God, family, church, and even government. Left on their own, the narrow, untamed self-interest of individuals would create social chaos everywhere.

Laissez-faire conservatism exalts human reason and intelligence and has unlimited faith in human ability, that is, the ability of individuals to control their own destiny.[6] Rather than emphasizing our imperfectibility and inability to control unruly passions and desires, laissez-faire conservatism embraces the ideas of human rationality, self-interest, and self-regulation. Individuals are self-interested (motivated by personal gain) and inherently competitive (more interested in their own good than that of others) and possess unlimited potential for self-improvement. Through reason, individuals can rationally assess a situation, weigh the alternatives, and choose the option that best suits their circumstances. If allowed to act independently without undue restraint from any external forces, individuals will maximize success.

Liberalism

Liberalism also contains two views of human nature: pragmatic liberalism, which has shaped the development of the welfare state in the United States, and humanistic liberalism, which has been more popular in Western Europe.

Pragmatic liberalism is an outgrowth of laissez-faire conservatism and shares its view of human nature, with one major difference.[7] Like laissez-faire conservatism, it holds a positive view of human nature as rational, autonomous, self-interested, competitive, capable of improvement, and motivated for success. However, the pragmatic liberals broke with laissez-faire conservatism when, in the early twentieth century, they lost faith in the capacity of the totally unregulated market to maximize human success. As more and more people failed to achieve the good life in the rapidly industrializing society, some laissez-faire conservatives gave up their belief in the notion of freedom as the absence of restraint. Instead, drawing on the belief that all humans are born free and possess the capacity to reason, pragmatic liberals conclude that all people merit an equal chance to pursue their own interests. Without denying that individuals are masters of their own fate, the new liberals reluctantly called on society to take greater account of the impact of social conditions on the capacity of individuals to compete for success.

Humanistic liberalism regards individuals as rational and autonomous but also as altruistic, dependent, and interdependent.[8] That is, individuals have interests, but they also have needs. Neoclassical conservatism forces a choice between autonomy and dependence. In contrast, humanistic liberalism argues that all human beings are born into a condition of dependence but eventually develop autonomy through their relationships with others. Yet autonomy cannot eliminate a person's dependence on or need to help others. Because we are interdependent, humanistic or social democratic liberalism sees human beings as social or communal creatures who live and work not in isolation, but in cooperation with one another.

Radicalism

Radicalism sees human nature as socially constructed through the historic interplay of human biology, the physical environment, and human society.[9] Whereas other ideologies define human nature in relation to the capacity to reason, radicalism draws on Marxism to emphasize human labor and our collective involvement in producing our means of subsistence: the food we eat, the clothing we wear, and the houses we live in. Human labor is central to this understanding of human nature because for radicalism, human nature is not fixed. Instead it is the product of human activity.

More specifically, whereas animals are governed by instinct and simply use what the world provides in order to survive, human beings consciously and intentionally engage in physical labor directed toward transforming the material world so it will satisfy basic needs. Humans produce the means of subsistence in an ongoing process that simultaneously fulfills our needs and transforms the material world.

Given its connection to the nature of productive activity, radicalism argues that human nature varies with specific historic conditions. In the words of Karl Marx, a father of radicalism, "All history is nothing but a continuous transformation of human nature."[10] Human nature reflects the existing mode of production (e.g., feudalism, capitalism, socialism, or communism) and the individual's location in society's class structure. Marx adds, "The mode of production of material life conditions the general process of social, political, and intellectual life. It is not the consciousness of men that determines their existence, but their social existence that determines their consciousness."[11] Thus, it is through production that men and women collectively create the society that in turn shapes them.

Feminism

Feminism criticizes each of the above conceptions of human nature for either reflecting only the life experiences of men or remaining silent on women. Feminism in general seeks to account for the experience of women as subordinate to men, but more than one version of feminism exists.

Liberal feminism accepts the beliefs of standard liberalism but argues that its acceptance of the view of women as irrational by nature and therefore inferior contradicts liberalism's mandate to treat all people the same, given that all humans possess the same capacity for reason.[12] Liberal feminism thus disputes the exclusion of women from the category of rational human being and instead insists that a common human nature exists beneath the surface of male/female differences. Any observed differences in the human nature of males and females reflect sex role socialization rather than the innate capacity of the individual. That is, human nature has no sex, and male/female differences should not be used to justify notions of female inferiority or the exclusion of women from mainstream institutions.

Cultural feminism, sometimes referred to as radical feminism, offers two views of human nature.[13] One school of thought holds that male/female differences and the subordination of women are rooted in nature, particularly in the biological division of labor. They call for changes in the latter.[14] The other school holds that patriarchy—the system based on male domination and female subordination—socially constructs human nature. That is, the sex/gender system transforms biological characteristics into social categories to explain human behavior. For example, in patriarchal society, certain facts about male and female physiology (anatomy, hormones, chromosomes) are linked to a set of expected masculine and feminine identities and behaviors. Thought of as "natural," these socially constructed identities define women as passive, obedient, weak, responsive, emotional, vain, kind, and friendly and men as assertive, competitive, strong, ambitious, and stoical. "Normality" becomes the ability of individuals to display the gender identity assigned to each biological sex. Cultural feminists argue that the existing categories of woman and man are neither natural nor eternal. Rather, they are used ideologically to define women as inferior and subordinated to men.

Socialist feminism represents an effort to incorporate the class analysis of standard radicalism and understanding of patriarchy introduced by cultural feminism.[15] Agreeing with radicals that human existence and productive activity determine our consciousness, socialist feminism concludes that the two deeply intertwined master systems of capitalism and patriarchy as well as racism play a role in shaping human nature. Just as a specific system of gender relations accompanied a feudal system of class relations, so a specific system of gender and race relations accompanied the capitalist class system. The capitalist system produces the means to satisfy basic material needs, and the patriarchal system produces the means to satisfy the human needs for reproduction, sexuality, and emotional gratification, among others. Racial hierarchies keep people divided. Like radicals, socialist feminists underscore the relationship between human labor and human nature. However, they add the impact of the gender division of labor on human nature—especially the systems of male domination and female subordination—in the organization of both economic production and social reproduction (procreation, socialization, caretaking, etc.).

The General Welfare: Individuals in Society

The various political ideologies offer different interpretations of how society best defines liberty and community and ensures the general welfare of all.

Social Conservatism

Social conservatism views human nature as flawed, that is, governed by uncontrollable impulses and selfish needs and not perfectible in this world.[16] Therefore, the well-being of individuals and society depends on restricting the freedom of individuals and controlling their behavior so that their unruly passions and desires will not endanger either themselves or the social peace. Security, support, and nurture require using the law, social norms, and the distribution of resources to enforce duty, proper behavior, and social obligation. Reflecting a notion of community that appeals to the belief in a prior golden era of order, hierarchy, and place, social conservatives believe that the general welfare depends on individual compliance with the moral authority of God, the patriarchal authority of the family, and the mandates of the state.[17] Liberty (which stems from the Latin word *liber* meaning "free") means freedom from original sin.

Laissez-Faire Conservatism

Laissez-faire conservatism (also known as neoclassical liberalism) views human beings as rational, competitive, self-contained, solitary units dedicated to the pursuit of self-interest.[18] Therefore, the well-being of individuals and society depends on ensuring individual autonomy and independence and maximizing individuals' ability to compete for success. Individuals must be left alone to operate in the market economy with a minimum of control or interference from others.

This unregulated competition ensures the greatest good (i.e., progress and wealth) for the greatest number because, in this view, the labor of each individual automatically adds to the entire wealth of the nation. The spontaneous outgrowth of thousands of self-seeking individuals each pursuing his or her own fortune without regard for the welfare of others automatically enhances the well-being of all. As described by Adam Smith, author of *The Wealth of Nations* (1776) and father of laissez-faire economics, an "invisible hand" automatically channels the selfish motives of many individuals into mutually consistent and complementary activities that best promote the welfare of all. Smith believed that in "pursuing his [sic] own interest [the individual] frequently promotes that of society more effectively than when he really intends to promote it."[19] In this world of autonomous, detached individuals, liberty refers to freedom from restraint, and community is limited to contracts based on the consent of naturally free and independent persons and freely chosen participation in voluntary community groups organized for mutual benefit.[20]

Pragmatic Liberalism

Pragmatic liberalism, like laissez-faire conservatism, regards individuals as rational beings dedicated to the competitive pursuit of self-interest.[21] At the same time, as noted earlier, pragmatic liberalism broke with laissez-fare conservatism due to concerns about the human implications of capitalism, particularly the fact that some people will enter the race for success with differences based on initial advantage, inherent talents, social circumstances, and sheer luck. For pragmatic liberals, large differences in income and wealth deprive the disadvantaged of the chance to pursue their self-interest to the fullest and to secure their fair share of what the market has to offer.

Whereas laissez-faire conservatives claim that leaving people alone will ensure equal opportunity, pragmatic liberals claim that society needs to make equal opportunity a possibility for the disadvantaged. Reflecting the underlying principle of liberalism—that all human beings merit equal treatment by society because they are born free and with the potential to reason—pragmatic liberals call on the government to offset liabilities of those with less.

The general welfare thus depends on the capacity or willingness of the state to provide the tools and to create the conditions that will enable disadvantaged individuals to enter the market and compete for success on an equal footing with others. Liberty refers to freedom from want, and community derives from a limited offer of help to the disadvantaged.

Humanistic Liberalism

Humanistic liberalism holds that individuals develop best in relationship to others, that autonomy follows a long period of dependence (childhood), and that we remain interdependent throughout our lives.[22] Because interdependence is part of the human condition, society must create the conditions for cooperation, not competition, among individuals; promote collective as well as individual welfare; and encourage sentiments of mutuality, altruism, and responsibility for others. That is, the general welfare rests on solidarity and social integration, both of which are furthered by greater equality than the market, left on its own, typically yields. More equality contributes to social integration. Why? Because large disparities of income and wealth lead the market to respond to the economic demands of affluent consumers, leaving unmet the basic needs of those with less. Inequality also generates social conflict, which breaks the bonds of community and prevents individuals from reaching their full potential.[23] Community or social integration depends on putting the common good ahead of one's private desires, and liberty goes beyond freedom from want to the freedom to become a fully engaged member of the community and to maximize one's potential.

Radicalism

Radicalism contains still another vision of the relationship between the individual and society, one that flows from its understanding of human nature as socially constructed through the interaction of human biology, human society, and the physical environment.[24] The fundamental problem of capitalism, according to Marx, is not the material deprivation it creates for many people, but rather the lack of community on which the ability to engage in socially productive labor depends. The built-in competition for scarce resources undercuts community by, among other things, turning people, friends, colleagues, and cooperators into enemies, competitors, or persons to avoid. In a stratified society, the strong emphasis on the individual pursuit of self-interest creates major social divisions along the lines of class, race, and gender, among others. The alienation of people from each other, their work, and their environment stemming from such divides diminishes the possibility of cooperative and socially productive labor.[25]

For Marxism, the general welfare is not possible except in an egalitarian classless society organized to satisfy human needs. Such a society would ask people to contribute according to their ability and receive according to their need. It would be structured to reduce the contrast of wealth and power, to promote participatory over elite democracy, and to minimize special privilege based on an unequal distribution of resources. No one would hold power over another and the needs of people would come first. In the words of David Gil, "All individuals should have the right to freely actualize their inherent human potential; to lead as fulfilling a life as possible within the reality of, and in harmony with, the natural environment but also to be free of exploitation, alienation, and oppression."[26] This liberty or freedom from the oppression found in a class society, depends on ensuring that people have the resources and capacity to control the conditions of their lives.

Feminism

Feminism posits a relationship between the individual and society that flows from its view of human nature as gendered. Liberal, cultural, and socialist feminisms offer different analyses of the gender basis of human nature and the underpinnings of the gendered structure of society. Yet they all concur that prevailing patriarchal arrangements disadvantage women. Each framework regards as flawed any notion of the common good that ignores the gender divide, and they agree that the general welfare cannot be attained until gender inequality disappears.

Liberal feminism focuses on sexism, or the differential treatment of people based on sex, as an arbitrary and oppressive constraint on the freedom of both women and men.[27] Sexism limits the capacity of women to maximize their autonomy and denies women equal opportunity to pursue their interests as they define them. Liberal feminists therefore stress that for women the general welfare rests on equal opportunity to participate fully in all societal institutions. This means eliminating sexist practices that bar women from public life as well as all male/female double standards.

Cultural feminism highlights the impact of patriarchal domination in all spheres of life.[28] Male control of women's bodies, labor, resources; of marriage, employment, and government; and of most other spheres of life deprives women of power and self-determination. Cultural feminism calls for organizing society around new values, transcending patriarchal dualisms of self and world, nature and spirit, reason and emotion. These feminists also believe that women will not be free until society gives up the glorification of motherhood for all women, the sexual objectification of women, homophobia, and many other oppressive structures. For cultural feminism, both the general welfare and freedom depend on eliminating the oppression of women based on male domination in all spheres of life.

Socialist feminism suggests that the relationship of individuals to society reflects the gender division of labor, which structures human nature and human productive activity.[29] It also reflects the prevailing structures of power: patriarchy (based on male supremacy), capitalism (based on class supremacy), and racism (based on white supremacy). Unlike liberalism and cultural feminism, socialist feminism argues that the individual's relationship to society is governed by the intersection of gender, race, and class. Therefore, for socialist feminists, the general welfare and freedom depend on altering or eliminating the current gendered division of labor within and between both workplace and the home, the ideology of women's roles, and all the forms of domination based on class, gender, and race.

The Ideology of the Definition of Need

The third major issue of great importance to social policy and the development of the welfare state concerns the concept of need. To a large extent, the history of social services and social welfare policy consists of the evolving recognition of social needs and the organization of society to meet them.[30] For years, philosophers and political theorists have tried to sort out the knotty questions of who and what determines people's understanding of what they need. In general, the answers offered by conservatism, liberalism, radicalism, and feminism correlate with their different perspectives on the size, shape, and cost of the welfare state.

"The Minimum Wage: Has She Earned It?" A question from 1913: Women carry the world on their shoulders and the right to vote is almost within their grasp. But do they need a minimum wage? Have they earned it?

Conservatism: Need as Individual Preference or Consumer Demand

Both social and laissez-faire conservatism define personal and societal needs by looking at the individual's role in the market. Drawing on neoclassical economic theory, conservatism presumes that people know what they need and have all the information required to make an informed choice. Because human decisions are shaped by nothing other than market forces,[31] the behavior of the individual in the market expresses actual need. That is, individuals reveal their needs or market "preferences" by virtue of how they spend their money. People buy what they need and need what they buy—and these choices accurately reflect their true physical and emotional requirements. Put in other words, consumer demand for goods and services backed up by the dollar translates into need.[32] The needs of society as a whole represent no more or less than the sum total of millions of individual preferences. Because people buy what they need, the gap between needs and resources—the liberal justification for the welfare state—does not exist. This individualized understanding of social needs also supports conservatism's opposition to nearly all forms of government intervention in the economy.

Pragmatic Liberalism: Need as a Social Minimum

Following laissez-faire conservatism, pragmatic liberalism relies on the individual's interaction with the market to define need. However, because pragmatic liberalism recognizes that many people do not have the financial wherewithal to buy what they need, it rejects the belief that market behavior alone represents an accurate mirror of what people must have to survive.[33] Without taking income differences into account, the equation of consumer preferences with real needs allows the community to wrongly conclude that poor people *prefer* less food, second-hand clothes, inferior education, and substandard housing. According to the liberal economist Robert Heilbroner, a central weakness of the market is "its inability to formulate public needs above those of the marketplace."[34]

Pragmatic liberals invite the government to define a standard of need—a minimum level of subsistence below which no one should be expected to live. According to the well-known economist John Kenneth Galbraith, "An affluent society that is also both compassionate and rational, would no doubt secure to all who needed it the minimum income necessary for decency and comfort" as a "normal function of society."[35] The Beveridge Plan implemented in Britain after World War II reflects a similar sentiment: "We want to draw a line below which we will not allow persons to live and labor, yet above which they may compete with all the strength of their manhood. We want to have free competition upwards; we decline to allow free competition to run downwards."[36] Pragmatic liberalism equates liberty with freedom from want defined as a basic minimum standard of living or survival. It calls on the government to make sure that all individuals reach this line without necessarily making great changes in the prevailing distribution of income and wealth.

Humanistic Liberalism: Need as the Right to Full Participation

Humanistic liberalism defines need more broadly, arguing that the free market system responds to economic demand (i.e., purchasing power), not to need. In this view, need goes beyond mere survival to access to social rights: the rights of citizenship that accrue to individuals by virtue of their membership in the community (not national origin). Community-defined social rights range from a minimum level of subsistence to the right to live a full life according to the standards prevailing in society. Without these resources, individuals are "in need" because they cannot think, compete for success, vote intelligently, develop relationships, enjoy leisure time, or otherwise pursue their own growth.[37]

Radicalism: Need as a Collectively Determined Civic Standard

Radicalism criticizes defining need in market terms and offers an alternative measure. It suggests that the meaning of need is socially constructed by the class structure and the profit motive. The dominant class is positioned to shape how individuals perceive their needs by virtue of its control of the system of production and cultural idea systems. One's location in the class structure also influences the perception of need, so that haves and have-nots develop different expectations for themselves. Those exposed to wealth and power tend to expect a relatively high standard of living, whereas marginalized and deprived people, having access to fewer possibilities, often settle for less. How many impoverished children even wonder if they can attend an Ivy League college? For years, many women did not consider becoming a doctor, a truck driver, or an engineer. Such low expectations serve individuals poorly. But radicalism holds that low expectations benefit the elite because rising expectations often lead deprived groups to demand a larger share of the economic and political pie.[38]

The profit-driven interests of business and industry also define need. The culture of consumerism that accompanied the rise of mass production in the early years of the twentieth century still encourages people to "need" whatever companies produce, including cigarettes, an extra dress, and a big car. With clever advertising, business and industry also induce people to realize their personal identity through what they consume and to "keep up with the Joneses" by having more. If keeping up with the Joneses entails moving from the central city to the suburbs, the competition creates the "need" for a new home along with new appliances and furniture to fill it, a new car, a barbecue grill, and a backyard pool.[39] Technological innovations such as the automobile, home computer, and cellular phone have produced "needs" unheard of before the new devices came on the market.

In addition to inducing people to buy what they may not need, radicalism holds that profit-driven consumerism also allows important needs to go unmet. The market does not "care" that its dynamics leave some people with too little income, food, housing, and health care. It does not falter if the economy produces more cake than bread or more yachts than low-rent housing. Nor does the market economy readily register the need for parks, schools, satisfying work, environmental protections, and other improvements in the quality of life that do not yield a profit.[40]

Instead of need determined by market dynamics, radicalism subscribes to a social or collective definition of need. Only after everyone is living up to this civic standard, which represents the resources needed by each member of society to participate fully, would society begin to deal with needs above this line. For radicalism, the distribution of societal resources according to need is a central social value, not a pragmatic way to achieve other ends. The main aim of production and distribution is the satisfaction of human needs.[41]

Feminism: The Need for Care

Feminism addresses need in relation to caregiving. Society still links care to women's character, based on the stereotypic belief that for women caring is a biologically or "natural" form of relating, but refuses to define caregiving as work. In social welfare policy, it is generally presumed that women—wives, mothers, and daughters—are primarily responsible for the care of family members. Because most social welfare policies also assume that the need for care should be met within the family, public sector care services remain underdeveloped. When caregiving is provided outside the home by government or social agencies, women, often for very low pay, do most of the work. Finally, for a host of reasons, including the gender division of labor, women are also the primary consumers of social service (care from others).[42]

Feminism broadens the meaning of need to include personal and societal needs for care. According to feminist scholar Deborah Stone, "Care is as essential as the air we breathe. Two centuries of myth-making about rugged individualism will not yield easily to the painful fact that dependence is the human condition."[43] Care is a universal aspect of human life. Echoing humanitarian liberalism, Stone adds that the need for care arises from the fact that not all humans are equally able at all times to take care of themselves or others. We all have needs that others must help us meet if we are to survive. We also need care to thrive and to develop our full capacities.

Why, then, is the need for care regarded as a sign of weakness and the work of care devalued and treated as private concern? Joan Tronto, a political scientist, suggests that those in positions of power gain ideologically by downplaying the need for care.[44] First, acknowledging the need for care discredits the myth of the "self-made man" as well as the belief in individual autonomy that it represents. Second, valuing care would reveal that caring work has always been underpaid and allocated to the least well-off members of society; in the past, this meant slaves, servants, and women; today it includes the working class, persons of color, and women. Third, recognizing the need for care would expose that the unequal distribution of who provided and who received care maintains and reinforces patterns of subordination. Fourth, talking about care would reveal that 41 million people lack health care, that we do not provide nearly enough child care outside the home, that children are overrepresented among the poor, and that our society is filled with profound failures of caring. By not noticing the centrality of the need for care in human life, the powers-that-be can continue to degrade the activities of care, exploit the caregivers, and fail to provide for the needs of both individuals and society as a whole.

The Ideology of the Role of the Government

At some point during the late nineteenth and early twentieth centuries, modern industrial societies, including the United States, recognized that they had to assist "the needy." A combination of mounting need, the development of resource capacity, and pressure from social movements led governments to begin to develop social welfare programs. However, because creating these programs represented a choice about how society uses its resources, the move toward a welfare state typically led to heated debates regarding the role of the government and the level of social provision.

The debate on the proper role of government often centers on which of three sites for resource distribution—the family, the market, or the government—should bear the heaviest burden in ensuring the well-being of people. We don't usually think of it this way, but all three systems play this role. The family distributes resources to its members by supporting those who do not work or otherwise cannot care for themselves. The breadwinner(s) supplies the wages needed to buy the food, clothing, shelter, medical care, and a host of other goods and services needed by family members. In exchange, adult women and other unpaid family members shop, cook, clean, care for children, and maintain the household. Conservatives believe that families can and should be self-sustaining. Liberals argue that from the start many families, especially those with limited income, have needed some kind of outside help to sustain themselves. Radicals hold that the operation of the system of production undercuts family maintenance.

The second and main system for distributing goods and services is the market.[45] The market economy produces goods and services as well as the jobs that provide people with the income needed to consume. Observers from all political camps agree that the market does not provide all people with the same degree of income and purchasing power. But they differ as to the importance of this uneven outcome and how society should respond to it. Conservatism holds that most needs can and should be met through market purchases. They believe that the need for goods and services stimulates people to work hard and to compete more vigorously for economic success (see section on ideology of work). Liberalism argues that the market favors the haves at the expense of the have-nots and leaves too many people out and too many needs unmet. It also faults the market for creating a surplus of luxuries alongside a shortage of basic goods and services.[46] The most ardent critic, radicalism, argues that the market economy thrives on a certain degree of inequality. The profit motive demands low wages, high unemployment, high prices, and the absence of unions.

However understood, the limitations of the market eventually led governments to mediate its uneven impact on the well-being of individuals and families. Given their different opinions regarding the capacity of the market to meet basic needs, conservatism, liberalism, and radicalism offer sharply different views regarding the appropriate role of the government in social welfare provision. Feminism adds a critique about the gender-blind nature of the welfare state.

Social Conservatism: The Welfare State as Means of Social Control

Social conservatives call on the government to intervene in some areas of social life while strongly opposing its activities in others. Given its view of individuals as ruled by an evil and uncontrollable human nature, social conservativism endorses greater use of the robust power of the state to control "irresponsible" behavior and to crack down on drugs, crime, abortion, divorce, single motherhood, homosexuality, undocumented immigration, the youth culture, and violations of family values. Unwilling to accept moral neutrality, they press the government to restrict abortion rights, require prayer in school, reverse judicial leniency, privatize Social Security, and reduce, if not eliminate, welfare rolls.[47]

At the same time, social conservatives deplore active government in other arenas. They believe that the welfare state rewards lifestyles and social practices that deviate from traditional religious values and blame its programs for promoting permissiveness that leads to moral laxity. They hold the liberal welfare state responsible for driving religion out of the schools, abetting the civil rights movement, liberating women, weakening our national defenses, and launching the War on Poverty. In other words, social conservatives ardently believe that "big government" condones what God condemns.[48] Further, they disparage the professionals who work in the welfare state as the "new class," "a liberal elite," "the intelligentsia," and "social engineers," who support the welfare state simply to further their own interests, not to help others.

Social conservatives also oppose big government on the grounds that it usurps the traditional authority of parents. They believe that the helping professions deprive parents of their legitimate functions by invading the family with therapeutic techniques and that the schools have imposed theories of evolution and sex education on children without consulting parents. Therefore, to reassert parental rights, social conservatives call for defunding advocacy groups, curtailing government intervention, and returning to local control.[49]

Ralph Reed, former director of the Christian Coalition, sums up the social conservative view of what smaller government would bring:

> America would look much as it did for most of the first two centuries of its existence, before the social dislocation caused by Vietnam, the sexual revolution, Watergate, and the *explosion of the welfare state*. Our nation would once again be ascendant, self-confident, proud and morally strong. Government would be small, the citizenry virtuous and mediating institutions such as churches and volunteer organizations would carry out many of the functions currently relegated to the bureaucracy. Instead of turning to Washington to solve problems, Americans would turn to each other.[50]

Laissez-Faire Conservatism: The Welfare State as a Necessary Evil

Laissez-faire conservatives lament America's departure from the principles of laissez-faire.[51] They believe that big government should stay out of the economic market—except to perform a few important oversight functions such as protecting national security, private property, and basic liberties.

Driven by economic rather than moral issues, laissez-faire conservatives believe that big government (equated with lumbering and self-serving bureaucracies) interferes with the unrestricted pursuit of self-interest, limits the ability of individuals to be self-determining, and stifles initiative and innovation. Social programs, in particular, undercut self-reliance, rob people of initiative, undermine the motivation of workers, weaken the two-parent family as a unit of consumption, and in general make people too dependent on the government.[52] Therefore, they call for local and limited welfare state programs targeted to enhancing self-sufficiency, not providing "handouts."

Laissez-faire conservatism opposes the welfare state, believing that programs are too redistributive and therefore promote equality over freedom. If government spending on social welfare did not absorb tax dollars, the reduced taxes of individuals and corporations would allow them greater choice over how to spend or invest their income.

Laissez-faire conservatives do not necessarily oppose abortion and child care services, which they define as individual decisions, as long as the services remain in private hands and do not interfere with personal liberty. The Republican position on adding a drug prescription benefit to Medicare reflected this thinking. According to the *New York Times*, "Republicans yearn for what they call the 'choice' and 'freedom' of a vigorous market-place of private health plans competing for the elderly's business."[53]

Despite these anti–welfare state views, laissez-faire conservatives have come to terms with government aid to the needy as a necessary evil. That is, they tolerate limited government provision as long as the aid is meager and assists only the "truly needy," that is those people who have temporarily fallen on hard times through no fault of their own and need help only until they get back on their feet. Harold Wilensky and Charles Lebeaux, social welfare researchers, refer to welfare states that provide such temporary and emergency aid as "residual" welfare states. The residual welfare state is

> based on the premise that there are two "natural" channels through which an individual's needs are properly met: the family and the market economy. These are the preferred structures of supply. However, sometimes these institutions do not function adequately: family life is disrupted, depressions occur. Or sometimes the individual cannot make use of the normal channels because of old age or illness. In such cases . . . a third mechanism of need fulfillment is brought into play—the social welfare structure. This is conceived as a residual agency, attending primarily to emergency functions, and is expected to withdraw when the regular social structure—the family and the economic system—is again working properly. Because of its residual or substitute characteristic, social welfare thus conceived often carries the stigma of the "dole" or "charity."[54]

To ensure that only the truly needy receive government assistance, conservatism favors the use of polices and practices that discourage people from applying for help. This includes shaming recipients by referring to them as lazy and irresponsible; stigmatizing benefits as charity, a handout, or the dole; setting benefits lower than the lowest prevailing wage so only the most needy will choose public benefits over work or family support; and in general denying the poor any dignified treatment.

In the mid-1970s, for a host of social, economic, and political reasons, laissez-faire conservatives became more hostile to the welfare state. With this development, the antigovernment arguments made by social and laissez-faire conservatives seemed to converge. Both groups concluded that the development of social programs had encouraged people to expect too much from the state. They held that the democratic aspects of our system—the surge of social movements in the turbulent 1960s and their demands for greater economic and political progress—had generated excessive expectations for new rights.[55] In a mid-1970s report, *The Crisis of Democracy: Report on the Governability of Democracies to the Trilateral Commission,* Samuel Huntington wrote, "Al Smith [former governor of New York] had remarked that 'the only cure for the evils of democracy is democracy.'" Huntington disagreed: "Applying that cure at the present time could well be adding fuel to the flames. Instead some of the problems of governance in the United States today stem from an excess of democracy."[56]

The report's call for "a greater degree of moderation in democracy" included smaller social welfare programs. Conservatives have supported tax cuts and then pointed to the resulting budget deficits to justify less social welfare spending. Since 1980, federal, state, and local governments have repeatedly cut taxes. The most recent and one of the largest on record, $1.35 trillion over the next ten years, was proposed by President Bush and passed by Con-

gress in January 2001. Like the Reagan administration's combination of tax cuts and high military spending, the Bush tax strategy combined with home land security and even higher military spending will fuel the contraction of the welfare state for years to come.

Conservatives also favor "devolution," or turning responsibility for social welfare from federal government back to the states. The conversion of the long-standing entitlement program AFDC into the state-run block grant TANF represents a major example of devolution.

A third conservative favorite is privatization. In the best of all possible worlds, conservatives would prefer that the private sector—nonprofit but also for-profit providers—own, operate, or manage social programs. During the 1970s, many state governments contracted out the provision of services to local nonprofit providers. In the 1980s, privatization expanded to include government subsidies to for-profit and faith-based organizations, including prisons, immigrant detention centers, and public schools as well as the privately managed schools and the use of publicly funded educational vouchers to pay for private school tuition. In the 1990s, conservatives began to call for the privatization of the Social Security retirement program, the linchpin of the U.S. welfare state.

Paradoxically, except for libertarian conservatives, who oppose all taxation, most laissez-faire and many social conservatives support the use of government dollars to help business. They rarely oppose government subsidies to business such as corporate bailouts, tax abatements, and a wide range of other benefits. Yet this "corporate welfare" violates the rules of free competition and free enterprise on which conservatism stands.[57]

Pragmatic Liberalism: A Reluctant Welfare State

Pragmatic liberalism endorses the market economy and limited government action. However, it recognizes that modern life is so complex that nearly everyone will need help at one point or another. Pragmatic liberalism assumes that living and working in a market economy regularly exposes individuals and families to risks over which they have little or no control. The hazards include the loss of income due to old age, illness, disability, unemployment, and family dissolution and lack of equal access to market-produced jobs, education, health care, and other necessities of life.

Because the market, the family, and the community cannot always protect or compensate people who suffer these dislocations, pragmatic liberalism holds that the government should—on a regular basis—both mediate the market's rough edges and make up for what these traditional institutions no longer can do. That is, as part of its normal functions, the government should be prepared to cushion or correct the negative impact of the market economy on individual and family well-being. While supporting the existing system, pragmatic liberalism calls on government to fix its flaws.

This more expanded role of government is what Wilensky and Lebeaux refer to as an institutional as opposed to a residual welfare state. In the name of equal opportunity to be cared for and to compete for success in the market, such a welfare state:

> implies not stigma, not emergency, not "abnormalcy." Social welfare becomes accepted as a proper, legitimate function of modern industrial society in helping individuals achieve self-fulfillment. The complexity of modern life is recognized. The inability of the individual to provide for himself or to meet all his needs in family and work settings is considered a "normal" condition; and the helping agencies achieved "regular" institutional status.[58]

In addition to an institutional welfare state, pragmatic liberalism also endorses government action to redress other market problems, including child labor, low wages, unsafe working conditions, environmental degradation, impure food and drugs, inadequate standards of housing, and public health. Pragmatic liberalism also calls on the government to stabilize and guide the overall economy against the wild yet reasonably predictable swings between periods of inflation and unemployment that are common in market economies.

The United States moved away from the residual and toward the institutional model of social welfare once the collapse of the economy in the 1930s made clear what the market could and could not do. From 1935 to 1975, political liberalism, economic growth, and the pressure of social movements fueled the expansion of the welfare state, which grew to include more people and to cover more needs. However, beginning with the election of President Reagan in 1980, laissez-faire and social conservatives who supported the residual model gained control of the government. Their tax and spending cuts have shrunk the welfare state, deepened poverty, and made life considerably more difficult for thousands of individuals and families. Even so, it is unlikely that the opponents of the welfare state will be able to eliminate it altogether given the chronic limits of the market, the continued widespread presence of social problems, and the ongoing pressure from advocacy groups and social movements.

Humanitarian Liberalism: The Social Right to Welfare

Humanitarian liberalism values what the welfare state can achieve in a capitalist nation, but argues that the government should do even more than what pragmatic liberalism supports. Humanitarian liberals fear that too large a gap between the haves and the have-nots both prevents social participation by individuals and poses a risk to the smooth functioning of wider society. Therefore, the government must create the social conditions for social integration by ensuring individuals' well-being, sense of belonging, and a chance to participate fully in wider society. The full participation of all members of society depends on the acquisition of three basic rights of citizenship: civil rights (the right to individual liberty and equality before the law), political rights (the right to vote and to run for political office), and social rights (the right to a community-defined adequate standard of living). Social rights, which correct, supplement, and supplant the market system, translate into a universal, comprehensive, and adequate system of government-provided benefits available to all as a right by virtue of membership in the community.

Humanitarian liberalism supports an extensive role for the government. Given the inequality built into a market system dedicated to private gain, it concludes that only the government has the capacity to adequately invest in people and to ensure a comprehensive distribution of benefits based on need. Such a program would reduce the social, economic, and political inequalities; lessen the power of one group over another; defuse the collective resentment and conflict that inequality breeds; and otherwise promote social integration.[59]

Radicalism: From the Welfare State to a Welfare Society

Radicalism holds that although a capitalist economic system may increase society's capacity to produce goods and services, the private ownership of production and the profit motive decrease society's ability to meet basic human needs.[60] For one, the dominance of the cash nexus, the reliance on competition, and the need for coercion undercut social solidarity. Furthermore, the government by definition must support the overall interests of the dominant class, mediate its internal rivalries, and contain the working class. In the Marxist tradition, radicalism remains skeptical about the welfare state. It argues that the welfare state was developed to meet the need of capitalism for a profitable economic environment and to maintain its core values and class structure. Social welfare provision helps to sustain business profits in various ways (see chapter 2). The capitalist welfare state is also the price or "ransom" paid for political security by the propertied class when confronted by social movements demanding an end to exploitation and oppression.[61]

Of course, it is not a one-way street. Because "the people" also have some influence on the government, radicals add that the state is not an unambiguous instrument of class domination. As shown in chapters 6 and 7, social movements have won a wide range of reforms that serve the interests of their members. However, radicals conclude that even though the state is forced to grant reforms, it minimizes redistribution to those with less. Indeed, radicals point out that the welfare state is financed in large part by taxes paid by the average family. Because most of the benefits circulate within the working and middle class rather than from the wealthy to the poor, some radical observers have facetiously described the welfare state as a self-help system.[62]

Radicalism concludes that as a social system, capitalism is antithetical to welfare. For one, the values and norms of welfare cannot make much headway in societies that do not make human well-being and meeting human needs core priorities. Further, given its ties to the survival of the dominant class, the capitalist welfare state can only go so far. Although social welfare policy may alleviate poverty and regulate the economy, it will not abolish the inequality built into the market economies, for to do so would undermine the wealth on which the power of the dominant class rests.

More recent radical analysts have added still another reason for the limitations of the welfare state. They point out that because most of society's economic surplus (revenues over expenditures) typically ends up in the private hands of wealthy individuals and major corporations, the government cannot raise the funds needed to sustain the cost of both creating the conditions for profitable economic activity (accumulation) and sustaining the social peace (legitimization). This eventually creates a "fiscal crisis" that forces the government to once again cut social programs.[63] In the final analysis, radicals believe that human liberation requires not a welfare state, but a welfare society that subordinates the market, that is, one that replaces private ownership of production and the profit motive with communal control over all areas of life.[64]

Feminism and the Welfare State

Feminism offers still another perspective on the role of government in social welfare. Given that the majority of social welfare clients and workers are women, feminism faults standard conservative, liberal, and radical thinking for their failure to look at the relationship between women and the welfare state. Feminists of all political stripes reject conservatism's limited view of women's roles and its opposition to government intervention in social welfare. They fault liberalism for ignoring women's rights and radicalism for focusing on labor, class structure, and capitalism but not gender, male domination, and patriarchy. These standard analyses cannot be applied to women, say feminists, unless they are broadened to include the relationship of the welfare state to the family, social reproduction, the gender division of labor, and women's political struggles.

Liberal feminists see government as a neutral arbiter of conflicting social interests and therefore an ally in their effort to extend liberty, equality, autonomy, self-fulfillment, and justice to women. Because liberal feminists expect the government to protect individual rights against the tyranny of any individual group, they take it for granted that the state is the proper and legitimate authority for expanding the rights of women.[65] Therefore, liberal feminism faults the state for its sexist social welfare programs.

Given their historic concerns about sex discrimination, liberal feminists were among the first to discover that social welfare programs were male-biased and gender-blind and treated women differently than men on the basis of their sex.[66] The male bias stems from social welfare policy's strong emphasis on work and wages, which reflects a male pattern of life and work (see section on ideology of work). The policies are gender- (and race-) blind because they generalize the male experience to women (and men of color) as if gender (and race) differences did not exist. For example, the strong employment focus on work as a condition of assistance makes it more difficult for women to receive benefits. Given their caretaking duties, women have a harder time than most men accumulating the years of work needed to qualify for full Social Security and Unemployment Insurance benefits. And given the male/female wage gap, women end up with fewer and lower benefits compared to men.

Finally, liberal feminism points out that although social welfare programs protect individuals and families from some labor market failures (e.g., loss of income due to old age, unemployment, illness), they rarely cover the unique risks faced by working women, such as the loss of income due to pregnancy and child-rearing and caretaking responsibilities. Nor does the welfare state protect women very well from failures of marriage (such as divorce, desertion, lack of child support from a noncustodial parent, and violence in the home), which impoverish women and leave them supporting children on their own.[67] Liberal feminists call on the state to recognize social welfare policy's male bias, to address the problems faced by working women, to improve women's labor market opportunities, and to ease the burden of the double day by legislating pay equity, paid maternal leave, universal health care, and quality child care, among other important supports.

Cultural feminism does not contain an explicit analysis of the role of government, although one can assume that it views the state as an arm of patriarchy.[68] At the outset, cultural feminism sparked a movement that emphasized self-defense and collective empowerment as the best way to combat male sexual violence against women. Volunteer programs taught women to fight, police their communities, support and advocate for victims, organize for increased social, economic, and political power, and challenge the cultural representations that sexually objectified women.

As the movement increasingly relied on state funding to protect women against male violence, the approach shifted from empowerment to paternalistic protections and repression of sexuality. The initial antirape hot lines and shelters for battered women run by the battered women's movement emphasized the empowerment of women.[69] However, once anticrime and victim's assistance monies replaced the original funding, the emphasis moved toward protection of women and sexual repression. Women are better protected against male violence today. More police departments have a pro-arrest policy for batterers and more states have simplified procedures for obtaining a restraining order. The rape laws of many states now prohibit cross-examination of the victim about her prior sexual history and no longer require corroboration by a witness or proof of physical violence. However, these more paternalistic programs do little to empower the women themselves.

More recently, right-wing women's groups that are hostile to feminism have formed their own programs to defend women and children against men's abuse of patriarchal power. This includes antiviolence programs but also government-funded programs to collect and improve child support payments and in some instances to reestablish alimony. Reflecting their roots in social conservatism, these right-wing organizations willingly use state power to discipline men as well as women, to impose traditional family structures on women, and to ensure that men provide protection and support to women who comply with traditional gender role behavior.

Socialist feminism has the most developed critique of the welfare state.[70] It holds that the welfare state, governed by the requirements of both capitalism and patriarchy, reproduces and reinforces the unequal power relations based on gender and race as well as class. Along with many other observers, socialist feminists note that social welfare programs often provide better benefits and service to the "deserving" middle class than to the "undeserving" poor. But socialist feminism criticizes these programs as well for favoring males and whites. Going beyond the problem of discriminatory treatment that liberal feminists identified, socialist feminists maintain that the welfare state also supports the social and economic basis for male domination of women. Its programs and policies endorse the gender division of labor, including traditional gender roles, social reproduction by women at home, and women's economic dependence on men. Social feminists also expose the racism that underpins social welfare provision, especially, but not only, for single mothers.[71]

Drawing on the cultural feminist analysis, socialist feminists argue that social welfare policy upholds patriarchal arrangements when it defines women in terms of their biological functions and uses state power to "protect" them as reproducers of the species and as mothers who socialize the next generation. For example, during the Progressive Era, many states passed protective labor laws that shortened the work day, limited night shifts, restricted the number of pounds workers could lift, and mandated that employers provide seats. The laws gained support on the grounds that women needed to be protected so as not to jeopardize their capacity to bear and raise children. The reformers could not convince lawmakers to extend these protections to equally exploited men. Compounding the problem, once it was passed, many employers used the law as an excuse not to hire women or to pay them lower wages than male workers. The 1935 Social Security Act, the core of the modern welfare state, also perpetuated the biological construction of womanhood by assisting most women in their roles as mothers and wives only as long as they were caring for children or a spouse.

The welfare state also shores up patriarchal controls by supporting traditional gender roles, especially women's economic dependence on men. As will be seen in the section of this chapter on the family, feminists point out that in addition to the work ethic, social welfare programs support the family ethic, which holds that women belong at home, married, raising children, and economically dependent on the male breadwinner.[72] The 1935 Social Security Act, along with most social welfare benefits and service programs, favor those who work over the jobless. Similarly, welfare state programs reward those women who comply with the family ethic and penalize those who fail to do so by choice or force of circumstance. The latter are considered able but unwilling to marry and responsible for a family's breakup.

As it evolved, socialist feminism moved from an analysis of the welfare state as an institution that enforced patriarchal controls to seeing it as a system that mediates the conflicts between patriarchy and capitalism—two interdependent systems that worked sometimes in concert and other times as rivals. The systems work in concert to the extent that the welfare state supports women's unpaid labor in the home. As discussed later in this chapter, the organization of women's household labor serves patriarchy because women provide individual men with a wide range of services for free. The arrangement also benefits capitalism because it provides employers with both a reserve pool of labor and mothers who keep the current and future workforce fit for laboring.

However, the two systems also compete in a tug of war over women's labor. As industrial capitalism advanced, its demand for low-paid females drew more and more women out of the home. Once women became permanent members of the workforce, they were less available to capital as a reserve labor pool that could be moved in and out of the labor market to replace absent male workers or to press down wages. Work outside the home by wives also weakened patriarchal controls in the home. It deprived individual men of their domestic services and increased women's economic independence. The welfare state helped to mediate the competing demands for women's unpaid home and low-paid market work by encouraging "deserving" women (those who complied with the family ethic) to stay home and forcing the "undeserving" group into the workforce using low benefits and stiff work rules.[73]

The controlling functions of the welfare state are well-known. However, socialist feminists also point to its emancipatory potential. As noted in chapter 2, by providing women with income outside of employment and marriage, the welfare state increases women's individual and collective leverage with both employers and male partners. Strengthening women's position to bargain for more independence in both arenas, social welfare provision weakens the power of both capitalism and patriarchy. A truly generous and comprehensive system that provided women with enough economic resources to maintain independent households would significantly reduce their economic dependence on men and allow them true autonomy.

Finally, socialist feminists point to the role played by women activists in the origins and development of the welfare state.[74] They identify the middle-class women reformers whose activism helped to launch the welfare state in the early 1900s as well as the less visible social welfare activism among poor and working-class women, both white women and women of color. The demands of the women activists in the early 1900s foreshadowed the needs that the developing welfare state would have to address. As the state increasingly underwrote the costs of family maintenance (social reproduction), women increasingly targeted the welfare state to provide more adequately for their families and communities.[75] Their activism contributed to the growth of the welfare state until the mid-1970s and then helped to defend it against the subsequent conservative assault.

The Ideology of Work and the Work Ethic

Ideas about work play a central role in social welfare policy. Indeed, people's access to most social welfare programs depends on their work history, the availability of jobs, and public attitudes regarding why people are not at work. Most ideologies place a high value on work; agreement disappears when it comes to defining work, its motivation, and its purpose.

Conservatism: Work as Necessity

Reflecting its view of human nature as selfish, conservatism holds that people avoid work unless driven to it by deprivation (or ambition). The view of work as a necessary evil dates back to feudal times, when society regarded the position of people at both the top and the bottom of the social order as preselected by God. Given this strong belief in predetermination, most people concluded that human effort made little difference. The Greek and Hebrew societies actually deplored work for the elite on the grounds that it brutalized the mind and stood in the way of prayer and contemplation of God. Other early societies regarded work as a punishment for original sin or as a painful humiliating scourge for the pride of the flesh. Spurning labor for the elite, these early societies accepted hard work as the God-given duty of serfs, slaves, and free laborers. Because the social status of laborers reflected God's will, society could disdain the poor without blaming them for their circumstances. Feudal society also discouraged the accumulation of wealth because the process interfered with the prevailing means for determining status, obligations, and duties.[76]

The emergence of the market economy, private enterprise, and wage labor in Europe after the sixteenth century undermined the feudal order and brought forward a new attitude toward work, as did the rise of Protestantism.

The idea that good deeds and hard work were the way to glorify God gradually replaced the prior beliefs of preordained salvation and of work as a punishment for original sin. According to a theologian who studied the shift from feudalism to capitalism, "The religious values [placed] upon constant, systematic, efficient work in one's calling as the readiest means of securing the certainty of salvation and of glorifying God became the most powerful agency in economic expansion."[77] The new work ethic praised hard work, self-discipline, and the successful pursuit of riches as ways to control unruly passions but also as a sign that one was destined for salvation. Thus, the thinking about work changed: from a route to religious salvation, the idea gradually emerged of work as the path to economic success. Once one's work status no longer reflected God's will, idleness became a deadly sin worthy of stigma, penalty, and punishment.[78]

The Puritans brought the Protestant work ethic to the New World. Over time, industrialization, the country's seemingly unlimited natural resources, and the sense of great possibilities led to the belief that no one who tried hard need be poor. At the same time, the new doctrine of individual responsibility held people responsible for their own economic situation and religious salvation. As the work ethic became part of American culture, the public repudiated those without work as unwilling to apply themselves—and became highly suspicious of and hostile to the poor.[79]

The repudiation of those not at work as lazy and unmotivated has a long history and strong impact on social welfare policy. The belief in human beings as rationally calculating choices that maximize pleasure and minimize pain (broadly defined) was also interpreted to mean that people tried at all costs to avoid work because it was undesirable (as pain vs. pleasure). In the late 1700s, the British economist Thomas Malthus concluded that individuals work only because they have to: "The savage would slumber for ever under his tree unless he were roused from this torpor by the cravings of hunger or the pinchings of cold and the exertions he made to avoid these evils." Malthus concluded that society must be organized to reflect a view of "man [sic] as he really is, inert, sluggish, and averse from labor, unless compelled by necessity. . . . Necessity has with great truth been called the mother of invention."[80] By "necessity," Malthus means that people work only to avoid the pain of hunger, poverty, and other basic deprivations.

These ideas about work eventually turned into disdain and penalties for those not at work. In the late 1800s, the science of eugenics held that people inherited the unwillingness to work. Social Darwinism argued that in the struggle for survival those who are strongest, smartest, and most fit for the competition will succeed and prosper. Those who are unfit will/should fail and suffer. Society's helping the downtrodden impeded individual freedom and retarded social progress.[81] In the early twentieth century, Sigmund Freud, the father of psychoanalysis, concluded that most people seem to have a "natural" aversion to work. Freud identified love and work as the major wellsprings of human happiness, but found that many individuals undervalued work as a source of satisfaction and worked only under the stress of necessity.[82]

The work ethic—one of the most enduring American ideologies—as portrayed on the cover of Horatio Alger's famous novel Strive and Succeed.

At the 1969 congressional hearings on Social Security and welfare reform proposals, Representative Wilbur Mills, former chair of the House Ways and Means Committee, declared that the poor needed to be coerced to work: "If you don't use a degree of compulsion, how do you get people to realize that they are so much better off if they get training and get into suitable employment?"[83]

In the mid-1980s, Charles Murray, then a senior policy analyst at the Manhattan Institute for Policy Research, a conservative think tank in New York City, concluded that "scrapping the entire federal welfare and income support structure for working age persons . . . would leave the working person with no recourse, whatsoever, except the job market." Murray added, "I am not suggesting that we dismantle income support programs for the working-age persons to balance the budget or punish welfare cheats. I am hypothesizing that the lives of large numbers of poor people would be radically changed for the better."[84] Writing in the mid-1990s, Lawrence Mead, a conservative scholar who refers to unemployment as "nonwork," stated, "Whatever outward cause one cites, a mystery at the heart of non-work remains—the *passivity* of the seriously poor in seizing the opportunities that apparently exist for them." Mead adds, "Seriously poor adults appear to avoid work, not because of their economic situation, but because of what they believe."[85]

The belief that people won't work unless driven by necessity or force has governed social welfare policy from the first colonial poor laws to the reauthorization of welfare reform in September 2002. In all this time, public policy directed to the poor has assumed that the poor are lazy, do not want to work, and need the strong arm of the government to force them to do so. Reflecting the view that deprivation motivates work, welfare policy has historically provided very low benefits (i.e., below the lowest prevailing wage), conditioned the receipt of benefits on the applicant's work history, and rewarded those with longer work records and higher wages while penalizing those with less. Policies have also stigmatized welfare recipients, closed welfare offices, and otherwise ensured that only the most desperate would choose welfare over work.

Liberalism: Work as Satisfaction

Conservatism's understanding of work did not go unchallenged. As early as the Renaissance (fourteenth to seventeenth centuries), some observers contested the ideas that individuals work only to overcome deprivation and that work is a necessary evil, valued only for its results. They argued that creative work could be a joy in itself. Some early utopians envisioned societies that matched work to people's character, experimented with different kinds of labor, and limited work to only part of the day.[86]

Drawing on twentieth-century social science, liberalism argues that people work because it serves a range of social, psychological, and economic needs. As proof, liberals point to studies showing that even when people come into unexpected wealth, they do not necessarily withdraw from paid work. Research has found that few people who inherit large sums of money or win the lottery stop working or fall into idleness. Studies also report that as people's income and wealth increases, they invest more time in their work.[87]

Social science offers a range of positive meanings of work for the individual and society. Economists tell us that work makes it possible for society to produce and distribute goods and services. It transforms raw nature into products that serve our needs and wants. Psychologists say that work provides people with a sense of mastery of themselves and their environment. Freud argued that work attaches people to reality, gives them a secure place in the human community, and provides important psychological functions, such as displacing a large amount of erotic, narcissistic, and aggressive libidinal impulses onto professional work and into human relations. Other psychologists add that producing something valued by others gives workers a sense that they have something to offer society. Sociologists emphasize the ways work brings people together, promotes social ties, confers social status, and gives one a place in society.[88] For better or worse, people become what they do. The question "Who are you?" typically evokes a response such as "I am a social worker" or "I work at the Middletown Mental Health Center." Work also provides us with a sense of order and structure that precludes chaos and confusion.

The discussion of the value of work to individuals intensified in the 1970s as the public became interested in the question of job satisfaction. The 1971 report of a Special Task Force to the Secretary of Health, Education and Welfare, *Work in America*, held that people need to earn a living, but they also need to have satisfying work. Dissatisfying work (or worse), it argued, risks setting off "severe repercussions" in other parts of the social system.[89] Drawing from programs already tried by some U.S. corporations, the report called for workplace reform and redesign. It recommended developing more flexible work schedules and rules, giving workers more autonomy and responsibility for production decisions, and promoting self-government, participatory management, and profit sharing. The report also called for government support for lifetime learning for workers, such as educational programs geared to worker self-renewal and a six-month sabbatical every seven years for all workers. Finally, *Work in America* recommended the creation of more and better jobs but also job security on the grounds that the absence of job opportunities, adequate wages, and safe working conditions undercuts the possibility of other sources of job satisfaction. These liberal ideas about work gained some currency during the 1970s, only to be pushed aside by the rising conservative tide that surfaced in the 1980s.

Radicalism: Work as Transforming Self and Society

Radicalism defines work as purposeful, sustained activity that allows individuals both to develop their human potential and to transform nature into useful products that fulfill human needs.[90] On a societal level, work is allocated to produce the goods and services needed by people for sustenance, clothing, shelter, defense, and luxuries. If employment as an income-producing effort is contrasted with idleness or volunteering, in this broader meaning work contrasts with leisure or rest.[91]

Radicalism regards individuals as naturally work-oriented and work as central to the human experience. Yet it concludes that the structure of work in capitalism creates a variety of problems. Conservatism holds that people avoid work because they are lazy and irresponsible; radicalism regards human beings as harmed by the social relations of work in a profit-driven economy.

More specifically, the structure of work is alienating for many people, the organization of work can lead to the exploitation and dehumanization of workers, and the distribution of work and its rewards are major sources of inequality. Alienation refers to the separation of human beings from each other, from themselves, and from the products they create. According to Marx, worker alienation arises because capitalist work arrangements deprive workers of control over their labor, create incentives for managers to manipulate workers, and require workers to do highly specialized repetitive tasks, often in large, impersonal settings. Allowed to use only a fraction of their talents, workers cannot develop pride in their creativity or the final product of their work, and so work loses its meaning and satisfaction. [92]

The free enterprise system also exploits workers by taking time and activity away from individuals and using it for the benefit of employers.[93] The radical theory of exploitation is based on the notion that workers labor for more hours than is needed to reproduce their "labor power." In any one eight-hour day, individuals may need to work only four hours to earn what is needed for their subsistence, broadly defined. For profits to be made, however, workers must labor for longer than this, perhaps for eight instead of just four hours. The dollar value of the four hours that exceeds the amount needed to ensure survival accrues to the employer as profit.[94] In other words, only part of the value of the daily labor of workers is returned to them in wages. Such exploitation creates the basis for class conflict. To ensure that people come to work every day, capitalist society has had to overcome the built-in disincentives by associating work with economic survival but also personal identity, wage hierarchies, and competitive consumption.[95] The organization of work in a profit-based economic system also creates incentives to keep wages down and invest little in working conditions, and otherwise poses a threat to human life.

Radicalism proposes that a system freed from capitalist alienation, exploitation, and workplace harms, one organized to meet human needs, would operate differently. It would not need to blame the victim, create false work incentives, or degrade, alienate, or exploit people. Rather, work would be a positive, growth-producing activity that allows human beings to develop their own capabilities, one that would transform society by converting the nonhuman world into a means for addressing human needs. The cooperation involved in such an endeavor encourages people to become and remain interconnected. Indeed, for Marx, the realization of all human potential is possible only as human beings as a group develop their powers; and these powers can be realized only through the cooperative action of all people over time.[96] In brief, work is the basis of human self-development and importantly beneficial for the entire society.

Feminism and Work

Conservatism decries the individual's lack of work motivation. Liberalism calls for more satisfying jobs to stimulate interest in work. Radicalism deplores the degradation of work. Despite its agreement with many of the ideas about work subscribed to by liberalism and radicalism, feminism had to change the question because the other schools of thought omitted women.

Feminism spends less time worrying about the work ethic than about who controls and benefits from women's labor in the home and on the job. Expanding the discussion of work to include the relationship of work to the subordination of women, feminism argues that women's unpaid labor in the home must be counted as work. Regardless of their political stripe, most feminists concur that the organization of work disadvantages women both at home and on the job.

Liberal feminists highlight sexism, both the unequal treatment of women in the workplace and the unequal distribution of household tasks among women and men. They argue that unequal pay for equal work is unfair and that, although women are just as capable workers as men, the commonly held belief that men are better leaders stymies women's advancement. Liberal feminists also believe that equal work opportunities will relieve men of the unfair responsibility for total financial support of the family. They focus attention on eliminating barriers to women and providing more opportunities for choice of employment by women and men.[97]

Cultural feminists view society through the lens of patriarchy, that is, the social relations of power that enable men to control women. In this view, although both men and women are injured by the demands of capitalism, due to patriarchy male roles bring them more prestige and financial rewards than do the roles assigned to women. Cultural feminists posit that the hierarchical organization of the workplace allows more powerful men to dominate and control other men. This relationship between men, in turn, allows all men to benefit materially and psychologically from the exploitation of women's labor. It also furthers a shared gendered interest in maintaining their position of dominance over women.[98] More specifically, because senior males have virtually total authority over subordinate males (and females), they can reward men economically and emotionally for obeying the authoritarian rules of the workplace. The economic rewards designed to ensure that subordinate men obey senior men also provide the less powerful men with the means to dominate women on the job and in their own homes. Therefore, cultural feminists call for altering or eliminating male-dominated hierarchies in the labor market and at home.

Socialist feminism developed its analysis by examining the relationship of women's work to both capitalism and patriarchy. Drawing on Marxism, socialist feminism values productive activity for its concrete results but also for its impact on human development and the wider society. Socialist feminists also agree with cultural feminists that men as a group benefit from women's labor on the job and at home. They argue that the lack of opportunity and choice decried by liberal feminism is a symptom, not a cause. The underlying problem is the gender division of labor that emerged with industrialization and continues to benefit both capitalism and patriarchy by disadvantaging women.

That nearly half the current workforce is women points to women's interest in employment, the family's need for women's earnings, and employers' demand for women workers as cheap labor. However, the organization of the workplace simultaneously supports capitalist profits and patriarchal arrangements. The existence of sex-segregated jobs, male-female pay differentials, and gendered power hierarchies justifies paying women less than men, which helps to lower employers' labor costs and sustain business profits.

The organization of women's labor also benefits capitalism. Assigned to the home, for years women served as a reserve army of labor that employers could move in and out of the labor market as needed. Employers typically recruited women workers when they wanted to replace absent men, undercut male skills, or press male wages down—only to send the women back home when their labor was no longer needed. Now that so many women work for wages outside the home, the shrunken reserve army of labor consists of stay-at-home moms and women employed only part-time.

The gendered labor market enforces patriarchal relations as well as capitalist profits. For one, it reflects patriarchal notions of women's "place" both in the cleaning, cooking, and service jobs that women do and in their lack of power in the workplace. The economic insecurity resulting from their low wages and lack of power (and the higher wages paid to men) creates the conditions for the subordination of women to men in the home and on the job by leaving women economically dependent on men and marriage for support.[99] As noted earlier, the emphasis on work and the work ethic has produced male-biased and gender-blind social welfare policies.

Feminists of color offer still another interpretation of work for women, by taking into account the impact of racism. Just as white feminists fault men for conceptualizing events on the basis of male experience and generalizing it to women as if no differences existed, so women of color fault white feminists for analyzing women's work based on the experience of white women and generalizing the conclusions to all women without accounting for racial differentials.

Feminists of color point out that many persons of color were either brought to this country or conquered to meet the need for a cheap and exploitable workforce. For much of the nineteenth and twentieth centuries, most women of color worked for low wages while middle-class white women remained at home.[100] First, women of color were employed as servants in white households, relieving white middle-class women of onerous aspects of domestic labor. Then they were disproportionately employed as service workers in private enterprise, where they also cleaned for and served others. So, while the feminist movement fought for the right of women to work outside the home, slavery, racial discrimination against men and women of color, and economic hardship forced women of color to work for wages outside the home—often against their will. In sum, racism prevented women of color from choosing to stay home. From the start, women of color experienced little or no separation of work and family. Instead, women's work outside the home was an extension of their family responsibilities.

The Ideology of Family

The word *family* entered the English language in the fifteenth century, when it was used to denote a household with servants. Today, most people use the term to refer to a set of people related by blood, marriage, or adoption. How the family is defined becomes key in social welfare policy because access to many, if not all, social welfare benefits depends on deep-seated assumptions about "deserving" and "undeserving" families.

Conservatism, liberalism, radicalism, and feminism all place a high value on the family as a social institution. But their agreement disappears when it comes to defining the family structure and the family's right to assistance. Conservatism favors the two-parent family unit over all others; liberalism validates diverse family arrangements; radicalism rarely addresses the family; and feminists, both white and women of color, look at the family for its impact on women. These different views about the family have coexisted for centuries. Yet the debate about what constitutes the "proper" family erupts periodically, typically during periods of social change when large numbers of people feel uncertain about the stability of their lives.

Such a debate occurred during the Industrial Revolution, when the agricultural economy gave way to market-based production. This dramatic shift created the need for someone to work in the new factories and someone else to remain at home. The resulting gender division of labor assigned women to caretaking in the home and men to breadwinning in the market. The debate surfaced again during the roaring twenties. This time the change in women's roles was marked by the enfranchisement of women, the expansion of service jobs, and the period's sexual revolution, which brought women short haircuts, short skirts, and bloomers.[101] After World War II, women's roles changed again, due first to the massive entry of married women into the workforce and then to the demands in the late 1960s of the women's movement.

The recent conflict over the definition of the family in the United States began in the late 1970s, fueled this time by a backlash to the gains made by the women's movement, the expansion of gay and lesbian rights, and the economic insecurity within the middle class generated by deindustrialization, downsizing, and the export of production abroad. In 1980, the White House Conference on Families foundered on the fundamental question of what constitutes a family and what makes for good family life.

Conservatism and "the Family"

Both social and laissez-fare conservatism regard the two-parent heterosexual family as a natural and unchanging social unit and the bedrock of society. Backed by mainstream social science, this definition of the family has provided the foundation for most ideas about the family and gender roles since the end of World War II.

The mainstream view of the family relies heavily on the work of Talcott Parsons, the influential American sociologist who defined the nuclear family as especially well-suited to the demands of an urban industrialized society. According to Parsons, as economic changes shifted production out of the home, the educational, economic, and protective functions of the older extended family were transferred to impersonal public institutions, including schools and later social welfare programs. Having lost its earlier purpose, the smaller, nuclear family came to specialize in raising children and meeting the needs of individual family members for love, security, loyalty, and companionship. The family also taught its members discipline, self-restraint, and self-control.[102]

Whether conservatives believe that the modern nuclear family structure is God-given, biologically destined, or essential to an efficient and productive society, they prefer it to any other arrangement. Therefore, its strength and stability must be protected and sustained at all costs. This includes preserving the gender division of labor considered to be functional for modern society. According to Parsons, the family contributes to social stability because fathers take on the "instrumental" role (e.g., earning income, participating in community affairs, maintaining family discipline) while mothers assume the "expressive" role (e.g., nurturance and socialization).[103] Most conservatives agree, especially social conservatives. They think that men—not women—should run the family, and that the social bonds among men, women, and children in the family ought to be regulated by traditional and religious morality. They oppose more egalitarian contractual relations worked out by the particular individuals involved. Indeed, in this view, sexual equality leads to promiscuity, lack of complementarity, and the collapse of the social bonds necessary for society.[104]

The standard two-parent heterosexual family is also key to social stability because it is regarded as an inherently harmonious and consensual unit. Given their mutuality of interests, husbands and wives agree as to what is best for each of them and for the family as a whole. The prescribed gender division of labor reduces the possibility of conflict by preventing competition between husband and wife within and outside the home. Public acceptance of this view of the stable and harmonious family peaked in the United Status during the 1950s. Television shows such as *Father Knows Best* and *The Adventures of Ozzie and Harriet* celebrated white breadwinning fathers and full-time homemaker mothers living harmoniously with their children in single-family suburban houses.[105]

Because this gendered pattern was regarded as "natural," best for the (always presumed heterosexual) modern family, and critical for social stability, any major change in gender roles or family structure was problematic. Change risked unleashing marital conflict, disrupting the household equilibrium, and challenging the moral foundation of society. By the mid-1960s, as the contest over the properly structured family surfaced, single-parent households came under a racialized attack as deviant and pathological. In 1965, Daniel P. Moynihan wrote of the black community:

> From the wild Irish slums of the nineteenth century Eastern seaboard to the riot-torn suburbs of Los Angeles, there is one unmistakable lesson in American history; a community that allows a large number of young men to grow up in broken families, dominated by women, never acquiring any stable relationship to male authority, never acquiring any set of rational expectations about the future—that community asks for and gets chaos.[106]

By the mid-1970s, leading conservatives declared that the family was in peril. Social conservatives viewed ongoing changes in family structure as evidence of moral decay and a fundamental attack on the family. They disliked

This photograph from the popular television show Father Knows Best *reflects the patriarchal family at its height after World War II.*

the rise of working wives, single mothers, divorced couples, gay parents, interracial marriages, test-tube babies, accessible abortions, and birth control. A conservative thinker touted the traditional family as

> situated apart from both the larger kin group and the workplace, focused on the procreation of children, and consisting of a legal, lifelong, sexually exclusive, heterosexual, monogamous marriage based on affection and companionship, in which there is a sharp division of labor (separate spheres), with the female as a full-time housewife and the male as primary provider and ultimate authority.[107]

Laissez-faire conservatives hoped to preserve the traditional family for other than moral reasons. They supported the traditional family because it promoted individualism and fostered self-assertion and the belief in the individual's ability to control the world through rational calculation. According to the authors of *The War over the Family*, "Put simply, the bourgeois family socialized individuals with personalities and values conducive to entrepreneurial capitalism on the one hand and democracy on the other."[108]

Both social and laissez-faire conservatives believe that big government, especially social programs and social service professionals, has weakened the family by usurping its traditional authority[109] and by supporting the single-parent household. When he was president, Ronald Reagan declared, "There is no question that many well-intentioned Great Society–type programs contributed to family breakups, welfare dependency, and a large increase in births out of wedlock."[110] In the mid-1990s, Robert Rector, a social analyst for the Heritage Foundation, a well-known conservative think tank, declared:

> Across the nation, the current welfare system has all but destroyed family structure in low-income communities. Welfare established strong financial incentives which effectively block the formation of intact, two-parent families. . . . Largely because of welfare, illegitimacy and single parenthood have now become the conventional "life-style" option for raising children in many low-income communities.[111]

The discussion of single motherhood and family breakdown became deeply racialized. Echoing Moynihan, contemporary conservatives repeatedly portray the African American family headed by a single mother as "broken." Heather MacDonald, a senior fellow at the Manhattan Institute, a New York City conservative think tank, has argued that single mothers should not be raising children. In such families, she declared, "there is no role model of somebody who is working living in the house." In the very next sentence and without offering a reason, MacDonald shifted from talking about single mothers in general to black families: "A lot of the problems we're seeing with young black males results from the fact that they have no positive male role models growing up. They're left out in the streets. They see nobody who works, who has gotten an education. There are simply jungle rules out there."[112] The use of the term *jungle* also evokes traditional stereotypes of blacks as uncivilized. Writing in the *Philadelphia Inquirer* about the high rate of nonmarital births in the black community, Charles Murray concluded that "the culture must be *Lord of the Flies* writ large, the values of unsocialized male adolescent-made norms—physical violence, immediate gratification, and predatory sex. That is the culture now taking over the black inner city."[113]

To deal with the changing family, social conservatives call on the government to exert moral leadership, to assert its influence over social and sexual mores, and to actively promote family values. The conservative strategy for restoring the "traditional family" includes

> a social movement whose purpose is "cultural education" in family values. It should point out the supreme importance to society of strong families, while at the same time suggesting ways that the family can better adapt to the modern conditions of individualism, equality and the labor force participation of both women and men. Such a movement could build on the fact that the overwhelming majority of young people today still put forth as their major life goal a lasting monogamous, heterosexual relationship which includes the procreation of children. It is reasonable to suppose that this goal is so pervasive because it is based on a deep seated need.[114]

New Right fund-raisers such as Richard Vigurie, religious leaders such as Jerry Falwell, and conservative political commentators such as George Gilder have called for reestablishing the traditional patriarchal family so that the nation can restore moral order, revitalize the economy, and strengthen itself at home and abroad.

Laissez-faire conservatives are less enthusiastic about using the state to patrol antifamily educational materials or to otherwise influence and control family behavior. They prefer to strengthen the traditional family by increasing choice, that is, by lowering the tax burden on married couples, providing child tax credits, providing educational vouchers for school choice, limiting access to abortion, and so on.[115]

Liberalism: From "the Family" to "Families"

Liberalism accepts the traditional family and its functions as depicted by Parsons. It sees the formation of families as a highly rational choice for meeting the needs it is intended to address. However, both pragmatic and humanitarian liberalism contain a more flexible attitude toward family structure. In the mid-1970s, if not before, some scholars, influenced by the women's movement, began to challenge the idealized version of "the family" as too narrow and not reflective of many of the country's households. These more liberal analyses recognized a range of family forms and began to employ the plural term *families* to denote this diversity. According to one historian:

> The one unambiguous fact which has emerged in the last twenty years is that there can be no simple history of *the* Western family since the sixteenth century because there is not, nor ever has there been, a single family system. The West has always been characterized by diversity of family forms, by diversity of family functions, and by diversity in attitudes to family relationships not only over time but at any one moment in time. There is, except at most trivial levels, no Western family type.[116]

Liberalism challenges the idea of the "traditional" nuclear family as natural and inevitable. Its proponents claim that the evidence points to the family as a social rather than a biological group and shows that a family's size, composition, boundaries, sentiments, and activities vary by culture, social conditions, and history. In 1990, *Newsweek* published a special edition on "The 21st Century Family: Who We Will Be, How We Will Live." A section entitled "Variations on a Theme" suggested that "the family tree of American society is sending forth a variety of new and fast growing branches." The branches included "gay and lesbian couples, unmarried heterosexual couples, married childless couples, single parent households, babies by donor inseminations, and grandparents raising their children's children." The news magazine backed up its observations with figures from a public opinion poll that asked twelve hundred randomly selected adults to define the word *family*. Only 22 percent picked the legalistic definition noted earlier: a group of people related by blood, marriage, or adoption. Almost 75 percent chose a much broader description: "a group of people who love and care for each other."[117]

Along with their belief in diverse families, both pragmatic and humanitarian liberalism argue for government policies to help all types of families from all walks of life carry out any functions they no longer can perform adequately. For many years, indeed since the New Deal of the 1930s, the welfare state has sustained families by replacing lost income due to old age, unemployment, illness, disability, or breadwinner absence; subsidizing the cost of food, housing, education, and health care; and providing for a range of social and mental health services. However, as changes in family life and structures mounted, especially with the rise of working mothers and single parenthood, liberals began to call for a broader "family policy."

"Our families may be different in the next century," declared the editors of *Newsweek* in 1990, "but we have an extraordinary opportunity to make them stronger."[118] The stronger family policy recommended by pragmatic liberals includes programs to make it easier for women (and men) to combine work and child rearing such as paid family and medical leave, more affordable child care services, flexible work hours, supportive housing, and other services to help adult children care for their aging parents. Humanitarian liberalism adds to this family policy agenda equal pay for equal work, the development of a family allowance, higher public assistance grants, afterschool programs, comprehensive health services including prenatal care, sex education in the schools, and programs for battered women.

Feminism and Families

Standard radicalism rarely analyzes gender or family issues. In contrast, given their concerns about the oppression of women, feminists place families center stage. Like standard liberalism, all the feminisms criticize the traditional view of the family as natural, biological, or "functional" in a timeless way. But they add the perspective of women. Most feminist schools of thought reject the idea of the nuclear family as natural or inevitable in favor of the notion of diversity described above. They believe individuals should be able to choose their preferred family structure without penalty and argue for a more inclusive definition of the family.

Despite important differences on "the family question," liberal, cultural, and socialist feminists and feminists of color conclude that the specifics of daily family living cannot be adequately understood without systematic attention to the underlying structures of gender.[119] This includes the allocation of household tasks, the experiences of work and leisure, and the giving and receiving of nurturance, but also conflicts, episodes of violence, and decisions about employment, moving, consumption, and family size.

Liberal feminism views women as individuals within the family rather than as mere components of it or anchors to it, as prescribed by the traditional model. Mirroring the emphasis on individual rights and equal opportunity in standard liberalism, liberal feminists call for women to have the same rights to autonomy and self-determination in the home as society grants to men. This more equal treatment of the sexes in the family, however, requires a restructuring of gender roles. These roles include breaking out of being just a wife and mother, demanding that men help with housework and child rearing, having access to divorce, and having a marriage contract that spells out equal rights and duties. Liberal feminism also calls for child care, equal pay, family medical leave, and other supports for balancing work and family that would put women as individuals on an equal footing with men in the family and in the labor market. Liberal feminists have resisted sex-role stereotyping in childhood socialization practices and oppose the sexual double standard for women and men and all other unfair rules and practices based on acceptance of male and female difference.

Cultural feminism challenges the traditional family in another way. It regards the family as patriarchal and predicated on heterosexuality, male authority, compulsory motherhood, and the domination of women by men—especially women's identity, body, and sexuality.[120] According to Gayle Rubin, the creation of two genders, the sexual division of labor, and compulsory heterosexuality are all parts of a sex-gender system that underlies family arrangements oppressive to women.[121]

Unlike liberal feminists, who seek individual rights and equal treatment with men in the family, cultural feminists affirm women as intrinsically different from—and superior to—men. They criticize capitalism for fostering individualism, competition, selfishness, and other traits associated with men and have no interest in endorsing the rules of a "man-made society" that do not reflect their interests. Instead, cultural feminists urge that the family and wider society be guided by cooperation, nurturance, and mutual caring—positive traits linked to women.

Rather than seeing the family as a safe haven in a heartless land, cultural feminists regard the male-dominated family as a potential site of oppression for women. The custom of a woman taking her husband's (and father's) last name emerged historically to signal women as the property of men. Cultural feminists also oppose using the titles *Miss* and *Mrs.* because they mark a woman's potential sexual availability (which led to use of the term *Ms.*).

Cultural feminists also counter the cultural glorification of motherhood by exposing its darker and unspoken experiences. They depict "compulsory motherhood" as an institution organized for and by patriarchy. Compulsory motherhood refers to (1) the assumption that because women can physically bear children all women are potential mothers; (2) cultural directives that all women become mothers; (3) sentimentalization of motherhood, the maternal instinct, and mother-child bonding; and (4) the pitying or stigmatizing of childless women. Patriarchy also determines the conditions of motherhood by denying women control over the processes of reproduction (contraception, birth control, abortion rights, sterilization); the conditions of giving birth (male control of medicine, hospitals, cesarean births, etc.); and sources of child-rearing advice.[122]

Cultural feminists also criticize compulsory heterosexuality, on the grounds that the assumption that women have an innate need for males is false and because the belief grants men personal power over women and keeps women divided from each other.[123] Compulsory heterosexuality also ensures that men, both individually and as a social group, benefit from women's unpaid work in the home. This domestic labor provides men with free housekeeping, shopping, child rearing, personal support, and sexual services, among other benefits. Men also benefit because, by staying home, women are less likely to compete with them for better jobs in the labor market.[124]

Instead of love and harmony between husband and wife, cultural feminists emphasize patterns of inequality and conflict in the family. Pointing to high rates of divorce, separation, incest, marital rape, and battering, they argue that irreconcilable differences between husband and wife, father and children turn some families into a site of conflict and violence. For those who so desire, cultural feminists call for the right to remain single and childless and to form partnerships with other women. They also put the issues of abortion, rape, and male violence against women on the public policy agenda.

Socialist feminism looks at how the interplay of patriarchy and capitalism structures the family life of women (and men). Cultural feminists stress male control over women's bodies and how men benefit from women's unpaid work in the home; socialist feminists emphasize men's control over women's domestic labor and the ways this household labor benefits both capitalism and patriarchy.[125]

Like the standard radical tradition from which they come, socialist feminists pay special attention to the role of productive activity in society. However, they expand the definition of productive activities to include women's unpaid household work. Defining work only as paid employment in the labor market, they say, ignores what women do for free for the family and for society. To replace a woman's services as cook, baby-sitter, and housekeeper, for example, her husband would have to hire several workers, thereby adding thousands of dollars to the GDP. In contrast, if a man married his housekeeper, he would cause the GDP to fall because she moved from paid to unpaid work.[126] Therefore, feminists argue, caregiving by women, which affects women throughout the life cycle, needs to be redefined from a natural female trait based on biology to work both in the home and outside.

Socialist feminism maintains that women's household labor benefits capitalism and patriarchy.[127] Most immediately, women's domestic services free employers from having to pay male workers enough to purchase the same services on the open market. Employers gain as well because workers are more productive on the job when they return each day fed, rested, and comforted by women's unpaid domestic labor. The food, clothing, socialization, and nurturance provided by women at home also supply employers with a fit and properly socialized workforce—services that employers would otherwise have to pay for out of their profits.

While cultural feminists emphasize the patriarchal institution of compulsory motherhood, socialist feminists suggest that the socialization of children done by mothers in the home serves the interests of both capitalism and patriarchy and generally contributes to the smooth functioning of the wider society. Mothers are expected to prepare children to fit into the social order by, among other things, accepting their "proper" adult roles as defined by class and race. The work women do at home ensures that children develop the attitudes, values, and behaviors they need to succeed, or at least survive, in the job market, such as respect for authority, punctuality, hierarchy, and competition. Mothering also teaches children how to behave as boys and girls and what to expect as women and men with regard to marriage, childbearing, and family relations.[128]

Women's work in the family also acts a bulwark of the market economy. For one, women's work in the home converts a given amount of wages into the consumption of the goods and services that industry produces. Second, as noted in the section on work, to the extent that women have been assigned to the home or work outside only part-time, they can be moved in and out of the workforce as needed by business and industry. Because women's labor helps to keep the wheels of industry turning in these and many other ways, some socialist feminists have called for it to be paid through wages or some form of public benefits.

Feminists of Color and Families

Feminists of color challenge the traditional ideology of the family in still another way. Their analysis highlights how the forces of domination work differently for different groups. Feminists of color argue that the so-called traditional nuclear family does not always reflect their family arrangement. They point to the presence of family forms in their communities that appear less often elsewhere, such as kinship caring, "othermothers,"[129] and single motherhood. They object when social observers label these family arrangements as deviant, implying that only one "good" or proper family type exists.

Feminists of color also take issue with white feminists who disparage the family as a site of women's oppression. They stress how racial stratification has shaped family life. For one, women of color experience the oppression of a patriarchal society but not the protections and buffering of a patriarchal family. The lack of social, legal, and economic support available to families of color has intensified and extended women's work in and outside the home. As a result, the family life of women of color has been less bound by the notion of separate male and female spheres. Nor has it been shaped as much by the idea of the family as an emotional haven separate and apart from the demands of the rough and tough economic marketplace.

Women of color experience little or no separation of work and family and no protected sphere of domesticity. Thus, they have a different view of unpaid work in the home than do many white women. Many women of color find unpaid housework less alienating than waged work because the combination of class, race, and gender discrimination in the labor market leaves them with the dirtiest, most dangerous, and lowest-paid jobs. Paid work may provide white women with a positive identity and material independence; for many women of color, however, waged work translates into low-paid drudgery, including the work done by women of color in the homes of white women.[130]

The wide range of pressure faced by families of color often strains their personal relationships. Yet the racialized circumstances also set the stage for a variety of creative adaptations. Despite the hardship imposed on family life by racial discrimination and the forced labor force participation of women, most families of color did not break down. Instead, they adapted as best they could to the forces of inequality in the wider society. Feminists of color do not consider these adaptations an exception to a "standard" family form. Although the white, middle-class family has become the model of "the family," it is neither the norm nor the dominant family type in other communities. It is, however, the measure against which society judges all other families.[131] Some feminists of color maintain that in their community, the family became a site of resistance to racism—a refuge from a racist society rather than a site of conflict and oppression. The solidarity and resistance to racial oppression it provided often overrode the oppression of women that the family may also entail.[132]

In sum, perhaps speaking for many feminists, Nancy Fraser, a feminist professor of philosophy, concludes, "The trick is to imagine a social world in which citizens' lives integrate wage earning, caregiving, community activism, and political participation—while also leaving time for some fun. This world is not likely to come into being in the immediate future, but it is the only imaginable post-industrial world that promises true gender equity."[133]

The Ideology of Racial Inequality

It is widely believed that social welfare programs have served mostly persons of color. It is also believed that the "races" vary widely genetically. Combined with the racialization of the welfare reform debate, these inaccuracies suggest a profound confusion and anxiety about the meaning of race. This section identifies the ideological perspectives on racial inequality that have become central in discussions of social problems and social welfare policy.

Social Conservatism: Racial Inequality as Biological/Cultural Inferiority

Social conservatism relies on theories of natural and fundamental differences to explain inequality. Throughout much of U.S. history, public policy and public opinion defined race as a biological category that separated groups of people in hierarchical and irreversible ways. As seen in chapter 2, national leaders historically treated skin color or other physical traits as given and immutable indicators of race. They regularly assigned social characteristics such as intelligence, temperament, morality, and culture to these so-called natural or inborn features and linked low intelligence, immorality, and so forth to dark skin, and dark skin to inferiority. This (mis)interpretation was then used to justify policies supporting racial segregation and discrimination.[134]

Contemporary conservatives have moved from the belief in biological inferiority to notions of cultural inferiority, which hold that existing inequities reflect moral or cultural rather than racial differences. Instead, cultural explanations attribute the failure of persons of color to attain economic success and social status to personal attitudes and community values, that is, to a culture of poverty that violates the traditional American values of hard work, thrift, deferral of gratification, and respect for marriage.[135]

A leading proponent of this view, Dinesh D'Souza, resident scholar at the American Enterprise Institute, a conservative think tank, and author of *The End of Racism: Principles for a Multiracial Society* (1995), has said, "What accounts for 'black failure' in America today is not genes and is not discrimination, but rather cultural dysfunctionalities in the black community. American blacks have developed a culture that was long adaptive to historical circumstances, including historical oppressions, but that in concrete ways is dysfunctional today. . . . some groups do not bring the same set of cultural orientations and skills to the race [for success]."[136] In addition to this "civilizational breakdown" in the black community, D'Souza, along with many conservative thinkers, suggests that blacks do not apply themselves as hard as more successful groups who get along despite racial discrimination and without the benefit of affirmative action (e.g., the model Asian minority). These conservatives also believe that *all* blacks are too dependent on the government: poor blacks on welfare, middle-class blacks in government jobs, and small black businesses on government set-asides. Instead of encouraging this dependency, black leaders should step up to the plate and address the community's problems. The government can play only a limited role in this kind of "civilizational restoration" project.[137]

Based on these arguments, social conservatives call for a return to race-neutral or color-blind social policy, defined as policies that do not "make any

special deference to blacks." D'Souza adds, "It is a policy that treats blacks like everyone else. The debate now is about whether blacks should be, in the eyes of the law, treated like everyone else or treated as special."[138] This thinking applies to affirmative action, which social conservatives oppose on several grounds. Some social conservatives believe that racism no longer exists and that more white people than persons of color now suffer "reverse" discrimination. Others hold that affirmative action has benefited middle-class women, disadvantaged minorities of color, and the poor *in that order* and that it insults persons of color by implying that they cannot make it on their own. They see the policy as divisive, opening social wedges in the basic American melting pot.[139]

Laissez-Faire Conservatism: Racial Inequality as Lack of Human Capital or Irrational Behavior of Firms

Lack of Human Capital

Drawing on neoclassical economic theory, some laissez-faire conservatives attribute racial inequality to individual differences in human capital. The theory holds that all blacks and whites will have equal opportunities so long as they possess the traits (motivation, behavior, ability, talent, etc.) and resources of human capital (health, education, income, wealth) that make them equally productive. Assuming equal opportunities and taking racial differences in human capital as given, the theory concludes that racial inequality reflects not race, but differences in the productive resources of the individual. The human capital model does not ask about the source of racial differences in the possession of productive resources or the unequal opportunities to employ them. As a result, it inevitably implies that unequal racial outcomes must be due to individual traits, choices, or behaviors (e.g., to a racial lack of motivation or other kind of inferiority).

Irrational Firms

A second laissez-faire explanation holds that some employers have a "taste for discrimination," but that this preference for hiring white people is irrational because it deprives their business of the profit-enhancing value of cheaper black labor. Because it is irrational and inefficient, racial discrimination cannot exist for long in a profit-driven market economy. Racial discrimination is lethal for business because it causes firms to lose the competitive advantage that comes from paying lower wages to persons of color and turning aside talented workers and paying customers just because of their race. Due to competition, the nondiscriminating firms will expand at the expense of those that discriminate. They will expand until all the inefficient discriminating firms go bankrupt. Left to its own devices, then, the market will ultimately eliminate racial discrimination.

Rational Odds

Still another view holds that discrimination is rational. This, a justification for racial profiling, holds that racial discrimination makes sense because the individuals in question belong to a group whose statistical pattern makes discriminatory judgments reasonable. The cab driver who is reluctant to pick up young black males, the police officer who collars a black teenager, the store clerk who keeps an extra eye on black customers—all are working on a rational assumption of criminal behavior based on the statistical odds.[140]

Pragmatic Liberalism: Racial Inequality as Racial Discrimination

Pragmatic liberalism's explanation of racial inequality emphasizes social rather than individual factors. Reflecting liberalism's view of human nature and equal opportunity, it argues that racial inequality stems from prejudice (beliefs, ideas, attitudes) and racial discrimination (actions and behaviors). A racially prejudiced person "prejudges" the individual or group on the basis of stereotypes. Racial discrimination refers to intentional and unequal treatment of individuals based on the social meaning attached to biological features such as skin color, hair type, and eye shape. The landlord who will not rent to persons of color, the judge who metes out unusually harsh sentences to blacks, and the employer who will not hire Latinos are all engaging in acts of racial discrimination. Racial discrimination, in turn, denies persons of color equal opportunities to pursue their self-interest and to succeed in the market economy and other spheres of life. Thus, pragmatic liberalism argues that racial inequality is the result of racial discrimination, not lack of motivation. It calls for legal equality, meaning equal treatment under the law, to reduce or eliminate barriers responsible for differential racial outcomes.

Humanitarian Liberalism: Racial Inequality as Lack of Human Rights

Humanitarian liberalism holds that despite considerable legislative, judicial, and constitutional progress in the United States, the nation contains a deeply entrenched racial divide that continues to result in systematic advantages to whites at the expense of persons of color. James Jennings, a professor of urban and environmental policy, explains the persistence of the racial divide as the product of a "well-ingrained racial hierarchy" that "involves a pervasive system of caste based on race . . . a 'vertical' order of domination."[141] Racism and racial discrimination emerge from and are facilitated by the existence of this racial hierarchy.

Racial inequality cannot readily be erased through conventional legal responses to racial discrimination because legally preventing racial discrimination does not necessarily alter racial hierarchies. The achievement of racial equality must be linked to human rights and the equality of result.[142] The United Nations International Convention on the Elimination of All Forms of Racial Discrimination provides a bridge to move society from simple legal responses to the more comprehensive approach to ending racial hierarchies. The U.N. document defines discrimination quite broadly as any "distinction, exclusion, restriction, or preference based on race, color, descent, or national or ethnic origin which has the purpose or effect of nullifying or impairing the recognition, . . . on an equal footing, of human rights and fundamental freedoms in the political, economic, social, cultural, or any other field of public life."[143] It places the issue of racial discrimination into an international context, encourages nations to consider the basic rights that should be available to all people regardless of national boundaries, and presses nations to deal with racial hierarchies as a fundamental cause of racial inequality.

The human rights model moves beyond the right of individuals to legal equality before the law to the right to nondiscrimination. To address racial discrimination, nations must accept the idea, the reality, and the interest of national minorities within their boundaries. They must incorporate collective as well as individual remedies to the problem. The solution requires equality of result, which means redressing the uneven outcomes produced by racial hierarchies of domination and subordination. In addition to breaking down the barriers of legal discrimination for individuals, nations must ensure full social rights, especially active participation in society. They must provide the needed health, education, employment, housing, and income resources without which many people cannot take advantage of equal opportunity.

Given the logic of equal opportunity, equality of result requires something additional. Equality of opportunity implies fair competition in which the participants have an equal chance to succeed. However, in most cases, those at the starting line do not possess equal resources. The children of past winners, for example, have big advantages in their own contests, including inherited wealth, good nutrition, opportunities to learn skills, useful business connections, and, in the case of race, the privileges associated with being white. Because those who start out with more tend to end up with more, winners and losers enjoy unequal prizes. It is true that being born rich does not guarantee success—but it helps. Amid all the unequal outcomes of the equal opportunity structure, achieving equality of result requires policies such as affirmative action that treat unequals differently. By providing something more to those with less, such policies address the initial imbalance among those on the starting line in the race for success.

Radicalism: Social Construction of Race and Institutionalized Racism

Radicalism argues that racial inequality reflects both the social construction of the meaning of race and the existence of institutionalized racism.[144]

Social Construction of Race

Race is a socially constructed label based on a belief in genetic variations among the races. However, modern genetic analysis (DNA) has found that such racial differences do not exist. Scientists report greater variation *within* racial groups than *between* them, leading to the conclusion that the races are not biologically distinct groups and that humankind consists of a single species. If race refers to the gene frequencies that give us our skin color, hair form, and eye shape, it is no more significant to our behavior than the color of our eyes. Although the notion of race does not explain group differences, racism and racial inequality still exist. Being born Latino, African American, or Native American in the United States has immediate and often negative and unequal outcomes.

If race is not a physiological category but racism flourishes, then, radicals argue, racial inequality must be socially or ideologically constructed by those in positions of power. That is, physiological racial categories acquire social, political, and economic meanings. Michael Omi and Howard Winant point out that historically the U.S. Census Bureau changed the racial designation of Japanese Americans several times: from nonwhite, to Oriental, to other, to one of the Asian and Pacific Islanders. Likewise, Mexican American, Jewish American, Italian American, and Latinos have been viewed, at different times and from different political standpoints, as white and nonwhite.[145] That these meanings have changed over time underscores the notion of social construction.

Institutional Racism

Radicalism also presumes that institutionalized racism produces racial inequality. Institutionalized racism refers to those established laws, customs, and practices that appear to be intrinsically free of racial bias (i.e., race-neutral or color-blind) but whose impact falls heavily and unfairly on persons of color. It denotes those patterns, procedures, practices, and policies that consistently penalize, disadvantage, and exploit persons of color because they ignore the consequences of past practices of prejudice, discrimination, and racial subordination. These built-in processes have become such a conventional part of the organization's bureaucratic rules and regulations that neither individual prejudice nor racial discrimination needs to be operative. Instead, racism is grounded in real hierarchies of power and domination. The resulting discrimination is subtle, informal, and therefore less obvious to wider society because the action may not be deliberate or intentional and because institutional racism is built into institutional structures.

A racist impact exists when a firm uses a practice or criterion that is race-neutral but that nevertheless adversely impacts persons of color as a group. It is racist if a race-neutral policy stems from or contributes to the perpetuation of overt racial discrimination—even if the person who administers the policy is not personally racist. Examples of such bias-free policies that have racist consequences include qualification standards such as "last hired, first fired" policies, the use of personal connections, and selection by seniority, all of which have ended up barring persons of color from more desirable jobs.[146] Likewise, for university admissions, a policy that admits only students who score high on tests designed primarily for white suburban students necessarily excludes blacks educated in poor urban schools. Unlike legal segregation or overt racial discrimination by a landlord or an employer, these admission criteria are not intended to be racist. Nonetheless, the university is pursuing a course that perpetuates institutional racism.

Social welfare policy also reflects institutionalized racism. The 1935 Social Security Act denied coverage to domestic and farm workers. While seeming race-neutral, these were the two main occupations open to African American men and women at the time. Excluded from the Social Security and Unemployment Insurance programs, the policy relegated black individuals and families to the more stigmatized and less generous public assistance programs. Once persons of color entered occupations covered by the Social Security Act, they continued to be disadvantaged because the work-related programs reproduced the unequal treatment of white and blacks in the labor market.[147]

In the 1940s, to implement its decision to insure only mortgages deemed to be economically sound, the Federal Housing Authority (FHA), along with most banks, drew a red line on maps around the areas of a city considered too risky. Until 1949, the FHA also refused to insure mortgages in integrated neighborhoods. Known as "redlining," this policy left most black families (and some poor whites) ineligible for federally insured loans. Nor would banks insure loans in the nation's ghettos—and due to residential segregation, few African Americans found housing outside of these neighborhoods. The FHA also located most public housing projects in racially segregated neighborhoods and, until 1949, encouraged the use of restrictive covenants that banned African Americans from living in given neighborhoods. The provision of public education also appears race-neutral. Yet, given ongoing residential segregation and the reliance on property taxes to fund education, public education continues as one of the most race-stratified institutions in the country.[148]

In sum, according to radicalism, racism begins with the creation and manifestation of race as social thought and practice. The process contains at least three elements: (1) imposition—the conquest of a people, together with the interruption, destruction, and appropriation of a people's history and productive capacity; (2) ideology—an elaborate system of pseudo-intellectual categories, stereotypic assumptions, and negative contentions that serve to justify racialized arrangements; and (3) institutional arrangements—a system of political, economic, and social structures that ensure white power and privilege over persons of color.[149]

Radicalism concludes that consideration of institutional racism, grounded in a system of racial domination of persons of color by white power structures, is key to understanding and ultimately eliminating racism and racial discrimination. Although not a radical document, *The Report of the National Advisory Commission on Civil Disorders* (issued in 1968 following the ghetto uprisings) concluded with a radical observation: "What white Americans have never fully understood—but what the Negro can never forget—is that white society is deeply implicated in the ghetto. White institutions created it, white institutions maintain it, and white society condones it."[150]

Radicals conclude that legal responses to prejudice and racial discrimination can mediate the impact of institutional racism at the level of social interaction. But eliminating institutionalized racism requires a redistribution of power that will enable persons of color (and others) to challenge white supremacy as well as the institutional arrangements that maintain it.

Ideologies of Professionalism

Though not directly related to the welfare state, the ideology of professionalism has had a strong influence on social work and the delivery of social services. From the early 1900s to midcentury, social work struggled to determine if it had become a bona fide profession, a status that it eventually claimed. Then, during the egalitarian struggles of the 1960s, some social workers began to question the value and benefits of professionalism for clients, social workers, and wider society. These critics contended that an undue emphasis on professionalism can make social work elitist, exclusionary, narrowly focused on guild issues, and apolitical. The ongoing debate among social work activists and the profession still influences social work thinking and social services.

The standard model of a profession identifies five distinguishing features: (1) *knowledge* based on a systematic body of theory acquired through training; (2) *authority* derived from specific professional expertise; (3) *a professional culture* consisting of values, norms, and symbols; (4) *community approval* to perform special services over which the profession has a monopoly; and (5) *a regulative code of ethics* that compels moral behavior and prevents the abuse of powers and privileges granted by the community.[151] The organized profession argues that complying with these mandates will result in the best service for people in need. Critics charge that the premises enforce problematic features of a capitalist society. These features include social values such as individualism and competition, an overemphasis on science and technology, and support for the market economy that favors profits over people. Still other critics argue that social workers should think of themselves as workers rather than professionals, join unions, and engage in social action.

The Social Work Knowledge Base

Professionalism rests on a systematic body of theory that informs practitioners about causes, effects, and treatment options for individual and social problems. Given its work with individuals, the social work knowledge base relies heavily on psychological theories of personality and human behavior. Critics maintain that this knowledge base leans too heavily toward individual explanations of social behavior, mainstream interpretations of social institutions, and an uncritical acceptance of social work's social control functions. The field's knowledge about groups and communities extends far less into the social work field.[152] John Ehrenreich, a social work historian, notes, "With rare exceptions the child's school problems, the adult's work problems, the housewife's marital problems are seen [by social workers] as a consequence of the individual's psychological or family problems." When social work takes the environment into account, he adds, "at best it highlights the most immediate environment, the child's particular school, or the adult's particular employer. It stops short of identifying the more systemic causes of problems such as unemployment, educational failure, community violence."[153] Further, social work's focus on the individual client sends a powerful message that the responsibility for personal distress lies with individuals and not the wider social structure.[154]

Authority Based on Technical Expertise

The service ideal holds that the possession of technical expertise ensures that clients receive informed and competent care. Having unique skills valued by society also provides professionals with a degree of discretion and autonomy and the freedom to do the job well without detailed direction. Professional expertise and autonomy also provide the profession as a whole with a basis for exerting influence in other arenas.

Critics worry that professional authority can turn into a rationale for controlling clients. Because people typically associate expertise with power in our society, professionalism endows the social worker with a disproportionate amount of influence over clients. Backed by theoretical knowledge and technical skills, this influence can allow social workers to take too great a lead in defining tasks and goals. It also positions social workers to encourage clients to conform to values and goals to which the clients may not subscribe. Those who disagree with workers risk being labeled resistant, lacking insight, or simply wrong. Class, race, gender, and sexual orientation differentials between worker and client can further aggravate these hierarchical dynamics.

Finally, critics maintain that the emphasis on technical competence favors working on a narrow set of issues and discourages dealing with the whole person. Too heavy a reliance on technique has political implications as well if it routinely implies that problem solving consists of a quick technical fix or other professional solutions to the exclusion of social change.[155]

Professional Culture

Professionalism rests on a culture of service backed by a set of values, norms, and symbols. The service ideal recommends three major behavioral norms: impersonality, objectivity, and impartiality. The norm of impersonality mandates social workers to remain emotionally neutral to balance the closeness needed for trust to develop and the distance needed to avoid over-involvement.[156] Social workers must not reveal themselves to or make friends with clients or see clients in nonneutral settings to ensure the emotional discipline needed to protect clients from judgmental reactions and undue intrusion into their lives. Critics claim that impersonality minimizes clients' role in decision making and reduces their overall self-determination.

Critics object to the call for professional objectivity because it encourages social workers to remain neutral about the social forces that contribute to individual and social problems and to separate professional work and social reform. To the critics, there is no such thing as apolitical social work. Instead, when social conditions undercut client well-being, "neutrality" represents "a political position." Social workers, they say, have precious little middle ground to stand on: they face the choice of siding with those who support the status quo or those who want to change it.[157]

Most critics support the norm of impartiality that mandates social workers to serve all persons regardless of age, race, religion, sexual orientation, or ability to pay. Service that is given or withheld on the basis of any of a client's personal characteristics undercuts confidence in the professional helping relationship. However, critics frequently fault social work and other professions for failing to honor impartiality to the fullest.

The Ethic of Service

The service ideal promotes an ethic of selflessness that mandates social workers to put the needs and interests of clients before their own or those of their agency. Trust falters in the client-worker relationship if clients believe that social workers care more about making money than providing good service or otherwise seek to use their client's confidences for personal gain. In the absence of such an ethic of selflessness, clients might also demand a guarantee of specific results—an outcome that most service professionals cannot promise—before any payment is made.

Critics argue that the drive to professionalize itself represents undue interest in personal gain. Matt Dumont, a community psychiatrist, sees professionals as motivated too much by the "personal dread of poverty, the insatiable appetite for wealth, the fascination with esoteric skill and complicated machinery, and the yearning for status. . . ." He criticizes the concept of professionalism, saying it has developed largely to protect and enlarge the status and prerogatives of the professionals.[158] In their history of the social work profession, Stanley Wenocur and Michael Reich reached a similar conclusion. Professionalization, they say, represents an institutionalized effort to gain occupational prestige, security, and financial rewards, and the need for professionals to gain and retain control over the market for their services competes with important service ideals.[159]

Community Approval

The service ideal holds that professions depend on community approval. In essence, communities permit professionals to perform their special services based on the profession's claim to technical expertise and its monopoly on a service. Critics concur that professions need community approval, but they argue that the need for community sanction, combined with the needs for paying clients, outside funding, and government support, induces professionals to abide by the goals and values of those with the most power. This, in turn, makes it harder for the profession to adopt alternatives that might better serve specific clients and communities.

Community approval can also mean licensing by the government as an exclusive provider of expertise and services. Supporters of licensing state that the process indicates proper training and protects clients against incompetence. Critics of licensing object to the idea embedded in licensing that only highly trained professionals can deliver effective social services. They believe that both paraprofessionals and community residents have valid expertise and that hiring them can reduce the client-worker social barriers that typically plague professionals. Critics also fear that in exchange for state recognition, licensing may require social workers to become more controlling or to otherwise align themselves with the interests of the state over those of their clients. Finally, by stressing academic credentials and a monopoly on expertise, licensing defines social workers as an exclusive group. This inevitably distances social workers from both their clients and other workers.[160]

Professionalization and Unionization

In addition to debate over the nature of professional practice, some in the field argue that social workers need to be unionized as well as professionalized. Social workers need to recognize that they are workers who have an economic as well as professional relationship to their place of employment. Advocates of unionization note that collective bargaining agreements would help social workers both to win salaries commensurate with their professional status and to maintain the personnel practices that support high professional standards. They historically have encouraged unionization among social workers, working with the labor movement, and engaging in political action with a wide range of relevant advocacy groups. They argue that promoting social change that improves the well-being of social work clients and wider society *is* good social work practice.[161]

Opponents of unionization argue that unionism conflicts with the notion of professionalism and public service, is unnecessary in nonprofit social agencies, undermines the notion of social workers as unbiased and value-free, and risks converting the image of the selfless professional into a self-interested worker more concerned about self than client. A more effective way to raise social work salaries is to improve professional practice, raise the profession's status, and otherwise convince employers and the community of the value of social work.

Interestingly, social work was one of the few professions to unionize before it became fully professionalized. From 1931 to 1945, unionization slowly gained ground in social work. For a while, it seemed that unionization might challenge professionalization as a way to protect the economic interests of social workers or that social workers might form unions that collaborated with professional associations. However, in the conservative political climate of the 1940s and 1950s, social work unions faded while professionalization expanded dramatically.[162] Unionization picked up again in the more liberal 1960s and 1970s, but most of the field remains nonunionized.

The tension between professionalism and unionization also applies to social action more generally. The profession boasts a long history of progressive activism directed toward individual and social change. At the same time, observers within and outside social work have often accused the profession of serving as a handmaiden of the status quo. Critics say that when social workers work for social change, they politicize a previously neutral, objective, nonpolitical profession. In contrast, social work activists contend that social work has always been political in that it deals either with human consciousness or the allocations of resources. Because social workers cannot avoid the political, they add, it is far better to address these issues than to pretend they do not exist. According to its advocates, this stance offers a more ethical option than claiming to practice nonpolitical social work.[163]

Feminism and Professionalism

Spurred by the women's liberation movement, feminism has also posed a challenge to the mainstream conceptions of professionalism. Regardless of its particular perspective, feminist social work stresses that women constitute the majority of social work clients and workers. Consequently, when working with women, the profession would benefit from valuing their contributions and emphasizing their strengths.

Feminist social work rejects patriarchy in favor of more egalitarian arrangements, sometimes called the empowerment approach.[164] It calls for expanding the profession's knowledge base to include material that focuses on the social construction of gender, male/female differences, the impact of gender inequality, and the effect of the wider social context (gender roles, sex discrimination, etc.) on the psychological and social problems faced by women.[165]

Feminist social work also urges the profession to recognize the historical and current leadership roles played by women. This recognition would include highlighting the major role played by women reformers, both white and black, in the formation of the profession as well as identifying the ongoing contributions to the field made by women leaders, theorists, scholars, and practitioners.

Finally, like the above noted critics, feminism urges social work to address the question of power. It supports a degree of self-disclosure by practitioners and favors client-worker cooperation with individuals, groups, and communities. Feminists believe that social workers should avoid an undue reliance on technical expertise and hierarchical structures, work to ensure client voice and involvement in the decision-making process, and recognize the political character of their work, especially the power inequities in interpersonal relationships and social institutions. Feminists do not define social action for social change as unprofessional. Instead, they call for more.[166]

6

Mimi Abramovitz

Social Movements and Social Change

Collective action—that is, the effort of people joining forces to create a better life for themselves and others—is central to the development of modern societies. Most of the time, however, individuals pursue their goals or seek relief from hardship on their own. We try to solve our problems by following the rules and not challenging the authorities. At certain moments in history, however, as some people link their private troubles to wider public issues, they find it necessary to join forces with others to meet unfilled needs and to change social conditions. The benefits of such collective behavior, whether the addition of a stop sign on the corner of a neighborhood street, outlawing racial discrimination, or fighting to end a war, extends beyond the needs of the immediate participants to large numbers of other people in similar circumstances.[1] Indeed, the world as we know it is, in part, the product of the effort of people working together to transform old social orders into new ones.

The social work profession believes that by acting in concert, people have the ability to affect and reshape the public realm. The NASW *Code of Ethics* urges social workers "to pursue social change, particularly with and on behalf of vulnerable and oppressed individuals and groups of people" and to focus these efforts "primarily on issues of poverty, unemployment, discrimination, and other forms of social injustice."[2] This stance is not surprising given that the social work profession itself arose, in part, from the broader social movements that called on the government to assume public responsibility for the well-being of individuals, families, and communities. The expansion of the welfare state reflects years of collective efforts by social reformers and/or oppressed groups who defined a social problem, developed a vision of its resolution, and fought for greater justice.

This chapter highlights the role of collective behavior as a force for social change. Collective behavior spans a continuum of activities, including the behavior of crowds, spontaneous protests, strikers on a picket line, advocacy by organized social movements, and violent uprisings. In each instance, groups of people pool their resources, including their own efforts, to achieve common ends.[3] If you have signed a petition, donated money, walked a picket line, attended a rally, marched on Washington, or joined a social change organization, you have been part of a social movement, if only in a small way. As social movements made up of ordinary people engage in conflict with an established adversary, their challenges to the system change attitudes, broaden citizenship, expand democracy, and secure needed structural changes.[4]

No discussion of modern history, the nature of industrial society, or the history of the U.S. welfare state would be complete without understanding the role of social movements in social change. The welfare state might have taken longer to materialize if the Progressive Era (1896–1914) coalition had not pressed the government to regulate big business, shorten the workday, support mothers' pensions and juvenile courts, and otherwise expand the social welfare obligations of state governments. By asking for more than what

Social theorists have long debated what causes people to organize social movements and demand social change.

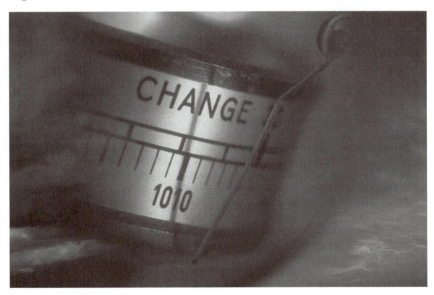

"society" would give, the Progressives left both a vision of what might be possible and much work undone. Most of all, it laid the foundation of a federally sponsored welfare state.

The emergency New Deal program put in place by Franklin D. Roosevelt during the Great Depression of the 1930s might have been less robust had it not been for protests at relief offices, the unionization of industrial workers, and the activism of political radicals. Without the ongoing pressure of the trade unions, women's organizations, the NAACP, and senior citizens groups, among others, the federal government may not have finally passed the landmark Social Security Act and assumed responsibility for social welfare provision.

Factories and offices would be different places today had not workers—male and female, black, white, and brown, young and old, native and foreign-born—risked their lives to form trade unions and used the power of their numbers in strikes, sit-downs, and collective bargaining to win better wages and working conditions. The growth of the civil rights movement of the late 1950s and its increased militancy in the 1960s led Congress to pass a host of antidiscrimination and affirmative action laws that improved the conditions of men and women of color. Lyndon B. Johnson promoted the War on Poverty and the Great Society in response to uprisings by the residents of the nation's ghettoized communities in the mid-1960s. Without the women's movement, we would not have the right to abortion, equal employment opportunities, protections against sexual harassment, battered women's shelters, and rape hot lines. The disability rights movement secured the Americans with Disabilities Act. The lesbian and gay rights movement forced the public and the government to pay attention to HIV/AIDS and the rights of lesbians, gay men, bisexuals, and transgender people. Since the 1980s, conservative forces led by the Moral Majority and Christian Right grew alongside the liberal movements. Their organized protests and movements bent U.S. social welfare policy to their agenda, which included weakening and undoing gains won by liberal activists in previous decades.

The historical record detailed in chapter 7 also shows that social movements have had direct and indirect but long-term effects. The movements politicized individuals, radicalized personal politics, altered the political culture, changed political institutions, and left lasting networks of activists ready to take up the next round. Most significant, the struggles contributed to the rise of the welfare state. The demands of the earliest groups foreshadowed the needs that the welfare state would ultimately have to address. Once the federal government took responsibility for social welfare, the efforts of social movements pressed for the expanded programs to keep up with new needs, a growing population, and a rising cost of living. In periods of contraction, such as the one that began in the early 1980s, liberal and conservative movements battled each other to win the day. Regardless of their ideological agenda, social movements—often referred to as collective action and collective behavior in the social science literature—have molded our contemporary institutions and continue to play a major role in social change.

Collective behavior can include panics, fashions, currents of opinion, cultural innovations, social protest, and social movements. This chapter focuses on collective behavior aimed at changing social policy. The historical record reveals that poor, working-class, and middle-class people have struggled for social change in various ways, including individual acts of resistance, social protest, and mass movements. So here we make note of the different ways a person can become active.

Individual Acts of Resistance

Individual acts of resistance are the small, personal, daily strategies resorted to by the most marginalized members of society in an effort to counter the ubiquitous forces of power that surround them. Locked outside of established institutions and deprived of power, subordinated persons frequently cannot afford the risk of more visible collective action such as strikes, protests, or movements. Instead, they create a hidden politics of life to protect their personal dignity and economic interests. This includes oppositional talk, walk, and dress; dissident messages embedded in songs, jokes, and folklore; and absenteeism, foot dragging, feigned ignorance, evasive actions, and petty theft.[5] These measures may not constitute activism in the standard sense of the word. Yet poorly positioned persons such as slaves, domestics, low-paid women workers, and welfare state clients have often fought back in these ways because their lack of power leaves them more vulnerable to retribution.[6] The long history of this type of resistance among low-income people reminds us that fear of losing one's job or one's life can curtail or deter action and that political confrontation is not always available or realistic.

But fears of penalty have not completely silenced the public voice of protest among poor and working- and middle-class people, who have also engaged in acts of resistance. Historically, black domestic workers resisted their working conditions by "pan-toting" (bringing home leftovers and other foodstuffs), leaving work early, or suddenly quitting to increase wages (similar to a strike). Through these actions, they sought to control the pace of work, compensate for underpayment, or seize more personal autonomy.[7] In the late 1960s, when millions of poor women applied for public assistance, they effectively resisted welfare officials, political authorities, and prevailing norms that prescribed self-reliance. Sharp increases in rent delinquencies may reflect defiance of the norms governing tenant-landlord relations. Even rising crime rates may represent defiance of civil order and property norms.[8] In the 1970s, auto plant workers threw soda bottles under the hoods of cars on the assembly line to express their alienation and resentment about their working conditions. In addition to such industrial sabotage, workers resisted their working conditions and tried to take control of the workplace through slow-downs, absenteeism, deliberate negligence, and other private actions.

Some observers regard the politicization of formerly intimate aspects of private life (i.e., middle-class identity politics) as another form of resistance to dominant cultural norms and prescriptions. In this view, all aspects of everyday life became expressions of one's political values and social commitments. For example, feminists insist that "the personal is political," pointing to the mechanisms of oppression that are intricately woven into personal identity, interpersonal relations, and the fabric of everyday life. For some women, abandoning bras and skirts constituted a political act. For others, it meant coming out as a lesbian. Similarly, during the 1960s and 1970s, many African Americans grew large Afro hairdos and wore clothes made from African fabric to denote that "black is beautiful." Equating the personal and the political fosters a politics of lifestyle that turns everyday life into a major political arena in which people seek the right to be different and the right to sustain community.[9]

Recognizing less visible acts of resistance as a force for social change challenges some of the assumptions found in the theories of social protest and social movements presented later in this chapter. These paradigms implicitly assume that people are passive, obedient, and acquiescent most of the time and that they become active only under extreme circumstances—and then only occasionally. In contrast, theories of resistance and rebellion highlight the chronic jostling and incessant actions among and between groups and classes, actions that do not necessarily appear on the political radar screen until they are writ large. But these acts of resistance can always be found among subordinate groups.

Personal resistance and rebellion may not directly threaten fundamental social structures. Yet the actions of many individuals acting separately can create a context of mass defiance or otherwise have collective outcomes that are not immediately apparent to others. This type of activism can also blunt the rough edges of the system and minimize its disadvantage for the individual resister. In *Weapons of the Weak*, James Scott suggests that individual acts of resistance may accomplish just enough material rewards and just enough social satisfaction to make life more bearable.[10] The record of resistance and rebellion suggests that the rise of more overt forms of collective action may signal the failure of these everyday forms of resistance and announce the existence of a wider crisis. The record also suggests that the very conditions that spawn individual acts of resistance at other times become the sparks that have mobilized large numbers of people for more organized collective action.[11] French historian George Rudé suggests that under certain conditions, such everyday collective actions may have far-reaching effects, paving the way for wider social movements and creating unanticipated possibilities for social change.[12]

Social Protest: Rapid, Short-Lived Actions

Social protest refers to rapid, short-lived, community-based activities such as marches, sit-ins, pickets, boycotts, and civil disobedience. In contrast to individual resistance, protests involve groups of people. Unlike social movements, discussed below, they do not depend on long-lasting, formal organizational structures.[13] Rather, protest activities tend to be spontaneous and characterized by showmanship and unconventional tactics.

Many observers dismiss protest politics as inconsequential and not worthy of notice. In contrast, based on their study of protest movements during the 1930s and 1960s, Frances Fox Piven, a professor of political science, and Richard A. Cloward, a professor of social work, conclude that social protest is a rational and political means of seeking social change, especially for the poor.[14] Although many groups and organizations turn to protest tactics as a form of activism, these actions represent an especially important political resource for those who lack access to other sources of political power, such as individual influence, organizational standing, foundation support, and political leaders. Often, the only resource available to the poor and the powerless struggling for social change is the power of protest, that is, the power to disrupt the status quo.

Piven and Cloward maintain that the type of political action available to low-income people is restricted by the structure of power in society, especially the concentration of power and wealth in the hands of the few, the obfuscation of the roots of this power, and the state's control of coercive force. That is, the ability to participate in the political process and the degree of influence available to groups varies, first and foremost, by their location in the class structure. Even when poor and working-class communities play by the rules, they cannot gain much political influence, given the political system's bias toward the haves over the have-nots.[15] Therefore, poor people's movements—those with few resources and limited access to centers of power—must resort to the politics of disruption that defy political norms to achieve their ends.

Piven and Cloward, along with other analysts, believe that protests, or the politics of disruption, are possible only under certain political conditions. For one, people have to be ready to question the legitimacy of the system. Like most people, the poor and working class tend to acquiesce to their plight most of the time, a political docility that "the system" reinforces with the belief that we all deserve our lot in life. However, during periods of crisis, these attitudes often shift. The destabilization, the increased hardship of people, mounting frustration, and a breakdown of social controls can alter the consciousness and behavior of people. As the masses awaken to their grievances, as more people question the current arrangements, they believe they can make a change. When this happens, the time is ripe for the poor to press their demands.

Because such periods of profound social dislocation are infrequent, those with less have few opportunities for mass protest. Therefore, when the opportunities arise, Piven and Cloward conclude, poor people's movements must create conditions to intensify the crisis, so that the elite become more willing to grant concessions. Disruptive tactics that expose contradictions in the system, create cleavages within the establishment, increase the vulnerability of the authorities, and otherwise threaten central social institutions can make it more difficult for the elite to ignore the insurgency or to forcefully repress it.[16] The historical record shows that protest politics has been a main resort of those who lack other institutional forms of political access and influence. It also shows that during major crises, political leaders confronted with mass protest have met the protestors' demands. The militant protests during the Great Depression, the massive strikes organized by the labor movement in its early years, and the disruptive sit-ins conducted by the civil rights movement to desegregate lunch counters, beaches, colleges, and most other public facilities are some of the better-known examples of how protest politics creates social change.

Piven and Cloward suggest several reasons why the politics of defiance and disruption works better than conventional strategies for the poor. First, given the workings of the political system, it is simply easier for the elite to ignore demands for change when protestors use conventional political strategies such as the vote and testifying at hearings. Second, disruptive rallies, sit-ins, boycotts, and rent strikes challenge the dominant group's vision of a satisfied public, polarize public opinion, and otherwise create problems for the elite. The protests mobilize discontent, galvanize public attention, force bystanders to take a stand on contested issues, fracture electoral coalitions, and create various divides that pose a threat to the established powers. Political leaders hoping to reduce the polarization and to quiet the unrest may feel compelled to offer a variety of concessions to restore order.[17]

While touting the successes, Piven and Cloward warn of victory's double-edged sword. On the one hand, success brings important reforms and needed gains. On the other hand, success also confronts movement leaders with powerful incentives to tone down their activities, to adopt less disruptive tactics, to reintegrate themselves into regular political channels, and to form traditional movement organizations. To the extent that poor people's movements respond to these incentives—and they, along with others, often do—the incentives act to co-opt its leaders, defuse the protest, legitimize the system, restore stability, and otherwise cause the movement to subside. In the end, many of the benefits of success accrue to the very establishment that the protests set out to change. Because the insurgency is always short-lived, Piven and Cloward conclude that sustaining it should be the top priority of those working with poor people for social change.[18]

Piven and Cloward also insist that building organizations, the more common means of working for social change, is inherently counterproductive for poor people's movements, which lack the resources needed to create and maintain oppositional organizations over time. When poor people's organizations do wrest concessions, "[the elite] are not actually responding to the organizations; they are responding to the underlying force of insurgency." Instead of building organizations and diverting energy from mass defiance, Piven and Cloward urge organizers to spend more time sustaining a politics of defiance and escalating the momentum of protests.[19]

Social Movements

Social movements represent another type of collective action in which individuals attempt to promote, control, or prevent social change. Sociologists say that a social movement exists when a loosely organized group of people challenges prevailing social norms and values to resist or to bring about changes that will affect many people. More specifically, social movements represent historically specific collective "challenges to existing arrangements of power and distribution by people with common purposes and solidarity, in sustained interaction with elites, opponents and authorities."[20]

The most widely studied type of collective behavior, the modern social movement, typically involves certain key elements. In addition to the readiness among people to get involved noted above, social movements are distinguished by the presence of formal organizations with an identified membership governed by rules and regulations and a degree of longevity. These organizations typically are staffed by professionals who have access to funding, the political process, and support from large numbers of people.

The social movement as a form of mass mobilization and means of social transformation emerged with the modern world and attempts to change it. It appeared in Western Europe during a long period of social, economic, and political turmoil known as the transition from feudalism to capitalism, which took place between 1500 and 1800. In addition to enormous economic shifts, the historic move into the modern age called forth the nation-state, turned the masses of rural folk into urban wage workers, and led to the development of science, which revealed the social order to be subject to change.[21]

The convergence of these social, economic, political, and intellectual currents altered the character of collective action. Up until this time, people saw the structure and operation of the social order as natural, God-given, and fixed. They engaged in collective action largely to protect or defend their existing rights and claims. The modern social movement took on its distinctive form once modernization (i.e., the development of capitalism) undermined the older social forms of collective action, and as people understood that *they* could change institutional arrangements through conscious collective action. The social movement emerged in the modern age as a general political force pushing for change; since then, various social movements have erupted during different historical periods. Indeed, it has been said that "contemporary societies bear the imprint of numerous past social struggles that have been inscribed in the contours and institutions of the modern world."[22]

Social Movements, Contradictions, and Social Change

Social movements do not emerge out of thin air. Rather, they embody conflicts arising from tensions or contradictions within wider society. Contradictions are the opposing forces within a system that cannot easily be resolved. The resulting tensions may remain submerged for a long time. However, when major events upset the prevailing equilibrium by creating undue hardship and revealing systemic inequities, the resulting crisis often leads people to join forces and demand change.[23] Business and the state seek to restore order either by making concessions or by repressing the angered masses. The concessions granted to social protestors and social movements over the years have contributed significantly to the rise and expansion of the welfare state. Repression typically sets back social policy and social movements.

Three key contradictions have sparked much of the activism in the United States during the twentieth century. Although the conflicts have been mediated by social reform, because the reform has been incremental, the underlying tensions remain unresolved. The contradictions that spark mobilization include the contradiction between (1) the democratic promise of equal opportunity and ongoing discrimination on the basis of class, race, gender, and other characteristics; (2) economic production for profit and the existence of unmet needs; and (3) the controlling and liberatory possibilities of the welfare state.

The Democratic Promise of Equal Opportunity and the Practices of Discrimination

A principal tenet of democracy promises individuals an equal opportunity (if not result) to compete for success in the marketplace. Yet nearly all societies condone practices that limit this option for some groups more than others. Alexis de Tocqueville in 1840, Gunnar Myrdal in 1944, the National Advisory Commission on Civil Disorders in 1968, and many other observers since then have found America to be beset by a social and moral paradox: "Of all the world's nations, the United States speaks eloquently of universal justice and equal opportunity. Yet its treatment of its principal minority belies those basic commitments."[24] This observation about the experience of African Americans speaks to a contradiction that applies as well to other powerless groups (Native Americans, women, impoverished workers, welfare mothers, the disabled, homosexuals, etc.) who have also responded to the failed promise of equal opportunities by mobilizing their forces for social change.

The Contradiction between the Production for Profit and Social Need

As any first-year business school text will tell you, the first priority of business in the market economy is to make a profit. Failing to do so, a firm risks going out of business because without profits to invest, the firm cannot expand. Writ large, the goal of economic production is to make profits rather than to meet basic needs. Indeed, meeting needs is not the job of the market. Business does not exist to provide adequate levels of income, food, housing, and care, if in the process profits fall. Instead, profits typically depend on low wages, high unemployment, high prices, replacing labor with machines—all of which make it harder for individuals and families to survive. Nor is it of any concern to the market economy whether profits come from building mansions or housing for the poor, planting seeds or turning crops under, conducting research on weapons of mass destruction or on how to prevent disease. The market does not register the need for parks, schools, clean air, or global warming unless profits can be made. The press for profits also leads firms to cut corners and to avoid paying for consumer protections, healthy workplaces, and safe highways.

According to the British historian E. P. Thompson, people become politically active when conditions violate widely held class or cultural norms about what the market should provide.[25] As a result, the contradiction between production for profits and social need has periodically generated social movements seeking to force the market and state to address unmet needs. The trade union movement arose to increase the bargaining power of labor versus capital and to secure adequate wages, better working conditions, and more control over the shop floor. The environmental movement erupted because people wanted a future with clean water, clean air, and abundant natural resources. The more recent antiglobalization movement protests global warming, lack of international labor standards, and policies that benefit banks and corporations at the expense of poor people around the world. And, in 2003, an antiwar movement coalesced quickly when the United States announced plans to bring about "regime change" by bombing Iraq.

The Welfare State as Site of Control or Site of Emancipation

A third contradiction also exists within the welfare state itself. The welfare state emerged in part to help people in need. However, its capacity to do so remained limited by the competing functions of social welfare policy discussed in chapter 2. That is, if social welfare provision became too generous, it would pose a threat to the prevailing subordination of workers, patriarchal family structures, racial hierarchies, and other structures of power. In other words, a more robust welfare state, one that offered genuine economic independence, would have a potential liberatory impact on individuals and families rather than its current controlling role. If fully developed, the welfare state would have the potential to increase the autonomy of the average person, reconfigure the balance of power between dominant and subordinate groups, and embolden individuals to form social movements or otherwise fight for greater social, economic, and political justice. As noted in the chapter 2, higher benefits and more comprehensive coverage function like a strike fund, providing an economic backup that reduces financial insecurity and enhances both the bargaining power of individuals and the political influence of social movements.[26] By fueling social movements, social welfare provision has altered the terms of political struggles between people and the state.[27]

As if to deny the liberatory potential of greater economic security, critics of the welfare state claim that social welfare provision does the opposite, that it fosters "dependency," that is, a poor work ethic, nontraditional families, and excessive reliance on government aid. To protect people and society from this invidious outcome, critics insist on a welfare state that is both limited and emphasizes social control of individual behavior. From the start, stigma, low benefits, undignified treatment, and strict penalties for not playing by the rules have been used to deter or punish those who turn to the government for help. The emphasis on policies of deterrence and punishment ensures that the welfare state will not exceed the limits of what the system is willing to absorb. When the pressure from social conditions or popular movements expands the welfare state too far, the powers that be typically begin to cut programs and attack social movements, hoping to push government assistance back to tolerable limits. The conflict between the liberatory possibilities of the welfare state and its social control functions has turned the welfare state into an arena of political struggle. As the next section reveals, even mainstream social science theories seeking to explain social movements became part of that struggle. Until the 1960s, they implicitly backed the state over the people by painting social movements as a negative and irrational force that disrupted the wider social order.

Theories of Social Movements

Given the long and varied history of social movements, social scientists have spent considerable time and energy trying to develop theories to explain them. A theory seeks to answer the question, Why? It points to causes of phenomena and tries to account for differences among them. In the case of social movements, scholars have asked, Who turns to social movements and why? How and why do social movements develop in any one historical period or moment in time? What dissatisfactions, conditions, or other forces stimulate their development? What are the most effective movement forms? What do movements accomplish?

Theories provide answers to such questions. But the answers have changed over time. New theories emerged in response to gaps in existing theories, the emergence of new social problems, contradictions within the existing paradigms, and the failure of theories to explain contemporary events. The varied and complicated set of explanations discussed below suggests that our understanding of the social movement itself is also influenced by the historical context in which the theory appeared and by the ideology of the times.[28]

The Classical Collective Behavior Theories: Social Movements as Deviance

The classical collective behavior theories shaped the thinking about social movements well into the twentieth century. Their specific hypotheses vary, but the *crowd, psychoanalytic, mass society,* and *structural strain theories* share several characteristics. They assume that movements arose in response to the grievances of people suffering from the dislocations that accompany rapid social, economic, and political change. Despite the terms *social* and *collective,* these theories focus on the motivations and behavior of individuals whom they see as impulsive and deviant. They also regard all forms of collective behavior as spontaneous (i.e., nonroutine), contentious, and socially pathological. If left unattended, this potentially dangerous form of noninstitutionalized activity could threaten a basically sound, stable, and established way of life.[29]

The understanding of individual behavior (viewed as rational, restrained, and normal) and collective behavior (viewed as irrational, impulsive, and deviant) begins with the theory of the crowd and early psychoanalytic thought. This thinking gained ground in the 1930s and 1940s. During this period, social scientists in Western Europe wanted to understand the rise of fascism and Stalinism as totalitarian regimes. In addition, from 1928 until 1941, when the United States entered World War II, militant social movements, especially the burgeoning labor movement, struggled for change that challenged the domestic status quo. While rejecting some of the more sweeping and overstated portraits of the irrational crowd offered by the earlier theories, the newer theories retained the view of collective behavior as irrational and deviant until the 1960s, when new activism forced a paradigm shift.[30]

The Crowd Theory

The crowd theory draws on the work of the French social theorist Gustave Le Bon. His negative interpretation of collective behavior stemmed from his dislike for the outcome of the 1789 French Revolution, which overthrew the ancien régime and established democratic rights for the average person. Writing in the late nineteenth and early twentieth centuries, during a period of rapid industrialization throughout Europe, Le Bon witnessed many spontaneous uprisings, street protests, and actions by discontented waged workers. He saw this as undesirable crowd behavior similar to that of the French Revolution. From this experience, Le Bon concluded that participants in "the crowd" are impulsive, suggestible, excitable, and easily manipulated by charismatic leaders. Even worse, the magnetic power of leaders and the hypnotic impact of the mob lead people to give up their individuality to the collective and do extraordinary things. Almost like animals in a herd, they sacrifice their rationality, morality, and personal interests to a uniform collective mentality that allows them to conduct irrational, violent, and barbaric acts that they never would consider on their own.[31]

Le Bon believed that civilization rests on the ability of a small intellectual elite to impose discipline and rationality on the rest of the people. Advanced by the French Revolution and other trends, democracy threatened this task because, to Le Bon, it unleashed the unruly mob whose irrational, destructive, and barbaric behavior could undermine civilization itself.[32] The irrational actions of the crowd point to the inherent dangers of democracy and the need to restore authoritative social control.

Psychoanalysis

Psychoanalysis also contained the idea that people become vulnerable to direct mobilizing appeals by charismatic leaders. Writing in the early twentieth century, Freud, like Le Bon, saw collective behavior as a threat to individu-

A crowd in New York's Grand Central Terminal. Even when crowds were not purposeful social movements, some social theorists worried that they could fall under the spell of a magnetic leader.

alism. He argued that individuals in groups become overemotional, give up their conscious individual personality, and otherwise show signs of regression to a state of primitive mental activity.[33] Others advanced the Freudian analysis of crowd leaders as surrogate fathers and of crowd followers as individuals who were libidinally attached to crowd leaders.

Psychoanalysis explained the mass attraction to fascist movements of the 1930s and 1940s in terms of "the authoritarian personality." In this tradition, Fromm saw the rise of fascism during the Depression of the 1930s as the mass response to magnetic leaders by individuals with an "authoritarian" character.[34] In Germany and other central European nations, he argued, patriarchal family structures promoted cultural propensities to either command or obey. Like the patriarchal head of the household, the Führer commanded the obedience that underpinned the mob mentality and offered protection in exchange for total submission. Fromm developed a personality inventory known as the F scale (for fascism), which probes for tendencies toward rigidity, exaggerated deference toward authority, sexual fears such as homophobia, conspiratorial thinking, and other traits that he said describe an authoritarian character structure. As late as the 1950s, Hannah Arendt described the rise of totalitarianism as a response to the economic crisis and "magnetic leaders" by individuals with a mob mentality.[35]

In the 1960s, psychoanalysis tried to explain the new student activism. Although these were not totalitarian movements, the explanations still saw social activism as somewhat irrational. For example, Lewis Feuer linked the student protests to intergenerational conflicts rooted in deep unconscious sources.[36] He believed that the protestors were young people with unresolved Oedipal complexes, subjected to harsh child-rearing practices and a conflicted relationship with their parents. They took out their hostile feelings on parental surrogates such as university administrators, police officers, and other authorities targeted by activists.[37]

Mass Society Theory

Mass society theory regards social movements as an extension of more elementary forms of collective behavior such as the crowd. Instead of resorting to the authoritarian personality, however, it defines collective behavior as the product of anomie and social disintegration associated with large-scale social change. During conditions of social breakdown, when marginalized people cannot reestablish ties to mainstream social institutions, they may turn to collective action to achieve a sense of community or solidarity. In this theory, social change appears to be the cause of the problematic disruptions, in contrast to later theories that see social change as something that social movements seek to achieve.

Drawing on the classical French theorist Emile Durkheim (1893) and William Kornhauser (1959), mass society theory argues that a stable society rests on strong class and group solidarities, on ties that bind people together and that control social behavior.[38] In periods of massive social change these mechanisms of social integration and social control break down. As a result of this breakdown, the uprooted masses become isolated, anxious, and frustrated. Unable to adjust to the changing times, the marginalized and alienated "riff-raff" without social ties become vulnerable to manipulation by the fanatic social movement leaders.[39] Similar thinking appears in relatively recent policy reports. For example, the McCone Commission described the people who participated in the 1965 riots in Watts, Los Angeles, as recent immigrants, poorly educated persons, and unemployed workers who lacked an organizational connection and who were not well-integrated in society.[40] The more recent "theory of the underclass" also depicts the poor as living outside of the mainstream and explains their poverty as a product of improper attitudes, values, and behavior.

Structural Strain Theory

Drawing on Talcott Parsons's theory of the social system and Neil Smelser's theory of social movements, structural strain theory represents still another explanation of collective behavior linked to the social instability created by social change.[41] This view of social movements is somewhat less negative than the picture painted in the prior theories.

Structural strain theory belongs to the broader school of thought known as structural functionalism that dominated sociology for many years following World War II. Structural functionalism compares society to a living organism consisting of interrelated parts that function together in a reinforcing way for the benefit of the whole. The theory places a high premium on harmonious relationships, integration, social consensus, and stability. Social stability rests on (1) the presence of a common set of values, which in the United States is often referred to as the American Creed; (2) the proper integration of well-functioning subsystems, each of which carries out a different but necessary role in the wider system; and (3) the capacity of societal structures and institutions to adapt to change, that is, to attain their goals, manage tension, and operate in mutually reinforcing ways.

Structural functionalism posits that stability prevails as long as the system and its parts exist in a state of equilibrium. As a corollary, a change in one part leads to changes in other parts. If the changes—which can stem from either internal inconsistencies or external intrusions—balance each other out, the system as a whole remains in the desired state of stability. If not, the change or conflict is likely to ripple through and disrupt the entire system. When the system responds to the resulting ambiguities by slowly and incrementally adapting new values and structures more suited to the altered times, the change is functional. That is, balance is restored without generating high levels of conflict or larger, more systemic modifications. In the final analysis, the structural functionalists believe that conflict and big change is necessarily destructive to social stability. Although these initial theorists did not take up social movements, conflict-generating movements were, by implication, regarded as problematic.

In the early 1960s, Smelser developed an elaborate theory of collective behavior but continued to see it as spontaneous, short-lived, disorganized, and composed of deviant actions taken by people who subscribe to irrational beliefs and who prefer to short-circuit appropriate channels of social action.[42] His theory, which includes social movements but also fads, panics, crazes, and revolutions, posits several structural prerequisites for the formation of a social movement.

The first prerequisite, structural conduciveness, refers to social arrangements that encourage or rule out specific kinds of social movements. A society with racial cleavages, for example, will be more likely to develop a civil rights movement than one without such a divide. The second precondition is a structural strain, such as the presence of perceived ambiguities, discrepancies, deprivation, and tensions. If a large number of people feel aggrieved by a specific strain (e.g., poverty, unemployment, racial conflict, or threats of war), a social movement might materialize. Third, people must be able to tap into generalized beliefs that supply interpretations and solutions, prepare potential participants for action, shape preferences for short-circuiting routine channels for political change, and otherwise reduce the ambiguity and tensions created by the strains. Such beliefs, which help to convert widespread strains into an ongoing movement, can range from major, encompassing, value-oriented ideologies (e.g., democracy, socialism, communism, fascism) to narrower, norm-oriented beliefs (e.g., organized labor's demand for better wages and working conditions, or the women's movement's demand for treatment equal to men's). Finally, the eruption of a social movement depends on the presence of several other precipitating factors or events that sharpen the focus of the strains, enable mass mobilization, weaken social controls, and otherwise catalyze action. If the resulting collective behavior compresses or circumvents established social change procedures, Smelser concludes that the movement is crude, excessive, eccentric, impatient—and irrational.

In the end, the negative assumptions that underpinned collective behavior theory from the 1930s to the 1960s prevented social scientists from anticipating or understanding the student, civil rights, antiwar, women's liberation, and other social movements that rocked the nation throughout the 1960s and 1970s. The dominant theories failed to understand "the sixties" because they saw collective behavior as a spontaneous, irrational, and noninstitutionalized response to abnormal conditions created by structural strain and social change. It did not help, either, that they viewed movement participants through the lens of class, gender, and race stereotypes.

The theories implicitly regarded middle-class students as too rational to risk their future careers by participating in movements for social change. In their view, American blacks were naturally different and culturally inferior, and poor people, women, and most people of color lacked the capability to advance their own interests through rational action and were therefore unable to effect, independently, changes on their own behalf.[43] In essence, the classical theories rendered movements of the 1960s inferior and invisible. Their out-of-date premises and explanations triggered a paradigm shift that dramatically changed the study and understanding of collective behavior.

Collective Behavior as Rational Activity

U.S. society underwent major changes in the 1960s and early 1970s. Among other things, as the political climate became more liberal, the nation began to pay greater attention to domestic problems. Inspired by the civil rights activism that began in the mid-1950s, newer social movements composed of students, women, the disabled, environmentalists, homosexuals, and others burst out in the 1960s. The resulting social turmoil in the United States and around the world elicited a new analysis of social movements. The presence of many progressive social movements, the period's openness to dissent, and researchers' own support for social change effectively discredited the earlier, pejorative interpretations and generated new ideas about both the activists and the movements.[44]

First and foremost, the new theorists rejected the view of social movements and their participants as irrational and deviant. Instead, they regarded the decision to join a social movement as a rational decision based on specific goals and a clear assessment of the costs and benefits of participation. Nor did the new theories denigrate pursuing social change outside of mainstream channels.

The Rational Crowd Theory

The rational crowd theory does not refer to social movements per se. It was, however, part of the effort to redefine collective behavior as a rational event. Theorists reconceptualized the crowd as a temporary gathering of people who share a common focus of attention and who influence one another, rather than as a mindless unruly mob. Though rational, the behavior of the crowd might be benign, dangerous, *or* a source of positive social change.

The rational crowd theory differentiates among types of crowd formations: the casual, the conventional, the expressive, the acting, and the protest crowd. The theory includes the crowd of people gathered in New York City's Times Square on New Year's Eve as well as the downtown celebration by sports fans after their team wins the Super Bowl. The mildly wild behavior in both instances has no purpose other than enjoyment or participation. Yet the theory calls it rational, adaptive, and normative because the individual's behavior reflects a choice of goals and means and conforms to a set of social expectations—which, in the case of New Year's Eve and team victories, tolerate pushing the edge of the envelope, though not too far.[45]

The rational crowd theory also defines certain civil disorders (also called riots) as rational events. It regards the uprisings in Watts, Detroit, and Newark during the 1960s and at Attica prison in the 1970s as rational and adaptive responses to anger and oppression. Rather than mindlessly following the crowd or a manipulative leader, as posited by the earlier collective behavior theories, the participants rationally calculated the relative benefits of the action (satisfaction of venting one's anger) and the costs (getting hurt, getting arrested), and their behavior followed a particular set of rules.[46]

Psychological Rationality

How to explain the student movements that exploded on hundreds of college campuses during the 1960s and 1970s? The press, mirroring the older collective behavior theories, often depicted the student protestors as riffraff or misguided victims of outside agitators and ideologies. Others, like Feuer, saw them as driven by irrational psychodynamics. Many observers regarded the campus protests as irrational because the anti-authoritarian students appeared to be risking lucrative future careers by subscribing to radical ideas and participating in disruptive social protest movements.

But the white middle-class student activists attending elite colleges did not easily fit into these traditional depictions of movement participants. Sympathetic psychologists saw the students as a new generation struggling for recognition by striking out against their elders and the establishment. They explained student activism as a *psychologically rational* response rooted in childhood socialization, parental values, or other developments.[47]

Kenneth Keniston, a well-known psychologist, explained New Left student activists as anti-authoritarian or rationally defiant because their liberal-leaning parents had socialized them to be skeptical about authority.[48] James Wood and Richard Flacks also pointed to the continuity between the values of their parents and those of the student activists.[49] In separate studies, they found that student radicals tended to have activist parents, although Flacks found that the views of the students often leaned further to the left than those of their elders. Flacks and other researchers also linked student activism to positive personality characteristics such as intellectuality, personal independence, and social responsibility. Moving beyond psychological rationality, Wood added that the students' opposition to the Vietnam War, racial discrimination, and educational inequality was rational because it sought to correct a problematic status quo.[50]

Other observers conceptualized the student movement as a rational response to the structural changes that were occurring in the higher education system, especially the tracking of students by class and race. The students opposed a system in which white, upper-class children attended expensive, private Ivy League universities, while working-class students of all races went to four-year public colleges or two-year community colleges. The tracking, which resulted from differential tuition costs and the advice of guidance counselors, functioned to place youth in jobs that corresponded to their place in the social structure. From this perspective, student activism did not stem from the student's psyche, family socialization, or desire for privilege. Rather, it reflected a rational political critique by a new group of social actors who questioned and wanted to redirect wider processes of social change.[51]

Social Psychological Rationality

Drawing on Robert Merton's role theory and Ralph Linton's concept of reference groups, the social psychological explanations of collective behavior focus on the relationship between psychological dispositions and social conditions.[52] Both *relative deprivation* and *status strain theories* (discussed next) explain why a category of people experiencing strain eventually defines itself as a group interested in fundamental social change. The analysis emphasizes subjective interpretations of social conditions and participation in social movements as a rational response to stress.

Relative deprivation theory emerged, in part, to explain why the most deprived people (i.e., those experiencing absolute material deprivation such as hunger, illness, and poverty) engage in collective behavior less frequently than better-off individuals and groups. Early theorists concluded either that the poor spend all their time trying to survive or that their personality characteristics and/or living conditions produce a culture of fatalism and passivity.

In contrast, relative deprivation theory asks why working- and middle-class people do become active. It suggests that social movements emerge in response to a sense of *subjective* (i.e., relative) rather than absolute deprivation. It explains that people act to reduce psychological pain when, regardless of their level of material want, they believe that they cannot sustain gains or attain further improvement or that they have made less progress than a comparable group. Collective action is one way people/groups address this perception of relative deprivation.[53] This thinking has been used to explain the rise of a more militant civil rights movement in the late 1950s and early 1960s. By the 1940s, structural changes began to loosen the grip of racial inequality and improve the conditions of black Americans. As the growing African American middle class increasingly compared its circumstances to middle-class whites rather than to poorer blacks, many African Americans decided to challenge the long-standing problem of racial discrimination. The contrast—the sense of relative deprivation in a context of rising expectations—politicized African Americans, who then joined or backed the increasingly militant civil rights movement.[54]

Status strain theory—another in the social psychological paradigm—argues that people join social movements when their symbolic position in society changes for the worse. It is a truism in political sociology that societies and middle-class groups in decline will often turn to leaders who offer oversimplified nationalist, chauvinist, racist, or fascist solutions to extremely complex problems. The classic case is the rise of fascism in Germany between the two world wars. Contemporary instances of anti-immigrant, anti-Semitic, and racist mobilizations have also appeared throughout Europe as reactionary responses to the relative decline of European dominance in the world.[55]

However, right-wing, often religion-based movements also arose in the United States during the first half of the twentieth century as people looked for ways to compensate for a fallen or falling social position or to deal with cultural discontent generated by changes in the wider social order. When demographic shifts, occupational restructuring, political realignments, and new waves of immigration led to an actual or feared loss of jobs, income, power, or prestige, the resulting status strain led some people to turn to right-wing groups promising to preserve or restore their once dominant status.

In the late nineteenth century, during a period of intense immigration by Catholics and Jews, various Protestant groups organized against the perceived threat to their religious dominance. In 1887, after an Irish Catholic candidate defeated a Protestant labor candidate in a local election, Protestants formed the American Protective Association, a secret anti-Catholic organization.[56] In the 1920s, as the political dominance of rural evangelical Protestants gave way to urban Catholic (and Jewish) immigrants, anti-Catholic sentiment fueled the rise of the Ku Klux Klan. To this day, each wave of immigration has given rise to anti-Catholic, anti-Jewish, antiblack, or anti-immigrant movements in the United States. These include the neo-Nazis, Aryan Supremacists, and young "skinheads" who seek to protect the white Anglo-Saxon Protestants or other groups from the growing influence of foreign immigrants.[57]

Changes in the structure of race and gender relations have also created status strain within the dominant group. After the Civil War (1861–1865), when the end of slavery and the potential end of segregation threatened the power of plantation owners and the Southern way of life, many whites joined the Ku Klux Klan to protect their privileges. In the 1960s and 1970s, when white ethnic working- and lower-middle-class groups faced school busing and racial integration, they formed neighborhood associations and other groups to exclude blacks. In the 1980s, the religious right appealed to Christian evangelicals, who feared the institutionalization of the gains made by the civil rights movement. Changes in gender roles (e.g., rising rates of divorce, teenage pregnancy, nonmarital births, and female employment and the right to an abortion) have also fueled the religious right and the antiabortion movement, both of which hold to the idea of male dominance. On a smaller scale, these gender changes led some men to form local groups that reasserted male domination.

The above-noted movements appealed to the status anxiety and class resentment of their members, who felt that their culture was under siege and who responded by negatively stereotyping the "other." Promising to curb challenges to core values ("culture wars") and to solve seemingly intractable problems ("social issues"), these movements have had highly political and, in some cases, dangerous consequences, ranging from lynching in the early part of the twentieth century to burning synagogues, bombing abortion clinics, and bashing gays today.[58]

Economic Rationality

Social movement theorists also turned to economic concepts as another way to override the notions of irrationality and deviance built into the classical collective behavior theories.

Rational choice theory presumes that individuals are autonomous reasoning beings whose decisions reflect narrow self-interest rather than common values and goals. When deciding to purchase a car (or join a social movement), individuals rationally weigh the relative costs and benefits of their options to determine if the benefits outweighed the costs.

Given this individualistic view of human nature, why would any rational person join a social movement? If an individual can secure the gains won by a social movement (e.g., higher wages, cleaner air, peace) without paying the cost of participation in time and money, why not simply "ride free," that is, enjoy the benefits without spending one's own discretionary time and funds? The economist Mancur Olson concluded that organizations could overcome the free-rider problem by offering special incentives to members.[59] If the rewards of participation exceed the costs, people will choose to become involved in social movements. Thus, trade unions and professional organizations provide members-only benefits; the 1960s welfare rights movement used the selective incentive of assistance in securing special cash benefits to mobilize welfare recipients.[60]

Without challenging the rationality of social movements, critics have challenged the idea that movements need incentives to recruit members. They argue that despite the opportunity to ride free, thousands of people have joined movements to express solidarity, to achieve urgent group interests, and to support principled commitments. The members of the civil rights and peace movements, for example, risked arrests, police beatings, and ruined careers to achieve their ends—without economic rewards.[61] Feminism, especially cultural (and radical) feminism, suggests that the incentive argument theory stems from the male bias of rational choice theory, with its emphasis on individualism, selfish motivation, and cost-benefit analysis. Feminists believe that discussions of the need to rely on incentives might disappear if movement theorists took women's experience as the prototype of human behavior and if they considered that the traits typically associated with women—connection, empathy, intuition, sharing, nurturance, and interdependence—motivated movement participation.[62]

Conflict Perspectives: Collective Behavior as Political Problem Solving

Conflict theories have a long history in the United States and around the world. They tend to gain popularity during periods of social upheaval such as the Great Depression (1930s), World War II (1940s), and the 1960s. The conflict theories resurface during these turbulent times because the upheaval polarizes opposing interests and exposes a lack of consensus. The lack of consensus, in turn, challenges the prevailing theories of society, which posit social stability as the natural order of things.

Like other theories, conflict theories define collective behavior as actions of individuals in crowds, groups, organizations, and communities as well as riots, strikes, protests, civil disorders, rebellions, social movements, and revolutions. Unlike other explanations, however, the conflict theories categorize collective behavior in political rather than psychological or behavioral terms.

Collective Behavior as Organizational Conflict: Resource Mobilization Theory

Resource Mobilization (RM) theory defines social movements abstractly as opinions or beliefs that represent participants' preferences for change in society, whether for clean air or greater equality. But the core of the theory dwells on a more concrete unit of analysis: the formal social movement organization (SMO). These complex, centralized, formal, highly developed professional organizations articulate the goals of the more general social movement and translate them into political action. By making organizations rather than individual motivation the center of its analysis, RM theory accepts collective behavior as a normal and rational part of the political process rather than defining it as deviant and irrational. This focus on organizational behavior places the RM analysis somewhere between the pre-1960s theories that dealt largely with individual motivation and the conflict theories that focus on social structural forces.

Drawing on the organizational theory developed by John McCarthy and Mayer Zald, RM theory analyzes the conditions that promote the growth and political effectiveness of SMOs. Earlier theories had argued that the burst of social movements in the 1960s reflected the breakdown of social control associated with social upheaval. Taking a more positive approach, RM theory linked the rise of formal SMOs (e.g., NAACP, National Organization for Women, ACT-Up, the National Right to Life Organization, Operation Rescue, the National Abortion Rights Action League) to the increased *capacity* of SMOs to mobilize a wider range of social, economic, and political resources.[63]

According to RM theory, by the 1960s several important changes had improved the capacity of SMOs. In response to political pressures, private foundations, religious organizations, and governmental agencies (e.g., Civil Rights Commission, the Commission on the Status of Women, the Office of Economic Opportunity) stepped forward to support/fund SMOs. Other new resources included the development of fund-raising and organizing technologies, the availability of young organizers who preferred the movement over traditional careers, and the growth of organizational networks, coalitions, and alliances. Finally, the reduction of cold war tensions allowed the media to devote more time to domestic social problems. In brief, access to new backers, new technologies, and greater media coverage provided SMOs with the resources needed to pursue success. As the organizations learned to mobilize these and other resources, they gained members, supporters, and legitimacy. Recognized for this by the more established players, SMOs became major forces in an increasingly contested political marketplace.[64]

Given its focus on organizational strength, mainstream legitimacy, and policy victories, RM theory concludes that large SMOs are inherently more effective than informal, decentralized, less well-endowed groups that rely on indigenous leadership, volunteer staff, and mass actions. Although Zald now includes enthusiasm and spontaneity as resources to be mobilized, critics maintain that RM theory continues to downplay poor people's movements, to dismiss the unconventional mass politics of the later 1960s and early 1970s, and to blur the important line between social movements and more conventional interest group politics.[65] Others complain that this midrange theory ignores both the smaller questions of individual motivation and social interaction and the larger role of social structures.[66]

Collective Behavior as Political Opportunity

Political opportunity structures (POS) theory highlights the role of political institutions rather than an organization's capacity to mobilize resources. Political opportunity refers to changing features of the political environment that raise or lower the costs of using collective action to secure social change. Drawing on the work of Charles Tilly and others who emphasize the wider political context, POS theory links the possibility of social movement activity to the growth and transformation of the state.[67]

Closely related to RM theory, POS theory lays out the dimensions of the political system that make it more or less receptive to the demands of social movements. It holds that social movements stand a better chance when prevailing political conditions reveal potential allies, exacerbate the vulnerability of the authorities, or otherwise create opportunities for collective action.[68]

POS theory outlines several types of political opportunities. The relative weight and independence of the judicial, legislative, and executive branches in the government can facilitate or hamper collective action. During the

1960s and 1970s, a strong, active, and relatively independent judiciary created political opportunities for social movements that often turned to the courts for redress. The 1954 Supreme Court ruling in *Brown v. Board of Education* outlawed racial segregation in public education. This historic civil rights victory swept away the legal grounds of Jim Crow, changed the rules of the game for African Americans, and contributed enormously to the growth and militancy of the civil rights movement. In the 1960s, as liberal Democrats became increasingly indebted to the black vote, they supported the Civil Rights Acts of 1964 and 1965, which enfranchised Southern blacks and dismantled the rest of the Jim Crow system.[69]

The women's rights and antitobacco movements also used the courts to change social policy.[70] In 1973, pressed by the women's movement, the courts granted women the right to an abortion. Similarly, the antitobacco forces successfully used the courts to extract millions of dollars from many cigarette companies after proving the lethal effects of nicotine on the health of individuals and the cost of health care.

A second type of political opportunity stems from the degree of cohesiveness among the governing authorities. Internal divisions within centers of power periodically undermine the influence of the ruling elite and create an opening for organized challengers. At its extreme, internal division can so paralyze the elite's capacity for action that it falls into crisis, becomes weak, or collapses. The war between France and England weakened the financial position of both kings, which improved the possibilities for the American and French Revolutions. Both the 1917 Russian Revolution and the 1949 Chinese Revolution occurred after a prolonged international war had weakened the state, World War I in the case of Russia and World War II in the case of China.[71] More recent government turmoil in Africa, Eastern Europe, the Mideast, and the former Soviet Union has also led to leadership contests.

Less explosive cleavages within the governing group may also increase the vulnerability of political leaders to outside groups wanting to "push" their agenda. The 1992 election of Bill Clinton as president of the United States shifted power from the Republicans, who favored the religious right and a strong military, to the Democrats, whose candidate had promised to end the ban on gays in the military. By exposing the division over family values among the political elite, Clinton's victory created an opening for the gay rights movement. The National Gay and Lesbian Task Force used the opening to build influential alliances with the women's movement, civil rights groups, and legislators in Congress and to press more strongly for their long-standing goal of ending the ban on gays in the military.[72]

A third type of political opportunity arises when elected officials legitimize social movements to build or rebuild their own popular support. Political leaders turn to outside groups when a recession, their endorsement of an unpopular policy, or other event costs them the support of their regular constituency.[73] For example, when business and other antigovernment forces attacked the Roosevelt administration, President Roosevelt, to win favor from organized labor for his New Deal programs, supported legislation that improved the climate for union organizing.[74] In the 1960s, to sustain the backing of African Americans, the Kennedy and Johnson administrations promoted funding for black causes, political appointments to blacks, and passage of anti-discrimination laws. President Kennedy also needed to hold on to the good-will of American women, who helped elect him to office. Unable to promote a women's rights agenda in the Republican-controlled Congress, Kennedy appointed women to high posts and created the first Presidential Commission on the Status of Women. Likewise, Johnson extended Executive Order 11246 mandating affirmative action to cover sex.[75] In the 1980s, to maintain the support of the growing Christian right, President Reagan appointed anti-abortion judges and limited women's right to choose.[76]

A fourth political opportunity structure for social movements depends on the degree of tolerance or repression found in the political climate.[77] The openness of the political context that shaped U.S. politics between the 1930s and 1960s, combined with postwar prosperity, contributed to the success of a wide variety of social movements.[78] In contrast, the repression of dissent following World War I and World War II stymied and repressed opposition. A firm, rather unyielding elite gained control of government institutions; demonized, prosecuted, and assaulted social movements, and periodically jailed, killed, or otherwise silenced dissenters. During the 1950s, for example, Senator Joe McCarthy (R-Wisconsin) used his control of the Congressional hearings on un-American activities to accuse activists of communist mem-bership or leanings. Many communists and noncommunists alike lost their jobs; those who refused to "name names" often went to prison. Although the political climate liberalized in the 1960s, the FBI infiltrated and repressed the militant Black, Red, and Brown Power groups, whose calls for deep changes in the power structure went beyond what the other social movements de-manded. These assaults both curtailed social movements and sent a strong message to all social critics about what might happen to them if they did not toe the line.

Shifts in the political climate may create political opportunities for pre-viously unsupported groups. In the 1980s, once conservatives gained the pres-idency, officialdom placed liberal social movements on the defensive while opening the door to right-wing organizations seeking to overturn hard-won liberal gains such as affirmative action, the right to abortion, and a higher minimum wage.[79] This conservative political climate also emboldened reac-tionary nationalistic and religious movements, such as White Aryan Resis-tance, the Ku Klux Klan, the neo-Nazi skinheads, right-wing survivalists, militias, and some fundamentalist religious organizations. These groups be-lieve that "racially pure" whites and Aryans are naturally superior to mixed or "hybrid" groups. Using the rhetoric of difference to code racist claims about the innate inferiority of particular peoples, they blame outsiders for a complex of social and economic problems (Jews run Wall Street, blacks use social program that waste tax dollars, etc.) and deal harshly with dissent. Groups espousing such neo-Nazi ideas have managed to infiltrate some of the more respectable organizations of the right and now participate in mainstream electoral politics. The political party formed by Lyndon Larouche, David Duke's election to the state legislature, and Pat Buchanan's campaign for the presidency have all left their mark on the political mainstream.[80]

The changes in the political climate do not wipe out the reforms won in earlier periods. Taking back policy change is not easy or fast. The new policies remain in place, at least in part, because the movements under attack tried to stem the tide by vigorously defending their gains and resisting the new regime. Thus, political struggle and social change remain on the agenda at all times.

Collective Action as Structural Conflict

The third group of conflict theories concentrates more explicitly on conflicts rooted in the unequal distribution of power. These structural theories explain social movements as a rational and instrumental response to great societal inequalities, especially those grounded in the class, race, and gender relations of power. The New Social Movement theory highlights the movements that target cultural oppression; Marxism and others focus on the conflicts grounded in the unequal power relations of class, gender and race.

New Social Movement Theory

New Social Movement (NSM) theory became and remains a main competitor to the more liberal RM and POS theories. Grounded in Western European social theory and political philosophy rather than the U.S. social sciences, NSM theory both builds on and critiques classical Marxism, the predominant school in much of European social movement theory prior to the 1960s. NSM theory contends that the new conditions of postindustrial society have undermined the old social movements, especially the labor movement, and stimulated new struggles (i.e., new social movements) more interesting to the middle class.

More specifically, beginning in the 1960s and early 1970s, changes in the political economy, especially the deindustrialization of the nation's central cities, globalization of the world economy, and the exportation of production abroad, undercut the U.S. labor movement by decimating the manufacturing base of many jobs and communities and fueling the expansion of the less unionized service sector. The breakup of jobs and industries scattered workers, dispersing the concentration that had fueled and strengthened the labor movement, and created new problems that the labor movement could not easily address. The conservative assault on labor rights beginning in the 1980s further limited the ability of unions to redistribute resources to their constituencies.

At the same time, social life was fractured by postwar surburbanization, rising immigration, and new race and gender divides. The loss of its base combined with the unions' resistance to fully incorporating other groups (e.g., youth, women, persons of color, unskilled workers) into their ranks cost the labor movement both members and power. Some of the groups poorly served by the trade unions gravitated to the NSMs that demonstrated greater concerns about issues of "difference," exclusion, and oppression. The new social movements appealed to these groups as well as to the middle class because the broader range of political goals stressed combating oppressive discrimination, cultural intrusions, bureaucratic domination, unrestrained militarism, and environmental devastation rather than just conflicts between labor and capital.[81]

The postindustrial trends, especially deindustrialization and fragmentation of social life, led NSM theory to define politics in cultural terms. NSM theorists struggled against a wide range of institutions that shape ideas, symbols, and meaning, especially the cultural and ideological institutions that dominate and control identities.[82] The movements reject authority structures in the family, the workplace, political parties, and the state. Self-consciously local, antibureaucratic, and antihierarchical, the NSMs hope to erode the power of the government. They envision a decentralized society with little or no regulation, intervention, or control and favor democratic participation, personal liberty, and civil rights as well as networks, collectives, communities, and other "free spaces" located between state and civil society.[83]

Many NSMs also contest the technological-scientific apparatus, the agencies of information and communication, and various institutions that also wield control over cultural definitions of self-worth and the overall "way of life." They challenge the role of experts and technocrats and the power of electronic communication technology that can control the personal (body, sexuality, affective relations), the subjective (cognition and emotional processes, motives, desires), and the biological (structures of the brain, the genetic code, reproductive capacity) features of life. NSM theory suggests that by concentrating on the political meanings contained in lifestyle, sexuality, interpersonal relations, and popular culture, the NSMs turn previously private domains into crucial political battlegrounds and open new spheres of political action.[84]

NSM theory's emphasis on other identity issues lead some observers to describe its agenda as one of "identity politics."[85] In this view, participants in the NSMs are searching for both an individual and a collective identity based on shared characteristics (e.g., sex, race, sexual orientation) acquired by accident of birth, in most cases, and over which individuals have little or no control. Thus, NSMs struggle to rescue ethnic, racial, gender, and other identities from their distortion or erasure by dominant culture. This process includes ridding oneself of the stereotypic ideas and beliefs that oppressed people uncritically and unconsciously often accept as true but that stand in the way of progress. Such ideas include the internalization by blacks of white values and racist attitudes, the acceptance by women of their place in the home, and guilt felt by homosexuals because they are not straight.

NSM theory also seeks to expand mainstream notions of "normality." The movement of differently abled persons, for example, tried to break with the traditional perception of disability as a sick, abnormal, and pathetic condition. The gay and lesbian movements struggled to depathologize homosexuality and promote recognition of diversity within the homosexual community.[86] The collective power of NSMs seeks to undo homophobia, sexism, racism, and ablism, to gain visibility and dignity for the group,[87] and to win the right to be different in a world that exerts strong pressure for conformity. As such, they pose a major challenge to the dominant logic of society, also thought of as the American Way of Life.

Some NSMs, especially the peace, environmental, and slow-growth movements, deal with identity issues but also with the economic logic of the market. These movements appeal to many educated middle-class individuals in search of continuity and stability in the fragmented and destructured social world. The particular struggles implicitly call for a reexamination of the self in relation to the world or universe, confront the economic logic of the market economy, remind society that the power to produce contains within it the power to destroy, and point to the need for humankind to understand its proper place in the natural order rather than operating as a race apart from or above nature.[88]

NSM theory suggests that struggles on the terrain of symbols of meaning and identity are highly political and that they may do more to expose contemporary forms of power ("points of antagonism") than more conventional political movements. NSMs represent a fundamental political challenge to the legitimacy of the central institutions of society and a cultural challenge to its core values.[89] Critics charge that neither the theories nor the movements are especially new. They argue that the classical collective action theories implicitly dealt with identity, if in negative terms. For example, the crowd and psychoanalytic schools grounded identity in biological, psychological, and social structures and held that primitive instincts or internal psychological structures produced panics, violence, riots, and other asocial or antisocial behavior. The early thinking about racial and ethnic identity often treated these as determined by some set of ascribed characteristics. Strain theories, relative deprivation, and status discrepancy theories claimed that maladaptive social structures create identities. More recent discussions regard identities as socially constructed, a product of an individual's interaction with society, one that is subject to continuous redefinition.

Critics also say that the traditional social movements also dealt with collective identity, derived from a shared sense of economic, racial, or gender injustice rather than the cultural oppression highlighted by the NSMs. The labor movement spoke to the identity of workers, and the union hall became a social space for participants. The nationalist impulses in the Black Power movement led to the slogan "Black is beautiful" to counter negative stereotypes and to validate black culture and its African roots.[90] Identity politics also loomed large in the cultural feminist and gay rights movements, which argued that "the personal is political" and stressed the right to be different, to realize one's own identity, and to form new social spaces.[91] It gets a little confusing at this point, because some observers think the above movements *are* the new social movements.

Critics decry the newness of the NSMs as well by showing that the middle class has always played a key role in social movements, including the abolition, prohibition, reproductive rights, and suffrage movements; that the youth, civil rights, feminist, and gay rights movements foreshadowed the demand for recognition, dignity, self-worth, and cultural control; and that the older social movements addressed the politicization of everyday life but with different targets.[92]

A second critique focuses on impact. Some observers see the NSMs as a force for multiculturalism and democratic insurgency; others fear the focus on difference is divisive. They worry that emphasizing identity and culture will reinforce divisions, ranging from intergroup hostility to "ethnic cleansing." They also worry that the politics of difference weakens the struggle for social change for all oppressed groups by preventing movements from joining forces around their common interests. Those fearing the NSM agenda call for building coalitions, seeking electoral power, and recreating a sense of public life through the state instead of privatizing it. They want to mobilize people based on a principled program that moves beyond narrow parochialism to social, economic, and political justice for all.

Marxism and Class Conflict

Conflict theories drawing on Marxism maintain that beneath the seemingly stable and harmonious social order depicted by most mainstream social scientists lie deep conflicts rooted in power differentials. In this view, dominant and subordinate groups structure society and the institutionalized relationships among them. The interests of the unequal groups inevitably clash because members of the dominant groups benefit materially and psychically from the prevailing structures, while members of powerless groups suffer the penalties and deprivations that accompany subordination.

Social movements appear when subordinated groups decide that authorities have appropriated an unfair share of societal status, privilege, wealth, or power. The movements represent the collective expression of discontent associated with the realities of oppression, marginalization, exploitation, and exclusion and are more or less necessary phases in long-term processes of social change.[93] In brief, those with less understand collective behavior as a struggle for greater equality—a highly rational effort intended to redress the social conflicts created by the market economy and systems of domination.

Karl Marx (1818–1883), whose ideas guided the early nineteenth- and twentieth-century socialist movements in Europe, put the issue of power conflict at the center of his work. Marxism provides a critique of bourgeois society, a historical analysis of exploitation, and a vision of a humane society that Marx and other Marxists believed the end of capitalism would produce. Much of the twentieth-century social movement theorizing by mainstream social scientists represents efforts to refute or elaborate on the Marxist analysis of capitalism and class conflict. From the 1930s to the 1960s, when the political silencing of dissent in the United States had a chilling effect on the social sciences, Marxism was largely ignored. Interest in Marxism and other power conflict theories resurfaced in the 1960s, if only marginally.[94]

The structural conflict theories also argue that social structures create the conditions that make social movements both necessary and possible. Marxism, for example, links the rise of modern social movements to the emergence of the capitalist system of production that destroyed the traditional basis of autonomy and influenced the development of modern society.[95] The historic shift from a feudal to a market economy uprooted masses of people and ushered in new economic arrangements favoring the owners of private property over others. The capitalist system of production brought into being a new class structure based on the owners of the means of production (land, labor, and machines) and the proletariat or waged workers who sold their capacity to work (i.e., their labor power) to the owners of plants and machinery. Those who owned and controlled the means of production had greater resources, power, and control than those who earned their livelihood in factories and offices. The owner's profits derived in large part from paying workers as little as possible for their efforts, demanding long hours of labor, investing minimally in improved working conditions, and excluding unions.[96] The class structures also determine the organization of production, the capacity for social reproduction, the distribution of resources, the content of cultural beliefs and values, and the class conflict that bred social movements.

The unequal class system eventually yielded class conflict. Because the wealth of the capitalist class (the owners of the means of production) and the relative poverty of the working class (the workers hired by capitalists) stemmed from the same economic process, the inevitable tension periodically spawned collective action by workers to improve wages and working conditions, if not transform capitalist society. The leverage of workers in this struggle rested on the fact that the means of production could not be operated without them.[97]

The development of the working class as a *potentially* oppositional force occurs logically and naturally, according to Marx. By itself, the advance of the market economy creates the conditions for the emergence of a workers' movement "at the point of production." The centralization of production into ever larger mines and factories concentrated a large number of employees in one place where they faced common grievances. As workers recognized their shared exploitation and the power of owners, they became more class conscious and motivated for collective action.

But the capacity of that class to act politically, to strive to win power and transform society, is not automatic. It depends on the emergence of organization, leadership, and intellectual activity; in fact, it requires a social movement.[98] At some point, under certain conditions, at least some exploited workers recognize that their misery stems from the workings of the capitalist system of production rather than from arduous machinery or an unrelenting boss. They realize that their physical survival and the meaning of their world depends on jointly resisting their condition. This increasing awareness (or consciousness) leads workers to organize themselves as a class to demand better wages and working conditions through unionization and the formation of labor-based political parities.

With the scope of their workplace expanding from local to national to international as the trade union movement gains strength, the demands of workers shift from defending their existing rights and resources to claiming additional rights and a greater share of societal resources. As workers replace their traditional groups with new solidarities, associations, and trade unions, collective action takes the form of strikes, demonstrations, and other forms of deliberate assembly. Banded together, workers gain power and set the stage for the creation of a rational society, defined as a fully realized democracy.[99] In most instances, workers faced ongoing resistance from employers who preferred to maintain control of the workers' labor and decision making on the shop floor.

A glimpse at U.S. labor history illustrates these points. Workers in the United States began to organize in the 1820s, as the Industrial Revolution began to expand factory production. In 1827, the Mechanics' Unions Trade Association in Philadelphia organized a wide range of skilled artisans. Ten years later, during the Depression of 1837, the early labor movement boasted five national trade unions. The unions and the workers' political parties that arose at the same time had a broad agenda. They called for equal and universal free education, public lands for settlement, restrictions on child and prison labor, better working conditions for women, the ten-hour day without a wage cut, governmental control of the currency, the right to organize workers, and the creation of public works jobs for the unemployed. In the 1840s, young daughters of farmers, employed in the early New England textile mills, organized the Lowell Female Labor Reform Association in Massachusetts. They published their own newspaper, *The Voice of Industry*, and fought for better wages and working conditions, including the ten-hour day, often walking off the job en masse to underscore their demands.[100]

The labor movement regained strength when, following the Civil War (1861–1865), the factory system incorporated more wage earners and exploitation intensified. Formed in 1869, the Knights of Labor enrolled 50,000 members by 1883 and claimed 700,000 by 1886. It demanded an eight-hour day, equal pay for equal work, an end to child labor, and cooperation among workers. Teachers, farmers, and housewives each formed their own locals.[101] But the American Federation of Labor (AFL) soon outpaced the Knights of Labor. Formed in 1881 to organize skilled white male workers, the AFL reached some 250,000 members in 1892, up from about 125,000 in 1886.[102] The depression of 1893 brought on a new wave of wage cuts, layoffs, and strikes. Between 1880 and 1900, more than 10 million workers participated in over thirty thousand strikes and lockouts.[103] AFL membership grew from 548,000 in 1900 to 1.6 million in 1904 and 2 million in 1914, rising from 3.2 percent of the employed labor force in 1900 to nearly 6.6 percent by 1920.[104]

During the Great Depression of the 1930s, with renewed labor militancy, the industrial unions joined forces to form the Congress of Industrial Organizations (CIO), which went on to achieve major victories in the steel, automobile, and other plants. Between 10 and 11 million workers, or about 7 percent of the labor force, belonged to a union by the late 1930s, half to the

In 1912, the military was called in to suppress a strike by factory workers in Lawrence, Massachusetts. The campaign to organize unions often brought trade unionists into direct and sometimes violent confrontations with armed troops. Courtesy of HarpWeek, LLC

older and more moderate AFL and half to the newer and more assertive and militant CIO. The stronger labor movement successfully pressed Congress to enact additional pro-labor laws, including the 1938 Fair Labor Standards Act, which required employers to pay a minimum wage of 25 cents an hour (rising to 40 cents in seven years), reduced the work week to forty-four hours (to reach forty hours in three years), and outlawed labor by children under age 16. The hourly pay rose for 300,000 workers and 2.3 million enjoyed a shorter work week.[105] The AFL and CIO merged in the mid-1950s to become the nation's largest labor federation. The AFL-CIO continues to represent most of the nation's unionized workers. In recent years, changed economic conditions, especially deindustrialization (the shift from manufacturing to service industries) and globalization (exportation of production abroad) have undermined the conditions that support unionization and cost the trade union movement both members and influence.

Marx paid nearly exclusive attention to class power and class conflict. He recognized the existence of other classes, but emphasized the fundamental split between a small group of owners and masses of struggling workers. Over the years, scholars have revised, revamped, and updated the Marxist understanding of class structure, the workings of capitalism, and the rise of social movements. As noted earlier, theorists have taken into account contemporary social, economic, and political conditions such as the expansion of the state, and new social divisions, including the social conflicts built into the hierarchical structures of gender and race.[106]

Gendered Conflict

Strict Marxists have analyzed gender and race in relation to capitalism and class conflict. They highlight the ways in which class patterns in capitalist societies have led to the subordination of women and people of color and argue that these groups enter social movements from their role as workers. Socialist feminists depart from an analysis that focuses exclusively on class issues. Instead, they define the relations of class, patriarchy, and racial domination as independent but interacting structures of power. All three make social movements both necessary and possible.[107]

Gendered arrangements—sex segregation of occupations, the economic dependence of women on men, women's near exclusive responsibility for the home—are so deeply embedded in our culture and social institutions that they often go unnoticed. Nonetheless, because gender operates as a fundamental principle of social organization, it has periodically spawned collective action by women seeking equal rights with men, greater access to societal resources, and economic justice, if not an actual end to patriarchal power relations.

The socialist feminist analysis highlights the conflicts arising from the gendered structures of power in society. More specifically, it argues that tensions arise from the power imbalance that enables men as a group to dominate women as a group. As noted in the discussions of ideology in chapter 5, socialist feminists conclude that gender inequality rests on the gender division of labor that assigns men to the market (public sphere) and women to the home (private sphere) and to separate gendered activities within each arena. The resulting exclusion of women from social, economic, and political centers of power provided men with the means to control women and ensured that women's place was in the home. The exclusionary practices also led women to organize on their own behalf.

Women's efforts to gain social, economic, and political equality in the United States are as old as the nation itself. However, given their attention to both capitalism and patriarchy, socialist feminists found that the nature of women's activism varies by class. Middle-class women have fought for equal rights with men; poor and working-class women demanded the opportunity to carry out their gendered obligations, which involved improving the economic circumstances of their families and communities at the "point of consumption."

In 1789, Abigail Adams urged her husband, John, who was attending the Constitutional Convention, "to remember the ladies," or "we are determined to foment a rebellion and will not hold ourselves bound by any laws in which we have no voice or representation."[108] In 1848, the rebellion predicted by Abigail Adams sixty years earlier erupted when Lucretia Mott and Elizabeth Cady Stanton convened the first women's rights convention, attended by three hundred people (including forty men) sparked by their lack of rights and the exclusion of women from the antislavery movement. Held in Seneca Falls, New York, the conference issued a Declaration of Sentiments modeled after the Declaration of Independence. The document proclaimed the self-evident truth that "all men and women are created equal," and its resolutions declared that the laws that placed women "in a position inferior to that of men are contrary to the great precept of nature and therefore of no force or authority."[109] After considerable struggle, married women gained the right to own their own property (1849), to keep their wages and inheritance, to make contracts in their own name, and to have joint custody of their children (1860). But women did not win the vote until 1919, when Congress ratified the Nineteenth Amendment to the Constitution. From 1920 to this day, sexism (the unequal treatment of women by men) has continued to spark activism by middle-class women.[110] For much of this time, African American and Latina women organized separately, first due to the laws of segregation that separated women racially and then because of unmatched agendas.

Poor and working-class women mobilized to fulfill their gendered obligations, which required them to carry out the expectations of women as defined by their community. Middle-class women rose up to protest that the democratic promise of equal opportunity for all did not apply to them; poor and working-class women protested that the workings of the market economy undercut their gendered family maintenance roles. The lack of family income made it difficult, if not impossible, for them to effectively carry out their part in the tasks of social reproduction assigned to the family and linked to women's role in the home.

The discrepancy between the profit-driven market's ability to produce enough income and jobs and the resources needed by the family to maintain themselves fueled activism among low-income women. They organized to ensure that they would be able to meet their gendered obligations at the point of consumption. For example, during the depression of the 1830s, working-class housewives organized flour riots. In the early 1900s, immigrant women on the Lower East Side of Manhattan and in other cities organized rent strikes to protest rising rents and butcher store boycotts to protest inflated meat prices. The action quickly spread to other neighborhoods and was the first of many other price-driven protests in cities around the nation in 1906, 1907, 1908, 1910, and 1914.[111] During the Great Depression of the 1930s, housewives around the country who lacked the ability to feed and clothe their families demanded government action. They supported strikes by men in their communities, blocked evictions, and organized consumer boycotts.[112] One of the largest boycotts took place in 1935, when housewives targeted butcher shops in many large cities, closing some forty-five hundred in New York City alone. Black working-class women formed their own housewives leagues and launched "Don't Buy Where You Can't Work" campaigns in numerous cities. Housewife activism peaked in an explosion of protests in the early 1940s after Roosevelt cut social spending in response to conservative critics. The protests stopped during World War II, but huge price increases in 1946–1947 and 1951 sparked two of the largest consumer strikes in U.S.

history.[113] During the civil rights movement, low-income women played key but highly unreported roles in local communities.[114] During the 1960s, they became active in the war on poverty and the welfare rights movements,[115] and to this day are involved in local campaigns against toxic waste, for neighborhood safety, and in support of many other community issues.

If the structure and operation of capitalist institutions, especially economic exploitation, created the conditions for collective action among workers at the point of production, so the structure and operation of patriarchal power relations, especially the gender division of labor, created the conditions for collective action among women seeking equal rights. Just as the rise of larger and larger factories concentrated male workers in one place and exposed conflicts between capital and labor, so the gender division of labor clustered women into female enclaves: housewives in neighborhoods, workers in "women's" jobs, and clients in social welfare programs.

But the capacity of women to act politically to try to change their circumstances is not automatic. It depends on the development of consciousness, leadership, and organizational capacity. In the case of women, the gender division of labor designed to keep women down and out paradoxically helped to create the conditions for the emergence of low-income women's activism and middle-class women's movements. The concentration of women in "women's places," whether low-paid jobs or local neighborhoods, made it possible for women to recognize their shared oppression. As some point, under certain conditions, women concluded that their problems were not individual but stemmed from the patriarchal devaluation of women, the differential treatment of women and men, the exclusion of women from major economic and political institutions, and women's inability to fulfill their gendered obligations. The perceptions of at least some women turned into a powerful critique of patriarchy, male domination, women's condition, and economic injustice. The increased awareness (i.e., consciousness) that their well-being depended on jointly resisting their condition eventually led some women to organize for social change.

The gender division of labor also generated the organizational capacity needed for collective behavior. Excluded from mainstream institutions and located in women's place in the home and on the job, women began to form their own clubs, associations, alliances, and organizations. The resulting networks became the infrastructure for collective action by women. Indeed, feminists point out that the shared experience of women denied basic rights, deprived of control over their bodies, and excluded from the centers of power fueled the first and second waves of feminism in the United States. The failure of the market to produce the income needed by low-income families sparked the collective action of low-income women throughout the twentieth century.[116]

Racial Conflicts

The structure and operation of racial domination, especially the process of racial formation and racialization, created the conditions for collective action among persons of color. Racial formation refers to the "process by which social, economic, and political forces determine the content and importance of racial categories and by which they are in turn shaped by racial meanings. Racialization is the extension of racial meaning to a previously racially unclassified relationship, social practice or group."[117]

Through these structural processes, race becomes, like class and gender, a fundamental organizing principle of social relationships. The racial divide in the United States has left blacks and whites living in what the political scientist Andrew Hacker has referred to as two separate, unequal, and often hostile nations.[118] Black domination by whites has periodically spawned collective action by persons of color seeking greater access to societal resources, if not the end of white supremacy.

Opposition to slavery began in the late 1700s and continued though the Civil War (1861–1865). In the 1830s, calls to end slavery were heard from David Walker, a free Negro in North Carolina whose widely circulated pamphlet preached insurrection and violence to right the wrongs suffered by blacks; the slave insurrections led by Nat Turner, among others; and the collectively organized Underground Railroad, a vast system of routes and safe houses that concealed runaway slaves and spirited them to freedom. In 1831, William Lloyd Garrison, a leader of the abolitionist movement, published *The Liberator*, a widely read antislavery newspaper. Others founded abolition groups such as the New England Anti-Slavery Society (which balked at admitting both women and blacks).[119]

After the Civil War, when the realities of segregation clashed with the democratic promise of freedom for all, black men and women founded their own movements. In 1896, drawing on the tradition of slave women's networks, deep roots in the black church, the free black women's associations, and antislavery work, black women formed the National Association of Colored Women (NACW), the oldest secular, national African American organization. By 1914, the NACW represented fifty thousand middle-class, educated black women in twenty-eight federations and over one thousand clubs.[120] While supporting much of the Progressive movement's agenda, the NACW platform also addressed the unique concerns of the African American community. It opposed the pseudo-scientific ideologies of black inferiority and sexual promiscuity; established settlement houses and social service programs for the young, old, and sick; and promoted women's suffrage, prohibition, and the civil rights agenda of the NAACP and the Urban League.[121] Other African American women joined the women's arm of the more separatist Universal Negro Improvement Association (UNIA), headed by Amy Jacques Garvey, wife of Marcus Garvey, founder of UNIA.

African American men and women formed the Niagara Movement (1905), organized by W. E. B. Du Bois (the first African American to earn a Harvard Ph.D.) and Monroe Trotter, the Urban League (1910), the NAACP (1911), and the United Negro Improvement Association (1914). The last attracted thousands of working-class and immigrant African Americans to the cause; the Urban League and the NAACP remain active today. The civil rights organizations fought an uphill battle for immediate recognition of the social, political, and economic rights of all black citizens. They made only limited headway until the late 1950s and early 1960s, when changing conditions broke the hold of segregation and fueled the next wave of the civil rights movement.[122] During the 1960s, the more racially integrated civil rights and Black Power movements made significant gains. But the African American fight for full civil rights has yet to be won.

These brief historical examples suggest how the structure and operation of racial segregation exposed the tension between the democratic ideal of equal opportunity for all and the realities of racial segregation, creating the conditions for collective action. The process parallels that for workers and for women. As noted earlier, the rise of larger and larger factories concentrated mostly male workers in one place and exposed conflicts between capital and labor. Similarly, the gender division of labor clustered women into female enclaves and exposed the conflicts between women and men and between the requirement of economic production and the gendered tasks of social reproduction. In a like manner, racism and racial segregation concentrated persons of color in neighborhoods and jobs and exposed conflicts between communities of color and the white power structure.

Racial oppression—the devaluation of persons of color, the differential treatment of white persons and persons of color, and the exclusion of the latter from major economic and political institutions—created the consciousness, political resources, and organizational capacity needed for collective behavior among persons of color. The shared experiences of being segregated into low-paid jobs, in underserved urban neighborhoods, and in unresponsive social welfare programs created anger and a set of racial grievances. Once the grip of racism loosened during the twentieth century, it became more possible for persons of color to act on their oppression. Their historic conflict with the white power structure for a fair, if not a controlling, share of resources and their ongoing exclusion from major economic and political institutions enabled some people of color to forge a powerful critique of racism and white supremacy. Denied basic rights, deprived of economic opportunities, and excluded from centers of power, this collective experience fueled the civil rights and Black Power movements and considerable grassroots activism by African American women.

Racial segregation designed to keep African Americans down and out also—paradoxically—created the organizational capacity for collective action. As blacks moved north after World War II, they secured better-paying jobs, enrolled in college, participated in black churches, and formed a variety of black organizations. Their isolation and exclusion from mainstream institutions controlled by white people led to the formation of black networks, clubs, church groups, federations, alliances, and organizations that became the basis for collective action in the African American community. Ironically, the concentration of the emerging black working class in racially segregated neighborhoods also turned them into a swing vote that helped to elect Democrats in more than a few presidential races. In response, however slowly, the

Democratic Party became more responsive to the needs of the black community, which, in turn, strengthened the hand of the civil rights movement. The early successes of the civil rights movement boosted the morale of other challengers, causing other social movements to surface in the late 1960s and early 1970s.

From Theory to Practice: Using Ideology When Seeking Social Change

Ideology plays a major role in social movements seeking social change. The ideological stance of a social movement inevitably defines the content, scale, and scope of the change it pursues. Also, because movements depend heavily on public support to secure their ends, they typically try to frame their message to resonate with cultural values and beliefs, a practice that can alter the movement's message and goals. Finally, movement organizers and other social change agents have to decide how much to insert ideological visions into direct practice. This chapter ends with a discussion of this practitioner's dilemma.

Social Movements, Ideology, and Social Change

Social movements represent various ideological agendas that parallel the ideological perspectives spelled out in some detail in chapter 5. Each represents belief in a different kind of social change.

Liberal Movements Call for Incremental Reform

The United States has witnessed liberal movements seeking to reform social institutions. These movements stand on a platform of individualism, citizens' rights, representative government, the merits of the market economy, private ownership of property, and limited government intervention in wider society. The major social movements in the United States—the trade union, civil rights, women's rights, gay rights, welfare rights, disability rights, peace, environmental, antiwar, and antinuclear movements—have accepted the capitalist economic system but have pressed the government to compensate for its limitations. They have fought with some success for small and large but mostly incremental reforms to increase equal opportunity and otherwise create a fairer society.[123]

Beginning at the turn of the twentieth century with the Progressive Era reformers, liberal movements gained strength during the Great Depression and after World War II, contributing to the expansion of the welfare state in both the United States and Europe. Since then, liberal social movements have fought for the right of workers to organize and against the exclusion of persons of color from full participation in society, including the right of African Americans to vote; the lack of access to market-produced goods and services by the poor and working poor; and ongoing discrimination against women, persons of color, immigrants, gay men, and lesbians. More recently, liberal movements have called on the government to extend Medicare coverage to prescription drugs for the elderly, protect Social Security against privatization, remedy political corruption, correct campaign finance distortions, limit environmental destruction, and increase consumer protection, among many other issues.

Conservative Movements Call for Restoring Tradition

Conservative movements seek to limit the role of government and to promote family values. They stand on a platform that protects private property, endorses inequality, and favors limited government intervention. Conservative forces held sway in the United States at the turn of the twentieth century, after World War II, and since the 1980s. Combining the beliefs of laissez-faire and social conservatism (see chapter 5), the New Right consists of organizations such as the Young Americans for Freedom, the National Conservative Political Action Committee, the Eagle Forum (which opposes the Equal Rights Amendment), the Christian Coalition, the Moral Majority, the John Birch Society, the Pro Family Forum, Right to Life (antiabortion movement), and numerous local antibusing, antitax, and anti–gun control initiatives.[124] These groups support traditional values and norms associated with the past and little, if any, social change. Their agenda, however, can be distinguished from that of the radical right and reactionary movements.

Reactionary Movements Call for a Homogeneous Society

The reactionary movements influenced by the doctrine of scientific racism subscribe to an ideology of domination, obedience, and homogeneity.[125] They regard leadership as the natural expression of individual superiority and glorify a strong, repressive, ethnically unified state as necessary to achieve their goals. They emphasize irreducible cultural differences, fear and loathing of strangers, and a wish to live among people of the same national group. Historically, when such ethnoracist movements gained control of the state, they coerced labor from the "others" (enslavement), forced the assimilation or expulsion of "foreigners" (ethnic cleansing), and exterminated "inferior races" (genocide). These horrific actions are taken in hopes of creating a society composed of only one, superior race.[126] Although less common in the United States than elsewhere in the world, groups such as the White Aryan Resistance, the Ku Klux Klan, neo-Nazi skinheads, and right-wing survivalists have gained a foothold at certain troubled points in our history.

Radical Movements Call for Transformative Change

Radical movements on the left seek fundamental social change. These social movements—including the Old Left, New Left, and some parts of the black, women's, and gay rights movements—stand on a platform that calls for the redistribution of wealth and power. They argue that the prevailing systems of inequality are untenable and call for a massive transformation of society. The radical movements regard liberalism as inextricably tied to capitalism and see liberal reforms as Band-aids rather than cures for the structural problems that impose harm on individuals and communities. Often organized as political parties, the radical movements criticize capitalism for using its inventiveness to put profits before people. They call for cooperation over competition, democratic decision making, and big rather than small social change.[127]

Instead of resisting or limiting change, radical movements encourage struggle over control of scarce resources as important and necessary engines of social change. Although the radical movements seek fundamental transformation, they often disagree with each other regarding the type of change needed and the strategies required to secure it. For example, social democratic and some socialist parties tend to support a gradual and peaceful evolution to the goal of a socialist society. In this evolutionary view, the socialist movement can achieve its egalitarian ends by slowly reforming capitalist institutions such as the welfare state, electoral processes, and the government itself. The market economy will gradually give way to a society organized on socialist principles by winning political democracy (universal suffrage), then creating social democracy (a welfare state that meets basic needs), and finally mandating economic democracy (public control over economic resources and the production process).

Other socialist and communist parties, mostly in Europe and Asia, have called for larger changes. They seek a sharp break with existing institutional arrangements and believe in more deliberate and overarching political struggle. The Russian Revolution (1917), the Chinese Revolution (1949), and the Cuban Revolution (1959) represent this kind of fundamental change.[128] These revolutionary movements and their political parties reject the possibility of reforming capitalism slowly from within. They argue that only class struggle, either peaceful or with the use of force if necessary, will transform society.

In addition to transforming society, some radical movements, especially liberation movements, aim to free people from certain beliefs and attitudes embedded in the dominant culture. Frequently but unwittingly accepted by subordinated people as true, these beliefs can stand in the way of securing freedom from oppression. As noted earlier, this includes blacks who have internalized white values and racist attitudes toward blacks, women who have accepted men's diagnoses and explanations of their situation, and homosexuals who have felt guilty because they are not straight. Liberation requires both raising consciousness to break the grip of these ideas and the decision to struggle with others, collectively, for social change.[129]

Social democratic and some socialist parties have long histories outside of the United States. During the years following World War II, Social Democrats became the democratically elected governing party in many Western European and Scandinavian nations, where they created a wide range of universal services, including health care, child care, family leave, stipends for university education, and other benefits available to individuals by virtue of their membership in that society. In most of these countries, parliamentary legislatures incorporate more than two political parties in the official legislature. Social Democratic, Socialist, and Communist Parties have also governed Canada,

Japan, Australia, and New Zealand as well as Cuba, China, Eastern European nations, the former Soviet Union, and many Latin American and East Asian countries.[130]

The United States is the only Western democracy that has never elected a social democratic, socialist, or communist political party representative to national office. Yet socialist and communist parties have been present on the political scene in the United States for a long time. Often calling for radical change while working within the system, they occasionally win seats in local elections. Their ranks tend to swell in more liberal periods and dwindle in more conservative times. One of the biggest, the U.S. Communist Party, played an important role in organizing industrial labor unions in the 1930s and in the early stages of the civil rights movement. But it never regained its strength after the "witch hunts" of the 1940s and early 1950s led by Senator Joe McCarthy delegitimized its work and decimated its ranks.[131]

During the 1960s, with the appearance of the New Left in both the United States and Europe, the traditional socialist and communist parties lost ground and became known as the Old Left. The New Left was not a single movement, organization, or centralized party. Instead, its organizations, such as the Students for a Democratic Society, consisted of national networks of loosely linked local chapters, collectives, and communities. The New Left movements—the student, civil rights, women's, environmental, and peace movements—challenged "the system" in new ways and on various fronts. Their shared critique of corporate and global capitalism called for greater equality, participatory democracy, anti-authoritarianism, peace, and social justice. It also drew on the Old Left traditions of radical democracy, populism, anarchism, and socialism. The networks of individuals, groups, and organizations supported local neighborhood organizing, militant protests, and mass demonstrations in Washington, D.C. The New Left also included hippies, "youth" groups, and others who merged the personal and the political in ways that challenged traditional cultural values and lifestyles while calling for "power to the people." The New Left as such no longer exists. Nonetheless, in many ways it was the prototype of the new social movements discussed elsewhere in this chapter.

Most recently, transnational globalization and antiwar movements from below have erupted on the scene. These new social movements are animated by human rights, environmental concerns, hostility to patriarchy, the negative impact of global capitalism, the desire for peace, and a vision of the human community based on the unity of cultures and the end of poverty, oppression, humiliation, and collective violence.[132] Directed against the elite and corporate-led "globalization from above," this diversely constituted opposition exists across borders and regularly targets the state in various nations. The movements connect a wide range of issues, activists, alliances, networks, and groups that oppose fiscal austerity, structural adjustments, and rollbacks of health care, education, housing, transportation, and other public sector programs.[133]

Conveying Ideological Messages

Given that social movements want to recruit as many people as possible to their efforts at social change, they hope their message will "make sense" to the wider public. To garner supporters, accumulate resources, and legitimize their cause, social movements identify themes that tap into local values, beliefs, and folk wisdom.

Students of social movements refer to the messages created by the movements as collective action frames. Erving Goffman defines a collective action frame as an action-oriented set of beliefs and meanings linked to a specific movement or issue. Building on existing cultural narratives, a frame gives meaning to events by underscoring or embellishing the severity of a social problem, pointing to causes, and suggesting corrective actions. Like most ideological explanations, the frame offers "an interpretative schemata that simplifies and condenses the 'world out there.' "[134]

Frames vary with the nature of social change. Movements pursuing small changes and staying close to prevailing values use frames to bridge, amplify, or expand existing cultural themes. Movements seeking more extensive change develop frames to transform belief systems. By definition, these collective actions depart from prevailing meaning systems.[135] Frames range from specific messages tied to the platform of a particular group or set of problems to generic master frames that cut across several organizations and movements. In either case, the effort to resonate with prevailing cultural values raises some problems for a movement whose agenda is out of synch with those beliefs. Do they change their message, or try to change public opinion?

Specific Frames

The debates between conservative and liberal movements often take the form of competing specific collective action frames. In the early 1980s, for example, the New Right appropriated the term *family values* to win public backing for its "personal responsibility" agenda. This powerful evocation of a highly familiar cultural image—the two-parent family—fueled support for cutting social programs, especially those serving single mothers and homosexuals. Failing to come up with an equally effective alternative, liberal movements insisted that their agenda honored family values more effectively than did the conservative proposals. Meanwhile, the conservative movements successfully reframed the term *liberal* to mean support for excessive tax and spending policies. Placed on the defensive, President Clinton billed the Democratic Party as "the New Democrats" representing a centrist "third way" somewhere between the goals of the liberals and the conservatives. Most observers agree that with this shift the Democratic Party changed its ideological stance, moving from a more liberal to a more conservative agenda. Some people think this was a winning strategy; others feel betrayed. Likewise, right-wing movements whose extremist beliefs lie outside the mainstream try to make their message acceptable to a more mainstream public. White separatists, for example, attempt to obscure the stigma of white supremacy by talking about love, pride, and "heritage preservation."[136] In the late 1990s, South Carolina groups opposed to removing the confederate flag from the dome of the state capitol drew on the heritage theme.

Numerous other political debates reveal specific collective action frames. Conservatives have framed affirmative action policies as unfair preference on the basis of race, whereas liberals see them as compensation for past wrongs and protection against future discrimination. Liberals have explained the nuclear threat as due to runaway technology at the same time that radicals blame the defense industry and capitalist profit motive.[137] Cultural conservatives call for "ending welfare as we know it" by arguing that because women on welfare are lazy and unmotivated, they need a temporary cash assistance program that forces work and discourages welfare "dependency." Liberal advocates support the idea of work but argue that it is both unfair and impractical to require women to leave welfare for work without providing education, training, social services, and other supports so that they can have an equal chance to compete in a market economy. The more radical full-employment coalition points to the lack of jobs and argues that welfare reform serves business interests by pressing wages down and flooding the labor market with too many low-wage workers. The feminist movement insists that child-rearing and homemaking activities done by women in the home are work, should be valued, and deserve government support.

Master Frames

Social movements also employ master frames such as choice, rights, injustice, and return to democracy. Because more than one movement has successfully adopted these generic, overarching concepts, their framing efforts have often inspired others to follow suit.

Choice

The emphasis on freedom and choice is basic to conservative and some liberal movements. The movement calling for the use of school vouchers and the privatization of public education argues that its programs promote greater educational choice. Although the liberal pro-choice movement also uses choice as a master frame, it originally campaigned for reproductive rights based on the right of women to control their body. In the more conservative 1980s, in an effort to resonate with public sentiment, the movement dropped the harder-hitting demand of a woman's right to control her body and took up the more moderate call for pro-choice. This new frame pleased some supporters but disappointed others.

Rights

Historically, the labor movement used the rights frame, linking unions to the protection and expansion of workers' rights. Early in the 1960s, Martin Luther King Jr. and the major civil rights groups adopted the civil rights frame, which mirrored the core liberal values of equal rights and opportunities for all regardless of personal characteristics. The frame linked racial injustice to the

A Wisconsin pro-choice march. In the more conservative 1980s, women reframed the demand for the control over their bodies and turned it into an issue of "choice."

discriminatory practices of societal institutions and called for integration through nonviolent means.[138] Since the 1960s, the master frame of rights has driven numerous liberal struggles, including that of gays and lesbians, women, the disabled, Native Americans, and farm workers. Defining themselves as victims of discrimination, these groups claim that they deserve expanded rights and protections under the law.[139]

Injustice

Social movements often emerge in response to or coalesce around ideologically defined perceptions of social injustice, such as a glaring contradiction between a cultural ideal and conventional social practices. For example, the contrast between the nation's promise of equality for all and the denial of the vote to women in the 1800s gave impetus to the women's suffrage movement. The ideological commitment to democracy and intense racial discrimination faced by black soldiers returning from the battlefields of World

During the 1960s, Martin Luther King Jr. framed racial injustice as a violation of civil rights.

War II fueled the civil rights movement. The contrast between the egalitarian rhetoric of both the nation and the New Left and the prevailing sexism in both arenas gave rise to the second wave of feminism in the 1960s.

Some groups defined injustice more radically as the outcome of a system of domination and subordination. The Congress of Racial Equality and the Student Non-Violent Coordinating Committee shifted their goals from racial integration and equal rights to a struggle against white privilege. They called for Black Power; a greater redistribution of social, economic, and political resources; and, in some instances, for a separatist movement.[140] Radical and cultural feminists fighting male domination and female subordination emphasized female superiority and supported a separatist women's movement. Likewise, left political parties regularly call for a redistribution of power from the haves to the have-nots.

Return to Democracy

Various movements in the former Soviet Union and in Eastern Europe called for "a return to democracy," first advanced by the Solidarity movement in Poland, in their effort to move from a socialist to a market economy.[141]

Organizers and Ideological Agendas

Although most social movements try to develop messages that resonate with the dominant culture, a debate exists among movement organizers regarding the explicit use of an ideological agenda when organizing for social change. The current debate about the use of ideological visions when organizing surfaced among progressive movements during the conservative 1980s and 1990s.

One side opposes ideological organizing. Social movement activists and theorists Harry Boyte and Sara Evans, for example, have argued that progressive social change depends on tapping the inherent ideology rooted in the particular histories, traditions, and inherited values of locally based groups rather than introducing new ideological perceptions into existing worldviews.[142] In this view, the inherent ideas, beliefs, and traditions of the common people are intrinsically, if not immediately, democratic and progressive. Their values grow from their family ties, ethnic groups, religious communities, civic and workers' organizations, and mutual aid societies and reflect a vision of popular democracy based on these experiences.

At crucial moments, family gatherings, religious sites, and other places become what Evans and Boyte call "free social spaces" where people gather to talk things over and where ancient beliefs in inherited rights can be transmuted into collective action. Free from a controlling elite or authoritative institutions, these free social spaces become the seedbed for ideas that lead to resistance, organization, and finally fundamental action for change. As people become active in defense of their rights, traditions, and institutions, their definition of what they are doing shifts from a protest against threats to old ways to a struggle for a new conception of rights and responsibilities.

Acknowledging that free spaces have nurtured reactionary as well as progressive efforts, Boyte and Evans see this fact as the exception rather than the norm. Others argue that correctives are needed for progressive activism because subordinated groups, suffering clear and identifiable grievances, often think about their position and their grievances in terms established by those in power. The historian George Rudé explains that traditional belief systems of working people and local communities are essentially self-protective rather than inherently progressive or reactionary. Because people mobilize largely to preserve or defend what they have rather than to change the social order,[143] social movements need a larger, more articulated social vision to ensure that they develop a progressive character. Social movements may arise when a community's rights and liberties come under attack, but reactionary political forms too can readily emerge from unmediated reliance on free communal spaces.

The well-known work of community organizer Saul Alinsky provides an example of this dilemma. Working in Chicago during the 1930s and 1940s, Alinsky himself was strongly pro-labor and antifascist but favored nonideological organizing. He believed in emphasizing tactics and strategies over ideology and maintained that people who banded together in neighborhood organizations could develop the power to meet their needs. One of Alinsky's most successful projects, the Back of the Yards Neighborhood Council (BYNC), occurred in a white working-class, ethnically mixed neighborhood. From the late 1930s through the end of World War II, BYNC unified the community and won major victories for the neighborhood. Yet, sometime after Alinsky moved on to other projects, BYNC shifted its agenda from antifascist and pro–social service to antiblack. It acted to bar African Americans who migrated from Chicago's North Side slums from living in their neighborhood—something Alinksy, a one-time radical, would have deplored.[144]

Rudé offers a way out of this either/or situation by distinguishing between two kinds of ideologies: traditional or inherent ideologies, composed of the commonsense beliefs of most people, and structured or derived ideologies, representing a coherent, systematic critique of conditions.[145] When the rights and liberties of a subordinated group come under attack, traditional ideology can nurture political resistance and defense of community rights. But such uprisings cannot guarantee the emergence of a movement seeking fundamental change. The resistance has transformative potential only when the traditional ideology has become strongly suffused with the derived or external ideology—one borrowed from others that can override a community's desire to protect its inherited sense of rights and immediate traditions.

Without the interplay of traditional democratic commitments and a coherent oppositional ideology, the moments of community resistance may check an immediate assault on a group's rights. But if the movement does not challenge the rules of the game ideologically, the rules remain unchanged. Thus, Rudé concludes that social movements develop transformative potential only when the group's or community's basic beliefs (inherent ideology) become strongly suffused with an external ideology.

Like most interesting debates, no clear answers exist. History reveals both the reactionary outcomes of nonideologically organized local movements and the limitations of rigid organizing along ideological lines. In the end, progressive social movements face the challenge of both tapping into the democratic impulse of local communities and creating a movement that moves beyond the defense of personal interests to struggle for basic social change.

7

Social Welfare History in the United States

What is the meaning of U.S. social welfare history? Can a look back at events, even of some centuries ago, help us understand the social welfare policy of today? This chapter answers these questions. Ultimately, we will find that history helps us identify some persistent themes in U.S. social welfare. Though these themes first surfaced in the English heritage of colonial America, they still shape our thinking about many current social welfare policies.

Let's remember, too, that social welfare history, the fifth and final factor in our policy analysis, is also different from the other factors. To be sure, the first four ingredients in our analysis are clearly interdependent—politics, for example, has a part that is economic, a part that is ideological, and a part involving social movements. Yet history is distinctive because it is the only factor that so neatly "contains" the other four. Of course, historical research usually focuses on the economics, politics, ideologies, and social movements of the period under study; after all, discussions of these topics go far toward explaining what makes each historical period unique. As we progress through the seven major periods in U.S. social welfare history, we too will examine these factors. Our examination, however, will not only illuminate each period; it will also illustrate our model of policy analysis and show its relevance for us as skilled social workers.

The United States promises equality: "We hold these truths to be self-evident, that all men are created equal, that they are endowed by their Creator with certain inalienable rights, that among these are Life, Liberty, and the Pursuit of Happiness." We all know the famous passage from the Declaration of Independence. But ever since this first, ringing declaration, the issue of equal rights has been one of the most hotly disputed questions in American history. From voting rights to property rights, from the right to free speech to the right to receive some income, the dispute about the pursuit of equality has always boiled down to two basic issues: How do we define equality? and Who is entitled to what?

Because social welfare gives people access to goods and services they would not otherwise have, you probably already sense that it reduces inequality. It will therefore come as no surprise to learn that equality has often been an important issue in debates about social welfare. Yet, for workers, women, people of color, gays, and other oppressed minorities, the gap between the promise of equality and the realities of American life has often loomed quite large. Charged with some of the responsibility for reducing this gap, social welfare has inevitably been pulled into debates about exactly how much equality we should have.[1]

When political philosophers discuss equality, they often divide the concept of rights into the civil, the political, and the economic. Civil rights involve liberties like freedom of speech and equality before the law. Do we have equal civil rights? In theory, we all enjoy freedom of speech, except that in an age of giant media empires, some opinions can circulate only among a small group of friends through word-of-mouth, while large corporations trumpet other ideas to millions through radio, television, and the Internet. Likewise, though officially we are all equal before the law, the implementation of capital punishment shows significant discrepancies that continue to exist on the question of who gets punished, how severely, and for which crimes.[2]

The notion of equal political rights also needs careful scrutiny. Every citizen is supposed to enjoy the right to vote, yet the universality of voting rights has been controversial all through U.S. history. Property requirements delayed universal white male suffrage until the 1840s. Women could not vote until passage of the Nineteenth Amendment in 1920. To apportion representation in Congress, the Constitution counted each African American slave as three-fifths of a person; in the South, law and custom effectively disenfranchised African Americans until the Civil Rights Act of 1964. Even more recently, after the presidential election of 2000, a congressional study found that the votes of the poor and minorities were more than three times as likely to go uncounted as the votes of the more affluent.[3]

Although the promise of economic equality was never as explicit as those for civil and political rights, this issue, too, underlies much of U.S. history. On the one hand, there is the myth (according to the era) that we are all moderately prosperous farmers or that we are all middle class. On the other, at the end of the nineteenth century, there were populist movements that raged at huge disparities of wealth, at robber barons like John D. Rockefeller and the power of monopolies like his Standard Oil Company. Similarly, today, many commentators have noted the dramatic increase in the ratio between chief executive officers' pay and what the lowest-salaried workers in their companies get. In other words, although Americans like to believe we all belong to one class, they do know differences exist but protest them only when they become too obvious.

This discussion of rights demonstrates the unrealized promise of equality in the United States. Much of U.S. history, however, has involved struggles around our efforts to realize this promise. Though one rather limited tradition defines social welfare as primarily concerned with the poor, this view is based on a misconception. Everyone needs community, nurturance, and support, and the institutions that meet these needs are components of social welfare. Indeed, the broader struggle to realize the promise of equality has addressed issues such as the persistence of poverty, the regulation of the economy to diversify its benefits, and the exclusion of women, Native Americans, African Americans, Latinos, gays, and other stigmatized groups. These efforts have brought together Americans of many different classes around issues of political and economic equality, especially when people who consider themselves middle class have begun to feel poor.

Problems of poverty have certainly intertwined with these political and economic issues, but in the past, when we have succeeded in improving the situation of broad groups within the population, the situation of the economically poor has also improved. At the same time, middle-class people's situation has usually gotten better when poor people became less poor. In short, although the expansion of social welfare has never been able to eliminate the inequalities produced by the larger political and economic system, reformers have repeatedly turned to it as a tool of democratization.

Social welfare measures to combat inequality have expanded and now include a wide variety of other measures like tuition assistance, affirmative action, and job training. In the beginning, however, social welfare in the United States simply meant direct aid to the poor, and it drew on a British tradition several hundred years older than the United States as an independent nation. Once we understand this original tradition, much of U.S. social welfare history follows quite logically.

What the British Brought

By the mid-1600s, Britain had established five policy traditions. Brought to the colonies, they soon became fundamental to American social welfare.

The first tradition comes from Calvinism and understands the poor according to their character. John Calvin (1509–1564) and the tradition he founded focused on the individual and stressed work as a divine vocation. The dutiful and hardworking could save money and improve their station in life.[4] If you worked hard and prospered, you were destined to be rich, but if you were poor and suffered, it meant you were destined to be poor, and your poverty reflected your moral failings. Because Calvinists believed that generous almsgiving rewarded the poor for their idleness, stinginess became an integral part of the British tradition. Putting down especially deep roots in New England, Calvinism taught us to understand poverty by examining the character of poor people.

Localism was the second notable British tradition. After Henry VIII broke with the Pope and put himself at the head of the Church of England (1534), parishes acquired even greater importance as units both of civil and ecclesiastical authority. New laws consistently charged them with the responsibility of caring for the poor, and they tried to ensure that only their own poor, and not some from another parish, got their help. The North American colonists secularized this administrative tradition. Dropping its association with the church, they held to the notion that local government should be responsible for the poor. As the discussion about the politics of social welfare in chapter 4 showed, this administrative structure remains the preferred method of aiding the poor to the present day.

Closely linked to localism, the third British social welfare tradition seeks to control the mobility of the labor force. If workers can get relief only in their own parish, then they must accept whatever jobs and wages are offered there. Assistance might be meager and wages might decline, but workers had no choice, knowing that another parish would turn them away. Limiting mobility of labor therefore served two purposes: it kept taxes down and prevented workers from outflanking their employers by getting better-paying jobs in other communities.

The English Law of Settlement (1662) loosened these rules but still retained a provision authorizing local authorities to expel, within the first forty days, any family renting a property for less than 10 pounds a year.[5] In effect, this law empowered officials to make a judgment about the likelihood of a family's success given the local demand for labor. If a family was industrious and employers needed them, they could stay. But if there were no jobs or they were likely to become a burden on the parish, they could be sent back to their previous residence. The British brought this tradition to the colonies, where it became an integral feature of social welfare policy. Indeed, it was not until 1969 in *Shapiro v. Thompson* that the Supreme Court officially recognized the existence of a national labor force by rejecting time limits for residency and allowing welfare clients to move to and, if necessary, collect benefits in any state in the country.

The British reliance on institutions such as the poorhouse and the workhouse was the fourth tradition. It derived from the single most important piece of British social welfare legislation, the Elizabethan Poor Laws of 1601, which allowed local parishes to tax property owners in order to care for the poor and authorized local authorities to build "convenient houses of habitation." Although this policy was ostensibly national, the tradition of localism offered communities enough independence from the central government for some to continue their practice of *outdoor relief*, aiding the poor in their own homes. New York City followed along with its first almshouse in 1693.[6] In the United States, as in England, the threat of assignment to an almshouse would hang over the poor for at least the next two hundred years.

The fifth British social welfare tradition is what has subsequently become known as *less eligibility*. In this context, eligibility refers not to whether the client qualifies for a benefit according to established criteria. Rather, the word derives from "elect," meaning to choose, and signifies that the recipient of relief should have no incentive to elect to receive public benefits. In other words, a poor person is always supposed to have a lower standard of living than the lowest-paid laborer. Although the term comes from the British Poor Law Reform of 1834, the practice emerged when a market economy in the late Middle Ages (fourteenth and fifteenth centuries) replaced feudalism, established the practice of work for pay, and made it necessary to distinguish between the wage earner and the unemployed. Because many market economies enforce work discipline by making this distinction, American social welfare might have arrived at this policy on its very own. But it did not need to: the British brought it with them. Americans then seized it with such enthusiasm that it became the governing principle of our social welfare policy.

These five British principles form the basis for development of our own policy tradition. We turn now to what the first colonists and then other Americans did with this tradition over the next three hundred years.

Social Welfare in the Colonies (1619–1783)

Colonial America exhibited the British social welfare tradition in its least modified form, but America was not Britain. It did not possess either England's landed aristocracy or its feudal tradition, and it had land and resources the British lacked. To be sure, divisions between classes grew sharper during the colonial period. Some men prospered through trade, and others received huge grants of land, so the position of the wealthy in the colonies was relatively secure. Still, because America's was a more fluid society, their position here was never as secure as their English counterparts'.

Ruling over colonies of free men, indentured servants, and slaves, colonial governments enacted poor laws that closely followed the British tradition. At first, they relied on the church, constructed almshouses whenever poor people became too numerous to be boarded in other people's homes, and sought to prevent the impoverished from moving from one place to another. Parallels in British and colonial treatment of the poor lasted long after their different economic circumstances began to pull the two societies apart. Indeed, the pace of this separation quickened as it became clear that America, much more than England, was a land of many possibilities.

The Economy

The colonial economy was predominantly agricultural. In rural areas, people produced for their own use: they farmed, fished, and consumed the goods they crafted, making candles, sewing clothing, grinding flour. The 5 percent living in the emerging cities of the eastern seaboard had a few more options. Although there was plenty of production for use in Boston, New York, and Philadelphia, it was also more common to sell goods produced at home on the open market. Moreover, workers in these cities could find jobs on the docks, in mercantile trade (the famous triangle route, which traded raw materials like lumber and livestock for Caribbean sugar, African slaves, and British manufactured goods), and as skilled craftspeople. Yet even in these cities, the economy remained largely preindustrial, with few enterprises including more than a master and an apprentice using hand tools.[7] Most important, in contrast to the relative stability of rural areas, trade and wars could alter economic conditions in the cities enough to increase the number of impoverished people.

The South had a different economy. About 1 million slaves were imported to or born in the colonies before the American Revolution; in fact, by the time of the Revolution, they made up about one-fifth of the total colonial population and about half the population in many southern states. The South's economy rested on the plantation, where its dependence on slave labor created an economy in which the master oversaw the workforce and fewer people worked for pay. Without a large class of free laborers, poor, unattached workers were less of a problem. Unlike in the North, where almshouses arose to address the most difficult cases of poverty, the southern gentry were more likely to take personal responsibility for the poor or allow them to receive assistance in their own homes.[8]

The colonial economy, then, was vigorous and enterprising. The northern merchant class prospered, and free laborers earned wages 30 to 100 percent more than workers in Britain.[9] Life, however, was hard for indentured servants, and harder still for slaves: they lived to serve a master and could not receive assistance on their own. The only people who received assistance were by definition unattached: single white women with children, widows of sailors who never returned, the sick, and the aged. With the widespread presumption that work was always available, aid to healthy male workers was correspondingly rare.[10]

Politics

The governor headed the English administration of each colony. As the king's representative, he implemented policy directives from London and responded to local problems. In colonial America, the governors devoted much attention to negotiating with local assemblies. Officially, governors could cancel any law the assembly enacted and dismiss the assembly at will. But as only the assembly could raise taxes and budget spending, discretion demanded very selective use of these powers. In an arrangement anticipating our own system of checks and balances, colonial assemblies had their own sphere of authority, and no governor could force them to pass a law.

Colonial politics focused on three main issues: relations with Britain, relations with the western settlements of each colony, and local laws, including administration of the poor. Relations with Britain revolved around taxes and tariffs on trade, which inevitably broadened into the issue of colonies' economic independence. Did the colonies engage in trade to benefit themselves or the mother country? Were they merely another economic outpost in the far-flung British Empire? If so, they had to subordinate their own economic interests and pay heavy taxes. If so, it also made sense to prohibit competition with English manufacturers, demand export of agricultural products even at the risk of food shortages, and require that English ships transport all goods.[11] Or, on the contrary, were the American colonies their own economic center? If they were, then they should keep more of what they gained for themselves and use that wealth as the basis for genuine political independence.

A second cluster of policies involved relations with the western settlements. As people moved west, they began to demand roads and protection in their encounters with Native Americans. These demands conflicted with the priorities of settlers in the east, who were more concerned with Britain and issues of local administration, including the poor laws. At first, easterners resisted the demands of their fellow colonists to the west. They relented, however, as the number of westerners grew and the political pendulum swung toward them.

The third issue, local administration, focused on domestic affairs in the east: issues of crime, construction of roads and wharves, and, of course, the poor laws. It was here that the principle of local administration was expressed most fully. Following the English Law of Settlement, colonial communities devoted much effort to deterring any immigration by the poor. In a hierarchical society, provision for the poor in their midst was evidence of "good works" and rightful stewardship by the wealthy. Because the presence of strangers threatened to raise taxes and disrupt each community's sense of itself as an organic whole, the first rule of colonial poor law administration was to make poor people who did not already live there somebody else's responsibility. Typically, local officials warned the poor out, ordering them to go back to their own community. This principle was so widely accepted that after Boston enacted a new poor law in 1735, local authorities could send someone away without the intervention of any court.[12]

Ideology

In the public sphere, where men predominated, an emerging republicanism was the prevailing ideology of the colonial era. The term *republicanism* reflects an implicit belief that the individual has a fundamental sense of expanding political rights and economic possibilities. Republicanism underlies the ideology of men neither indentured nor slaves, who expect to benefit from their own hard work. Filled with energy and optimism, this ideology simply did not recognize any circumstance in which an able-bodied man could not support his family.

Colonial society also developed an ideology for and about women. Families were economically productive units, and all members were important participants in the necessary work. Men were in charge, and woman, children, servants, and slaves subordinate. Of course, the husband in this stereotype had to be of a certain class—at a minimum, a free laborer. Nevertheless, the ethic that arose from this particular kind of family served as a standard for the behavior and respectability of women from other classes. For white women, as for white men, those who failed to meet this standard were classified with women of color as the unworthy poor.[13]

An ideology about colonial society bound together men and women in their respective roles. Largely Calvinistic, this ideology affirmed a hierarchy whose parts all fit neatly together. Like most justifications of hierarchy, this ideology assumed that these arrangements were natural. From the successful merchant to the slave, all had well-ordered roles, tasks, and responsibilities. Slaves and indentured servants were to work for their masters, free laborers to apply themselves and improve their station in life without challenging the elite merchant class, and the elite merchant class to attend to the system's smooth functioning. On its own terms, the system worked well, but its success required stigma and punishment for those who stood outside it: religious dissenters, women who did not conform to the family ethic, and the unworthy poor.[14] By themselves, these groups were not powerful enough to confront the dominant ideology. Instead, that challenge fell to the expanding class of free laborers, whose resentment of the merchant elite fed many of the social movements in colonial society before the Revolution.

Social Movements

Most portrayals of colonial society focus on just one social movement: the fight against "taxation without representation" that led to the Revolutionary War and independence from the British Crown. This picture is misleading, implying a tranquility not really prevalent in the colonial era. In fact, rebellions and slave uprisings erupted frequently because the character of colonial society was constantly at issue.

Hostility to the wealthy merchant class drove most rebellions. In 1676, Nathaniel Bacon led a revolt in Virginia against the upper class that blended resentment at their privileges with anger at their failure to support western settlers against the Native Americans. When the governor imprisoned Bacon, two thousand Virginians marched on Jamestown to demand his release. It took a British military expedition with a thirty-gun ship cruising the York River to put the rebellion down. Likewise, for two years in New York City (1689–1690), Jacob Leisler led a movement that for the first time enabled ordinary working men—bakers, bricklayers, and carpenters—to hold office.

A Leisler-dominated Assembly raised taxes, prohibited monopolies, and ended trade regulations that had long favored the merchant elite. The merchants countered by persuading King William that Leisler represented a threat. After a British expeditionary force besieged the city's fort, a court hastily convicted Leisler of treason and sent him to the gallows at the eastern edge of what is now City Hall Park.[15]

Slavery rebellions were also frequent. Historians have counted some 250 rebellions or conspiracies of ten or more slaves. During the slave rebellion in Stono, South Carolina, in 1739, slaves stole guns and gunpowder from a warehouse, burned buildings, and killed those in their way until the militia suppressed them. In 1712, New York City experienced the first major slave revolt in the colonies; slaves set fire to a building and killed whites who intervened. When mysterious fires occurred in New York twenty-nine years later, memories of the earlier rebellion prompted accusations that the slaves were conspiring with poor whites. After forced confessions and trials, thirty-one slaves and four whites were executed.[16]

These social movements illustrate some of the contradictions of colonial society. The merchant elite wanted to duplicate the rigid class structure of England, but this vision did not sit well with the rest of the population. Although colonial poor laws were too deeply entrenched in the society to be an explicit target, these social movements did seek to remedy the conditions that created a need for the poor laws. But even this question of poverty became temporarily moot when much of the merchant elite combined with the mass of the population in a great social movement to demand independence from Britain.

History

Patterning their legislation on the Elizabethan Poor Laws, the colonies soon acknowledged a public responsibility for the poor. In 1642, the Plymouth colony became the first to adopt such provisions; Virginia in 1646, Connecticut in 1673, and Massachusetts in 1692 gradually followed. Originally, as New Amsterdam, New York channeled its assistance through voluntary contributions raised by officials of the Dutch Reformed Church. When the British took over in 1664, however, taxation became compulsory, and New York's poor laws fell in line with the rest of the English colonies.[17]

Colonial society offered three primary methods of poor relief. The first was *farming out*, whereby the poor went to live with other families in town. In some arrangements, the poor went from one family to another, spending several weeks in each home. In other circumstances, however, the assignments were more permanent: a poor family might live in someone else's home for as long as thirty years. Although towns usually supplied clothing and medical care and paid a fixed sum for each person, they also held auctions: bid the lowest amount, and responsibility for the family was yours. Naturally, with so little money coming in, it was only worthwhile if the caretakers limited what they provided or extracted a lot of work from their charges.[18]

"You know, the idea of taxation with representation doesn't appeal to me very much, either."

A second significant form of aid was *outdoor relief*, or relief in the family's own home. Once again, it is important to emphasize that this form of assistance was only for town residents and not strangers. Otherwise, the principle of providing relief within the home fit neatly with the colonial conception of families as the society's core institution. Most often offered to sick, disabled, or old whites who conformed to definitions of the deserving poor, outdoor relief included food, clothing, firewood, medical care, and sometimes a small weekly cash payment. In 1747, for example, the Newport, Rhode Island, Town Council supplied two cords of wood to each of four widows; in 1754, Charleston, South Carolina, paid a midwife to care for the wives of two absent soldiers. Although public officials authorized this assistance, religious institutions and mutual benefit societies gradually arose to supplement their efforts. Founded in New York in 1754, the Scots Charitable Aid Society was one of the first: it provided outdoor relief while employing poor Scottish women in the spinning trades. But regardless of whether aid came from a public authority or a private voluntary institution, outdoor relief enabled the deserving poor to uphold the family ethic by continuing to live in their own homes.

For those who did not follow the family ethic, *indoor relief* was the preferred form of assistance. Indoor relief required recipients to enter a workhouse or almshouse. Established in some eastern cities during the late seventeenth and early eighteenth centuries, these institutions mixed efficiency and deterrence. Officials calculated that it might be more efficient to centralize aid for a growing number of poor people in one institution, but they also thought putting less-deserving poor people in an institution deterred others from deviating from the family ethic. If these early almshouses did not treat the poor as harshly as during the rapid industrialization of the mid-nineteenth century, the rise of indoor relief did nonetheless sharpen the distinctions between the worthy and unworthy poor.[19]

Throughout the colonial era, the cost of poor relief spiraled upward. In Boston, it rose from 500 pounds per year in 1700 to 2,000 pounds in 1715 and 10,000 pounds by 1753. Expenditures climbed similarly in New York. Historian Gary Nash estimates that in Philadelphia by 1772, poverty trapped one-quarter of the free men in the city. All told, in the North and South alike, municipalities devoted between 10 and 35 percent of their budgets to the poor. As the city's largest single outlay, expenditures on the poor "eroded the allegiance of many urban dwellers to the British mercantile system and also to their own internal social systems." In this respect, the spread of poverty contributed significantly to the American Revolution.[20]

Independence to the End of the Civil War (1783–1865)

The eighty-year period from the end of the Revolutionary War to the conclusion of the Civil War is when the United States established a national political identity and a national culture. As the country began to industrialize, production shifted from inside to outside the home, from production for domestic use and some outside sales to production in factories of modest size. In the colonial era, slavery and indentured servitude made the free laborer a rising but still noteworthy phenomenon. By the mid-nineteenth century, in the North at least, the free laborer had become the predominant type of worker. This change not only led to the first signs of a trade union movement but also spurred a national debate about slavery in the South, where a plantation economy had little need for the free laborer. One nation could not contain two such different economies, and as the clash between them intensified, the nation hurtled toward a bitter civil war.

Perhaps nothing is more indicative of this period's rapid change and tumult than the sudden turn toward institutions as a method of managing dependent people. In addition to a growing reliance on workhouses as a deterrent to the idle poor, the states also constructed the first asylums for the mentally ill, who previously had been ridiculed, isolated, and locked in cellars. As David Rothman argues in *The Discovery of the Asylum*, these early psychiatric hospitals constituted an important social reform that arose out of a very particular notion about the causes of insanity.[21]

At the same time as Americans celebrated the new republic's energy, they also mourned an older, more stable social order. Attributing the instability of mental patients to the instability newly evident in the larger society, they tried to restore the old order with asylums in rural areas and rigid schedules for every detail of the patient's day. This initiative certainly revealed anxieties about change that Americans were experiencing. Nevertheless, the institutional approach was doomed, because isolation in asylums can no more cure mental illness than workhouses can cure poverty. Still, the interest in reform and the presumption that these new institutions could be a significant part of that reform effort are suggestive of the desire to control this period's new economic and political forces.

The Economy

The years from 1783 to 1865, from the end of the Revolutionary War to the end of the Civil War, is the period when the Industrial Revolution came to America. In quick succession, inventions like the spinning jenny, the water frame, and the power loom enabled water power to make cotton from cloth in large factories. These inventions brought about the Industrial Revolution and an accompanying leap in production: the number of cotton bales soared from 6,000 in 1794 to 3,841,000 in 1860. Soon after came a still more fundamental change, the fabrication of products with interchangeable parts, which formed the basis for mass production. Railroads (from none in 1790 to 3,300 miles of track by 1840) and new canal construction (100 miles in 1816 to 3,300 miles in 1840) drove down the cost of transporting and distributing these goods.[22] The economy did not yet exhibit the monopolies that would come to dominate it later, in the nineteenth century. But even in this small business competitive capitalism, an observer could discern the first outlines of a truly national economy.

The social relations of work changed profoundly with this expansion of economic activity. Once, labor for wages was comparatively rare: assessment rolls designated just 6 percent of New York City workers as laborers in 1750; one hundred years later the proportion had climbed to 27 percent. By that time, most trades had ten or eleven workers for every proprietor, and the largest, the Novelty Iron Works at Twelfth Street and the East River, employed as many as twelve hundred. With labor for wages more common, jobs lost the unique qualities of a craft, and workers became as interchangeable as the parts they assembled. In both Philadelphia and New York, this loss of power led to the formation of trade unions. Resisted by employers in the printing and construction trades, these unions collapsed in the financial panic of 1837.[23]

With industrialization and the spread of wage labor, social welfare policy changed, too. In New York, Secretary of State John Yates's 1824 report on the poor laws proposed a system of almshouses that would effectively outlaw relief in people's own homes. In Massachusetts, Secretary of State Josiah Quincy had already reached the same conclusion three years earlier. Although neither New York nor Massachusetts completely abolished poor relief, Philadelphia did from 1827 to 1839, and further west, so did Chicago, from 1848 to 1858.[24] As a means of forcing workers to accept the prevailing wage, the insistence of the British Poor Law Reform of 1834 on indoor relief is probably better known. These laws therefore indicate exactly how much industrialization had spread in the United States, because even before the British reform, the practice of denying relief to workers in their own homes was well established in this country.

Politics

At first quietly, and then with rising clamor, the issue of slavery dominated U.S. political life in this period. Slavery affected everything it touched. It affected trade because northern banks offered credit for southern cotton picked by slaves and shipped to England in exchange for British manufactured goods. It affected the frontier, where new states formed as their settler populations increased. Despite several attempts to strike a balance—such as the Compromise of 1850, which passed a strict Fugitive Slave Law while admitting California as a free state—the single most important question about every new state was always whether it would be slave or free. And it brought on the Civil War, when the South finally seceded because the North's distaste for slavery had culminated in the election of Abraham Lincoln as our sixteenth president.

The debate about slavery was twofold. It was the great moral issue of the era and a conflict about what kind of labor system the country would have. Would it be one where employers owned their workers, or one in which workers were ostensibly free because their employers paid them a wage? Employers in the South and the North profited from different kinds of enterprises, so they answered this question differently. Production of cotton demanded plantations and a large, permanent workforce to labor year-round. Textile factories in the North needed less land, hired and fired in response to changing economic conditions, and took no responsibility for their workers when they did not actually pay them. When Northerners expressed outrage at the idea that one person could own another, Southerners condemned work for wages that used laborers when it was convenient and then dismissed them to fend for themselves. By contrast, as an apologist remarked, slavery is a "system of labor which exchanges subsistence for work. . . . slavery makes all work, and it insures homes, food, and clothing for all. It permits no idleness, and it provides for sickness, infancy, and old age. It allows no tramping or skulking, and it knows no pauperism."[25]

This debate had critical implications for social welfare. If the new states grew cotton and had slaves, then their economic system could not absorb the poor and the unemployed of the eastern cities. To Northerners of the employing classes, the frontier was supposed to function as a safety valve, defusing discontent and offering a chance at upward mobility.[26] The South did not have much of a public welfare system because the wealthy accepted responsibility for taking care of poor white people. Were slavery allowed in the new states, poor white people in the east would have nowhere to go, and pressure for substantial social reforms would intensify. As the great political issue of the era, then, slavery was closely linked to social welfare.

Ideology

Two related ideologies, one for men and another for women, gathered increasing strength during these years. The first is the ideology reflected in the title of historian Eric Foner's book, *Free Soil, Free Labor, Free Men: The Ideology of the Republican Party before the Civil War*. Drawing on the expanding pool of free laborers, this ideology combined commitment to work for wages, upward mobility, abolitionism, devotion to the Union, and a desire to export the wage system to each new state. In this conception, workers are workers only temporarily. Because they too are on their way to becoming small business owners, they are not a separate class whose interests conflict with their employers. Indeed, by the time the Republican Party was founded in 1856, becoming a small business owner was thought to be the destiny of all free white men.[27]

The industrial family ethic was the logical counterpart to this ideology. Splitting the world of work from the home, this ethic assigned work to men and domesticity to women:

> It was a virtual prerequisite for middle-class (and for upperten [the top tenth of the population] status) that the male breadwinner spare his wife from work outside the household. She was instead installed as priestess of the home, where her task was to provide a serenely pastoral sanctuary from the urban jungle. In theory, this was achieved by effortless emanations of her character; in fact, it took a tremendous amount of hard work.[28]

By nature, women were supposed to be weaker, more delicate, and more vulnerable. Often accompanied by an overdose of sentimentality, this characterization inflated women's dependence on men and perpetuated their consignment to a lesser sphere. At a time when ever larger numbers of men had to work for somebody else, the dependence of women exalted the importance of their work: with their whole family relying on them, they had to earn a "family wage." Or, as the *New York Post* put it in 1829, "The only way to make husbands sober and industrious was to keep women dependent upon them."[29]

These ideologies are critically important as much for what they include as for what they exclude. The roles break down by gender, but the division mostly occurs between men and women of the middle and upper classes, whose conduct became an ideal and a norm. The very strength of the ideal suggests the stigmatization that might befall men and women of the lower classes who could not conform to these roles. A man would be stigmatized either for his lack of work or, if he did work, for earning too little to support his family. And by definition, the cutthroat world of commerce soiled any women who worked there. Between prescriptions for the correct roles of men and of women, the dominant ideology in this period severely disdained the poor of either gender.

Social Movements

The most significant social movements of this era speak to the issues of race, gender, and class. At the same time that abolitionists like William Lloyd Garrison, Frederick Douglass, and Sojourner Truth addressed the issue of race by trying to eradicate slavery, western expansion depended on the subjugation of Native Americans and the belief that their land rightfully belonged to white men. Meeting at Seneca Falls during the summer of 1848, the New York Women's Rights Convention led by Susan B. Anthony and Elizabeth Cady Stanton put the demand for women's suffrage on the public agenda for the very first time. In the cities, upper-class social reformers, frightened by the trade union movement and the widening chasm between rich and poor, initiated new social welfare organizations like the Association to Improve the Condition of the Poor, founded in New York by some of its wealthiest merchants in 1843.

These movements all contested the notion that only white men of a certain class are full-fledged citizens who can participate in public life and earn a decent living from their labor. In 1858, during the first of his great debates about slavery with Abraham Lincoln, Stephen Douglas offered an unambiguous statement of this disputed idea: "I believe this government was made on a white basis. I believe it was made by white men, for the benefit of white men and their posterity for ever, and I am in favor of confining citizenship to white men, men of European birth and descent, instead of conferring it upon Negroes, Indians, and other inferior races."[30]

Douglas's need to make this statement is an indication that on many fronts, a previously unquestioned assumption was now under serious attack. Although few doubted white men's right to take land from Native Americans, the abolitionist cause had gradually gained strength. Starting in the 1830s with a few outspoken people like Garrison, Douglass, and the sisters Sarah and Angelina Grimké who believed in immediate emancipation of slaves, this social movement led a growing number of Americans to doubt the morality of slavery. Although many, to be sure, just wanted slavery not to spread any further, it proved difficult to contain the idea that one person should not own another. Eventually, these misgivings placed the North in firm opposition to the South and brought on the Civil War.[31]

The mid-nineteenth-century women's movement stirred similar doubts about the issue of gender. Why couldn't married women own property, control bank deposits in their name, divorce, or have custody of their children? Why couldn't they enter the professions of law and medicine? And, above all, why couldn't they vote? With men contending that women's tasks outside the home violated the natural division of roles, positive answers to these questions were slow in coming: they delayed women's suffrage until passage of the Nineteenth Amendment in 1920. Yet, merely by raising them, the women's movement steadily undermined the presumption that only men could be full economic and political citizens.

Besieged on issues of race and gender, white men of the "right" classes sought ever more aggressively to manage the poor. The growing reliance on workhouses and almshouses was actually just part of a broader social movement for temperance, religious revival, and newer forms of social welfare organizations. Frightened by the effects of a rapidly industrializing society, especially by evidence of the mounting social disorder in the cities, the middle and upper classes launched campaigns in the 1820s to ban alcohol and sell biblical tracts. Assuming that the presence of alcohol and the absence of religion spread social disorder, they initially insisted that only moral behavior would eliminate poverty.[32]

When these efforts failed, some upper-class reformers established new social welfare organizations. Perhaps the leading example of this development is New York's Association to Improve the Condition of the Poor (1843). In the aftermath of the depression of 1837 and the hard winter of 1842–1843, leading New Yorkers decided that social conditions demanded more aggressive outreach. Visiting poor people in their own homes, Association staff were the first social welfare visitors to classify the poor according to their dutifulness and industry. The sober and appreciative got "sympathizing counsel which rekindles hope" and perhaps a little aid; alcoholics got only disapproval. Over time, however, the Association did soften its insistence that only personal defects cause poverty. Out of this newer understanding of the poor came its sponsorship of a pure milk law as well as construction of New York City's first model tenement (1855).[33] But, as with its response to both abolition and the nineteenth-century women's movement, the elites' initiatives could modify but not halt the impact of sweeping social movements.

History

In our discussion of economics, politics, ideology, and social movements, we have already touched on many of this period's most significant milestones in social welfare history. Most of these events were on the state level and involved whites who were at least eligible for aid. But there were also African American communities, largely ineligible for aid, as well as a federal government that throughout this era disclaimed it had any responsibility for social welfare.

At the beginning of the Civil War in 1861, there were approximately five hundred thousand free blacks in the United States. Most white charities excluded them. African Americans instead drew on a long tradition going back to Africa and the cooperative practices of family and tribe. Following the model of the African Methodist Church (1787), organizations like the Black Masons, the Negro Oddfellows, and the African Female Union established benevolent mutual aid societies to supply medical, educational, and burial services. As a community under siege, it was not wealthy, but what individuals had, they usually shared.[34]

Restrictions on the federal government contributed to the need for communities to help their own. In a key statement of nineteenth-century social policy, President Franklin Pierce vetoed a bill pushed through both houses of Congress in 1854 by Dorothea Dix that would have provided 10 million acres of public lands for construction of mental asylums. Horrified at the treatment of the mentally ill (existing facilities could shelter just one-twelfth of the population), Dix had already helped to establish mental hospitals in nine states. But some sixty thousand miles of traveling throughout the United States convinced her that the problem demanded federal intervention. The federal government often distributed land to land speculators: why shouldn't it distribute land for social welfare? Although it took six years of determined advocacy to persuade Congress, President Pierce rejected the legislation on the grounds that it would establish a precedent for other kinds of federal responsibility. Social welfare henceforth remained a state responsibility until the Depression of the 1930s and the advent of the New Deal.[35]

The End of the Civil War to the Progressive Era (1865–1900)

The Civil War decided the issue of slavery. Thereafter, the northern rather than the southern labor system would prevail, and the economy of the United States would rest on labor for wages. This determination settled one crucial debate about the economy, but left many aspects of the social welfare system unresolved. Work for pay did permit some people to improve their standard of living. Still, without adequate provisions for social welfare, a system of paid labor that did not enable some people to support themselves could well resemble the southern apologists' frightening portrait of an uncaring "wage slavery."

The Economy

Between 1865 and 1900, the basis of the U.S. economy shifted from small to large businesses. Large businesses had been rare, but now a new institution, the corporation, sold shares in the enterprise and could, when it successfully outmaneuvered its competitors, come to dominate an industry. Soon, near monopolies existed in many major industries: oil (Standard Oil, led by John D. Rockefeller), steel (Andrew Carnegie, Ford Frick, and the company that would eventually become U.S. Steel), railroads (the New York Central, led by Cornelius Vanderbilt and later J. P. Morgan, who controlled the rails in the Northeast), sugar (the Sugar Trust and Henry Havemeyer), and communications (Western Union for the telegraph, the American Telephone and Telegraph Company for the telephone).

Great economic competition had produced some victors, and these, in turn, propelled the economy to new heights of wealth and productivity. From 1860 to 1900, for example, investment in manufacturing plants rose from

$1 billion to $12 billion. The value of their products surged from under $2 billion to over $11 billion, and the number of industrial workers more than quadrupled, from 1.3 to 5.5 million. It was an astonishing transformation. As historians Charles Beard and Mary Beard wrote, "Twenty-five years after the death of Lincoln, America had become in the quantity and value of her products, the first manufacturing nation in the world. What England had once accomplished in a hundred years, the United States had accomplished in half the time."[36]

This was the age of laissez-faire, of robber barons and a largely unregulated capitalism. As a result, it was also a period of boom and bust. Frenetic investments in the new industries created booms. The busts typically came when profits did not flow and Wall Street's leading financial titans could not scramble successfully to cover their losses. In 1873, the first of these long pauses in the rapid pace of economic expansion occurred when bankers on Wall Street refused to loan additional money to Jay Cooke and Company's Philadelphia investment house. Cooke had tried to peddle shares in his Northern Pacific Railway by hiring public relations experts who touted the railroad's right of way through the desolate Dakota and Minnesota territories as a "vast wilderness waiting like a rich heiress to be appropriated and enjoyed." When Cooke's investment house failed, it set off the Panic of 1873. Banks closed, half of all American railroads defaulted on their bonds, and the total number of bankruptcies rocketed from 51 in 1873 to 10,478 five years later. Within a year, 3 million people were unemployed.[37]

Other panics, perhaps somewhat less severe, followed in 1884 and 1893, extending the era's economic instability for much of its last thirty years. This economic uncertainty intensified because wage tightening was one of business's primary responses to competitive pressures. Perhaps the most dramatic illustration of this response occurred in the midst of the 1877 depression, when the Baltimore and Ohio Railroad cut wages 10 percent at a time when brakemen earned just $1.75 a day. Railroad workers struck throughout the Northeast and Midwest. In Martinsburg, West Virginia, strikers and their sympathizers clashed with militia and federal troops, then spread to Baltimore, Pittsburgh, and Harrisburg, where the fighting peaked in some of the nineteenth century's bloodiest labor strife. By the time the great railroad strike of 1877 had failed, one hundred thousand people had refused to work, one hundred people were dead, and one thousand had been jailed.[38]

For social welfare, the consequences were consistent with the historic pattern. As the boom-and-bust cycle spun out of control, political and economic elites leaned hard on what they thought they could manage—not only labor, but once again, any evidence of too generous social assistance. They tried to align a decline in welfare with the decline in wages through another fierce attack on outdoor relief, which was completely successful for a time in Brooklyn and partly successful in many other towns and cities.[39] Cheap labor and even cheaper welfare: together, these two campaigns were the two pillars of the rising corporate order in the post–Civil War economy.

The Republican Party dominated politics for most of this period. As the party of Lincoln, the martyred president who had saved the Union, Republicans consistently denounced the Democrats as the party of the South and its defeated institution of slavery. For a brief period during the era of Reconstruction, federal troops were stationed in the South and Republicans even supported the vote for African Americans. Voting in large numbers, Republicans elected blacks to southern state legislatures, two U.S. Senators (Hiram Revels and Blanche Bruce, both from Mississippi), and twenty congressmen. The same Republican coalition enacted the Thirteenth, Fourteenth, and Fifteenth Amendments to the Constitution, outlawing slavery, guaranteeing citizenship for everyone "born or naturalized in the United States," and extending the vote to all male citizens.[40] In social welfare, it initiated the Freedmen's Bureau, which, from 1865 to 1872, distributed food and shelter, opened four thousand schools for both black and white children, and offered land (at a minimal cost) to a predominantly African American population.[41]

The 1876 presidential race between Samuel Tilden, the Democratic governor of New York, and Rutherford Hayes, the Republican governor of Ohio, ended this cycle of reform. Tilden won the popular vote by 250,000 and seemed to have emerged victorious in the electoral vote, 203 to 165. But then Republicans noticed that if enough votes shifted in Louisiana, Florida, and South Carolina—the three southern states they still controlled—Hayes could slip by with a one-vote lead in the electoral college, 185 to 184. The Republicans disallowed enough ballots in these three states, a specially appointed commission voted eight to seven along purely partisan lines, and in the Compromise of 1877, Hayes became president. Concerned about the need for federal troops to combat growing labor militancy in the North and persuaded that the South would not actually reenslave African Americans, Republicans agreed to this compromise because they felt it was time for men of property in both regions to reach an understanding. By withdrawing its troops from the South, the North could deal effectively with rebellious workers and the South could regain political and economic control over the freed slaves.[42]

In addition to hostility from the executive branch, reformers also confronted the conservativism of the courts. Because the U.S. government of the late nineteenth century had not yet developed much of a bureaucracy, many scholars describe the government in this period as "court-dominated." The power of courts came both from the ideology of judges and the courts' position in the government. This position allowed them to declare unconstitutional reforms that state legislatures had passed and state governors had signed. Relying on anticonspiracy doctrine and the presumption of equal power in any contractual relationship between workers and owners, they repeatedly struck down most labor legislation. In the typical case of *In re Jacobs* (1885), New York's highest court overturned the new union-sponsored law that prohibited the manufacture of cigars in tenement buildings.[43] Nor were the courts any better on racial issues: it was, after all, the Supreme Court that established in *Plessy v. Ferguson* (1896) the doctrine of "separate but equal" that would persist into the second half of the twentieth century. Thus, in every branch of government and at both the federal and state levels, the politics of this period hindered social reforms.

Ideology

The post–Civil War era needed an ideology to justify competition, declare the winners of the competition to have triumphed by right, and oppose any interference in economic and social affairs. It found just such an ideology in Social Darwinism.

Charles Darwin published *The Origin of Species* in 1859; it proclaimed that "survival of the fittest" governed the animal kingdom. In the late 1860s, British social philosopher Herbert Spencer applied this concept to human societies. Popularized in the United States by William Graham Sumner, Social Darwinism assumed that competition was natural and that the principle of survival of the fittest had the status of a scientific law. If, like the animal kingdom, society had laws that governed its functioning, then social reforms constituted a foolish attempt to meddle with the natural order. Social Darwinists believed that those who objected to the power of monopolists like Rockefeller and Carnegie had simply refused to recognize the scientific fact that survival of the *unfittest* was the only possible alternative to survival of the fittest.

Social Darwinists feared this prospect: they thought that survival of the unfittest would threaten the social order if weak-minded reformers coddled the poor with charity and enacted social legislation to soften the hard edge of economic competition. Throughout the late nineteenth century, whenever, in their judgment, reformers acted foolishly, Social Darwinists fought to prevent them from tampering with natural law as they imagined it.[44]

Social Movements

The labor militancy of the late nineteenth century flourished in the cities of the Northeast and Midwest. But labor was hardly the only social movement. In the South, the rise of the Ku Klux Klan helped to reestablish the dominance of a white political conservative elite that curbed both federal and state social reforms until the 1960s. In the Midwest, angry farmers organized a Populist movement that challenged mainstream politics. Although it never won its demands for nationalization of railways or plentiful silver coinage, its fights for an eight-hour day, direct elections of senators, and a graduated income tax influenced Progressives well into the twentieth century.

The Ku Klux Klan rose in the aftermath of the Civil War. Through raids, lynchings, and burnings, it terrorized blacks in the South. In Kentucky alone between 1867 and 1871, the National Archives records 116 acts of violence: "Sam Davis hung by a mob in Harrodsburg, May 28, 1868 . . . Negro killed by Ku Klux Klan in Hay County January 14, 1871." As the violent arm of

TWO MEMBERS OF THE KU-KLUX KLAN IN THEIR DISGUISES.

After the Civil War, the Ku Klux Klan enforced racial oppression in the South.

the white oligarchy, the KKK worked to ensure that African Americans returned to the bottom rung of southern society, segregated in every aspect of their lives and, after 1900, barred by statute from voting in every southern state.[45] Their suppression gave a free hand to the white planter class. Using race to divide poor whites from poor blacks, they retained control over state governments and through seniority rose rapidly in the congressional leadership. From the latter position, they anchored a powerful conservative bloc that doomed universal social legislation, most particularly by excluding African Americans from any source of income independent of their jobs as field hands and domestics.

Populism goes back to the industrial economy's effects on the farmer. Caught between falling prices for farm products and monopolies that set the prices of seed, fertilizer, railroads, and interest rates, the Populists envisioned a federal income tax, public ownership of major industries like the telegraph and the railroad, and, in an effort to ally with industrial workers, an eight-hour day. In 1892 they offered a third-party platform; in 1896 Populist William Jennings Bryan ran as the Democratic candidate for president with his memorable speech "You shall not crucify mankind upon a cross of gold." They also campaigned for a policy of "easy money," a monetary policy based on both silver and gold that would expand the supply of money and make it easier to pay off loans. Although Populists made some gains in the South, they never succeeded in breaking southern racism's hold on the small white farmer. And when white urban workers rejected their appeal for a farmer-worker alliance, the Populist movement disintegrated in the face of a corporate constituency mobilized by Ohio industrialist Mark Hanna during Republican William McKinley's 1896 presidential campaign.[46]

History

The post–Civil War era marked the establishment of the first charity organization societies (COSs), the first settlement houses, and, just before the turn of the century, the beginnings of what we would recognize today as the first example of formal social work education. The COSs represented the conservative wing of the charity movement; the settlement house movement constituted the liberal wing. From the beginning, social work education tried to bring knowledge to bear that would bridge the gap between the two.

The charity organization society dates to London in 1869. The political and economic turmoil of the 1873 depression soon gave COSs considerable appeal in the United States. Once Buffalo founded the first American COS in 1877, the societies spread rapidly; by 1892, there were ninety-two such organizations in cities with a total population of 11 million people.

The COS claimed to represent a new approach to the poor: it relied on "friendly visitors" to investigate poor families and kept a single list of all names so that poor people could not get help from several different neighborhood sources. Nevertheless, its claim of scientific innovation could not really obscure the old social welfare ideology of individual responsibility, elimination of outdoor relief, and the repression of pauperism. Although some leaders of COS such as Josephine Shaw Lowell, the American author of the leading COS book, *Public Relief and Private Charity* (1884), broke with this perspective to advocate for trade unions and higher wages, the broad COS movement adhered to a belief that charity ruined the recipient.[47]

By contrast, the settlement house movement in the United States began in the late 1880s. Modeled after London's Toynbee Hall (1884), the movement offered a vehicle for some of the best-known female social reformers of the late nineteenth and early twentieth century, including Jane Addams at Hull House in Chicago and Lillian Wald at the Henry Street Settlement on New York's Lower East Side. Typically, settlement house workers used a building in an immigrant neighborhood to provide nursing, English instruction, and other social services to their poor neighbors. The movement departed from the mainstream social welfare tradition by stressing social and economic conditions without making the usual distinctions between the worthy and unworthy poor. Settlement house leaders believed that principles of rationality, objectivity, and democracy could be used to "combat reactionary politics, judicial bias, social injustice, intolerance of political difference, and antidemocratic impulses—features they associated with the social dislocations of the industrial era."[48]

One should not exaggerate the differences between the settlement house and the COS approaches. Both drew volunteers from the privileged classes who sought to reduce the gap between rich and poor. In addition, although some settlement house reformers saw the strength in poor people, others patronized them, moving into their neighborhoods in the hope of modeling what it meant to be an American. Yet the settlement house movement did gather facts about the poor, and it did use these facts to interpret the poor to other people. In this respect at least, it represents a significant change from prior social welfare organizations.

By the late 1890s, volunteers had accumulated some knowledge about assessing clients as well as about social conditions. This knowledge gave more experienced practitioners confidence that they had something to teach. So, in the summer of 1898, the New York Charity Organization Society offered the first course to volunteers. In 1904, this summer course turned into a yearlong program that eventually became the basis for the Columbia University School of Social Work. With organizations in other cities like Boston and Chicago establishing similar courses, the newly emerging profession of social work could now look back to the beginnings of formal social work education at the end of the nineteenth century.[49]

The Progressive Era to the New Deal (1900–1932)

Most accounts of the Progressive Era stress the importance of this period's reforms. The federal government passed antitrust legislation such as the 1902 Clayton Act, which barred interlocking directorates and prevented directors of corporations from fixing prices. It enacted a federal income tax (1913) based on the ability to pay. In social welfare, it organized the first White House Conference on Children (1909), established a Children's Bureau (1912) to advocate for the well-being of children, and even, for a brief period (1921–29), sponsored the Sheppard-Towner Act, which funded some medical care for mothers and infants. At the state level, legislators provided workers' compensation; for the first time, they also authorized mothers' pensions, which anticipated by twenty years the welfare provisions of the 1935 Social Security Act (Aid to Dependent Children). By the standards of the preceding era, all these initiatives were downright interventionist.

From another perspective, however, the broad pattern of these initiatives broke less dramatically with the past. Although reformers in the Progressive Era passed laws to eliminate the period's worst excesses, this legislation was emphatically *corporatist*. Preserving the fundamental political and economic hierarchies, corporatist social policy stabilizes the marketplace and leaves a smaller target for reformers. Instead of an economy dominated by monopolies like Rockefeller's Standard Oil, these policies used antitrust legislation to create oligopolies, where four or five large companies now ruled in the place of one. Social welfare reforms trace a similar pattern: workers' compensation limited the risk of an injured employee's winning a big judgment in court, and child welfare legislation made businesses less vulnerable to charges of exploitation and improved the health of future workers. Because these reforms demonstrated that interventions could have positive effects, it would be wrong to minimize their consequences. A closer look, however, belies the popular belief in the Progressive Era as a time that changed the economic structure.[50]

If the Progressive Era was not a period of structural change, this failing at least partly derives from the "middle-class" outlook that gave it its distinctive character. The new corporate economy swept through the United States, transforming the class structure of small towns, where a majority still lived, particularly those whose ancestry reached some generations back. A traditional middle class of small farmers, independent businessmen, and self-employed professionals had long thrived in these communities. Nudging these people aside, the new economy created an educated and salaried stratum of teachers, doctors, journalists, engineers, managers, and administrators. Caught between the demands of workers and the disruptions brought about by this new corporate economy, the "professional managerial classes," including many women with no other outlet for their talents, tried to carve out a place for themselves. Luckily, for the first time, it was possible to open up such a place, one fostered by the need that concentration and centralization had created for long-term economic and social planning. Mediating between business and workers, the professional managerial classes secured their own position. In the process, they also introduced the long list of moderate reforms that historians have since called progressivism.[51]

The Economy

"This," said President Theodore Roosevelt in 1905, "is an age of combination [trusts], and any effort to prevent combination will not only be useless, but in the end vicious, because of the contempt for law which the failure to enforce law inevitably produces. . . . [Hence, we need] not sweeping prohibition of every arrangement good or bad, which may tend to restrict competition, but such adequate supervision and regulation as will prevent any restriction of competition from being to the detriment of the public."[52] This quotation illustrates perfectly the Progressives' attitude toward reform of the economy. Trapped between public opinion and their belief that tight regulations would damage industry, Progressives enacted just enough reform to forestall harsher measures. In short, both the economy and public opinion were the targets of this legislation.

The breakup of the Standard Oil monopoly in 1911 typifies this pattern. The Supreme Court dissolved the company into thirty-four distinct concerns, including Standard Oil of California, of Ohio, and of New Jersey. Although the decision aimed to curb their power in the marketplace, the companies soon extended their production and marketing activities beyond their original territories. To avoid the label "Standard Oil," they gave themselves new names, such as Mobil (for Standard Oil of New York) and Chevron (for Standard Oil of California).[53] Nearly a century later, these companies again dominate the energy market, and though antitrust policy certainly slowed the process, it would be difficult to contend that it significantly diminished their power.

This is the economic environment of social welfare policy during the Progressive Era. Indignant about the economy's worst features, reformers enacted the first controls on what business could do. Included in these controls was a new appreciation for social welfare. They understood that as long as it went unregulated, the economy would pass from crisis to crisis, devouring human resources and antagonizing ever larger segments of the population. Antitrust legislation, a federal income tax, workers' compensation, and mothers' pensions—these reforms were all worthwhile if some reform could secure peace.

Politics

Much of the politics of the Progressive Era focused on corruption. In the abstract, of course, everyone opposes corruption, but when social reformers in this era raised this issue, they also had another, plainly self-interested motive. To reformers, corruption often meant control of city or state politics by an ethnically based political machine. Typically immigrant and Democratic, this machine delivered votes, jobs, and payoffs in cities like Boston, New York, and Chicago, which it used to gain considerable power in state politics. Frightened by the prospect of a political machine with a working-class base, reformers either demanded that neutral, technically competent city managers run the city government, or they launched mayoral campaigns under the "good government" banner. In both cases, they had dual goals: end corruption and end the domination of city politics by immigrants who wanted more from government than urban elites thought government should give.

The issue of corruption proved especially crucial in slowing social welfare reform. Although the most far-seeing reformers of the Progressive Era, like Isaac Rubinow, director of the American Association for Labor Legislation, wanted to enact some form of national social security legislation, the experience of Civil War pensions created a major obstacle. As Harvard sociologist Theda Skocpol explains in *Protecting Soldiers and Mothers*, pensions for Civil War veterans started out as a small program. Then it grew rapidly. By 1893, the federal government was devoting 41 percent of its revenue to such pensions; by 1910, 28 percent of all elderly men and 8 percent of all elderly women received them. Although there were laws governing eligibility, getting a pension often depended on a veteran's connections with a politician or an influential lawyer. With opponents criticizing the pensions as a corrupt national patronage scheme, they could not serve as the model for a well-designed social security system.[54]

The issue of corruption, then, delayed social reform in the Progressive Era. But this was also the first time that the structure of state government served to hamper social reform. As companies became larger, the political decentralization of the U.S. government heightened the power of businesspeople, who claimed that too much social legislation in any single state would put that state at a competitive disadvantage. This contention was particularly persuasive in the industrialized Midwest and Northeast. There, governors who otherwise might have wanted to test new social policies by turning their states into "laboratories of experimentation" found that other, less generous states could easily underbid them.[55] At first nationally, and now on a global scale, social reformers have struggled with this issue ever since.

Ideology

The ideology of progressivism combined moralism and empirical analysis (analysis based on observation) in equal measure. Determined to resurrect the role of the individual at a time when the individual was increasingly dwarfed by larger political and economic forces, progressive ideology brought a fierce indignation to bear on behalf of a world that was already lost. In Jacob Riis's photographs of the New York's Lower East Side tenements and in muckraking exposés like Ida Tarbell's on U.S. Steel and Upton Sinclair's on the Chicago stockyards, reformers could give full expression to their distaste for the conditions under which great fortunes were made. For the most part, though, when the indignation they stirred up gave rise to actual legislation, the changes it brought about were restrained.

Moralistic feelings also influenced social welfare reform. As historian Linda Gordon stresses in her book *Pitied but Not Entitled*, the female reformers of the Progressive Era were determined to preserve a separate domestic sphere for women as the source of their special power. Shielded from the crude hurly-burly of the masculine marketplace, women were viewed as the potential caretakers of the nation. Yet, at the same time that female reformers highlighted women's unique capacity for caretaking, they also subjected women from the poorer classes to moralistic condemnation. Such women were to be saved from their environment, but they were to be saved through a process of victim blaming that was often "preachy, rigid, inflexible, [and ignorant of their] actual universe of choice[s]."[56]

Progressive ideology was also empirical, however. Observing the poor, progressives were the first group of social reformers who actually ventured out to collect data about them. Many of the reformers who collected these data came out of the settlement house movement. Alice Solenberger conducted a demographic analysis of one thousand homeless men in the Chicago Loop district; likewise, social worker Robert Hunter, who wrote *Poverty* (1904), one of the first sociological studies of the poor, worked at Jane Addams's Hull House in Chicago and University Settlement in New York.[57] Reformers in the Progressive Era gathered information about the poor in the hope of explaining them to the larger society. They believed that if enough people understood some basic facts about the poor, more would share in their own reforming fervor.

Social Movements

Three social movements created a large part of the context for the social reforms of the Progressive Era: the rise of a radical left, the first national movement for black people, and the women's suffrage campaign that won women the right to vote. Each in its own way shaped what did and did not happen in social welfare policy.

The radical left experienced a notable rise during the Progressive Era. As Theodore Roosevelt complained in 1906, "The dull purblind folly of the very rich men; their greed and arrogance . . . and the corruption in business and politics, have tended to produce a very unhealthy condition of excitement and irritation in the public mind, which shows itself in the great increase in the socialistic propaganda."[58]

Roosevelt was right to be worried. The Industrial Workers of the World (the IWW, or Wobblies), which aimed to organize all workers regardless of sex, race, or skills into one big union, had just been founded. Militant but never large, the IWW could nonetheless command thousands of supporters for demonstrations and other labor conflicts. Its pamphlets contained such statements as "The worker on the job shall tell the boss when and where he shall work, how long and for what wages and under what conditions." Statements like these terrified employers.

Drawing on surprising strength in the Midwest and West, membership in the Socialist Party also grew. This growth culminated in the presidential election of 1912, when Socialist Party candidate Eugene Debs received a record high 6 percent of the presidential vote, and some twelve hundred Socialist public officials, including seventy-nine mayors in twenty-four states, were elected nationwide.[59] The fevered state of public opinion helps to explain what progressive reformers were so worried about: in the absence of some moderate reforms, much more radical proposals might have carried the day.

Despite such rare exceptions as settlement house leaders Addams and Wald, progressive reformers were not very attentive to race relations. For this reason, the Progressive Era was probably the twentieth century's low point in the treatment of African Americans. Whatever their views about the need for other kinds of social legislation, most reformers assumed that African Americans were, and properly should continue to be, second-class citizens, barred from any participation in the nation's political life and restricted to the most menial jobs. Nine million of the 10 million African Americans lived in the South. There, the Ku Klux Klan, to which one of every eight white American males belonged at its peak, beat or lynched African Americans who tried to break out of their subordinate role. Nor were conditions much better in the North, where bloody race riots erupted in twenty-eight cities, including St. Louis (1917) and Chicago (1919).[60]

Faced with these obstacles at the turn of the century, some African Americans rejected the placating strategy of blacks like Booker T. Washington and began to push for a national organization. Led by W. E. B. Du Bois, the first African American to receive a Ph.D. from Harvard University, they formed the National Association for the Advancement of Colored People (1909); among its white leadership, Du Bois was the only African American.[61] Using education and lawsuits to advance its cause, the NAACP pressed on for more than forty years before it was able to win the 1954 landmark desegregation case *Brown v. Board of Education*. Although progress on civil rights was slow and incremental, its roots go back to the African American social movement, which found its first national expression in the NAACP during the Progressive Era.

The women's suffrage movement also grew rapidly in this period. Leading up to the Nineteenth Amendment granting women the right to vote (1920), marches and protests spread through major cities. In debates with men who complained that women voters would lose their femininity, suffragettes like Rose Schneiderman of the Garment Workers Union replied,

> Women in the laundries . . . stand for thirteen or fourteen hours in the terrible steam and heat with their hands in hot starch. Surely these women won't lose any more of their beauty and charm by putting a

"A Woman's Work is Never Done." Women were at the forefront of many campaigns for social reforms in the Progressive Era.

ballot in a ballot box once a year than they are likely to lose standing in foundries or laundries all year round.[62]

Yet the women's suffrage movement has an ambiguous relationship to social welfare. The suffragettes wanted equality; most female social welfare reformers wanted protective laws to regulate the conditions in which women worked. They hoped that the maintenance of separate spheres for men and women would give reformers the moral leverage to create the basis for a maternalist welfare state, one that was more attentive to women's special needs. But it is also misleading to make too much of this trend. The programs that helped poor women were very meager; even by 1931, mothers' pensions served just 93,620 of the 1.5 million female-headed households in the United States.[63] In retrospect, then, the suffrage movement grew partly because the moral leverage gained from a separate sphere did not bring women enough real benefits.

History

The Progressive Era was the period during which social work crystallized as a profession. This process of professionalization was not easy and came at a considerable price. The trade-off was simple and clear: if social workers aspired to professional status, they had to minimize their commitment to social reform. Upper-class funders of settlement houses, COSs, and other community agencies did recognize the need for some social change. What they could not accept was the idea that an entire profession might be devoted to it.

The first milestone in the debate about professionalism occurred when Abraham Flexner, a Carnegie Foundation official who had successfully pushed for recognition of medicine as a profession, spoke at the National Conference of Charities and Corrections in 1915. He was asked whether social work was a profession. Much to the dismay of the conference organizers, Flexner responded with a firm no. Social workers, Flexner contended, did not need a specific body of skills; all they had to do was coordinate the activities of other professionals. And then there was the problem of our enthusiasm for social reform. Flexner somewhat haughtily insisted that if social work were a true profession, it would understand that "vigor [in these matters] is not synonymous with intelligence."[64]

Aspiring to professional status, social workers scrambled in reaction to Flexner's comments. At a time when leading social workers like Addams, Wald, and Florence Kelley were among the few opponents to U.S. participation in World War I, the profession as a whole tried to address Flexner's concerns by distancing itself from politics.[65] A crucial step in the process was the publication of Mary Richmond's *Social Diagnosis* (1917), the first book that social work as an emerging profession could truly claim as its own. From her work at the COSs in Baltimore, Philadelphia, and New York, Richmond sought to distinguish the skills and knowledge base of trained social workers from the well-meaning efforts of volunteers. Blending old and new views about charity, she transformed the COS's commitment to investigation into the new social work skill of diagnosis. As one part of the three-step procedure "study-diagnosis-treatment," diagnosis was to be a rational scientific process, similar to that which lawyers and doctors employed in their own professional work. If social work could lay claim to it, then perhaps it really was on its way to becoming a profession.[66]

Other factors contributed to the professionalization of social work. After the 1917 Russian Revolution magnified the mainstream's fear of communism, the post–World War I "red scare" spurred Attorney General A. Mitchell Palmer to round up four thousand "radicals" in thirty-three states on one night in January 1920. In this atmosphere, it is not surprising that some of the social workers who founded the American Association of Social Workers (one of the predecessors of the National Association of Social Workers) were eager to avoid the taint of politics, lest they seem unprofessional. Instead, some leaders in social work turned to the internal focus of psychoanalysis, which first captivated the profession in the 1920s. No wonder that by the end of the decade, Porter Lee, director of the New York School of Social Work, could address the annual meeting of social work leaders known as the Milford Conference and report with satisfaction that social workers had shifted their energies from "cause to function"—from a concern with politics to a concern with the efficient day-to-day administration of a social welfare bureaucracy.[67] Lee's speech accurately reflected the popular mood. The reforming impulse of the Progressive Era had long been spent, and it would take a new crisis to galvanize the nation.

The New Deal to World War II (1933–1945)

In the fall of 1929, the stock market crashed. Combined with a prior decline in farm prices, the entire economy soon faltered. Even from a distance of three-quarters of a century, it is difficult to underestimate the effect of this economic collapse. A stock market frenzy had driven stocks upward in the spring of 1928. General Motors, which had sold at $99 a share in 1925, hit $212 a share three years later. RCA nearly doubled its share price, from $94.50 to $178, in little more than two weeks. The swift appreciation of stocks gave rise to a host of rags-to-riches stories: of the peddler who turned $4,000 into $250,000 and of the speculator whose initial investment of $1 million quickly ballooned to $30 million. Nor was the end of this boom anywhere in sight. Shortly before leaving office in early 1929, President Calvin Coolidge declared that stocks were "cheap at current prices."

The Crash quickly dispelled these illusions. Between September and November 1929, the value of industrial stocks on the New York Stock Exchange fell 50 percent. With one hundred thousand workers laid off every week for three years and industrial production down 54 percent, the national unemployment rate peaked at 25 percent in 1933. Conventional theory held that the economy would eventually right itself. When it did not, President Herbert

The economic consequences of the Depression
dramatized the need for social welfare reforms.

Hoover's optimism and insistence on private relief seemed completely inadequate. In the presidential election of 1932, Hoover lost in a landslide to the patrician governor of New York, Franklin Delano Roosevelt, who promised a New Deal.[68]

The New Deal lacked the moral fervor of the Progressive Era. Although its social policies cut deeper into the U.S. political and economic core, its reformers were, at heart, practical and experimental. Faced with a society on the verge of collapse, they did whatever they thought they needed to do to bring the country back from the brink. As Franklin Roosevelt said in 1932, "It is common sense to take a method and try it. If it fails, admit it frankly and try another. But above all, try something."[69]

A widespread myth tells us that Keynesian deficit spending pulled us out of the Depression. In truth, however, though New Deal policies were beneficial in myriad ways, their influence on economic recovery was mixed. Unemployment, which declined to 14 percent in 1937, shot back up to 19 percent in 1938, so it was actually the arms buildup for World War II, and not the New Deal itself, that ended the Depression.[70] Yet the social welfare legislation the New Deal enacted—most prominently, the Social Security Act (1935); the Wagner Act (1935), recognizing the right to join a union; and the 1937 Housing Act—permanently altered the relationship of Americans to their government. From now on, when they tried to cope with economic insecurity, at least some federal programs would be on their side.

Economics

There is a significant ambiguity in the economics of the New Deal. If the Depression signified anything, it demonstrated the failure of an unregulated corporate system. Corporations, however, were the cornerstones of modern private enterprise: it was their investments that made the system run. To preserve private enterprise, therefore, required preservation of the role of the corporation within it. Without that preservation, the whole system might collapse.

New Deal economics tried to bridge this contradiction by resurrecting the economy and keeping large corporations profitable. In an unofficial sense, the New Deal motto was "The corporation's dead, long live the corporation," and it did everything in its power to make this motto come true. When Roosevelt assumed power in 1933, he declared a four-day bank holiday. One-third of the banks had failed, and the banking system was in such desperate straits that he could have nationalized it. But Roosevelt instead simply proposed laws to regulate the banking system and restore faith in the securities market.

The impetus for Keynesian deficit spending arose out of the same premise. If the economy slumped because consumers were not buying enough goods, New Dealers reasoned that the government should go into debt to stimulate the economy. Corporations stood at the top of the economic pyramid in this system; the system was failing because their goods did not sell. But if people bought their goods, the sales would restore the system, and the corporations' role within it, to good health. In this sense, New Dealers practiced an early version of the trickle-down economics that has prevailed ever since.

The National Industrial Recovery Act (1933; later, simply the NRA, the National Recovery Administration) was the centerpiece of this strategy. The NRA was a monopolist's dream. Under it, business would get government approval for price fixing and production quotas, with the understanding that it would allow workers to organize and would treat poor workers more kindly. But until the U.S. Supreme Court ruled it unconstitutional in 1935, the NRA gave short shrift to labor while allowing corporations unchallenged freedom in the marketplace. As with the other policies, the premise was that if the Roosevelt administration was going to pull the country out of the Depression, corporations would lead the way.

Especially after 1935, in what historians often call the Second New Deal, Roosevelt switched strategies. Emboldened by the Democrats' victories in the 1934 congressional elections, he tried to stimulate the economy by moving to the left. Instead of the more corporate version of trickle-down, Roosevelt turned to social welfare legislation to put more money in people's hands. That was Roosevelt's genius: he reorganized the system so that for the first time, everybody got something. Nevertheless, it is crucial to our understanding of the New Deal that even as it made more people stakeholders in U.S. society, its goal of restoring the market system required it to be especially attentive to the business corporation as the biggest stakeholder of them all.

Politics

Even more than in the Progressive Era, the politics of social welfare in the New Deal accentuated the division between the state and federal governments. At the time when the Social Security Act established the modern U.S. welfare state, decentralized government exacted a tremendous price. In chapter 8, we discuss the three main parts of the Act: ADC, the ancestor of TANF; Social Security retirement; and Unemployment Insurance benefits. But we will understand it much better as a whole if we start by recognizing that the federal structure of the United States, by its very nature, imposes severe handicaps.

ADC, the welfare provision in the Social Security Act, allowed each state to establish its own basic need and grant levels. Although an early version of the Social Security Act would have provided a single uniform standard of payment, southern opposition defeated it. Not only did the provision raise the specter of equal pay for whites and blacks, but it also threatened to free African American women in the South from having to work as field and domestic laborers. As one southern public assistance supervisor commented soon after the Social Security Act was passed, "There is hesitancy on the part of lay boards to advance too rapidly over the thinking of their own communities, which see no reason why the employable Negro mother should not continue her usually sketchy seasonal labor or indefinite domestic service rather than receive a public assistance grant."[71]

Old Age Survivors Insurance, today called Social Security, suffered similarly. To be sure, unlike public assistance, OASI does provide a uniform national benefit. But until 1951, the OASI program also excluded domestic and agricultural workers. And until President Nixon created SSI in 1972, separate means-tested programs for the aged, blind, and disabled also existed in every state. During the New Deal, then, states' rights proved most powerful in limiting programs for the very poor.

Unemployment Insurance faced comparable obstacles. Although some states were concerned about the wage differences, most policy experts probably favored a national unemployment benefit system, with equal benefit payments all across the country. President Roosevelt, however, was afraid of the politically difficult issues surrounding these benefits, including how much employers would contribute and whether those contributions would be pooled into one reserve fund. Retreating in the face of these concerns, Roosevelt enacted a program in which the states determined benefits but the federal government offset the cost of the unemployment tax.[72]

These concessions to states' rights contributed to one of the New Deal's most significant and troublesome social welfare legacies: its essentially residual character. As chapter 2 explained, residual benefits are the opposite of universal ones and are available to individuals who can demonstrate that they lack something most people are presumed to have, whether it is money, health, or sanity. If you think back, you will realize that the history presented in the earlier parts of this chapter show residualism and its necessary corollary, the means test, to be an enduring feature of U.S. social provision.

The Social Security Act maintains the legacy of residualism by making a sharp distinction between welfare and social insurance programs. Welfare programs for the poor tend to be means-tested, stingy, stigmatizing, and administered by the states. Social insurance programs such as Social Security are more likely to be federal, universal, and relatively generous. Although many social welfare advocates in the 1930s were acutely aware of this pattern, conservatives who opposed the New Deal were able to deploy the power of states' rights and use it to derail any federalized, and universal, welfare legislation.

Ideology

The pursuit of greater inclusiveness was the dominant ideology of the New Deal. The system had broken down, and the New Deal's architects knew it. They realized that any successful new system would require the political and economic enfranchisement of trade unions and the poor. Although this enfranchisement would not ensure the system's stability, not even a minimum of stability could be achieved without it.

This inclusiveness should not be exaggerated. The Roosevelt administration did not depart significantly from mainstream opinions of the period on the position of African Americans or the assumption that women belonged in the home. Nor, as we have indicated, did the New Deal challenge the central economic role of the private corporation. Yet, these qualifications aside, the inclusiveness of New Deal ideology did represent something novel in American life.

Roosevelt thought of the New Deal as establishing an "economic declaration of rights." Once, when he was away for the summer, contractors undertook a long overdue renovation of the White House. Roosevelt drew a pointed analogy: "The architects and builders are men of common sense and artistic American tastes. They know that the principles of harmony and of necessity itself require that the new structure shall blend with the essential lines of the old. It is this combination of the old and the new that marks orderly peaceful progress, not only in building buildings but in building government itself."[73]

And so, to a political and economic structure that had rarely recognized anyone but the entrepreneur, the ideology of the New Deal acknowledged several new groups. Farmers got help through the Agricultural Adjustment Administration, which provided subsidy payments and production controls. Trade unions got the right to organize from the Wagner Act. The elderly, the poor, and the unemployed got the Social Security Act. A consistent ideology

Blending promises of substantial change with a sense of political continuity, President Franklin D. Roosevelt used the new medium of radio to reassure the nation.

was implicit in all these initiatives. By designing programs for these groups, the New Deal demonstrated that it was including them; from now on, farmers, trade unionists, the elderly, the poor, and the unemployed would all be part of its ideological vision.

For the first time, this ideological vision included social welfare, which the federal government would now use to gain the allegiance of previously unrecognized groups. To be sure, this addition was but a limited gain as long as the conflict within social welfare remained unresolved, and the old division between the unworthy and the worthy poor persisted in the distinction between public assistance and social insurance, respectively. But this impasse aside, it is apparent that by the 1930s, federal social welfare programs had risen sufficiently in importance so that the need for them had become a prominent part of the dominant ideology.

Social Movements

When people look around and see that neither they nor their neighbors can meet the most basic needs for food, clothing, and housing, it impels them to think collectively about what to do. Such thinking inspired the extraordinary variety of social movements that proliferated in the 1930s. These movements include those for expanded social welfare such as the Unemployed Councils, the Townsend movement, and the social work rank and file; organizers fighting to establish trade unions; and, on the other side, the major business opponents of the New Deal. Each had a significant effect on social welfare policy.

Popular movements for social welfare had perhaps the most direct and explicit consequences. As local organizations of the unemployed, the Unemployed Councils spread rapidly through the country. In Chicago, they succeeded in raising relief payments to one of the highest levels in the nation. Pressured by the twelve thousand-member Seattle Unemployment League, the Seattle municipal government gave the organization $500,000 to administer relief. The Councils were militant and disruptive in their tactics, leading mass resistance against evictions of miners in New Mexico and sending thousands to support strikes in Toledo, Ohio, and Milwaukee, Wisconsin. The success of these efforts led to the formation of a national organization, the Workers Alliance of America, in 1935, but the organization and much local protest declined rapidly soon thereafter. The existence of the Unemployed Councils drove home the absolute necessity of including some form of unemployment insurance in the Social Security Act. Once that benefit was secured, the Councils no longer seemed quite so necessary.[74]

The Townsend movement had a similar impact on old age pensions. Francis Townsend was a physician who moved from Illinois to California only to be left unemployed by the Depression. In 1933, he proposed the Townsend Plan. Funded by a transaction tax (essentially, a sales tax on each transaction), the plan offered adults over 60 years of age $200 a month provided they did not work and spent the money in the same month they got it. Most policy experts dismissed the plan as ill-considered, but some 25 million people signed petitions supporting it. When the Committee on Economic Security—whose members included social workers Edith Abbott, Frances Perkins, and Harry Hopkins—drafted the Social Security Act, they did so knowing that the movement loomed in the background. Although Townsend did not get his plan, its existence certainly persuaded many more people in Congress that they had to pass Social Security.[75]

Unlike the Unemployed Councils and the Townsend movement, the social work rank and file movement did not influence any specific piece of legislation. For a time, however, in the 1930s, it did carry considerable weight within the profession. The rank and file movement engaged in a broad range of activities. Beginning with discussion clubs in 1931, the movement diversified to organize unions—mostly of public service workers in the larger cities—and later to found *Social Work Today*, a journal published and distributed by the New York Discussion Club from 1934 to 1942. Led by radical social workers such as Bertha Reynolds, Harry Lurie, and Mary Van Kleeck, rank-and-filers provided pressure from the left on many issues, advocating closer alliances with labor unions and a more adequate federally funded relief program and opposing racial discrimination throughout social welfare. Although they did not win everything they sought, they pushed more mainstream organizations like the American Association of Social Workers to be more vigorous and expanded the consciousness of the profession.[76]

The impact of labor unions on New Deal social legislation was also indirect. Although trade unionists supported most of it, they were primarily concerned with clearing a path to aid in union organizing. They faced a difficult situation, because as companies laid off employees in the early 1930s, the number of union members dropped to 2.7 million mostly urban workers concentrated in the railroad, printing, building, coal, and clothing industries.

Nevertheless, the CIO, which was originally a subdivision of the AFL, fought to energize the labor movement with a series of strikes among assembly line and other unskilled workers around the country. Amid a general upsurge of labor activity headlined by the 1934 San Francisco general strike on behalf of the longshoremen and the fifty thousand people who turned out for a funeral of two unionists slain in Minneapolis, some liberal senators such as Robert Wagner (D-New York) pushed for legislative recognition of the right to form a union. When the Wagner Act passed in 1935, it changed the broad, general endorsement of unions contained in the NRA into an enforceable right. With the law behind it, a newly separate labor organization—the CIO, led by John L. Lewis—swept through the industrial sector. Sitting in at factories—most prominently, the forty-day takeover of the Fisher Body Plant in Flint, Michigan—the organizing drive boosted union membership to 6 million each for the AFL and the CIO by 1945. In the midst of this drive, it also spurred the passage of the first minimum wage law in 1938.[77]

Business organizations mostly opposed these social movements. Although business had initially supported early New Deal legislation like the NRA that permitted price fixing and some reform-minded elites continued to participate in drafting the Social Security Act, most business leaders turned away from Roosevelt as he moved leftward. Before the 1934 congressional elections, some prominent executives, such as Alfred P. Sloan of General Motors, Edward F. Hutton of General Foods, and the members of the Dupont family, formed the Liberty League to resist "radicalism" and protect property rights. Although the Democrats gained seats anyway, talk of a social security act galvanized business once again. Sloan complained that "industry has every reason to be alarmed at [its] social, economic, and financial implications," and the National Association of Manufacturers disputed the very notion of taxing industry to pay for the social security of its employees.

Even after passage of the act, many businesses tried to prevent the January 1937 implementation of the payroll tax. In the 1936 congressional elections, they inserted messages in workers' pay envelopes saying, "You're sentenced to a weekly pay reduction for all your working life. You'll have to serve the sentence unless you help reverse it November 3rd." Treating this business opposition as selfish and shortsighted, Roosevelt usually triumphed over it. Yet, even when a law was passed and the business coalition lost, it won something, because the law was often less progressive than its proponents wanted.[78]

Historians often divide the New Deal into two distinct periods. During the first period, from 1933 to 1935, the Roosevelt administration experimented with a host of emergency programs. Designed to salvage a collapsing economy, these programs are frequently remembered as the alphabet soup of the New Deal. In addition to the NRA, they included FERA (the Federal Emergency Relief Administration, 1933–1935) to supplement local relief efforts; the CCC (Civilian Conservation Corps, 1933–1942), which paid unemployed young men $30 a month to conserve forests, control floods, and develop state parks; the CWA (Civil Works Administration, 1933–1934), which provided work to get the country through the bottom of the Depression; and the WPA (Works Progress [later Projects] Administration, 1935–1942), which employed people to construct buildings, roads, and airports.

We discuss these programs in greater detail in chapter 9, but it is revealing that these New Deal work programs focused so clearly on white men. In fact, just 12 percent of all WPA workers were female, and they got jobs because Eleanor Roosevelt so actively lobbied her husband.[79] New Deal policies often effectively barred women because, between 1932 and 1937, the Federal Economy Act prohibited more than one member of the same family from civil service employment. With popular opinion firmly set against married women's holding jobs, private employers like Northern Pacific Railway and New England Telephone and Telegraph also dismissed their female employees.

Nor was the New Deal any kinder in its treatment of African Americans or Latinos. The WPA was reluctant to place African American women; they held little more than 2 percent of all such jobs in 1939. The programs discriminated against African Americans and Latinos on the grounds that they were already accustomed to a lower standard of living. Faced with racial quotas and deliberate delays in processing applications, racial minorities complained to the Roosevelt administration. The complaints, however, had little effect, and the policy remained fundamentally unchanged throughout the New Deal.[80]

The second New Deal extended from 1935 to 1937. Unlike the transient programs of the first period, the second spans most of the era's landmark legislation: the Social Security Act, the Wagner Act, and the 1937 Housing Act, authorizing the federal government to construct public housing. But although this social legislation created a safety net and tied constituent groups to the Democratic Party, neither it nor New Deal economic policy ended the Depression. As we emphasized at the outset, only the coming of World War II could do that.

The war transformed U.S. society. It raised issues of race that led to the desegregation of the armed forces and reverberated into the decades ahead. For a brief moment, through the Lanham Act, it also created modern day care. Enacted in 1943, the Lanham Act is the legislation that made "Rosie the Riveter" possible. With the men off to war and a labor shortage in the factories, it funded day care facilities in factories so women could work. Then,

With the Lanham Act providing day care, women replaced men in wartime production.

when the war ended, Congress cut funding and women had to return home; between 1945 and 1947, 2.7 million women lost their jobs in industry.[81] The Lanham Act demonstrated that, like other kinds of social needs, no fixed rules govern the provision of day care. As the New Deal demonstrated and as our subsequent history confirms, social welfare legislation frequently responds to the needs of the labor market.

Post–World War II to the Great Society (1946–1968)

The cold war frames the period 1946–1968. Emerging from World War II as the world's dominant superpower, the United States faced the challenge of the Soviet Union, which detonated an atomic bomb in 1949, only four years after the United States had. Over the next twenty years, the United States desegregated public schools, enacted civil and voting rights legislation, and launched a War on Poverty. Social movements pushed hard for all this domestic legislation. At the same time, however, foreign policy considerations pervade much of it.

American opinion makers often said during this period that we were engaged in a struggle for the "hearts and minds" of nonaligned people throughout the world. When they made these statements, they usually referred to newly independent countries in Asia and Africa, where former colonies of England and France were now trying to chart a political and economic course for themselves between the private enterprise model of the United States and the communism of the Soviet Union. Although they admired some parts of the U.S. model, African and Asian leaders also knew that if they visited Washington and took a drive into the Virginia countryside, they would have to drink out of "colored only" water fountains. In the great battle between capitalism and communism, this experience was hardly calculated to win their hearts and minds.[82]

From this perspective, then, the social legislation of this period had an additional dimension. As always, it responded partly to social movements, to the labor market, and to the needs of a changing economy. But it also was something more: an attempt to eliminate segregation as the most obvious blemish on U.S. society. In this instance, at least, foreign policy concerns made domestic reform possible.

Quite apart from civil rights, the cold war had one other overriding effect on social legislation. The Soviet Union presented another model of how an economy could operate, one in which almost everything was top-down, nationalized, and collective. Although the United States rightly rejected this model, the mere fact of its existence opened up more possibilities for the public sector. Even as the United States sought to distinguish its mixed public/private economy from the purely national ownership of Soviet communism, its own social policies went in a more liberal direction.

The Economy

One feature, in particular, distinguishes this period of the twentieth century: it was the time when income gains were most broadly shared. In the postwar era, U.S. production workers' real wages grew 2.5 to 3 percent per year. Benefits spread, too. In 1950, union contracts provided pensions to just 10 percent of all production workers, and just 30 percent included insurance. Only five years later, 45 percent of all contracts offered pensions, and 70 percent offered health insurance.

Pent-up demand catapulted the economy forward. When GIs returned to start families, they got a college degree through the GI bill, bought houses with government-subsidized loans, and then filled the houses with dishwashers, washing machines, televisions, and refrigerators—all the new consumer goods of the postwar era.[83] Admittedly, the path upward was not unbroken: recessions in 1949, 1958, and 1961 drove the unemployment rate to unacceptable levels (5.9 percent in 1949, 6.8 and 6.7 percent in 1958 and 1961). Still, these downturns were brief enough that more than ever before, many Americans reveled in their feelings of a shared prosperity.

The key to this prosperity was deficit spending. Coming out of World War II, many U.S. political leaders were concerned that demobilization of the military would return the United States to the high unemployment of the 1930s. Deficit spending had been used in the Depression and throughout the war; in fact, by the end of the war, the United States was spending more than double its actual revenues (received $45 billion; expended $95 billion). It was, however, an entirely new policy to rely on peacetime deficits in a reasonably well-functioning economy. But faced with the political and economic risks of another depression, the federal government could no longer rely on spending by American consumers. If they did not spend enough to keep the economy going, the government would go into deficit. And it did, not only for most of this period, but for almost all of the next thirty years.[84]

This deficit spending had another aspect. From World War II on, deficit spending in the United States is closely intertwined with what some call the warfare/welfare state.[85] They contend that the federal budget, particularly the deficit, comes from spending on warfare or welfare. Of course, as chapter 3 explained, in a multibillion-dollar budget, any part of the budget could be defined as extra, and there is no way to determine exactly what the deficit pays for. Nevertheless, the extent of military and/or welfare spending does seem to have performed a critical function in ensuring the economy's health.

Before the Great Society legislation of 1964–68, the tilt was emphatically toward military spending. For example, during the Korean War (1950–53), the government reduced unemployment from 5.9 percent in 1949 to 2.9 percent. One year after the war ended, the unemployment rate immediately shot back up to 5.5 percent. Similarly, while unemployment reached 6.7 percent in 1961 before the buildup to the Vietnam War, the combination of spending on both warfare and Great Society welfare programs reduced it to 3.6 percent in 1968.[86] It is not, then, just that the government engaged in deficit spending, but that the content of deficit spending seems to have had such a decisive effect on whether the economy performed well or badly.

The feeling of prosperity arising from the combination of military and social welfare spending also had psychological consequences. For the first time in a generation, most Americans felt reasonably secure. The primary menace came not from economic insecurity, but from overseas: the Korean War, the cold war with the Soviet Union, and after the Soviet Union exploded its first nuclear bomb in 1949, the constant threat of nuclear holocaust. Nevertheless, by the 1950s and early 1960s, a comfortable feeling of normality had settled over many homes and communities: work was regular, and there were baby boomers to raise. Whatever unruly feelings lay underneath, Americans felt secure enough to extend some of the benefits they enjoyed to previously excluded racial minorities. This psychology explains, in part, the timing of the Great Society. For a brief moment in the mid-1960s, the economy made people feel that giving to others took very little away from themselves.

Politics

When political scientists talk about periods of dominance by one party, they usually describe the postwar period as part of an extended New Deal coalition, one that lasted from 1932 to 1968. Just as the Republicans dominated from

1896 to 1932, interrupted only by President Woodrow Wilson (1912–20) as the one two-term Democrat, so the postwar period following on the New Deal was predominantly Democratic, except for President Dwight D. Eisenhower (1952–60) as the one two-term Republican. Although these political signposts are accurate, they do not really reflect the political challenges from right and left that helped frame the politics of the period.

The challenge from the right came in the form of McCarthyism. Named after Senator Joseph McCarthy (R-Wisconsin), McCarthyism's heyday began in 1950, when he claimed to have a list of 205 communists (which he never showed) currently working in the State Department. It ended in 1954, when the Senate censured him after the Army-McCarthy hearings.

McCarthy himself was the most visible symbol of a "red scare" that made anyone who spoke about poverty or racism vulnerable to the charge of being a communist. In the years after World War II, the scare silenced key elements of the progressive coalition, especially unions, eleven of which were expelled from the CIO. The largest of these unions, the United Electrical Workers, saw its membership drop from 300,000 to 50,000. In addition, under pressure from President Harry Truman's Federal Employee Loyalty Program and government investigators such as the House Un-American Activities Committee, thousands of teachers, screenwriters, and social workers lost their jobs. At the University of Pittsburgh School of Social Work, for example, a long-running campaign led to the resignation of prominent faculty members, including Grace Marcus, Ruth Smalley, and Marion Hathway. With anticommunism, conservatives could keep the more liberal tendencies of the Second New Deal out of the politics of the postwar era.[87]

While, from the right, anticommunism limited the politics of social reform, internal conflicts within the Democratic Party finally drove it to address racial issues. Although a majority of the black electorate voted Democratic for the first time in 1936, most blacks still lived in the South, where they could not vote at all. But as agriculture in the South modernized, blacks lost agricultural work and moved north. By 1960, 90 percent of all northern blacks were located in the ten northern states with the largest number of electoral votes. This development put the southern, white part of the Democratic Party—the "Solid South"—in direct conflict with its northern, urban, and increasingly black counterpart.

Local politics further complicated this dilemma because white ethnics provided the political base for the Democratic machine in northern cities like Boston, Chicago, New York, Detroit, and Philadelphia. Unsure that he could count on southern Democrats wary of his Catholicism during his 1960 bid for the White House, John F. Kennedy turned to the black vote in the northern cities. Doubts about his seriousness held their vote down to 69 percent, but the turnout in many northern cities did tip some key states into the Democratic column. Cautious throughout his administration, Kennedy eventually signed an executive order barring discrimination in federally subsidized housing, but he never sent a civil rights bill to Congress.[88] Still, his pursuit of electoral votes blended with President Lyndon Johnson's Great Society civil rights legislation to tie African Americans to the Democratic Party for the rest of the century.

Until the rise of a powerful movement against the Vietnam War in the mid-1960s, McCarthyism on the right and the civil rights movement on the left defined the basic contours of domestic politics. Like other domestic issues, social welfare policy existed within those limits. To be sure, there were some new legislative initiatives. The most notable of these include the enfeebled Full Employment Bill of 1946 (discussed in chapter 9), which did not guarantee full employment; the Housing Act of 1949 (discussed in chapter 10), which cleared slums in the cities and subsidized the growth of the suburbs; the addition of disability insurance to the Social Security Act in 1956 (see chapter 8); and the 1962 amendments to that Act, which, for the first time, authorized the federal government to reimburse states for the provision of social services. At a time when the very notion of a welfare state sounded "socialistic," the politics of the era inevitably limited these new programs.

Ideology

Cold war liberalism was this era's dominant ideology. While the liberalism of the New Deal was experimental, if flawed, the liberalism of the postwar era was careful and muted. Believing that the history of the Soviet Union demonstrated that socialism meant totalitarianism, cold war liberalism reasoned that a few well-chosen policies could preserve the private enterprise system. These policies included use of Keynesian deficit spending to promote growth and prosperity, collective bargaining, and a modest welfare state. Growth would propel the private sector; business profits would finance increased wages; workers would buy more; and with everyone integrated into a state-supervised capitalist economy, the United States could embark on an unending cycle of material progress. As long as these policies produced a great middle-class democracy, there was no need to do anything more.[89]

As the 1950s wore on, however, the emergence of a democratic left began to challenge cold war liberalism. Supported by students—at first, primarily those at the elite schools, young people under the influence of Beat writers such as Jack Kerouac and Allen Ginsberg, and literary intellectuals like Norman Mailer and Irving Howe—this ideology pressed for genuine racial equality, criticized the arms race with the Soviet Union, and insisted that additional social programs would make the United States more, not less, of a democracy. For them, cold war liberalism was a cramped ideology offering a narrow range of policy options. Tentatively at first, and then with increasing confidence, they tried to carve out an ideology to compensate for what they saw as the defects of both capitalism and communism.[90]

In social welfare, the call for a new political consciousness came in the form of Michael Harrington's classic volume, *The Other America*. Published in 1962, the book exploded the postwar myth that the United States had vanquished poverty. Amid the constant refrains about the United States as a middle-class society, it was easy to overlook the 40 to 50 million Americans who were still poor, including the low-income elderly, miners in Appalachia, African Americans in the cities, and Mexican Americans in the Southwest. Harrington was probably naïve in his assumption that if Americans just knew about poverty, they would do something about it. Nor was he very explicit in his belief that doing something about poverty would require government planning and social investment—the kind of policies pioneered by Sweden and other advanced European welfare states. But despite these drawbacks, *The Other America* stimulated public interest in the issue and created an opening for discussion of some new approaches. When President Kennedy read it and declared the abolition of poverty a major domestic goal, it became the book that launched the War on Poverty.[91]

Social Movements

The struggle for racial equality, the women's movement, and opposition to the Vietnam War were the three great social movements of this period. The struggles for racial quality led to such social welfare legislation as the Civil Rights Act of 1964, the Voting Rights Act of 1965, and, for a short time to quiet the tumult, a significant expansion of public assistance. Although women were also guaranteed equality under the Civil Rights Act—southern congressmen actually added this provision in an effort to defeat it—genuine enforcement of the Act awaited founding of the National Organization for Women (1966) and the maturation of the women's movement into an organized constituency focusing on equal pay, reproductive rights, and ending domestic violence. The third great social movement, against the Vietnam War, addressed a foreign rather than a domestic issue. Money spent on the war was money not spent on poverty, race relations, and social welfare. By itself, this glaring fact angered and politicized a large segment of the population.

The modern civil rights movement dates from the NAACP's successful 1954 suit, *Brown v. Board of Education*, which desegregated schools and thereby called into question the legality of racial segregation in every other public facility. Drawing on its base, first in African American churches and later in black colleges, the movement deepened and spread. In late 1955, Rosa Parks, a seamstress who had recently attended workshops on organizing at the Highlander School in Tennessee, refused to give up her seat for a white man on a Montgomery, Alabama, bus. Her refusal set off a 381-day bus boycott that led to desegregation of the entire system and gave Martin Luther King Jr., the minister of a local church, his first national platform. Four years later, four freshmen at Agricultural and Technical College in Greensboro, North Carolina, sat in at a whites-only lunch counter. Their protest resulted in the formation of the Student Non-Violent Coordinating Committee, the 1961 Freedom Rides to desegregate public transportation facilities throughout the South, and a flurry of national indignation about southern racial policies.[92]

The early civil rights movement practiced nonviolence. Gandhi had used nonviolence to win India's independence from Great Britain; King, heavily influenced by Gandhi, adopted the strategy for the United States. To some extent, the strategy worked, but as the movement met resistance, younger blacks in urban areas took to the streets. In the summer of 1964, as riots swept through New York, Jersey City, Rochester, Chicago, and Philadelphia, President Johnson began the War on Poverty, funded job training and community action programs within a newly established Office of Economic Opportunity, and signed the Civil Rights Act. These legislative initiatives were the first time that the federal government devoted substantial resources to racial issues. Looking at Head Start (early education for children), Job Corps (job training for inner-city youth), and rising welfare payments in the inner city, some social welfare historians of the civil rights movement have drawn a pointed conclusion: although nonviolence gained political sympathy, only disruption produced legislation that was really worthwhile.[93]

The feminist movement of the 1960s traces its origins to two different sources. The first group consisted of women who gravitated toward the more traditional form of social organization, with elected officers, bylaws, and established democratic procedures. Influenced by Betty Friedan's 1963 classic *The Feminine Mystique* and its critique of the "happy homemaker," these are the women, including Friedan herself, who founded the National Organization for Women in 1966. Less formally organized, a second, somewhat younger group of mostly white women and typically recent college graduates met in small groups that initially stressed consciousness-raising. Excluded from the civil rights movements by the shift to Black Power and from the antiwar movement by the fact that only men could resist the draft, they looked to women's liberation as the place to express themselves politically.[94]

Through 1968, the women's movement had little to show for its efforts; concrete results would come later, during the next thirty years. Nonetheless, without yielding actual legislation, the movement did succeed in placing gender alongside race on the national agenda. The women's movement as an organized political force would soon pose the question of whether, in the midst of the war in Vietnam, it was possible to address the concerns of either constituency.

The antiwar movement underscored the importance of this question. Students were the first identifiable group to oppose intervention in Southeast Asia. Led by newly formed groups like Students for a Democratic Society, the movement organized teach-ins on campus to oppose the war and spearheaded the first antiwar march on Washington in 1965.[95] Gradually, as opposition spread to other segments of U.S. society, some national leaders began to emphasize the explicit conflict between domestic and military spending. As King said, if the country could spend "35 billion dollars a year to fight an unjust, evil war in Vietnam, and 20 billion dollars a year to put a man on the moon, it can spend billions of dollars to put God's children on their own two feet right here on earth."[96]

In their respective ways, then, these three major social movements of the 1960s all focused on social welfare spending. African Americans and Latinos had a more developed movement, so they could talk explicitly about demands for jobs, housing, and education. By contrast, the early stages of the women's movement stressed divorce law reform, equal pay for equal work, and passage of the Equal Rights Amendment. Each of these reforms offered women more economic independence, but if women were not successful on their own, they also implied a greater need for social welfare. Finally, though the antiwar movement ostensibly pointed to issues of foreign policy, one of its underlying principles was that the United States could not squander great sums of money on a war in Asia and still respond adequately to emerging domestic needs. Each of these social movements made some headway in the 1960s. It is hardly surprising, then, that for the rest of the twentieth century, Americans would debate the public policy implications of their success.

History

The history of the postwar era subdivides neatly into three distinct periods. In the first period, roughly 1946–53, conservatives squelched the notion that the postwar era would simply continue New Deal social policies. This is the time of the 1946 Full Employment Act, which business successfully stripped of any enforcement powers; the antiunion Taft-Hartley Act (1947), penalizing workers for unauthorized strikes and allowing them to get a job without joining a union; and the red scare that silenced political dissent. In 1946–48, the Republicans were actually in control of Congress, but even when they were not, the political climate was unfavorable to major social welfare legislation.[97]

In 1954, however, *Brown v. Board of Education* desegregated the public schools and the Senate censured McCarthy. The mood began to change. As the civil rights movement grew and McCarthyism began to decline, the pace of social change quickened. In 1956, Congress added disability payments to the Social Security Act. In 1957, President Eisenhower sent the National Guard to Little Rock, Arkansas, to desegregate Central High School and signed a modest Civil Rights Act, the first since Reconstruction, that Senate Majority Leader Lyndon Johnson had skillfully steered through Congress.[98] The early 1960s witnessed the success of the Freedom Rides, the 1962 Social Security legislation liberalizing federal reimbursement for social services, and in 1963, Martin Luther King Jr.'s famous "I Have a Dream" speech on the steps of the Washington mall. By then, the Kennedy administration, which had waffled on civil rights before, understood that significant social welfare legislation would be necessary to satisfy the movement's demands.

During the third period, Kennedy's assassination created the political momentum that made this legislation possible. In quick succession over four years, Congress enacted and President Johnson signed the 1964 Civil Rights Act; food stamps (1964); the 1965 Voting Rights Act; federal aid to education (1965); Medicaid (1965); Medicare (1965); and many War on Poverty programs, including the Office of Economic Opportunity, Head Start, Model Cities, and Job Corps. Though expectations ran high and poverty did decline from 1960 to 1972, the War on Poverty was not designed to redistribute welfare or restructure the economy, and its first budget was only $800 million. Caught up in a bureaucratic tangle of federal, state, and local agencies and subject to withering criticism from many quarters, it stumbled so badly that by the early 1970s, not much except Head Start and Job Corps was left of its programs.[99]

The history of social work as a profession parallels this history of social welfare. Through the early 1960s, the profession emphasized a casework model whose counseling orientation viewed the client's behavior apart from a social context. With material on alcoholism, delinquency, and school problems filling the journals, *Social Work*, the organ of the NASW, published just two articles on the civil rights movement and one on the threat of nuclear war before 1963. In 1957, Marion K. Sanders's article for *Harper's* magazine nicely captured the professional concerns of social work at midcentury. "The day after the bomb fell," she wrote, "the doctor was out binding radiation burns. The minister prayed and set up a soup kitchen in the ruined chapel. The policeman herded stray children to the rubble heap where a teacher had improvised a classroom. And the social workers wrote a report; since two had survived, they held a conference on 'Interpersonal Relationships in a Time of Intensified Anxiety States.' "[100]

When Johnson declared a War on Poverty, however, the profession did an about-face. Suddenly, community organizing courses appeared in social work schools, and new groups like the National Welfare Rights Organization challenged the whole concept of professionalism as a means of maintaining power and enforcing social control. With the feminist movement questioning male dominance of a largely female profession and black social workers establishing separate organizations, social work broadened to include social action, social change, and social policy.[101] Although a strong commitment to this diversification would not last long, it would, like the War on Poverty, echo throughout the next generation.

1969–Present: The Conservative Response

The period after 1969 seems quite diverse. After all, it includes the conservative Republican presidencies of Richard Nixon (1969–74), Ronald Reagan (1981–89), and the two George Bushes (the father, 1989–93, and the son, 2001–), as well as two Democratic presidents, Jimmy Carter (1977–81) and Bill Clinton (1993–01). Because Reagan ran against Carter, Clinton ran against George Bush, and Clinton's vice president Al Gore ran against George W. Bush, the distinctions between the parties' social policy positions are often exaggerated. But in fact, there has been considerable continuity throughout this period, because it was a time when the market had a freer hand and both Democrats and Republicans took a step back (one smaller and one larger) from the social policy gains of the 1960s.[102]

A review of our five factors clarifies the enormous consequences for social welfare policy. The orientation of economics became more conservative.

Swayed by campaign contributions and influenced by conservative foundations and think tanks, politics turned to the right as well. Ideology justified this rightward drift, fragmenting the social movements of the 1960s and fostering conservative groups on issues like abortion and taxes to counter them. As a result, when we look back at the history of this period, social welfare policy seems, at best, to have stalled.

Economics

Mainstream economics returned to the belief that markets are self-adjusting and operate best with the least interference. It set out six principles to guide economic policy in this period: (1) globalization and free trade; (2) tax relief; (3) privatization and deregulation; (4) labor flexibility; (5) restraints on social welfare; and (6) the commercialization of social costs. All six principles flow from the notion that only the unimpeded market should establish a price for goods and services. Recent economic policy will seem a lot clearer once you understand the basis for this reasoning.

Globalization and free trade involve price setting because they rest on the premise that goods and services should be made where they can be produced most efficiently. If one country can produce video monitors for less money than another, then that is where video monitors should be made. Presumably, other countries will be more efficient making different products, and the countries will all trade with one another. In theory, then, this whole system is a true model of efficiency, because every nation is doing what it does best.

As we explained in chapter 3, the problem with this theory is apparent in its practice. Although some countries have natural resources such as oil or gas that others do not, much of the new information technology depends more on the availability of a cheap and willing labor force. By playing one national workforce off against another, corporations can choose the country in which they want to invest. In effect, it is their power to influence the government's economic policy on wages, working conditions, and the environment—not the "natural" operation of the market—that determines how much multinational corporations pay a particular workforce to produce a particular product.

Tax relief is a second guiding principle. Why, this theory contends, should businesspeople risk their investments if the profits get taxed away? What right, some people argue, does the government have to take my hard-earned money? Relying on these premises, policymakers have effectively slashed the highest rate of taxes on income in half, from 70 percent in 1981 down to 35 percent under George W. Bush in 2001. With the exception of Clinton's tax hike in 1993, the system over the past thirty years has become steadily less progressive.

Mainstream economic theory has argued for privatization and deregulation on similar grounds. The premise is that environmental and oversight regulations place an undue burden on business enterprise and interfere with the market's natural functioning. What this argument overlooks, of course, is that

In a conservative era, Bill Clinton felt he had to compromise with conservatives on issues like welfare reform and deregulation.

in the past, the "natural functioning of the market" engaged in unethical business practices, despoiled our environment, and sold adulterated foods and medicines that threatened our health; that is why we enacted the regulations in the first place, and why, after Enron, we will probably enact some of them again. Likewise, over the years, some services such as education, fire protection, and sanitation have become public services because everyone needs them, and it is difficult for the private sector to profit from them. In recent years, mainstream economic theory has dismissed all of these objections. As a result, Republicans at every level of government have sought to privatize and deregulate, and Democrats have, at best, tried half-heartedly to stop them.

The fourth cornerstone of economic policymaking has been the push for labor flexibility. Arising out of intensifying competition in the global marketplace, labor flexibility typically has meant that workers should be more flexible—in other words, more willing to give back benefits and accept lower wages. The international labor market has expanded now to include countries where the wages are as low as $2 or $3 a day, and mainstream economists contend that American workers have to accept lower wages if they want to keep their jobs. Hence, economic theory has justified and businesses have implemented policies to hold down wages for most of the past thirty years.

The fifth and perhaps most directly relevant economic principle of the modern period has been the campaign to contain social welfare. This campaign has taken several different forms. Some see social welfare as a simple matter of too much federal spending. They maintain that when the federal government runs a deficit, it competes with the private sector for capital and drives up the interest rate on borrowed funds. Others contend that the existence of social welfare disrupts the marketplace's natural capacity for price setting because it requires employers to pay higher wages to attract a labor force. From this perspective, when unemployment benefits are too generous, the salary workers demand may exceed the actual value of their contribution to the firm. All these conflicts between social welfare and the market have led to a fundamental principle of modern policymaking: whenever social welfare and the market clash, social welfare must give way.

Yet, while the new economy tries to erase the old forms of social welfare, new forms of social welfare have reappeared in their place. The most prominent of these involves the delivery of social services to the imprisoned. Prisons house and feed some 2.1 million people. Prison is the place where they get their mental health services and are treated for their physical ailments. For many, it is also the site of some additional schooling. Prison inmates receive services inside a jail that other poor people receive outside. In short, the jail has replaced the poorhouse. It is the new form of indoor relief, an old institution put to additional uses.

At 700 incarcerations per 100,000 people, the United States has the highest per capita prison population in the world. This population is heavily black and Hispanic. Overall, almost 5 percent of African American men are incarcerated; among males 25–29 years old, the proportion reaches 10 percent. The rate is about 3 percent for Hispanic males of the same age, but little more than 1 percent for whites.[103] The war on drugs has significantly inflated these numbers, imprisoning blacks and Hispanics at two to three times their actual rate of drug use.[104]

Two significant economic facts stand out about this population. In the past, policymakers have often deployed social welfare to discipline the workforce. By cutting benefits, social welfare policy pressured workers to accept lower wages. Now, however, the discipline of prison has partly replaced the discipline of social welfare. Where social welfare used to be employed to discipline the workforce, now prison disciplines the workforce—or, perhaps more accurately, the less employable portion of the workforce—before it is eligible for social services.

The second critical fact about this policy is that although imprisoning more than 2 million people is expensive, it is not, in economic terms, only a social cost. Instead, through the trend toward privatization of prisons, the social cost of housing the incarcerated has been converted into a profitable business. In fact, the leading private corrections company, Corrections Corporation of America (CCA), now operates sixty facilities with fifty-nine thousand beds in twenty-one states, making it the sixth largest prison system in the country.[105] CCA and its allies claim that it costs less to imprison people in a privately run institution. Opponents dispute this contention and further insist that only the state has a right to administer punishment. Yet the fundamentals of this debate go far beyond prisons. The notion that criminals should not be the only people to make money from crime illustrates the sixth and final principle of the modern U.S. economy: if the first five principles have harmful consequences, even those consequences have commercial possibilities.

Politics

For most of the past thirty years, two key political issues—the politics of taxes and the politics of race—have pervaded social welfare. Indeed, in some conservative politicians' skillful hands, these issues are intimately linked. Facing a decline in their living standard, many white lower- and middle-income workers have been especially receptive to racial appeals. Even though AFDC typically accounted for just 1 percent of the federal budget, they imagined their taxes were high because so much money went to welfare programs for people of color.

This argument is appealing for two reasons. It is appealing to the workers themselves, because, though they cannot do much to control the businesses that pay them less, their votes do give them some control over their government. Their votes, in turn, have great appeal for conservative politicians. If, as a conservative, you believe that tax rates on those with the highest income should be low, you must tackle the obvious problem that the top 1 or top 5 percent of the population do not make up a voting majority. To cut taxes on the richest Americans, you must identify a larger group of people and convince them that they will benefit, too. As part of this strategy, it always helps to claim that some important social welfare programs subsidize mostly racial minorities.

The first salvo in the campaign to tie taxes to racial minorities came in 1978, when voters in California enacted Proposition 13. By slashing property taxes, this proposition kindled a national revolt against taxation for welfare spending. Ronald Reagan, the former governor of California, supported the proposition and frequently repeated the argument when he became president.[106] When he and other conservative politicians attacked "welfare queens," no careful listener could think that they were talking about white women.

Several decades of these arguments had a powerful cumulative effect. Again, with support from professional economists, angry white voters created a political climate that made it possible to reduce taxes. At the same time, many of these same voters clamored for changes in our social welfare system. Even though African Americans and whites usually constitute about the same proportion of the total program, this constituency believed the racial myths about public assistance and insisted on the social welfare cutbacks that led to the 1996 welfare reform.

Since passage of that Act, the linkage of taxes and welfare seems to have weakened. The September 11, 2001, attack on the World Trade Center and the Pentagon may even speed up this process. In its aftermath, public opinion polls show a big leap in favorable attitudes toward government: 64 percent of Americans now say they trust the federal government "nearly always" or "most of the time." At double what it was a year before, this percentage is the highest level of trust in government since 1966.[107] To be sure, this jump in confidence could simply reflect a temporary turn to government when the nation has been attacked. At the same time, since both warfare and welfare involve mobilization of resources, it is possible that the mobilization for war may bolster some social welfare programs.

Ideology

It is hardly surprising that several fundamentally conservative ideologies should dominate a fundamentally conservative period. The emphasis here is on the plural, because the dominant conservatism has actually taken several different forms. In fact, since the 1970s, the dominant conservatism has been different in each decade: Nixon's standard Republicanism for the 1970s, Reagan's Social Darwinism for the 1980s, and "market populism" in the 1990s. All these ideologies share a preference for the marketplace, but they diverge substantially in their attitude toward social welfare.

Nixon's conservatism in the late 1960s and early 1970s grew out of a critique of the Great Society programs. His particular variety of conservativism rested on a strong federal government, one that could turn on its own anticommunism and make a strategic alliance with China, while simultaneously using social policy to build a "silent majority" of whites resentful of the 1960s. Although Nixon's New Federalism did begin to shift social welfare services to the states, he is also the only president who ever seriously tried to legislate a national guaranteed income (the Family Assistance Plan, in 1969). Nixon also enacted (in 1972) a 20 percent increase in Social Security benefits, which he then indexed to inflation; established the Supplemental Security Income program that federalized state benefits to the aged, blind, and disabled (1972); and passed the Comprehensive Employment Training Act (1973). Nixon played on resentment of the programs for the poor, but he was never a right-wing populist denouncing Washington, mostly because he relished deploying the power of Washington for his own ends.

Reagan's conservatism was harsher. Building up the military and condemning most social welfare programs, Reagan's approach expressed his Social Darwinist philosophy: the successful deserve to succeed and those who fail get what they deserve. Whereas Nixon shifted resources to build his political coalition, Reagan cut social welfare, slashing the public housing program, tightening eligibility for AFDC, and reducing spending on food stamps.[108] This shift in conservative ideology reflects a new attitude toward the poor. Nixon's ideology assumed that although too much money had been spent on the poor, they were still part of U.S. society; according to Reagan, however, poor people are little more than a drain on the budget and something less than full citizens.

The third variety of conservative thinking arose during the stock market boom of the 1990s. Best described as market populism, this ideology equates markets with democracy and assumes that they express the will of the people better than the political process. In its vision, the corporate CEO is actually a populist statesman acting on behalf of "the common man." Though business is organized hierarchically and its decision making is not democratic, the market populist makes much of all the new choices people can enjoy, with the one large exception that there is no alternative to the market itself. And because all social policy is market-based, it has little to do except to privatize, deregulate, and ensure a healthy environment for business.[109] Most significant, because poor people are barely visible in this environment, market populism does not even bother to attack them. If, in the 1970s, conservatism saw the poor as citizens and in the 1980s it viewed them as lazy and deficient, in the 1990s, market populism treated them as if they were just not there.

Social Movements

The social movements of the past thirty-five years present an ambiguous picture. Some social movements, such as those for women and African Americans, seem to have lost momentum. Others, such as the gay and lesbian movement, have overcome great obstacles to make substantial progress. Most recently, after a long period without new progressive social forces, the anti-globalization movement has arisen to offer a glimmer of hope for the development of an international social policy.

The women's movement and the civil rights movement followed similar paths. Through the early 1970s, each was strong with powerful groups behind it. The feminist movement had the National Organization for Women, plus many local women's liberation groups. The civil rights movement had the NAACP, the Urban League, and countless black churches and local political organizations providing activists. Each of these movements succeeded in legitimizing its respective cause, so that most women today see themselves as equal to men, openly racist statements are increasingly unacceptable, and both women and African Americans have assumed ever more prominent positions in our public life. In this process, however, both movements stopped functioning as *organized social movements*. Partly, they ran into conservative opposition, with campaigns against the Equal Rights Amendment, the pro-choice movement, and every example of affirmative action, from college admission to government money for minority businesses. But they also came apart internally: from programs for battered women to job training in the inner cities, each won enough to take the edge off people's anger and make the militancy go away.[110]

The modern gay rights movement began with the 1969 Stonewall Rebellion. When New York City police raided the Stonewall, a gay bar in Greenwich Village, the patrons fought back, sparking a riot that lasted for two days. The Gay Liberation Front, the Lambda Defense and Educational Fund, and the National Gay and Lesbian Task Force were all established in the next couple of years. But conservatives and the religious right mobilized as well, successfully repealing gay rights ordinances in several states and cities. Nevertheless, despite the ongoing threat of violence and the murders of people like Harvey Milk, a gay member of the San Francisco Board of Supervisors, and Matthew Shepard, a 21-year-old student who was beaten and tied to a fence outside Laramie, Wyoming, in 1998, the movement has made slow but steady progress. Gays and lesbians can adopt children in some localities, discrimination based on sexual orientation is now illegal in a number of states, and many employers, especially in the public sector and some large corporations such as Disney, give spousal benefits to gay and lesbian partners.[111] As a result of these changes, though three-quarters of gays, lesbians, and bisexuals report some experience with discrimination, the same percentage say that they feel more accepted than they did several years ago.[112]

Apart from the hard-won successes of the gay and lesbian movement, social activists have not had much to celebrate over the past thirty years. So the antiglobalization movement of the late 1990s seemed a harbinger of changing political times. The antiglobalization movement criticizes free trade policy and protests international organizations such as the World Bank and the International Monetary Fund that loan money to countries only if they reduce public spending on social needs. In demonstrations at Seattle in 1999, Washington, D.C., in 2000, and Quebec in 2001, it has contended that the capacity of the multinational corporation to bend the global economy to its own needs demands the establishment of social policies that are both international and democratic. With this criticism, the antiglobalization movement became a vehicle for activists to air opinions otherwise ignored in recent years.

Perhaps you have participated in one of these contemporary social movements. Even if you have not, you may well identify with the issues they raise. Social movements always raise policy issues, but these seem an especially apt demonstration of how much social movements can define the public agenda. By reshaping popular opinion and applying pressure on decision makers, they have consistently helped to produce a different policy outcome.

History

The history of social welfare policy since 1969 defines the framework of your social work practice today. If you deal with income security programs, it is important to know that after Nixon increased Social Security in 1972, two other social security "crises" followed within a decade, in 1977 and 1983, both of which increased Social Security taxes. This information places the current debate about privatization of Social Security in a broader historical context. So, too, it is helpful to know about the long-term decline in the value of public assistance, which led to the welfare reform bill of 1996, as well as a parallel decline in the value and use of unemployment benefits. We discuss all these issues at greater length in the next chapter.

The last third of the century has not been kind to the reputation of employment programs either. As chapter 9 highlights, Nixon's passage of the Comprehensive Employment Training Act in 1973 was the high point of public sector job training in the post–World War II period. But after Reagan enacted the Job Training Partnership Act in 1983, job training turned away from the public sector to emphasize workfare for welfare clients. This model lasted fifteen years, until Clinton's Workforce Investment Act of 1998 established the possibility for some diversification in our job training programs.

If you want to help your clients get housing, the recent history of housing policy gives you very little room to maneuver. The 1974 Housing and Community Development Act, with its famous provision for Section 8 subsidized housing, marked the first turn away from the public sector. After Reagan slashed housing subsidies by 75 percent between 1981 and 1988, housing for the poor became ever scarcer and homelessness proliferated. For several years in the mid-1990s, Congress even refused to fund any new Section 8 housing. When it did focus on housing again, Congress broadened the income eligibility requirements for admission to public housing, making it likely that the 1998 Housing Reform Act will reduce the number of units available to poor people. Chapter 10 covers this history in more detail.

As a social worker, it is hard to avoid encountering our health care system, with all that its recent history says about its successes and failures. As we discussed in chapter 1, the explosion of costs in Medicare for the elderly and Medicaid for the poor drove the Reagan administration to experiment with diagnostic related groupings. Relying on the profit motive, DRGs allot a specific amount for each diagnosis, enabling hospitals to pocket the difference if their patients leave early. Together with the rise of for-profit HMOs, this health care model has contributed to a conception of health care as a market commodity, with the best health care in the world for those who can afford it existing alongside some 41 million Americans who have no health coverage at all. And, as chapter 11 spells out, when Clinton in 1994 made a major effort to address some of these problems, his health care reform bill became his first term's most prominent legislative failure.

The recent history of food policy is closely tied with the growth of hunger and homelessness. If you have clients who need to supplement their income with food stamps or rely on a food pantry or soup kitchen for some meals, our patchwork system of voluntary food programs may seem quite inadequate. As chapter 12 explains in the final policy analysis, after the establishment of the food stamp program in 1964, the number of recipients climbed so rapidly that Reagan discontinued the public outreach program. Reports of growing hunger among the poor appear to be true: religious and other nonprofit organizations have been swamped in their efforts to address the need.

This history has had a cumulative effect on contemporary social work practice. You are not studying social welfare policy in the 1960s, when there were heightened possibilities. Instead, you are learning about it in the first decade of the twenty-first century, when the potential for an activist social welfare policy and an expansive social work practice has shrunk. Trends since the 1960s, such as the decline of the feminist and civil rights movements, the rise of corporate-dominated politics, and social policy's subordination to the marketplace, are key factors in explaining this shrinkage. To be sure, there are always difficult clients who reject your help. But the chances are that when you want to help and do not have the resources, a good deal of the frustration you experience comes out of what has happened in social welfare policy during the past thirty years.

The Historical Patterns

Understanding the history of U.S. social welfare is useful for two reasons. First, it enriches our social work practice to identify a distinct historical pattern, to learn that the issues with which we grapple are not unique to our individual work but instead have deep historical roots. Second, understanding these roots is particularly important because at a time when there are more limits on social work practice, you as a new member of the profession can help to figure out how to push those limits back.

So, exactly what have we learned from this history of social welfare? Seven distinct patterns seem evident:

1. The oldest and most persistent stereotype is that poverty is the individual's own fault—that poor people have weaker moral fiber than other, hardworking citizens. This belief divides working people as a class into two distinct groups. Whether they have been labeled the worthy and the unworthy poor, the working and nonworking poor, or the working poor and the underclass, U.S. social welfare history illustrates an apparent need to retain this illusory distinction. As a result, only in a few historical periods have a majority of Americans recognized that poverty comes out of the organization of our political and economic life.

2. Issues of gender and race pervade the history of U.S. social welfare policy. The "family ethic" has defined women's roles, rewarding those who conform and punishing those who do not. In the process, it has also demonstrated how, depending on political and economic needs, social welfare policy has funneled woman's labor into either the workplace or the home. Likewise, on the issue of race, social welfare policy has stigmatized and controlled people of color, defining them as separate and reinforcing distinctions between the white (worthy) and black and Latino (unworthy) poor. This racialized division has been a key factor in keeping working people fragmented, legitimizing residualism, and consistently blocking universal social policies.

3. Social welfare policy has often been punitive, and punitive policies are part of a strategy of social discipline. By deterring poor people from relying on welfare, they are forced to accept the available wage. Political and economic elites often rely on this strategy in times of transition (an agricultural to an industrial economy, or an industrial to a service economy) because elites can best manage this change when workers cannot easily fall back on social programs.

4. Federalism has defined much of social welfare policy's evolution. The fragmentation of the U.S. government into federal, state, and local organizations has consistently retarded policy development. The South's official pol-

icy of racial segregation was probably the single most important factor in this fragmentation.

5. Progress in social welfare policy is reversible. There is nothing inevitable about the evolution of social welfare policy and the welfare state. Policies have been more generous at some times, less generous at others, and will be so again.

6. The state has always been involved in social welfare policy. Although there has long been a mixture of public and private contributions, there has never been a golden age of voluntarism, and voluntarism has never been adequate to the depth and complexity of social welfare–related problems.

7. The activity of the poor on their own behalf has been critical to progress in social welfare policy. The poor have gained through social movements, coalition, and conflict, but rarely through the disinterested benevolence of individuals or the state. That is why, when the poor have been quiet, they have seen little progress, but when they have organized, some breakthroughs have been made.[113]

These seven patterns define U.S. social welfare history. Now that you have reviewed them, you will undoubtedly recognize them in your practice. To start, you can look for them in the policy analyses of the next five chapters. At the same time, you can begin to think about these patterns as impediments to good social work. How do you think their effects might be limited even if they cannot be completely overcome?

III

Policy Analyses: Applying the Policy Model

8

Income Support: Programs and Policies

Income support programs provide cash—not services—to supplement the income of individuals and families. The United States does not provide many of the income support programs offered in other countries. For example, the United States does not guarantee a minimum income, a monthly allowance for each child regardless of the family's earnings, or paid family leave. But the United States does offer a cluster of smaller, and mostly less adequate, income programs. These programs include (1) Social Security retirement (OASI); (2) disability insurance (DI); (3) Supplemental Security Income (SSI); (4) Unemployment Insurance (UI); (5) Temporary Assistance for Needy Families (TANF); (6) workers' compensation; (7) the Earned Income Tax Credit (EITC); (8) general assistance; (9) experimental Individual Development Accounts (IDAs); and (10), still in its formulative stages, the Basic Income Grant (BIG), a novel guaranteed income program. The first eight programs constitute the primary sources of income assistance in the United States; the ninth (IDAs), however, has gained increasing attention. The tenth (BIG) would uproot the most fundamental principles of U.S. social welfare.

This chapter describes each of these programs. It begins by exploring the social change triggers that brought them into existence. Next, it reviews their provisions and benefits. Finally, following the policy model developed in the preceding chapters, it looks at income support programs through the lens of economics, politics, ideology, social movements, and history. By examining each program from all of these different angles, we should be able to obtain a full portrait. From the beginning, however, one important point needs to be remembered. Although we are going to treat each program separately, they do not exist separately, and, in fact, interact with other forms of social support in at least three different ways.

The first way they interact is as *coentitlements*. In a coentitlement, the use of one benefit automatically entitles you to another. Hence, eligibility for TANF automatically makes you eligible for food stamps and Medicaid. The premise is that once you have demonstrated sufficient poverty, you should have access to all those programs serving the poorest of the poor.

The second interaction, *automatic disentitlements*, is the exact opposite. To prevent duplication, it prohibits the receipt of benefits from similar programs at the same time. For example, if you are a disabled worker, the government deducts your workers' compensation benefits from your disability insurance.

The third interaction involves an *unintended coentitlement*, which mistakenly authorizes people to get money from several different sources. Armed Forces and civil service personnel used to get a military or civil service pension and then, if they wished, work for ten years to vest in Social Security. By bringing them into the Social Security system in the mid-1980s, Congress ended this dual eligibility.[1]

The larger point is that in the absence of a single large cash program like a guaranteed annual income, people who need money may try to get it from many different sources. Amid the maze of U.S. income supports, it is inevitable that these sources will both supplement and conflict with one another.

Poverty rate since 1960. Income support programs are supposed to reduce poverty. Looking at this chart, to what extent do you think they have succeeded?

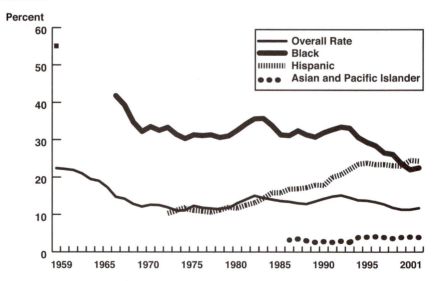

Try an experiment: ask a group of friends to explain what has led to the development of new income support programs. Depending on their political views, they would probably tell you either that people needed them, or that some group made a lot of noise. They would not be completely wrong, but they would not be completely right, either.

It is true that most poor and working people do not get assistance unless they *need* assistance. But who defines that need? And of all the needs out there, how does their particular need come to receive the necessary political attention? The answers to these questions suggest that the trigger for new income programs is a lot more complicated than one might initially think.

In fact, four different social change mechanisms prepared the way for the passage of these income support programs. Reflecting the functions of social welfare policy detailed in chapter 2, the first involves an effort to *stabilize the marketplace;* it explains a great deal about the spread of workers' compensation. The second mechanism closely relates to issues of *government structure and political control*, such as the desire for centralization; hence, in 1972, the federal government took over the states' individual programs for the aged, blind, and temporarily disabled and combined them all into SSI. The third mechanism arises when *instability in the labor market* requires more direct government intervention. First enacted in 1975, the EITC offered cash to supplement low-wage work. Finally, there is the classic trigger of social change that Frances Fox Piven and Richard Cloward describe in their 1971 book, *Regulating the Poor*, whereby *an increase in social protest* brings about a growth in social programs.[2] Enacted in response to social movements during the Great Depression, the 1935 Social Security Act illustrates this mechanism. With the understanding that none of these programs has a single cause as the trigger for social change, let's discuss each of these mechanisms in more detail.

Marketplace Instability

The impetus for workers' compensation came from a desire to stabilize the marketplace. Death and injury on the job constituted a very serious problem in early twentieth-century America. In 1904, 28 of every 10,000 railroad workers died in an accident; in 1916, 1 of every 10 was injured. Similarly, in 1906, 48 of every 10,000 coal miners were killed. All told, 35,000 workers were killed and 536,000 injured in U.S. industry each year from 1888 to 1908.[3]

Initially, workers sued but found it difficult to collect. Employers took refuge in a variety of legal defenses. They blamed accidents on the worker's own negligence; they invoked the "fellow servant" doctrine, whereby other workers were at fault; or sometimes, they simply contended that workers had accepted employment under conditions they knew to be dangerous. By 1908, however, sixteen states had outlawed the fellow servant rule, and workers began to win lawsuits. As their success in the courtroom forced employers to buy more liability insurance, the total value of that coverage skyrocketed from $200,000 in 1887 to $35 million in 1912.[4]

When workers die or are injured on the job, their families need some income assistance. In the case of workers' compensation, however, the trigger for social change was less the injury and death of workers than the financial uncertainty that a flood of lawsuits produced. As this uncertainty became intolerable, one state after another enacted workers' compensation. Minnesota, Wisconsin, and New York were the first, beginning in 1909, but by 1920, forty-three states had passed legislation requiring employers to compensate their employees for injuries sustained at work. Typically, the legislation mandates employers to purchase insurance from either private insurance companies or a state insurance fund. Once again, the impetus for this legislation was not the injuries themselves, but the desire to stabilize what had become an increasingly unstable marketplace.[5]

Government Structure and Political Control

The second trigger for social change has more to do with government structure and political control. When President Franklin Roosevelt's administration passed the Social Security Act in 1935, it allocated responsibility for different social programs to different levels of the government. The retirement part of Social Security went to the federal government; unemployment insurance went to a mixed federal/state arrangement; and welfare, known as Aid to Dependent Children along with assistance to the aged, blind, and disabled, got assigned to the states.

As circumstances changed over the next thirty years, this division of responsibility made less sense. The mechanization of southern agriculture meant that employers did not have to depend on cheap African American farm labor and the state-run welfare programs that helped to supply it. In addition, as the Social Security system matured, it assumed responsibility for a larger number of aged, blind, and disabled people who might otherwise have been eligible for state aid. Faced with less state opposition to a comparatively small program, the federal government could opt for administrative efficiency and centralize responsibility for the aged, blind, and disabled. As another by-product, the resulting program, SSI (1972), had the not so incidental consequence of turning those still receiving welfare from the states into the even less worthy poor.[6]

Labor Market Instability

Instability in the labor market is the third trigger of social change. When Congress authorized the EITC in 1975, the median American wage had just begun a twenty-five-year-long slide. Although the program, which provides a tax refund to low-wage workers, started quite small, Presidents Reagan, Bush, and Clinton all expanded it. These expansions served two functions: they subsidized the income of low-wage workers and kept labor costs down for employers. With liberals approving of the subsidy to workers and conservatives approving of the subsidy to business, the EITC helped to manage the transition from a manufacturing to a service economy. Without the government's intervention, the pressure for higher wages might have intensified. Instead, a quarter-century of instability in the labor market brought forth the EITC. There is just one problem with this system: taxpayers must foot the bill for industry's inability or unwillingness to pay a decent wage.

Social Unrest

Social unrest is the fourth and perhaps best-known trigger for change in welfare programs. According to this theory, the political and economic system depends on the silence of poor people. Because poor people do not customarily engage in disruption, their marches and demonstrations alter the ordinary rhythms of public life. Typically, officials both condemn these actions and increase their spending on welfare. Often, when the tumult dies down, this spending is then cut back.[7]

Social unrest certainly helped to trigger the passage of the Social Security Act in 1935. In the midst of the worst depression the United States has ever experienced, the poor and unemployed took to the streets. When World War I veterans launched the 1932 Bonus March on Washington to demand early payment of monies promised eight years earlier, it took U.S. Army tanks under the command of General Douglas MacArthur and Colonel Dwight D. Eisenhower to disperse them. Likewise, as councils of the unemployed formed in many cities, crowds of neighbors would sometimes block marshals trying to evict tenants who could not pay the rent. In a prelude to Social Security, the Townsend movement proposed a pension scheme in which everyone over 60 would receive $200 a month on the condition that they spent it immediately. With his platform of taxing the rich, some commentators thought that Louisiana Governor Huey Long's Share the Wealth campaign could threaten the reelection of President Franklin Roosevelt. It was, in short, a time when the popularity of radical ideas called into question the reluctance of the federal government to address the failures of the private sector.[8]

An inclusive Social Security Act constituted one response to this turmoil. Shaped by the Roosevelt-appointed Committee on Economic Security, the Act provided retirement pensions for the aged, unemployment benefits to workers who lost their jobs, and assistance to children through ADC (later, AFDC). As a federal intervention, the Act broke with previous U.S. social policies. But it also represented the most conservative version of all the available policy options. It preserved the states' rights to determine their own eligibility standards in unemployment and welfare, financed pensions with a regressive payroll tax, and excluded health care and housing. Still, even though the conservative tilt made its impact less sweeping than it otherwise might have been, there is no denying its significance. By providing poor and working people with some federal support, it effectively proclaimed that they were citizens, too. In the process, it also demonstrated the influence of social unrest as a trigger of change in social policy.

Yet, the subsequent history of the Social Security Act does not completely fit the theory. In the 1960s, the welfare rights movement initially produced a rapid growth in the welfare rolls, followed, when the movement declined, by a sudden tightening. But there were no cutbacks in the aftermath of Social Security. Several factors explain this difference. First, as an omnibus bill, the pension/social insurance part of the Act provided some initial protection for the welfare provision. Second, a return to normalcy usually precedes the cutback phase of the cycle. The late 1930s witnessed continued social unrest, marked most dramatically by a surge in union organizing; at the same time, the nation mobilized for war. In these anything-but-normal circumstances, the classic pattern just did not hold.

Looking over this list of the triggers for social change, one theme stands out: need alone is never enough. Except in social insurance programs like Social Security that provide benefits nearly universally, people do not receive money unless they are needy. Nevertheless, the need for money is a necessary but not sufficient explanation for the decision to introduce a new income support program. Whether it was rationalizing the marketplace, greater administrative efficiency, subsidizing business and labor, or responding to social unrest, in every instance, some other political or economic factor has also been required. It is useful to keep this point in mind as we describe these programs

Social Security

Officially designated OASDI (Old Age, Survivors, and Disability Insurance), the Social Security program includes both an old-age pension and disability insurance. We first discuss the old age pension and analyze the George W. Bush administration's proposals for reform through privatization. In the next section, we describe disability insurance.

The Social Security retirement program is the single largest social program in the United States. Social Security covers more than 154 million workers and currently provides benefits to some 46 million people (39 million in pension benefits to retired workers and their survivors, and 7 million through disability). In 2002, the average monthly Social Security benefit for all retired workers was $874 a month. As a maximum, however, a single worker could get $1,660 a month, and an aged couple could receive as much as $1,454 each. To be eligible for these benefits, you must have the equivalent of forty quarters (ten years). Since 1978, individuals receive credit on an annual basis by earning a preestablished minimum up to a maximum of four quarters a year. Raised annually in step with the average wage, this minimum is currently set at $870.[9]

Every year, the government increases Social Security benefits through cost-of-living adjustments keyed to the previous year's inflation rate. In addition, as a result of the Senior Citizens' Freedom to Work Act of 2000, while $1 in Social Security benefits is still deducted for every $2 in earnings above $11,280 for those aged 62–65, there is no longer any limit on how much retired persons can earn once they reach their sixty-fifth birthday.[10]

Payroll taxes fund the Social Security program. Both employers and employees pay 6.2 percent of the worker's salary up to the income ceiling to fund Social Security, and another 1.45 percent on all earnings to fund Medicare. In 2003, the income ceiling is $87,000. That is why if you look for deductions on your paycheck under FICA (the Federal Insurance Contributions Act), you will see that 7.65 percent (6.20% + 1.45%) has been deducted up to that ceiling. The ceiling rises almost every year, but does not apply to the 1.45 percent Medicare tax, which is collected regardless of income. The self-employed shoulder responsibility for both the worker and employer contribution; their tax rate is 15.30 percent.

Employers forward these taxes to the government to be placed in the Social Security Trust Fund, where they are turned over to the U.S. Treasury in exchange for interest-accruing government bonds. Boosted by the earnings of the baby boomers, this trust fund had a 2001 balance of more than $1.21 trillion.[11] But contrary to popular myth, the Social Security Administration does not have a safe deposit box with your name and number on it. Instead, the program might best be described as a chain letter stretched out over time. When you work, your contributions pay for the people who are now retired. All you can hope for is that this financial compact continues to hold, so that when you retire, contributions from subsequent generations will be sufficient to take care of you.

Because the benefits that Social Security provides are earnings-related, workers who earn more—white, male, educated, and professional—get more. Historically, as chapter 7 pointed out, Social Security has underpaid people of color because domestic and farm labor was not covered in the original Act, and those who were eligible got fewer benefits as a result of their shorter average life span. For those who do earn more, however, the larger dollar amount makes up a lower percentage of their old salary. Social insurance experts refer to this figure as the replacement rate. For example, the Social Security Administration projects that the low-wage worker born in 1973 will enjoy a replacement rate of 56 percent, considerably higher than the average earner's 42 percent or the maximum earner's rate of 27 percent.[12]

It is true that the Social Security tax is regressive because both low and high earners pay the same rate. Nevertheless, the progressive distribution of benefits partly offsets its regressive financing. Progressive in its benefits, regressive in its taxes, the Social Security program reflects the U.S. political electorate's desire to ensure that its major social insurance program engages in some, but not too much, redistribution.

Yet within these limits, Social Security remains a good deal. For those retiring in 2010, it will take only thirteen years for benefits to equal their contributed taxes and interest. Because men have a life expectancy of another sixteen years past retirement and women more than nineteen, the value of

Old Age Survivors Insurance (OASI), 1935

Number of recipients:	39 million retirees
Who offers the benefit or service:	The public sector through the federal government
What form does it take:	A monthly cash payment
To whom is it provided:	Retired workers, their survivors, and dependents
At whose expense:	In 2002, OASI cost $382 billion. The payments are an earned entitlement funded out of the Social Security payroll tax. In effect, however, because each retiree soon exhausts what he or she contributed, every generation of retirees depends on the next generation of workers to pay for their retirement.

Disability Insurance, 1956

Number of recipients:	7 million
Who offers the benefit or service:	The public sector through the federal government (the Social Security Administration)
What form does it take:	A monthly cash payment
To whom is it provided:	Disabled workers and their dependents
At whose expense?	In 2002, the program cost $69 billion. It is funded through the Social Security payroll tax.

Supplemental Security Income (SSI), 1974

Number of recipients:	6.4 million
Who offers the benefit or service:	The public sector through the federal government (the Social Security Administration)
What form does it take:	A monthly cash payment
To whom is it provided:	Poor people who are aged, blind, or disabled
At whose expense?	The program costs $28 billion. Funded by general revenue, it replaced the original state programs for the aged, blind, and disabled.

Unemployment Insurance Benefits, 1935

Number of recipients:	Typically, between 7 and 10 million, depending on economic conditions
Who offers the benefit or service:	The states
What form does it take:	A weekly cash payment
To whom is it provided:	Unemployed workers who are actively looking for work
At whose expense?	UIB costs $25 billion ($21 billion in benefits and $3.6 billion in administrative costs). Employers fund it through a 6.2 percent federal tax on the first $7,000 of each employee's income. Usually, this tax is partly offset by a 5.4 percent rebate, making the effective federal tax rate 0.8 percent.

Temporary Assistance to Needy Families (TANF), 1996: replacing Aid to Families with Dependent Children (AFDC), 1962, and Aid to Dependent Children, 1935

Number of recipients:	5.4 million
Who offers the benefit or service:	The public sector, through the states

(continued)

What form does it take:	A monthly cash payment for food, rent, and other basic necessities
To whom is it provided:	Poor people, mostly female-headed households and their children
At whose expense?	TANF costs $18 billion. Tax revenues (a federal block grant and a state contribution) fund the program.

Workers' compensation, 1908 (first state program)

Number of recipients:	126 million workers are covered
Who offers the benefit or service:	The states
What form does it take:	A monthly cash payment + medical benefits
To whom is it provided:	Workers injured on the job
At whose expense:	In 2000, $46 billion was paid in workers' compensation. Employers must obtain insurance coverage, which costs them a total of $54 billion.

Earned Income Tax Credit (EITC), 1975

Number of recipients:	18 million families
Who offers the benefit or service:	The federal government
What form does it take:	A cash tax refund
To whom is it provided:	Low-income families who work
At whose expense:	In 2000, the federal government spent about $30 billion on EITC.

General assistance (1935)

Number of recipients:	Because of the variation among these programs, there are no exact numbers, but probably more than 1 million people
Who offers the benefit or service:	35 of the 50 states and some localities
What form does it take:	Cash, clothing, or funds to obtain medical care
To whom is it provided:	Individuals under the age of 65 who do not qualify for other social welfare programs
At whose expense:	Taxpayers, through payment of state and local taxes

Individual Development Accounts (IDAs), 1990s

Number of recipients:	Few: the program is still in its experimental stages
Who offers the benefit or service:	The federal government
What form does it take:	Cash to build assets, in the form of a 2:1 matching grant for money that participants save
To whom is it provided:	Poor people, particularly those in the TANF program
At whose expense:	The federal government has funded the experiments so far, at a cost (in the 2002 budget) of $25 million.

Basic Income Grant (BIG); not yet established

Number of recipients:	All U.S. citizens
Who offers the benefit or service:	The federal government
What form does it take:	A universal monthly cash allowance
To whom is it provided:	All U.S. citizens
At whose expense:	The federal government would fund this program, through a progressive income tax.

their benefits will substantially exceed their contributions. These benefits extend even to the next generation. Without Social Security, nearly half—48 percent—of the elderly would be poor, or four times the actual rate.[13] Of course, if the poverty rate among the elderly were that much higher, most of the additional financial burden would fall on their adult children.

Led by President George W. Bush, doubts have nonetheless been raised about the long-term solvency of Social Security generally, particularly about its value for African Americans, Latinos, and women. Conservatives have claimed that privatization would be better for these groups. They have also asserted that it would improve the system's overall financial integrity.

As part of the campaign for privatization targeting key electoral groups, a report by the Heritage Foundation, a conservative Washington think tank, contended that African Americans and Latinos would have more money for their retirement if they were allowed to invest their Social Security contributions in private accounts containing a mix of stocks and government bonds.[14] Such a provocative claim received a good deal of attention, until critics zeroed in on the report's assumptions. The Social Security Administration found that the authors had overstated the payroll taxes that workers pay and underestimated the benefits they receive. African American and Latino workers are more likely to have a low income, so that Social Security actually provides them with a better return on their investment. Furthermore, the Heritage report excluded disability and survivor benefits, more of which flow to African Americans. It also failed to factor in the cost of paying for current and soon-to-be-retired workers during the transition to a private system. This omission notably distorts the returns to young, low-wage African American and Latino workers, who would otherwise have to bear these costs.[15]

Arguments about Social Security shortchanging women rest on firmer ground. When the Social Security program became law in 1935, the family structure was quite different: men worked and women stayed home to raise children. When the worker reached retirement age, the family received benefits equal to the earner's full pension plus half that amount for the spouse. If the earner died, the surviving spouse got the earner's full share.[16] Now that most women work, this benefit system produces inequities. Employed women still cannot receive any more than 50 percent of their husband's benefits. With the family getting just 150 percent of benefits, this provision is heavily biased against dual-earner households, especially those where the husband and wife make comparable salaries so that the wife would receive her full benefits if she lived alone.

Nor is this provision the only inequity. Women who divorce after less than ten years cannot claim survivor insurance. They get paid just 74 percent of what the average full-time male employee receives and work an average of just twenty-seven years when the benefit formula assumes an average of thirty-five. And when her husband dies, Social Security payments can drop precipitously. Depending on whether or not she was drawing her own benefit, a widow receives a monthly check that is two-thirds or one-half of the couple's combined benefit. All these inequities suggest that changes such as increasing divorced women's spousal benefit from 50 to 75 percent are essential to feminist reform of the Social Security system.[17]

By itself, however, privatization is more likely to worsen than resolve these problems. Not only do older women have a higher poverty rate than older men, but 25 percent of older women living alone rely on Social Security as their only source of income. With lower salaries and less money to invest, privatization would penalize women. It would also cost them life and disability insurance, which provide benefits to spouses caring for children if a worker retires, becomes disabled, or dies.[18]

Despite all these doubts about privatization, it is appealing to some people who fear that the Social Security system is going to run out of money. The demographic trends are certainly indisputable. Because taxes on the earnings of current workers pay for the retirement of former workers, the ratio declines as the number of beneficiaries rises. In 1960, for example, the worker:beneficiary ratio was 5:1, but it dropped to 3:4 in 2000 on the way down to a projected 2:5 in 2020 and 2:1 in 2040. Proponents of privatization contend that shifting the Social Security system into the stock market is the best way we can help American workers shoulder this heavier burden.[19]

Although this argument sounds seductive, it actually has many problems. By law, the Social Security system must plan seventy-five years ahead—an extremely long time frame. At this distance, small percentage differences in growth, productivity, and wages make a huge difference in the size of the Social Security Trust Fund. Just three years of economic growth pushed back the day of reckoning in the Social Security system—the time when it will no longer have enough money to fulfill all its financial obligations—from 2029 to 2041. And over the full seventy-five-year span, the total deficit is just 1.87 percent of projected receipts. Surely, even in the worst-case scenario, we should be able to figure out how we can provide the fund with this additional income.[20]

Besides, the idea of privatization has some serious problems. Administrative costs for Social Security presently run at less than 1 percent of its budget. If privatization creates 150 million separate accounts that must be managed individually, administrative costs will surge to 15 or 20 percent. Such an increase would redirect another $60 to $80 billion a year to Wall Street portfolio managers.

Perhaps most significant, privatization cannot guarantee workers a secure income. After all, as the corporate scandals of 2002 have proved once again, stock markets go up and stock markets go down. Even without touching a penny of his or her assets, someone who was born in 1901, retired in 1966, and died in 1982 would have suffered a 44 percent drop in the value of his or her portfolio, reflecting the market's decline during those sixteen years of retirement.

Indeed, the whole promise of rapid growth in stock values may well be illusory. For the past seventy-five years, a 3.5 percent growth rate has produced a 7 percent annual increase in the value of stocks. For the next seventy-five years, however, the Social Security Trust Fund projects a growth rate of just 1.5 percent. The stock market of an economy expanding at less than half its historic rate cannot continue to appreciate at the same speed. If, as some plans propose, the transition to privatization directs some portion of each worker's taxes—say 2 percent, or about $75 billion—into individual accounts, there will be less money than now for surviving spouses, retirees, and the disabled.[21]

But President Bush is committed to privatization, so he appointed a commission to respond to these criticisms and point the way toward Social Security reform. Although every member of the commission favored privatization, the best they could do was put forth three tentative plans. All three substantially reduced Social Security benefits (depending on circumstance, the reduction might range from 17 to 41 percent), and none specified the source of any additional money or restored long-term balance to the Social Security system. Together with growing doubts about the stock market, the commission's failure to produce a serious reform proposal has slowed privatization's momentum.[22]

Social Security is a social contract across generations. You do not ask for a high rate of return on your fire insurance; you just expect it to be there in case your house burns down. Social Security operates on the same premise. If you compare administrative costs and include the expense of paying for all current dependents, its rate of return is similar to what privatization promises. With a little tinkering—a faster growth rate, an increase in the ceiling on taxable income, or a further delay in retirement—a public Social Security program will be around for years to come.

Disability Insurance

Disability insurance is one of a series of supplements to the original Social Security Act. Enacted in 1956, this supplement extended assistance to disabled workers between ages 50 and 64. Subsequent amendments expanded these benefits to the dependents of disabled workers (1958) and then to workers below the age of 50 (1960). Generally, these benefits are slightly lower than those for retirees. In 2002, the average payment to all disabled workers was $815 a month; for a disabled worker with a spouse and one or more children, it was $1,360.[23]

The definition of disability is the key to this program. The law defines disability as an inability to engage in "substantial gainful activity" due to a physical or mental impairment that has lasted five months and is expected to last for at least twelve months or result in death. In 2002, the standard for substantial gainful activity was $780 a month, except for blind individuals, who can earn up to $1,300. Federally funded state agencies make these determinations. Workers are eligible if they have a total of twenty quarters of coverage (five years) in the preceding forty quarters (ten years).[24]

Except for a very controversial decline during the early 1980s under President Reagan, the number of recipients in the disability program has climbed fairly steadily. From 1970 to 1980, the number on people receiving disability insurance grew from 2.6 to 4.6 million. This upward leap prompted a Social Security Administration audit, which found that as many as 20 percent of all recipients might actually be ineligible. Relying on this audit, Congress authorized triennial reviews, a mandate that the Reagan administration used to throw almost a half million people off the rolls. Reports even documented instances of rejected cardiac cases who died in Social Security Office waiting rooms, as well as a surge in the number of mentally ill who lost their benefits and became homeless. Finally, in 1986, the Supreme Court denounced the reviews as "arbitrary and capricious." The disability rolls soon resumed their upward rise, so that by 2002, 7 million people were receiving benefits. Disability insurance is not means-tested. But as many of these new recipients were low-skill workers who had turned to disability benefits in the absence of other options, the new influx may well test the premise of whether social insurance used in this way can maintain its standing with the public.[25]

Supplemental Security Income

SSI is the federal means-tested income support program for the aged, blind, and disabled. Although both SSI (Title XVI) and disability insurance (Title II) come out of the Social Security Act, SSI is a residual welfare program funded out of general revenues and not a form of social insurance financed by payroll taxes. In 2002, SSI paid $545 a month (76 percent of the poverty line) for an individual, and $817 a month (91 percent of the poverty line) for a couple. Like Social Security, these figures rise annually through a cost-of-living adjustment. About 6.4 million people were recipients in 2002, when SSI disbursed about $28 billion. In addition, all but seven states and jurisdictions offer their own optional state supplementation of the SSI program.[26]

Eligibility guidelines place stringent resource limits on SSI recipients. An individual may not have more than $2,000 in resources; a couple, not more than $3,000. Other eligibility criteria include either U.S. citizenship or legal resident status attained by the date of the passage of the welfare reform bill in August 1996, and a monthly income less than the SSI payment. Although the original provisions for SSI permitted payments to people with alcohol and drug addictions, Congress revoked this authorization in 1996. Now, substance abusers cannot receive SSI unless they also have another disabling condition; in these circumstances, the government sends the check to a representative payee, preferably an organization. By contrast, SSI does assume that anyone with a medical condition such as AIDS or severe mental retardation is automatically eligible.[27]

Because SSI is a welfare program, these rules are complicated, and just 55 to 60 percent of those who could receive SSI actually do so (this is called "the take-up rate"). In part, the take-up rate is low because SSI was originally designed more for physical than mental disabilities. If you can work some of the time—which is true of people with bipolar or schizophrenic disorders—then you are not eligible. In addition, eligibility determinations often demand substantial medical documentation. With as much as one year required for all the paperwork, the relatively low take-up rate is hardly surprising.[28]

The eligibility of children for SSI is one of the most important recent developments in the program. In a famous Supreme Court case, *Sullivan v. Zebley* (1990), the Court ruled that the definition of disability for children was more restrictive than for adults and thus had to be struck down. In the aftermath of this decision, the number of children receiving benefits rose rapidly, and Congress looked to tighten eligibility requirements for the program. As a result, the 1996 welfare reform law eliminated all references to maladaptive behavior for children and required SSI to evaluate their condition every three years.[29]

Even as a federal program, then, SSI embodies the contradictions of welfare in the United States. The federal government's takeover of responsibility for the aged, blind, and disabled helped to overcome some of the administrative problems associated with a state-run welfare system. But while the aged, blind, and disabled are the worthy poor from whom little work can be expected, SSI is still a means-tested welfare program with high barriers to eligibility and low monthly benefits. Ultimately, although it is better that the federal government administers SSI, it must still operate within the limits established for all welfare programs.

Unemployment Insurance Benefits

Unemployment insurance (UI) is another income support program that traces its origins to the Social Security Act of 1935. By law, UI has two objectives: (1) to provide temporary assistance to workers whom employers have laid off, and (2) to increase the purchasing power of the unemployed and thereby help to stabilize the economy during recessions. In 2000, UI offered coverage to 125 million workers, or about 97 percent of all wage and salary employees and 89 percent of the civilian workforce. Although maximum benefits varied widely by state, from $190 a week in Mississippi and Alabama to $646 a week in Massachusetts, the average benefit was just $215 a week. Since 1986, all unemployment benefits have been taxable.[30]

In creating the UI program, policymakers faced the persistent political question of the federal-state relationship. A purely federal program would violate deeply held American views about states' rights; a program run individually by fifty states would be an administrative nightmare. These extremes framed some critical policy issues. Should Washington or the states retain the funds collected by a payroll tax on employers? Should the federal government determine the amount and duration of UI and levy taxes accordingly? Should employers' participation be mandatory or voluntary?

Policymakers came up with a resourceful compromise to address these issues. Although each state would levy what is, in essence, a federal payroll

*Before unemployment insurance,
the unemployed sometimes took
any job to bring in a little income.*

tax (currently, 6.2 percent of salary up to $7,000), the states would also get a tax credit (now 5.4 percent), making the actual federal tax rate 0.8 percent. After the states collect this tax, they send the money to Washington, where the federal government maintains a separate fund for each state. Because the states also set eligibility and benefit levels, UI represents a very creative blend of states' rights with federal financing.[31]

This hybrid administrative structure has fostered significant diversity in the states' eligibility rules. These rules focus on three major factors: (1) the amount of recent employment and earnings; (2) demonstrated ability and willingness to accept appropriate employment; and (3) disqualification related to the claimant's last employment termination. On the second and third factors, there is little disagreement: most states insist that UI applicants should be willing to work and disqualify individuals for leaving work without good cause. The states do diverge, however, on the first issue. Although most states require six months of employment within the prior year, eligibility for the minimum weekly benefit varies from annual earnings of just $130 in Hawaii to $4,280 in Florida. Likewise, for the maximum weekly benefit, the threshold ranges from $5,850 in Nebraska to $30,888 in Colorado.[32]

States usually provide coverage for twenty-six weeks. In the aftermath of the September 11, 2001, attacks, however, the government extended benefits for an additional thirteen. A second thirteen-week extension may be available in those states already experiencing high unemployment. Although the first thirteen-week extension technically has been available since the early 1980s, the relatively low unemployment rates of the late 1990s limited the number of workers eligible for it in recent years.[33]

UI worked best in an industrial economy, where it provided some financial support during periods of unemployment at the same job. If the demand for steel dropped or orders slowed at the Chevy plant, UI could help to tide workers over until the factory needed them again. In this kind of economy, the percentage of unemployed who received benefits rose quickly during recessions, reaching a high of 75 percent in 1975.

Then the economy changed. With the shift from industry to service, the number of permanent layoffs increased and workers were no longer able to return to their old jobs. Many states also tightened their eligibility requirements. Between 1992 and 1997, for example, fourteen states added provisions to disqualify eligible persons discharged for refusing to take a drug test, and another thirteen states disqualified employees of temporary help agencies whose assignments ended but who did not report back to their agency before they filed for UI. The combination of a changing economy and tightened eligibility requirements drove down the percentage of unemployed workers receiving benefits, so that currently, only about 40 percent get some financial help.[34]

In addition to the declining percentage of workers receiving assistance, the UI program has some other problems. Because the program pays for unemployment, not retraining, it wastes an opportunity to prepare some workers for jobs in the new economy. The program also discriminates against women because those who leave for lack of child care cannot easily reestablish eligibility. Finally, the extra taxes employers pay as the cost of laying off another worker are usually less than the cost to the UI program of paying the worker's benefits. As a result, employers tend to lay off too many workers, leading a number of states to experiment with prorated benefits (half of benefits for half a week's work) for workers on shortened time.

Clearly, UI continues to perform a valuable service by tiding workers over during slack periods. Nevertheless, the existence of these problems suggests that some reforms are necessary to keep the program in tune with the needs of an increasingly female workforce and a changing economy.[35]

Temporary Assistance for Needy Families

In 1996, TANF replaced AFDC as the main U.S. welfare program. TANF ended the guarantee of federal assistance embodied in AFDC. Instead, for the period of TANF's original authorization (1997–2002), each state received a fixed amount in the form of a block grant. Setting a five-year lifetime limit on the receipt of public assistance (except for the 20 percent of each state's caseload that is eligible for a hardship exemption), TANF demands that the

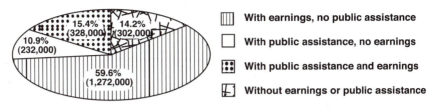

15.4% (328,000)	14.2% (302,000)
10.9% (232,000)	
59.6% (1,272,000)	

▥ With earnings, no public assistance

☐ With public assistance, no earnings

⊞ With public assistance and earnings

⊡ Without earnings or public assistance

Distribution of poor children by source of family income. Popular myths to the contrary, very few poor families with young children rely exclusively on public assistance.

head of the household—typically, a female caretaker—work within two years of receiving benefits. It also barred aid to legal immigrants who entered the United States after the August 22, 1996, passage of the law.[36]

Because social policy experts use different standards to evaluate welfare reform, they have come to different conclusions about its success. For those looking primarily at national caseload levels, TANF brought about a decline between 1996 and 2001 of 57 percent, with Wisconsin leading the way at more than 90 percent. Improved economic conditions undoubtedly explain part of this drop. Indeed, early on, President Clinton's Council of Economic Advisors suggested that the economy might explain as much as 44 percent. Still, as most studies show that about half of those who left welfare are now working, many policy experts have hailed TANF's success.[37]

Building on this consensus, the Bush administration has proposed a 2002 TANF reauthorization that expands the work requirement from thirty to forty hours a week. During TANF's first five years, many states failed to spend their block grant monies and, in particular, failed to provide enough day care. Ten hours of additional work will further strain this limited day care capacity,

Chart—Number of welfare recipients since 1960. Between workfare and a tightening of eligibility rules, the welfare rolls have dropped in recent years.

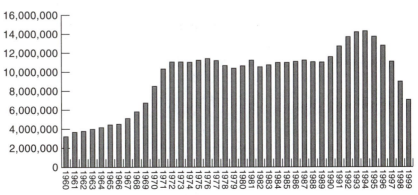

especially as states seeking to meet the caseload workfare quota may be forced to shift money out of day care and invest it in make-work programs.[38]

The Bush proposal also emphasizes marriage. For the Bush administration, marriage combined with work points the way out of poverty. In some respects, this position makes sense, because two married people can combine their incomes and share housing costs. Yet for poor women, the reality does not quite match the theory. Poor women are less likely to meet men who earn enough to raise the family out of poverty. They have little incentive to marry an adult for whom they are going to have to care, and no reason to do so if, as up to 30 percent of women on welfare report, that adult is abusive. Violating a basic principle of equity, the Bush administration singles out women on public assistance as the subject of governmental marriage promotion, while ignoring those receiving student loans and Social Security checks. Finally, and perhaps most significant, the marriage proposal stumbles on the contradiction between the economic independence of female workers and the economic dependence of wives. As studies in Connecticut and Iowa have shown, women who get jobs after welfare are less likely to get married for the simple reason that once they have obtained an independent source of income, they become more selective about their prospective partner.[39]

Seeing TANF as a success, both these Bush administration proposals seek to further reduce the welfare rolls. But while this interpretation of TANF guides many policy analysts and is popular in the media, others raise a broader question: Was the purpose of TANF to get people off welfare, or to end poverty? If TANF has done well by the first standard, it has lagged badly on the second.[40]

Most studies have found two distinct groups of recipients who have left welfare. By any standard, one group has clearly done worse. Its predicament appears in reports of spikes in the size of the homeless population and in longer food lines at neighborhood kitchens. In 1999, for example, 47 percent of the families that recently left welfare for full-time, full-year employment experienced one or more critical hardships, such as going without food, shelter, or necessary medical care. Despite the improving economic conditions of the late 1990s, this figure represents a 10 percent increase over just two years earlier.[41]

Another group of approximately equal size represents the official "successes." These are the people who average about $7 an hour in the typical post-welfare job and with intermittent employment typically earn less than $10,000 annually. By the first standard, they are employed, productive citizens; by the second, they are still unquestionably poor. Furthermore, as they are now working harder outside the home, they may well be less able to raise a family and take care of their children. Indeed, in the aftermath of welfare reform, researchers have noticed a sudden spike of 600,000 more children (and 200,000 additional urban African American children) living in no-parent families.[42]

This is perhaps the most striking outcome of the TANF experiment: low-paid work may lead to a decline in a family's standard of living. The key to understanding this outcome lies in a groundbreaking study about the real

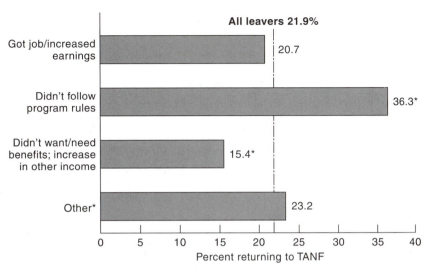

All leavers 21.9%

	Percent returning to TANF
Got job/increased earnings	20.7
Didn't follow program rules	36.3*
Didn't want/need benefits; increase in other income	15.4*
Other*	23.2

Return rates by reason for leaving TANF. Last hired, first fired: because the jobs former recipients get are often transient, a surprisingly large number have returned to welfare.

spending patterns of welfare mothers, conducted by sociologists Kathyrn Edin and Laura Lein. They discovered that recipients spent an average of $876 a month, $311 more than they received from welfare and food stamps. They got the additional money from a combination of sources: boyfriends, relatives, and babysitting and other off-the-book jobs. When they secured a regular paying job, their income did rise to $1,243 a month, but unfortunately, by the time they totaled up the cost associated with working—clothing, transportation, and child care—their standard of living had actually declined. As Edin and Lein demonstrate, the issue is not whether welfare mothers work, but the terms of that work—in particular, whether the wages and benefits they receive actually improve their lives.[43]

It is not hard to sketch a route out of poverty for former welfare recipients. They need good jobs, health care, day care, job training, and education. Some TANF programs have focused on these elements. For example, Portland, Oregon, has stressed job quality, substantially increased participation in education and training, and helped more participants obtain both a GED and an occupational certificate.[44] Overall, however, such programs have been the exception. TANF is a success because it cut the welfare rolls, but it is a failure because it has substituted this goal for a reduction in poverty.

Workers' Compensation

Workers' compensation provides cash and medical benefits to workers injured on the job, as well as survivors' benefits to the dependents of those whose death was work-related. Although there are federal programs for federal employees, maritime and railroad workers, and victims of black-lung disease, federal involvement in the workers' compensation program is actually quite minimal. Instead, there are different programs in each of the fifty states and the District of Columbia. What all these programs share is a conception of workers' compensation as a form of no-fault insurance, where workers do not have to take legal action to receive benefits for a work-related injury.

In 2000, workers' compensation covered about 126 million workers, or about 90 percent of the civilian labor force. Uncovered workers include domestic and agricultural employees, casual laborers, and workers in many nonprofit, charitable, and religious institutions. The same year, cash and medical benefits totaled about $46 billion.[45] Typically, cash benefits constitute about three-fifths of this amount, with 70 percent of cash benefits going for permanent partial disabilities and a much smaller amount, 5 to 8 percent, awarded to survivors for work-related deaths.

Although cash compensation is usually set at about two-thirds of weekly pretax earnings at the time of the accident, the range of maximum benefits is considerable, from $1,494 in 2000 for federal employees, to $1,031 for Iowa, down to $316 for Mississippi.[46] Payments for workers' compensation are not means-tested, but they can be limited by time, amount, or extent of disability (temporary or permanent). Some states pay for total length of disability, including life, and some pay medical benefits. Some have a maximum number of weeks for temporary disability. Medical services, rehabilitation, and job training may be provided, but these too may be restricted at the states' discretion.

Commercial insurance companies provide employers with this insurance coverage. Employers, however, may also self-insure by demonstrating their capacity to carry their own risk, purchase insurance through a state-administered fund, or buy insurance commercially from a high-risk insurance pool established by the state. Two states, North Dakota and Washington, require employers to purchase insurance from the state fund; four states, Nevada, Ohio, Washington, and West Virginia, require either a purchase from the state fund or self-insurance. Although insurance costs exceed the payout every year, the difference is worth it to employers, because workers' compensation protects them from unexpectedly large court judgments and purchases peace of mind.[47]

Earned Income Tax Credit

Enacted in 1975 and expanded in 1986, 1990, and 1993, EITC offers a tax refund to supplement the wages of low-income workers. In 2001, workers who earned less than $28,281 and supported one child could receive a check from the federal government for as much as $2,428. With two children and a family income up to $32,121, the refund reaches as high as $4,008. Married workers without children and incomes below $10,170 can receive a smaller check of $364. Because the benefits of EITC taper off as workers earn more money, it provides the most help (i.e., the largest refund as a percentage of income) for families earning between $10,000 and $15,000 annually. Since 1987, EITC supplementation has been inflation-adjusted, so the rate rises every year.[48]

In 2000, the federal government spent $30 billion on the EITC program. By most yardsticks, this money is well spent. Because it aids more than 18 million families, EITC is currently the nation's most effective program against childhood poverty. That may not be saying much: the reduction in childhood poverty is only about 14 percent, but without it, another 4.8 million people, including 2.6 million children, would still be poor.[49]

Following on the success of the federal program, thirteen states and the District of Columbia have implemented their own EITC programs. Most of these piggyback on top of the federal tax, offering additional credit calculated as a percentage of the federal refund. Depending on the state, this additional credit ranges from 5 to 50 percent. Eight states and the District of Columbia offer refundable credit. In these circumstances, a family receives the full amount of the credit even if that amount exceeds the amount they owe on income taxes. Another five states limit the state tax to the family's income tax liability.[50]

As the number of working families using EITC has grown, concern about abuses has produced a crackdown. In the 1997 Taxpayer Relief Act, Congress tightened the rules relating to EITC and enacted some punishments against those who obtain it fraudulently. The Act specifies a two-year ban on those who claim eligibility as a result of a reckless or intentional disregard for the rules and provides a ten-year ban for cases of clear fraudulence. In addition, the Act also holds paid tax preparers to the standard of "due diligence" in preparation of the EITC and requires the sharing of information regarding child support orders among various governmental authorities.[51]

Quite apart from the issue of potential fraud, three primary criticisms have been directed at the EITC program. First, by providing a tax refund on top of wages, the EITC subsidizes low-wage employees and thereby defuses the pressure on their employers to pay higher salaries. Second, EITC restricts its help to the working poor. This focus probably accounts for the popularity of the program among both liberals and conservatives, but it does little to assist the unemployed and other, presumably even more desperate poor people. Third, although EITC offers a bigger refund for a second child, it does not provide additional aid to those with still larger families. These are all serious criticisms, but, for the moment anyway, they have hardly lessened the widespread public support for the program.

General Assistance Programs

General assistance programs provide locally administered and locally financed help to individuals under the age of 65 who are not otherwise eligible for aid. The Social Security Act authorized these programs but specified that they could be implemented only at the locality's option, without any federal monies. Given the nature of this mandate, it is hardly surprising that only thirty-five states now offer general assistance, including just twenty-four that have uniform statewide rules, and that in recent years, most have been discontinued or cut back.[52]

States and localities offer different forms of aid. Some offer a simple cash grant, usually even less than what TANF provides. Others give food, clothing, or funds to obtain medical care. Modeling themselves after the requirements in TANF, GA programs are increasingly likely to demand some work. Above all, GA programs are a prime example of administrative discretion, where a local unit of government, a neighborhood welfare center, and even sometimes an individual caseworker has considerable freedom to offer or withhold aid.

Cutbacks in GA programs have occurred all over the country. Of the thirty-eight states with programs in 1989, twenty-seven have tightened eligibility, especially for able-bodied adults without dependent children. In 1991, Michigan cut 82,000 able-bodied adults from the rolls. The next year, Illinois terminated its program for 66,000 recipients, and Ohio followed in 1995 when it removed 50,000. Where states like New York and California have retained their GA programs, they have instituted time limits. And while state programs for the disabled have suffered fewer cutbacks, seven states implemented time limits, another seven further restricted the definition of disability, and four completely eliminated their GA disability program.[53]

Overall, GA programs are skeletal, meager in the assistance they provide, and a perfect illustration of the principle that the smallest administrative unit usually provides the least aid. Although other programs have always provided more, the link between general assistance and local administration does not bode well for the current trend to shift social welfare responsibility to the states.

Individual Development Accounts

IDAs do not yet exist at the national level, but they have been proposed, most prominently perhaps, in President Clinton's 2000 State of the Union address. With forty-four state policy initiatives, including twenty-seven states that have established IDAs for welfare recipients, they may well become a significant new tool for social policy.[54]

IDAs differ from the other programs we have discussed in this chapter because they are about assets, not income. Under most IDA proposals, the government would match savings by the poor with its own contribution. In the best circumstances, the ratio for the poorest families might even approach 9:1, with the government adding $9 to every $1 a poor person saved. The resulting assets could be used for any worthwhile purpose: buying a home, getting a college education, or starting a small business. Indeed, there is some evidence that the poor would save. In one large demonstration project sponsored by eleven foundations, participants put away about $27 a month. Multiplied through a 2:1 matching grant, a total of about $900 a year went into their IDAs.[55]

The trend toward IDAs reflects a widespread disenchantment with the ineffectiveness of income-based antipoverty programs. The programs we have described, especially the ones that are means-tested, have had limited success in reducing poverty. Their failure doubtless stems from lack of funding, as well as from their inability to pay more than the bottom rungs of the job market. The IDA's proponents do not dispute this criticism, but they prefer to emphasize all the ways in which the government offers tax breaks to the more affluent through individual retirement accounts (IRAs) and 401(k)s. With 93 percent of these tax benefits already going to households earning over $50,000, they believe it is time the government developed a similar instrument for the poor.[56]

IDAs will complement, rather than replace, income support programs. Their proponents believe that they will lead to greater household stability, promote long-term planning, increase self-esteem, and enhance political involvement and community participation. They might well have these results; they certainly have focused attention on policies that funnel tax breaks to the affluent. In the meantime, however, one significant policy question hovers over the whole premise of IDAs.[57]

IDAs hinge on an individualist philosophy. The assumption is that your needs will be met if you get some capital. The role of government is to help you acquire this capital. Then, as someone with assets—a home owner or perhaps a small businessperson—you will acquire a stake in society. Admittedly, this vision mirrors the modern American social ethic that holds citizens personally responsible for their financial well-being. But by subtly deemphasizing the structural origins of poverty, look at what IDAs and this vision omit: in a society dominated by large businesses that strive to contain wages, IDAs focus not on better salaries, more generous income supports, or other group-related benefits, but on the size of each individual's nest egg. Even with a government subsidy, the savings of wealthier people will routinely dwarf the $25 a month that poor people can put away. At this rate, the hopes for IDAs seem excessive: whatever their other virtues, they will not reduce political and economic inequalities or substantially enhance the financial leverage of poor people.[58]

The Basic Income Grant

BIG is an idea, not a program. It is, however, an idea with the power to upend the other cash programs. BIG's advocates propose a universal guaranteed income that would replace all other forms of public income support. Better known in Europe, BIG has nonetheless begun to provoke discussion as a long-term response to poverty in this country.[59]

Although there are many variations on the fundamental idea, the core of BIG is an annual grant given to everyone and taxed at a progressive rate. For example, suppose we set BIG at $15,000 a year. A family with an income of $500,000 a year would now have $515,000. Taxed at 50 percent, the extra $7,500 would simply add to their discretionary income. For those earning $12,000 a year, however, a $15,000 BIG grant, especially one that goes largely untaxed, ensures a minimally decent standard of living.[60]

Critics usually raise two main objections to such proposals: first, they worry about its effects on the work ethic; second, they contend that BIG would be unduly expensive. These concerns are legitimate, but both seem overdrawn. Although BIG does establish a floor under all other income, additional paid work would continue to offer a higher standard of living. If some did choose more leisure time, that choice must be balanced against a universal grant that prevents others from living in stigmatized poverty.

As for BIG's finances, although it undoubtedly would be expensive, the elimination of many other programs (TANF, SSI, GA, EITC, and perhaps even UI) would help to keep costs down. These programs are all expendable if everyone has already attained an adequate standard of living. In this respect, BIG represents a down payment on greater equality. But because it will not be enacted in the near future, we have a long time to consider whether the price is worthwhile.

We have now reviewed the main features of ten income support programs. Applying our model of policy analysis, we next turn to economics, politics, ideology, social movements, and history. Looking at income support programs through each of these lenses, we will be able to understand not only what the programs do, but how they came to be what they are today.

Economics

From an economic viewpoint, income support programs represent a direct challenge to one of U.S. society's most fundamental principles: the notion that individuals are supposed to work for a living. Two key assumptions are implicit in this notion. One is the idea that those who can earn more have a right to live better. The second is that those who cannot or will not work for a living must earn less than those who are able to do so.

As discussed, these conflicting ideas create a dilemma. On the one hand, it is awkward, morally wrong, and sometimes even politically dangerous to let people starve; on the other, people who do not work, for whatever reason, cannot be allowed to live as well as those who do. A careful review of these income support programs illustrates the way out of this dilemma. Arranged from top to bottom, their generosity depends on their relationship to the job market and perceptions of the recipients' eligibility. In essence, as we will discover when we look through the lens of ideology, the worthiness of the recipients combines with economics to determine how much less than the

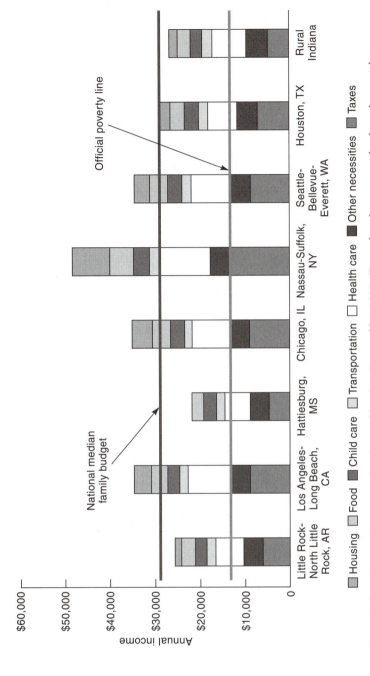

Family budgets for a single parent with a 4-year-old and an 8-year-old in 1999. Even when they are considered together, social programs rarely bring recipients up to the poverty line, much less to a standard that could be considered a safe and decent standard of living.

wage of the lowest salaried worker an income support program will have to pay.

From this perspective, it is easy to understand why the workers' compensation program is probably the most generous. Workers' compensation is an insurance program without any federal financing that pays for individuals who are injured on the job. As a form of no-fault insurance, it does not attribute responsibility, protects businesses from potentially larger lawsuits, and aids beneficiaries who may not even be poor. In the absence of the constraints that hamper some of the other income programs, these factors enable workers' compensation to pay as much as two-thirds of the average weekly wage.

The Social Security retirement and disability programs are next on the list. Both programs require that someone once worked for an extended period of time, and the benefits they offer stem from either their subsequent retirement or a disability they have acquired through no fault of their own. Unlike workers' compensation, however, Social Security presumes that because its beneficiaries have saved money for retirement, they need only some supplementary aid. As a consequence of all these factors, Social Security pays less than work but is nonetheless a fairly generous income support program.

The UI benefits program falls below Social Security. Its recipients are still in the prime of working life, but, unlike those receiving workers' compensation, can return to a job. Because UI is temporary, benefits that are too generous would create an incentive to remain unemployed. Recent cutbacks have further restricted the reach of the program. Nevertheless, within the limit of a program that must necessarily pay less than a worker would otherwise earn on the job, the average UI benefit still treats its recipients better than any of the welfare programs.

As a tax credit, the EITC program is different. For most working families, it provides no more than an extra couple of thousand dollars annually. Unlike Social Security and unemployment benefits, it is not a form of social insurance. And even though it is less generous than the welfare programs (SSI, TANF, GA), it lacks their strict eligibility requirements and close surveillance of behavior. As it is, properly speaking, neither social insurance nor welfare, it belongs in its own, in-between category.

The welfare programs are still easier to sort. Not only is there a descending order of generosity—SSI to TANF to GA—but this order closely parallels the scope of governmental authority. SSI is federal; TANF is state-run with block-granted federal monies; and GA is local, sometimes even down to the county level. The perceived worthiness of the poor also mirrors this descending order. SSI helps the aged, blind, and disabled—the quintessential worthy poor; TANF usually aids single mothers, whose children only partly offset popular perceptions of their mother's unworthiness; and GA offers minimal benefits to unworthy single adults. All recipients of welfare, then, get less than the lowest wage, but how close they can come to this lowest wage depends on the government authority that administers the program and beliefs about the recipients' worthiness.

In different ways, both IDAs and BIG try to sidestep both the concept of worthiness and the principle of less eligibility. IDAs seize on the notion of asset building as a form of social insurance—something that is there without conditions placed on it, which a family can turn to in time of need. In practice, however, despite significant government supplementation, the amount a family is likely to save may well mark them as poor, even if that poverty simply means fewer assets and not just a smaller monthly public assistance check. Of course, a BIG program would go even further. By guaranteeing income regardless of a private salary, it seeks to retire, permanently, the distinction between the worthy and unworthy poor.

Quite apart from any ranking by adequacy, all these income support programs perform several other important economic functions. Perhaps the most classic is that they increase the purchasing power of their recipients and thereby expand aggregate demand. This function is especially helpful in a recession, when wages stagnate and people have less money to spend. Imagine what it would be like in these circumstances if governments at every level did not redirect some money into the hands of those who have the least to spend. Not only would poor people find it harder to cope, but in the absence of this additional spending, the economy would lack a necessary economic stimulus and the recession might well go on for much longer.

In their performance of another economic function, these income support programs also socialize, to varying degrees, the cost of maintaining poor people in poverty. Social insurance programs do not perform this function as much as welfare programs because their financing comes from both the employer and the worker. In the case of Social Security, for example, the existence of the Social Security Administration may make a political statement about the importance of the public sector's administering Social Security, but workers contribute half the revenue, so they are really sharing the cost of maintaining themselves.

By contrast, UI involves an employer contribution with a federal tax rebate against a state unemployment tax. Whether it is calculated at the state or federal level, socializing the cost through the public sector is clearly evident here. It is even more evident with welfare programs, which use revenues from the general tax fund for this purpose. In sum, the United States relies on Social Security programs funded by a dedicated tax for individuals who are unlikely to return to work, but turns to general revenues to maintain those whom we hope will eventually get a job.

From an economic perspective, this division between social insurance and welfare extends even further. The existence of social insurance encourages older workers to retire and hence allows for an influx of new workers. At the same time, however, meager welfare benefits push recipients, especially poor female recipients, into the workforce. Given the little that welfare pays, these women's search for any paying job is a real boon to the service industries and to employers' need for cheap labor. As with most other interactions between social welfare policy and economics, the relationship ultimately comes down to the specifics of the link between a particular social program and the market for labor.

We have already mentioned one important political dimension underlying income support programs: the way the size of the government institution—federal, state, or local—seems to parallel the adequacy of the social benefit. Programs such as Social Security operated by the federal government customarily pay more than those administered by the states or localities. As discussed in chapter 4 in the section on federal-state structures, decentralizing program administration means that states often try to compete by underbidding each other on their welfare programs. State programs with lower average benefits are the inevitable result.

Social welfare programs also perform a variety of other functions. Welfare programs defuse political antipathy among recipients while offering nonrecipients a suitable target for their anger. Social insurance programs build political loyalties. As a group, social welfare programs reassure people about the soundness of U.S. political institutions. They convey the message that we will care for the poor, even if, in the end, we cannot do very much about the existence of poverty.

The first significant political component arises from means-tested welfare programs. These programs serve a dual function: they give just enough to poor people to undercut political organizing, and at the same time, they offer a wealth of opportunities for scapegoating. Welfare programs group recipients and set them up as the legitimate targets of other people's anger. Because the recipients in these programs are usually weak and vulnerable, those who are not in the program can attack them with impunity. And precisely because they can be attacked with impunity, some individuals are likely to express anger against them instead of at other, more powerful people. In effect, by grouping recipients together in one program, authorities both defuse the recipients' anger and create a safety valve for the discontent of nonrecipients that might otherwise be expressed in more politically threatening ways.

If social insurance programs did not exist, this would arouse anger, too. But once they do exist, they help to cultivate political loyalty. The elderly, for example, are a key voting bloc. In some states, like Florida and Arizona, with large retirement communities, their votes may even be decisive. For them, Social Security is a critical issue, so presidential candidates touring these states always stress what they will do to maintain the program's integrity. Both in these states and in the nation at large, candidates who succeed in this task gain the elderly's allegiance, and this allegiance, in turn, can help to catapult them to the presidency.

This cultivation of loyalty is actually only part of a broader political function, because the existence of income support programs sends such an important message. This message says that the United States is a society that takes care of everyone, where no one has to starve for the lack of funds. The spillover effect of this message is to legitimize U.S. political institutions. By implication, the existence of income support programs says that although poverty exists, we will always take care of our own.

Yet, hidden in this reassurance is another political meaning. If housing and feeding poor people demonstrates that our institutions are sound, then poverty itself must be stubborn and persistent. And as we cannot apparently eliminate such a stubborn and persistent poverty by working within our political institutions, then we are going to have to become resigned to its presence among us for a long time.

Ideology

Ideology ties together the political and economic functions of income support programs. Ideology justifies the principle of less eligibility. Instead of ensuring adequate treatment for those who do not work, income support programs convey the belief that work must pay more than welfare. From this ideological perspective, people don't work because they want to, either as an expression of who they are or of their desire to contribute to society. Instead, the only reason to work is to avoid the fate of those whose lack of work consigns them to a lower standard of living. Without the ideological message embodied in the principle of less eligibility, this whole narrow system of reward and punishment risks collapse.

Put in more sociological terms, the ideological function of income support programs is to enforce work norms. Lack of these programs might provoke political outrage; with too generous programs, the principle of less eligibility would evaporate. Set at the proper midrange level, however, income support programs do neither too little nor too much. Instead, at this level, income support programs go a long way toward enforcing the idea that everyone should work.

Income support programs also perform an ideological function by distinguishing between the worthy and unworthy poor. While social insurance programs serve the worthy poor—those who have had some significant connection to the job market—welfare programs aid the unworthy: those who are shiftless, lazy, and deficient in character. Income support programs help to carry out this elaborate system of classification. Not only do they make an ideological statement about the importance of this distinction, but they also help to mark the unworthy poor for easy scapegoating.

Grouping the unworthy poor together prepares them for public declarations about the necessity of reforming their character. This is an important ideological task. It suggests that there are good poor people and bad poor people, and that the bad poor people need careful supervision to change their ways. Justification of this careful supervision demands regular statements about the need for work programs, critiques of the poor's sexual misbehavior as a cause of single motherhood, and speculations about what—apart from more money—would make poor people better behaved. The clear ideological premise is that the poor need to be reformed for their own sake. In the process, however, many people get to feel better about themselves precisely because they are not poor.

Enforcement of the family ethic is the final ideological function. The fam-

In recent years, U.S. income support programs have increasingly tended to classify female-headed households as the unworthy poor.

ily ethic rewards women who conform to the accepted female roles of homemaking and child rearing, while punishing those who act independently. Income support programs mix ideological justification for the family ethic with the other functions we have already described. Just look at the justifications for the principle of less eligibility, classifying the worthy and unworthy poor, and the goal of improving the poor's character: each of these functions takes on a new meaning when we think of them in connection with poor single mothers. According to the family ethic, poor women who try to live independently must be worse off than those who work; belong, by definition, to the group known as the unworthy poor; and need help from others to make some positive changes in their character. The family ethic ties all these justifications together and applies them to the female poor.

Social Movements

Some of these income support programs have their origins in social movements. Social movements usually take the form of a powerful grassroots demand for a particular kind of income support. Labor unions, women's groups, and community activists push these demands until they become visible enough to attract the attention of political and economic elites. Compromising with the organized power from below, these elites then revise the demands and turn them into a more moderate program.

The best example of this pattern is the Social Security Act. For thirty or forty years before the Act, workers campaigned for unemployment insurance, women's groups demanded public assistance for mothers who were widowed, separated, or divorced, and activists from many different groups insisted that social insurance for the retired elderly was the best possible remedy for poverty in old age. Political and economic elites strongly rejected these demands until the Depression of the 1930s provoked such turmoil that giving in seemed wise. Although public assistance, unemployment benefits, and social insurance for the retired were all incorporated into the Social Security Act, President Roosevelt's elite Committee on Economic Security defused many of the original demands. The result was a weaker Social Security Act, one that redistributed less money downward, often bowed before states' rights even when those states practiced segregation, and further sharpened the distinctions between the worthy and unworthy poor.[61]

Yet, many of the income support programs we have described did not originate in this way. Instead, for programs like workers' compensation, EITC, and SSI, elites themselves provided the major impetus. Although they were not the only groups, these programs did not, for the most part, have strong mass movements behind them. In some instances, such as workers' compensation, elite groups wanted to rationalize the marketplace by protecting themselves from potentially costly lawsuits. In other instances, EITC, for example, tax credits to low-income workers reduce the need for employers to raise wages. And with SSI, policymakers favored federalization of state programs for the aged, blind, and disabled because it helped to streamline the bureaucracy. It may be just a question of degree, but compared with the programs in the Social Security Act, these policy initiatives had more elite origins.[62]

TANF, the most recent major program initiative, adds several new twists to this distinction between the grassroots and elite origins of social policy. To begin with, TANF arose out of a social movement that sought to cut rather than expand welfare. This movement also had many sources, both elite and nonelite. Conservative think tanks such as the Heritage Foundation, the American Enterprise Institute, and the Manhattan Institute used a flood of corporate contributions to prepare policy analyses about welfare reform and to publish books like Charles Murray's *Losing Ground*, which argued for its abolition.[63] At the same time, with wages declining and American families under stress, many people were genuinely angry that welfare mothers were allowed to stay at home and take care of their children. Conservatives may have skillfully directed this rage, but they did not create it. For all these reasons, TANF is a wonderful illustration of the complexity of the relationship between the grassroots and elite origins of social policy.

What can we learn from the history of these income programs? Arranged in chronological order, some patterns do emerge.

The oldest of the contemporary programs is workers' compensation, which dates back to 1909, when the first three states enacted laws. Eight more states followed the next year, and by the end of the decade, almost every state had one.[64] Workers' compensation had no federal involvement; it was simply a state-mandated program that provided insurance and protected businesses. That is why workers' compensation was the first of these income programs: none of these arrangements broke with existing U.S. political and economic institutions.

The programs authorized by the 1935 Social Security Act are next chronologically. They include social insurance for the elderly, which requires the involvement of the federal government; public assistance (ADC), which, until it was replaced by TANF, was also a federal entitlement; UI, a federal-state hybrid; and general assistance, to be offered only at the local government's option. Although the origins of general assistance extend back to Elizabethan Poor Laws of 1601, the Act's other provisions, especially federal involvement and socialization of the responsibility to maintain the poor, do mark an important milestone.

In 1956, the government added disability insurance for people 50 and over with a permanent disability. In 1960 and 1965, it extended these benefits to disabled workers of any age solely on the basis of their inability to work for at least one year.[65] SSI followed in 1974. Although neither program was notable for its generosity, both increased the federal government's responsibility. In the final quarter of the twentieth century, this alone made them the last of their kind.

The remaining three current programs—EITC (1975), TANF (1996), and IDAs (now in its experimentation phase)—all reframe this commitment. EITC is a federal program with an optional state supplement, but it uses tax refunds to assist low-income workers rather than the poor. TANF strips the federal government of direct responsibility for the poor, and IDAs assume that the federal government should help the poor accumulate a nest egg for investment in themselves as "human capital."

So what is the historical pattern in this odd mix of programs? Through the mid-1970s, there is a fairly steady pattern of growth. This growth occurs in bits and pieces, adding a category of the needy first in one group and then in another. Underlying it all, though, is a sense, first, that government is the only collectivity that can compensate for the failings of the market, and second, that responsibility for addressing these failings should be vested in the *federal government* whenever our political and economic institutions allow.

In the past quarter century, this federal responsibility has ebbed. Global competition has created a competitive free-for-all, where people are responsible for themselves and the new social ethic limits broader concerns. Diminished federal responsibility for the poor has been one primary outcome of this change. Though even at its height, this federal responsibility never reached the point of providing a guaranteed annual income or other universal benefit, now more than ever, an income support program must resemble the market to win political acceptance. After almost three-quarters of a century of steady if haphazard growth, this historical trend has held for the past twenty-five years.

By focusing on economics, politics, ideology, and social movements, we have had ample opportunity to familiarize ourselves with the reasons for these trends. In the next chapter, we explore the question of the extent to which these same historical patterns have shaped the development of employment policy.

9

Jobs and Job Training: Programs and Policies

People who do not want to rely on income support programs have another option: they can try to get into a job training program or perhaps obtain a publicly created job. Yet those pursuing this alternative face many obstacles. Few programs rank as an unqualified success; the actual number of vacancies has never amounted to more than a small fraction of potential trainees, perhaps one of every twenty workers,[1] and the programs themselves have always targeted the poor. So, not only is it hard to get into a program and the programs help only a little, but the skills participants gain usually come with a stigma.

These difficulties share a common origin. Unlike in European countries, employment policy in the United States has never tried to match the needs of business for a labor force with the employment needs of all workers. Instead, it has left that task to the job market, making just a modest investment in the training of workers—the "disadvantaged" and people of color—who could not find work on their own. As a consequence, although some U.S. employment programs involve workfare and many are linked to welfare, most bear the marks of a residual social policy.

In training programs, as in so many other matters, modest investments have produced modest gains: too few slots, very brief training periods, and, except for those workers who were retrained after losing well-paying jobs, salaries that rarely rose much above the poverty line. During the second

Clinton administration, these results prompted another attempt at reform of U.S. employment policy, the 1998 Workforce Investment Act (WIA). As we shall see, however, although this Act does offer some hope for improvement, it too is unlikely to overcome the limitations that have been placed on the development of employment policy.

The Context for Employment Policy

Economic changes have transformed the job market. In 1960, 31 percent of U.S. workers labored in manufacturing. By 1997, that percentage had been cut in half. The decline in agricultural employment has been steadier but even more dramatic: in the 1870s, 70 percent of all Americans worked on farms; today that figure has declined to 3 percent. A dramatic surge in service employment has accompanied this drop. Although workers in service industries constituted 10 percent of all employment in the 1870s, now they make up 81 percent of the workforce.[2]

Service employment includes a wide variety of jobs and salaries. At the high end are architects, lawyers, computer programmers, and successful psychotherapists. Hotel employees, fast food workers, home health aides, and retail sales clerks lie at the other extreme. The high end of service employment gets more publicity, but the low end produces more jobs.

Although no one would have thought of offering government-sponsored job training for agricultural workers in the 1870s, success in a globalizing economy depends on competitive skills. By 2006, the labor market is expected to produce 15 million new jobs.[3] Many of these jobs are low wage, and low-wage workers have lost the most income over the past twenty-five years. In a different political environment, this trend could become the basis of a renewed emphasis on federal employment programs.

Classifying Federal Job Programs

Federal job programs fall into two main categories. The first and by far more common category includes programs that offer training to workers. These initiatives originated during the Great Society with the enactment of legislation such as the 1962 Manpower Development and Training Act and the Job Corps program (1964). Subsequently, programs like the Job Training Partnership Act (JTPA; 1983) and, most recently, the WIA belong to the same policy tradition.

Although these programs may provide a stipend, they mostly focus on training for the private sector. In fact, from 1981 until the enactment of the 1996 welfare reform law, the government did not authorize the expenditure of any money for the creation of public sector jobs. Workers got training, some counseling, and perhaps a job referral, but they had to get a real paying job on their own.

The second category of employment programs dates back to the Great Depression of the 1930s. Here, the training comes from a government-provided job and employs people who could not otherwise find work. Included in this category are New Deal initiatives such as the Civilian Conservation Corps and the Work Projects Administration, as well as the Nixon administration's Comprehensive Employment Training Act (CETA, 1973). In each case, the training occurs in the public sector, either through direct federal expenditures to create jobs, as it did during the Depression, or, in the case of CETA, to fund state jobs the local government can no longer afford.

The first kind of federal job program is more common. During the past forty years, some training program has always existed, even when interest in training has declined. By contrast, the second kind, paid work in the public sector, has been less consistently available. Faced with long-standing conservative opposition to the federal government's funding of jobs, it must surmount a still bigger hurdle.

The Triggers for Social Change in Federal Job Programs

Five different triggers for social change have brought about new federal job programs. Blending political and economic concerns, they all seek to coordinate the existing pool of labor with the workforce that business needs now and might foreseeably require in the future. Although these concerns are fairly constant, sometimes they intensify to the point where policymakers feel they must modify the employment training system.

The first and perhaps most common trigger for social change occurs when policymakers believe that employment training could upgrade the workforce. This trigger is evident in the 1962 Manpower Development and Training Act, when policymakers worried about the effects of automation, and in 1998, when concerns about the overall competitiveness of the workforce in a globalized economy led to passage of the WIA. Doubts about the preparedness of the workforce for coming economic changes were key in both instances.

The second trigger for social change in employment programs involves issues of poverty and welfare. Like other aspects of U.S. social welfare, employment policy has usually focused on means-tested programs for the poor. Depending on the political climate, this attention has produced two distinct kinds of job legislation. In more generous periods like the Great Society, policymakers have recognized that lack of education and training interfere with poor people's getting and keeping a well-paying job. Now in its fourth decade, the Job Corps program for "disadvantaged youth" reflects this orientation.

At other times, however, policymakers have shifted their attention from the structures that prevent poor people from succeeding to the poor people themselves. Emphasizing the poor's personal deficiencies, these policymakers have tied receipt of welfare to a burdensome set of workfare requirements and devised employment programs, like the 1983 JTPA, that skimped on the

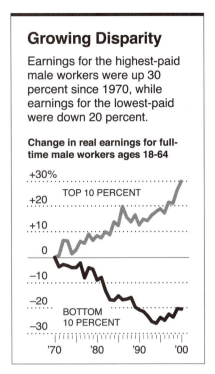

Growing Disparity

Earnings for the highest-paid male workers were up 30 percent since 1970, while earnings for the lowest-paid were down 20 percent.

Change in real earnings for full-time male workers ages 18-64

+30%

TOP 10 PERCENT

+20

+10

0

−10

−20

BOTTOM
10 PERCENT

−30

'70   '80   '90   '00

Disparity between highest and lowest wage for paid workers. The 1998 Workforce Investment Act reflects a desire to upgrade the workforce and halt the growing disparity between high- and low-wage workers.

provision of day care and stipends. Whatever the usefulness of these initiatives, policymakers enacted these programs in a political environment that required any new employment training to improve the poor's character.

The prevention of social unrest among inner-city youth is the third impetus for social change in job training programs. Until the 1998 WIA consolidated funding into a broader youth employment program, Congress would go through an annual ritual about providing money for youth during the summer months. Proponents would threaten a long, hot summer full of crime and rioting unless Congress came up with adequate support. The urban violence of the 1960s and the 1992 riots in Los Angeles all lent support to these threats, which were so effective that the federal response extended beyond summer youth programs to include just about every employment program ever put forth for the inner city. Although consolidated funding in the WIA changed the need for separate annual appropriations, underneath the desire to fund some inner-city training programs the fear always remains of what youth might do without them.

Employment programs have also served to grease the passage of controversial legislation. The best recent example of this phenomenon occurred during the fight to enact the 1993 North American Free Trade Agreement. Most U.S. trade unions strongly opposed NAFTA because they thought that cheaper imports would cost jobs. Nevertheless, when the lawmakers agreed to provide job training for workers displaced by imports, the trade agreement

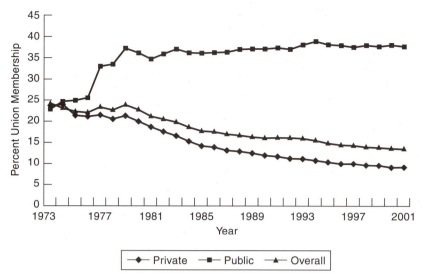

Union membership density among U.S. wage and salary workers, 1973–2001. Even though the number of workers in unions has declined, trade unions remain influential in job training and have been able to obtain some new employment programs for workers displaced by legislation like the North American Free Trade Act (NAFTA).

gained enough support to ensure its passage. In this case, the trigger for social change is not some larger economic concern, but simply the political use of employment programs as a way of making the legislative machinery run more smoothly.

The final trigger of social change in employment programs occurs when either high unemployment or rapid transformation of the labor market has created obstacles that no job training program can overcome. Under these circumstances, policymakers set aside their usual opposition and authorize the federal government to engage in job creation. High unemployment prompted the labor-absorbing legislation of the New Deal like the Civilian Conservation Corps and the Works Progress Administration. But in an interesting twist at a time of relatively low unemployment, the WIA also grants the states some latitude to fund their own job creation programs.[4] Although this concession is just a small, optional, state-operated experiment, it does suggest that some wariness about turmoil in the job market lies just under the surface.

These five triggers, then, suggest the primary impetus for social change in employment policy. But what is it that they have brought about? To answer this question, we first outline some general themes in employment training, then review the programs themselves.

How much does it cost to educate students and prepare them for a career? When students are talented and have already received a good education, it might cost $140,000 over four years to attend a prestigious college. At the other extreme, suppose a young woman is poor and undereducated and left high school to work in a series of unskilled and unstable jobs. If she is lucky and can get into one, the remedy for her problems in the job market is likely to be a four-month training program that costs $2,500. Because she started at a much lower level of skill, such a modest investment cannot possibly compensate for her long-term deficits.

Yet employment programs do try. They provide on-the-job training, classroom training, or job search assistance. On-the-job training benefits workers who need skills for a particular job in a particular kind of company; classroom training is best for those whose skills are outdated. Job search assistance is generally the cheapest, but because it targets those who are already job ready, that may not be saying much. All these programs help a little. The evidence suggests, however, that they do so more because participants retain jobs and work longer at them than from any significant increase in their hourly wages.[5]

In the mid-1990s, Congress began to look at these results and wonder whether we could do better. It asked the U.S. General Accounting Office, the monitoring arm of the federal government, to conduct a review. The GAO found that although the federal government had never committed to a comprehensive employment policy, it nonetheless funded 125 different employment programs. Sixty-five of these programs served the "economically disadvantaged" and forty-eight targeted out-of-school youth. In addition, there were eighteen programs serving veterans, ten programs for Native Americans, and four for homeless people.[6] Although Congress did not address the issue of resources, it did decide to do something about the duplication. After several years of legislative compromise, this resolve led to the enactment of the latest omnibus employment training law, the Workforce Investment Act of 1998.

The Workforce Investment Act

WIA instigated many changes in employment policy. Legislatively, it replaced the 1983 JTPA provision for economically disadvantaged adults, youth, and dislocated workers with three new programs, Adult, Dislocated Worker, and Youth. These programs de-emphasize the categorical nature of JTPA and make the general public eligible for a broader range of services. To improve access to these services, communities must consolidate delivery and offer them in one-stop shopping centers.

WIA authorizes three tiers of service. The core first tier provide job search assistance. At this level, staff provides the worker with some help looking for a job, searching the classified pages or a list of job vacancies, or perhaps offering some hints on dressing for the interview. If the worker fails to get a job, he or she becomes eligible for the next tier. This tier includes more intensive services such as assessment and case management to help workers get jobs on their own. Only when they fail to do so are they eligible for job training in the third tier.[7]

This service delivery system reveals a lot about the intent of policymakers. Although the system is supposed to universalize services, the need for job training is nonetheless associated with failure. WIA therefore remains the trainer of last resort, and using it to get a job will still carry a stigma.

As an umbrella employment act, WIA also retains most of the programs funded under previous policies. Although the Act does end the existence of a separate summer youth program, the funded programs otherwise are not that different. These programs include those for adults; dislocated workers; youth; an employment service program; trade adjustment assistance programs, veterans' employment, and training programs; Job Corps, welfare-to-work grant-funded programs; Senior Community Service Employment Programs; and employment and training for migrants, seasonal farm workers, and Native Americans.[8] This list may cover nearly everyone, but it is still training by category.

Officially, five main principles shaped the development of WIA: (1) "work first"; (2) greater coordination; (3) increased reliance on market mechanisms; (4) the provision of universal services; and (5) increased accountability. From our review, however, it will soon become clear that the Act enforces some principles more closely than others.

The first principle of WIA, and the one that is perhaps most emphatically enforced, is "work first." This term means that WIA looks to the job market to evaluate the pool of workers who are seeking employment and training assistance. In effect, this emphasis on work de-emphasizes training. It suggests that instead of the government's investing in training, workers should train themselves through work. Under WIA, only those who lack the capacity to develop their skills through work can progress through the three service tiers and become eligible for job training vouchers.[9]

In an effort to improve service delivery, WIA also strongly encourages increased coordination among the various programs, especially at the state and local levels. From unified state-level planning across job training programs to common performance indicators, WIA rewards collaborative efforts without calling for actual program consolidation or integration. Indeed, even as the Act retains numerous restrictions on eligibility and many allowable services persist as quasi-block grants, it does show some promise by offering states greater leeway to prepare long-term unified plans for their workforce programs.[10]

The third guiding principle of WIA comes from its reliance on market mechanisms. In keeping with the market model, WIA requires the use of an individual training account (ITA) to deliver services. ITAs represent the individual referral model, one that assesses and counsels individuals before referring them to a qualified service provider. To enhance informed consumer choice, WIA also demands that providers offer accurate, up-to-date performance information, so that participants will know who has the best record for helping people in their situation.[11] WIA therefore resembles other social policies adhering to a market model. WIA may offer more choice, but it is a choice defined by the modest U.S. investment in employment and training programs.

Universal service is the fourth principle. WIA replaced the JTPA programs for economically disadvantaged and dislocated workers with programs for adults, dislocated workers, and youth. This shift represents a move toward universalism because it de-emphasizes the differences among groups needing assistance. As part of this change, WIA also established Workforce Investment Boards to substitute for the Private Industry Councils that matched participants with the need for training in specific local industries under JTPA. Because, in theory, the Workforce Investment Boards are responsible for overseeing all government training programs in their region, they have a broader mandate and might, over time, foster greater universality and coordination.[12]

The fifth principle demands increased accountability. Consistent with this principle, WIA calls for the establishment of a performance accountability system whose purpose is to maximize return on investment and promote continuous improvement. Distinctive features of this new system include requiring indicators of performance, distributing the information widely, and applying the standards at the state and local levels.[13] The thinking behind this principle is that participants are customers who are entitled to the most accurate data possible about the system's functioning.

Although no one would dispute the worthiness of these principles, many critics have suggested that WIA will not bring about that many important changes. For starters, despite implications to the contrary, WIA does not unify the nation's employment programs. As the late Senator Paul Wellstone (D-Minnesota) said,

> The [Act] incorporates adult and vocational education *without* threatening those programs' separate funding streams. [I]t will also include reauthorization and improvement of vocational rehabilitation programs, again *without* threatening separate funding for vocational rehabilitation programs. It assures *separate funding* to adults, to youth, and to dislocated workers according to state formulae, and also according to formulae within states. . . . It does not block grant job training, adult education, and vocational education programs.[14]

In short, as an umbrella program, WIA says it is unifying all the programs under it, but retains their source of funding and keeps the programs distinct. This new packaging may dress up the programs somewhat differently; it does not, however, alter their content.

The maintenance of separate funding streams offers just one example of how difficult it will be to achieve some of WIA's stated goals. The centerpiece of WIA is one-stop shopping. But how do you share costs in a one-stop shopping center? Suppose there are three different programs in one office space: without a common budget, it is unclear how the expense of adminis-

Workforce Investment Act (WIA), 1998

Number of recipients:	Adult Employment Service, 300,000; Dislocated Worker, 937,000; Youth, 476,000; NAFTA, 37,000; Job Corp, 100,000
Who offers the benefit or service:	Employment counseling and job training agencies, both public and private, by contract
What form does it take:	Job counseling and training
To whom is it provided:	Anyone can get help looking for a job, but job training is limited to those who have not been able to obtain a job on their own
At whose expense:	The federal government spent about $5.6 billion on job training in 2002.

tration and utilities can be shared. How, then, do you allocate the costs for electricity, heat, and phones? Each program has restrictions on how its money can be used, as well as specific requirements for reporting. WIA mandates that the programs work together, but the way the funds are distributed makes genuine cooperation difficult.[15]

The same criticism applies to WIA's goal of universal service. It is a fine idea in theory, but without adequate funding, it is fanciful to talk about universalism as a serious possibility. We have never spent much money on workforce services, never more than 0.85 percent of the GDP, or 2.4 percent of federal budget outlays. WIA does provide core services that are universal, such as outreach, intake, initial assessment, job search, and provider performance information. But in the absence of greater financial support, WIA only gives welfare recipients and the poor priority for training services. Once again, the lack of money turns universalism in theory into selectivity and stigma in practice.[16]

Although it is too early to render even a preliminary judgment, these criticisms suggest that the WIA has been oversold. Its principles may be admirable, but it will not be able to carry them out. Some might contend that merely stating the principles is a step forward, and that if WIA fails to attain its goals this time, perhaps it will with further refinements. Others dispute this contention, arguing that lofty goals without the resources to achieve them sets up another failure that sows further doubts about the possibilities for effective social policy. Whichever side you come down on depends on your understanding of employment policy and, in particular, of the individual programs that have now been incorporated into new pieces of legislation.

Adult Employment Service

Adult Services fall under Title 1 of WIA. The Act defines age eligibility for core services as 18 years or older. It grants priority for training to recipients of public assistance and other low-income individuals. In keeping with one of the leading features of WIA, most services for adults will be offered in one-stop shopping centers, and most participants will rely on their ITAs to figure out which provider and which training program best fit their needs. Once again, participants move through WIA's three tiers of core, intensive, and training services, receiving employment training only after all their previous efforts have failed. The states administer this adult program through a combination of formula grants to state and local entities. In fiscal year 2002, the program allocated $950 million.[17]

Dislocated Workers

Title 1 of WIA also authorizes assistance to dislocated workers. Typically, these workers have been fired in a major layoff; despite considerable experience, there is little likelihood that the company will recall them to their old jobs. Between their union membership and their relatively high prelayoff earnings, they are usually unemployed for a long time—often, until they accept a lower salary in another industry.[18]

Relying on a separate Title 1 funding stream, WIA makes provision for dislocated workers through a state-operated program that replaces the dislocated worker assistance authorized under JTPA. This provision offers reemployment services and retraining assistance to individuals who are permanently separated from their employment. In addition, the states may use these funds to respond quickly to workers seriously affected by mass layoffs and plant closures. In fiscal year 2002, the total appropriation for this provision was $1.55 billion, enough for an estimated 937,000 participants.[19]

Youth

Youth employment programs constitute the third key component of Title 1 in WIA. No longer is there a separate training program for summer youth. Instead, WIA consolidates the summer youth program into a broad, general youth training program. This program emphasizes long-term development by providing social, educational, and employment services to eligible youth, ages 14–21, a comprehensive statewide system.[20]

Ninety-five percent of these youth services retain their focus on the poor. In addition, however, if youth face specific barriers to employment or completion of school, Title 1 does reserve the remaining 5 percent for those who are not poor. This provision opens the program up to those who are school dropouts, offenders, pregnant or already parents, have a basic literacy deficiency, or, in the broadest category, need help completing an educational program and getting a job.[21]

To link academic and occupational learning, WIA providers must have strong ties with employers. The programs stress tutoring, study skills training and dropout prevention, paid and unpaid work experience, mentoring and leadership development, as well as appropriate support services. Participants receive guidance and counseling plus at least one year of follow-up services. Nationally, there are over six hundred local workforce investment areas assisting an estimated 476,000 youth annually. In fiscal year 2002, the federal government appropriated $1.13 billion dollars for their activities.[22]

The NAFTA–Transitional Adjustment Assistance Program

The federal government also assists workers adversely affected by foreign trade. The most recent version of this policy, the NAFTA–Transitional Adjustment Assistance program, combines provisions from two older laws—the Economic Dislocation and Worker Assistance Adjustment Act (from the 1983 JTPA) and the Trade Adjustment Assistance program (from the Trade Act of 1974)—under the auspices of NAFTA (1993). The program helps workers who lose their jobs or get less work and lower wages as a result of trade with Mexico or Canada. It offers participants a quick response to the threat of unemployment and the opportunity to receive income support while engaging in long-term training.[23]

The Department of Labor rules on all applications. Eligible workers can benefit from reemployment services such as career counseling, skills assessment, job placement assistance, job search assistance, and job referrals. The worker may also receive up to two years of approved training in occupational skills, basic or remedial education, training in literacy, or English as a second language. After exhausting six months of unemployment benefits, a worker participating in an approved full-time training program is also eligible for fifty-two weeks of a cash trade adjustment allowance. Although this arrangement sounds generous, six months of unemployment benefits and one year of an allowance still leaves the two-year trainee six months short of cash.[24]

During 1999, the Department of Labor certified 129,000 such workers, 37,000 of whom received a trade adjustment allowance averaging $269 a week. Including administration, the total cost of the program was $94 million.[25]

Trade certainly provides cheaper goods for consumers, but at the cost of some domestic jobs. The major policy question about this program, then, is whether a budget of $94 million fully accounts for the economic dislocation that trade causes.

Job Corps

Job Corps is the largest and most comprehensive intervention for youth sponsored by the federal government. Job Corps provides youth with education, training, health, and other services in a residential setting under continuous supervision and away from their old neighborhoods. In the classic study of the program's effectiveness, evaluators found that Job Corps improved educational attainment and increased annual earnings by 28 percent.[26]

There are 111 Job Corps centers in forty-six states, the District of Columbia, and Puerto Rico. Because it is a residential program featuring a comprehensive array of training, education, and supportive services, Job Corps is comparatively expensive: with a budget of $1.46 billion and 100,000 enrollees in 2002, it costs almost $15,000 a person. To reach young workers most other programs overlook, it relies on strict behavioral standards, prohibiting drugs and violence, and expelling people for violations.[27]

Eligibility for Job Corps is limited to those between 16 and 24 years of age. Although participants must be high school dropouts who come from a disruptive environment, they should not be on probation or parole and must have no serious medical or behavioral problem. The program trains them in occupational trades such as construction, computers, clerical skills, automotive mechanics, and the health occupations. Once the program has been completed, it also provides placement services.

The typical Job Corps student is an 18-year-old high school dropout who reads at the seventh-grade level, belongs to a minority group (57 percent are African American, 16 percent Latino, and 4 percent Native American), and has never held a full-time job. He or she (60 percent of all Job Corps participants are male) will remain in the program for about seven months. The Department of Labor estimates that upon completion, about 70 percent of all participants get jobs, and another 10 percent go elsewhere to continue their education or attend another training program. This positive termination rate of 80 percent is often cited as evidence of Job Corps' effectiveness.[28]

Native American Job Program

Another national program authorized by the WIA offers job training, work experience, and other employment-related services to Native Americans. Consistent with the prior definition of Native American under JTPA, WIA identifies Indians, Eskimos, Aleuts, and Native Hawaiians as potential recipients of these services. The Department of Labor administers this section of WIA by awarding grants to Indian tribes and reservations. The program, however, is relatively small; in fiscal year 2000, it expended just $58 million.[29]

Competition for these grants occurs every two years, though once an organization receives a grant and demonstrates that it has done what it has promised, the Department of Labor may renew the grant on receipt of a satisfactory plan for the next two-year cycle. According to WIA regulations, satisfactory plans first identify the population to be served and assess its needs. Then they explain how the activities will strengthen the capabilities of the individuals who are served to get and keep unsubsidized employment. Finally, they specify the performance standards to which they should be held. The All-Indian Pueblo Council of New Mexico typifies the successful applicant. In this community, WIA pays for twenty-five individuals and sixty youth to obtain some work experience.[30]

Lack of investment persists as one of the major causes of the economic problems in Native American communities. For this reason, it is unfortunate that WIA specifically forbids any money to be spent on employment-generating projects. WIA may well enhance the occupational skills of Native

Americans, but as a principle of social policy, it errs in assuming that it need not address the demand for workers, because no amount of skill enhancement will ever be enough if local businesses do not want to hire them.

Migrant and Seasonal Farm Workers Program

The National Farm Workers Job Program traces its origins to the Economic Opportunity Act of 1964. Currently authorized under Section 167 of WIA, it is designed to address the chronic seasonal unemployment and underemployment experienced by migrant and seasonal farm workers. These are the low-paid workers who harvest the fruits and vegetables that other Americans eat. The program offers assistance to help them and their families achieve economic self-sufficiency.

Like the rest of WIA, this program offers three different kinds of services. The core level includes skills assessment, job search, eligibility determination, and access to other essential services available at the local one-stop shopping center. A second level of intensive services relies on case management to develop a strategy for further education and skill development. The third level provides actual training.

In addition to these three levels, however, WIA actually goes one step further. Recognizing the low wages and difficulties of farm labor, the program also offers some direct short-term assistance. The intensive and training services enable workers to upgrade their employment in the agricultural sector or to get another job outside farming. The direct cash assistance is intended to tide them over during winter or when work is otherwise scarce.

To be eligible for this program, an individual must be a citizen of the United States or a lawfully admitted permanent resident who has registered for military duty with the Selective Service and who has worked as a farm laborer during twelve of the preceding twenty-four months. By law, the worker's family must also have been disadvantaged for twelve months in the preceding twenty-four.

In fiscal year 2000, the budget for this program was about $74 million.[31] Although it is a small program that costs only slightly more than services to Native Americans, the cash assistance it provides remains its most distinctive feature. Most people are familiar with the hard life that farm workers lead: they have low wages and little power. Their employers resist paying more because higher wages would cut into profits and might modestly increase the cost of food. But because these wages are often insufficient to support their families, the government uses money that you have paid in taxes to retain them as part of the agricultural workforce. This cash assistance subsidizes both workers and employers: the workers because they get public money, and the employers because they do not have to pay a living wage.

Veterans

Although Title 1 of WIA included a provision for veterans' programs, the federal budget for fiscal year 2001 transferred the account from the Department of Labor to the Office of Veterans' Employment and Training. This account encompasses two different programs, one for disabled veterans outreach and another for local veterans' employment representatives. In fiscal year 2000, WIA's budget for these two initiatives amounted to a little more than $7 million.[32]

Specialists staff the Disabled Veterans Outreach Program. By developing job and training opportunities for veterans, especially those with service-connected disabilities, these specialists offer direct services that enable them to compete in the job market. These services include the promotion of community and employer support for apprenticeships and on-the-job training as well as linkages to likely governmental and community organizations such as the Department of Veterans Affairs and local veteran groups.[33]

Local veterans' employment representatives are state employees who provide a full range of employment assistance. They counsel and test veterans, identify training and employment opportunities, and monitor job listings from federal contractors to ensure that eligible veterans get referral priority. They also cooperate with the Department of Veterans Affairs to identify and aid those who need prosthetic devices or other special equipment to improve their employability.[34]

The veterans' employment program illustrates one of the fundamental dilemmas of U.S. employment policy. In the absence of an organizing principle such as comprehensiveness and universality, employment policy wavers between delivering services through a bureaucracy devoted to employment services (the Department of Labor) and delivering services by demographic category, as it does with veterans. The Department of Labor has the expertise; in most European countries, its counterparts run the nation's employment programs. But because we have never completely reconciled ourselves to employment programs, we sometimes place them in agencies that serve populations with special needs. The result is that our employment programs suffer from considerable decentralization and do not have a single controlling authority.

Public Job Creation Programs

When the Reagan administration terminated the Comprehensive Employment Training Program in 1981, it ended public job creation programs in the United States for the next fifteen years. With the passage of welfare reform in 1996, however, public job creation programs have returned as a supplement to welfare-to-work initiatives. Now states have the opportunity to use federal welfare funds for low-income families who meet state eligibility requirements. Nor is this the only avenue: programs focused on economic or community development can also generate jobs in the public sector.[35]

These jobs have three primary federal sources: the TANF block grant, the welfare-to-work program, and WIA. Under TANF, state welfare departments can, at their own discretion, earmark funds for job creation, either through direct allocation or by other state, local, or nonprofit agencies. Used to subsidize wages, these TANF monies do not even count against the five-year federal lifetime limit. The second option, welfare-to-work funds, are grants available to the states that the states can pass on to local agencies for programs that could include public job creation. Finally, WIA authorizes job creation as a third-level, intensive employment service in either the private or the public sector.[36]

Both TANF and the welfare-to-work programs are limited, because they cannot be used for individuals without children. That restriction aside, some publicly funded job creation experiments have shown positive results. In Milwaukee, the New Hope project operated as a community-based nonprofit organization funded by a consortium of local, state, and national organizations. New Hope offered child care subsidies, affordable health insurance, assistance to raise participants' income to the poverty level, and full-time employment working in local nonprofit organizations for those who could not otherwise find a job. Although, with under $12,000 in wages, the participants remained poor, the program did raise earnings by 13 percent. Equally significant, community service jobs seem to have smoothed the path to unsubsidized employment, as 62 percent of those employed in such positions held a regular job in the following quarter.[37]

This new willingness to experiment with public job creation suggests that we have at least temporarily overcome public perception about the failures of previous job creation efforts. These efforts suffered both from charges of "make-work" (e.g., for raking leaves) and for their inability to offset the substantial job losses in a faltering economy.[38] Yet this opportunity may not last long, because the linkage of public job creation with welfare-to-work programs limits its potential. When poverty and welfare are tied to public job creation, they stigmatize the programs, which are then sure to be abandoned at the first sign of failure.

We have now reviewed the major U.S. employment programs, highlighting, in particular, their most prominent strengths and weaknesses. To clarify their place within the larger field of social policy, however, we must now look at them through the lens of our policy model.

Economics

The economic functions of employment programs depend on the kind of program. So far, we have identified two types, job training and job creation, each of which has a different set of economic dynamics. In addition, even though none currently exists, a third kind of program, for full employment, has a sufficiently distinct group of economic functions to warrant an analysis of its own.

In theory, job training programs improve the workforce's competitiveness. If more people are trained, then American workers should have better skills to compete in the global economy. Nevertheless, it does make a difference

In recent years, employment training programs have had to retrain industrial workers for jobs in the service economy.

exactly what workers are trained to do: if the primary purpose is to teach former welfare recipients to prepare fast food, then their training does not increase the skills of the American workforce in the way that it would if training emphasized information-age skills in computers and technology.

Job training programs also possess two complementary functions. From the perspective of business, they use public dollars to provide the private sector with a trained workforce; from the perspective of labor, training improves workers' skills and helps them to get better jobs.

Employers always need a trained workforce. But it saves them money to have the public sector train workers and certify that they possess the necessary skills. When there is a shortage of skilled help, job training programs can supply the workers that increase competition and keep wages down. In effect, by organizing the orderly flow of labor, job training programs are another example of how the public sector subsidizes the private.

For displaced or unemployed workers, the role of job training is equally vital. No longer discarded and unproductive, they gain the skills that make them more employable. Although graduates of job training programs do not get much higher wages, their annual earnings increase because they work more. Hence, for the worker who can get into one, a job training program does offer some hope for a higher standard of living.

If job training programs supply businesses with trained workers at the same time that they help workers secure better jobs, then they serve to match the needs of business with the needs of labor. Mind you, such a description does not specify how well they perform this function, because mismatches occur all the time. If a recession looms, job training could produce too many skilled workers. Or, if the economy turns upward, skilled workers could be in short supply. Yet even granting the possibility of these mismatches, the existence of job training programs ensures that the marketplace is no longer solely responsible for matching business and labor.

The second kind of employment programs, public job creation, serves a different economic function. By putting additional money into the hands of workers, these programs help to stimulate the economy. Moreover, the stimulus they provide is much greater than with job training, because although job training provides employment for the workers who run the program, it does not channel any extra money to the participants. They only get extra money later, if they succeed in obtaining a better-paying job on their own.

The explicit goal of public job creation programs is to create jobs and reduce unemployment. These functions are comparatively incidental to job training, which have these outcomes only if a business decides that it can make more money by hiring another skilled worker. This difference matters. Job training expands the supply of skilled workers, increases competition, and contains wages; new public sector jobs stimulate the economy, reduce competition, and raise wages. Should we have a job training or a job creation program? As we shall see in the next section, this difference in their functions makes the decision a highly political one.

One shared function does emerge from all these differences. Although politics shapes the way they handle the issue, both job training and job creation programs perform the function of managing the relationship between the workers and the unemployed. Job training programs make the move from unemployment to work a matter of the workers' own skill and initiative; the transition is automatic with job training programs. In both cases, however, the issues are how many people should be employed, how many people should be unemployed, and what is the effect of the supply and demand for workers on the wages that businesses pay. In effect, by tilting one way or the other, employment programs' management of the relationship between workers and the unemployed has significant implications for these questions.

The third kind of program, full employment, resembles a single public job creation program, with one crucial difference: in the typical full-employment program, the public sector creates jobs until everyone has one. By its very definition, then, full employment makes workers scarce and tends to raise wages. To the extent that it manages the workforce, it does so on terms favorable to workers. It is for this reason that business fought and enfeebled the only two full-employment acts (the 1946 Full Employment Bill and the 1978 Humphrey-Hawkins law) that Congress ever passed. In each instance, it took a law with the teeth to reach full employment, stripped it of its enforcement powers, and turned it into largely symbolic legislation.

In sum, employment programs have the economic functions of stimulating the economy and modifying the supply and demand for labor. But to understand exactly how circumstances shape their performance of these functions, we must turn to the politics of employment programs.

The Politics of Employment Programs

A political analysis of employment programs helps to explain the scarcity of public job creation programs, the absence of a full-employment program, and the reason why job training programs are so often described as "modestly successful." The essence of this explanation is rooted in the federal structure of the U.S. government, a structure that promotes considerable fragmentation and decentralization.

As we discussed in chapter 4 on the politics of social welfare policy, power in the federal government is divided among the executive, legislative, and judicial branches. An uneasy tension also exists between the federal government and the states.

This tension has significant consequences, because large-scale employment programs are a major administrative undertaking. In most European countries, the Ministry of Labor runs them. In the United States, however, the fragmentation of government has never allowed the Department of Labor to build up the expertise—what some social policy critics term "the institutional capacity"—that would enable it to run a large-scale employment program. Instead, it administered some employment programs but shifted the responsibility for others to agencies like the Department of Commerce and the Veterans Administration. Programs can fail for a variety of reasons, but when they are established reluctantly and distributed among several different bureaucracies, they operate at cross-purposes and make failure more likely. In a never-ending cycle, critics then cite this failure as further confirmation that a federally funded employment program cannot succeed.[39]

This opposition also has another dimension. Although business interests may benefit from employment programs that improve workers' skills, they are generally wary of the public sector and even more opposed to public job creation programs that make workers scarce and drive up wages. National business organizations such as the U.S. Chamber of Commerce and the National Association of Manufacturers can therefore be counted on to oppose most new job training initiatives. In fact, just two circumstances cause businesses to soften their opposition: when they need more skilled workers and when high unemployment jeopardizes political stability.

Besides the general distaste for employment programs, the pay scale and the nature of public sector jobs often arouse political controversy. Admittedly, it is difficult to establish the pay scale for public sector employment. If its purpose is to provide extra jobs and pay people enough to survive, then salaries should be set higher. Set a salary too high, however, and every low-wage employee will flood into the program.

The nature of public sector work feeds this controversy. The private sector relies on profit as a rough index of success, and it calculates salaries accordingly: star in a blockbuster movie or rebound for a winning basketball team, and the business will reward your contribution. But how do you quantify the value of a public service like day care, education, or help for an aging parent? If you can't, it not only makes it much harder to determine a salary, but also encourages the stereotype that many public sector jobs are not that far removed from raking leaves.

The final political issue embedded in employment policy is a dilemma that many other social programs share. As chapter 2 explained, the United States has a categorical system of social welfare, which devotes a lot of time and energy to classifying the poor. Those who are not poor get some subsidies because they can deduct expenses like additional dependents, child care, and college tuition from their taxes. But with the prominent exception of the Social Security Act, there are few other universal programs. Instead, most social welfare programs benefit poor people, offering them meager, means-tested assistance that requires them to follow specific regulations and behave in a particular way. Employment programs follow this model. Largely reserved for the poor, they are anchored in the U.S. political framework of "poor programs for poor people." Consequently, it would violate this tradition if they were more than modestly successful.

Ideology

The economics and politics of employment policy have their expected ideological underpinnings. As with other social programs, these underpinnings promote individual initiative and enforcement of the work ethic, justify minimum government intervention, and blame those who fail.

If the attempt to develop employment programs seems half-hearted, that is because mainstream U.S. ideology firmly believes that the market is the best mechanism for matching business and labor. Bringing this abstract principle down to practice, imagine that Ms. Olson owns an environmental recycling firm that needs more plant workers. Mr. Lestan is a 24-year-old man with one year of college who needs a job. How are Ms. Olson and Mr. Lestan going to find each other on the job market so that one can purchase the other's labor? How can Ms. Olson be assured that Mr. Lestan knows his job? Mainstream ideology usually says that these things will happen in the marketplace, without any government intervention.

The underlying ideological principle here is individual initiative. In theory, it is individual initiative that kindled Ms. Olson's entrepreneurship, and it will be individual initiative that propels Mr. Lestan's search for a job. Ms. Olson might have inherited ownership of her company from her father; Mr.

Lestan might be more productive if training enhanced his skills. Yet neither possibility affects the durability of this ideology, which continues to define the availability and adequacy of employment programs.

This ideology has its consequences. Certainly, it pushes people to try harder, to get up in the morning and find a job out of a desire to avoid any suggestion of laziness and irresponsibility. But there is a structural problem. If you cannot find a job and seek to gain access to a training program, you will soon discover that, on average, only one vacancy exists for every twenty eligible people. That's 5 percent, a tantalizing percentage. It suggests that a few people in your neighborhood are probably getting into a job program, but the odds are not high that you will. When you do not get into a job program, you might remember that there are just not enough slots. It is, however, at least as likely that you will simply blame yourself: What did you fail to do? Could you have done something differently? When employment programs are inadequately funded, an ideology that encourages individual initiative becomes closely linked with an ideology of self-blame.

The ideologies that frame employment programs are not inviting. Nevertheless, from time to time, this ideological discouragement has not stopped people from demanding more jobs and better training. There is no single form for these demands because a variety of social movements have made them. It is to these social movements in all their diversity that we now turn.

Social Movements

Many employment training programs, especially those that do not involve actual job creation, have not emerged from social movements. Their origins lie instead with policy experts and government officials, and they follow a consistent pattern. First, these experts become increasingly concerned about either some aspect of the job market or some dimension of the employment training system. Perhaps the economy is changing as a result of automation, as it did in the years preceding the passage of the 1962 Manpower Development Training Act. Or perhaps the fragmentation and duplication of the employment training system itself has become excessive, as it did in the mid-1990s prior to the enactment of the 1998 Workforce Investment Act. In either case, though trade unionists may lobby in support of the reform, it is policy experts in and around the government who are the primary advocates for this new legislation.

Urban riots lie at the other extreme. From bombings by the most militant protestors to outright repression by the police, U.S. social movements have sometimes involved violence. By their very nature, riots lack the organization that goes into developing a social movement. Nevertheless, because social movements express anger about some unmet need, riots are often their by-product. This was certainly the case in the 1960s, when the civil rights movement focused mounting indignation on discrimination and unemployment in the job market. The result was programs such as Job Corps and the Neighborhood Youth Corps that specifically targeted those "disadvantaged" youth in the inner city who were most likely to engage in rioting.

Recessions and depressions have also produced social movements that fought for jobs and job training programs. The classic example of this phenomenon occurred during the Great Depression, when the official unemployment rate reached 25 percent and for a moment, at the time of Roosevelt's 1933 inaugural, every bank in the country was closed.

Naturally, this crisis precipitated a rash of organizing. That same year saw the formation of the Federation of Unemployed Workers Leagues of America, a continental Congress of Workers and Farmers, a Chicago Conference of the Federation of the Unemployed, and a convention of the Unemployed Leagues of Appalachia. The following year, another series of conferences led to the establishment of the Workers Alliance of America, which by 1936 could claim some sixteen hundred locals in forty-three states with an estimated dues-paying membership of three hundred thousand people. New Deal work programs such as the Works Progress Administration arose at least in part as an explicit response to this organizing.[40]

Another kind of social movement draws heavily on the mobilization of trade unions and specifically involves full-employment campaigns. In 1946 for the Full Employment Act and again in 1978 for the Humphrey-Hawkins full employment legislation, a law would have charged the federal government with the responsibility of ensuring full employment. Although liberal congressmen from the Northeast joined some Western progressives in support of these bills, trade unions demanding jobs for their members were the most powerful single interest fighting for their passage. Yet business interests succeeded in defeating the 1946 bill and stripping Humphrey-Hawkins of its enforcement powers, until full employment became a nice, if largely symbolic, goal.[41]

Social movements for job creation take a somewhat different form. Trade unions are certainly active here too, but as most job creation initiatives have occurred in the community on a local level, government trade unions have tended to be more dominant. This visibility is especially evident in the case of job creation programs for local government functions, where government workers in the American Federation of State, Municipal and County Employees have been most active. From the Comprehensive Employment and Training Act of 1973 to the Workforce Investment Act of 1998, if the job involves day care, social work, or another human service, government workers have fought for programs that would add to their ranks.

Employment programs, then, have their origins in many different kinds of social movements. An overview is useful because it suggests all the various routes that brought them into being. At the same time, however, the history of employment programs is easily fragmented when we review them in this way. To end that fragmentation, we need to look at a more chronological history.

The idea of putting the unemployed to work in tough economic times did not originate in the New Deal. When President Thomas Jefferson pushed through the Embargo Act of 1808, prohibiting foreign trade, a flood of unemployed sailors prompted New York City to initiate the nation's first work-relief program. Under the auspices of this program, the unemployed filled in the Collect Pond in downtown Manhattan and dug the foundation for City Hall. From 1817 to 1825, New York State also employed thousands of workers to construct the Erie Canal.[42] For a century, however, projects like these were exceptions. Although local governments might embark on major public works projects or find some worthwhile tasks for work relief, it was not until the 1930s that employment programs became a fixture of federal policy.

The subsequent history of employment programs divides into three stages. In the first stage, during the 1930s and 1940s, employment programs were initially on the upswing. This period starts with programs for work and relief and ends with the failure of a universal full-employment bill in 1946. The second stage begins in the 1960s with concerns about the effects of automation (the Manpower Development Training Act of 1962) but soon narrows its focus during the Great Society to racial minorities. It concludes with the Comprehensive Employment and Training Act of 1973 and the failure of the Humphrey-Hawkins full-employment bill five years later. The third phase takes the focus on racial minorities and turns it into an increasingly exclusive emphasis on workfare. With its orientation to the private sector, the Job Training Partnership Act of 1983 marks the beginning of the third phase. Now, as the 1998 Workforce Investment Act broadens potential eligibility, the third phase may be undergoing a significant modification.

The first stage began in 1933 with the enactment of the Federal Emergency Relief Administration. FERA was the first major grant-in-aid program to the states, which were required to establish an emergency relief administration that would distribute federal and state funds to localities. FERA was means-tested, and most projects were in construction and production for use (goods produced for use by relief recipients). By the time it ended in 1935, FERA had distributed more than $3.25 billion. But with businesses fighting to keep wages down, only a small portion of this money went to promote work relief for wages.[43]

The Civilian Conservation Corps made more headway on this issue. Also enacted in 1933, the CCC deployed men in forestry, erosion, flood control, and other conservation projects, where they were paid $30 a month. The CCC divided administrative responsibility for supervision among the Departments of Labor, War, Agriculture, and Interior. Mobilization by the army was central to its effectiveness. Projected to employ 275,000 men, the CCC reached this quota within several months of its establishment.[44]

The next New Deal work program, the Civil Works Administration, did not last very long. Set up in November 1933 to defuse another winter of need and protest, the CWA employed 4.26 million by January. About half of CWA's workers came from FERA's relief rolls. It hired professionals, artists, and white-collar workers, as well as craftsmen and unskilled laborers, and it paid them wages, not a relief dole. Nevertheless, it was exactly these positive attributes about the CWA that intensified the political pressure on it. Lobbied by business groups and Southern Democrats who were concerned about its effect on wages and worried about the potential for creating a large social welfare apparatus, Roosevelt ended CWA after just four months and FERA the year after.[45]

The Works Progress Administration (after 1939, the Works Projects Administration) replaced them. It lasted from 1935 until 1943, when mobilization for World War II eliminated unemployment. Within one year, it employed 3 million people for all kinds of work: repairing highways, cataloguing archives, and recording the stories of former slaves. Unlike the CWA, which permitted more than one family member to hold a job, the WPA limited participation to one person per family at any time and paid just 65 to 70 percent of the prevailing wage. Because family size, composition, and monthly budgets determined eligibility, it relied on social workers to conduct investigations.[46]

The first phase concluded with the Allied victory in World War II. Fearful that demobilization of the military would bring back Depression-era levels of unemployment, liberals and trade unionists introduced the Full Employment Act of 1946. Conservatives and business interests quickly rejected this proposal. Defining the New Deal work programs as a one-time exception, they rebuffed efforts that committed policymakers to low levels of unemployment. In the aftermath of this failure, work programs disappeared from the federal government for the next fifteen years.

They returned with the Manpower Development and Training Act in 1962. Enacted out of concerns about the effects of automation, the MDTA provided both classroom and on-the-job training. Classroom training paid an average of just $35 a week stipend for up to one year at skill centers that often operated out of public schools. This pay was below the minimum wage, so that when the economy improved, many men left the program for higher-wage jobs. By contrast, on-the-job training offered a subsidy to employers as a hiring incentive. MDTA averaged over 209,000 participants during the 1960s. But in a move foreshadowing the era's trend toward racial targeting, its 1966 amendments stipulated that in the aftermath of urban rioting, 65 percent of its funds were to be spent on the hardcore unemployed.[47]

The programs that followed in its wake were cut from the same cloth. In 1964, the Economic Opportunity Act added the Neighborhood Youth Corps, which was designed to keep youth in school or increase their employability if they dropped out, and the Job Corps, with its residential centers for the least employable youth. Subsequently, in 1972, the passage of the Work Incentive Program signaled the first shift in emphasis. Born out of an increasing apprehension about growth in the number of welfare recipients, it marked the real beginning of a thirty-year effort to get them off the rolls.

The second phase culminated in the passage of the 1973 Comprehensive Employment and Training Act. CETA provided work in socially useful jobs: screening programs in hospitals, additional personnel for law enforcement agencies, community programs in arts and recreation, staffing battered women shelters and child care centers. In 1978, the national CETA wage maximum was $10,000 with an additional $2,000 permitted for high-wage areas, but the average national wage was supposed to be just $7,200. In effect, CETA consolidated all the major job programs into a single administrative structure that relied on public employment to ease the effects of economic downturns.[48]

The existence of a significant public employment program emboldened trade unionists, liberal members of Congress, and other progressive forces. Building on CETA, they tried to enact another full-employment bill, the 1978 Humphrey-Hawkins Act. In its initial version, the Humphrey-Hawkins bill established a goal of 3 percent unemployment. But, just as in the end of the first phase during the 1940s, the prospect of a full-employment bill aroused conservative fears about the power of labor unions and the possibility of excessive government intervention. The subsequent mobilization of conservative forces enfeebled the Humphrey-Hawkins legislation and signified the end of the second phase.

The third phase of this history began in 1983 with the passage of the Job Training Partnership Act. Two prominent features distinguish it. The first is the orientation to the private sector that JTPA embodied and that other programs would reflect in subsequent years. The second is the heavy emphasis on workfare programs for welfare recipients.

JTPA was the model employment program of the Reagan era. Rejecting CETA's commitment to the public sector, JTPA turned to private industry councils (PICs) composed of community businesspeople who were responsible for allocating training funds according to local business needs. By law, JTPA could not train participants for work in the public sector. Moreover, because JTPA paid contractors based on their success rate, it also favored the easily placed worker over the hardcore unemployed. Eventually, this absence of public oversight led to PICs misdirecting funds and created a serious problem of accountability.[49]

The focus on work for welfare recipients intensified during this period. When President Reagan's first budget, the Omnibus Budget Reconciliation Act of 1981, authorized the states to experiment with workfare, many turned to the Community Work Experience Program, which either forced recipients to "work off" their welfare grants in public or community jobs or converted those grants into wage subsidies for employers. In 1988, the passage of the Family Support Act and the Job Opportunities and Basic Skills Training Program (JOBS) ended this experiment. Expanding the workfare population to those on welfare with no children under 3 years, the Family Support Act instructed the states to target those who were less likely to leave welfare on their own and required them to fund a broad array of employment-related services. Although the states often underfunded social supports like day care, some 13 percent of adults on AFDC were participating in the JOBS program by 1995.[50]

This emphasis on work for welfare recipients crystallized in the Personal Responsibility and Work Opportunity Act of 1996. From the perspective of the preceding sixty years, this Act collapses welfare policy into employment policy, so that a disproportionate part of employment policy is now focused on welfare recipients. For these people, training may be necessary for work, but work is at least implicitly a punishment, something demanded of recipients when they will not get a job on their own. This conception of employment policy makes little allowance for workers who are laid off in a turbulent labor market or those who simply want to get their skills upgraded. At this point in the history of U.S. employment policy, these tasks are each individual's own responsibility.

Yet the Workforce Reinvestment Act of 1998 does suggest some other possibilities. Not only does it begin what could become a more drastic process of program consolidation, but building on the welfare reform act of 1996, it extends the possibilities for job creation in the public sector. To be sure, the Act is hardly a universalist piece of social legislation: anyone can get counseling, but only those who fail to obtain a job through any other means are eligible for public employment training. Nevertheless, from a more optimistic perspective, at least counseling is now universal and perhaps one day soon, other services will be also.

The third historical stage of employment programs ends, then, just the way it should: on a very ambiguous note. The United States has largely adhered to a restricted conception of the role of employment programs, one that de-emphasized full-employment policies while providing training for people in great financial need. Only on comparatively rare occasions has it assisted workers who were simply laid off or displaced. From economics to politics, from ideology to social movements, all the factors we have discussed suggest that it will not be easy to move beyond what this history outlines. And yet, there is this ambiguity, the hint of potential and possibility in the Workforce Investment Act, which points to the prospect that employment policy might yet acquire an expanded role.

10

Housing: Programs and Policies

Income support programs give people money; employment programs help them to increase their income. Both these programs operate on the *demand* side of the economic equation; that is, they work to put more money in people's pockets. But on what do people spend this money? The answer is that they spend a lot of it on housing, health care, and food, the basic human needs that are the subject of this and the next two chapters.

People certainly spend a growing percentage on housing. Housing costs have spiraled upward because an affluent segment of the population has created a tight market for the better housing stock. Space is also scarce in the older cities, especially in the Northeast, where a developer cannot so easily extend the city onto previously undeveloped land. Gentrification, real estate speculation, and the increased cost of new construction have also taken their toll. All these factors have intensified pressure on the market for more reasonably priced housing—the kind that poor people, those just out of college, and workers earning less than $25,000 a year can afford.

The withdrawal of the federal government from the housing market has reinforced these trends. Despite the existence of some subsidies for the poor, such as public housing projects and Section 8 housing vouchers, the federal government has never provided direct public assistance to more than 6 percent of U.S. households. Moreover, as the budget for the Department of

Housing and Urban Development has declined in recent years, the role of the federal government has diminished still further.

Given the relative roles of the private sector and the federal government, one might well ask whether the United States has a housing policy. That would be a reasonable but ultimately misleading question. The United States has a clear, if not always clearly articulated, housing policy, one that is largely market-based. Looking to the private sector as the source of most housing, this policy assumes that the vast majority of Americans will be able to rent or buy housing on their own. But just in case their inability to do so should ever call that private sector source into question, the federal government quietly offers two crucial tax subsidies for home owners. These two subsidies allow home owners to deduct local property taxes and the interest on their mortgage from their federal tax obligation. Indeed, so strong is the federal government's commitment to the marketplace that the combined value of these hidden subsidies is actually several times the value of the assistance it provides to poor people who need housing.

We will talk more about these subsidies later in the chapter. For now, it is important to remember what these subsidies suggest about U.S. housing policy: it is rooted in the market, kind to the real estate industry triangle of banks, landlords, and developers, and gives more help to wealthier people. Any assistance that housing policy in the United States tries to offer the poor always runs up against these entrenched priorities.

Part of the problem with housing policy, then, is that it has many other purposes besides the provision of housing. Because shelter against the elements is a basic human need, housing is central to our lives. Housing policy affirms the importance of the market, but it also subsidizes the poor, perpetuates racial divisions by residential location, and shapes the development of neighborhoods. In addition, for individuals, perhaps its most significant economic function is to expand home ownership and thereby add to personal wealth: 72 percent of families with an income between $40,000 and $50,000 a year have more equity in their home than in the stock market. Even at an income of $100,000 a year, 40 percent still have greater equity in their home.[1] With so many families banking on their home as an important component of their total assets, housing policy has always sought to ensure the economic health of the real estate industry on the assumption that it must remain profitable if families are to build wealth.

The Context for Housing Policy

The context for housing policy has many dimensions, including home ownership, the shortage of affordable housing and the spread of homelessness, the role of the suburbs, and the crucial impact of race. Each of these factors interacts with the development of housing policy, and we will discuss them in turn.

There are roughly 100 million households in the United States. Sixty-eight percent of these are home owners; 32 percent are renters. Such a high ownership rate is unusual by international standards. In Germany, France, Great Britain, and Norway, just 33 percent of the population own their own homes. Only Canada, New Zealand, and Australia—all countries with small populations, a frontier tradition, and a traditional British dislike for cities— have equally high rates of home ownership.[2]

Like every other economic indicator, home ownership rates mirror divisions of class and race. Eighty-six percent of households in the top quarter of income own their homes, compared to 48 percent in the bottom quarter. Consistent with these figures, the median income of owners was almost $44,000. Renters, by comparison, earned just 52 percent of owners' income, or less than $23,000. The median was brought down by the substantial segment of very poor people who rent, the 27 percent of renters with income below 30 percent of the median.[3]

The racial difference is equally clear. In 2002, the home ownership rate for whites reached 74 percent, while it is 48 percent for blacks and 47 percent for Hispanics. These statistics mean that even though the rate for people of color has been increasing, whites are still almost 60 percent more likely to own their homes.[4]

Nationally, the home ownership rate in 2002 reached an all-time high of 68.7 percent. This growth in home ownership, however, is primarily attributable to people over 55, who purchased their housing when it was more affordable. Nowadays, many younger adults cannot buy a house because with a national median price in 2002 of more than $153,000 (up 7 percent from the preceding year), the down payment is too high and the carrying costs (mortgage, taxes, and upkeep) are excessive. In 1978, more than 62 percent of all 30- to 34-year-olds lived in their own homes. By 1998, however, the share had dropped to just 53 percent.[5]

Home ownership data, then, paint a deceptively rosy picture of the health of the U.S. housing market. In fact, one in every seven U.S. families, 13.7 million people, has a critical housing need, including 51 percent of all working families who own their own homes.[6] According to the National Low Income Housing Coalition, a family living on a minimum wage cannot rent a typical apartment in any U.S. city.[7] To compensate for this lack of income, minimum wage workers in seventy of the nation's metropolitan areas would have to work one hundred hours a week to pay for an apartment at the fair market rent (the Department of Housing and Urban Development term for reasonably priced housing in a particular region). They would have to work so hard because in 2001, the national minimum housing wage—the wage a household should receive to afford a two-bedroom apartment at the fair market rent—was $13.87 an hour, or more than 2.5 times the minimum wage.[8]

With prices like these, the housing shortage is hardly restricted to the poorest people. Further up the income scale, 2.4 million working renters with incomes under $25,000 spend more than half of their income on housing or live in substandard housing.[9] In thirty-nine states, 40 percent or more of renters cannot afford the fair market rent for a two-bedroom unit. And across

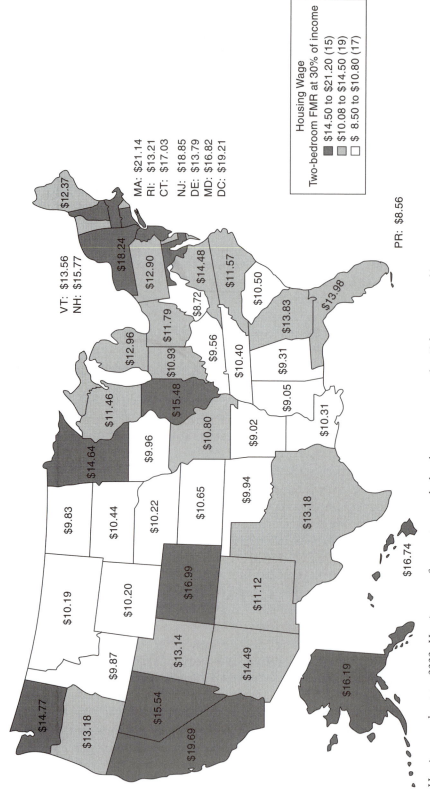

VT: $13.56
NH: $15.77

MA: $21.14
RI: $13.21
CT: $17.03

NJ: $18.85
DE: $13.79
MD: $16.82
DC: $19.21

Housing Wage
Two-bedroom FMR at 30% of income

■ $14.50 to $21.20 (15)
▨ $10.08 to $14.50 (19)
□ $ 8.50 to $10.80 (17)

PR: $8.56

$12.37
$18.24
$12.90
$8.72
$14.48
$11.57
$10.50
$13.83
$13.98
$11.79
$12.96
$10.93
$9.56
$10.40
$9.31
$9.05
$10.31
$15.48
$11.46
$10.80
$9.02
$14.64
$9.96
$9.94
$13.18
$10.19
$10.20
$9.83
$10.44
$10.22
$10.65
$16.99
$11.12
$9.87
$13.14
$14.49
$16.74
$14.77
$13.18
$15.54
$19.69
$16.19

Housing wage by state, 2002. Housing wage figures represent the hourly wage necessary (at 40 hours per week) to earn enough income to afford the fair market rent for a two-bedroom unit at 30% of income.

the country, at least 220,000 teachers, police, and public safety officers spend more than half of their income on housing. All told, in 2000, 5.4 million families paid half of their income on housing or lived in severely distressed housing.[10]

To calculate the overall shortage of affordable housing, experts have developed an indicator. This indicator measures the number of affordable housing units relative to the number of households who need them. In 1970, for example, there were 6.5 million low-cost units and 6.2 million low-income renters. With a surplus of some 300,000 units, the low-income housing market was tight, but renters could still find affordable housing. By 1995, however, the market had tightened so much that 10.5 million poor people were competing for 6.1 million units. This shortfall of 4.4 million units documents the mounting severity of the housing affordability gap.[11]

Homelessness

The most visible evidence of the housing affordability gap arises from the growth of a sizable homeless population. Before the 1970s, homelessness in most U.S. cities was contained in Skid Rows. These neighborhoods were typically downtown areas populated by single adult men, often alcoholics, who lived in cheap, single-room hotels. When they were unable to pay the rent, they turned to voluntary agencies such as the Salvation Army for food, shelter, and clothing. Skid Row residents were very poor, and they usually had little contact with the rest of the urban population.

But then homelessness began to spread. As wages declined, the government cut benefits, and the housing shortage deepened, people with the least financial and emotional resources lost their housing. Unlike the residents of Skid Row, this new homeless population included families, youth, and single women as well as single men. Because homelessness among families was generally well hidden, street begging by single adults became the public face of homelessness in the United States. As a visible social problem in many U.S. cities, the existence of such public poverty created an ideological problem. Much more than private poverty, public poverty needed to be explained away.

Drawing on a long-standing U.S. political tradition, critics quickly contended that homeless people should be blamed for their predicament. A purely demographic analysis, one that looks only at the people's characteristics, suggests they might well be right: after all, many homeless people do suffer from alcoholism, drug addiction, and mental illness. A structural perspective, however, puts these demographic characteristics into another context. From this perspective, personal traits are merely the visible symptoms of the housing affordability gap already described. If there are too few housing units for the number of poor people—if, in essence, the search for housing is really a desperate game of musical chairs—then it is the most troubled people who will fail to find shelter. Given the housing shortage, who else would you expect to become homeless?

For more than two decades now, the growth of the homeless population

Beginning in the 1980s, homeless people became the visible poor whose presence needed to be explained away.

has prompted a vigorous debate about its causes, size, and persistence. Conservatives blame individual deficiencies, a rash of irresponsible behavior stemming from the permissiveness of the 1960s, single motherhood, the discharge of patients from mental hospitals, and even the "ready" availability of temporary shelter.[12] On the opposite side of the political spectrum, progressives cite the housing shortage; the decline in wages, especially among low-paid workers; and cutbacks in social welfare. Acknowledging the role that individual decisions play, they stress that poor people face a narrower range of options, leading them to engage in behavior, including aggressive panhandling and eating out of garbage cans, that others may view as annoying or repugnant.

The size of the population has also been the subject of considerable controversy. When the Department of Housing and Urban Development conducted the first census of the homeless population in 1984, they came up with a figure of just 250,000 people who were homeless on any given night. Advocates mocked this number. Insisting that the Reagan administration deliberately designed the study to minimize the size of the problem, some maintained that 3 million people were actually homeless during the course of the year. More careful analysis has subsequently disproved both figures. By the late 1980s, this research had established 500,000 to 600,000 as the accepted number. In the most recent studies, researchers counted 842,000 people who

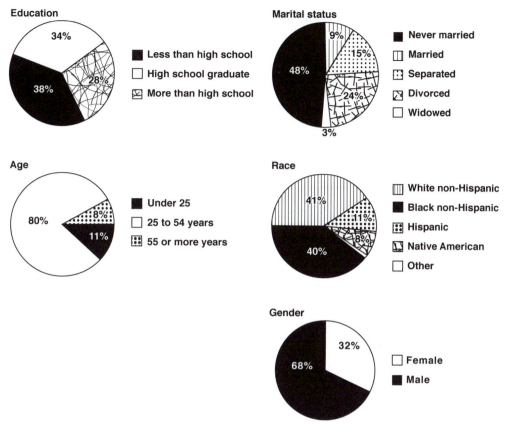

Education

- ■ Less than high school
- □ High school graduate
- ▨ More than high school

34%
38%
28%

Marital status

- ■ Never married
- ⊞ Married
- ⦂ Separated
- ⊠ Divorced
- □ Widowed

9%
15%
48%
24%
3%

Age

- ■ Under 25
- □ 25 to 54 years
- ⦙ 55 or more years

80%
8%
11%

Race

- ▥ White non-Hispanic
- ■ Black non-Hispanic
- ⦂ Hispanic
- ◩ Native American
- □ Other

41%
11%
8%
40%

Gender

- □ Female
- ■ Male

32%
68%

Demographic characteristics of homeless clients in 2000.

were homeless during one week in February 1996, and 2.3 million adults who were likely to be homeless during the course of the year.[13]

Homelessness has proven to be an unusually stubborn problem. As the population grew, the nation's homeless assistance network expanded by 220 percent, from 275,000 beds in 1988 to almost 608,000 in 1996. From these figures alone, it appears that the United States has done a lot to address this issue. This expansion, however, merely represents an increase in the number of temporary shelter beds, which does nothing to address the causes of homelessness. At the same time, the expenditure of considerable sums on a bigger temporary shelter system does help to explain why so many people have lost patience. They feel that because homeless people still approach them on the street, the only solution is to criminalize behavior like begging and sleeping on park benches.[14]

Even if their reaction is understandable, a closer analysis suggests that U.S. policies have actually been quite limited: fewer people may live on the streets, but they still do not have a home. To be sure, other services for counseling and employment have also expanded, but the problem of homelessness persists because its causes prevent its elimination.

We could virtually eliminate widespread homelessness if wages were higher, cash benefits were increased, social services were readily available, and poor people had easy access to affordable housing. These are the deficits that cause homelessness, and yet in every instance, powerful political and economic forces obstruct any attempt to provide more. Businesses do not want to raise wages, nor would they allow the value of social welfare benefits to rise above current wage levels, because then people would lose their incentive to work. Likewise, conservatives object to the higher taxes that comprehensive social services demand. And even though a shortage of affordable housing is a primary cause of homelessness, the softening of prices brought about by any significant expansion of government-subsidized housing would encounter strong opposition from the real estate industry. Looking at this array of political and economic forces, it is no wonder that the policies of the past two decades have not made much headway. Although no one set out to make anyone homeless, the causes of homelessness continue to obstruct a cure.

The Suburbs

The American dream is to own a home, and the most likely place for this dream to be realized is in the suburbs. Until the development of the railroad in the nineteenth century, big cities were densely populated and not very spread out. But as cities became manufacturing centers and railroads allowed the more affluent to flee the soot and noise, some people began to commute from outside the most populated parts of the city to their place of work. Suburbs such as Lake Forest outside of Chicago and along Philadelphia's Main Line arose in this period.

Mass production of the automobile quickened the pace of suburban development. By 1927, in part due to Henry Ford's development of the Model-T, one of every five Americans owned an automobile. Following the first construction of modern highways in the 1920s, a growing number of them used their cars to get away from big cities. The adoption of gasoline taxes (by 1929, every state had one) provided an ample source of revenue for this great surge of road construction.

Nevertheless, the real explosion of suburban growth did not occur until after World War II. The mass production of housing, especially as pioneered by people like William and Alfred Levitt, the developers of Levittown, New York, combined with federally guaranteed mortgages and an influx of returning veterans to produce a market for the detached, single-family home on a small plot of land that distinguishes the modern suburb. Critics denounced this housing for its "cookie-cutter" design, but for families leaving ethnic working-class neighborhoods in the major cities, it represented the fulfillment of a lifelong dream.[15]

Through the 1990s, more than 70 percent of city dwellers who obtained a mortgage did so to buy a suburban home. Included in this trend were many people of color from the inner city, who bought suburban homes at only a slightly lower rate than their white counterparts.[16] This development is certainly a welcome trend, but it has not yet matured enough to alter the extent to which housing policy, the phenomenon of single-home ownership, and the growth of the suburbs all remain profoundly entangled with the issue of race.

Race

Racial segregation has long been an essential component of U.S. housing policy. Until the 1960s, it was automatically assumed that whites and blacks lived in separate neighborhoods. Under the Jim Crow laws, the states enforced this policy in the South, while in the North, few challenged the racial covenants and informal understandings that directed whites to one neighborhood and blacks to another. In deference to the power of Southern Democrats, President Roosevelt slighted racial issues to enact many otherwise progressive New Deal programs.

The mechanization of Southern agriculture, however, triggered a massive migration north. This migration intensified the contradictions of U.S. social policy and created enormous pressures for change. When African Americans migrated to assembly lines in Detroit, for example, they found restrictive covenants; between 1940 and 1947, builders attached these covenants to the deeds in every Detroit subdivision. A typical covenant on the northwest side stated simply that the house "shall not be used or occupied by a person or persons except those of the Caucasian race."[17] Even Levittown, New York, that model development of mass-produced housing, had its own racially exclusionary policies.

In the cities, public housing tended to reinforce these arrangements. Public housing projects could be constructed only with the approval of the local public housing authority, which was always extremely vulnerable to each community's racial politics. Because public housing policy restricted eligibility for public housing to poor people, race and class combined to funnel poor African Americans into public housing. In most urban areas, it was just too hard to get housing anywhere else. As a result, by 1967, black families occupied 50 percent of all public housing.[18] And in a sad but seemingly inevitable downward spiral, this increasing concentration of African Americans in the inner cities further spurred the flight of whites to the suburbs.

Faced with a critical mass of African Americans in the Northern industrial states, the Democratic Party shifted its position on race during the 1960s. Despite considerable opposition from many white working-class ethnics who were closest to blacks on the job and in neighboring communities, Democrats led by President Lyndon Johnson enacted the Civil Rights Act of 1964, which prohibited racial discrimination in housing, employment, and all public facilities.[19] Over the next four decades, however, we have learned that, though passing a law may make something illegal, it does not necessarily end the practice.

Several studies have demonstrated that housing discrimination still exists, though more for blacks than Hispanics. When matched pairs of buyers looked for a home, real estate agents showed blacks about 25 percent fewer houses than their white counterparts. African Americans were also less likely to receive special incentives to rent or to be offered help in finding financing for purchases, but they were more likely to be steered toward particular neighborhoods and higher interest loans. In addition, a 1991 study found that even after factors like credit history were taken into account, loan applications by black and Hispanic customers were 82 percent more likely to be turned down.[20]

The most apparent effects of housing discrimination include greater concentrations of poverty, a significant difference in home ownership rates, and poorer schools.[21] In fact, housing discrimination is so powerful that by one estimate, its elimination would lead to a 14 percent drop in the poverty rate among African Americans.[22] Although few issues in housing can be considered apart from race, the persistence of housing discrimination offers the most explicit testimony about the role of race in U.S. housing policy.

Social Change Triggers

What, then, triggers social change in housing policy? On the surface, with more than two-thirds of all Americans living in their own homes, it appears as if most people are reasonably well-housed. Nevertheless, as our review suggests, this appearance of comfort and security obscures some serious problems that lie just under the surface. In the past, housing policy has changed when these problems become too serious to ignore.

Perhaps the most common trigger of change in housing policy is so widely assumed that we tend to overlook its implications. That trigger is, of course, the prime interest rate set by the Federal Reserve. This is the interest rate that the Federal Reserve charges its member banks, who then charge you about 2 percentage points more for your mortgage. High mortgage rates can quickly put a moderately priced home out of the reach of a typical family. When inability to buy a home causes a slowdown in the real estate and construction industries, pressure builds on the Federal Reserve to ease the prime rate and make housing more widely affordable.

Fannie Mae (the Federal National Mortgage Association) and Freddie Mac (the Federal Home Loan Mortgage Corporation) are two public/private institutions that can also help to put home ownership within reach of the average family. Congress chartered Fannie Mae and Freddie Mac to create a market for secondary mortgages, so that once you arrange a mortgage with your bank, your bank can sell it to someone else. As housing costs spiked in the 1990s, the Department of Housing and Urban Development increased the percentage of low- and moderate-income housing units in which Fannie Mae and Freddie Mac could trade. Like a reduction in the Federal Reserve's prime rate, these actions reflect a concern that housing costs have risen beyond the reach of the average home buyer.[23]

Sometimes, concerns about the ability of a particular category of people to get housing—World War II veterans, for example—come together with an economic objective such as development of the suburbs. These were two of the most powerful triggers behind the 1949 Housing Act, in which the government guaranteed the mortgages that emptied the cities, enabled veterans to buy in the suburbs, and permitted banks and real estate developers to arrange risk-free financing. World War II veterans were the honored soldiers of the last good war. Their victory created a sense of possibility, and their status combined with the economic potential of the suburbs to smooth the way for the passage of a new housing law.

In housing for the poor, the social change triggers are both similar and different. They are similar because the issue of housing affordability is even more troublesome for the poor than it is for moderate-income families. But while moderate-income people have easier access to political power, the housing problems of the poor are usually more conspicuous. Historically, crime, riots, and the spread of homelessness have been the triggers for policy changes in their housing.

Hence, concern for housing affordability among the poor rarely stands alone. Instead, during more liberal eras like the Great Society, slum conditions breed concern about crime and civil unrest, leading to demands for more public housing. In 1965, these demands brought about the establishment of the Department of Housing and Urban Development. Three years later, the newly enacted Housing and Urban Development Act set numerical goals for the construction of 26 million units over the next ten years, with 6 million units allocated for low- and moderate-income families.[24] In a liberal era, then, slum conditions had to be linked to crime and unrest for change to occur, but at least the poor got some additional housing.

In more conservative periods, concern about the level of crime in public housing is expressed in a different way. Perhaps the most recent example of this trigger for social change is the enactment of the Quality Housing and Work Responsibility Act of 1998. Although this Act sought to prevent crime by bringing some tenants of moderate income into public housing, it failed to provide any additional housing for the poor. In fact, by reallocating housing from the poor to those with a higher income, crime among the poor actually brought about their further displacement.

As we discussed earlier, homelessness too can be an important trigger for social change. Once again, the trigger here is public poverty, the poverty that you encounter on your daily commute. Private poverty in the United States is usually acceptable as long as it is hidden. Indeed, for the most part, poverty in this country does remain hidden, and you do not suspect that someone is poor unless you pass through a poor neighborhood or see someone use food stamps to pay for groceries at a supermarket.

Yet neither of these experiences is as jarring as regular and unwilling encounters with public poverty. We all know that many people look down on public poverty, so we intuitively understand how desperate some poor people must be to display their poverty in public. Because such public displays contradict the usual message that all is well with almost everyone, they must be managed. For the past twenty years, we have managed them through the

Connecting poor housing with crime and unrest, policymakers in more liberal periods have advanced proposals for additional public housing.

construction of an elaborate shelter system. This system does not make homeless people any less poor, but at least it gets them off the streets and out of public view.

Another trigger of change in housing policy is the perceived need for urban renewal. Twice in the second half of the twentieth century, the private sector saw significant potential for new investment in the urban centers and pressured government for policies that would enable this potential to be realized. In the first case, as part of the 1949 Housing Act (the same Act that provided government-guaranteed mortgages for suburban development), the government authorized the destruction of city slums to eliminate their negative effects on downtown business areas. The National Association of Real Estate Boards, the United States Savings and Loan League, and the Mortgage Bankers Association of America all supported this act. Once again, it was not housing conditions that prompted this concern about slums, but the expectation that the land on which they were located might be put to more profitable use.[25]

Gentrification sparked the second period of urban renewal in the 1970s and 1980s. Although reconstruction of the downtown area in this period was less widespread than in the first phase, it still destroyed 1 million units of single-room occupancy housing, which previously had housed casual laborers and the deinstitutionalized, people who could not afford a full-size apartment but could pay $25 a week for a room. Nevertheless, as the economic base of cities shifted from dirty industries such as auto and steel to clean services like computer technology, real estate in the downtown center became more attractive for both business and residential uses. Encouraged by a variety of new municipal incentives, real estate interests displaced poor people and gentrified the downtown.[26]

From crime to gentrification, all these triggers of change in housing policy share a common thread. In no case do the living conditions of the poor alone bring about a change in housing policy. Instead, for a change to occur, the effect of these living conditions must spill over into some other social, economic, or political issue. Whether it is the safety of nearby residents, the economic potential of the housing if it were redirected to other uses, or the threat that tenement-related unrest poses to political stability, changes in housing policy come about because other, more powerful people have been affected. By themselves, the living conditions of the poor rarely matter enough.

Housing Programs

Over the years, the federal government has enacted a variety of housing programs. A few deal with the needs of special populations such as people with AIDS or those in rural areas. Some stress community investment and redevelopment. Others grapple with the ongoing question of how to give housing assistance to the poor. Although a few comprehensive programs might be more effective than many small ones, no combination of housing programs can be effective, regardless of their size, when HUD's budget has plunged from about $85 billion in 1978 to just $29.4 billion in 2002 in inflation-adjusted terms.[27]

Housing Opportunities for People with AIDS (HOPWA)

Enacted as part of the 1990 National Affordable Housing Act, this program is intended to encourage states and localities to develop strategies for meeting the housing needs of persons with HIV/AIDS and their families. Grants are made to the states and local jurisdictions; more than one hundred jurisdictions qualified for assistance in 2002. Recipients of the grant may use the funds for short-term rental assistance and to develop community residences for people with AIDS, as well as for housing information and technical assistance. Independent of any housing activity, they may also provide services

Housing Opportunities for People with AIDS (HOPWA), 1990

Number of recipients:	62,000
Who offers the benefit or service:	States and local jurisdictions
What form does it take:	Grants for short-term rental assistance and development of community housing
To whom is it provided:	People with AIDS/HIV, their families, and the agencies that serve them
At whose expense:	In 2002, the federal budget for HOPWA was $277 million. States and local jurisdictions receive this money as a federal grant.

Community Development Block Grant (CDBG), 1974

Number of recipients:	Since its inception, grants have been awarded to more than 4,000 communities
Who offers the benefit or service:	The public sector through the federal government
What form does it take:	Grants for housing and expansion of economic opportunity
To whom is it provided:	Local jurisdictions
At whose expense:	CDBG is funded from federal tax dollars and is usually budgeted for between $4 billion and $5 billion annually.

Section 202 (Housing for the Elderly), 1959

Number of recipients:	The residents of 300,000 housing units benefit from the program
Who offers the benefit or service:	The public sector through the federal government
What form does it take:	Grants for building and operating housing for the elderly
To whom is it provided:	Nonprofit agencies that serve qualified tenants of at least 62 years of age, with an income less than 50% of their area's median income
At whose expense:	In 2002, the federal government budgeted $783 million for this program.

Home Investment Partnership Program (HOME), 1990

Number of recipients:	589 jurisdictions
Who offers the benefit or service:	The public sector through the federal government
What form does it take:	Grants
To whom is it provided:	60 percent to urban areas, 40 percent to the states
At whose expense:	In 2002, the federal government spent about $2 billion for the HOME program.

Hope VI, 1990

Number of recipients:	So far, 146 communities in 37 states and territories
Who offers the benefit or service:	The public sector through the federal government
What form does it take:	Grants to demolish, and sometimes replace, public housing
To whom is it provided:	Local communities
At whose expense:	Altogether, the federal government has allocated $4.7 billion for these purposes.

(continued)

Low Income Housing Tax Credit (LIHTC), 1986

Number of recipients:	About 1 million units of low-income housing
Who offers the benefit or service:	The state housing agency, from federal tax credits that are passed on through the state
What form does it take:	Tax credits
To whom is it provided:	Individual and corporate sponsors of low-income housing
At whose expense:	Because the federal government offers these credits, taxpayers must pay additional taxes to compensate for the uncollected revenue.

Native American Housing Assistance and Self-Determination Act (NAHASDA), 1996

Number of recipients:	583 tribes or their designated housing authorities (2002)
Who offers the benefit or service:	The federal government
What form does it take:	Block grant
To whom is it provided:	Native American tribes or tribally designated housing authorities
At whose expense:	In 2002, the federal government allocated $648 billion for this program.

Section 8, Housing and Community Development Act, 1974

Number of recipients:	1.3 million in project-based housing assistance (directly to landlords), and more recently, 1.5 million in tenant-based housing (through a voucher)
Who offers the benefit or service:	The public sector through the federal government
What form does it take:	A rental subsidy in the form of a voucher
To whom is it provided:	75 percent of vouchers go to tenants with 30 percent or less of the area's median income; the remaining 25 percent go to those with up to 80 percent of the area's median income
At whose expense:	In 2002, the federal government allocated $15 billion for expiring project-based housing and $144 million for 26,000 new vouchers.

Rural Housing Programs (Sections 502, 515, and 521), 1949

Number of recipients:	15,600 units (direct loans) and 38,555 units (guaranteed loans) through Section 502; 452,000 units through Section 515; 245,000 units through Section 521
Who offers the benefit or service:	The public sector through the federal government
What form does it take:	Low-interest loans or loan guarantees (Section 502); project-based housing assistance (Section 515); and tenant-based housing assistance (section 521)
To whom is it provided:	Poor rural households (Sections 502 and 521) or rural landlords (Section 515)
At whose expense:	The 2002 federal budget for these programs were $1.1 billion in loans and $3.1 billion for Section 502; $114 million for Section 515; and $712 million for Section 521.

Public Housing (1937)

Number of recipients:	3 million people in 1.3 million units
Who offers the benefit or service:	The public sector through the federal government

(*continued*)

PROGRAM CHART	Housing Programs (*continued*)
What form does it take:	Low-cost housing in a public housing project
To whom is it provided:	Mostly the poor, but recently with some diversification from people with higher incomes
At whose expense:	In 2002, the federal budget for public housing projects was $3.5 billion.
Tax Expenditures (1913)	
Number of recipients:	32 million
Who offers the benefit or service:	The federal government
What form does it take:	A tax deduction for local property taxes and the interest on mortgages
To whom is it provided:	All home owners, but heavily tilted toward the wealthy
At whose expense:	In 2002, tax expenditures cost $102 billion, or 3.5 times the entire HUD budget.

such as counseling, nutrition, and intensive care. The fiscal year 2002 budget for HOPWA was $277 million.[28]

Among federal housing programs, HOPWA is unusual because it is the only one targeting a specific disease. This distinction has made the program vulnerable to criticism. Some critics say that we should not allocate housing assistance on this basis. To complicate the issue, the new AIDS drugs have enabled people to live longer, lengthening the waiting list for HOPWA housing. Perhaps, some experts suggest, the money should not be spent on housing after people have contracted the disease; perhaps it should be spent early on, to stop its spread.[29]

For those who already have AIDS, however, stable housing is essential to the drug regimen necessary for the disease's control. HOPWA-funded residential facilities are 80 to 90 percent cheaper than acute-care hospital beds. Because the cities hardest hit by AIDS often have five-year waiting lists for other forms of public housing, AIDS patients do not have another alternative. The 1996 National AIDS Strategy stated that "without stable housing, a person living with HIV has diminished access to care and service and a diminished opportunity to live a productive life." Questions may be raised about the HOPWA program, but under these circumstances, it clearly qualifies as essential health care.[30]

Community Development Block Grants (CDBG)

First authorized in 1974, CDBGs constitute the most flexible method of bringing federal community development money into low-income communities. This money can be spent to provide decent housing, to create a suitable living environment, and to expand economic opportunity. Some examples of eligible activities include housing rehabilitation, down payment assistance and other first-time home buyer activities, lead-based paint detection and removal, construction of public facilities such as shelters, and the purchase of land and buildings. By law, cities with more than fifty thousand residents and urban counties with more than two hundred thousand are designated "entitlement jurisdictions." They automatically receive 70 percent of CDBG funds. Smaller cities and counties receive the remainder.

Since the establishment of the program, more than four thousand communities have received grants. Total CDBG funding has recently ranged between $4 billion and $5 billion, but such a sum thins out rather quickly when it is spread all across the United States. Nevertheless, in the communities where it has been available, CDBG money does serve an important function.[31]

The Community Reinvestment Act (CRA)

Enacted in 1977, CRA is designed to address the practice known as redlining, in which banks refused to grant mortgages for homes in some poor and often black and Latino neighborhoods. Because banks are major suppliers of mortgage credit to home buyers, the denial of this credit significantly worsened the prospects for sale of these homes. This practice persisted despite evidence that part of the money the banks loaned came from the deposits of residents in these neighborhoods.

Four federal banking agencies—the Federal Reserve Board, the Office of the Comptroller of the Currency, the Federal Deposit Insurance Corporation, and the Office of Thrift Supervision—retain supervisory authority over depository lenders. Under the CRA, these agencies must evaluate the extent to which banks and savings institutions have helped to meet local credit needs. These evaluations are taken into consideration when these agencies review requests for financial mergers and acquisitions. Only 2 percent of all banks receive a low rating, but as a bank's CRA rating is a matter of public record, the threat of a low rating has been a useful tool for activists to extract more community investment from local bankers.

Since its enactment in 1977, community groups have used the law to win more than $100 billion of credit. They have also succeeded in reducing the loan costs and establishing more flexible credit standards for low- and moderate-income borrowers. The CRA has even been helpful in the affirmative action marketing of banking services, as well as in the development of special business and community development loan programs.

Despite these successes, a major piece of new legislation, the Financial Services Modernization Act of 1999, casts a large shadow over the future of the CRA. For the first time since the 1930s, this legislation allows banks, insurance companies, and securities firms to own one another and to enter into each other's businesses. Although the Act does prohibit bank holding companies without a satisfactory CRA rating from acquiring insurance or security firms, it implicitly shifts the burden of proof: mergers may still require permission, but now they are presumed desirable. In this environment, some conservatives have accused community groups of using the CRA's provision for public disclosure as a weapon of blackmail and extortion. Consequently, its future is very much up for grabs.[32]

Housing for the Elderly (Section 202)

Housing programs for the elderly date back to 1959, when Congress authorized Section 202, a direct loan program designed to provide rental housing and related facilities for the elderly. By law, these projects could also include new or rehabilitated structures such as dining facilities, community rooms, and infirmaries. The loans, which were initially limited to 98 percent, were later extended to cover the entire development costs and could be repaid over a period of as long as fifty years.

In 1990, a change in the law turned the loans into grants, on the condition that the organization complies with affordability requirements (30 percent of income) for forty years. But while this change ends the need to repay the money, it does not address the fundamental problem of a housing shortage for the elderly. Limited by a 2002 budget of just $783 million, Section 202 can assist only about three hundred thousand housing units. According to the American Association of Retired Persons, this figure is just one-ninth of the elderly who have severe housing needs.

Section 202 funding will therefore have to be significantly expanded if we are to keep pace with a rapidly growing elderly population. In addition, advocates for the elderly believe that the growth of the population warrants other, more far-reaching measures. These might include a greater emphasis on assisted living facilities, some additional monies for an augmented service coordinator program, and even intergenerational learning centers to share Internet technology while providing both affordable senior services and affordable child care.[33]

Housing Discrimination and the Fair Housing Act

Title VI of the Civil Rights Act of 1964 prohibited discrimination in federally assisted housing. Four years later, the Fair Housing Act (originally, Title VIII of the Civil Rights Act of 1968) became law; it barred discrimination in the rental and home ownership markets. To address incidents of discrimination on the basis of race, color, religion, national origin, and (after 1974) sex, the Act authorized three methods of enforcement: private lawsuits, administrative complaints to HUD, and civil actions by the attorney general. HUD itself, however, had no enforcement powers until Congress overhauled the Fair Housing Law in 1988.

Revisions to the law in 1988 added handicapped and family status to the existing law, leading to much better protection for foster children. It also extended from 180 days to one year the period during which an administrative complaint may be filed, removed the previously existing limit of $1,000 on monetary and punitive damages in civil actions, and gave HUD greater authority to resolve FHA complaints.

Despite the new penalties written into the law, housing discrimination remains a serious problem. Recent studies report that as many as 2 million incidents of housing discrimination occur in a single year. People of color seeking rental housing in cities encounter discrimination as much as 80 percent of the time. A survey of housing complaints filed with local housing agencies suggests that discrimination is also quite common against people with disabilities and those with an unusual family status. The law has doubtless reduced the incidence of discrimination, but once again, it can achieve just so much with a 2002 budget of less than $50 million.[34]

The Federal Housing Administration

The Federal Housing Administration guarantees mortgages on health care facilities as well as both single and multifamily housing. These guarantees reassure lenders, who would otherwise be reluctant to loan money to low-income, higher-risk home buyers. Under its 2002 single-family insurance program, FHA can offer insurance for mortgages up to $144,000 in lower-cost communities and up to $261,000 in communities where housing costs are higher. This insurance allows people to obtain a mortgage with a minimal down payment. It can also be used to cover some portion of the up-front fees. Over the years, these provisions have made the program a major source of support for lending to minority and first-time home buyers.[35]

FHA operates a parallel program for multifamily dwellings. In this instance, HUD insures mortgages for construction or renovation of a variety of multifamily dwellings with more than five units. The insurance will cover 90 percent of the mortgage for private sector investment and 100 percent of the mortgage for nonprofits. In recent years, HUD has insured loans for about forty thousand units of housing annually through this program.[36]

Home Investment Partnerships Program (HOME)

HOME is another federal program that helps to finance and support low-income housing. As the most prominent part of the National Affordable Housing Act of 1990, HOME seeks to facilitate home ownership as well as to expand rental assistance for low-income families. A broad interpretation of these goals enables governments to pay for security deposits, help home buyers with down payments and closing costs, acquire property, and assist in demolition, rehabilitation, and new construction.

HUD allocates HOME funds according to a formula that measures a jurisdiction's share of the total need for affordable housing. Sixty percent goes to urban areas, 40 percent goes to the states.[37] To receive HOME funds, a jurisdiction must submit a Consolidated Plan to HUD and provide a 25 percent matching share.[38]

Strict eligibility guidelines govern the use of HOME funds. Most target either poor renters or less prosperous home buyers. Typically, the funds are blended with monies from other sources such as low-income housing tax credits and community development block grants to place homes and apartments within the reach of assisted families. By leveraging $2.40 for every dollar of HOME funds, the program helps to bridge the gap between the subsidies that already exist and what some families need.

In 1999, a total of 589 jurisdictions participated in the HOME program. Since the program began, about half the units have been rehabilitated, a little less than one quarter is new construction, and a little more than one quarter involves the purchase of existing property. Housing advocates were very enthusiastic about the passage of the HOME program in 1990. With a budget of under $2 billion a year, however, the HOME program may have helped a little, but it is hard to argue that it has had significant impact on the problem of housing affordability.[39]

HOPE VI

HOPE VI is the latest in a sequence of HOPE programs dating back to the National Affordable Housing Act of 1990. In its original conception, these programs worked to enable public housing tenants to become owners of their housing projects. Hence, HOPE I targeted public and Indian housing projects; HOPE II focused on multifamily dwellings owned by HUD or other federal agencies; and HOPE III authorized the sale of government-owned single-family homes to low-income families. Proponents of these programs argued that in their new role as owners *and* residents, the inhabitants of public housing would take better care of the property, try harder to become economically self-sufficient, and raise their self-esteem.

Yet the sale of public housing proved difficult to implement. Not only did the process take a long time, but the sale often burdened residents with high rehabilitation costs relative to the value of their property. Some critics even went so far as to question whether it was appropriate to encourage people with little real estate experience to purchase apartments that were poorly built or poorly located. As a result, no money has been authorized for these versions of HOPE since the 1995 federal budget.[40]

Nevertheless, HOPE VI has arisen in their place. Instead of money to buy public housing projects, HOPE VI provides grants to demolish them. The purpose of this demolition is to change the physical shape of public housing by replacing the worst projects with apartments that can blend in better with their communities. In addition, HOPE VI also seeks to reduce concentrations of poverty by diversifying the income mix among public housing residents and granting vouchers to the former tenants so that they can move into Section 8 housing. To supplement these initiatives, the Act combines support services to help public housing residents get and keep their jobs with high standards of personal and community responsibility.[41]

So far, 146 communities in thirty-seven states and territories have shared more than $4.7 billion dollars. These communities have already demolished 115,000 units of public housing. Although the program has replaced or plans to replace 66,000 units, another 49,000 have been lost. Admittedly, families who move into the new public housing units will have higher incomes than the people who were displaced. But although income mixing deconcentrates poverty in public housing projects, it may well worsen the affordability crisis for the poorest tenants. If there is less public housing, and as a practical matter displaced residents cannot use the vouchers either because they provide too little assistance or landlords will not accept them, then where are the poor to go except into other neighborhoods with high concentrations of poverty? Unless HOPE VI targets new units with income guidelines that are consistent with the old, the program may simply shift the concentration of poverty from public housing units into neighborhoods with a mix of the worst public and private housing.[42]

Low-Income Housing Tax Credit (LIHTC)

LIHTC is the nation's primary tool for building low-income housing. Each state receives tax credits based on their population, and housing finance agencies in each state award the credits to the sponsors of low-income housing developments. These sponsors then sell the tax credits to individual and corporate investors. Although these investors may not have any interest in housing, they make the investment because the law permits them to deduct the tax credits against unrelated income over the next ten years. By reducing the housing development's long-term debt, the availability of this money lowers rents by 20 to 30 percent below the market rate for new apartments. Still, it requires other, additional subsidies to bring down rents to a level the lowest-income families can afford.

Enacted in 1986, the LIHTC has already helped to finance about 1 million units of low-income housing. After a decade and a half that depressed the value of the housing credits, legislation in 2000 finally increased the credit and beginning in 2003, indexed it to inflation. But while the demand for housing credits has subsequently risen 40 percent, many analysts question whether it is the most efficient method of lowering rents for low-income tenants. Because syndicating, underwriting, and developer fees absorb a full 20 percent of its value, federal grants to reduce the cost of developing the project might well be a cheaper form of aid. Nevertheless, for the moment, at least, Congress prefers tax credits as a more indirect and less visible method.[43]

Native American Housing

As much as 40 percent of the housing in which Native Americans live is inadequate, and the home ownership rate is 30 percent, less than half that of the United States as a whole. To address this issue, Congress enacted the Native American Housing Assistance and Self-Determination Act (NAHASDA) of 1996, based on principles that acknowledge the unique status of Indian tribes. The underlying premise is that public housing projects designed for urban Americans should not be imposed on Native Americans, most of whom live in rural areas.

To maintain the government-to-government relationship between Washington and the Indian tribes, NAHASDA established the Indian Housing Block Grant, which gives tribes the right to plan their own community development through a single block grant that is allocated under a needs-based formula. In 2002, Congress allocated $648 million for these grants.

Yet the underlying problem remains. Native Americans living in tribal areas suffer from unemployment and underemployment. Although some can get work with the government, on farms, and in the tourist industry, the lack of roads, telephone lines, and other utilities do not provide much of a foundation for investment. Deterred by these inadequacies, banks and other lending institutions are reluctant to make residential and commercial loans in Native American areas. Moreover, because the tribal community holds land in trust, bankers cannot foreclose on properties when lenders default on their mortgages. NAHASDA tries to be respectful of Native American autonomy on the issue of housing, but underneath the purely economic problems lies a clash of cultural values that has not yet been successfully resolved.[44]

Section 8 Housing

Perhaps the most famous part of the 1974 Housing and Community Development Act, Section 8 originally included two methods of providing housing. One, usually termed "project based," funded substantial rehabilitation and new construction; the other, called "tenant based," typically paid for the difference between 30 percent of the tenant's income and the fair market rent. Soon after assuming office in 1981, the Reagan administration withdrew HUD's authority to rehabilitate and construct housing. Except for units that had already been approved, this decision left tenant-based housing the only remaining part of the Act.[45]

Beginning in the early 1990s, however, the project-based units presented a critical problem. Under the initial arrangement, HUD contracted with owners to provide housing to tenants for fifteen or twenty years. Subsequently, the owners could charge whatever the market would bear, even if that meant evicting their tenants in the process. Between 1993 and 2002, the expiration of these contracts put an estimated 900,000 units and 1.4 million people at risk, with another 396,000 units due for renewal in the next three years.[46]

To address this problem, Congress authorized special annual expenditures. In 2002, for example, HUD requested $15 billion for expiring Section 8 contracts, or more than half of its $29 billion budget for that year.[47] But because the money does not add to the stock of affordable housing, housing policymakers are essentially running faster to remain in place.

Tenant-based housing has faced similar difficulties. The number of net new rental commitments peaked in 1977 at 354,000, only to decline to 54,000 under President Reagan by 1983. For the next ten years, it stabilized at between 50,000 and 85,000. After the election of a Republican Congress in 1994, however, HUD funded no additional vouchers from 1995 to 1998. When Congress did fund 50,000 vouchers again in 1999, they were strictly designated for welfare-to-work families. But by 2002, the number had slipped down again to just 26,000. Obviously, it would require a commitment many times this size to make much of a dent in the housing shortage.

Proponents may prefer vouchers because they are cheaper than new construction, but vouchers do not add to the supply of housing, and, by adding to the number of possible renters, may actually bid up the price. In addition, voucher holders encounter low vacancy rates, landlords who refuse to participate because they do not want to be bothered with the paperwork, and landlords who discriminate based on race or ethnicity. As with so many other U.S. social welfare programs, it is better for poor people that vouchers exist, but their existence actually makes a very modest contribution to helping them obtain affordable housing.[48]

Rural Housing Programs

When we think about the issue of housing, most of us picture housing problems in a big city. This image is misleading. Almost one-quarter of all rural households pay more than 30 percent of their income for housing, including 2.1 million who pay more than 50 percent of their income for shelter, and another 2.5 million who spend between 30 and 50 percent. Rural housing for African Americans is, on average, worse than their urban counterparts; Hispanics in rural areas are twice as likely as other rural inhabitants to reside in poor housing; and rural Native Americans face some of the worst housing conditions in the United States. All told, some 1.8 million rural households live in physically inadequate housing, and another 465,000 are overcrowded. Usually, when we think about the problem of housing, we imagine a dilapidated big-city tenement; these statistics remind us to remember the migrant farm worker's shack and the run-down family farm.[49]

Because agricultural services are more widely dispersed than HUD offices in rural areas, it is the U.S. Department of Agriculture Rural Housing Service, not HUD, that is responsible for addressing rural housing problems. The RHS administers one program for direct loans that help families buy or repair modest houses (Section 502). It also administers two programs for rental housing, one for landlords (Section 515) and another for tenants (Section 521). All three initiative programs closely parallel programs that HUD operates.

Section 502 requires applicants to show that they have been unable to get loans elsewhere or on reasonable terms. But for those families who do demonstrate their eligibility, the interest on loans can be as low as 1 percent. By law, these loans must go to families with less than 80 percent of the area's median income. Within this group, however, 40 percent of the loans must target those with very low incomes, less than 50 percent of the area median. Section 502 also offers a loan guarantee for purchasers of moderate priced homes. That program caps eligibility at 115 percent of the area's median. For fiscal year 2002, the budget allocated about $1.1 billion for loans and $3.1 billion in loan guarantees.

The rental housing program (Section 515) resembles the project-based part of Section 8. When project owners of some of these subsidized apartments wanted to repay their mortgages so that they could put their homes into the unsubsidized rental market, the government placed restrictions on who could purchase these buildings and offered inducements to keep them available for low-income tenants. Reduced in recent years, the 2002 budget provides about $114 million, which will produce just fifteen hundred new units of affordable housing.

The Department of Agriculture's rural rental assistance program (Section 521) also mirrors Section 8. It provides subsidized housing to about 245,000 households, virtually all of whom resided in Section 515 multifamily housing, some while also receiving Section 8. In fiscal year 2002, the federal government budgeted $712 million for this program.

Altogether, these programs suggest that the RHS is the Department of Agriculture's version of HUD. Like HUD, it tries to channel money to poor people living in rural areas who have difficulty obtaining housing, but does so under budgetary constraints that are less than adequate for the task. In addition, however, it also encounters some distinctive problems. For example, 80 percent of the rural elderly are home owners rather than renters, some of whom need help fixing and maintaining their property. Yet, because the elderly are often unable or reluctant to assume responsibility for long-term mortgage payments, one of RHS's major programs has limited usefulness for this significant group.[50] Like HUD itself, the RHS would benefit from a larger budget and greater flexibility in addressing the problem of rural housing.

Public Housing

Public housing, or what is popularly known in many cities as "the projects," dates to the Housing Act of 1937. The Roosevelt administration sponsored this Act to boost construction in the real estate industry. The Act was a public works project to create housing for tenants—unemployed workers who were temporarily down on their luck. Just to make sure that the intervention of the government did not increase the supply of housing and disrupt the private real estate market, the Act promised to destroy one substandard unit of housing for every new unit it constructed. These conflicting goals have dogged the public housing arena ever since.

To build public housing, a state must establish a local public housing authority (PHA). Although officially the PHA is independent of other local governments, in practice the county and the municipality must grant approval to any project. The need for this approval explains much of the criticism that has since been directed at public housing projects. Because the real estate industry, private owners, and many neighborhood groups wanted to maintain a clear distinction between public and market-based housing, they demanded that local governments build large projects and place them on the "other side of the tracks"—sometimes literally, in other cases, across the highway or near an industrial zone. Clearly marked by its design and neighborhood as public housing, the projects inevitably came to embody the principle of less eligibility in the housing field.

Today, public housing authorities manage almost fourteen thousand projects containing 1.3 million units that house about 3 million people. Over the years, however, the demographics of public housing have changed dramatically, so that what was once housing for workers has gradually become the main source of housing for the poorest of the poor: in one 1998 study, the average income of public housing tenants was $9100 annually, or just 18 percent of the U.S. household median. Because residents usually pay only 30 percent of their income in rent, the declining income of public housing tenants has reduced the income available to PHAs for operating expenses. As a result, the federal government's average monthly subsidy, $187, almost equals the $193 a month that the typical resident pays. Yet because the housing is so cheap and, for the most part, comparatively sound, the waiting list for public housing averages thirty-three months in the biggest cities and extends to as long as ten years in Newark and Los Angeles.

A 1998 law, the Quality Housing and Work Responsibility Act, represents the most recent attempt to address many of the issues that have long troubled public housing. Under the law, public housing authorities must diversify the residents of public housing by admitting people with higher income. Moreover, in what are perhaps the most controversial sections of the law, Congress demanded that all able-bodied adults in public housing contribute eight hours each month to community service. And in what some critics contend is a violation of confidentiality, applicants must also sign an authorization for the release of information from local drug treatment centers. The emphasis on drugs takes on special importance in light of a 2002 U.S. Supreme Court decision evicting a tenant of Oakland public housing because her mentally disabled daughter had been arrested on charges of possessing cocaine three blocks away.[51]

Perhaps most revealing, if a PHA does not correct severely distressed housing, the 1998 law allows HUD to remove the units from its jurisdiction; it may even demolish or replace them. The law therefore reflects a sense of frustration and exhaustion with the whole idea of public housing.[52] The failures of public housing certainly warrant some experimentation with new methods of providing shelter for families who cannot afford the market rate. Nevertheless, two issues continue to loom over the new law. First, there will be no improvement in housing for the poor if, in the interests of income diversity, they are not allowed to live there. Even more important, while lawmakers focus exclusively on the deficiencies of public housing, they ignore the context in which public housing operates. As long as this context prevents public housing from becoming attractive enough to compete with the private housing market, it is unlikely the 1998 law can alter the requirement that it remain "poor housing for poor people."

Tax Expenditures

While policymakers struggle to find some method of helping poor people obtain affordable housing, the single most expensive government housing program is the indirect aid that comes in the form of government tax expenditures. If you remember, a government tax expenditure is a provision in the tax code that allows the taxpayer to forgo payment of taxes that would otherwise be due. The deduction for each dependent child is a tax expenditure: you pay lower taxes because society recognizes the social value of parents raising their children. Likewise, in housing policy, the single biggest government housing program is the provision that allows home owners to deduct local property taxes and the interest on their mortgage from their taxable income. In 2002, the value of these subsidies cost the federal government almost $102 billion, or approximately 3.5 times the entire HUD budget.[53]

But there is a further catch: as the single largest government housing program, tax expenditures mostly benefit the wealthy. In fiscal year 2000, the wealthiest 2.2 percent of all taxpayers—those earning $200,000 or more—received more than 20 percent of all these subsidies. In fact, almost 70 percent of the wealthiest families received this subsidy, and the subsidy averaged more than $13,600 per family. Further down the income ladder, only 12 percent

"Sure, we need affordable housing—just so long as it doesn't come at the expense of unaffordable housing."

of families earning \$30,000–\$40,000 a year received any help, and only 9 percent of families earning \$40,000–\$50,000 got this aid: their subsidies average just \$859 a year. Of course, poor home owners do not qualify for a tax break, and poor renters are completely excluded from this system.[54]

The whole policy of tax expenditures highlights what is perhaps the most fundamental issue in the housing field. Although it is indirect (through the tax code) as opposed to a direct (cash) benefit, tax expenditures channel public funds to the wealthy for market-based housing. Tax expenditures have undoubtedly contributed to the high rate of home ownership in the United States. Yet, amid complaints about the subsidies that the poor receive in their search for affordable housing, we would be wise to consider what it says about U.S. housing policy that the wealthy actually receive a significantly disproportionate share of all federal housing assistance.

National Housing Trust Fund

What's ahead in housing policy? To remedy the disarray and constant underfunding, the most recent initiative seeks to establish a National Housing Trust Fund. Financed with profits from housing programs operated by the Federal Housing Administration, Ginnie Mae, and matching funds from the states, the goal of this initiative is to build and preserve 1.5 million units of low-income rental housing over the next ten years. By 2002, twenty-four senators and 169 members of Congress had signed on to support the bill, which at this time probably represents the best hope for reforming housing policy.[55]

Program Summary

This list of housing programs is lengthy, but, as with many other arenas in social welfare policy, the number of programs may well signal weakness rather than strength. To be sure, it is helpful that distinct demographic groups such as the elderly, Native Americans, and people with AIDS all have their own program. At the same time, however, many of these programs seem underfinanced and comparatively ineffectual. Their weakness stems from their inability to overcome the major structural issue in the housing field. That issue is the question of how we provide housing for the poor in a society that values housing for profit, when the poor, by themselves, do not possess the resources to ensure a profit for the owners of this housing. If Americans have yet to offer a satisfactory answer to this question, we can nevertheless get a better sense of these issues by once again turning to the primary factors in our policy analysis: the economics, politics, ideology, social movements, and history of U.S. housing policy.

Economics

It costs a lot of money to build a house. When the federal government helps people to build housing, it stimulates the housing market. When it assists people in renting or buying housing that is already built, it puts money into the economy that otherwise might not circulate. This is the first, and perhaps most fundamental, economic function of federal housing policy.

Just consider for a moment the long list of groups and institutions that derive economic benefit from the government's intervention. Whether it is the direct aid of cash and vouchers for the poor, assistance to landlords, or the indirect benefit of tax expenditures such as the deductibility of the property tax and interest on mortgages, housing policy adds to property values. This increase makes home ownership more attractive and brings extra business to construction companies that build housing as well as to banks and mortgage lenders that finance it. It also inflates the value of the individual home, which is the vast majority of families' single most important financial asset.

Federal housing policy cements its ties to the marketplace by increasing the value of the overall housing market. This contribution to the nation's overall economic development has both a private and a public component. The private component relies on a variety of tools such as tax expenditures, subsidized mortgages, and the Federal Reserve Bank to boost the growth of a privately owned infrastructure: the single and multifamily dwellings in which most Americans live. The public component is smaller but nonetheless crucial. Although this component is most evident in the federal government's financing of a public housing project, it actually extends to any subsidy of poor people who otherwise would not have enough income to cover the rent. In this role, the federal government serves to supplement the demand for housing. As with other issues in social welfare, however, any policy that aids the poor by giving them money must negotiate a policy minefield.

In the United States, significant minorities of people do not make enough money to pay for their own housing. Ignoring their plight and allowing them to become homeless would advertise the failure of the economic system and create an unacceptable political problem. The federal government must therefore intervene. But its intervention means that the federal government is giving poor people money they did not earn. The existence of this federal benefit therefore creates a problem that is just as unacceptable as the inability of too many people to obtain housing. Because U.S. policymakers had to find a route out of this dilemma, they tried hard to distinguish between the quality of private and of public housing. Then it would be easy to tell who obtained their housing through hard work on their own and who required a direct cash subsidy.

This distinction in the quality of housing is crucially important, because although public housing may be structurally sound enough to bring people inside, it has rarely been designed to be appealing. In purely economic terms, it is enough for it to be functional, so that it can perform the essential economic task of social reproduction for a limited number of poor people. Once they are provided with adequate housing, these poor people are more likely to reproduce and raise healthy children who, in turn, might some day become workers in their own right.

Ordinarily, we would assume that social reproduction is inherently valuable. After all, every society needs a next generation of workers. In recent years, however, cutbacks in housing and other social welfare programs have begun to qualify this assumption. Suppose the economy does not need workers in the United States because it is going to rely instead on workers in other countries. If that were true, then poor people in the United States are economically superfluous, and it is not nearly as important for them to be housed and healthy. To judge by the contraction in housing programs, it is fair to say that under these circumstances, the importance of social reproduction has diminished significantly.

Politics

Although the politics of housing are complex, five basic elements are essential to understanding the primary political dynamics: (1) the question of how much must be given to the real estate industry to get them to house poor people; (2) the idea that public housing is, in some sense, a benefit to politically influential groups; (3) the politics of the federal housing bureaucracy; (4) the opposition to public housing as an example of localism in U.S. government; and (5) the politics of housing and race.

The first question is a perennial one: How much must be given to real estate owners for them to house poor people? In this country, housing is a valuable commodity that is marketed for profit. As poor people do not have enough money to enable the owners of housing to profit from selling or renting to them, the federal government must always grapple with the issue of how it can get the owners of real estate to treat people who are poor just like those who are not. Its usual response to this issue has been to ensure adequate profit for landlords, either by giving them enough money or supplementing the poor sufficiently so that they had as much as a poor working family. The political power of the real estate industry has always been extremely effective in enforcing this demand.

The second political component follows from the first. Among its many other political dimensions, public housing is a financial benefit to the real estate industry. It is expensive to finance and build public housing. Perhaps that is why there is a hitch. If the federal government is going to intervene on behalf of poor people, then business and professional people must benefit. But because federal monies do not go to everyone, the question of who benefits naturally becomes a very political issue. In the end, however, the money is likely to be distributed, as with any other federal dollar, to the most politically connected lawyers, banks, and construction firms.

The Department of Housing and Urban Development, and public housing generally, also has a reputation for an elaborate and complex bureaucracy. If you currently receive or want to apply for public money from any HUD program, for example, as a member of a community development group that is seeking to acquire a building for renovation, the paperwork and red tape are daunting. The difficulties of this bureaucracy flow from the politics of public housing.

Bureaucracies develop to simplify routine tasks. They become complex when their goals conflict. If housing in the United States were either completely public or completely private, the bureaucracy would be relatively simple to administer. When, however, the administrative task requires a bureaucracy to fit a small public system into a predominantly private housing market, the public sector must be careful not to offend private interests, and the details of who can do what under which circumstances have to be written up in extraordinary detail. The politics of this bureaucracy requires many volumes of instruction for the operation of housing programs, not the least of which is a lengthy set of rules for both tenants and landlords.

The tradition of localism is the fourth political ingredient in housing policy. To construct a public housing development, local officials must establish a public housing authority. But because the creation of a PHA signals that the locality is willing to accept public housing, the political opposition from home owners and local real estate interests is often intense. In cities where the poor are concentrated, supporters of public housing can usually overcome this opposition. In many suburban areas, however, residents perceive public housing as a problem of the cities they have just fled. As a result, even though these suburban areas might have a sizable number of poor people, the tradition of localism prevents the establishment of PHAs and hinders the construction of any public housing.

Of course, like the politics of housing generally, this localism has a strong racial component. The whites-only policy of post–World War II suburbs like Levittown, New York, converted this localism into housing policy by blocking the establishment of PHAs, thereby stopping people of color—increasingly, the typical residents of public housing—from moving into their communities. Cities, by contrast, were generally less explicit; they authorized the construction of public housing projects but usually placed them in segregated neighborhoods. In both the suburbs and the cities, then, the power of localism barred public housing from becoming a tool for racial integration. Instead, the politics of housing intertwined with the politics of race to channel different racial groups to different communities, one with a private and one with a public housing system.[56]

Ideology

Some elements of the ideology of housing policy parallel the ideologies underlying other social policies. In organizing housing policy around what the private sector is willing to deliver, it prizes the marketplace as the best way of distributing goods and services. In addition, like many income support programs, it clearly embodies the principle of less eligibility, so that housing obtained through a direct public subsidy will be less attractive than housing that workers earn on their own. This principle, in turn, helps to uphold the work ethic because it sends a message to workers that their hard work will be rewarded. By themselves, however, these beliefs do not get at what is distinctive about the ideology of housing policy. That demands thinking about the United States as a nation of home owners and about home ownership as perhaps the fullest expression of the American dream.

We have already cited the most pertinent statistic: more than two-thirds of all Americans own their own homes. Admittedly, given the heavy mortgage debt, this ownership may well be in name only. Nevertheless, regardless of how much they owe on their mortgages, Americans who live in their own homes tend to think of themselves as home owners. This self-image shapes their individualist psychology and nurtures the ideology of home ownership.

At its root, this ideology of home ownership harks back to President Thomas Jefferson's vision of the United States as a country of small farmers. In Jefferson's conception of a democracy, people have relatively equal amounts of wealth, and no one has a disproportionate amount of power. The United States is no longer a predominantly agricultural country; it has great inequalities of wealth and equally large differences in power. But the notion of a nation of home owners remains potent because it tries to reassure us about the relevance of this vision. Moreover, if that vision becomes too hard to maintain, at least home owners possess a "haven in a heartless world," a place to which they can retreat with their families when they feel tired and vulnerable.

These associations help to explain the ideological power of housing policy. U.S. housing policy is focused on the two-thirds of the population who help to sustain the vision. It even grants them significant tax breaks so that they can continue to do so. Yet there is very little place in this vision for those who cannot afford private sector housing. Because they are dependent and do not belong to the self-sufficient housing community, the ideology of U.S. housing policy intimates that they are somehow less than full-fledged political citizens. And as less than full-fledged citizens, that same ideology substantially restricts the help they can receive.

Social Movements

Two kinds of organizations have shaped the housing agenda. One is an elite reform coalition, typified by the National Housing Conference. Since its founding in 1931 by Mary Simkhovitch, a social worker in New York City's Greenwich Village, the NHC has brought together a diverse group of bankers, state and local officials, community development specialists, and social reformers to work on housing issues. The NHC does not engage in community organizing. But by combining its expertise with its contacts in government, it has been able to influence virtually every major piece of housing legislation that has been enacted during the past seventy years.[57]

The second kind of housing organization exists at the grassroots, where tenant movements have predominated. Organizations of tenants have fought to defend rent control, get better-quality services from landlords, and instigate rent strikes like those in Harlem during 1934 and the winter of 1963–64. At their most successful, these displays of tenant power have won greater protections for tenants and created a new body of law.[58] But housing organizing is never easy, and over the past twenty years, it has fallen on ever harder times.

That the United States is a nation of home owners creates a major obstacle for organizers, because private ownership fuels an individualist outlook. Hence, at least two-thirds of the population is hard to organize on housing issues, and some portion of the other third is difficult to reach because they are so focused on obtaining their own homes. This potential constituency dwindles still further because tenants live in different buildings with different landlords. A small landlord with a few apartments is likely to react differently from a landlord with one large building or, for that matter, a real estate company that owns property all over the city. Quite apart from their own internal conflict, such a diverse and fragmented opponent makes it difficult for tenants to identify their common interests.

Despite these obstacles, the tenant movement did grow throughout the 1970s, reaching its peak in about 1980, with the founding of the National Tenants Union. The NTU had ambitious goals: a clearinghouse for information, development of model programs, and the creation of a lobby presence on Capitol Hill. But the movement soon fizzled out. Its decline paralleled the overall decline in movement organizing, as well as the aging of the organizer population and the shift from specifically tenant organizing to development of affordable housing. In addition, the Democratic Party, which had once sided with tenant groups, became a much less reliable ally. And although some state groups like the New York State Tenant and Neighborhood Coalition were successful enough to obtain money from the Department of Housing and Urban Development, this new source of funding may have helped to defuse their militancy. As a result, tenant groups are now engaged in a holding action, trying to figure out how they can link their organizations with others engaged in progressive labor and community campaigns.[59]

History

The history of housing policy is a history of attempts to tame the housing market. Although none of these attempts has been an unqualified success, they have undoubtedly helped to house millions of people. Nevertheless, a history of housing policy suggests that every attempt encounters the same dilemma: If housing in this country is a for-profit enterprise, how do people who do not earn enough for landlords to make a profit get housing of acceptable quality? The answer is that although government must always pay, other factors (politics, economics, ideology, and the strength of social movements) determine the terms and quality of the housing that poor people have been able to obtain. In their own way, the Progressive Era, the New Deal through to the Great Society, and the conservative drift of the past thirty years each offer different illustrations of this pattern.

In the early twentieth century, a fear of disease mixed with concern about conditions in immigrant slums like those on New York's Lower East Side to turn housing into a prominent issue. Reformers focused on housing conditions because they thought that better housing could remedy both disease and the radical political ideologies that spread quickly in such tight quarters. Influenced by books like Jacob Riis's *How the Other Half Lives* and led by prominent advocates such as Lawrence Veiller, they pushed a program of regulation that sought to ensure that tenements had adequate fire escapes, windows, and plumbing. Although real estate interests strenuously objected to these new laws and dismissed reformers like Veiller as far too radical, their program was actually committed to the marketplace and quite moderate. Firmly opposing any construction by the public sector, they believed that the housing problem should be addressed only through government inspection and regulation. But despite their hopes, this belief soon proved to be mistaken. The best new tenements continued to remain out of reach of the very poor, and even after a generation of reform, no one could honestly contend that poor New Yorkers were well housed.

The same pattern held elsewhere in the country. In Chicago, housing reform rose to prominence in the aftermath of the 1919 race riots, which killed thirty-eight people and injured 537. There, the most progressive housing reformers featured pioneers of the settlement house movement like Jane Addams, Sophonsiba Breckenridge, and Florence Kelley. The settlement house movement rooted itself in particular neighborhoods, each of which had its own distinctive racial and ethnic mix. It is hardly surprising, then, that the housing reformers who emerged from this movement never had a vision extending beyond the goal of better, though segregated, market-based housing.

From the shacks of the nineteenth century to the model tenements of the twentieth, housing reformers in the Progressive Era helped to modernize U.S. cities. They introduced regulations for building conditions, established minimal standards of sanitation, and upgraded the worst tenements. They did not, however, challenge the assumption that only the private sector could provide housing. Regulation of the private sector did help to improve the existing housing stock. By itself, however, it could not significantly expand the supply of housing for the poor.[60]

Regulation also had other limitations. Despite efforts to upgrade housing, a 1933 national survey demonstrated that there was still much work to be done. The survey found that 50 percent of all homes had no bath or central heat, 33 percent had no inside toilets, and 18 percent were found to be unfit for use. In the midst of the political and social turmoil of the Depression and the New Deal, these data demanded a new and more interventionist set of policies. As Secretary of the Interior Harold Ickes put it, "One of the most pressing and important tasks in the establishment of this new social order is a revolutionary improvement in housing conditions in the United States. We want, and we must have attractive low cost housing for those in the lower income groups."[61]

Acting on this principle for the next thirty-five years changed the terms of the relationship between the private and public sectors. Now the government would actually build housing. The legislative hallmarks of this period were the 1937 Housing Act, the 1949 Housing Act, and the Great Society laws that added to the supply, supplemented rent, and enacted fair housing laws. By carving out a role for government beyond mere regulation, this legislation acknowledged that housing for profit could not house a large segment of the poor.

This shift in housing policy was significant. Yet, focusing solely on this commitment to the construction of housing for the poor can be misleading. Although housing the poor was surely one important purpose, other goals of this legislation demonstrate how respectful it remained of the private sector. Passage of the 1937 Housing Act, the first federal legislation to authorize the construction of public housing, depended on the understanding that this construction was a public works project that would engage restless unemployed workers and revive the construction industry. Likewise, the 1949 Housing Act boosted the private sector by funding urban renewal projects in the cities and guaranteeing mortgages, so that lenders could finance development of the suburbs risk-free. Even during the 1960s, Great Society housing legislation built public housing, stimulated the economy, and amid the turmoil of the period, brought a greater measure of social peace. The importance of the expansion of public housing should not be underestimated. But neither should we ignore the way that each piece of legislation directed enough business to the private sector to soften its strongest opposition.

By the late 1960s, however, the terms of the relationship between the public and private sector began to change again. Amid an urban housing shortage created by segregation of the suburbs and the migration of African Americans to the North, two federal commissions, the National Commission on Urban Problems and the President's Committee on Urban Housing, agreed on the need to produce 26 million units of new and rehabilitated housing in the next ten years. With the Vietnam War draining the federal budget, however, the cost of such a program was prohibitive. President Johnson therefore turned to the banking lobby, which favored an interest subsidy program. The lobby figured that if the government helped to pay the interest on mortgages, it would keep the interest rate high. From their perspective, this policy was far preferable to direct government aid on behalf of the poor.[62]

Yet, despite the heavy involvement of the private sector, the commitment goals were never met. Although public housing did reach its all-time record of ninety-one thousand completions in 1971, real estate investors took advantage of lax government regulations to buy and sell private housing for the poor at a quick profit. The resulting scandal fed the mounting discontent toward the very idea of public housing as hotbeds of poverty, crime, and waste. As a result, in 1973, President Nixon called a halt to all federally subsidized housing programs.[63]

This halt marked the beginning of the third phase. The history of housing policy in this phase is a history of the public sector in retreat. From the passage of the 1974 Housing and Community Development Act to the present, the terms of the relationship between the public and private sectors have shifted to become even more favorable to private interests. During the period from the New Deal to the Great Society, the public-private partnership on housing showed the public sector to be making slow but steady inroads. But as crime became a more prominent issue and public housing became stigmatized housing, policymakers turned once again to the private sector. Instead of expanding the housing supply or directly subsidizing the poor, the new housing policy asked a newer and even more deferential question: What did the government need to do for the private sector so that it would agree to house the poor?

The legislation in this period tries to answer this question ever more respectfully. To obtain landlords' participation in Section 8, the Housing and Community Development Act of 1974 allowed direct payment to landlords for the first time. The same Act authorized vouchers, which, though they ostensibly gave poor tenants greater choice, were hard to obtain, paid just a small portion of the actual rent, and did not add to the total number of housing units. When President Reagan came into office, he squeezed public subsidies by raising the tenant's portion of the rent from 25 to 30 percent of income. He also slashed the HUD budget by about 75 percent.

More recent legislative initiatives have been no more favorable to the public sector. Hopes for the National Affordable Housing Act of 1990 fizzled amid a lack of funds and an emphasis on home ownership. Predictably, such a private sector model helps fewer people, most of whom are the better-off among the poor. Likewise, the Quality Housing and Work Responsibility Act of 1998 pursues the admirable goal of income diversification within public housing projects but without providing any new housing. In a similar vein, the Act permitted landlords to rent to just one Section 8 tenant when, until 1996, a rental to one tenant obligated them to rent to others; by barring the "endless lease," it also allowed them to evict a tenant at any time.[64] Together with the complete elimination of Section 8 certificates for several years in the mid-1990s, the clear implication of this housing policy is that enough government money may enable a modest number of poor people to obtain housing, but as long as landlords can make more money from other tenants, even these poor people will never have anything but a very precarious foothold in the private housing market.

Conclusion

Although the recent history of housing policy may not be uplifting, it is instructive. By trying to find a small niche in the marketplace for poor people, it has highlighted that market's historic dominance. Housing policy struggles with this dominance by relying on many small and only partly effective programs. But backed by political and economic power, the dominance persists. In turn, it has ensured that from tax expenditures for the affluent to the severe limits placed on direct assistance for the poor, U.S. housing policy is largely focused on helping those who are best able to help themselves. The poor do not really fit into such a market-based policy. For this reason, the policy has always struggled awkwardly and without much success to find them enough satisfactory housing.

11

Health Care: Programs and Policies

Everyone gets sick. This fact of life injects a very personal emotion into discussions of health policy. You may be indignant about public assistance programs, think job training should be available to all, and fume at the cost of housing in your community. But few other topics in social welfare policy get people going as much as the experience of racing to a hospital emergency room, only to be asked how they intend to pay for the necessary treatment. Perhaps that is why, more than any other issue, health care is something that grips everyone.

These feelings arise from the paradox of U.S. health care. On the positive side, health care in the United States has many admirable features. Patients who have some potentially life-threatening diseases are very lucky to be patients in the United States: with their access to advanced medical technology, American women who have breast cancer do better than women with breast cancer in Australia, France, Germany, or Japan.[1] But if you do not have health insurance, spend hours trying to straighten out your medical bills, or must fight your health maintenance organization (HMO) to get the next treatment, then the U.S. health care system is likely to make you quite angry.

It is not hard to identify some good reasons for this anger. U.S. social welfare policy treats health care as a commodity. Whether it is housing, cars, or health care, a commodity typically has a price in the marketplace, with more affluent people able to purchase a better-quality good or service. To

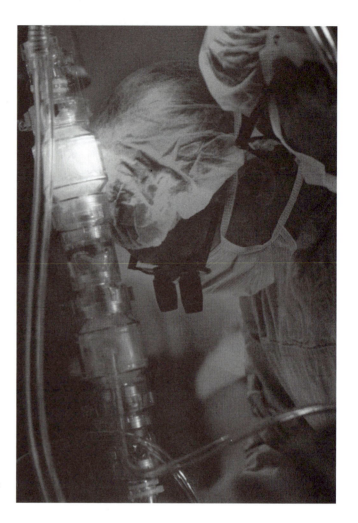

Advanced medical technology is one of the U.S. health care's most notable features.

illustrate the extent of this commodification, investors are able to purchase shares in companies that are part of the "health care industry"; in effect, third parties speculate about whether more or less health care will be bought and sold. This system works quite well for people who have money: they usually get reasonably good care. But for those who do not have money, or for those who think that good health care is every citizen's right, the conception of health care as a marketplace commodity involves inequitable rationing.

Every country rations health care; otherwise, it could be infinitely costly. And certainly, rationing through the market, where ability to pay determines access to resources, is hardly the only kind. Implicit strategies are equally common, and though these strategies seem to offer access, they limit facilities, restrict referrals to specialists, and erect subtle barriers to care. Both market- and government-oriented systems can employ this strategy.

There is also a third, formal type of rationing, one that is public and explicitly democratic. In this kind of rationing, public officials ask the critical policy questions: What should be the national hospital budget? Would it be better to train specialists or family physicians? Should we spend money on additional nurses, or should we invest in more medical technology?[2] The United States employs the first and second, but not the third, kind of rationing. Although our health care debates sometimes touch on these issues, we usually subcontract a large measure of responsibility for them to private individuals and institutions. In a for-profit system, they set our rationing policies.

Most critically, Americans do not like to admit that they ration health care. Such a public admission would collide with our modern sense of entitlement. When we want something, we believe that we deserve it *now*. Perhaps that is why we have opted for rationing by price and other, less visible methods of managing scarcity. Even as our demand for immediate health care drives spending upward, we allow rationing by price to disguise a system that provides health care for some people while denying it to others.

Another distinctive feature of our market-based system involves its ties to the workplace. In 2002, some 166 million people, or two-thirds of the population, obtained their health insurance from their employer. Employer-based health care spread after a 1943 Internal Revenue Service ruling that employees did not have to pay taxes on their employer's contributions to group health plans. Although this ruling enabled employers to supplement wages in wartime and compete for the best employees, it also helped to foster a two-tier system.[3] In this system, your employer is supposed to offer you health care insurance. If your employer does not offer health insurance, your insurance is inadequate, or you are unemployed, you must either buy coverage yourself or get it through a public program like Medicaid or Medicare. Many workers in low-wage jobs do not receive health care from their employer. As a result, in 2001, more than 41 million people, or 14 percent of the population, had no health insurance.[4]

The third notable feature of the U.S. health care system is its cost. We spend $3,858 a person for health care; Canada, which has the next most costly system, spends just $1,899. American consumers shoulder 17 percent of the total U.S. bill, private health insurance covers 38 percent, and direct public spending assumes responsibility for 45 percent.[5] Although many policymakers expected that a reliance on HMOs would cut costs, the period of 2 percent inflation in health insurance premiums lasted just four years, from 1994 to 1998. Health care premiums then jumped 8 percent in 2000 and rose another 11 percent in 2001. Moreover, among those covered by private insurance, rising health care costs have prompted employers to shift more of the burden to their employees. In turn, these employees must now pay larger premiums, higher deductibles (the amount for which the employee is responsible before insurance coverage begins), and bigger copayments.[6] Despite hopes to the contrary, the cost of drugs, medical technology, and a complex, profit-oriented, private sector bureaucracy continues to drive insurance costs upward.

The expense of U.S. health care would be justifiable if the benefits clearly exceeded the costs. Yet comparative health statistics offer little evidence to support this contention. The United States places seventeenth in life expectancy and ranks twenty-first in both infant and maternal mortality rates.[7] At least when Canada spends money, it gets a significantly longer life expectancy rate for both men (76, compared to 73) and women (82, compared to 80). Even more striking, Sweden's national health care system, whose health care budget is little more than 33 percent of ours and 70 percent of Canada's, has the lowest infant mortality record, with a rate less than half that of the United States.[8]

The U.S. health care system, then, combines health care as a commodity in the marketplace with costly employer-based insurance that fails to cover one-seventh of the population and yields what are, at best, by international standards, mediocre health outcomes. To be sure, much of its research and medical technology is pace-setting. But the system as a whole is wasteful and inefficient. Emphasizing the treatment of disease instead of prevention, it does not provide particularly good health care for the average person. The existence of such a curious system raises a pointed question: What social change triggers brought such a hybrid into being?

Social Change Triggers

Since the late nineteenth century, policymakers in every nation attaining a moderate level of economic development have expressed an interest in health care. The reasons for this interest are easily understandable: industrialization and urbanization created potential public health hazards on an unprecedented scale. Given the intensely social dimension of public health, even the most affluent individuals could not be completely safe with an epidemic raging around them. Care of the destitute sick and young widows with children also put an extra burden on relief services. At the same time, modern armies needed a reliable supply of physically able recruits, just as modern industrial societies required a healthy labor force. Last, as medical technology lengthened life spans, the growth of an aging population produced a respected political constituency that could press for attention to its health care needs. Compared to all these powerful political and economic factors, humanitarian concerns were distinctly secondary.[9]

The triggers for change in U.S. health care hew closely to these broad patterns. In the early twentieth century, reformers worried about diseases like cholera and tuberculosis spreading through urban slums; AIDS and hepatitis would provide a similar impetus less than a century later.[10] When, during the Progressive Era, illness or injury interfered with ability to work, the loss of productivity also attracted concern. In the Depression, attention to health care reform arose from the major health care expenses that could break the finances of uninsured families.

The triggers changed somewhat after World War II. Then, breakthroughs in medical research held the promise that an investment in health care could reduce mortality from preventable diseases. In subsequent years, Americans have witnessed a breakdown of coverage for the poor, retired, and chronically ill, leading to the enactment of Medicaid and Medicare and the spectacle of rising health care costs, which underlay Nixon's and Carter's efforts at reform.

Medicare and Medicaid are fee-for-service programs: the government reimburses health care providers for each service they provide. This method of reimbursement creates a built-in incentive to offer as many services as possible. Naturally, with such an unlimited market, health care costs spiraled rapidly upward. As costs spun out of control, policymakers turned first, under Reagan, to fixed reimbursement systems like the DRGs, and then to even more explicitly market-based reforms such as HMOs and managed care.[11]

These systems, however, have not improved health outcomes or made much headway against the ranks of the uninsured. Instead, they have created an elaborate private sector bureaucracy and ignited another round of health care inflation. As the baby boomers age, the next bout of health care reform will emerge from the public indignation about these failures. In the process, it will also, inevitably, spotlight questions about the adequacy of U.S. social welfare programs.

Social Programs

The primary health care programs are Medicaid, Medicare, and the Children's Health Insurance Program of 1997 (CHIPs). Along with income supports, U.S. health care programs are perhaps the leading example of a categorical social policy. There is Medicaid for the category of people deemed poor, Medicare for the category of those deemed elderly and/or disabled, and CHIPs for poor, medically underserved children. The uninsured adult who is not poor cannot get any help from this list.

We will review each of these programs. First, though, let's discuss managed care and HMOs. Although these are not programs, they are the methods of health care financing and delivery on which government programs increasingly rely.

Managed Care and Health Maintenance Organizations

Faced with spiraling costs, policymakers have shifted to managed care. In managed care, insurers try to balance the need for cost containment with access and quality of service. To understand how managed care broke with the traditional method of health service delivery, it is only necessary to go back as far as the early 1980s, when patients had to find a doctor on their own, and the insurance company paid the doctor's or hospital's bill. Now, under most managed care plans, the insurer contracts with a group of health care providers, monitors the care (through utilization review) to determine whether it is really needed, and demands the approval of a primary care physician before a patient can see a specialist.

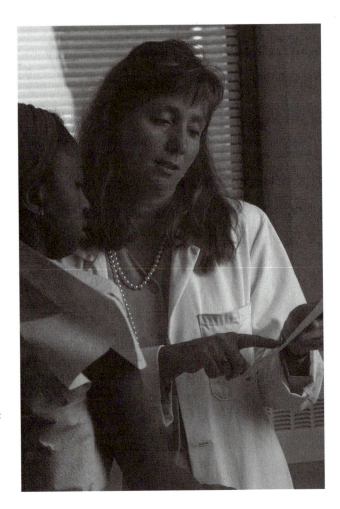

Because they value the doctor-patient relationship, many Americans resented it when health maintenance organizations (HMOs) questioned their doctors' recommendations for medical treatment.

There are three major kinds of managed care plans: health maintenance organizations (HMOs), preferred provider organizations (PPOs), and point-of-service plans (POS). HMOs are prepaid managed care networks that guarantee patients a range of health care services for a fixed monthly fee. HMO plans are supposed to reduce unnecessary and inappropriate care. Their supporters also contend that by coordinating care for a fixed fee, HMOs have an incentive to keep patients healthy. PPOs are different. In a PPO, physicians and hospitals provide a discounted fee for service to groups enrolled in the program. If patients want to venture outside the network, they must pay a greater share of the cost. Essentially, PPOs provide a volume discount, and physicians see more patients to compensate for their lower fees. POS plans combine features of the HMO and the PPO models. POS is a managed care system in which a primary care physician, a "gatekeeper," controls access to the rest of the network. If they are willing to shoulder a higher percentage of the costs, patients venturing outside the network can receive partial reimbursement.[12]

In the mid-1990s, when growth in costs slowed for a brief period, proponents of these models could make a plausible argument that managed care had reduced spending. But now that the market revolution in health care has passed and inflation has returned, the evidence is building that our reliance on managed care detoured policymakers from the path to a more sensible system. For one thing, managed care is not cheaper. It may reduce utilization rates and compel suppliers to offer discounts, but direct patient costs are not total costs, especially when the high administrative overhead of managed care is factored in. And though premiums may be lower, these savings often reflect cost shifting and "cherry-picking"—accepting only the healthiest patients into the plan.[13] Finally, managed care mostly offers a different method of delivering health care service to the insured population. Although this method did make delivery of these services more market-oriented, it did little to extend coverage to the uninsured.

Managed care plans are also under pressure. Many have begun to lose money, and smaller ones, in particular, are having difficulty raising the capital for on-line information systems that cost $200 million to $300 million. Doctors object to inadequate payments, employers resist rate increases, and hospitals are merging to fight back.[14] At a time when patients in forty-one states can appeal denials of care to independent outside reviewers and two-thirds of HMOs no longer require approval from a health plan nurse before a patient can be admitted to the hospital or see a specialist, managed care's efforts to cut costs have also fallen on hard times.[15] No wonder that initiatives seeking to funnel patients into government programs like Medicare HMOs have instead led the HMOs to shed more than 2.4 million patients between 1999 and 2003.[16]

The key question about managed care is whether it is rationing care for rational or self-interested motives. Although most of us would dispute the claim that we ever receive unnecessary care, we would probably agree in the abstract that we cannot all see every specialist and have every possible lab test. When managed care tries to enforce this principle, it arouses the suspicion of many of the 80 million Americans in managed care. An increasing number of these participants are asking the question: Has my care been denied for a good reason, or has it been denied because the financial stakeholders in managed care—shareholders and investors—will benefit monetarily? As David Lawrence, the chief executive of the Kaiser Foundation Health Plan and Hospitals, summarized it:

> The managed care movement of the last decade was really a financing system that was attempting to influence the way a group of fragmented, unintegrated physicians and hospitals practiced medicine. What was discovered was that when one uses financial tools to change the delivery of health care, A, they are not very powerful, and B, they make people mad.[17]

For now, managed care seems well entrenched. Yet this position may be deceiving. If managed care cannot solve the problems of the health care system and it makes people mad, it will not go unchallenged for long.

Authorized under Title XIX of the Social Security Act, Medicaid is a federal-state program that provides medical assistance to low-income people. This category of eligible participants includes the aged, blind, disabled, and members of families with dependent children. Because each state designs and administers its own program within federal guidelines, the coverage, benefits, and amount of payment for services all vary. These differences are so large that a poor single mother whose income is 75 percent of the poverty line may receive no coverage in one state, full coverage in another, and partial coverage but difficulty finding a provider in a third.[18]

Federal guidelines, however, do specify some services that states must offer to the medically needy. These services include inpatient and outpatient hospital services; laboratory and X-ray services; nursing facility care for those over 21 years; home health services for those entitled to nursing care; screening, diagnosis, and treatment for those under 21 years; family-planning services and supplies; and physician and nurse-midwife services. Exercising their option under the regulations, thirty-two states also cover drugs for the medically needy.[19] The federal government pays for these services using a formula that it adjusts annually. Called the federal matching rate, the formula ranges from 50 to 83 percent and is inversely related to each state's per capita income, so that the poorer states get the most help.

In 2001, Medicaid rolls totaled about 36 million people, or about 13 percent of the entire population, down from more than 40 million in 1998. At the same time, although Medicaid is supposed to provide health care to poor people, only 40 percent of the total population in poverty actually received Medicaid. But because children under the age of 18 years face less stringent eligibility requirements, their rate of participation is somewhat higher, at 55 percent. The program's total costs run about $199 billion dollars, with $112 billion coming from the federal government and the rest spent by the states.[20]

Medicaid policies have changed considerably in recent years. Between 1984 and 1990, eligibility expanded to include low-income pregnant women, infants, and children. But as the push for welfare reform gained strength in the early 1990s, the national AFDC caseload dropped. Medicaid had previously been linked to the receipt of cash benefits like AFDC and SSI. Worried that Medicaid gave public assistance recipients another reason to stay on welfare, policymakers enacting the 1996 welfare reform act disconnected Medicaid from public assistance. The Act gave the states greater flexibility to expand eligibility beyond the traditional limits of welfare. At the same time, however, it also barred most legal immigrant children and pregnant women from nonemergency services through Medicaid during their first five years in this country.[21]

More reform followed the next year. The 1997 Balanced Budget Act repealed federal requirements for state reimbursement of nursing homes, hospitals, and community health centers. In another move with wide-ranging consequences, it eliminated the need for states to obtain waivers to enroll

Medicaid recipients in managed care organizations.[22] Acting on the premise that Medicaid managed care would enhance access for beneficiaries, improve the quality of care, and reduce program costs, the states moved to embrace this option. By 2001, nearly 57 percent of all Medicaid recipients had been enrolled in managed care, up from 40 percent just five years earlier.[23]

Yet serious doubts have been raised about the appropriateness of managed care plans for Medicaid recipients. Managed care plans have had little previous experience with the high-risk, multiproblem, inner-city clients who need supportive services such as outreach, case management, and transportation. Managed care networks will do little to expand the supply of health services in the poorer neighborhoods; indeed, when linking existing providers to their network, they are more likely to select those providers who keep costs down. Also, for the first time, Medicaid managed care asks that participants select a health plan and primary provider, curtail the use of other providers, and obtain approval before seeing a specialist or visiting an emergency room. These decisions all require a telephone, access to plentiful information, and the ability to make prudent choices. If the system of Medicaid managed care cannot address these issues, it and the population it serves may prove to be poorly matched.[24]

The shift to Medicaid managed care is one of many factors that depressed the Medicaid rolls by 4 million people after 1998. Problems with the welfare reform law also contributed. Despite the requirements of the Act, many states did not provide transitional medical assistance, causing 1 million parents to lose their benefits. Other factors in the decline include the heightened stigma associated with the receipt of benefits from any welfare program, the confusion of rules about who is eligible, and the belief of some immigrants, even children who are citizens, that a Medicaid application could disqualify their parents from citizenship. In addition, many poor people simply assume that they are in good health and can get Medicaid if they need it. Observers nonetheless predict that if the economy falters, it could offset all these factors and drive the total number of people on Medicaid back up to 40 million.[25]

Of course, Medicaid continues to be the primary source of coverage for long-term care. The cost of one year in a nursing home now averages $55,000, and most people stay in a nursing home for about two and a half years. Low wages and inadequate staffing actually help to keep these prices down. According to a report prepared by the Department of Health and Human Services, more than 90 percent of the nation's nursing homes are understaffed, and it will require another $7.6 billion to bring the care up to adequate levels. Fearing the additional expense of federally mandated staffing, the George W. Bush administration has instead decided to publish data on the number of workers in each nursing home, in the hope that an informed public can pressure nursing homes to hire enough workers.[26]

To pay for care at current levels, disabled elderly people either rely on their own resources, collect on private long-term insurance, or spend down their assets to establish their Medicaid eligibility. Some 68 percent of nursing home residents are dependent on Medicaid to cover part of their long-term

Medicaid, 1965

Number of recipients:	36 million
Who offers the benefit or service:	The states, under federal guidelines
What form does it take:	Medical coverage
To whom is it provided:	Low-income people, including the aged, blind, disabled, and members of families with dependent children
At whose expense:	From 50 to 83 percent of each state's Medicaid budget comes from the federal government's general tax revenue; the states absorb the rest. In 2001, total costs for the Medicaid program amounted to $199 billion.

Medicare, 1965

Number of recipients:	40 million
Who offers the benefit or service:	The federal government
What form does it take:	Insurance for hospital stays (Part A) and optional coverage for doctor's services (Part B)
To whom is it provided:	The elderly and/or disabled
At whose expense:	In 2001, the Medicare program cost $238 billion, minus the premiums the elderly pay, for a net federal outlay of $215 billion. Federal revenues for this program come from a 1.45 percent tax that is part of your Social Security deduction, but that unlike Social Security, does not have an income ceiling.

State Children's Health Insurance Program (SCHIP), 1997

Number of recipients:	4.7 million children were enrolled in SCHIP at some time during 2001
Who offers the benefit or service:	The states
What form does it take:	Medical coverage
To whom is it provided:	Children in families with income up to 200 percent of the poverty line
At whose expense:	$4 billion a year has been allocated for SCHIPs, with the states paying 70 percent of the share they assume for Medicaid and the federal government picking up the rest. The revenue comes from an increase in the tobacco tax.

care; they account for about 35 percent of all Medicaid spending nationwide. Moreover, as the baby boomers age, this percentage is projected to climb upward, so that by 2018, the inflation-adjusted cost of Medicaid's long-term care expenditures will be twice what it was just twenty-five years earlier.[27] If we do not have a national health insurance system by that date, baby boomers flooding into the Medicaid program might well constitute a strong enough political force to demand better treatment in long-term care.

Medicaid also functions as a crucial backup for poor elderly people receiving Medicare. Some 7 million people are beneficiaries of both programs; most Medicare-Medicaid enrollees are eligible for full benefits under their state's eligibility criteria. The need for Medicaid arises because, as we shall see next, the Medicare program has so many gaps that its beneficiaries spent 22 percent of their income on health care. Medicaid steps into these gaps by assisting with Medicare's high out-of-pocket expenses, such as the monthly premium for doctor's services ($54 in 2002), or, in the absence of a catastrophic cap on beneficiary's expenses, the possibility of a financially ruinous medical condition. Medicaid also pays for the cost of services that Medicare does not cover. Besides long-term care, these services can include prescription drugs, transportation for medical purposes, eyeglasses, hearing aids, and dental appointments. For poor older people on Medicare, Medicaid is the last bulwark against sickness and impoverishment.[28]

Medicare

If you have clients who are elderly or disabled, you will have to deal with Medicare. Enacted in 1965 as Title XVIII of the Social Security Act, Medicare is the national insurance program for almost 40 million elderly and disabled people. Medicare insurance comes in two parts. Part A covers inpatient hospital services, up to one hundred days of posthospital care in a skilled nursing facility, some home health services, and hospice care. Patients must pay a deductible equal to the cost of one day in the hospital ($812 in 2002) each time they enter a hospital and begin a benefit period (a benefit period starts when the patient enters a hospital and ends when he or she has not been in a hospital or a skilled nursing facility for sixty days). Part A pays for the next sixty days of hospital care. Beyond that sixty days, patients are again subject to additional charges.

Part B, the second form of insurance under Medicare, is an optional program for all those Part A–eligible Medicare recipients who also want coverage for physician and laboratory services. Recipients pay the annual monthly fee of $54 (or, as described above, Medicaid pays it for them). After a $100 deductible, Part B covers 80 percent of Medicare's fee schedule for each service. The recipient must then pick up the remaining 20 percent.[29]

In 2001, the Medicare program cost about $238 billion, minus premiums collected, for a net federal outlay of about $215 billion. Part A is financed from the 1.45 percent payroll tax that is part of Social Security (7.65 percent is taxed, with the remaining 6.2 percent going to Social Security). Because employers contribute an equal amount, Part A receives 2.9 percent of payrolls. By law, Part B premiums are supposed to cover 25 percent of its costs, with general tax revenues financing the rest.[30]

Although the financing for Part B remains secure, projections about the long-term health of the insurance trust fund fluctuate wildly. In 2002, the fund's trustees announced that Medicare would remain solvent until 2030, the longest period of projected solvency in the program's history. Yet only nine years before, Medicare was supposed to be bankrupt by 1999; as recently as 1997, the money was supposed to run out in 2001. Then, a reduction in the rate of Medicare spending combined with improvements in the economy to push back the date of financial reckoning, so that five years of elapsed time delayed its projected bankruptcy by twenty-nine.[31]

Yet, despite this improving outlook, issues of adequacy and efficiency continue to plague the program. As a result of copayments, deductibles, and a fee schedule that sometimes runs below market, the average beneficiary, excluding long-term care, spends more than $3,000 annually on out-of-pocket expenses. The benefit package is also inadequate because it leaves beneficiaries responsible for nearly half the cost of their acute care. To fill these gaps, some 85 percent of beneficiaries have supplemental insurance. Medicaid and employer-sponsored retirement plans do a reasonably good job of boosting coverage, but employer plans, which cover about one-third of all Medicare beneficiaries, have become less available. At the same time, the cost of Medigap policies from private insurance, which serve one-quarter of all beneficiaries, has risen beyond the means of those with average income. For example, in Dallas, a 65-year-old purchasing a Medigap policy with minimal drug coverage would pay between $1,500 and $3,900.[32]

Caught between demands for services and demands for efficiency, policymakers have experimented with a variety of private sector solutions. The most common solution has been a growing reliance on HMOs, especially the Medicare+Choice (M+C) program initiated by the Balanced Budget Act of 1997. M+C's sponsors hoped to expand the health plan options available to beneficiaries, with the expectation that they would become more actively involved in their own health care. Yet a report from the U.S. General Accounting Office—the monitoring arm of the federal government—found that although the federal government has increased payments to HMOs and some 5.6 million, or 14 percent of all Medicare beneficiaries have joined them, the money has largely gone to hospitals and other health care providers and not for enhanced services to the elderly.

In fact, not only have the number of choices been diminished, but HMOs have canceled coverage for more 2.1 million people over four years, including 536,000 in 2002. At a time when hospitals need money to offset lower reimbursement rates and policymakers insist that insurance plans should offer more choices, the M+C option has been charged with the responsibility of reducing costs. By 2005, the Bush administration wants to double participation in M+C to 30 percent of all Medicare beneficiaries. The experience so far raises serious questions about the wisdom of this goal.[33]

Medicare, like Medicaid, represents a very partial solution—one to the health problems of the elderly and disabled, the other to the health problems of the poor. Concerns about costs, conflicts between health providers and patients, and a growing faith in the private sector's delivery of health care hamstring both programs. To address one of their most conspicuous failings, Congress recently enacted a program to reduce the number of poor children without health coverage. As we shall see next, however, this program has also stumbled on some administrative hurdles that prevent it from attaining its ostensible goals.

State Children's Health Insurance Plan—Title XXI of the Social Security Act

Enacted as part of the 1997 Balanced Budget Act, the State Children's Health Insurance Program provides matching funds to expand coverage to children in families with income up to 200% of the federal poverty level. Financed by an increase in the tobacco tax, it was expected to cover an additional 2 to 3 million children. Funds are allocated in proportion to the states' share of the nation's uninsured children, and the states receive higher federal matching payments than under Medicaid. The design of SCHIP reflected constraints that policymakers faced during the balanced budget debate of 1997. Because they wanted to target new funds to needy children, they thought they would get the largest reduction in the number of uninsured by focusing their attention on those who were not Medicaid-eligible.[34]

The total allocation for SCHIP is $20 billion for five years. During the first three years, states received their annual allotment based on the number of low-income, uninsured children in their state. During the past two years, the formula broadened to include more low-income children, regardless of whether they have health insurance.

As indicated earlier, the federal government pays for Medicaid according to a formula that ranges from 50 to 83 percent and is inversely linked to each

In an attempt to reduce the number of uninsured, the Clinton administration enacted the State Children's Health Insurance Plan, which expands coverage to children.

state's per capita income. Under SCHIP, states pay 70 percent of their Medicaid matching rate, so that a state that pays 50 percent of its Medicaid costs finances 35 percent of SCHIP. The states must also submit a plan to the Department of Health and Human Services explaining which option they choose as the means for disbursing the funds. They can use their grants to expand Medicaid coverage, enroll children without coverage in new plans, or experiment with a combination of these approaches.[35]

By now, you can probably guess what happened. In another typical example of the mismatch in federal-state relations, about 45 percent of the first year's $4.2 billion allocation went unused, and forty states had to return some funds. The states offered a number of reasons for this failure. Many took a year or more to enroll children; some were reluctant to spend matching funds; and a few complained about complex application forms or could not find enough eligible uninsured children to use the full allotment. Louisiana, the worst-performing state, had to return almost 64 percent of its grant.[36]

Conscious of the inadequacies of U.S. health care, policymakers implemented SCHIP to remedy one of its most flagrant problems: the lack of insurance coverage for some poor children. Unfortunately, it addressed this problem with the same set of policy tools that had created the problems in the first place. Although these tools enabled the states to insure some additional children, they also restricted the progress that could be made.

The Inadequacies of the U.S. Health Care System

Although Medicaid, Medicare, and SCHIP try to fill the gaps left by employer-based insurance, they are, at best, partial remedies for some large systemic problems. Examining the U.S. health care system as a whole, we can identify five distinct issues that deserve careful attention: (1) inequality; (2) the uninsured; (3) prescription drugs; (4) mental health policy; and (5) the need for a national health care system. We first address these issues, then filter the issue of health care through our model of policy analysis.

Inequality

Inequality is one of the hallmarks of the U.S. health care system. Men with less than twelve years of education (using education as a broad indicator of low income) are more than twice as likely to die of chronic ailments such as heart disease and nearly twice as likely to die of communicable diseases than those with more than thirteen years of education. Women with family income under $10,000 are more than three times as likely to die of heart disease and nearly three times as likely to die of diabetes than those with income above $25,000.

The racial division is consistent, too. African Americans are more likely than whites to die of AIDS, heart disease, diabetes, and cancer. For many years, research downplayed racism and attributed these outcomes to a lack of access to care. But a major study by the National Academy of Sciences Institute of Medicine reaffirms the crucial importance of race. In New York State, African Americans were 37 percent less likely to undergo state-of-the-art cardiovascular treatments like angioplasty; nationally, African American Medicare beneficiaries with diabetes are 3.6 times more likely to have their legs amputated. Minorities receive poorer medical treatment because their insurance places stricter limits on services, and they are less likely than whites to have a long-standing relationship with the same doctor. In addition, a subtle racism often lowers the expectations of the doctors they do see, leading them to discount the possibility that patients of color will participate in follow-up care.[37]

Combining class and race, the health policy literature has firmly established the principle that inequality kills, irrespective of the riskier health behaviors in which poor people sometimes engage.[38] This effect of inequality on health is unsurprising. After all, a poor adult with a health problem is only half as likely to see a doctor as a high-income adult, and adults living in low-income areas are twice as likely to be hospitalized for a health problem that could have been treated with prompt outpatient care. Moreover, from a broader perspective, the wider the income gap between rich and poor, the less inclined the affluent are to pay for vital health services such as public hospitals on which they do not rely. And, because the level of income inequality relates closely to the degree of social cohesion, communities with a wide range of income are less likely to offer the social networks that help to keep people alive.[39]

This text has emphasized that social welfare policies usually develop out of the influence of a nation's particular values and institutions. Because economic inequality is so much a part of American society, a health care system stressing equality would constitute a decisive break; in effect, it would have to exist as a separate system. On this issue especially, then, it is important to know the odds: at the same time that the dynamics of social policy development make such a system unlikely, the human cost of inequality makes its pursuit worthwhile.

The Uninsured

In 2001, the number of uninsured reached 41.2 million people, or about 14 percent of the U.S. population. The lack of health insurance for this group is probably the U.S. health care system's most flagrant deficiency.[40] Although policymakers often stress the expense of providing the uninsured with coverage, they usually underestimate the less visible costs of leaving them uninsured. The most prominent of these costs include work productivity lost to illness, greater vulnerability to communicable diseases, and an excessive reliance on emergency rooms, the most expensive form of care. Because 37 percent of unemployed people are uninsured, and more than 33 percent of the workers who lose their jobs also lose their health insurance, all these factors are sure to gain importance when layoffs rise, as they did in the aftermath of the 1990s economic bubble.[41]

Who are the uninsured? Because of the crazy-quilt U.S. health care system, the demographics are not so neat. With Medicaid covering the poorest people, many of the uninsured are not poor. Over one-third (35 percent) are families with income above 200 percent of the poverty line. Just under one third (29 percent) are families with income between 100 and 200 percent of the poverty line. Only a minority of 36 percent are actually poor.[42]

Crosscut by race, age, and employment status, the uninsured encompass just 14 percent of non-Hispanic whites but 24 percent of African Americans and 37 percent of Hispanics. Eight million are between the ages of 18 and 24; 11 million are children under the age of 18 (even while two-thirds are eligible for SCHIP or Medicaid); 60 percent live in families where one worker is employed year-round; and another 24 percent reside in families with a part-time or part-year employee.[43]

As a result of the 1996 welfare reform law, immigrants arriving in the United States after August 1996 cannot get Medicaid for five years. The consequences of this regulation are evident among low-income immigrants, 46 percent of whom lacked health insurance in 1999. In particular, because so many recent immigrants are Latinos, they are more than twice as likely to lack health insurance as the rest of the population. They do not have this coverage because they work for employers who do not offer it, labor in low-paying jobs excluded from the firm's health plan, or simply believe that high-premium, high-deductible health insurance is a bad deal.[44]

Mothers are another noteworthy group among the uninsured. In 1999, some 5.9 million mothers—including 4.3 million, or one-third, of all low-income mothers—lacked health insurance coverage. These mothers risk going without pap smears, mammograms, and other necessary preventive and primary care. Their lack of health care has especially wide ramifications, because it endangers them, their capacity to care for their children, and the health of any other babies they might have.[45]

The consequences of an absence of health coverage extend to the uninsured population as a whole. Those without coverage are less likely to have a regular doctor (53 percent uninsured vs. 18 percent insured) and to have received preventive services (45 percent vs. 23 percent). Compared to 18 percent of the insured, 49 percent of the uninsured are more likely not to see a doctor when they need one, to ignore a prescription because of its cost, or to skip a medical treatment.[46] These are all risky health practices. Together, they serve to remind us that, as with other aspects of the U.S. health care system, policy deficiencies have real, personal consequences.

Prescription Drugs

The third major problem with the U.S. health care system involves the cost of prescription drugs and their omission from the Medicare plan. In 2002,

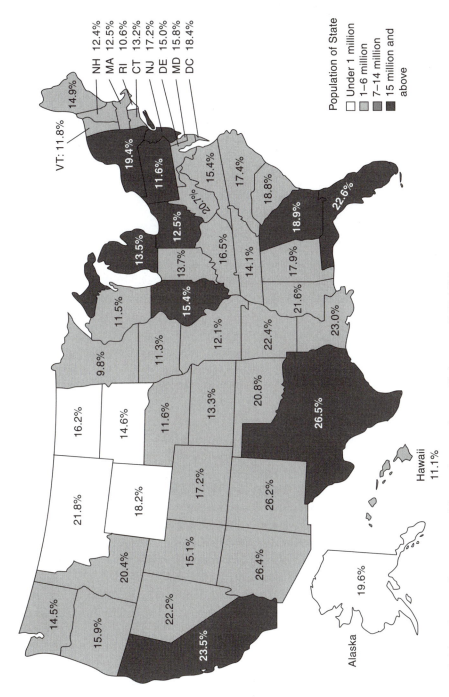

Probability of persons being uninsured for population under age 65, by state, 1997–1999.

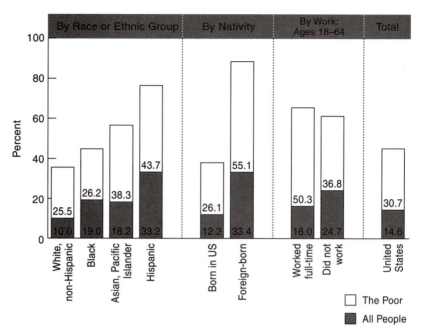

| | By Race or Ethnic Group | By Nativity | By Work: Ages 18–64 | Total |

Percentage uninsured as compared to percentage in poverty: Who has and who does not have health insurance.

the average Medicare beneficiary spent $1,051 for drugs out of pocket, a figure that is pushed up by the 38 percent who have no insurance to pay for drugs outside the hospital.[47] Drug prescriptions make up just 9 percent of all health care costs, but they constituted 44 percent of the growth in costs in 1999 and overall remain the fastest growing part of health care expenses. The resulting financial burden can quickly devastate the elderly. A *Families USA* report noted that a widow who has acid reflux disease and lives on $12,525 a year (150 percent of the poverty level) would spend $1,455, or 12 percent of her income, on medicine.[48]

By 2002, the spectacle of rising drug costs led to the introduction of bills in thirty-seven state legislatures. Some states have already enacted legislation. In Pennsylvania, policymakers simply used state money to pay for part of the cost of prescriptions. California and Florida limited the prices that pharmacies can charge elderly customers. Michigan and Missouri created tax credits to offset amounts spent on prescription drugs. Iowa, Washington, New Hampshire, and West Virginia established buyer clubs or purchasing cooperatives, and Maine and Vermont have received federal approval to use Medicaid funds for drug discounts to those who would otherwise be ineligible. In the absence of firm national legislation, the states are developing a diverse mix of local policies.[49]

The conflict about prescription drugs revolves around two different conceptions of public need. The drug companies contend that they spend billions on drug research. They assert that when just one of every five thousand compounds tested becomes a marketable drug, the price they charge for it must recoup their investment on all the other failures. Critics respond that a breakdown of drug company spending shows that research is actually a relatively small portion of the total drug bill. Hence, although we spend $106 billion on drugs, $16 billion goes to research, $20 billion is profit, and the drug companies allocate much of the remainder on expensive advertising and political campaigns.[50]

Although drug companies have undoubtedly developed some breakthrough medicines, drugs in other countries sell for one-quarter of their U.S. price. For example, the breast cancer drug Tamoxifen sells for $241 in the United States and $34 (86 percent less) in Canada; glucophage, a drug to treat diabetes, costs $64 in the United States and just $14 (78 percent less) in Canada. Such a large differential leaves critics wondering whether there might be some way of separating cutting-edge drug research from the advertising, political influence, and high profits that appear to characterize the modern U.S. drug industry.[51]

The critics know that it will be difficult. To preserve their position, drug companies have paid manufacturers to keep generic drugs off the market. In one typical case, Abbott Laboratories struck a deal with Zenith Goldline pharmaceuticals. Zenith produced a generic drug that would replace Abbott Lab's Hytrin, a blood pressure medication. Abbott made $500 million a year from Hytrin and agreed to pay Zenith $2 million a month to delay the introduction of a cheaper substitute. The deal lasted for a year and half, until an antitrust investigation scuttled it.[52]

Drug companies have other strategies for extending their patents. One study found that two-thirds of all drugs approved between 1989 and 2000 were actually modified or identical versions of existing medicines. For example, Clarinex, an allergy drug, is a reformulation of Claritin, and Sarafem, which treats premenstrual irritability, is Prozac, the antidepression drug, repackaged in pink and lavender capsules. To be sure, drug companies did develop some genuinely new medicines, including Fosamax for osteoporosis, Avanida and Actos for diabetes, and Viagra for erectile dysfunction. But without enough real breakthroughs in the pipeline, companies have frequently relabeled old drugs to protect patents and ensure adequate revenues.[53]

For critics, these strategies serve to confirm their belief that the industry is committed to high and rising drug prices. But what should be done? Conservative proposals usually advocate tax incentives for the industry or offer block grants to the states in the hope that they will subsidize benefits for the most needy seniors. But as subsidies do not change the pricing structure and the money from block grants has often been redirected away from the poor, the adequacy of these proposals remains in doubt.[54] Policymakers continue to debate the key provisions of the most likely reforms: How generous should the benefit be? Should it be available to all Medicare beneficiaries or only those with the lowest income and the greatest need? Should the benefits be provided by private insurance companies or added to Medicare?

Much drug research traces its origins to public funding sources like the National Institutes of Health (NIH), as well as to private charitable foundations. When drug companies turn this research into profitable drugs, they maintain the long-standing division in public policy that makes costs public, that is, absorbed by the taxpayer, and profits private. It certainly does not address the issue of the impoverished older woman who needs her heart medication now, but perhaps the longer-term solution to cheaper drugs demands that we build on this public system and invest more money in the NIH.[55] Although the drugs developed from this research would not replace the private sector, at least they would ensure a greater public benefit from the taxpayers' investment.

Mental Health Policy

Many social workers offer counseling. It is therefore of critical importance to the profession that U.S. health care policy so severely de-emphasizes the importance of mental health. Because mental health policy has never had parity with policies to maintain physical health, it narrows its focus to the most serious psychiatric diagnoses. If you are depressed but not suicidal, or if your marriage is in trouble but you are not actually threatening your spouse, you may have a psychological problem, but it is not one that public policy recognizes.

Yet, just because we downplay the problems of the worried well is not to suggest that we adequately address the difficulties of those with psychiatric diagnoses. Although HMOs do treat psychiatric diagnoses such as schizophrenia and depression, patients often face higher copayments and deductibles than they would if they were treated for physical ailments like diabetes or cancer.[56] Mental health policy is therefore consistent with the broad outlines of U.S. social policy: it is categorical rather than universal, but even when it concentrates resources on the neediest, it does not bring them up to the standard of the rest of the population.

Within the federal government, primary responsibility for mental health policy resides with the National Institute of Mental Health, established as part of the 1946 National Mental Health Act. Since 1992, NIMH has also included two other institutes: the National Institute on Drug Abuse and the National Institute on Alcohol Abuse and Alcoholism. Through their research, these institutes determine the broad outline for the direction of mental health policy, while administrative responsibility lies with the Substance Abuse and Mental Health Services Administration.[57]

In 1980, at the end of President Carter's term, his administration enacted the Mental Health Systems Act. With its national orientation, the Act was designed to support the ongoing activities of community mental health centers, to recognize the special needs of chronically mentally ill persons, and to mandate the NIMH to design national goals and priorities for the prevention of mental illness. But the legislation did not last long. When Reagan became president, he block-granted mental health funds and moved them to the states. Instead of spearheading the development of national mental health policy, the State Comprehensive Mental Health Services Plans Act of 1986 merely requires states to submit comprehensive plans to receive special funding.[58]

The increasing reliance on managed care threads its way through this history. Managed care first began to cover mental health in the 1970s, when the 1973 HMO Act stated that to qualify as an HMO, a program had to offer treatment for physical disorders as well as crisis intervention mental health services.[59] HMOs have stuck to this principle ever since, rationing coverage for counseling and psychotherapy. The system is so pervasive that nowadays, to provide mental health services, the vast majority of clinical social workers in private practice must belong to a managed care network. But despite this pervasive need, HMOs have refused to grant parity to mental health. Indeed, faced with the strongest legislative effort yet to end the disparity between the treatment of mental and physical illnesses, managed care organizations were instrumental in defeating a 2001 bill, which they claimed would spur a new round of health care inflation.[60]

The failure of this latest effort leaves two key issues looming over mental health policy. The first issue continues to be parity. As a simple matter of equity, policymakers have so far failed to acknowledge that someone with schizophrenia, like someone with cancer, suffers from a disease. At an even broader level, we have yet to come to grips with the pain and emotional suffering that less serious psychological ailments can cause, despite their considerable social and economic consequences in lost productivity, unstable marriages, and destructive parenting.

This issue poses a second, closely related question: Should mental health policy be framed as a part of general health policy, or as a separate domain? The argument for a separate domain arises from the contention that unless mental health acquires a distinctly independent status, it will always be subordinate. It is true that the fragmentation of policy into discrete domains is more consistent with U.S. policy tradition. Yet this same tradition demonstrates that, by itself, a policy's independent status does not guarantee either respect or adequate funding. For this reason, though it may be visionary, there is in principle no reason why we should not define health care policy broadly and treat policies involving mental health as one of its essential ingredients.[61]

The Lack of National Health Care

The fifth and perhaps overriding deficiency in U.S. health care policy is the lack of a national health care system.[62] This deficiency makes the United States unique among its peers: every other developed country has one. Although this contrast certainly accentuates the lack of a national health care system in the United States, it also enables us to choose from some existing models.

The first distinction that should be made among these models involves the difference between a national health service and national health insurance. In a national health service—England's, established in 1948, is the best known—the government pays a salary to doctors, nurses, and other medical personnel. Under the English system, medical personnel are government employees, health care is financed out of general revenues, and the service is free. Although Prime Minister Margaret Thatcher encouraged the development of a second, private tier and the government has starved the public system in recent years, the National Health Service persists as an integral component of the British welfare state.[63]

In the national health insurance model, by contrast, both medical institutions and medical personnel retain their private status. Hospitals do not have to become public hospitals and doctors do not have to become government employees. Instead, all that changes is the funding mechanism. The particulars of this funding mechanism can vary, from payments from many private insurance companies supplemented by government programs to guarantee universal coverage, to the Canadian single-payer model, where the government negotiates with the health care system and serves as sole insurer. President Clinton designed his 1993 health care proposal along the lines of the first option. Further to his left, more than ninety members of Congress and many grassroots organizations pushed for a U.S. version of the Canadian single-payer system.[64]

In recent years, the Canadian system has fallen on hard times. Underfinanced like the British, it has moved to enforce still stricter rationing, especially of expensive medical technology, resulting in crowded emergency rooms and long waits for some operations. The Canadian system does not cover drugs, dentistry, or most eye care, and the taxes that pay for the provincial share of its costs are sometimes regressive, for example, a sales tax on most consumer goods. But Canadians like their health care system: two-thirds rate it highly, and for some American reformers, its obvious virtues offset correctable deficiencies. In Canada, health care is free; that is, Canadians simply flash their health identification card and pay nothing at the point of service. Furthermore, because Canada lacks a bloated private bureaucracy that devotes its time to bill collection, evaluating insurance risks, and marketing competitive health insurance policies, the costs of health care administration add up to just one-fifth of those in the United States. In fact, the General Accounting Office once estimated that the implementation of a single-payer system in the United States would save enough money to provide health care coverage for all the uninsured.[65]

One large political obstacle looms over the debate about the single-payer model. As its proponents all admit, it would probably require a tax increase. In exchange, however, there would be no insurance premiums, free health care at the point of service, and much less hassle about who paid how much to whom. In short, a simpler public tax would substitute for a complex system of private financing.[66]

Americans' antipathy to government has always given them pause about this idea. As a result, incremental pathways to national health insurance are probably more likely. Such a plan might offer automatic enrollment in the

Federal Employees Health Benefits Plan (which provides health insurance to 9 million federal workers and their families) for the working uninsured; extend Medicare down to 55 years of age and/or those with overwhelming medical expenses; and expand Medicaid to everyone with income less than 100 percent of the poverty line.[67] Cobbled together from these three programs, the plan is not a particularly neat or efficient method of covering the uninsured. It would, however, cover almost everyone.

These five deficiencies—inequality, the uninsured, the cost of prescription drugs, the lack of coverage for mental health, and the need for a national health care system—tarnish the positive achievements of the U.S. health care system. The system consequently lies poised between its sometimes miraculous cures of lethal diseases and its inability to provide decent quality mental and physical health care at a reasonable cost to all Americans. Once again, our policy model can help to explain why U.S. health care seems to be perpetually caught in such a striking contradiction.

Economics

U.S. economics and U.S. health care are terribly mismatched. Although the U.S. economic system values markets, profits, and competition, the interaction of these values with our health care system often tends to distort it. Markets treat the affluent well and the poor badly. This is a distinction that people accept in the contrast between a luxury and a battered car; they are much less willing to maintain it in matters of life and death. In one national survey, 91 percent of respondents agreed that "everyone should have a right to the best possible health care—as good as a millionaire gets."[68]

Americans also respect the profit motive, but they ask probing questions when HMOs seek to maintain their profit margin by rationing medical procedures. Applied to health care, competition too is a dubious concept: would you price-shop if you were recovering from a heart attack or treating a malignant tumor? Most health consumers would spend anything to save themselves or a loved one. Yet, unlike in other competitive markets, few of us have any knowledge—apart from what a doctor tells us—about our medical options. Indeed, because expensive advertisements for medical services such as drugs, health technologies (CT scans and MRIs), and hospitals become part of everyone's health care bill, it is easier to argue that competition keeps competitors on their toes than it is to demonstrate that it actually saves money for the whole system.

What are the practical consequences of this mismatch between market values and the provision of good quality health care for all? Although it is a fundamental principle of market economics that every individual's pursuit of enlightened self-interest will bring about the best possible outcome, this principle hardly seems to hold in the health care marketplace. Employers want to keep costs down to protect profits; doctors and hospitals will not perform services at a loss; drug and insurance companies seek the largest possible profits for their shareholders; and the less money people pay out of pocket, the more expensive treatment they will demand. When each of these participants in the health care market pursues economic self-interest, our health care system malfunctions.

In tracing the economic origins of the system's problems, analysts calculate that managed care insurers devote about 80 to 85 percent of their premiums to reimbursing providers; the rest covers administration, marketing, and profits. Together with the profits of other medical services—labs, hospitals, drug companies, and physician groups—plus the marketing of their services and the burden of bill payments throughout the system, it is estimated that up to one-third of all health care spending consists of profit and waste. The population is aging; American doctors rely on medical technology that is less available in other countries; and we have an excess of expensive specialists instead of primary care physicians. Still, if there is one reason we spend twice as much as the Japanese but live, on average, four years less, the most likely explanation is the profit and waste that is built into the U.S. health care system.[69]

Politics

The politics of health care flow from its economics. The problem is that although profit and waste may be the major reason for our excessive health care spending, that excess is usually somebody's job and somebody's standard of living. We may all agree that the system has some serious problems. At the same time, it is hardly surprising that much of the politics of health care goes toward perpetuating the benefits that some people receive from misallocation of resources in the existing system.

Campaign spending by the drug companies is perhaps the preeminent example. In the 1999–2000 election cycle, drug companies shaped public policy by spending $230 million on lobbying, campaign contributions, and issue ads. This investment was designed to prevent the Republican-controlled Congress from providing prescription drug coverage through Medicare. The money included $170 million in lobbying, $35 million in campaign ads for the drug industry group Citizens for Better Medicare, and $10 million funneled to the U.S. Chamber of Commerce. To conduct this campaign, the drug companies employed 297 lobbyists, more than one for every two members of Congress.[70]

Following up in the next Congress, the Pharmaceutical Research and Manufacturers of America also paid for all the advertising in a special health issue of *Newsweek* magazine. This violation of journalistic ethics sparked a protest from five national consumer groups, who noted that the issue's editorial content matched the positions preferred by the manufacturers' lobby.[71] Soaring drug prices may anger the elderly, but it is hard for consumer groups to keep pace with the financial and political clout of such a powerful, ongoing campaign.

Other sectors of the health care industry also exercise great political influence. Large health insurers like Aetna and Humana advance their viewpoint through the Coalition for Affordable Quality Health Care, while small and medium-size insurance companies rely on the Health Insurance Association of America. To pursue higher Medicare and Medicaid reimbursement rates, hospitals depend on the American Hospital Association. The organizations representing the nursing home industry, the Alliance for Quality Nursing Home Care and American Health Care Association, try to reduce the burden of federal regulations. Likewise, although the American Medical Association has lost influence among younger doctors, it still seeks to defend the profession's income and autonomy. Employers both large and small join in organizations such as the Business Roundtable, the Chamber of Commerce, and the National Association of Manufacturers to fight the rapid inflation in health care costs. The National Alliance for the Mentally Ill serves as an advocacy group for that population. And finally, as their representative, the elderly have the 35 million members of the American Association of Retired Persons.[72] With these organizations all out to protect their own interests, the result is a political free-for-all.

This political free-for-all leads to a policy paralysis. By the standards of what needs to be done—universal coverage, affordable drugs, parity for mental health—very little gets done. This is not to say that the paralysis of policy is never broken. But unfortunately, these breakthroughs often ride a wave of money and influence on behalf of the very organizations that created the problem in the first place. Under these circumstances, it has always been very difficult to squeeze the waste out of the U.S. health care system.

Ideology

The ideology underlying the U.S. health care system reflects the most basic American values. It values self-reliance and work, treats health care as a commodity, and prefers private insurance to government programs. Although these values often pervade our social welfare policies, they assume an even greater prominence in health care.

U.S. health insurance is work-based. Historically, this association began in World War II, when companies seeking a way around wage and price controls used health insurance as a fringe benefit to attract workers in a tight labor market. This link with work parallels the orientation of other social policies and conforms to established American values.

Yet the work ethic component of social policy ignores a problem: not everybody works. In the 1960s, the federal government legislated Medicaid for the poor and Medicare for the elderly to address this problem. But as the poor and the elderly represent just two of the categories of people who do not have a job (or at least, in the case of the poor, a job that offers a fringe benefit like health care), the system has corroded. Now, although many low-paid service jobs do not offer health insurance, U.S. health policy is tied to a system that revolves around the vagaries of the individual job. As a result, because the ideology linking work and health insurance leaves the government to fill in the gaps, it acts as a major impediment to the development of a national health care system.

The second ideology associated with health policy assumes its commodification. The commodification of health care flows from the idea that it, like any other consumer good, should be purchased on the open market. You can get a stove at an appliance store, pay to see a movie at your local theater, and buy a plane ticket on an airline's Web site. By analogy, health care is a commodity just like a stove, entertainment, or a vacation. People can purchase it, and indeed investors can speculate on the difference between the price consumers pay and the amount it actually costs to deliver the service. It is true, of course, that in the United States, we also commodify other basic human needs such as food and housing. Nevertheless, our willingness to accept the consequence of putting a price on what is often a life-and-death need demonstrates just how far we are prepared to embrace this ideology.

For the third ideological ingredient in health policy, we reach bedrock: Americans are suspicious of and even dislike their federal government. This attitude envelops every health care policy issue. Hospitals and insurers developed Blue Cross and Blue Shield in the 1930s as an alternative to national health care, long after most European countries had already implemented a national insurance system. When the issue of a national system arose again in the 1960s, Medicaid, one of the two categorical programs put forth as a compromise, avoided centralization of authority in Washington to confer significant power on the states. Likewise, in the 1990s, the opposition to a tax increase undermined support for the Canadian single-payer model, even as many policymakers contended that the taxes paid would probably amount to less and produce a better system than the premiums paid to private insurers.

Although the fear of big government always straitjackets social welfare policy reforms, there are usually other factors at play. Perhaps the population is stigmatized, or, on the surface at least, the reforms might actually be more expensive. In the case of health care, however, the issue affects everyone, and though a national system would redistribute resources, it would likely save money. Setting the other factors aside, we are left with an antipathy to the federal government as the primary ideological bulwark against a national health care system. The contradiction is irreconcilable: although Americans desire a national health insurance system, they just do not want the federal government to provide it.

Social Movements

It fits the historic pattern: when powerful interests paralyze social welfare policy at the federal level, reformers turn their energy to the states. This is exactly what happened after the failure of President Clinton's 1994 health care bill. At the national level, various coalitions tried to expand existing programs, lobbying for a patients' bill of rights and getting more funding for Medicare. But as it has become clear that a system of managed care will not cut costs or reduce the number of uninsured, advocates have also championed more fundamental changes in the hope that they might be able to establish universal coverage in some states. Although it has not been an easy process, perhaps now, as in the past, the success of universal coverage in one state can serve as a precedent for the whole country.

Already, reformers have succeeded in introducing single-payer legislation in about ten states: Maine, Missouri, Minnesota, New Mexico, Connecticut, Rhode Island, Montana, Michigan, Massachusetts, and Oregon.[73] The political dynamics follow the same pattern. In most cases, while the number of legislators supporting the single-payer model has risen each year, in states as on the federal level the coalition remains a distinct minority.

In Maine, proponents of a single-payer system got a boost in 2001, when, despite Anthem Blue Cross/Blue Shield's $382,000 advertising campaign, a nonbinding referendum carried the city of Portland by 52 to 48 percent. In 2000, single-payer legislation passed the Maine House of Representatives but failed in the Senate. Maine progressives are hoping that the Portland referendum will help to tip the balance.[74]

Single-payer's trail in Vermont is even longer. Beginning in 1987, Burlington's independent mayor (and subsequently congressman) Bernie Sanders convened a task force of academic and medical professionals to analyze the problems of Vermont health care. After study by various committees and much political intrigue, lawmakers finally introduced the first version of a single-payer bill into the Vermont legislature in 1992. By 1994, the bill had evolved into a proposal that relied on a 7.8 percent payroll tax (after an exclusion of the first $20,000 of income) and added a 3 percent tax with a similarly progressive exclusion on both adjusted gross income and income from self-employment. Although the bill failed to win a legislative majority, the prospect of a single-payer system continues to loom over the Vermont legislature. Organizers may not have been wholly successful, but they have been able to extract a number of smaller reforms.[75]

Single-payer campaigns have also reached the West Coast. Californians undertook a $3.2 million ballot initiative in 1994, but lost in the face of a multimillion dollar advertising campaign. Similarly, after failing several times to pass the Oregon legislature in the 1990s, the Oregon Health Action Campaign combined with Health Care for All–Oregon to introduce a ballot initiative. Like any number of states that have single-payer proposals in various stages of study and development, its passage is probably a long shot. National groups such as Physicians for a National Health Program and the Universal Health Care Action Network will continue to fight for a federal single-payer system, and all the grassroots organizing suggests that in the meantime, at the state level, the issue is not going to go away.[76]

In 1917, Isaac Rubinow, one of the leaders of the reform-minded American Association for Labor Legislation, wrote, "Whether this legislative year will see actual health insurance legislation or not is not a matter of very great importance. . . . I think even the most bitter opponents of the health insurance movement are willing to admit that the best they can achieve is a certain postponement."[77] Rubinow was overly optimistic. After many failed attempts to legislate national health insurance, that postponement has lasted more than eighty years.

Other chapters have already discussed three noteworthy attempts to enact health insurance: the New Deal, the Great Society, and Clinton's doomed National Health Security Act of 1994. But the twentieth century witnessed at least three other significant campaigns: during the Progressive Era, under President Truman in the late 1940s, and again during the 1970s. They also faltered, for reasons similar to their more famous counterparts.[78]

The first major presidential candidate to endorse the concept of national health insurance was Theodore Roosevelt, who announced his support even before Rubinow's statement, when he campaigned on the Bull Moose Ticket in 1912. Like many others during the Progressive Era, Roosevelt looked to workers' compensation as the model for health insurance. Surely, the far-seeing businessman could understand that just as workers' compensation pro-

"Protected!" Social reformers have pursued their goal of national health insurance since the first quarter of the twentieth century.

(Courtesy New York Women's Joint Legislative Conference.)

"PROTECTED!"
This workingman's family is ready for the inevitable "rainy day" caused by sickness.

tected employers from large damage suits, some form of national health insurance would improve the health of workers and strengthen the country. Although this mix of moral compassion and appeal to economic efficiency was typical of the Progressive Era's reformers, it could not overcome the campaign against health insurance waged by a motley alliance of doctors, employers, insurance companies, and even some labor unions who did not want the issue taken off the bargaining table. Labeled as "Made in Germany" during World War I and "Made in Russia" in the aftermath of the Russian Revolution, the drive for national health insurance sagged to the point where it could not even get state legislation enacted in New York and California.[79]

When Harry Truman assumed the presidency in 1945, he too proposed national health insurance as a way to fill the biggest omission in New Deal social policy. Building on the Wagner-Murray-Dingell bill that had previously been introduced in 1943, Truman sought to incorporate health insurance into Social Security. It was the proper means, he said, to protect people from the "economic fears" of sickness.

The counterattack began soon thereafter. Even though Truman offered more money to doctors and promised continuity of care, the American Medical Association wrote an editorial contending that national health insurance would make doctors "slaves." At a time when the AMA dominated U.S. medicine, its opposition stopped the proposal in its tracks. Truman's focus on health care did help to enact the 1946 Hill-Burton Act for hospital construction and contributed to the establishment of the National Institutes of Health. But though the proposal for national health got a brief boost from Truman's surprise reelection in 1948, Republicans continually tagged it as "socialized medicine," and it vanished as a serious political option amid the mounting anticommunism of the late 1940s.[80]

After the passage of Medicare and Medicaid in the mid-1960s, national health insurance returned to the public agenda in the 1970s. This era of health care reform divided into two periods. On the heels of the social movements of the 1960s, the early 1970s featured an expansive conception of health care reform. Led by Senator Edward Kennedy, this conception favored a model of national health insurance with the government acting as a consumer cooperative to bargain with organized medical providers. With opinion shifting to the right, however, this political moment did not last long. Countered first by Nixon's plan to mandate health care at the workplace, and later by a variety of Carter administration proposals to cut costs and streamline the health care bureaucracy, the campaign for national health insurance once again faded from view, only to return, and fail again, under President Clinton in the 1990s.[81]

This history, then, does not provide much uplifting news for those committed to health care reform. Fears of increased taxes, the federal bureaucracy, and the loss of choice have repeatedly derailed the movement for some kind of national health insurance. And with labor unions reluctant to give up their administrative control over health coverage as a negotiated benefit, reformers have never been able to count on organized labor as a reliable ally.[82]

Without a crucial part of the reform coalition, the movement for national health care has always fallen to the enduring myths that shield its powerful opponents.

The next battlefield may be different. In the process of reforming health care, the health care industry has created an odd parallelism. As premiums have soared, the HMO bureaucracy has thickened, and fewer patients can choose their doctors, the industry has begun to acquire the defects, but not the virtues, of a government plan. In effect, the issues of cost, bureaucracy, and choice, which have been used to defeat any government plan, now apply with equal force to managed care. Although the outcome may still not be any different, what might happen next is at least somewhat unpredictable on this more level playing field.

12

Food and Hunger: Programs and Policies

U.S. food policy revolves around a great paradox. Just as the United States has a significant number of poor and near poor people in a nation of great wealth, it has hunger and food insecurity in a land of extraordinary abundance. The connection between poverty and hunger might seem quite natural in other countries, where famines, civil wars, and frequent crop failures disrupt the supply of food and reduce a largely agricultural population to desperation. In the United States, however, an abundance of food accentuates the paradox underlying the existence of hunger. After all, the United States is the world's breadbasket—the biggest exporter of wheat and corn and the third biggest exporter of rice. So abundant is our food supply that even while retailers, consumers, and restaurants discard 25 percent of their produce, Americans still spend less on their food—8 percent of income—than anyone else.[1] The implications are dismaying. In a land where food is cheap and plentiful, the paradox of hunger amid abundance looms even larger than the paradox of poverty amid wealth.

Yet hunger is different from other social problems. At some point on the route to becoming a social problem, crime, drugs, and unprotected sex produce a payoff or pleasure. But hunger has no payoff, and no one, apart from panic dieters, ever seeks to be hungry. Unlike other social problems, then, the hungry do not have to contend with uncontrollable impulses or addictions. Even while the hungry continue to be stigmatized for their poverty, most people can relate to hunger and are consequently less prone to see it as a personal fault. Perhaps that is why 94 percent of those surveyed in one poll said that "it's not right to let people who need welfare go hungry."[2]

The hungry elicit personal sympathy. Less stigmatized but plainly needy, they have become the objects of charitable aid from the neighborhood pantries that have sprung up as the federal entitlement to food has slipped away. For conservatives, the beauty of this charitable enterprise comes from its reliance on individual goodwill. In this respect, emergency food assistance models the way they believe all social welfare should be.

Some, however, have their doubts. Sociologist Janet Poppendieck, for example, wonders whether individual goodwill is "kinder, but less just." In her opinion, the proliferation of food charities acts as a moral safety valve that creates the illusion of effective action by reducing the most visible evidence of hunger. Like others who respect the work of volunteers, she believes that as a matter of social policy, the growth of a charitable food network actually undermines the goal of feeding the poor.[3]

This argument frames the policy discussion of this chapter. But it also

Along with other social welfare cutbacks, many critics contend that the shift from entitlement programs to charity has led to a rise in hunger.

means we are getting a little ahead of ourselves. Before we can really discuss the issue of food policy, we must first define hunger, estimate the size of the population that is hungry, and talk about the consequences of hunger on physical and psychological health. Then, after analyzing the triggers for social change, we describe the public and private programs that nourish those at risk of consuming inadequate or insufficient food. Last, after putting these programs through our policy model, we will be able to take a more informed position on the debate about entitlements versus charity.

Definition

Hunger should be simple to define. If you do not eat enough food, you get hungry. But try to estimate the magnitude of hunger as a social problem and the answer becomes a lot more complicated. Most people get hungry when they skip a meal, dieters try to tolerate hunger to lose weight, and some poor people scavenge for food out of garbage cans. If leftover fried chicken is all that the garbage contains, whoever eats it will not be hungry, but few would maintain that a person engaged in such behavior should not somehow be included in any count of hungry Americans.

These definitional issues bedeviled policymakers for many years. In 1977–78, however, the U.S. Department of Agriculture (USDA) distributed a food consumption survey that, for the first time, asked whether people always had enough to eat. The questionnaire was worded as follows:

Which of the following statements best describes the food eaten in your household?
1. Enough and the kinds of food we want to eat
2. Enough, but not always what we want to eat
3. Sometimes not enough to eat, or
4. Often not enough to eat

The intuitive good sense of these questions soon became the basis of most subsequent surveys.

Three years later, another USDA study introduced the concept of *potential hunger*. Incorporated into the 1984 *Report of the President's Task Force on Food Assistance*, the concept helped to distinguish between the clinical/medical condition of hunger—insufficient caloric intake—and circumstances in which someone cannot obtain enough food, even if the condition does not lead to a health problem.[4] In subsequent years, these ideas have become the basis of a standardized eighteen-question survey. Developed by the USDA's Food and Nutrition Service and refined by a federal interagency Food Security Measurement Project, this survey is specifically designed to gauge the prevalence and severity of various food insecurity indicators.[5]

Food policy research has also produced its own unique vocabulary. The term *food security* refers to assured access to enough food at all times for an active and healthy life. At a minimum, food security includes the availability

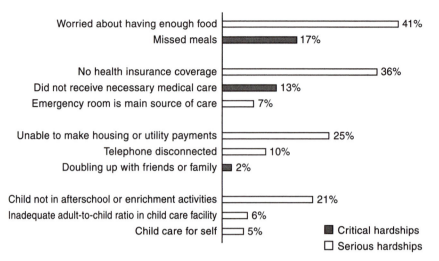

Worried about having enough food ⊏━━━━━━━━━━━━⊐ 41%
Missed meals ▓▓▓▓▓ 17%

No health insurance coverage ⊏━━━━━━━━━━⊐ 36%
Did not receive necessary medical care ▓▓▓ 13%
Emergency room is main source of care ⊏━⊐ 7%

Unable to make housing or utility payments ⊏━━━━━⊐ 25%
Telephone disconnected ⊏━⊐ 10%
Doubling up with friends or family ▓ 2%

Child not in afterschool or enrichment activities ⊏━━━━⊐ 21%
Inadequate adult-to-child ratio in child care facility ⊏⊐ 6%
Child care for self ⊏⊐ 5%

■ Critical hardships
□ Serious hardships

Food insecurity. Of all the hardships faced by families who earn less than twice the poverty rate, food insecurity is the most common.

of nutritionally adequate and safe foods and a guaranteed ability to acquire acceptable foods in socially acceptable ways (without stealing, scavenging, or resorting to emergency food supplies). Its opposite, *food insecurity,* occurs whenever the availability of nutritionally adequate and safe food, or the ability to acquire acceptable foods in socially acceptable ways, is limited or uncertain. *Hunger* is defined as the uneasy or painful sensation caused by a recurrent or involuntary lack of food and is a potential, though not necessary, consequence of food insecurity. Over time, hunger may eventually lead to malnutrition.[6]

This terminology now appears everywhere that policy analysts discuss hunger. Still, its widespread acceptance does not mean that questions do not continue to linger. Because people often fudge answers about how much they eat, analysts at conservative think tanks such as the Heritage Foundation have raised reasonable questions about the validity of surveys based on self-reporting. The problem is, however, that because people get hungry before they become malnourished, even the most expensive study of nutritional intake will always underestimate the level of hunger. And then there is the trade-off between the social science precision of a term like *food insecurity* and the emotional power of a word like hunger. To test the effect of this trade-off, just imagine that your social agency asked you to put together a fund-raiser. In your leaflet, would you refer to "hungry children" or to children who are "food insecure"?[7]

Nevertheless, these reservations cannot seriously diminish the accomplishments of food policy analysts over the past twenty-five years. They have developed a widely employed questionnaire and created a new vocabulary for talking about the problem of hunger in the United States. Using their questionnaire and this vocabulary, we can now estimate how many people in the United States have difficulty obtaining enough food.

Prevalence

Most studies are remarkably consistent. According to the best available research, about 10 percent of all American households face some degree of food insecurity, and about 4 percent experience actual hunger. Most poignant, of the 30 million people who live in food-insecure households, 12 million, or 40 percent, are children.[8]

The hunger and food insecurity of this population are not strictly limited to those in poverty. The USDA reported that nearly 40 percent of all households whose income was less than half of the poverty line experienced food insecurity, and 17 percent sometimes went hungry. But even up to twice the poverty line, 50 percent of all families also worried about food shortages or had difficulty finding food. Of course, a larger income did reduce the likelihood that someone in the household would actually experience hunger: at 185 percent of the poverty line, the rate of those who were hungry fell to 1.4 percent. Still, when they lost food stamps, got fired from a job, or gained a household member, even those above the poverty line often found themselves in a situation where they had to skimp on meals.[9]

The evidence of hunger and food insecurity shows itself however it is examined. To be sure, states do exhibit some disparities, from a low in North Dakota, where 5.1 percent of the population is food insecure, to a high in New Mexico, where food insecurity affects nearly 14 percent. In many U.S. metropolises, however, hunger seems to have intensified: the 2001 U.S. Conference of Mayors' annual twenty-seven-city survey estimated that requests for emergency food assistance had risen 23 percent. Indeed, the need was so acute that in 85 percent of these cities, the emergency food network had to limit either the frequency or quantity of their handouts.[10] Nor were conditions any better in rural areas, where 12 percent of households reported uncertainty about their ability to obtain enough food, and 3.4 percent said they experienced hunger.[11]

Some studies using the food security questionnaire on at-risk groups have found hunger prevalence rates that are five to ten times the national average.[12] Within the low-income population, those at high risk include Mexican Americans, families without health insurance, and those whose head has not completed high school. In one study among Asian and Mexican legal immigrants in California, Texas, and Illinois, 40 percent were food insecure without hunger and 41 percent were food insecure with hunger. Since about half of food-insufficient individuals live in employed families, the lack of a job does not, by itself, explain their food insecurity.[13]

Partly because of welfare reform, women represent a disproportionate share of those who receive emergency food aid. In one study by Second Harvest, a national network of nonprofit food banks, two-thirds of the recipients were women. No survey has yet documented how many of these women used to be on public assistance, but almost 15 percent of former welfare recipients have reported that it was often true food did not last, and almost 40 percent said it was sometimes true. Unable to increase their income, one group of former welfare recipients has apparently ended up on food lines.[14]

Yet, even if these studies have all established that some Americans do indeed go hungry, a cynic might ask another, still more hard-headed question. That some people are hungry is an unpleasant fact, but what difference does their hunger make for social policy? The short answer is that hunger leads to nutrient deficiencies and severe discomforts, which affect health, interfere with productivity and learning, and foster feelings of worthlessness and inadequacy. By almost any standard for social policy intervention, these are worthy concerns.

Nutrient Deficiencies

The consequences of hunger are most evident in children. The proportion of poor children with substandard intake of food energy is more than two and a half times the rate for children who are not poor. Inevitably, this food deficit shortchanges their nutrient intake. Between 1 and 4 million children take in too few calories and too little B_6, C, E, iron, and zinc. Poor children are six times as likely to consume insufficient vitamin A and magnesium. No wonder that, given these deficits, low-income food-insufficient children are more than three times as likely to have a poor health status as their high-income peers.[15]

Hunger is linked to an inability to concentrate at school. In one study, food-insufficient children ages 6–11 had significantly lower arithmetic scores. In addition, they were more likely to repeat a grade, struggle to get along with other children, and see a psychologist. Food-insufficient teenagers behaved similarly, except that schools usually suspended them instead of demanding that they repeat a grade. Besides disrupting other students' learning, hunger in children may also lead to a pervasive feeling of worthlessness.[16] Even if they cannot fully articulate their own deprivation, they may always carry with them the feeling that they never got—and perhaps did not truly deserve—adequate parental care.

Among adult women, food insufficiency has been closely linked to low intake (less than 50 percent of the recommended daily amount) of calories and eight essential nutrients. And while the food-insufficient elderly also suffer from inadequate consumption of some essential vitamins, they do not consume enough protein and calcium either. Overall, the members of food-insufficient households consume just a small fraction (8 to 18 percent) of thirteen different nutrients eaten in households that have enough food.[17]

For both children and adults, hunger has both physical and psychological consequences. Its social costs include the poorer health status of the people who are hungry as well as the effects of their plight on other, better-fed people. From education to health, from the effects of hunger on children to the effects of hunger on the elderly, any listing of these costs should have sufficed to trigger instant changes in food policy. In fact, however, the social costs of hunger have rarely played the decisive role in altering food policies because other important factors have instead held sway.

Social Change Triggers

Three different types of change have spurred developments in food policy. Rooted in the genuine social movements, the first type is most closely tied to entitlement programs like food stamps. It usually came about when many people noticed that some Americans were hungry and resolved to do something about it. But, like so many other changes in social policy, human need alone has rarely been sufficient. Instead, at other times, farm overproduction (an excess of agricultural goods) has been influential enough to qualify as a distinct second trigger of social change. On these occasions, the hungry were fed because agricultural interests pressured the government to dispose of their surplus food. Finally, there is the third and perhaps most contemporary model, in which the decline in government-sponsored food entitlement programs has created a vacuum in public policy that private charities have rushed to fill.

The classic example of the entitlement model comes out of the 1960s. The ferment of the era heightened people's awareness of hunger and poverty. Influenced by this new public mood, Senators Joseph Clark (D-Pennsylvania) and Robert Kennedy (D-New York), leaders of the Senate Subcommittee on Employment, Manpower, and Poverty, took an April 1967 tour of the Mississippi Delta, where they saw children with obvious signs of malnutrition. A May 21, 1968, CBS documentary, *Hunger in America*, aroused further interest. Soon thereafter, both houses of Congress held hearings, which led to the formation of the Senate Select Committee on Nutrition and Human Needs. The child care and summer food programs were established the same year, and two years later, amendments mandated uniform national eligibility standards for the food stamp program.[18] In the most straightforward and direct way, a social movement to address hunger and poverty did bring about social change.

Yet, even when social movements have brought about change in food policy, agricultural interests have often exercised a decisive influence. Federal commodity distribution began in 1933, after the Agricultural Adjustment Act came under heavy criticism for its slaughter of 6 million piglets to reduce pork supplies. Established in 1935 to streamline distribution, the Federal Surplus Commodities Corporation distributed various commodities until 1974, but, naturally, what it handed out depended on what was in surplus. Likewise, one of the early versions of the food stamp program in 1939 enabled relief recipients to obtain $1.50 of food stamps ($1 of orange stamps plus a $.50 bonus of blue stamps) for $1. Consumers could use the orange stamps for any food; blue stamps could be used to purchase only commodity surplus. The initial list of approved items included butter, eggs, flour, cornmeal, oranges, grapefruit, prunes, and dried beans. Later, during the Reagan administration, huge dairy surpluses led to the distribution in 1982 of 150 million pounds of cheese and 50 million pounds of butter. In all these examples, the hungry got food, but they got food because there was a surplus and their interests happened to correspond with the interests of farmers.[19]

Private charities distinguish the third kind of social change. Several factors contributed to the growing prominence of these charities. In 1981, Reagan ended funding for food stamp outreach programs, so that fewer people knew of this entitlement. While poverty among the poorest of the poor led to greater homelessness and hunger, the Republican presidents—Reagan, George Bush, and George W. Bush—have all encouraged charitable giving and "one thousand points of light" as the solution to the nation's social problems. Ironically, the one Democratic president, Bill Clinton, who did not emphasize "one thousand points of lights" was the president who ended an entitlement to public assistance. In this political environment, an extraordinary array of secular and religious institutions has sprung up to collect and distribute food. Yet the more this system develops, the more the pendulum swings from food provision as a government entitlement to the voluntary sector. In this instance, although a gap in social provision has served as a trigger for social change, many people interested in food policy continue to worry about whether it is social change of the right kind.[20]

These three types of social change—social movements leading to entitlement, the power of agricultural interests, and the rise of private charities to address a gap in social welfare—account for the primary changes in food policy that have occurred since the New Deal. In turn, these policy changes have resulted in the establishment and subsequent modification of eight major food programs. We describe these programs in the section that follows.

Food Programs

Of all the food programs, the food stamp program is doubtless the most famous; after all, it costs the most and benefits the largest number of clients. Yet by feeding people who would otherwise eat less or perhaps not at all, seven other food programs also perform a crucial function. These programs are the Supplemental Nutrition Program for Women, Infants, and Children (WIC); the National School Lunch Program; its close relative, the National School Breakfast program; the Summer Food Service Program for Children; the Child and Adult Care Food Program; the Emergency Food Assistance Program (TEFAP); and, spurred by TEFAP, the rise of a private food assistance network. The following brief summaries highlight the differences among them.

Food Stamps

Operating in all fifty states, food stamps supplement the food purchases of about 19.3 million low-income people. The program makes up the difference between the 30 percent of income that is supposed to be spent on food and

Food Stamps, 1964

Number of recipients:	19.3 million people (2002)
Who offers the benefit or service:	The state and local government are primarily responsible for the day-to-day administration of the program
What form does it take:	A voucher for food
To whom is it provided:	Households with gross incomes below 130 percent of the poverty line, which means that most TANF, SSI, and general assistance recipients are automatically eligible
At whose expense:	The federal government assumes responsibility for the cost of all food stamp benefits and half of the state's administrative costs. In 2001, total federal expenditures reached $17.5 billion.

Special Supplemental Nutrition Program for Women, Infants, and Children (WIC), 1972

Number of recipients:	7.5 million people
Who offers the benefit or service:	The federal government
What form does it take:	A voucher for specific foods
To whom is it provided:	Pregnant women, new mothers, infants, and children up to 5 years of age with income less than 185 percent of the poverty line
At whose expense:	The federal government pays for the total cost, which is currently budgeted at about $4.4 billion annually.

National School Lunch Program, 1946

Number of recipients:	27 million children
Who offers the benefit or service:	98,000 public and private nonprofit elementary and secondary schools and residential child care institutions
What form does it take:	Lunch at free or reduced prices
To whom is it provided:	Schoolchildren from families with gross income below 130 percent of the poverty line receive lunch for free; those between 130 and 185 percent of the poverty line receive reduced-price lunches
At whose expense:	The federal government pays for the program, which costs about $5.56 billion.

National School Breakfast, 1966

Number of recipients:	7.9 million children
Who offers the benefit or service:	72,000 schools and residential centers
What form does it take:	Free or reduced-price breakfasts
To whom is it provided:	Schoolchildren from families with gross income below 130 percent of the poverty line receive breakfast for free; those between 130 and 185 percent of the poverty line receive it at a reduced price
At whose expense:	The federal government pays for the program, which cost $1.49 billion in 2001.

Summer Food Service, 1968

Number of recipients:	2.1 million children, plus 1.1 million for lunches
Who offers the benefit or service:	Public and private nonprofit institutions

(continued)

Summer Food Service, 1968

What form does it take:	Free or reduced-price summer breakfasts and lunches
To whom is it provided:	Schoolchildren, according to the same eligibility standards as in the National School Breakfast and National School Lunch programs
At whose expense:	The federal government, at a cost of $298 million.

Child and Adult Care Food Program (CACFP), 1968

Number of recipients:	2.5 million children and 67,000 elderly daily
Who offers the benefit or service:	Day care centers, private nonprofit adult day facilities, homeless shelters, Head Start, and afterschool programs
What form does it take:	Free or reduced-price meals and snacks
To whom is it provided:	Children, according to the same eligibility standards as in the National School Breakfast and National School Lunch programs, and adults who are either functionally impaired or over age 60
At whose expense:	The federal government relies on grants to the states to pay for CACFP. The states then distribute this money to local social agencies. In 2000, the program's budget was $1.6 billion.

The Emergency Food Assistance Program (TEFAP), 1981

Number of recipients:	4 million households annually
Who offers the benefit or service:	The emergency food assistance network: community kitchens and food banks
What form does it take:	Surplus commodities
To whom is it provided:	Poor people who meet state guidelines that determine eligibility for surplus food
At whose expense:	The federal government spends about $200 million annually on TEFAP.

Private Food Assistance Network (early 1980s)

Number of recipients:	At least 23 million people annually (the number Second Harvest, one of its umbrella organizations, served)
Who offers the benefit or service:	Community kitchens and food pantries
What form does it take: food:	More than 2 billion pounds annually
To whom is it provided:	Poor people who cannot afford to pay the market price for food
At whose expense:	Everyone who donates food or money to a food charity.

the cost of a marginally nutritional diet (the Department of Agriculture Thrifty Food Plan). The Department of Agriculture's Food and Nutrition Service administers food stamps and gives direction to state welfare agencies. These agencies then establish whether clients meet the eligibility standards, calculate benefits, and issue the appropriate allotment. The federal government provides 100 percent funding of food stamp benefits and, in most cases, half of the state's administrative costs. In fiscal year 2001, total federal expenditures for the program reached $17.5 billion.[21]

Until recently, the food stamp program provided monthly coupons to eligible low-income families so they could purchase food. Now, however, some forty-four states, Puerto Rico, and the District of Columbia have replaced these coupons with an EBT (electronic benefit transfer) system. The EBT system offers participants a benefit card that is just like a bank card. In 2002, the maximum benefit that can be drawn on this card is $356 a month for three people and $452 monthly for four.

Eligibility for the program depends on both financial and nonfinancial factors. Most TANF, SSI, and general assistance recipients are automatically eligible. This rule is consistent with the regulation that all households except those including the elderly or disabled must have a gross income below 130 percent and a net income (after specified allowable deductions) below 100 percent of the poverty line. Households may also have up to $2,000 in countable assets, with a $3,000 exemption for the elderly (age 60 and up) and disabled.

After the 1998 Agricultural Research, Extension, and Education Act lifted the 1996 welfare reform ban against the provision of food stamps to all legal immigrants, children, the elderly, and disabled who were legal immigrants living in the United States when the law was passed (August 22, 1996) can receive benefits, though other legal immigrants and all undocumented immigrants remain ineligible. In addition, the work requirements from the 1996 Act, which restricted food stamp eligibility to between three and six months

Tightened food stamp eligibility requirements have made it harder for some poor people to obtain the necessary food.

for all able-bodied adults without dependents (unless they are working half time or engaged in some training activity), continue to apply.[22]

The amount of food stamps to which a household is entitled requires a simple calculation. Once you know the number of people in the household, its net monthly income, and the maximum monthly benefit levels, you determine the benefit by subtracting the expected contribution (30 percent of net income) from the maximum allotment. If, as we indicated, the maximum allotment for four people in 2002 was $452, and a household's net income was $600 a month, then the household would receive $272 a month in food stamps ($452 minus $180 [30 percent of $600] = $272). This budget is tight, and its tightness shows up in surveys of food stamp recipients, who often report that they exhaust their monthly benefits during the third week.[23]

The demographic characteristics of food stamp participants match those of most other programs for the poor. In 2000, 89 percent of all food stamp households lived in poverty, including 33 percent whose gross income was equal to or less than half the poverty line. Slightly more than 50 percent of all food stamp recipients were children, 39 percent were nonelderly adults, and 10 percent were elderly people. Food stamp households with children were somewhat larger than the national average, with 3.4 people compared to 2.3 people nationally. A single adult usually ran these households, almost half of whom received TANF aid.[24]

Until rising unemployment reversed the trend, the number of food stamp recipients had declined since the last recession, from 28 million people in 1994 (72 percent of the poor population) to 17 million, or about 52 percent, in 2000. This decline is not hard to explain. Forty-four percent of the decline occurred because fewer people were eligible to participate, 35 percent due to rising income and assets, and the remainder because of changes in eligibility rules. The rest of the decline may be attributed to confusion in the implementation of TANF, leading to unjustified denial of some applications, and the heightened stigma associated with food stamps as a welfare program in the wake of the 1996 reform.[25]

An ever more burdensome application process is perhaps the best example of the rising barriers to food stamp eligibility. Although food stamps have often been targets of fraud and abuse charges, repeated studies have found, at most, very little real evidence of fraud. Nevertheless, the states keep erecting higher hurdles. Food stamp applications within the fifty states now average twelve pages in length. California, New York, and twenty-seven other states ask applicants if they own a burial plot. Nevada and Nebraska want to know if applicants have sold their blood and for how much. Hawaii demands garage sale receipts, South Dakota totals bingo winnings, and on page twenty of a thirty-six-page application, Minnesota checks to see if anyone earns money from a paper route. Such a daunting application process surely gives pause to even the most eligible applicant.[26]

Although a wobbly economy has reversed the decline in program participation, the food stamp program remains extremely vulnerable. Born of a compromise between agribusiness interests who want to expand food consumption and urban liberals interested in obtaining more food for the poor, the program has suffered from the delicate arrangements required to sustain this coalition. That food stamps have always been a welfare program run out of the Department of Agriculture is perhaps this arrangement's most telling illustration. Lodged in a bureaucracy that was never designed to serve the poor, the program has suffered from charges of fraud and abuse, a failure to conduct outreach, and an intimidating and needlessly complex application process. The purpose of food stamps is surely to feed the poor. This list of impediments, however, suggests that there is a problem, and the problem is that as with other social welfare programs, helping the poor is not its only or even its primary goal.

Special Supplemental Nutrition Program for Women, Infants, and Children

The WIC program provides nutritious food, nutrition education, and access to health care for low-income pregnant women, new mothers, and infants and children at risk of poor nutrition. Piloted by Congress in 1972 and established as a national program two years later, WIC served about 7.5 million people in 2002. The federal government absorbs the total cost, currently budgeted at about $4.4 billion annually.[27]

The WIC program is different from food stamps. To begin with, it has a narrow target population: poor, pregnant women and their children up to 5 years of age who are at nutritional risk, rather than those who are at nutritional risk among the population as a whole. In addition, unlike food stamps, program recipients are not households, but individual women, infants, and children. WIC also provides vouchers that can be redeemed only for the purchase of specific food items; that is, assistance does not come in dollar amounts but in quantities of specific foods. Once income eligibility has been established, the size of the benefit is fixed: more income within the range of income eligibility does not reduce how much a participant receives. Finally, unlike food stamps, WIC is not an entitlement program, limiting its budget to what the federal government allocates in any given year.[28]

Four criteria determine WIC eligibility. At 185 percent of the poverty line, the WIC program has the highest income ceiling of any food program. Participants must be pregnant, postpartum breast-feeding women, or under 5 years old. A health care professional must certify the participant to be at nutritional risk, a standard that includes medical conditions such as inadequate diet, abnormal weight gain during pregnancy, and child growth problems like anemia, stunting, and underweight. In addition, any poor pregnant woman, mother, or young child at nutritional risk who already gets food stamps or Medicaid, or is a member of a family in which a pregnant woman or child gets Medicaid, is automatically eligible.[29]

Most women enrolled in WIC are 18 to 34 years old, prime childbearing years. Mothers of WIC infants are a little older, with fewer than 5 percent under age 18 and 16 percent over age 35. About 25 percent of the women are employed, and 44 percent are married. A majority complete high school.

The most notable change in WIC demographics during recent years has been the caseload's rapid expansion in the Western states. This regional shift reflects the rising share of Latinos receiving WIC, from 22 percent in 1988 to 32 percent in 1998. It also mirrors a small but significant number of Native Americans; hungry or food insecure at twice the rate of the population as a whole (22 percent), they now have fifty-seven thousand women, infants, and children in the program.[30]

Like many other food programs, WIC has always had to address the concerns of those who wonder if its benefits justify its costs. Admitting that WIC has increased the intake of some nutrients, such as iron, they have doubted the health effects of this increased consumption. In response, other food policy experts have insisted that iron deficiency is an important public health problem, because too little iron leads to long-term cognitive and behavioral delays. Much research supports their contention. In fact, the first thorough analysis of WIC found that women in the program had longer pregnancies, lower levels of fetal mortality, fewer premature births, and larger babies. Subsequently, a General Accounting Office study reported that $1 spent on WIC saves $3.50, mostly by avoiding low birthweights.[31] In this country, doubts about the value of social welfare programs never totally subside, yet, because WIC can offer documented proof of its success in helping a vulnerable and sympathetic population, it has been better able than most to withstand criticism.

National School Lunch Program

The National School Lunch Program (NSLP) was the first of the federal school food programs. In the aftermath of World War II, Congress became concerned that serious nutritional deficiencies had contributed to the high rate of rejection among draftees. That is why it enacted the NSLP in 1946 as a "measure of national security." Its passage was intended to ensure that American children ate at least one healthy meal every school day.[32]

Nowadays, the NSLP operates in almost ninety-eight thousand public and nonprofit private schools and residential centers. Together, these centers provide lunches to more than 27 million children. The institutions get the lunches through cash subsidies and USDA-donated commodities. Like the school breakfast program, the lunches must meet official dietary guidelines: no more than 30 percent of calories from fat, less than 10 percent from saturated fat, and 33 percent of the recommended daily allowance for calories, protein, iron, calcium, and vitamins A and C. In fiscal year 2000, the whole program cost the federal government $5.56 billion.[33]

The lunch program and the breakfast program have the same eligibility requirements: it is free for families with income up to 130 percent of the poverty line ($23,535 for a family of four in 2002), reduced for those between 130 and 185 percent ($33,492), and full price (though slightly subsidized) for students above that level. Although the program also offers afterschool snacks on the same basis, areas where at least 50 percent of all students receive free or reduced-price meals may serve all of their snacks for free. Under this system, during the school year 2001–02, the federal government paid $2.09 for each free meal, $1.69 for reduced-price meals, and a $.20 subsidy for meals served to students above the 185 percent ceiling. The subsidy for snacks was set at $.57, $.28, and $.05, respectively.[34]

The NSLP has received uniformly positive evaluations. Students ate more and better-quality food and, despite the concerns of some agricultural interests, there was no evidence that giving free food reduced their families' overall food expenditures. Participation in the program was relatively high, too: 79 percent of those eligible for free meals and 71 percent of those eligible for meals at a reduced price. Nevertheless, even these comparatively high percentages still mean that between 5 and 7 million children who are eligible for school lunches are not receiving them.[35]

School Breakfast Program

The School Breakfast Program is a federal entitlement program that offers cash assistance to the states for nonprofit breakfast programs in seventy-two thousand schools and residential children's facilities. The program began as a pilot project in 1966; when the government made it a permanent program in 1975, it gave administrative authority to the Food and Nutrition Service (FNS). The FNS drafts the regulations that require all school meals to meet official dietary guidelines. Under these rules, school breakfasts must provide one-fourth of the recommended caloric intake as well as an equivalent amount of protein, calcium, iron, and Vitamins A and C.[36]

Like the lunch program, the breakfast program offers three different levels of assistance. The first tier includes children from families with income at or below 130 percent of the federal poverty guidelines; these children receive free breakfasts. In the second tier, children from families with income between 130 and 185 percent of the poverty line get their breakfast for no more than $.30. Except for those school districts with universal free breakfast programs, children from families above this level fit into the third tier and pay most of their meal costs, minus the subsidy all student meals receive from the federal government. During the 2001–02 school year, the federal government reimbursed schools $1.15 for each free meal, $.85 for all reduced-price meals, and $.21 for every paid meal. Schools in Alaska, Hawaii, and severe-need districts (where at least 40 percent of the children receive free or reduced-price meals) receive a little more. On a typical school day in 2001, the program fed about 7.9 million children at an annual cost of $1.49 billion.[37]

The beneficial effects of the school breakfast program are rarely disputed. Once breakfast is defined not as fifty calories but as a substantial meal—for instance, intake of food energy greater than 10 percent of the RDA—the likelihood of eating breakfast is significantly greater for low-income elementary students attending schools with the school breakfast program than for those who do not (82 vs. 66 percent). Researchers at Boston Medical Center also reported that participants scored higher on achievement tests and had lower rates of tardiness and absenteeism. Likewise, Harvard Medical Center discovered that children who participated in the school breakfast program improved both academically and psychosocially.[38]

These positive benefits suggest that service gaps constitute the program's main problem. In this respect, there may well be lessons to be learned from Arkansas, Kentucky, Mississippi, Oregon, and West Virginia, the five best-performing states. If the school breakfast program performed as well in the other forty-five states, another $300 million would be become available for additional food and staff. This measure would constitute a helpful interme-diate step. Although it is unlikely that the school breakfast program will ever reach a point where it feeds every needy child, advocates do believe that we could take some major strides toward that goal if eligibility for school break-fasts were better integrated with the receipt of food stamps and TANF. To increase participation, they also recommend greater outreach to parents, stu-dents, and the general public.[39]

Summer Food Service Program for Children

As the Second Harvest National Food Bank Network has reported, 47 per-cent of the food banks experiencing seasonal changes in requests for emer-gency food found that children's need for emergency food spikes during sum-mer vacation.[40] Policymakers designed the Summer Food Service Program with this need in mind.

Congress established the program in 1968. Administered by the USDA, Summer Food Service is an entitlement program that enables public and private nonprofit institutions to provide nutritious meals when school is not in session. A wide variety of institutions are eligible for sponsorship, including schools, residential camps, and units of local, tribal, or state government. In the summer of 2000, the program fed 2.1 million children daily, plus another 1.1 million through the summer extension of school lunches. The combined programs therefore reach about 21 percent of those served free or reduced-price lunches during the regular school year at a cost of about $298 million.[41]

Children receive one or two meals a day at most sites, though FNS may authorize a full complement of three meals at camps that serve migrant work-ers. In summer 2002, the maximum reimbursement rate for these meals was $1.32 for breakfast and $2.30 for lunch or supper, plus $.53 for a snack. Administrative costs of $.13, $.24, and $.06, respectively, supplement these allowances.[42]

The Summer Food Service Program has twice been subjected to significant scrutiny. It was first tarnished by rumors of mismanagement in the mid-1970s, when three-quarters of the sponsors were nonprofit groups such as churches and neighborhood organizations, many of which were poorly equipped to handle food. Their problems gave Reagan a chance to end the program. Although he did not succeed, his Omnibus Reconciliation Act of 1981 did bar nonprofits from participation. As a result, between 1981 and 1982, 30 percent of sponsors left the program and the number of children served dropped from 1.9 to 1.4 million. It took another ten years to rebuild.[43]

In 1996, welfare reform targeted the program again. Cutting reimbursement rates by 10 percent (at the time, about $.19 a meal), the cuts may partly explain why from 1999 to 2000, enrollment in the Summer Food Service Program declined by 3 percent while enrollment in the National School Lunch Program climbed by 7 percent. Responding to a Food Research and Action Center report about this decline, Congress authorized a pilot program that reduces paperwork and simplifies cost accounting for sponsors in thirteen states and Puerto Rico. The District of Columbia, Nevada, and California rank as having the highest level of participation in the Summer Food Program. If, boosted by this congressional initiative, all the other states performed at the average of the top three, another 3.1 million children would be able to eat better meals in the summer.[44]

Child and Adult Care Food Program

The Child and Adult Care Food Program (CACFP) funds meals and snacks for children in licensed child care facilities including day care centers, Head Start, recreation centers, settlement houses, and afterschool programs; public and private nonprofit adult day facilities are also eligible if they provide services to nonresidential adults who are at least 60 years old or functionally impaired. In addition, after breaking with its 1999 prohibition against services in residential facilities, CACFP began to allow reimbursement for up to three meals served to children of families who reside in homeless shelters.[45]

CACFP is administered through grants to the states. Although most states designate the state department of education as the responsible authority, several others rely on another agency such as health or social services. Like other food programs, CACFP subsidies have the same subsidy thresholds: up to 130 and 185 percent of the poverty line for free and subsidized meals, respectively. By law, day care facilities in low-income areas merit a Tier I designation, which makes all children eligible for free meals. Those facilities that are not in a low-income neighborhood must identify low-income children eligible for free meals on an individual basis; otherwise, the meals they serve are merely reduced in price.[46]

Larger than the Summer Food Program but smaller than food stamps, WIC, or the two meals-in-school programs, CACFP served 2.5 million children daily and 67,000 elderly people in fiscal year 2000, for a total of 1.6 billion meals and snacks. The program's budget was $1.6 billion.[47]

The Emergency Food Assistance Program

Begun in 1981, TEFAP distributes commodities to the hungry. At the time, the USDA stored more than 1 billion pounds of surplus food nationally, including 200 million pounds that were either frozen or refrigerated in underground tunnels beneath Kansas City. The cost of storing this food combined with the recession of the early 1980s to spawn a Temporary Emergency Food Assistance Program. Subsequently, in 1988, the Hunger Prevention Act committed the Department of Agriculture to purchase additional commodities for distribution to low-income households and the local emergency food network. To acknowledge this changed role, the 1990 farm bill then renamed the program the Emergency Food Assistance Program.[48]

In the first few years of TEFAP, the program distributed surplus food—mostly dairy products such as cheese and nonfat milk, but also wheat flour, cornmeal, and honey—to as many as 19 million people per month. In recent years, however, those numbers have diminished, to the point where TEFAP distributes surplus food worth more than $229 million to about 4 million households annually. Each state determines eligibility for the program and adjusts income standards according to statewide needs. These standards may include participation in existing food or assistance programs that use income as an eligibility criterion.

TEFAP is one of the smaller federal food programs. In 2002, its total federal budget amounted to about $200 million.[49] TEFAP also fits well with the conservative drift of policy. Administered by a private food network using federal funds, it is the federal food program that most resembles charity. It distributes food, not money, which appeals to those worried about the misuse of food stamps. It pleases farmers by moderating the supply of farm products and providing price stability. It soothes antihunger activists, who are angry about the failure of other food programs to reach the needy. Even the food industry likes it, because when they donate excess food to local food banks, they get goodwill instead of a bill for its disposal. In effect, spreading its benefits so widely has garnered broad support for TEFAP to institutionalize a private food distribution network.[50]

The Private Food Assistance Network

With government funds from TEFAP spearheading its development, the private food assistance network has mushroomed. According to Second Harvest, one of its umbrella organizations, just its own network served more than 23 million people in 2001, including 7 million different people each week, and now gives away between 2 and 2.5 billion pounds of food each year. Sixty-four percent of these recipients have an income at or below the official federal poverty line, and 10 percent are homeless. Thirty-nine percent of the families include at least one employed adult; the same percentage consists of children under 18 years of age. The racial composition of those served was 45 percent white, 35 percent African American, and 17 percent Latino.[51]

The spread of this charitable food network depends on individual acts by a large number of Americans. In one recent study, 79 percent of all Americans claimed to have helped the hungry, a plausible number if people simply mean that they donated a can of soup to their local food bank. The system certainly invests single acts of charity with enormous personal appeal, uplifting the

Founded in 1981, City Harvest is the world's oldest and largest food rescue program, delivering food to community food programs throughout New York City.

charitable by giving them the feeling that they have made a difference. Nevertheless, advocates estimate that between 1995 and 2002, they would have had to increase their food acquisition by 425 percent just to keep pace with food stamp cuts. Individual acts of charity shrink before a problem of this size.[52]

The charitable network is more informal and flexible than a government program. It certainly makes people feel better than paying taxes to fund an entitlement to food. Yet charity lacks consistent funding and may require submission to some religious auspices. It promises Thanksgiving turkey and Christmas ham, but cannot ensure enough different kinds of the right foods the rest of the year. Because charitable organizations cannot guarantee an adequate supply of volunteers, the network itself grows topsy-turvy; for example, the two wealthiest city council districts in Manhattan have more soup kitchens than the two poorest, because that is where the churches and synagogues with resources are. Compare a cash entitlement with collecting food and taking it to a collection point, then to a local pantry, and then to an individual person, and it is also notably inefficient. Add the indignity of waiting in line to get meals and the power differential embodied in the charitable relationship between givers and receivers, and the case for a charitable solution to the problem of hunger gets even weaker.[53]

The problem of poverty and insufficient income for food dwarfs the efforts of an army of even the best-intentioned volunteers. The feeling that they can do something about a serious social problem is empowering; it provides volunteers with some necessary moral relief. Charity, however, is supposed to be about the material needs of the poor and not about the emotional needs of the charitable. The emergency food network may feed the hungry, though inadequately. In the meantime, however, serious questions remain about whether its existence sidetracks policymakers from a public entitlement to food that would constitute a more effective approach to the issue of hunger.

Classifying Food Programs: Who, What, to Whom, and at Whose Expense

Before we apply the policy model, let's first classify these programs. One helpful system of classification groups the programs by asking four specific questions: *who, what, to whom,* and *at whose expense. Who* refers to the sector that delivers the benefit: Is it public, private, or some combination? *What* refers to the content of the benefit, in this case, whether participants receive cash, a voucher, or food. *To whom* speaks to the issue of eligibility; it asks about the population served, both its economic status, poor or near poor, and its age (children and/or adults). *At whose expense* inquires after the source of the money: Does it come from taxpayers, or from private charity? Together, the responses to these questions offer a new perspective on the food programs.[54]

Most food programs operate under public auspices. Food stamps, the WIC program, and the school breakfast, lunch, and summer programs all fall in this category. CACFP is also public, except both it and the summer food program permit a variety of public and private nonprofit agencies to distribute the food. The balance finally shifts with TEFAP, which combines government surplus with charitable contributions into a privately administered network of food pantries and community kitchens.

But what form does this assistance take? Food stamps come in dollar amounts and are almost like cash, although the program does prohibit recipients from purchasing liquor, tobacco, and hot foods prepared for immediate consumption. WIC is stricter: it offers a voucher that is good only for specific food items. The rest—all the school programs, CACFP, and TEFAP—offer food, though the programs that deliver food through institutions like schools and child care centers provide more balanced meals than TEFAP and the private assistance network, which may offer just random commodities. The food programs may now be largely public, but their emphasis on in-kind benefits carries on a tradition dating back to early nineteenth-century America, when the first organized charities begin to give food because they thought that money given to the poor would only be drunk and gambled away.[55]

And to whom are these programs directed? Poor people, but poor people defined according to several different standards. The food stamp program defines the eligible population as all poor people with income up to 130 percent of the poverty line. WIC expands this definition to those with income up to 185 percent of the poverty line but restricts the population to women, infants, and children. Although CACFP, the two programs at school, and the summer food program also set a limit of 185 percent, they differ in other respects. The school and summer programs serve children, and CACFP serves children in child care centers and adults in nonresidential facilities. Finally, TEFAP targets the poor but lets the states establish eligibility standards. Food programs are clearly categorical programs for the poor, but they put different people in this category.

As to who pays for these programs, except for the private food network, the taxpayer foots the bill in every instance. The one distinction is that food stamps, the school and summer food programs, and CACFP are entitlements, where the federal government must cover all eligible people, in contrast to WIC and TEFAP, which have budgetary limits.

Overall, then, food policy consists of publicly funded programs overseen by the public sector but delivered in part by a mixed public/private system. The programs target the poor and near poor, giving them some cash-like stamps, restricted vouchers in the WIC program, and a lot of food. This summary helps us understand food policy and prepares the way for our use of the policy model.

Economics

After pharmaceuticals, food is the second most profitable industry in the United States.[56] But because the cost of food lies beyond the reach of some poor people, the economics of food policy has always reflected the uneasy conflict between helping farmers and feeding the poor. By restricting the kind of aid provided, the business of agriculture has usually triumphed in this conflict.

Three different restrictions have been placed on this assistance. The first restricted the circumstances under which it was given; the second insisted that the aid should always help, rather than harm, the industry's profitability; and the third influenced the nature of the aid so that agricultural interests would always benefit.

The restriction on circumstances helped the food industry retain political control and rationed the provision of aid. This control has remained unchallenged for the past seventy years, except for two brief periods during the 1930s and 1960s, when social movements elevated the importance of feeding the hungry to a position of equality with the interests of commercial agriculture. Once the social movements subsided, however, these commercial interests reasserted their dominance. Marking this return to normal, a 1940 USDA report about an early food stamp program stated that the program's "principal objective is to raise farmers' income by increasing the demand for their products and so to use food surplus to improve the diets of undernourished families in this country."[57] Likewise, attacks on fraud in the food stamp program began in the 1970s, after the social movements of the previous decade had died down.

Because of their economic power, agricultural interests were also able to insist that food policy must always boost farm income. Even when the urban poor were hungry, farm subsidies kept prices high. Surplus food might be distributed if it could not be sold, but the distribution had to be carefully managed to limit it to random commodities. Cheese and nonfat milk do not amount to a balanced meal; that is one reason why both could be given away in 1981, because there was too much to sell, and with price supports, giving it away would not depress farmers' income.

The third economic principle restricts the type of aid to food-specific purchasing power (food stamps) or commodities. Food stamps can be used to deepen the market for food. Although agricultural interests like food stamps for this very reason, they recognize that if a surplus develops, the market, even a market supplemented by food stamps, cannot absorb it. Then they turn to commodities.

Commodity distribution can take several forms. The USDA gives surplus food to day care centers. Companies producing tomato sauce donate the mislabeled cases to the community food pantry, where it may sit on the shelf next to the three-day-old bread from the local bakery. Of course, a straight cash subsidy would enable poor people to purchase whatever they need. But if existing income support programs do not enable people to buy enough food, the food industry consistently influences the form the aid takes.[58]

These three restrictions demonstrate that the economics of food policy closely resembles the economics underlying many other social welfare issues. In each instance, some basic human need, such as housing, health care, or food, is organized as a for-profit enterprise. Poor people, who do not have enough money to enable the producers to make a profit, lie outside this self-enclosed system. The question then becomes how we preserve this system while addressing their needs. As always, the answer is that the core of the for-profit system continues unchanged, and that in food policy, we feed the poor with what are, at least programmatically, the leftovers.

Politics

The politics of food policy are largely rooted in the structure of the U.S. government. Once again, the key fact is that our Congress has two houses: a House of Representatives in which seats are allocated by population and a Senate in which every state regardless of population has two members. This arrangement gives rural states disproportionate power. In a classic example of this power, the rural states have worked to ensure that the food stamp program always reflects their interests.

Because farmers often had large surpluses, these became a major problem for a Democratic Party dominated by rural Southerners. But as the mechanization of Southern agriculture freed Southern Democrats from the necessity of defending an economy based on tenant farmers and the plantation system, they became willing to accept the food stamp program in exchange for an extension of commodity subsidies. Admittedly, their hands were forced on this issue, because as the New Deal aged, some urban Democrats also gained enough congressional seniority to challenge them.[59]

Politics and administration go hand in hand. As agricultural politics have always dominated food policy, the Department of Agriculture has run food programs ever since 1935, when food distribution was shifted from the Federal Surplus Relief Corporation. The Department of Agriculture represents different interests from those of the Department of Health and Human Services; it is concerned not with the welfare of the poor, but with the welfare of farmers. If the Department of Health and Human Services administered food stamps, the program would not have stuck quite so closely to its origins as a farm subsidy.

This agricultural dominance has other political consequences. In Congress, food stamps fall under the jurisdiction of the agricultural committees, where, as the welfare program in their midst, it must compete with price supports and other farm initiatives. Separated from committees like House Ways and Means, it is hard to coordinate its operation with other income maintenance programs. And lacking a real political home in Congress, food and hunger policy has had to depend on the establishment of select committees. Although these committees have conducted special investigations of this issue, their temporary status often undercuts their capacity to muster long-term political support.[60]

Food is therefore a policy orphan. Lacking both administrative protection within the federal bureaucracy and a political protector in Congress, it rivals welfare in its lack of political clout. Both have some urban liberals behind them; the difference is that the Department of Health and Human Services oversees some unpopular welfare programs, while food for the poor is attached, however weakly, to the Department of Agriculture and its support of farming as a commercial enterprise. In this less than hospitable environment, it is hardly surprising that food policy should seek to gain some political traction by falling back on the ideological appeal of voluntarism.

Ideology

Have you ever donated clothing? Have you ever donated food? When you participate in some charitable enterprise, do you feel better about yourself because you believe you are making some small dent in the world's social problems? The belief that charitable enterprises are the best way of handling our social problems is called voluntarism. With the decline of an entitlement to food, it has once again claimed its place as a guiding American ideology.

President Reagan evoked this tradition when he commemorated the one hundredth anniversary of United Way in 1986. Reagan said,

> Since earliest times, we Americans have joined together to help each other and to strengthen our communities. Our deep-rooted spirit of caring, of neighbor helping neighbor, has become an American trademark—and an American way of life. Over the years, our generous and inventive people have created an ingenious network of voluntary organizations to give help where help is needed.[61]

Food as charity reflects Reagan's sentiments. We give food to people who are hungry, and we glory in this tradition. It is the tradition of one-on-one, of localism and direct assistance that circumvents those unwieldy government bureaucracies. And in some ways, of course, it makes a lot of sense. If your neighbors are hungry, shouldn't you feed them?

The people who engage in charitable enterprises are, by and large, sensitive, compassionate, and well meaning; a critique of the ideology of voluntarism is not meant as a personal criticism of them. Nor is it intended to deny that across a whole range of issues, from shelter to food, the voluntary sector does provide some significant help. Reflecting on this help, however, we are also obligated to note that the United States trails behind most other advanced industrial countries in its treatment of the poor. Indeed, the indicators of this lag—no national health insurance, no family allowance, a high rate of poverty and infant mortality, record levels of imprisonment and frequent capital punishments—have been amply demonstrated throughout this book. For critics of reliance on the charitable, the question then arises of whether there is a connection between this charitable tradition and the prominence of these indicators.

This connection exists as "repressive benevolence." Originally Christian in its orientation, charity as repressive benevolence makes giving conditional on the poor's gratitude and willingness to change. Do what your betters want, and they will offer to feed, clothe, and shelter you. But reject the virtues of civilization, and punishment—a punishment often accompanied by violence—will soon follow. Although the history of Native Americans surely constitutes the leading example of this pattern, the treatment of the poor belongs to the same tradition. Repeatedly, charity has combined with sentimentalization of the poor to obstruct the passage of new public programs.[62]

Food fits this ideology well. We can all relate to hunger, most of us can share something from our plate or cupboard, and we can all take pleasure in doing a good deed. Advocates of voluntarism say this list is sufficient. Its critics count the number of hungry people and say otherwise.

Because the prospect of hunger is so emotionally affecting, diversity is the hallmark of the social movement against it. The major antihunger organizations and the dates of their establishment include the Food Research and Action Center (1970), Bread for the World (1973), Interfaith Impact for Peace and Justice (1974), World Hunger Year (1975), Second Harvest (1979), the Center on Budget and Policy Priorities (1981), and the Tufts (now the Brandeis) Center on Hunger and Poverty (1990). In addition, a number of religious organizations such as Catholic Charities, the Lutheran Office for Governmental Affairs, the Presbyterian Hunger Program, and Mazon ("the Jewish response to hunger") also do antihunger work.

Three differences distinguish a movement of such diversity. The first is the divide between the secular (e.g., Food Research and Action Center) and the religious (e.g., Catholic Charities); the second, between local research-based institutes (e.g., the Brandeis Center on Hunger and Poverty) and national umbrella organizations (e.g., Second Harvest); and the third between advocacy (e.g., Center on Budget and Policy Priorities) and service (e.g., Second Harvest and Catholic Charities). Although the division among these organizations is not absolutely fixed, some patterns do appear. At one extreme, no major religious organization targets the root causes of poverty; at the other, no research institute functions as a service organization. In between, there are a host of national organizations that, to varying degrees, try to blend education, advocacy, and service.[63]

The social movement against hunger therefore appeals to both religious and secular organizations that wish to render service in the face of such dire need. While their primary purpose is to feed hungry people, more militant advocacy groups gravitate to the issue of hunger for other reasons. To them, the existence of hunger dramatizes income inequality, documents the effects of cutbacks in entitlements, and creates solidarity with those whose plight is most desperate.[64] In short, whether your interest is in preventing human suffering, investing in the labor force of tomorrow, or criticizing what your organization identifies as blatant injustices in the social structure, hunger in the United States is multilayered enough in its implications to provide a cause for almost everyone.

History

The public provision of lunch was the first of all U.S. food programs. The program began locally in the Philadelphia school system during the early twentieth century. New York City's Board of Education followed in 1919, when it assumed responsibility for school lunches in the Bronx and Manhattan. But federal involvement did not began until 1933, when reaction to the Agricultural Adjustment Agency's slaughter of 6 million pigs led to the creation, in 1935, of the Federal Surplus Commodities Corporation. Transferred to the Department of Agriculture, it soon shifted its focus from unemployment relief to surplus disposal.[65]

World War II brought further program developments. The Federal Surplus Commodity Corporation distributed produce to schools, employing people in lunchrooms and, in the aftermath of the war, establishing a precedent for passage of the National School Lunch Act of 1946. Conceived as another alternative to commodity distribution, food stamps also made their first appearance in 1939. Offering a broader range of food than those stockpiled by the Federal Surplus Commodities Corporation, this program benefited grocery stores and provided a more varied diet for the hungry. But despite involving 4 million people in half of all U.S. counties, it lasted only until wartime employment eliminated the need.

In the 1950s, some senators, such as George Aiken (D-Vermont), Robert La Follette Jr. (R-Wisconsin), and Leonor Sullivan (D-Maryland), pushed to restore the food stamp program. It was not until 1959, however, that the secretary of Agriculture was granted authority to experiment, and another two years before President Kennedy piloted a program in five states. Although the administration moved to shift funding to a permanent appropriation in 1963, the urban Democrats and rural Southerners could not come to agreement until after the Kennedy assassination, when they brokered a deal for a wheat and cotton bill in exchange for a food stamp program. President Johnson signed the bill in August 1964.

In social welfare policy as well as in other matters, President Nixon liked to centralize authority. Replacing an optional program that had widely varying regulations in the states, his administration enacted the 1970 amendments that mandated uniform national resource and eligibility standards. The initial program also required participants to make a cash purchase of food stamps at face value, based on family income and size. But this policy did not work because some people did not have enough cash, and others (in the rural South) rarely used money. Still, the cash purchase requirement was not eliminated until 1977.

The same law also severed automatic food stamp eligibility for those receiving AFDC or SSI. Although Reagan did reestablish this linkage in 1985, his administration reduced program benefits and eliminated eligibility for strikers and college students.[66] In 1996, the welfare reform bill instituted further cutbacks with its prohibition on legal immigrants (since partially rescinded) and its limits on the receipt of food stamps to three months out of every thirty-six for single unemployed individuals between 18 and 50 years old.[67]

The history of the other programs parallels the history of food stamps. From the breakfast program (1966) to the Child and Adult Care Food Program (1968) and WIC (1972), most were established during the social movements of the 1960s or their immediate aftermath. Although some of the programs for children have demonstrated greater resiliency, government cutbacks have spurred the shift to a network of charitable food providers. The containment and trimming of these programs demonstrates once again that inside the larger patterns of expansion and contraction, the durability of some welfare programs depends, in part, on their recipients' perceived worthiness.

Conclusion

Charity or entitlement? Food programs represent a clear test of this basic policy issue. Although the testing has gone on for some time, Americans do not yet seem to have agreed on a standard for evaluating the results. By all accounts, while the number of hungry Americans continues to grow, this evidence does not necessarily lead us to rethink our attitude toward charity. In a world beset by a multitude of intractable social problems, the presence of so many poor people is paradoxically empowering: feed them, and we feel better. Yet it is also possible to evaluate food policy by another standard. Because this standard holds that banishing hunger requires comprehensive public policies, it is one that in recent years Americans have been reluctant to adopt.

IV

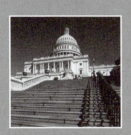

Conclusions

13

If You Want to Analyze a Policy . . .

In the first chapter of this book, we stressed that every form of social work practice embodies a social policy. Twelve chapters later, does what we have learned confirm this statement?

To answer this question, consider the human service jobs you have had in the past and what you are doing now in your school field placement. Picture the kind of social work you hope to do in the future. In all these settings, most of your clients probably got help from the income support programs detailed in chapter 8. Some may participate or hope to participate in the job training programs analyzed in chapter 9. If they are not actually homeless, they may still have the housing problems that chapter 10 addresses or face the health issues discussed in chapter 11. Perhaps the most desperately poor among them are even experiencing hunger, which chapter 12 described.

A look at this list supports one of our most basic contentions: no matter how hard you worked before, it always helps to learn about social welfare policies because they frame the social problems your clients face and pay you to do your job.

Learning about social welfare policy, we have repeatedly encountered five cardinal themes. The first is the premise that because practice embodies policy, knowledge about policy is essential to ensure that our practice is conscious and informed. We need this knowledge to solve problems for our clients, to maintain our own job satisfaction, and to participate as members of the social work community in the development of social welfare. Inevitably, this principle evokes a still broader conception of our role as true public citizens, who care about social welfare policy, understand its effects on people, and can speak from experience on a wide range of policy issues.

Another theme that runs through this text is social change. Because social policies are never permanent, it is predictable that one social policy will inevitably replace another. But what causes these changes in U.S. social welfare policy? Do we have any control over them? Do some triggers of social change have a more positive effect on social welfare? Our analysis of these questions has found that although social change has many different political and economic causes, the biggest leaps in the development of social welfare policy have always involved the active participation of many people in great social movements. When participants in these movements demonstrated, protested, and took to the streets, social policy moved ahead. Although social change certainly continued after these movements subsided, economic elites dominated the politics of these periods, and they used the quiet to contain or even roll back the advances made in the preceding era.

The next three themes all revolve around the policy model. Each time we turned to our model, we learned about the five basic factors that influence

How do we allocate resources? The answer to this question changes with each powerful social movement.

policy development in the U.S. welfare state. Knowledge about these factors help us to understand the often hostile policy environment in which social workers operate. It not only explains why the development of social welfare policy here lags behind other countries but also suggests what strategies for social change have been most successful in this environment.

The policy model also maintained the continuity of two other themes. The first taught the content of policy issues, so that when we applied it to the five areas of income support programs, job training, housing, health, and food, we learned some important information about social policy. A second theme emerged in this process: learning the content gave you practice in the uses of the methodology. The idea is that once you see the model applied to these five issues, you will be able to apply it, too.

When you do apply it, it is critical to give full weight to two opposing forces: those resisting and those propelling social change. It is important to give the forces resisting social change their full weight; otherwise, if you are trying to alter public policy, something you did not expect will surely blindside you. As we have consistently found, Americans have a default preference for markets and fragmented government and an ideology of individualism, residualism, and blame for the "unworthy poor." From health care reform to job training, we are also graced with a social welfare history that does not sparkle with successes. Social workers who ignored these factors would be more than merely naïve. They would do so at their peril.

Yet there is no reason to get too depressed. As the policy model demonstrates, significant changes in social policy have occurred in the past, and social workers have often played a crucial role in bringing them about. Here is where the policy model can be most useful, because it helps to highlight those occasions during which Americans have changed both their economics and politics in pursuit of a more authentically democratic national community.

Draw, then, on the model to analyze social welfare policy whenever you encounter it. Use it in your everyday practice with clients, as well as in broader contexts. In particular, use it to pinpoint the factors that have furthered positive social changes, and perhaps you, in your future role as a social worker, will be able to make such changes again.

Notes

Chapter 1

1. The National Association of Social Workers, *Code of Ethics*, revised 1999, http://www.naswdc.org/Code/ethics.htm, accessed March 15, 2003.
2. Piotr Sztompka, *The Sociology of Social Change* (Malden, MA: Blackwell, 1993), 99–100.
3. Ibid., 101, 113.
4. Charles Harper, *Exploring Social Change: America and the World* (Upper Saddle River, NJ: Prentice-Hall, 1998), 78–80.
5. Sztompka, *The Sociology of Social Change*, 155.
6. See, for example, Charles Tilly's critique of nineteenth-century theory building in *Big Structures, Large Processes, Huge Comparisons* (New York: Russell Sage Foundation, 1984).
7. For example, Neil Gilbert and Paul Terrell, *Dimensions of Social Policy*, 4th ed. (Boston. Allyn and Bacon, 1998); Donald E. Chambers, *Social Policy and Social Programs: A Method for the Practical Public Policy Analyst*, 3d ed. (Boston. Allyn and Bacon, 2000).
8. For a fuller discussion of this conflict, see James O' Connor, *The Fiscal Crisis of the State* (New York: St. Martin's Press, 1973), 6.
9. For a discussion of these dynamics, see Gary T. Marx and Douglas McAdam, *Collective Behavior and Social Movements: Process and Structure* (Englewood Cliffs, NJ: Prentice-Hall, 1993).
10. For the origin of this phrase, see Harold Wilensky, introduction to Harold Wilensky and Charles M. Lebeaux, *Industrial Society and Social Welfare* (New York: Free Press, 1965), xvi–xvii.

Chapter 2

1. Bruce S. Jansson, *Becoming an Effective Policy Advocate: From Policy Practice to Social Justice* (Pacific Grove, CA: Brooks/Cole, 1999), 13.
2. Elizabeth A. Segal and Stephanie Brzuzy, *Social Welfare Policy, Programs and Practice* (Itasca, IL.: F.E. Peacock, 1998), 9.
3. Martin Rein, *Social Policy: Issues of Choice and Change* (New York: Random House, 1970), 3.
4. *Webster's New Universal Unabridged Dictionary*, 2d ed, (New York: Simon & Schuster, 1983), 2077.
5. Richard Titmuss, *Essays on the Welfare State* (Boston: Beacon Press, 1963), 16.
6. Howard Jacob Karger and David Stoesz, *American Social Welfare Policy: A Pluralist Approach* (Boston: Allyn and Bacon, 2002), 3.
7. Walter Friedlander, *Introduction to Social Welfare*, 5th ed. (Englewood Cliffs, NJ: Prentice-Hall, 1961), 4.
8. The term *social work* differs from social welfare policy and social services. Social work refers to a professional occupation.
9. Philip Popple and Leslie Leighninger, *Social Work, Social Welfare and American Society*, 4th ed. (Boston: Allyn and Bacon, 1999), 68–69; John H. Ehrenreich, *The Altruistic Imagination: A History of Social Work and Social Policy in the United States* (Ithaca, NY: Cornell University Press, 1985), 121–122; Stanley Wenocur and Michael Reisch, *From Charity to Enterprise: The Development of Social Work in a Market Economy* (Urbana, IL: University of Chicago Press, 1989), 147–166.
10. Neil Gilbert, *Capitalism and the Welfare State: Dilemmas of Social Benevolence* (New Haven: Yale University Press, 1983), 7–8.
11. Michael B. Fabricant and Steve Burghardt, *The Welfare State Crisis and the Transformation of Social Service Work* (Armonk, NY: M.E. Sharpe, 1992), 118–119.
12. About 82 percent of all nursing homes operate for profit; about half of these are recipients of public Medicaid funds. Neil Gilbert and Paul Terrell, *Dimensions of Social Welfare Policy*, 5th ed. (Boston: Allyn and Bacon, 2002), 53.
13. Mimi Abramovitz, "Privatizing the Welfare State: A Review," *Social Work* 31 (July/August 1986), 257–265; Mimi Abramovitz and Irwin Epstein, "The Politics of Privatization: Industrial Social Work and Private Enterprise," *Urban & Social Change Review* 16.1 (winter 1983): 13–19.
14. Karger and Stoesz, *American Social Welfare Policy*, 168–170.
15. U.S. Joint Committee on Taxation, *Estimates of Federal Tax Expenditures for the Fiscal Year, 1999–2003* (Washington, DC: U.S. Government Printing Office, December 1998).
16. Mimi Abramovitz, "Everyone Is Still on Welfare: The Role of Redistribution in Social Policy," *Social Work* 46.4 (October 2001): 297–308.
17. Ibid.
18. Peter Dreier, "The Truth about Federal Housing Subsidies: Socialism for the Rich, Capitalism for the Poor," in Chester Hartman, Rachel Bratt, and Michael Stone, eds., *Housing: Foundation of a New Social Agenda* (Philadelphia: Temple University Press, forthcoming), table 5.
19. National Low Income Housing Coalition, *2002 Advocates' Guide to Housing and Community Development* (Washington, DC: National Low Income Housing Coalition, 2002), 10, 56.
20. Congressional Budget Office, *The Budget and Economic Outlook: Fiscal Years 2002–2011* (Washington, DC: U.S. Government Printing Office, 2001), 148–151.
21. Daniel Bartlett and J. Steel, "Corporate Welfare." *Time* November 8, 1998, 38.
22. R. D. Hershey, "A Hard Look at Corporate Welfare," *New York Times*, March 7, 1995, D1.

23. Robert J. McIntrye, *The Hidden Entitlements* (Washington, DC: Center for Tax Justice and the Institution for Taxation and Economic Policy, 1996), appendix.

24. Congressional Budget Office, *The Budget and Economic Outlook: Fiscal Years 2003–2012* (Washington, DC: Government Printing Office, 2003) 160.

25. Peter Bachrach and Morton S. Baratz, *Power and Poverty* (New York: Oxford University Press, 1979), 7.

26. Peter Bachrach and Morton S. Baratz, "Decision and Non-Decisions: An Analytic Framework," *American Political Science Review* 57 (1963): 632, 642.

27. Richard Harris, *A Sacred Trust: The Story of Organized Medicine's Multi-Million Dollar Fight against Health Insurance* (Baltimore: Penguin, 1969).

28. Amanda Smith Barusch, *Foundations of Social Policy: Social Justice, Public Programs and the Social Work Profession* (Itasca, IL: F.E. Peacock 2002), 326–332; Bruce S. Jansson, *The Reluctant Welfare State: American Social Welfare Policies Past, Present and Future* (Belmont, CA: Wadsworth/Thompson Learning, 2000), 51–52, 264.

29. August Meier and Elliott Rudwick, *From Plantation to Ghetto* (New York: Hill and Wang, 1976); Harvard Sitkoff, *The Struggle for Black Equality, 1954–1980* (New York: Hill and Wang, 1981).

30. Smith Barusch, *Foundations of Social Policy*, 332–344; Jansson, *The Reluctant Welfare State*, 402–403.

31. Nancy E. McGlen and Karen O'Connor, *Women's Rights: The Struggle for Equality in the 19th and 20th Centuries* (New York: Praeger, 1983).

32. Smith Barusch, *Foundations of Social Policy*, 352–366; Jansson, *The Reluctant Welfare State*, 402–403.

33. Mimi Abramovitz, *Regulating the Lives of Women: Social Welfare Policy from Colonial Times to the Present*, 2d ed. (Boston: South End Press, 1996); Mimi Abramovitz, *Under Attack, Fighting Back: Women and Welfare in the United States*, 2d ed. (New York: Monthly Review Press, 1999).

34. Phyllis Day, *A New History of Social Welfare* (Boston: Allyn and Bacon, 2000), 34–35.

35. Abramovitz, *Regulating the Lives of Women*.

36. Paul Corrigan and Peter Leonard, *Social Work Practice under Capitalism: A Marxist Approach* (London: Macmillan, 1978), 99–102.

37. Ian Gough, *The Political Economy of the Welfare State* (London: Macmillan, 1979), 53.

38. James O'Connor, *The Fiscal Crisis of the State* (New York: St Martin's Press, 1973).

39. Ibid., 5–10; Gough, *The Political Economy of the Welfare State*, 44–54.

40. Frances Fox Piven and Richard A. Cloward, *Regulating the Poor: The Functions of Public Welfare* (New York: Pantheon, 1971), 124–146, 147–180.

41. J. Brenner and B. Laslett, "Social Reproduction and the Family," in Ulf Himmelstrand, ed., *The Social Reproduction of Organization and Culture* (London: Sage Publications, 1986); J. Dickinson and B. Russell, *Families, Economy and State* (New York: St. Martin's Press, 1986).

42. O'Connor, *The Fiscal Crisis of the State*, 5–10; Gough, *The Political Economy of the Welfare State*, 4, 7, 69–70.

43. Alan Hunter, "The Ideology of the New Right," in Kenneth Fox, Mary Jo Hertzel, Thomas Riddell, Nancy Rose, and Jerry Sazama, eds., *Crisis in the Public Sector* (New York: Monthly Review Press, n.d.), 309–332; Barbara Ehrenreich, "The New Right Attack on Social Welfare," in Fred Block, Richard A. Cloward, Barbara Ehrenreich, and Frances Fox Piven, eds., *The Mean Season: The Attack on the Welfare State* (New York: Pantheon, 1987), 161–196.

44. Frances Fox Piven and Richard A. Cloward, *The New Class War: Reagan's Attack on the Welfare State and Its Consequences* (New York: Pantheon, 1982).

45. Mimi Abramovitz, "Social Work and Social Reform: An Arena of Struggle," *Social Work* 43.6 (November 1998): 512–527.

46. Popple and Leighninger, *Social Work, Social Welfare and American Society*, 436–453; Gilbert and Terrell, *Dimensions of Social Welfare Policy*, 50–51.

47. Diana M. DiNitto, *Social Welfare: Politics and Public Policy*, 5th ed. (Boston: Allyn and Bacon, 2000), 103–107; Ralph Dolgoff and Donald Feldstein, *Understanding Social Welfare*, 5th ed, (Boston: Allyn and Bacon, 2000).

48. Smith Barusch, *Foundations of Social Policy*, 58–60; DiNitto, *Social Welfare*, 122–123; Dolgoff and Feldstein, *Understanding Social Welfare*, 205–209.

49. Smith Barusch, *Foundations of Social Policy*, 64–65, 137–139; DiNitto, *Social Welfare*, 257–258; Dolgoff and Feldstein, *Understanding Social Welfare*, 239–244.

50. DiNitto, *Social Welfare*, 231; Smith Barusch, *Foundations of Social Policy*, 287–291.

51. Dolgoff and Feldstein, *Understanding Social Welfare*, 259–263; Popple and Leighninger, *Social Work, Social Welfare and American Society*, 47–48; Smith Barusch, *Foundations of Social Policy*, 132.

52. Mimi Abramovitz, "Temporary Aid to Needy Children," *Encyclopedia of Social Work*, 19th ed., 1997 supplement (Washington, DC: NASW Press, 1997), 311–330; Abramovitz, *Regulating the Lives of Women*, 313–343; Dolgoff and Feldstein, *Understanding Social Welfare*, 104; Abramovitz, *Under Attack, Fighting Back*.

53. Popple and Leighninger, *Social Work, Social Welfare and American Society*, 47.

54. DiNitto, *Social Welfare*, 216–225; Popple and Leighninger, *Social Work, Social Welfare and American Society*, 48; Dolgoff and Feldstein, *Understanding Social Welfare*, 250–252.

55. DiNitto, *Social Welfare*, 225–229; Popple and Leighninger, *Social Work, Social Welfare and American Society*, 49.

56. DiNitto, *Social Welfare*, 229–220; Popple and Leighninger, *Social Work, Social Welfare and American Society*, 49.

57. DiNitto, *Social Welfare*, 252–256; Dolgoff and Feldstein, *Understanding Social Welfare*, 244–249.

58. Popple and Leighninger, *Social Work, Social Welfare and American Society*, 48; Smith Barusch, *Foundations of Social Policy*, 105.

59. Popple and Leighninger, *Social Work, Social Welfare and American Society*, 48; Smith Barusch, *Foundations of Social Policy*, 105–106.

60. Popple and Leighninger, *Social Work, Social Welfare and American Society*, 48; Smith Barusch, *Foundations of Social Policy*, 103.

61. Popple and Leighninger, *Social Work, Social Welfare and American Society*, 49–50.

62. DiNitto, *Social Welfare*, 343–347.

63. Popple and Leighninger, *Social Work, Social Welfare and American Society*, 48.

64. Smith Barusch, *Foundations of Social Policy*, 173–177; Popple and Leighninger, *Social Work, Social Welfare and American Society*, 49–50.

65. Popple and Leighninger, *Social Work, Social Welfare and American Society*, 50

66. DiNitto, *Social Welfare*, 296; Martha Davis, *Brutal Need: Lawyers and the Welfare Rights Movement, 1960–1973* (New Haven: Yale University Press, 1993).

67. Popple and Leighninger, *Social Work, Social Welfare and American Society*, 50.

68. Winifred Bell, *Contemporary Social Welfare* (New York: Macmillian, 1983), 22–27; Gilbert and Terrell, *Dimensions of Social Welfare Policy*, 93–97; Dale Tussing, "The Dual Welfare System," *Society* 11.2 (January/February 1974): 50–57.

69. Alfred J. Kahn, *Social Policy and Social Services* (New York: Random House, 1979), 14–18; Louise C. Johnson and Charles L. Schwartz, *Social Welfare: A Response to Human Need*, 4th ed. (Boston: Allyn and Bacon, 1997), 13.

Chapter 3

1. Paul A. Samuelson and William D. Nordhaus, *Economics*, 16th ed. (New York: Irwin McGraw-Hill, 1998), 4.

2. Samuel Bowles, David Gordon, and Thomas Weisskopf, *After the Wasteland* (Armonk, NY: M.E. Sharpe, 1990), 59–60.

3. Samuelson and Nordhaus, *Economics*, 27.
4. Robert Heilbroner and Lester Thurow, *Economics Explained* (New York: Touchstone Books, 1998), 12–14.
5. Gosta Esping-Andersen, *Social Foundations of Postindustrial Economies* (New York: Oxford University Press, 1999).
6. Charles Noble, *Welfare as We Knew It* (New York: Oxford University Press, 1997), 7.
7. Howard Sherman, *Radical Political Economy* (New York: Basic Books, 1972).
8. Robert Kuttner, *Everything for Sale* (New York: Knopf, 1997), 181.
9. Heilbroner and Thurow, *Economics Explained*, 314.
10. Just among the major television networks, Disney owns ABC, Viacom owns CBS, General Electric owns NBC, and Rupert Murdoch's News Corporation owns the Fox Network.
11. Sarah Anderson and John Cavanagh, *Top 200: The Rise of Global Power* (Washington, DC: Institute of Policy Studies, 2000), 3.
12. *Statistical Abstract of the United States 2001* (Washington, DC: U.S. Department of Commerce, 2001), 473, 483, 486; *Fortune*, April 15, 2002.
13. See, for example, Joseph Stiglitz, *Globalization and Its Discontents* (New York: Norton, 2002); Dani Rodrik, *Has Globalization Gone Too Far?* (Washington, DC: Institute for International Economics, 1997); Gary Teeple, *Globalization and the Decline of Social Reform* (Aurora, Ontario: Garamond Press, 2000).
14. See Bowles, et al., *After the Wasteland*, 8–9.
15. Social workers particularly interested in the subject of microeconomics would benefit from reading Michael Lewis, *Economics for Social Workers* (New York: Columbia University Press, 2001).
16. Robert J. Barro, *Macroeconomics*, 5th ed. (Cambridge, MA: MIT Press, 1998), 169–170.
17. N. Gregory Mankiw, *Principles of Economics* (Orlando, FL: Dreyden Press, Harcourt Brace, 1998), 69, 74.
18. Ibid., 694–695.
19. Heilbroner and Thurow, *Economics Explained*, 154.
20. Congressional Budget Office, *The Budget and Economic Outlook: Fiscal Years 2003–2012* (Washington, DC: U.S. Government Printing Office, 2002), 154.
21. Marc L. Miringoff, Marque Luisa Miringoff, and Sandra Opdycke, *The Social Health of the Nation: How America Is Really Doing* (New York: Oxford University Press, 1999).
22. David Leonhardt, "Long-Term Jobless Rose by 50 Percent over the Last Year," *New York Times*, September 9, 2002; and U.S. Department of Labor, Bureau of Labor Statistics, *Labor Force Statistics from Current Population Survey* [http://www.bls.gov/cps.homehtm, accessed March 16, 2003].
23. Samuelson and Nordhaus, *Economics*, 566–567.
24. U.S. Bureau of Labor Statistics, *Employment Situation Summary*, June 2002, http://www.bls.gov/news.release/empsit.nr0.htm, accessed July 18, 2002.
25. U.S. Bureau of Labor Statistics, *Contingent and Alternative Employment Arrangements*, February 2001, www.bls.gov/news.release/conemp.nr0.htm, accessed July 18, 2002.
26. Fox Butterfield, "1% Increase in U.S. Inmates Is Lowest Rate in Three Decades," *New York Times*, August 1, 2002.
27. U.S. Bureau of Labor Statistics, *12 Month Percent Change*, http://www.bls.gov.serlet.surveyOutputServlet?/data_tool=latest_n, accessed July 18, 2002.
28. Samuelson and Nordhaus, *Economics*, 587–588.
29. Congressional Budget Office, Appendix E, "Changes in Calculating the Consumer Price Index," in *The Budget and Economic Outlook: Fiscal Years 2000–2009* (Washington, DC: U.S. Government Printing Office, January 1999), 119–121; Dean Baker, "The Measurement of Inflation," Appendix C, in Lawrence Mishel, Jared Bernstein, and John Schmitt, *The State of Working America, 1998–1999* (Ithaca, NY: Cornell University Press, 1999), 400–402.

441

30. Phineas Baxandall, "Is the 'New Economy' More Productive? Sorting Fact from Fiction," *Dollars & Sense*, no. 241 (May–June 2002): 9; Joel Blau, *Illusions of Prosperity: America's Working Families in an Age of Economic Security* (New York: Oxford University Press, 1999), 20; Dean Baker, *The New Economy Goes Bust: What the Record Shows* (Washington, DC: Center for Economic and Policy Research, October 29, 2001), 3.

31. U.S. Census Bureau, *Poverty Rate Rises, Household Income Declines, Census Bureau Reports*, September 24, 2002, http://www.census.gov./Press-Release/www/2002/cb02-124.html, accessed September 24, 2002.

32. Barbara R. Bergmann, "Deciding Who's Poor," *Dollars & Sense*, no. 228 (March–April 2000): 36–38, 45; Louis Uchitelle, "Devising New Math to Define Poverty," *New York Times*, October 18, 1999.

33. U.S. Census Bureau, Foreign Trade Division, *U.S. Trade—Balance of Payments*, June 20, 2002; Bank of International Settlement, "Currency Breakdown of Reporting Banks' Cross Border Positions," *Quarterly Review* (June 2002): A-16; Louis Uchitelle, "Foreign Investors Turning Cautious on Spending in the U.S.," *New York Times*, August 4, 2002.

34. Congressional Budget Office, *The Budget and Economic Outlook, 2003–2012*, 168; Richard W. Stevenson, "Budget Deficit Is Said to Be $159 Billion," *New York Times*, October 25, 2002.

35. Congressional Budget Office, *The Budget and Economic Outlook, 2003–2012*, 168.

36. Ibid., 12.

37. Samuelson and Nordhaus, *Economics*, 434.

38. U.S. Census Bureau, "Share of Aggregate Income Received by Each Fifth and Top 5 percent of Household, 1967–2000," *Money Income in the United States: 2000*, table A-2, p. 21.

39. Mishel, Bernstein, and Schmitt, *The State of Working America, 2000–2001*, 259.

40. Sarah Anderson, John Cavanagh, Chris Hartmann, and Betsy Leondar-Wright, *Executive Pay 2001* (Washington, DC: Institute for Policy Studies, 2001), 1.

41. U.S. Census Bureau, "Share of Aggregate Income Received," table A-2, p. 21.

42. Cited in Tom Redburn, "Honoring, and Paying, All Those Who Serve," *New York Times*, October 28, 2001.

43. Kuttner, *Everything for Sale*, 16–18.

44. Samuelson and Nordhaus, *Economics*, 439.

45. Mankiw, *Principles of Economics*, 603–604.

46. Internal Revenue Service, *Personal Exemptions and Individual Income Tax Rates, 1913–2002*, p. 216, table 1, p. 219; Richard W. Stevenson, "Congress Passes Tax Cut, with Rebate This Summer," *New York Times*, May 27, 2001; Citizens for Tax Justice, *Year-by-Year Analysis of the Bush Tax Cuts Show Growing Tilt to the Very Rich* (Washington, DC, June 12, 2002).

47. Congressional Budget Office, *The Budget and Economic Outlook, 2003–2012*, 160; Joel Friedman, Iris Lav, and Peter Orszag, "Would a Capital Gains Tax Cut Stimulate the Economy?" Center on Budget and Policy Priorities, September 20, 2001; Blau, *Illusions of Prosperity*, 196–197.

48. Congressional Budget Office, *The Budget and Economic Outlook, 2003–2012*, 3, 164, 166.

49. Congressional Budget Office, *The Budget and Economic Outlook: Fiscal Years 2000–2009*, 61.

50. Richard Rose, "Common Goals, but Different Roles: The State's Contribution to the Welfare Mix," in Richard Rose and Rei Shiratori, eds., *The Welfare State East and West* (New York: Oxford University Press, 1986), 16–17.

51. Karl de Schweinitz, *England's Road to Social Security* (New York: A.S. Barnes, 1961).

52. *Statistical Abstract of the United States 2001*, 370, 376.

53. Theodore R. Marmor, Jerry L. Marshaw, and Philip L. Harvey, *America's Misunderstood Welfare State* (New York: Basic Books, 1990), 142–143.

54. Martin Feldstein, "Social Security, Induced Retirement and Aggregate Capital Formation," *Journal of Political Economy* 82 (September–October 1974): 905–926.

55. Arthur Okun, *Equality and Efficiency: The Big Trade-Off* (Washington, DC: Brookings Institution, 1975).

56. Bowles, et al., *After the Wasteland*, 221–222.

57. A. B. Atkinson, *The Economic Consequences of Rolling Back the Welfare State* (Cambridge, MA: MIT Press, 1999), 37.

58. Ibid., 184.

59. See James O' Connor, *The Fiscal Crisis of the State* (New York: St. Martin's Press, 1973), 8–9.

60. Jacob M. Schlesinger, "Did Washington Set the Stage for the Current Business Turmoil? Seeking Growth, Policy Made Free Markets Freer, Shot Down Naysayers," *Wall Street Journal*, October 17, 2002.

61. See Baker, *The New Economy Goes Bust*, 9, for data about the rise of the stock market; for data on the appreciation in the value of the five hundred corporations and the thirty largest fortunes, see Kevin Phillips, *Wealth and Democracy: A Political History of the American Rich* (New York: Broadway Books, 2002), 111–112.

62. Phillips, *Wealth and Democracy*, 112; Mishel et al., *The State of Working America, 1998–1999*, 131; Blau, *Illusions of Prosperity*, 114; Committee on Ways and Means, U.S. House of Representatives, *1998 Green Book* (Washington, DC: U.S. Government Printing Office, 1998), 431.

63. Blau, *Illusions of Prosperity*, 57–59.

64. U.S. Department of Labor, Bureau of Labor Statistics, *Union Members Summary, 2001*, 1.

65. Ibid., 2.

66. Holly Sklar, "Minimum Wage: It Just Doesn't Add Up," August 29, 2001, Common Dreams News Center [http://commondreams.org/viewso1/0829-08.htm], accessed July 29, 2002.

67. Blau, *Illusions of Prosperity*, 71–74, Jared Bernstein and Chauna Brocht, *The New Minimum Wage and the Old Opposition* (Washington, DC: Economic Policy Institute, 2000). For the conservative argument, see Donald Deere, Kevin Murphy, and Finis Welch, "Sense and Nonsense on the Minimum Wage," *Regulation* 1 (1994): 47–56. For the liberal position, see Alan Kreuger and David Card, *Myth and Measurement: The New Economics of the Minimum Wage* (Princeton: Princeton University Press, 1995).

68. Mishel et al., *The State of Working America, 2000–2001*, 5.

69. Margaret Webb Pressler, "A Workforce Divided: Rising Use of Temps Is Creating Two Classes of Employees," *Washington Post*, June 23, 2002; Mishel et al., *The State of Working America, 2000–2001*, 250–251.

70. Mishel et al., *The State of Working America, 2000–2001*, 248.

71. David Moberg, "Business as Usual in the Disinformation Economy," *In These Times*, March 4, 2002, 14–15; David Barboza, "Officials Got a Windfall before Enron's Collapse," *New York Times*, June 18, 2002.

72. Majorie Kelly, "Waving Goodbye to the Invisible Hand: What Enron Teaches Us about Economic System Design," *San Francisco Chronicle*, February 24, 2002; David Leonhardt, "The Long Boom's Ugly Side," *New York Times*, May 12, 2002.

73. Paul Zielbauer with Michael Brick, "Connecticut Feels Fallout from Enron," *New York Times*, February 22, 2002.

74. James K. Gailbraith, "Enron May Spark Revolt of the Professionals," *Newsday*, January 25, 2002; Peter G. Gosselin, "Enron a Rerun of History," *Los Angeles Times*, February 22, 2002.

75. Robert l. Borosage, "The Conservative Bubble Boys," *Washington Post*, July 9, 2002; David Wessel, "Why the Boardroom Bad Guys Have Now Emerged en Masse," *Wall Street Journal*, June 20, 2002.

76. Robert Borosage, "Articles," *The Nation*, February 4, 2002, 12; Alex Berenson, "Tweaking the Numbers to Meet Goals Comes Back to Haunt Executives," *New York Times*, June 29, 2002.

77. David Stout, "Bush Signs Broad Changes in Business Laws," *New York Times*, July 30, 2002; Louis Uchitelle, "Broken System? Tweak It, They Say," *New York Times*, July 28, 2002.

Chapter 4

1. Theodore J. Lowi and Benjamin Ginsberg, *American Government: Freedom and Power*, 5th ed. (New York: Norton, 1998), 426–427.

2. Christopher Ham and Michael Hill, "The Role of the State," in *The Policy Process in the Modern Capitalist State* (New York: St. Martin's Press, 1986), 26–29. The classic pluralist work is Robert Dahl, *Who Governs?* (New Haven: Yale University Press, 1961).

3. Edward S. Greenberg and Benjamin Page, *The Struggle for Democracy* (New York: HarperCollins, 1999), 217–218.

4. E. E. Schattschneider, *The Semi-Sovereign People* (New York: Holt Rinehart and Winston, 1960), 35.

5. Demetrius Iatridis, *Social Policy: The Institutional Context of Social Development and Human Services* (Pacific Grove, CA: Brooks/Cole, 1994), 94–95.

6. Ham and Hill, "The Role of the State," 28.

7. See James Buchanan and Gordon Tullock, *The Calculus of Consent* (Ann Arbor: University of Michigan Press, 1965), and the discussion in Diane M. Johnson, "Public Choice Theory, Conservativism and the Development of the American Welfare State," unpublished paper, School of Social Welfare, Stony Brook University, spring 1999.

8. Johnson, "Public Choice Theory," 7, 13–14.

9. Kenneth Janda, Jeffrey M. Berry, and Jerry Goldman, *The Challenge of Democracy* (New York: Houghton Mifflin, 1999), 44; C. Wright Mills, *The Power Elite* (New York: Oxford University Press, 1956).

10. See Martin Carnoy, *The State and Political Theory* (Princeton: Princeton University Press, 1984). On the left, the classic debate about this issue took place between Ralph Miliband, *The State in Capitalist Society* (London: Weidenfield and Nicholson, 1969), and Nicos Poulantzas, *State, Power, Socialism* (London: Verso, 1978).

11. Janda et al., *The Challenge of Democracy*, 33–37.

12. Iatridis, *Social Policy*, 90–92

13. Greenberg and Page, *The Struggle for Democracy*, 8–12.

14. Ibid., 14.

15. Morris P. Fiorina and Paul E. Peterson, *The New American Democracy* (Needham, MA: Allyn and Bacon, 1999), 316.

16. Ralph Dolgoff and Donald Feldstein, *Understanding Social Welfare* (Needham Heights, MA: Allyn and Bacon, 2000), 122; Joel Blau, *Illusions of Prosperity* (New York: Oxford University Press, 1999), 180.

17. Greenberg and Page, *The Struggle for Democracy*, 65–67.

18. Daniel L. Elazar, "The Evolving Federal System," in Richard M. Pious, ed., *The Power to Govern* (New York: Academy of Political Science, 1981), 5–19.

19. Linda Greenhouse, "Justices Expand States' Immunity in Federalism Case," *New York Times*, May 29, 2002. The cases are *Alden v. Maine* (1999) and *Federal Maritime Commission v. South Carolina Ports Authority* (2002).

20. Janda et al., *The Challenge of Democracy*, 100–101.

21. Fiorina and Peterson, *The New American Democracy*, 81.

22. Greenberg and Page, *The Struggle for Democracy*, 62–64.

23. Charles Nobel, *Welfare as We Knew It: A Political History of the Welfare State* (New York: Oxford University Press, 1997), 29–30.

24. Lowi and Ginsberg, *American Government,* 52.

25. Greenberg and Page, *The Struggle for Democracy,* 46. The Jefferson quote comes from his *Notes on the State of Virginia,* ed. Thomas Perkins Abernathy, (New York: Harper & Row, 1964), 120.

26. Clinton Rossiter, *The American Presidency,* revised ed. (New York: Harcourt Brace Jovanovich, 1960); Rexford G. Tugwell and Thomas Cronin, eds. *The Presidency Reappraised* (New York: Praeger, 1974), 235.

27. Stephen J. Wayne, *The Legislative Presidency* (New York: Harper & Row, 1978), 22–23.

28. Elizabeth A. Segal and Stephanie Brzuzy, *Social Welfare Policy, Programs, and Practice* (Itasca, IL: F.E. Peacock, 1998), 223.

29. Fiorina and Peterson, *The New American Democracy,* 360.

30. Lowi and Ginsberg, *American Government,* 189; Wayne, *The Legislative Presidency,* 5.

31. Fiorina and Peterson, *The New American Democracy,* 398.

32. *Fact Sheet,* Center for American Women and Politics, Eagleton Institute of Politics, Rutgers University, May 2002; Laurent Belsie, "Redistricting Forces Black Democrats to Pick Sides," *Christian Science Monitor,* June 21, 2002; Maria Travierso, "Number of Hispanics Growing Rapidly," *Hispanic Magazine.Com,* April 2001, http://www. hispanicmagazine.com/2001/apr/Panorara/journal1.html, accessed June 26, 2002.

33. Lowi and Ginsberg, *American Government,* 354.

34. Donald L. Horowitz, *The Courts and Social Policy* (Washington, DC: Brookings Institution, 1977), 2.

35. Donald E. Chambers, *Social Policy and Social Programs* (Needham Heights, MA: Allyn and Bacon, 2000), 53.

36. Fiorina and Peterson, *The New American Democracy,* 489–490.

37. Lowi and Ginsberg, *American Government,* 277.

38. U.S. Office of Personnel Management, *Federal Civilian Workforce Statistics,* May 2001, table 1.

39. Lowi and Ginsberg, *American Government,* 293.

40. See, for housing, Joel Blau, *The Visible Poor: Homeless in the United States* (New York: Oxford University Press, 1992), 68, and, for employment policy, Blau, *Illusions of Prosperity,* 119.

41. Greenberg and Page, *The Struggle for Democracy,* 451.

42. Ibid., 283–293.

43. Margaret Weir, Ann Shola Orloff, and Theda Skocpol, *The Politics of Social Policy in the United States* (Princeton: Princeton University Press, 1988), 16.

44. Nobel, *Welfare as We Knew It,* 28.

45. Frances Fox Piven and Richard Cloward, "Structural Constraints and Political Development: The Case of the Democratic Party," in *The Breaking of the American Social Compact* (New York: New Press, 1997), 423.

46. See Stephen Skowronek, *Building a New American State: The Expansion of National Administrative Capacities 1877–1920* (Cambridge: Cambridge University Press, 1982).

47. Weir et al., *The Politics of Social Policy in the United States,* 18–19.

48. Fiorina and Peterson, *The New American Democracy,* 255–256; Lowi and Ginsberg, *American Government,* 507–511.

49. Demetrios James Caraley, "Ending Welfare as We Know It: A Reform Still in Progress," *Political Science Quarterly* 116.4 (winter 2001–2002): 546.

50. Fiorina and Peterson, *The New American Democracy,* 255–258.

51. Cited in "Soundbites," *Extra! Update,* the newsletter of F.A.I.R. (Fairness and Accuracy in Reporting), April 2002, 2.

52. See the data at the Web site of the Institute for Democracy and Electoral Assistance, http://www.idea.int/vt/intro/introdo3.cfm, accessed July 5, 2002.

53. E. J. Dionne, *Why Do Americans Hate Politics?* (New York: Simon & Schuster, 1991).

54. Gallup poll, June 6–9, 1998, http://www.pollingreport.com/institut.htm, accessed July 5, 2002.

55. Greenberg and Page, *The Struggle for Democracy*, 318–319; Weir et al., *The Politics of Social Policy in the United States*, 19.

56. Lowi and Ginsberg, *American Government*, 463–464.

57. Cited in Nelson P. Valdes, "American Democracy—A Lesson for Cubans," *Radio Progreso*, July 4–10, 2002, http://www.rpregreso.com/RPWeekly/052302/usvaldes democracy, accessed July 3, 2002.

58. Data from *New York Times*, November 21, 1998.

59. Nathan Newman, "The Campaign Finance Limit Illusion: We Need Public Financing, Not Fake Reform," *The Progressive Populist* (March 1, 2002); Ellen S. Miller, "With Victories Like These . . ." *The American Prospect* 13.6 (March 25, 2002): 14–15.

60. Arnold Heidenheimer, Hugh Heclo, and Carolyn Teich Adams, *Comparative Public Policy: The Politics of Social Choice in Europe and America* (New York: St. Martin's Press, 1975), 258–259.

61. Weir et al., *The Politics of Social Policy in the United States*, offer probably the most cogent examples of this perspective.

62. Morris Janowitz, *Social Control of the Welfare State* (Chicago: University of Chicago Press, 1976), 87.

63. James Morone, *The Democratic Wish* (New York: Basic Books, 1990).

64. Ibid., 333.

65. See Seymour Martin Lipset, *American Exceptionalism: A Double-Edged Sword* (New York: Norton, 1996); Byron E. Shafer, ed., *Is America Different? A New Look at American Exceptionalism* (Oxford: Clarendon Press, 1991).

66. See Lipset, *American Exceptionalism*, 84–86. The classic treatment of these issues is Louis Hartz, *The Liberal Tradition in America* (New York: Harvest Edition, 1991).

67. Heidenheimer et al., *Comparative Public Policy*, 262.

68. Iatridis, *Social Policy*, 100.

69. Weir et al., *The Politics of Social Policy in the United States*, 437.

70. Ibid., 17.

Chapter 5

1. Terence Ball and Richard Dagger, *Ideals and Ideologies: A Reader*, 3d ed. (New York: Longman, 1998), 1.

2. David Gil, *Confronting Injustice and Oppression: Concepts and Strategies for Social Workers* (New York: Columbia University Press, 1998), 43–44.

3. Robin D. G. Kelly, *Race Rebels: Culture Politics and the Black Working Class* (New York: Free Press, 1994); Tera W. Hunter, *To 'Joy My Freedom: Southern Black Women's Lives and Labors after the Civil War* (Cambridge, MA: Harvard University Press, 1997); Jacqueline Jones *Labor of Love, Labor of Sorrow: Black Women Work and Family, from Slavery to the Present* (New York: Basic Books, 1985); David Katzman, *Seven Days a Week: Women and Domestic Service in Industrializing America* (New York: Oxford University Press, 1978).

4. Rebecca E. Klatch, *Women of the New Right* (Philadelphia: Temple University Press, 1987), 34, 198; Terence Ball and Richard Dagger, *Political Ideologies and the Democratic Ideal*, 3rd ed. (New York: Longman, 1999), 94–95, 114, 119.

5. Klatch, *Women of the New Right*, 24–25, 61–64, 197–200.

6. Ball and Dagger, *Political Ideologies and the Democratic Ideal*, 48; Alison M. Jaggar, *Feminist Politics and Human Nature* (Totowa, NJ: Rowman & Allenhead, 1983), 15–23, 33; Jeffry H. Galper, *The Politics of Social Services* (Englewood Cliffs, NJ: Prentice-Hall, 1975), 36.

7. Ball and Dagger, *Political Ideologies and the Democratic Ideal*, 7.

8. Joan C. Tronto, *Moral Boundaries: A Political Argument for an Ethic of Care* (New York:

Routledge, 1993), 162–165; Ball and Dagger, *Political Ideologies and the Democratic Ideal*, 123.

9. Rosemarie P. Tong, *Feminist Thoughts: A More Comprehensive Introduction* (Boulder, CO: Westview Press, 1998), 94–95; Jaggar, *Feminist Politics and Human Nature*, 52–59.

10. Cited in Jaggar, *Feminist Politics and Human Nature*, 130.

11. Cited in Tong, *Feminist Thoughts*, 95.

12. Tong, *Feminist Thoughts*, 12–44; Jaggar, *Feminist Politics and Human Nature*, 27–50.

13. Tong, *Feminist Thoughts*, 45–93; Jaggar, *Feminist Politics and Human Nature*, 83–122.

14. Shulamith Firestone, *The Dialect of Sex: The Case for Feminist Revolution* (New York: William Morrow, 1971).

15. Tong, *Feminist Thoughts*, 94–129, Jaggar, *Feminist Politics and Human Nature*, 123–168.

16. Ball and Dagger, *Political Ideologies and the Democratic Ideal*, 98; Klatch, *Women of the New Right*, 197–200; Johanna Brenner, *Women and the Politics of Class* (New York: Monthly Review Press, 2000), 188–189.

17. Raymond Plant, Harry Lesser, and Peter Taylor-Goodby, *Political Philosophy and Social Welfare: Essays on the Normative Basis of Welfare Provision* (Boston: Routledge & Kegan Paul, 1980), 222.

18. E. K. Hunt, *Property and Prophets: The Evolutions of Economic Institutions and Ideologies* (New York: Harper & Row, 1981); 41–42; Gordon Scott, *Welfare, Justice and Freedom* (New York: Columbia University Press, 1980), 54; Klatch, *Women of the New Right*, 34; Ball and Dagger, *Political Ideologies and the Democratic Ideal*, 76, 86.

19. Cited in Hunt, *Property and Prophets*, 43.

20. Plant et al., *Political Philosophy and Social Welfare*, 227–230.

21. Tong, *Feminist Thoughts*, 11; Ball and Dagger, *Political Ideologies and the Democratic Ideal*, 48, 77; Jaggar, *Feminist Politics and Human Nature*, 33.

22. Anne Phillips, *Democracy and Difference* (University Park: Pennsylvania State University Press, 1993), 40; Tronto, *Moral Boundaries*, 162–165; Robert Mullaly, *Structural Social Work: Ideology, Theory and Practice* (Toronto: McClelland & Stewart, 1993), 87–88; Ball and Dagger, *Political Ideologies and the Democratic Ideal*, 74, 123.

23. Vic George and Paul Wilding, *Ideology and Social Welfare* (London: Routledge & Kegan Paul, 1984), 67, citing Richard M. Titmuss, *Commitment to Welfare* (London: Allyn and Unwin, 1968), 151.

24. Mullaly, *Structural Social Work*, 41–42; Tong, *Feminist Thoughts*, 94–101; Hunt, *Property and Prophets*, 85.

25. Hunt, *Property and Prophets*, 86; Tong, *Feminist Thoughts*, 99.

26. David Gil, *Unravelling Social Policy: Theory, Analysis and Political Action towards Social Equality*, 4th ed., revised (Rochester, VT: Schenkman Books, 1990), xviii.

27. Jaggar, *Feminist Politics and Human Nature*, 27–50, 173–206.

28. Ibid., 83–122, 251–302.

29. Ibid., 123–171, 303–350.

30. Plant et al., *Political Philosophy and Social Welfare*, 20.

31. Len Doyal and Ian Gough, *A Theory of Human Need* (New York: Guilford Press, 1991), 10; Jaggar, *Feminist Politics and Human Nature*, 28–29, 43; Randy Albeda, Robert Drago, and Steven Shulman, *Unlevel Playing Fields: Understanding Wage Inequality and Discrimination* (New York: McGraw-Hill, 1997), 124.

32. Kathleen Jones, John Brown, and Jonathan Bradshaw, *Issues in Social Policy* (London: Routledge & Kegan Paul, 1983), 28.

33. Andre Gorz, *Strategy for Labor: A Radical Proposal* (Boston: Beacon Press, 1968), 76–99.

34. Robert Heilbroner, *The Making of Economic Society*, 3d ed. (Englewood Cliffs, NJ: Prentice-Hall, 1970), 213.

35. John Kenneth Galbraith, *The Affluent Society*, 2d rev. ed. (New York: New American Library, 1960), 249–250.

36. George and Wilding, *Ideology and Social Welfare*, 58, citing W. S. Churchill, *Liberalism and the Social Problem* (London: Hodder & Stoughton, 1909), n.p.
37. Doyal and Gough. *A Theory of Human Need*, 51–54; Ramesh Mishra, *Society and Social Policy: Theories and Practice of Welfare* (London: Macmillan, 1987), 27, 32.
38. Plant, et al., *Political Philosophy and Social Welfare*, 106–107.
39. Ibid., 154–155, 157; Albeda et al., *Unlevel Playing Fields*, 125–126.
40. Plant, et al., *Political Philosophy and Social Welfare*, 155, 152; Gorz, *Strategy for Labor*, 100–133.
41. Mishra, *Society and Social Policy*, 135; Mullaly, *Structural Social Work*, 104.
42. Carol Baines, Patricia Evans, and Shelia Neysmith, "Caring: Its Impact on the Lives of Women," in Carol Baines, Patricia Evans, and Shelia Neysmith, eds., *Women's Caring: Feminist Perspectives on Social Welfare* (Toronto: McClelland & Stewart, 1991), 11–36.
43. Deborah Stone, "Why We Need a Care Movement," *The Nation*, March 13, 2000, 13.
44. Tronto, *Moral Boundaries*, 111.
45. Heilbroner, *The Making of Economic Society*, 6.
46. Demetrius Iatridis, *Social Policy: Institutional Context of Social Development and Human Services* (Pacific Grove, CA: Brooks/Cole, 1994), 138.
47. Klatch, *Women of the New Right*, 6.
48. Ibid., 90; Barbara Ehrenreich, "The New Right's Attack on Social Welfare," in Fred Block, Richard A. Cloward, Barbara Ehrenreich, and Frances Fox Piven, eds., *The Mean Season: The Attack on the Welfare State* (New York: Pantheon, 1987), 161–196.
49. Klatch, *Women of the New Right*, 90–99.
50. Ralph Reed, *Politically Incorrect: The Emerging Faith Factors in American Politics* (Dallas: Word Publishing, 1994), 35–36, emphasis added.
51. Klatch, *Women of the New Right*, 102–116.
52. Ibid., 108.
53. Robin Toner, "Why the Elderly Wait . . . and Wait," *New York Times*, June 23, 2002, section 4, p. 1.
54. Harold L. Wilensky and Charles N. Lebeaux, *Industrial Society and Social Welfare* (New York: Free Press, 1965), 139.
55. Frances Fox Piven and Richard A. Cloward, *The New Class War: Reagan's Attack on the Welfare State and Its Consequences* (New York: Pantheon, 1982), 122–124.
56. Cited in Edward S. Greenberg, *Understanding Modern Government: The Rise and Decline of the American Political Economy* (New York: Wiley, 1979), 16–17.
57. Mimi Abramovitz, "Everyone Is Still on Welfare: The Role of Redistribution in Public Policy," *Social Work* 46, 4 (October 2001): 289–384.
58. Wilensky and Lebeaux, *Industrial Society and Social Welfare*, 139–140.
59. Mullaly, *Structural Social Work*, 88.
60. Mishra, *Society and Social Policy*, 68–98; Mullaly, *Structural Social Work*, 101–114.
61. Ian Gough, *The Political Economy of the Welfare State* (London: Macmillan, 1979), 39–54; James O'Connor, *The Fiscal Crisis of the State* (New York: St. Martin's Press, 1973), 1–12; Mishra, *Society and Social Policy*, 75.
62. Mishra, *Society and Social Policy*, 73, 76.
63. O'Connor, *The Fiscal Crisis of the State*, 9.
64. Mishra, *Society and Social Policy*, 71.
65. Jaggar, *Feminist Politics and Human Nature*, 199–200.
66. Mimi Abramovitz, *Under Attack, Fighting Back: Women and Welfare in the United States* (New York: Monthly Review Press, 1996), 98–102.
67. Ibid.
68. Brenner, *Women and the Politics of Class*, 59–82; Robyn Rowland and Renate Klein, "Radical Feminism: History, Politics, Action," in Diane Bell and Renate Klein, eds.,

Radically Speaking: Feminism Reclaimed (North Melbourne, Australia: Spinifex Press, 1996), 11–36.

69. Susan Schecter, *Women and Male Violence* (Boston: South End Press, 1982).

70. Mimi Abramovitz, *Regulating the Lives of Women: Social Welfare Policy from Colonial Times to the Present* (Boston: Massachusetts: South End Press, 1996); Abramovitz, *Under Attack, Fighting Back.*

71. Dorothy Roberts, *Killing the Black Body: Race Reproduction and the Meaning of Liberty* (New York: Pantheon, 1997).

72. Abramovitz, *Regulating the Lives of Women*, 7–10.

73. Abramovitz, *Regulating the Lives of Women.*

74. Abramovitz, *Under Attack, Fighting Back*, 109–141; Mimi Abramovitz, *Gendered Obligations: The History of Social Welfare Activism among Poor and Working Class Women in the Twentieth Century*, manuscript.

75. Mimi Abramovitz, "Toward a Framework for Understanding Activism among Poor and Working-Class Women in Twentieth Century America," in Gwendolyn Mink, ed., *Whose Welfare?* (Ithaca, NY: Cornell University Press, 1999), 214–248.

76. Stanley Parker, *The Future of Work and Leisure* (New York: Praeger, 1971), 34, 35; Hunt, *Property and Prophets*, 9.

77. Cited in Hunt, *Property and Prophets*, 33.

78. Philip Popple and Leslie Leighningher, *Social Work, Social Welfare and American Society* (Boston: Allyn and Bacon, 1999), 463.

79. Ibid.

80. Cited in Jaggar, *Feminist Politics and Human Nature*, 210.

81. Ball and Dagger, *Political Ideologies and the Democratic Ideal*, 76.

82. Cited in Popple and Leighningher, *Social Work*, 461–462.

83. Cited in Lawrence Mead, *The New Politics of Poverty* (New York: Basic Books, 1992), 159.

84. Charles Murray, *Losing Ground: American Social Policy 1950–1980* (New York: Basic Books, 1985), 228–229.

85. Mead, *The New Politics of Poverty*, 12.

86. Parker, *The Future of Work and Leisure*, 36.

87. Ibid., 3–10.

88. Popple and Leighningher, *Social Work*, 461; *Work in America: Report of a Special Task Force to the Secretary of Health, Education and Welfare* (Cambridge, MA: MIT Press, 1971), 4–5.

89. *Work in America*, xv.

90. Jaggar, *Feminist Politics and Human Nature*, 208.

91. Parker, *The Future of Work and Leisure*, 19.

92. D. Stanley Eitzen and Maxine Baca Zinn, *Social Problems* (Boston: Allyn and Bacon, 2000), 311.

93. Jaggar, *Feminist Politics and Human Nature*, 209; Iris Marion Young, "Five Faces of Oppression," in Thomas E. Wattenberg ed., *Rethinking Power* (Albany: State University of New York Press, 1992), Nancy C. M. Hartsock, *The Feminist Standpoint Revisited and Other Essays* (Boulder, CO: Westview Press, 1998), 45.

94. Pierre Jalee, *How Capitalism Works* (New York: Monthly Review Press, 1977), 22–30.

95. Hunt, *Property and Prophets*, 85; Jaggar, *Feminist Politics and Human Nature*, 208, 587; Ball and Dagger, *Political Ideologies and the Democratic Ideal*, 140.

96. Hartsock, *The Feminist Standpoint Revisited*, 48.

97. Rachel Kahn-Hut, Arlene Kaplan Daniels, and Richard Colvard, "Unresolved Questions: Three Feminist Perspectives," in Rachel Kahn-Hut, Arlene Kaplan Daniels, and Richard Colvard, eds., *Women and Work: Problems and Perspectives* (New York: Oxford University Press, 1982), 268–269.

98. Natalie J. Sokoloff, *Between Money and Love: The Dialectics of Women's Home and Market Work* (New York: Praeger, 1980), 154, 237.

99. Harriet Bradley, *Men's Work, Women's Work: A Sociological History of the Sexual Division of Labour in Employment* (Minneapolis: University of Minnesota Press, 1989); Sokoloff, *Between Money and Love*, 238, 175.

100. Maxine Baca Zinn, "Feminist Rethinking from Racial Ethnic Families," in Maxine Baca Zinn and Bonnie Thorton Dill, eds., *Women of Color in U.S. Society* (Philadelphia: Temple University Press, 1994), 303–314; Evelyn Nakano Glenn, "From Servitude to Service Work: Historical Continuities in the Racial Division of Paid Reproductive Labor," *Signs: Journal of Women in Culture and Society* 18, 1 (1992): 1–43.

101. Estelle Freedman, "The New Woman: Changing View of Women in the 1920s," in Lois Scharf and Joan M. Jensen, eds., *Decades of Discontent: The Women's Movement, 1920–1940* (Boston: Northeastern University Press, 1987), 21–44.

102. Steven Mintz and Susan Kellogg, *Domestic Revolutions: A Social History of American Family Life* (New York: Free Press, 1988); Klatch, *Women of the New Right*, 24, 246.

103. Michèle Barrett, *Women's Oppression Today: The Marxist Feminist Encounter*, rev. ed. (London: Verso, 1988), 88–189.

104. Alan Hunter, "The Ideology of the New Right," in Kenneth Fox, Mary Jo Hetzel, Thomas Riddell, Nancy Rose, and Jerry Sazama, eds., *Crisis in the Public Sector* (New York: Monthly Review Press, n.d., 155.

105. Mintz and Kellogg, *Domestic Revolutions*, 197.

106. Daniel Patrick Moynihan, *Family and Nation* (New York: Harcourt Brace Jovanovich, 1986), 9.

107. David Popenoe, "The Family Transformed," *Family Affairs* 2, 203 (summer/fall 1989): 1.

108. Cited in Sanford M. Dornbusch and Myra H. Strober, *Feminism, Children and the New Families* (New York: Guilford Press, 1988), 38.

109. Klatch, *Women of the New Right*, 90.

110. Cited in Mintz and Kellogg, *Domestic Revolutions*, 215.

111. Robert Rector, "Combating Family Disintegration, Crime, Dependence: Welfare Reform and Beyond," *Heritage Foundation Backgrounder*, April 8, 1994, 10.

112. "Dependent on the Kindness of Strangers: Two Views on Children and the Welfare System," *CultureFront* (summer 1995): 10.

113. Charles Murray, "The Emerging White Underclass and How to Save It," *Philadelphia Inquirer*, November 15, 1993.

114. Popenoe, "The Family Transformed," 5.

115. Dornbusch and Strober, *Feminism, Children and the New Families*, 28–29.

116. Cited in Michèle Barrett and Mary McIntosh, *The Anti-Social Family* (London: Verso, 1987), 81.

117. *The 21st Century Family: Who We Will Be, How We Will Live* (special issue), *Newsweek*, winter/spring, 1990, 4, 38, 40.

118. Ibid., 3.

119. Barrie Thorne, "Feminist Rethinking of the Family: An Overview," in Barrie Thorne with Marilyn Yalom, eds., *Rethinking the Family: Some Feminist Questions* (New York: Longman, 1982), 11.

120. Rowland and Klein, "Radical Feminism," 31.

121. Cited in Thorne, "Feminist Rethinking of the Family," 9.

122. Jaggar, *Feminist Politics and Human Nature*, 255–260; Tong, *Feminist Thought*, 80–87.

123. Adrienne Rich, "Compulsory Heterosexuality and Lesbian Existence," *Signs: Journal of Women in Culture and Society* 5.4 (1980): 647–650.

124. Sokoloff, *Between Money and Love*, 166–174.

125. Sokoloff, *Between Money and Love*; Catherine A. MacKinnon, *Toward a Feminist Theory of the State* (Cambridge, MA: Harvard University Press), 61–65; Rayna Rapp, "Family and Class in Contemporary America: Notes toward an Understanding of Ideology," in Thorne and Yalom, *Feminist Rethinking of the Family*, 172.

126. *Work in America*, 2–3.

127. Sokoloff, *Between Money and Love*; MacKinnon, *Toward a Feminist Theory of the State*, 61–65; Rapp, "Family and Class in Contemporary America," 172.

128. Mimi Abramovitz, "Poor Women in a Bind: Social Reproduction without Social Supports," *Affilia: A Journal of Women and Social Work* 7.2 (summer 1992): 23–44.

129. Patricia Hill Collins, *Black Feminist Thought: Knowledge, Consciousness and the Politics of Empowerment* (London: HarperCollins, 1991), 119–122.

130. Sylvia Walby, *Theorizing Patriarchy* (Cambridge, MA: Basil Blackwell, 1991), 76.

131. Zinn, "Feminist Rethinking from Racial Ethnic Families," 303–314; Evelyn Nakano Glenn, "From Servitude to Service Work," 1–43.

132. Sylvia Walby, *Patriarchy at Work* (Minneapolis: University of Minnesota Press, 1986), 48.

133. Nancy Fraser, *Justice Interruptus: Critical Reflections on the Post-Socialist Condition* (New York: Routledge, 1997), 63.

134. Charles Reasons and William D. Perdue, *The Ideology of Social Problems* (Sherman Oaks, CA: Alfred Publishing, 1981), 568, 580.

135. Paula Rothenberg, "The Construction, Deconstruction and Reconstruction of Difference," *Hypathia* 5.1 (spring 1990): 42–57.

136. Nicholas Lemann, "The End of Racism? An Interview with Dinesh D'Souza," in *Annual Editions: Social Problems 99/00* (Guilford, CT: Dushkin/McGraw-Hill, 2000), 54–65.

137. Ibid., 61, 62.

138. Ibid., 63.

139. Clarence Page, "Supply Side Affirmative Action," in *Annual Editions: Social Problems 99/00* (Guilford, CT: Dushkin/McGraw-Hill, 2000), 90–94.

140. Lemann, "The End of Racism? An Interview with Dinesh D'Souza," 61.

141. James Jennings, "International Convention on the Elimination of All Forms of Racial Discrimination: Implications for Challenging Racial Hierarchy," *Howard Law Review* 40.3 (spring 1997): 603.

142. Ibid.

143. Cited in ibid., 604.

144. Reasons and Perdue, *The Ideology of Social Problems* 568, 580; Louis L. Knowles and Kenneth Prewitt, *Institutional Racism in America* (Englewood Cliffs, NJ: Prentice-Hall, 1969), 9.

145. Karen Brodkin Sachs, "How Did Jews Become White Folks?" in Stephen Gregory and Roger Janjek, eds., *Race* (New Brunswick, NJ: Rutgers University Press, 1994), 78–102; Ruth Frankenberg, *White Women, Race Matters: The Social Construction of Whiteness* (Minneapolis: University of Minnesota Press, 1991), 13; Evelyn Nakano Glenn, "Race, Gender and American Citizenship: Historical Change and Regional Variation," University of California, Berkeley, unpublished manuscript, May 1996; and Michael Omi and Howard Winant, *Racial Formation in the United States: From the 1960s to the 1980s* (London: Routledge, 1986).

146. Gertrude Ezorsky, *Racism and Justice: The Case for Affirmative Action* (Ithaca, NY: Cornell University Press, 1991), 9–27.

147. Michael Brown, "Race in the American Welfare State: The Ambiguities of Universalistic Social Policies since the New Deal," in Adolph Reed Jr., ed., *Without Justice for All* (Boulder, CO: Westview Press, 1999), 93–122.

148. Dennis Judd, "Symbolic Politics and Urban Policies: Why African Americans Got So Little from the Democrats," in Reed, *Without Justice for All*, 123–150.

149. Maulena Karenga, "Introduction to Black Studies," in Ellis Chasmore and James Jennings, eds., *Racism: Essential Readings* (Thousand Oaks, CA: Sage, 2001), 209–216.

150. The National Advisory Commission on Civil Disorders, *Report of the National Advisory Commission on Civil Disorders* (New York: Bantam Books, 1968), 2.

151. Ernest Greenwood, "Attributes of a Profession," *Social Work* 2.3 (July 1975), cited in Neil Gilbert and Paul Terrell, eds., *Dimensions of Social Welfare Policy* (Boston: Allyn and Bacon, 1998), 168; Popple and Leighninger, *Social Work*, 56.

152. Galper, *The Politics of the Social Services;* Malcolm Payne, *Modern Social Work Theory: A Critical Introduction* (Chicago: Lyceum, 1991), 204–205.

153. John H. Ehrenreich, *The Altruistic Imagination: A History of Social Work and Social Policy in the United States* (Ithaca, NY: Cornell University Press, 1983), 228.

154. Galper, *The Politics of Social Services*, 97.

155. Ibid., 92.

156. Wilensky and Lebeaux, *Industrial Society and Social Welfare*, 299–300.

157. Mimi Abramovitz, "Social Work and Social Reform: An Arena of Struggle," *Social Work* 43.6 (November 1998): 512–527; Paul Wilding, *Professional Power and Social Welfare* (London: Routledge & Kegan Paul, 1982), 99–100.

158. Mathew Dumont, "The Changing Face of Professionalism," *Social Policy* (May/June 1972): 32.

159. Stanley Wenocur and Michael Reisch, *From Charity to Enterprise: The Development of American Social Work in a Market Economy* (Urbana, IL: University of Chicago Press, 1989), 4–5.

160. Mullaly, *Structural Social Work*, 193.

161. Ann Withorn, "Professionalism vs Radicalism and the Future of BCRS," *BCR Reports* (fall/winter 1996–1997): 1–2.

162. Wenocur and Reisch, *From Charity to Enterprise*, 202–207.

163. Abramovitz, "Social Work and Social Reform," 512–527.

164. See Barbara Bryant Solomon, *Black Empowerment: Social Work in Oppressed Communities* (New York: Columbia University Press, 1976); Barbara Levy Simon, *The Empowerment Tradition in American Social Work: A History* (New York: Columbia University Press, 1994); Elaine Pinderhuges, "Empowerment for Our Clients and for Ourselves," *Social Casework* 64 (1983): 331–338; Elaine Pinderhuges, *Understanding Race, Ethnicity and Power: The Key to Efficacy in Clinical Practice* (New York: Free Press, 1989); Lorraine M. Gutierrez, "Working with Women of Color: An Empowerment Perspective," *Social Work* 35 (1990): 97–192.

165. Nan Van Den Bergh, ed., *Feminist Practice in the 21st Century* (Washington, DC: NASW Press, 1995); Mary Bricker Jenkins and Nancy Hooyman, eds., *Not for Women Only* (Silver Spring, MD: NASW Press, 1986) Elaine Norman and Arlene Mancuso, eds., *Women's Issues and Social Work Practice*, (Itasca, IL: F.E. Peacock, 1980); Ann Weick and Susan T. Vandiver, eds., *Women, Power and Change.* (Washington, DC: NASW Press, 1981).

166. Van Den Bergh, *Feminist Practice in the 21st Century*, xi–xxix; Helen Land, "Feminist Clinical Social Work in the 21st Century," in Van Den Bergh, *Feminist Practice in the 21st Century*, 3–19; Karen Haynes and Karen Holmes, *Invitation to Social Work* (New York: Longman, 1994), 21–29.

Chapter 6

1. Anthony Oberschall, *Social Movements: Ideologies, Interests and Identities* (New Brunswick, NJ: Transaction, 1995), 1.

2. National Association of Social Workers, www.naswdc.org, accessed August 13, 2002.

3. Prudence S. Posner, "The American Working Class and the Community-Workplace Dichotomy: Selections from the Writing of Ira Katznelson," in Joseph L. Kling and Prudence S Posner, eds., *Dilemmas of Activism: Class, Community and the Politics of Local Mobilization* (Philadelphia: Temple University Press, 1990), 56.

4. Charles L. Harper, *Exploring Social Change* (Englewood Cliffs, NJ: Prentice-Hall, 1993), 139; Roberta Garner, *Contemporary Movements and Ideologies* (New York: McGraw-Hill, 1996). 86; Steven M. Buechler, *Social Movement in Advanced Capitalism: The*

Political Economy and Cultural Construction of Social Activism, (New York: Oxford University Press, 2000), 5–6, 11.

5. Robin D. G. Kelly, *Race Rebels: Culture Politics and the Black Working Class* (New York: Free Press, 1994); Tera W. Hunter *To 'Joy My Freedom: Southern Black Women's Lives and Labors after the Civil War* (Cambridge, MA: Harvard University Press, 1997); Jacqueline Jones, *Labor of Love, Labor of Sorrow: Black Women Work and Family, from Slavery to the Present* (New York: Basic Books, 1985); David Katzman, *Seven Days a Week: Women and Domestic Service in Industrializing America* (New York: Oxford University Press, 1978).

6. N. S. Perl, "Resistance Strategies: The Routine Struggle for Bread and Roses," in Karen B. Sachs and D. Remy, eds., *My Troubles Are Going to Have Trouble with Me* (New Brunswick, NJ: Rutgers University Press, 1984), 93–209; Doris E. Janiewski, *Sisterhood Denied: Race, Gender and Class in a New South Community* (Philadelphia: Temple University Press, 1985); Virginia R. Seitz, "Class, Gender and Resistance in the Appalachian Coal Fields," in Nancy Naples, ed., *Community Activism and Feminist Politics: Organizing across Race, Class and Gender* (New York: Routledge, 1998), 213–236.

7. Kelly, *Race Rebels*, 17.

8. Frances Fox Piven and Richard A. Cloward, *Regulating the Poor: The Functions of Public Welfare* (New York: Pantheon, 1993), 464–465.

9. Buechler, *Social Movement in Advanced Capitalism*, 47, 150–151.

10. James C. Scott, *Weapons of the Weak: Everyday Forms of Peasant Resistance* (New Haven: Yale University Press, 1985).

11. Daniel Brook, "The Continuum of Collective Action" unpublished manuscript, n.d., available at Brook@bankok.com.

12. George Rudé, *The Crowd in History* (New York: Wiley, 1964).

13. Michael Lipsky, "Protest as a Political Resource," *American Political Science Review* 62(1968): 1144–1158.

14. Frances Fox Piven and Richard A. Cloward, *Poor People's Movements: Why They Succeed, How They Fail* (New York: Vintage Books, 1977), xix–xxix; Piven and Cloward, *Regulating the Poor*, 456.

15. Piven and Cloward, *Poor People's Movements*, xxiii, 2, xix–xxiv.

16. Frances Fox Piven and Richard A. Cloward, "Movements and Discensus Politics," in Sidney Tarrow, ed., *Power in Movement: Social Movements, Collective Action and Politics* (Cambridge: Cambridge University Press, 1996), 235–249.

17. Piven and Cloward, *Poor People's Movements*, xxi, 3; Richard A. Cloward and Frances Fox Piven, *The Politics of Turmoil: Poverty, Race, and the Urban Crisis* (New York: Vintage Books, 1975), 85; Frances Fox Piven and Richard A. Cloward, "Normalizing Collective Protest," in Aldon D. Morris and Carol McClurg Mueller, eds., *Frontiers in Social Movement Theory* (New Haven, CT: Yale University Press, 1992), 319.

18. Piven and Cloward, *Poor People's Movements*, 28, 452–453.

19. Ibid., xxi.

20. David S. Meyer and Sidney Tarrow, *The Social Movement Society: Contentious Politics for a New Century* (Lanham, MD: Rowman & Littlefeld, 1998), 4.

21. Buechler, *Social Movement in Advanced Capitalism*, 5–10.

22. Ibid., 16.

23. P. Jalee, *How Capitalism Works* (New York: Monthly Review Press, 1977).

24. Andrew Hacker, *Two Nations: Black and White, Separate, Hostile, Unequal* (New York: Scribner's, 1992). See Alexis de Tocqueville, *Democracy in America.* (New Rochelle, NY: Arlington House, 1966); G. Myrdal, *An American Dilemma: The Negro Problem and Modern Democracy* (New York: Harper and Brothers, 1944).

25. E. P. Thompson, "The Moral Economy of the English Crowd in the 18th Century," *Past and Present* 50(1971):71–136.

26. For more details, see Mimi Abramovitz, *Under Attack, Fighting Back: Women and Welfare in the United States* (New York: Monthly Review Press, 1996), especially ch. 2.

27. Gosta Esping-Anderson, *The Three Worlds of Welfare Capitalism* (Princeton: Princeton University Press, 1990); Ann Orloff, "Gender and the Welfare State," *American Review of Sociology* 22(1996): 51–78; Frances Fox Piven and Richard Cloward, *The New Class War: Reagan's Attack on the Welfare State and Its Consequences* (New York: Pantheon, 1982).

28. Garner, *Contemporary Movements and Ideologies*, 42, 64–65; James L. Wood and Maurice Jackson, *Social Movements: Development, Participation, and Dynamics* (Belmont, CA: Wadsworth, 1983), 31–32.

29. Harry H. Bash, *Social Problems and Social Movements* (Atlantic Highlands, NJ: Humanities Press, 1995), 149; J. Craig Jenkins, "Resource Mobilization Theory and the Study of Social Movements," *American Review of Sociology* 9 (1983): 538; Mayer N. Zald, "Looking Backward to the Future: Reflection on the Past and Future of the Resource Mobilization Research Program," in Morris and McClurg Mueller, *Frontiers in Social Movement Theory*, 328.

30. Wood and Jackson, *Social Movements*, 36.

31. Ibid.

32. Gustave Le Bon, *The Crowd* (1895; New York: Viking Press, 1960); Oberschall, *Social Movements*, 4–6.

33. Sigmund Freud, *Group Psychology and the Analysis of the Ego* (New York: Liveright, 1951), 91.

34. Marc Edelman, "Social Movements: Changing Paradigm and Forms of Politics," *Annual Review of Anthropology* 30 (2001): 285–317, citing Eric Fromm, *Escape from Freedom* (New York: Holt, Rinehart & Winston, 1941).

35. Edelman, "Social Movements," citing Hannah Arendt, *The Origins of Totalitarianism* (New York: Harcourt Brace & World, 1951).

36. Lewis S. Feuer, *The Conflict of Generations* (New York: Basic Books, 1969).

37. Wood and Jackson, *Social Movements*, 33, 103–105.

38. Jenkins, "Resource Mobilization Theory," 529. See Emile Durkheim, *The Division of Labor in Society* (1893; New York: Free Press, 1964); William Kornhauser, *The Politics of Mass Society* (New York: Free Press, 1959).

39. Buechler, *Social Movement in Advanced Capitalism*, 27; Oberschall, *Social Movements*, 18; Harper, *Exploring Social Change*, 144.

40. Wood and Jackson, *Social Movements*, 66.

41. Talcott Parsons, *The Social System* (Glencoe, IL: Free Press, 1951); Neil Smelser, *Theory of Collective Behavior* (New York: Free Press, 1962).

42. Buechler, *Social Movements in Advanced Capitalism*, 25–27; Wood and Jackson, *Social Movements*, 41–44; Harper, *Exploring Social Change*, 151–152.

43. Aldon D. Morris, "A Retrospective on the Civil Rights Movement: Political and Intellectual Landmarks," *Annual Review of Sociology*, (1999): 571, Info Trac Wed electronic collection A64263021.

44. Buechler, *Social Movement in Advanced Capitalism*, 30–31; Harper, *Exploring Social Change*, 145, 148; Wood and Jackson, *Social Movements*, 33; Sidney Tarrow, Introduction, in Sidney Tarrow, ed., *Power in Movement: Social Movements, Collective Action and Politics*, viii; Garner, *Contemporary Movements and Ideologies*, 48.

45. Oberschall, *Social Movements*, 12.

46. Ibid., 13–25.

47. Ron Eyerman and Andrew Jamison, *Social Movements: A Cognitive Approach*, 20.

48. Kenneth Keniston, *The Uncommitted: Alienated Youth in American Society* (New York: Harcourt Brace, 1965).

49. Wood and Jackson, *Social Movements*, 113; Richard Flacks, "The Liberated Generation: An Exploration of the Roots of Student Protest," *Journal of Social Issues* 23 (July 1967): 52–75.

50. Wood and Maurice Jackson, *Social Movements*, 36, 116.

51. Eyerman and Jamison, *Social Movements*, 21.

52. Harper, *Exploring Social Change*, 145. See Robert Merton, *Social Theory and Social Structure* (New York: Free Press, 1968); Ralph Linton, *The Study of Man* (New York: Appleton-Century-Crofts, 1936).

53. Buechler, *Social Movements in Advanced Capitalism*, 28–29; Wood and Jackson, *Social Movements*, 37.

54. Harper, *Exploring Social Change*, 146; Wood and Jackson, *Social Movements*, 37; Garner, *Contemporary Movements and Ideologies*, 48, 53.

55. Buechler, *Social Movements in Advanced Capitalism*, 76.

56. Wood and Jackson, *Social Movements*, 128.

57. Garner, *Contemporary Movements and Ideologies*, 297.

58. Ibid., 215–216.

59. Mancur Olson, *The Logic of Collective Action* (New York: Schocken, 1965).

60. Jenkins, "Resource Mobilization Theory," 537.

61. Bruce Fireman and William Gamson, "Utilitarian Logic in the Resource Mobilization Perspective," in Mayer N. Zald and John D. McCarthy, eds., *The Dynamics of Social Movements* (Cambridge, MA: Winthrop, 1979), 8–44; Wood and Jackson, *Social Movements*, 33; Harper, *Exploring Social Change*, 144, 148; Oberschall, *Social Movements*, 20–21, 57; Edelman, "Social Movements," 285–317.

62. Nancy Hartsock, "Exchange Theory: Critique from a Feminist Standpoint," in Scott McNall, ed., *Current Perspectives in Social Theory, 1985*, vol. 6 (Greenwich, CT: JAI), 57–70 cited in Steven M. Buechler, "Beyond Resource Mobilization," *Sociological Quarterly* 34, 2 (1983): 227; Paula England, "Feminist Critique of Rational Choice Theory: Implications for Sociology," *American Sociologist* 20 (1989); Myra Marx Feree, "The Political Context of Rationality: Rational Choice Theory and Resource Mobilization," in Morris and McClurg Mueller, *Frontiers in Social Movement Theory*, 29–52; J. Ann Ticker, "Feminist Perspectives on Security in a Global Economy," in Caroline Thomas and Peter Wilkin, eds., *Globalization, Human Security and the African Experiences* (Boulder, CO: Lynne Riener, 1999), 47–48.

63. John D. McCarthy and Mayer N. Zald, "Resource Mobilization and Social Movements: A Partial Theory," *American Journal of Sociology* 82, 6: 1212–1241; Harper, *Exploring Social Change*, 154; Edelman, "Social Movement," 289.

64. Sidney Tarrow, " 'The Very Excess of Democracy': State Building and Contentious Politics in America," in Anne N. Costain and Andrew S. McFarland, eds., *Social Movements and American Political Institutions*, (Lanham, MD: Rowman & Littlefield, 1998), 7–19.

65. Edelman "Social Movement," 289; Zald, "Looking Backward to the Future," 326–348.

66. Garner, *Contemporary Movements and Ideologies*, 49–51; Harper, *Exploring Social Change*, 155; Buechler, "Beyond Resource Mobilization," 218; Carol McClurg Mueller, "Building Social Movement Theory," in Morris and McClurg Mueller, *Frontiers in Social Movement Theory*, 17–18.

67. Charles Tilly, *From Mobilization to Revolution* (Reading, MA: Addison Wesley, 1978).

68. Doug McAdam, "Culture and Social Movements," in Enrique Larana, Hank Johnson, and Joseph R. Gusfield, eds., *New Social Movements: From Ideology to Identity* (Philadelphia: Temple University Press, 1994), 36–57; Marcy Darnovsky, Barbara Epstein, and Richard Flacks, *Cultural Politics and Social Movements* (Philadelphia: Temple University Press, 1995), 18; Andrew McFarland, "Social Movements and Theories of American Politics," in Costain and McFarland, *Social Movements and American Political Institutions*, 11; Eyerman and Jamison, *Social Movements*, 36.

69. Aldon D. Morris, "A Retrospective on the Civil Rights Movement: Political and Intellectual Landmarks," *Annual Review of Sociology* (1999): 517–541; Jenkins, "Resource Mobilization Theory," 532, 548; Garner, *Contemporary Movements and Ideologies*, 53.

70. Garner, *Contemporary Movements and Ideologies*, 52.

71. Harper, *Exploring Social Change*, 156; Garner, *Contemporary Movements and Ideologies*, 51.

72. Darnovsky et al., *Cultural Politics and Social Movements*, 18.

73. Jenkins, "Resource Mobilization Theory," 547; Harper, *Exploring Social Change*, 157; Piven and Cloward, *Poor People's Movements*.

74. Garner, *Contemporary Movements and Ideologies*, 52.

75. Douglas W. Costain and Anne N. Costain, "The Political Strategies of Social Movements: A Comparision of the Women's and Environmental Movements," *Congress and the Presidency* 19.1 (spring 1992): 1–27.

76. Garner, *Contemporary Movements and Ideologies*, 80.

77. Harper, *Exploring Social Change*, 157.

78. Garner, *Contemporary Movements and Ideologies*, 53; McFarland, "Social Movements and Theories of American Politics," 11.

79. Garner, *Contemporary Movements and Ideologies*, 92, 109–123; Wood and Jackson, *Social Movements*, 6; Rebecca Klatch, *Women of the New Right* (Philadelphia, PA: Temple University Press, 1987), 14.

80. Wood and Jackson, *Social Movements*, 6; Garner, *Contemporary Movements and Ideologies*, 297; Edelman, "Social Movement," 303.

81. Buechler, *Social Movement in Advanced Capitalism*, 48; Bob Fisher and Joseph Kling, "Popular Mobilization in the 1990s: Prospects for New Social Movements," *New Politics* 3 (1991): 76.

82. Ralph Turner, "Ideology and Utopia after Socialism," in Larana et al., *New Social Movements*, 94.

83. Buechler, *Social Movement in Advanced Capitalism*, 438; Robert Fisher and Joseph Kling, "Community Organization, New Social Movement Theory, and the Condition of Postmodernity," in David J. Tucker, Charles Garvin, and Rosemary Sarri, eds., *Integrating Knowledge and Practice: The Case of Social Work and Social Science* (Westport, CT: Praeger, 1997), 105–115; Fisher and Kling, "Popular Mobilization in the 1990s," 106–109; Garner, *Contemporary Movements and Ideologies*, 76, 99.

84. Edelman, "Social Movement," 289; Tarrow, *Power in Movement*, introduction, xiii, xiv; Alberto Melucci, "A Strange Kind of Newness: What's 'New' in New Social Movements," in Larana et al., *New Social Movements*, 102.

85. Fisher and Kling, "Community Organization, New Social Movement Theory, and the Condition of Postmodernity," 105–115; Fisher and Kling, "Popular Mobilization in the 1990s," 110.

86. Edelman, "Social Movement," 299.

87. Hank Johnson, Enrique Larana, and Joseph R. Gusfield, "Identities, Grievances, and New Social Movements," in Larana et al., *New Social Movements*, 10.

88. Melucci, "A Strange Kind of Newness," 104.

89. Buechler, *Social Movement in Advanced Capitalism*, 33; Edelman, "Social Movement," 289.

90. Turner, "Ideology and Utopia after Socialism," 89–90.

91. Johnson et al., "Identities, Grievances, and New Social Movements," 10–11.

92. Ibid., 12; Edelman, "Social Movement," 296–297.

93. Joe R. Feagin and Clairece Booker Feagin, *Social Problems: A Critical Power-Conflict Perspective* (Upper Saddle River, NJ: Prentice-Hall, 1997), 17.

94. Buechler, *Social Movement in Advanced Capitalism*, 14; Feagin and Feagin, *Social Problems*, 18.

95. Feagin and Feagin, *Social Problems*, 18.

96. Richard Flacks, "Marxism and Sociology," in Bertell Ollman and Edward Vernoff, eds., *The Left Academy: Marxist Scholarship on American Campuses* (New York: McGraw-Hill, 1982), 22.

97. Ibid., 23; Eyerman and Jamison, *Social Movements*, 2; Buechler, *Social Movement in Advanced Capitalism*, 108.

98. Flacks, "Marxism and Sociology," 9–52.

99. Tarrow, *Power in Movement*, introduction, viii; Wood and Jackson, *Social Movements*, 34–35; Oberschall, *Social Movements*, 52.

100. Barbara Wertheimer, *We Were There: The Story of Working Women in America* (New York: Pantheon, 1977), 72–78; Abramovitz, *Under Attack, Fighting Back*, 117.

101. Phyllis J. Day, *A New History of Social Welfare* 3d ed. (Boston: Allyn and Bacon, 2000), 3, 194; William H. Whitaker and Ronald C. Federico, *Social Welfare in Today's World* (New York: McGraw-Hill, 1997), 159.

102. Day, *A New History of Social Welfare*, 195.

103. John M. Blum, Bruce Catton, Edmond Morgan, Arthur M. Schlesinger Jr., Kenneth M. Stampp, and C. Vann Woodward, *The National Experience: A History of the United States* (New York: Harcourt, Brace & World, 1968), 455–460.

104. June Axinn and Mark J. Stern, *Social Welfare: A History of American Response to Need* (Boston: Allyn and Bacon, 2001), 131–132; Blum et al., *The National Experience*.

105. Axinn and Stern: *Social Welfare*, 178.

106. Feagin and Feagin, *Social Problems*, 18–20; Buechler, *Social Movement in Advanced Capitalism*, 107–116.

107. Buechler, *Social Movement in Advanced Capitalism*, 107–116.

108. Nancy E. McGlen and Karen O'Connor, *Women's Rights: The Struggle for Equality in the 19th and 20th Centuries* (New York: Praeger, 1983), 1.

109. Cited in George Brown Tindall, *America: A Narrative History*, 499–502.

110. Annelise Orleck, *Common Sense and a Little Fire: Women and Working-Class Politics in the United States, 1900–1965* (Chapel Hill: University of North Carolina Press, 1995): Abramovitz, *Under Attack, Fighting Back*, ch. 3.

111. Orleck, *Common Sense and a Little Fire*; Abramovitz, *Under Attack, Fighting Back*, 122–123.

112. Mark Naison, "From Eviction Resistance to Rent Control: Tenant Activism in the Great Depression," in Ronald Lawson, ed., *The Tenant Movement in New York City, 1904–1984*. (New Brunswick, NJ: Rutgers University Press, 1986).

113. Ann Stein, "Post War Consumer Boycotts," *Radical America* 9 (July–August 1993): 156–161; Orleck, *Common Sense and a Little Fire*; Abramovitz, *Under Attack, Fighting Back*, 126.

114. Jo Ann Gibson Robinson, *The Montgomery Bus Boycott and the Women Who Started It* (Knoxville: University of Tennessee Press, 1987).

115. Naples, *Community Activism and Feminist Politics*; Guida West, *The National Welfare Rights Organization: The Social Protest of Poor Women* (New York: Praeger, 1981).

116. Mimi Abramovitz, "Learning from the History of Poor and Working-Class Women's Activism," *Annals of the American Academy of Political and Social Science* 577 (September 2001): 118–130.

117. Howard Winant, "Race: Theory, Culture and Politics in the United States Today," in Tarrow, *Power in Movement*, 174–188; Howard Winant, "Race and Race Theory," *Annual Review of Sociology* (2000): 169, Info Trac Web electronic collection A67051605.

118. Hacker, *Two Nations*.

119. Tindall, *America: A Narrative History*, 560–564.

120. Anne Firor Scott, "Most Invisible of All: Black Women's Voluntary Associations," *Journal of Southern History* 56.1 (February 1990); 3–22.

121. Belinda Robnett, *How Long? How Long? African American Women in the Struggle for Civil Rights* (New York: Oxford University Press, 1997); Lillian Serece Williams, "National Association of Colored Women," in Wilma Mankiller, Gwendolyn Mink, Marysa Navara, Barbara Smith, and Gloria Steinem, eds., *The Readers' Companion to U.S. Women's History* (New York: Houghton Mifflin, 1998), 392.

122. Whitaker and Federico, *Social Welfare in Today's World*, 163; Axinn and Stern: *Social Welfare*, 146.

123. Garner, *Contemporary Movements and Ideologies*, 92; Harper, *Exploring Social Change*, 134.
124. Garner, *Contemporary Movements and Ideologies*, 92, 109–123; Wood and Jackson, *Social Movements*, 6; Klatch, *Women of the New Right*, 14.
125. Garner, *Contemporary Movements and Ideologies*, 271–304.
126. Klatch, *Women of the New Right*, 104–106.
127. Robert Mullaly, *Structural Social Work: Ideology, Theory, and Practice* (Toronto: Canadian Publishers, 1993), 82.
128. Garner, *Contemporary Movements and Ideologies*, 159; Mullaly, *Structural Social Work*, 185.
129. Terrence Ball and Richard Dagger, *Political Ideologies and the Democratic Ideal* (New York: Longman, 1988), 220–221; Prudence S. Posner, introduction, in Joseph M. Kling and Prudence S. Posner, eds., *Dilemmas of Activism*, 3–20.
130. Garner, *Contemporary Movements and Ideologies*, 134.
131. Ibid., 172.
132. Richard Falk, "The Making of Global Citizenship," in J. B. Childs, J. Brecher, and J. Cutler, eds., *Global Visions: Beyond the New World Order* (Boston: South End Press, 1993), 39, cited in Edelman, "Social Movement," 304.
133. Edelman, "Social Movement," 307–308.
134. Erving Goffman, *Frame Analysis: An Essay on the Organization of Experience* (New York: Harper, 1974); David A. Snow and Robert D. Benford, "Master Frames and Cycle of Protest," in Morris and McClug Mueller, *Frontiers of Social Movement Theory*, 133–156.
135. Carol McClurg Mueller, "Building Social Movement Theory," in Morris and McClurg Mueller, *Frontiers in Social Movement Theory*, 3–26.
136. Robert D. Benford and David A. Snow. "Framing Processes and Social Movements: An Overview and Assessment," *Annual Review of Sociology* (2000): 611, electronic collection A6705111623.
137. Ibid.
138. Snow and Benford, "Master Frames and Cycle of Protest," 133–156.
139. McAdam, "Culture and Social Movements," 36–57.
140. Snow and Benford, "Master Frames and Cycle of Protest," 133–156.
141. McAdam, "Culture and Social Movements," 36–57.
142. Harry Boyte, *The Backyard Revolution: Understanding the New Citizen Movement* (Philadelphia: Temple University Press, 1981); Sara Evans and Harry Boyte, *Free Spaces: The Sources of Democratic Change in America* (New York: Harper & Row, 1986).
143. Evans and Boyte, *Free Spaces*.
144. Robert Fisher, *Let the People Decide: Neighborhood Organizing in America* (Boston: Twayne, 1984), 46–59; Robert Fisher and Joseph M. Kling, "Leading the People: Two Approaches to the Role of Ideology in Community Organizing," in Kling and Posner, *Dilemmas of Activism*, 74–76
145. George Rudé, *Ideology and Popular Protest* (New York: Pantheon, 1980).

Chapter 7

1. See J. R. Pole, *The Pursuit of Equality in American History* (Berkeley: University of California Press, 1993), for an authoritative discussion of this issue.
2. See the special issue of *Monthly Review, Prisons & Executions: The U.S. Model* (July/August 2001).
3. David Stout, "Study Finds Ballot Problems Are More Likely for Poor," *New York Times*, July 9, 2001.
4. Ralph Dolgoff and Donald Feldstein, *Understanding Social Welfare* (Needham Heights, MA: Allyn and Bacon, 2000), 46–47.
5. Karl de Schweinitz, *England's Road to Social Security* (Philadelphia: University of Pennsylvania Press, 1943), 40.

6. Nels Anderson, *The Homeless in New York*, unpublished manuscript, completed for the Welfare Council of New York, February 1934, 71–72.

7. Bruce Jansson, *The Reluctant Welfare State*, 4th ed. (Belmont, CA: Brooks/Cole, 2001), 40; Mimi Abramovitz, *Regulating the Lives of Women* (Boston: South End Press, 1996), 50–51.

8. Jansson, *The Reluctant Welfare State*, 54; June Axinn and Mark Stern, *Social Welfare: A History of the American Response to Need*, 5th ed. (Needham Heights, MA: Allyn and Bacon, 2001), 27.

9. Phyllis Day, *A History of Social Welfare*, 3d ed. (Needham Heights, MA: Allyn and Bacon, 2000), 133.

10. John A. Garraty, *American History* (New York: Harcourt, Brace, Jovanovich, 1986), 94.

11. Jansson, *The Reluctant Welfare State*, 40.

12. Dolgoff and Feldstein, *Understanding Social Welfare*, 65.

13. Abramovitz, *Regulating the Lives of Women*, 52.

14. William Appleman Williams, *The Contours of American History* (Chicago: Quadrangle Books, 1966), 93–102.

15. Howard Zinn, *A People's History of the United States* (New York: Harper Perennial, 1980), 39–41; Edwin Burrows and Mike Wallace, *Gotham: A History of New York to 1898* (New York: Oxford University Press, 1999), 100–101.

16. Zinn, *A People's History of the United States*, 35–36.

17. Walter Trattner, *From Poor Law to Welfare State*, 6th ed. (New York: Free Press, 1999), 17.

18. Ibid., 18.

19. Abramovitz, *Regulating the Lives of Women*, 86–89.

20. Trattner, *From Poor Law to Welfare State*, 30–31.

21. David Rothman, *The Discovery of the Asylum* (Boston: Little, Brown, 1971).

22. Axinn and Stern, *Social Welfare*, 41–42; Garraty, *American History*, 296–300, 309–312.

23. Michael B. Katz, *In the Shadow of the Poorhouse* (New York: Basic Books, 1986), 4; and Burrows and Wallace, *Gotham*, 659.

24. David M. Schneider, *The History of Public Welfare in New York State, 1609–1866* (Chicago: University of Chicago Press, 1938), 228; Katz, *In the Shadow of the Poorhouse*, 22; Abramovitz, *Regulating the Lives of Women*, 148.

25. Axinn and Stern, *Social Welfare*, 40–42. The quotation is from William J. Grayson, *The Hireling and the Slave*, xiv–xv, cited in Vernon Louis Parrington, *Main Currents in American Thought* (New York: Harcourt Brace, 1930), 2:104.

26. Eric Foner, *Free Soil, Free Labor, Free Men* (New York: Oxford University Press, 1970), 58.

27. Ibid.

28. Burrows and Wallace, *Gotham*, 731.

29. Cited in Abramovitz, *Regulating the Lives of Women*, 127.

30. Cited in Pole, *The Pursuit of Equality in American History*, 176.

31. Garraty, *American History*, 388–393.

32. Katz, *In the Shadow of the Poorhouse*, 60–61.

33. Blanche Coll, *Perspectives in Social Welfare: A History* (Washington, DC: U.S. Government Printing Office, 1973), 36–37.

34. Dolgoff and Feldstein, *Understanding Social Welfare*, 67–68; Wilma Peebles-Wilkins, "Effectively Teaching African-American Social Welfare Historical Developments," *Journal of Sociology and Social Welfare* 21.1 (March 1994): 145.

35. Trattner, *From Poor Law to Welfare State*, 64–67.

36. Cited in ibid., 81–83.

37. Burrows and Wallace, *Gotham*, 1020–1022.

38. Zinn, *A People's History of the United States*, 240–250.

39. Katz, *In the Shadow of the Poorhouse*, 46–52.

40. Zinn, *A People's History of the United States*, 193–195.
41. Day, *A History of Social Welfare*, 191.
42. Garraty, *American History*, 509–510; Burrows and Wallace, *Gotham*, 1034–1035.
43. Theda Skocpol, *Protecting Soldiers and Mothers: The Political Origins of Social Policy in the United States* (Cambridge, MA: Harvard University Press, 1993), 70, 227.
44. Richard Hofstadter, *Social Darwinism in American Thought* (Boston: Beacon Press, 1955).
45. Zinn, *A People's History of the United States*, 198–199, 203.
46. Lawrence Goodwyn, *The Populist Moment* (New York: Oxford University Press, 1978).
47. Coll, *Perspectives in Social Welfare*, 44; Katz, *In the Shadow of the Poorhouse*, 68–69.
48. Patrick Selmi, "Social Work and the Campaign to Save Sacco and Vanzetti," *Social Service Review* 75.1 (March 2001): 115–134.
49. Linda M. Shoemaker, "Early Conflicts in Social Work Education," *Social Service Review* 72.2 (summer 1998): 182–191.
50. Gabriel Kolko, *The Triumph of Conservatism* (Chicago: Quadrangle Books, 1963); James Weinstein, *The Corporate Ideal in the Liberal State, 1900–1918* (Boston: Beacon Press, 1968).
51. John Ehrenreich, *The Altruistic Imagination: A History of Social Work and Social Policy in the United States* (Ithaca, NY: Cornell University Press, 1985), 26–29.
52. Cited in Weinstein, *The Corporate Ideal in the Liberal State*, 71.
53. Elmer Smead, *Governmental Promotion and Regulation of Business* (New York: Appleton-Century-Crofts, 1969), 123.
54. Skocpol, *Protecting Soldiers and Mothers*.
55. Charles Noble, *Welfare as We Knew It* (New York: Oxford University Press, 1997), 44–45.
56. Linda Gordon, *Pitied but Not Entitled: Single Mothers and the History of Welfare* (Cambridge, MA: Harvard University Press, 1994), 16–17.
57. Alice Solenberger, *One Thousand Homeless Men* (New York: Russell Sage Foundation, 1911); Robert Hunter, *Poverty* (New York: Macmillan, 1904).
58. Quoted in Richard Hofstadter, *The American Political Tradition* (New York: Vintage Books, 1948), 224.
59. Zinn, *A People's History of the United States*, 322–324; James Weinstein, *The Decline of Socialism in America, 1912–1925* (New York: Vintage Books, 1969), 93, 103.
60. Michael Reisch and Janice Andrews, *The Road Not Taken: A History of Radical Social Work in the United States* (Philadelphia: Brunner-Routledge, 2001), 33–34; Tony Platt and Susan Chandler, "Constant Struggle: E. Franklin Frazier and Black Social Work in the 1920s," *Social Work* 33.4 (July–August 1988): 294.
61. Zinn, *A People's History of the United States*, 340.
62. Cited in ibid., 336.
63. Gordon, *Pitied but Not Entitled*, 49.
64. Cited in Ehrenreich, *The Altruistic Imagination*, 58.
65. Ehrenreich, *The Altruistic Imagination*, 58; Reisch and Andrews, *The Road Not Taken*, 35.
66. Michael Reisch, "The Sociopolitical Context and Social Work Method, 1890–1950," *Social Service Review* 72.2 (June 1998): 161–181.
67. Ehrenreich, *The Altruistic Imagination*, 58, 47; Roy Lubove, *The Professional Altruist: The Emergence of Social Work as a Career, 1880–1930* (New York: Atheneum, 1980), 157.
68. William Leuchtenberg, *The Perils of Prosperity, 1914–1932* (Chicago: University of Chicago Press, 1958), 243–247.
69. Quoted in Richard Hofstadter, *The Age of Reform* (New York: Vintage, 1955), 307.
70. Philip Harvey, *Securing the Right to Employment* (Princeton: Princeton University Press, 1989), 15.
71. Cited in Abramovitz, *Regulating the Lives of Women*, 318–319.

72. Ann Shola Orloff, "The Political Origins of America's Belated Welfare State," in Margaret Weir, Ann Shola Orloff, and Theda Skocpol, eds., *The Politics of Social Policy in the United States* (Princeton: Princeton University Press, 1988), 71–72.

73. The phrase "economic declaration of rights" is quoted in Hofstadter, *The Age of Reform*, 330; the second quotation comes from Kenneth S. Davis, *FDR: The New Deal Years, 1933–1937* (New York: Random House, 1979), 373.

74. Frances Fox Piven and Richard A. Cloward, *Poor People's Movements: Why They Succeed, How They Fail* (New York: Vintage, 1977), 69–77.

75. Edwin Amenta, *Bold Relief: Institutional Politics and the Origins of Modern American Social Policy* (Princeton: Princeton University Press, 1998), 112–114; Frances Fox Piven and Richard A. Cloward, *Regulating the Poor* (New York: Vintage, 1971), 101.

76. Jacob Fisher, *The Response of Social Work to the Depression* (Cambridge, MA: Schenkman, 1980), 92, 237–239.

77. Williams, *The Contours of American History*, 445; Amenta, *Bold Relief*, 109; Zinn, *A People's History of the United States*, 386–393.

78. Noble, *Welfare as We Knew It*, 25–27; Piven and Cloward, *Regulating the Poor*, 87–99. The Sloan quote comes from Piven and Cloward, *Poor People's Movements*, 93.

79. For the relationship between Eleanor and Franklin Roosevelt on social policy issues, see Blanche Wiesen Cook, *Eleanor Roosevelt: The Defining Years, 1933–1938* (New York: Penguin, 2000), and Doris Kearns Goodwin, *No Ordinary Time* (New York: Simon & Schuster, 1994).

80. Abramovitz, *Regulating the Lives of Women*, 224, 283.

81. Ehrenreich, *The Altruistic Imagination*, 147.

82. See Mary L. Dudziak, *Cold War Civil Rights: Race and the Image of American Democracy* (Princeton: Princeton University Press, 2002); Thomas Borstelmann, *The Cold War and the Color Line* (Cambridge, MA: Harvard University Press, 2001).

83. Robert Reich, *The Work of Nations* (New York: Vintage Books, 1992), 56–57, 45.

84. U.S. Department of Commerce, Bureau of the Census, *Statistical Abstract of the United States 1989* (Washington, DC: Government Printing Office), table 489, p. 303.

85. See the special issue of *Journal of Sociology and Social Welfare* on this topic, 15.2 (June 1988).

86. Harvey, *Securing the Right to Employment*, 15.

87. Ehrenreich, *The Altruistic Imagination*, 140–141; Reisch and Andrews, *The Road Not Taken*, 101–106.

88. Piven and Cloward, *Regulating the Poor*, 250–256.

89. Todd Gitlin, *The Sixties: Years of Hope, Days of Rage* (New York: Bantam Books, 1987), 60–61.

90. The 1962 Port Huron statement, the founding document of Students for a Democratic Society, is a fine example of this perspective. For a discussion, see Gitlin, *The Sixties*, 114.

91. See Michael Harrington, *The Other America: Poverty in the United States* (New York: Simon & Schuster, 1997); Trattner, *From Poor Law to Welfare State*, 316–325.

92. Jo Freeman, "On the Origins of Social Movements," in Jo Freeman, ed., *Social Movements of the Sixties and Seventies* (White Plains, NY: Longman, 1983), 10–13.

93. See Jill Quadagno, *The Color of Welfare* (New York: Oxford University Press, 1994), 30, and, of course, Piven and Cloward's *Regulating the Poor*, which was the first to offer this interpretation.

94. Freeman, "On the Origins of Social Movements," 17–21.

95. Kirkpatrick Sale, *SDS* (New York: Vintage Books, 1974), 169–172.

96. Cited in Michael B. Katz, *The Undeserving Poor* (New York: Pantheon, 1989), 54.

97. Beth Stevens, "Blurring the Boundaries: How the Federal Government Has Influenced Welfare Benefits in the Private Sector," in Weir et al., *The Politics of Social Policy in the United States*, 138–139.

98. See Robert Caro, *The Years of Lyndon Johnson: Master of the Senate* (New York: Knopf, 2002).

99. Quadagno, *The Color of Welfare*, 175.

100. Cited in Ehrenreich, *The Altruistic Imagination*, 187–190.

101. Ehrenreich, *The Altruistic Imagination*, 190–205.

102. Louis Uchitelle, "Clinton Policies Find a Home with Bush," *New York Times*, July 5, 2001.

103. Roy Walmsley, *World Prison Population List* (London: Home Office Research, Development and Statistics Directorate, 2002), 1; Paige M. Harrison and Allen J. Beck, *Prisoners in 2001* (Washington, DC: U.S. Department of Justice, 2002), 12.

104. See *Drug War Facts*, http://www.drugwarfacts.org/racepris.htm, p. 2, accessed November 13, 2002.

105. Corrections Corporation of America, *Investor Relations*, http://www.shareholder.com/cxw, accessed November 14, 2002. The five larger systems are Texas, California, the Federal Bureau of Prisons, New York, and Florida.

106. Trattner, *From Poor Law to Welfare State*, 358.

107. Robin Toner, "Now, Government is the Solution, Not the Problem," *New York Times*, September 30, 2001.

108. Joel Blau, *The Visible Poor* (New York: Oxford University Press, 1992), 52–58, 71.

109. Thomas Frank, *One Market under God: Extreme Capitalism, Market Populism, and the End of Economic Democracy* (New York: Doubleday, 2000).

110. Barbara Epstein, "What Happened to the Women's Movement," *Monthly Review* 53.1 (May 2001): 1–13.

111. Wallace Swan, ed., *Gay/Lesbian/Transgender Public Policy Issues* (New York: Haworth Press, 1997).

112. "Gays Report a Rise in Public Acceptance," *New York Times*, November 13, 2001. The report was based on a study conducted by the Henry J. Kaiser Family Foundation.

113. This section draws on the list in Michael Katz, *Poverty and Policy in American History* (New York: Academic Press, 1983), 239–241.

Chapter 8

1. Donald E. Chambers, *Social Policy and Social Programs: A Method for the Practical Public Policy Analyst*, 3d ed. (Boston: Allyn and Bacon, 2000), 223–230.

2. Frances Fox Piven and Richard A. Cloward, *Regulating the Poor* (New York: Random House, 1971).

3. Michael B. Katz, *In the Shadow of the Poorhouse* (New York: Basic Books, 1986), 192.

4. Ibid.

5. Ibid., 191, 199; Charles Noble, *Welfare as We Knew It* (New York: Oxford University Press, 1997), 25; Chambers, *Social Policy and Social Programs*, 135.

6. Margaret Weir, Ann Shola Orloff, and Theda Skocpol, "The Future of Social Policy in the United States: Political Constraints and Possibilities," in Margaret Weir, Ann Shola Orloff, and Theda Skocpol, eds., *The Politics of Social Policy* (Princeton: Princeton University Press, 1988), 430; Karen S. Haynes and Karen Holmes, *Invitation to Social Work* (White Plains, NY: Longman, 1994), 94.

7. Piven and Cloward, *Regulating the Poor*.

8. John Ehrenreich, *The Altruistic Imagination: A History of Social Work and Social Policy in the United States* (Ithaca, NY: Cornell University Press, 1985), 84–100.

9. John Schwartz, "Social Security Checks to Rise 2.6%, an Average of $22 a Month," *New York Times*, October 20, 2001; Social Security Fact Sheet, *2002 Social Security Changes* http://www.ssa.gov/cola/cola2002.htm, accessed June 4, 2002; "Number of Social Security Beneficiaries," http://www.ssa.gov/OACT/ProgData/icpGraph.html, accessed June 4, 2002; Committee on Ways and Means, U.S. House of Representatives, *2000 Green Book* (Washington, DC: Government Printing Office), 16.

10. Social Security Fact Sheet, *2002 Social Security Changes*.

11. *2002 Social Security Trustees' Report*, http://www.ssa.gov.OACT, accessed March 27, 2002.

12. Committee on Ways and Means, *2000 Green Book*, 57.

13. Ibid., 94; Kathyrn H. Porter, Kathy Larin, and Wendell Primus, *Social Security and Poverty among the Elderly* (Washington, DC: Center on Budget and Policy Priorities, 1999), 1.

14. William W. Beach and Gareth G. Davis, "Social Security's Rate of Return," Washington, DC: Heritage Foundation, January 1998.

15. Kilolo Kijakazi, "African-Americans, Hispanic Americans, and Social Security: The Shortcoming of the Heritage Foundation Reports," Washington, DC: Center on Budget and Policy Priorities, October 8, 1998.

16. Rochelle Stanfield with Corinna Nicolaou, "Social Security: Out of Step with the Modern Family," Washington, DC: Urban Institute, April 2000, 4.

17. Ibid., 6; Susan B. Garland, "Commentary: Making Social Security More Women-Friendly," *Business Week*, May 22, 2000, 101–104.

18. Catherine Hill, "Privatizing Social Security Is Bad, Particularly for Women," *Dollars & Sense*, no. 232 (November/December 2000): 17–19, 35–36.

19. Committee on Ways and Means, *2000 Green Book*, 75.

20. *2002 Social Security Trustees' Report*.

21. Dean Baker and Mark Weisbrot, *Social Security: The Phony Crisis* (Chicago: University of Chicago Press, 1999); Joel Blau, *Illusions of Prosperity: America's Working Families in an Age of Economic Insecurity* (New York: Oxford University Press, 1999), 213–215.

22. Henry Aaron, Alicia Munnell, and Peter Orszag, "Social Security Reform: The Questions Raised by the Plans Endorsed by President Bush's Social Security Commission," New York: Century Foundation and Center on Budget and Policy Priorities, November 30, 2001; Peter A. Diamond and Peter R. Orzag, "Reducing Benefits and Subsidizing Individual Accounts: An Analysis of the Plans Proposed by the President's Commission to Strengthen Social Security," New York: Century Foundation and the Center on Budget and Policy Priorities, June 2002, 6.

23. Committee on Ways and Means, *2000 Green Book*, 2–36, Social Security Fact Sheet, *2002 Social Security Changes*.

24. Committee on Ways and Means, *2000 Green Book*, 17, 28, 29; Social Security Fact Sheet, *2002 Social Security Changes*.

25. Joel Blau, *The Visible Poor: Homelessness in the United States* (New York: Oxford University Press, 1992), 56; Chambers, *Social Policy and Social Programs*, 159; Committee on Ways and Means, *2000 Green Book*, 79; Louis Uchitelle, "Laid Off Workers Swelling the Cost of Disability Pay," *New York Times*, September 1, 2002.

26. Elizabeth A. Segal and Stephanie Brzuzy, *Social Welfare Policy, Programs, and Practice* (Itasca, IL: F.E. Peacock, 1998), 115; Social Security Fact Sheet, *2002 Social Security Changes: Annual Report of the Supplemental Security Income Program*, May 2002, p. 2, http://www.ssa.gov.cgi-bin/cqxgi/@ssi.env, accessed June 6, 2002; Committee on Ways and Means, *2000 Green Book*, 212–213, 233.

27. Linda P. Anderson, Paul A. Sundet, and Irma Harrington, *The Social Welfare System in the United States* (Boston: Allyn and Bacon, 2000), 95, 108.

28. Chambers, *Social Policy and Social Programs*, 151.

29. Anderson, et al., *The Social Welfare System in the United States*, 13.

30. Committee on Ways and Means, *2000 Green Book*, 280, 293.

31. Bruce Jansson, *The Reluctant Welfare State*, 3d ed. (Pacific Grove, CA: Brooks/Cole, 1997), 174–75.

32. Committee on Ways and Means, *2000 Green Book*, 287.

33. "Temporary Extended Unemployment Compensation," http://workforcesecurity.doleta.gov/unemploy/factsheetteuc.asp, accessed June 7, 2002; Committee on Ways and Means, *1998 Green Book* (Washington, DC: Government Printing Office), 341.

34. Blau, *Illusions of Prosperity*, 120; Wayne Vroman, *Effects of Welfare Reform on Unem-*

ployment Insurance (Washington, DC: Urban Institute, 2000), 4–5; David Leonhardt, "Georgia Finds Itself in Jobless Benefits Bind," *New York Times*, January 16, 2002.

35. Katharine G. Abraham and Susan N. Houseman, *Job Security in America* (Washington, DC: Brookings Institution, 1993), 5; Saul J. Blaustein, *Unemployment Insurance in the United States: The First Half Century* (Kalamazoo, MI: Upjohn Institute, 1993), 62–63.

36. Sheila Collins and Trudy Goldberg, *Washington's New Poor Law: Welfare Reform and the Roads Not Taken 1935 to the Present* (New York: Apex Press, 2000).

37. Robert Pear, "Federal Welfare Rolls Shrink, But Drop Is Smallest Since '94," *New York Times*, May 21, 2002; Jason DeParle, "Bold Effort Leaves Much Unchanged for the Poor," *New York Times*, December 30, 1999; Council of Economic Advisors, *Explaining the Decline in Welfare Receipt, 1993–1996*, May 9, 1997; Office of the Assistant Secretary for Planning and Evaluation, Health and Human Services, "Interim Status Report on Research on the Outcomes of Welfare Reform," 1999, 4.

38. Tami J. Friedman, "How States Are Spending Their Welfare Money—Or Not," *Dollars & Sense*, no. 240, (March–April 2002); 46–47; Sharon Parrott, Wendell Primus, and Shawn Fremstad, "Administration's TANF Proposal Would Limit—Not Increase—State Flexibility," Center on Budget and Policy Priorities, March 18, 2002; Peter Edelman, "The True Purpose of Welfare Reform," *New York Times*, May 29, 2002.

39. Heidi Hartman and M. K. Tally, "Welfare, Poverty, and Marriage: What Does the Research Say?" *Institute for Women's Policy Research Quarterly Newsletter* (winter/spring 2002): 1, 4–5; Nina Bernstein, "Strict Limits on Welfare Benefits Discourage Marriage, Studies Say," *New York Times*, June 3, 2002.

40. Neil DeMause, "Declaring Victory in the Welfare Debate," *Extra* 15.3: (June 2002): 17–18.

41. Heather Boushey, "Former Welfare Families Need More Help," Economic Policy Institute briefing paper, http://www.epinet.org/briefingpapers/bp123.html, accessed April 17, 2002.

42. Timothy Bartik, "Employment as a Solution to Welfare," *Upjohn Institute Employment Research* 7.1 (April, 2000). 1–4; Sharon Parrott, *Welfare Recipients Who Find Jobs: What Do We Know about Their Employment and Earnings?* Center on Budget and Policy Priorities, 1998), 1–2; Nina Bernstein, "Side Effect of Welfare Law: The No-Parent Family," *New York Times*, July 29, 2002.

43. Kathyrn Edin and Laura Lein, *Making Ends Meet* (New York: Russell Sage Foundation, 1997), 111.

44. Karin Martinson and Julie Strawn, *Built to Last: Why Skills Matter for Long-Run Success in Welfare Reform* (Washington, DC: Center for Law and Social Policy and the National Council of State Directors of Adult Education, 2002), 4.

45. See Daniel Mont, John F. Burton Jr., Virginia Reno, and Cecili Thompson, *Workers' Compensation: Benefits, Coverage, and Costs, 2000 New Estimates* (Washington, DC: National Academy of Social Insurance, June 2002), 1.

46. See U.S. Department of Labor, *State Workers' Compensation Laws* (Washington, DC: Department of Labor, January 2001), tables 6, 7, 8.

47. Committee on Ways and Means, *2000 Green Book*, 983–987.

48. Nicholas Johnson, *A Hand Up: How State Earned Income Tax Credit Helps Working Families Escape Poverty in 2000: An Overview* (Washington, DC: Center on Budget and Policy Priorities, June 9, 2000), 5–6; Center on Budget and Policy Priorities, *Facts about the Earned Income Tax Credit* (Washington, DC.: Center on Budget and Policy Priorities, 2001), 3.

49. The White House, Office of the Press Secretary, "President Clinton Proposes to Expand the Earned Income Tax Credit in Order to Increase the Reward for Work and Family," January 12, 2000, 3; Committee on Ways and Means, *2000 Green Book*, 812; Collins and Goldberg, *Washington's New Poor Law*, 314; Johnson, *A Hand Up*, 1.

50. Johnson, *A Hand Up*, 1.

51. Committee on Ways and Means, *2000 Green Book*, 808.

52. L. Jerome Gallagher, *A Shrinking Portion of the Safety Net: General Assistance from 1989 to 1998*, Urban Institute, Series A, No. A-36, September 1999, 1.

53. Ibid., 2, 5.

54. Center for Social Development, George Warren Brown School of Social Work, Washington University, *Research at Center for Social Development Influences President Clinton's Proposal for Matched Saving*, 2000; Michael Sherraden, "Building Assets to Fight Poverty," *Shelterforce* 22.2 (March–April, 2000): 26–27, 30.

55. James Midgley, "Debate: Can an Asset-Based Welfare Policy Really Help the Poor?" in Howard Karger and James Midgley, eds., *Controversial Issues in Social Policy* (Boston: Allyn and Bacon, 1994), 283; Center for Social Development, *Savings and Asset Accumulation in Individual Development Accounts* (St. Louis: Center for Social Development, Washington University, 2001), iii.

56. Sherraden, "Building Assets to Fight Poverty," 26.

57. Michael Sherraden, "Debate: Can an Asset-Based Welfare Policy Really Help the Poor?" in Karger and Midgley, ed., *Controversial Issues in Social Policy*, 278.

58. Ibid., 283–286.

59. The first U.S. Congress on BIG was held in New York City in spring 2002.

60. Karl Widerquist and Michael A. Lewis, "An Efficiency Argument for the Guaranteed Income," Working Paper no. 212, Jerome Levy Economics Institute at Bard College, November 1997; Guy Standing, *Beyond the New Paternalism: Basic Security as Equality* (London: Verso, 2002).

61. Linda Gordon, *Pitied but Not Entitled* (Cambridge, MA: Harvard University Press, 1994); Theda Skocpol, *Protecting Soldiers and Mothers* (Cambridge, MA: Harvard University Press, 1992).

62. Katz, *In the Shadow of the Poorhouse*.

63. Charles Murray, *Losing Ground: American Social Policy 1950–1980* (New York: Basic Books, 1984).

64. Katz, *In the Shadow of the Poorhouse*, 199.

65. Ibid., 286.

Chapter 9

1. Garth Mangum, "Reflections on Training Policies and Programs," in Burt S. Barnow and Christopher T. King, eds., *Improving the Odds: Increasing the Effectiveness of Publicly Funded Training* (Washington, DC: Urban Institute, 1999), 296.

2. U.S. Department of Commerce, Bureau of the Census, *1989 Statistical Abstract of the United States*, 397; Frank Bennici, Stephen Mangum, and Andrew M. Sum, "The Economic, Demographic, and Social Context of Future Employment and Training Programs," in Barnow and King, *Improving the Odds*, 19; Lawrence Mishel, Jared Bernstein, and Heather Boushey, *The State of Working America 2002–2003* (Ithaca, NY: Cornell University Press), 177.

3. Bennici et al., "The Economic, Demographic, and Social Context of Future Employment and Training Programs," 23.

4. Clifford M. Johnson and Steve Savner, *Federal Funding Sources for Public Job Creation Initiatives* (New York: Center for Law and Social Policy, December 1999), 3–6.

5. Duane Leigh, *Does Training Work for Displaced Workers?* (Kalamazoo, MI: W. E. Upjohn Institute, 1990), 3; W. Norton Grubb, *Learning to Work: The Case for Reintegrating Job Training and Education* (New York: Russell Sage Foundation, 1996), 69–70, 95. For more specific detail, see also U.S. Department of Labor, *What's Working (and What's Not): A Summary of Research on the Economic Impacts of Employment and Training Programs* (Washington, DC: U.S. Department of Labor, Office of the Chief Economist, January 1995).

6. U.S. General Accounting Office, *Multiple Employment Training Programs: Overlapping Programs Can Add Unnecessary Administrative Costs* (Washington, DC: U.S. GAO, 1994).

7. Cynthia M. Fagoni, Director, Education, Workforce, and Income Security Issues, Health Education and Human Services Division, *Testimony before the Subcommittee on Human Resources of the House Committee on Ways and Means and the Subcommittee on Postsecondary Education, Training, and Life-Long Learning of the House Committee on Education and the Workforce*, Joint Hearing on One-Stop Career Centers, June 29, 2000, 2–4, http://waysandmeans.house.gov/humanres/106cong/6-29-00/6-29fagn.htm, accessed September 20, 2000.

8. Ibid.

9. National Governors' Association, *Workforce Investment Act of 1998*, August 1998, 2.

10. Burt S. Barnow and Christopher T. King, "Publicly Funded Training in a Changing Labor Market," in Barnow and King, *Improving the Odds*, 7.

11. Ibid., 8.

12. Stephen A. Woodbury, "New Directions in Reemployment Policy," *Employment Research* 7 (October 2000): 1–4.

13. Barnow and King, "Publicly Funded Training in a Changing Labor Market," 9.

14. U.S. Senate, May 1, 1998, *Congressional Record*, p. S4024.

15. Fagoni, *Testimony*, 8–9.

16. Barnow and King, "Publicly Funded Training in a Changing Labor Market," 9; Ann Lordeman, "The Workforce Investment Act: Training Programs under Title I at a Glance," *Congressional Research Service*, March 9, 2000, 2.

17. "Key Features of the Workforce Investment Act as Compared to Current Law," August 10, 1998, http://usworkforce.org/sideby810.htm, accessed September 15, 2002; Lordeman, "The Workforce Investment Act," 2; U.S. Department of Labor, Employment Training Administration, *Fiscal Year 2002 Conference Appropriations Action*, www.doleta.gov/budget/02appsum.pdf, accessed May 6, 2002.

18. Duane Leigh, "Training Programs for Dislocated Workers," in Barnow and King, *Improving the Odds*, 227; Bruce C. Fallick, "A Review of the Recent Empirical Literature on Displaced Workers," *Industrial and Labor Relations Review* 50 (October 1996): 5–16; Lori G. Kletzer, "Job Displacement," *Journal of Economic Perspectives* 12 (Winter 1998): 115–136.

19. Lordeman, "The Workforce Investment Act," 2; U.S. Department of Labor, *Fiscal Year 2002 Conference Appropriations Action*.

20. U.S. Department of Labor, "Youth Training Programs," p. 1, www.doleta.gov/programs/trn.htm, accessed November 22, 2000.

21. U.S. Department of Labor, Employment and Training Administration, *Workforce Investment Act of 1998*, September 1998, pp. 6–7, http://usworkforce.org/Runningtext2.htm, accessed September 20, 2000.

22. U.S. Department of Labor, *Workforce Investment Act of 1998*, p. 7; U.S. Department of Labor, "Youth Training Programs," p. 1; Lordeman, "The Workforce Investment Act," 1; U.S. Department of Labor, *Fiscal Year 2002 Conference Appropriations Action*.

23. U.S. Department of Labor, Employment and Training Administration, *NAFTA Transitional Adjustment Assistance*, 1–3, http://www. doleta.gov/programs/factsh/nafta.htm, accessed September 20, 2000; Committee on Ways and Means, U.S. House of Representatives, *2000 Green Book* (Washington, DC: Government Printing Office, 2000), 337–349.

24. U.S. Department of Labor, *NAFTA-Transitional Adjustment Assistance*, 1; Joel Blau, *Illusions of Prosperity: America's Working Families in an Age of Economic Insecurity* (New York: Oxford University Press, 1999), 126.

25. Committee on Ways and Means, *2000 Green Book*, 339, 342, 345.

26. Charles Mallar, Stuart Kerachsky, Craig Thornton, and David Long, *Evaluation of the*

Economic Impact of the Job Corps Program: Third Follow-Up Report (Princeton: Mathematica Policy Research, 1982).

27. U.S. Department of Labor, *Job Corps Fact Sheet,* http:www.doleta.gov/individual/job corps.asp, accessed May 6, 2002; U.S. Department of Labor, *Fiscal Year 2002 Conference Appropriations Action.*

28. U.S. Department of Labor, *Job Corps Fact Sheet;* Committee on Ways and Means, *2000 Green Book,* 968.

29. Lordeman, "The Workforce Investment Act," 2.

30. The Workforce Investment Act of 1998, Section 166, Native American Programs, http://www.wdsc.org/dinap/html/lwiasec166. html, accessed November 22, 2000, All-Indian Pueblo Council, WIA Program Fact Sheet, Pueblo, NM, http:edge1. ecommercesys.com/CE/Cedge.dll?catalog?merchant=AIPCINC&page=21, accessed November 22, 2000.

31. U.S. Department of Labor, *The National Farm Workers Jobs Program,* 1–3, August 2000, http:www.wdsc.org/msfw/html/facts.htm, accessed November 22, 2000; Lordeman, "The Workforce Investment Act," 2.

32. Employment Training Administration, *FY 2001 Budget,* 4, http:www.doleta.gov/budget/01burqsum.htm, accessed November 22, 2000; Lordeman, "The Workforce Investment Act," 2.

33. U.S. Department of Labor, *Fact Sheet No. OASVET-97-2 Employment Services for Veterans,* 1, http://www.dol.gov/vets/public/programs/fact/vet97-2htm, accessed November 22, 2000.

34. Ibid., p. 2.

35. Clifford M. Johnson and Steve Savner, *Federal Funding Sources for Public Job Creation Initiatives,* Washington, DC: Center for Law and Social Policy, December 1999, 2.

36. Ibid., 3–6.

37. See Hans Bos, Aletha Huston, Robert Granger, Greg Duncan, Tom Brock, and Vonnie McLoyd, *New Hope for People with Low Incomes* (New York: Manpower Demonstration Research Corporation, 1999).

38. Clifford M. Johnson and Ana Carricchi Lopez, *Shattering the Myth of Failure: Promising Finding from Ten Public Job Creation Initiatives* (Washington, DC: Center on Budget and Policy Priorities, 1997), 1–3.

39. See Margaret Weir, *Politics and Jobs: The Boundaries of Employment Policy in the United States* (Princeton: Princeton University Press, 1992).

40. Frances Fox Piven and Richard Cloward, *Regulating the Poor: The Functions of Public Welfare* (New York: Vintage Books, 1971), 107–108.

41. Weir, *Politics and Jobs,* 45–46, 135–136.

42. Edwin G. Burrows and Mike Wallace, *Gotham: A History of New York City to 1898* (New York: Oxford University Press, 1999), 411–412, 430–431.

43. Edwin Amenta, *Bold Relief: Institutional Politics and the Origins of Modern American Society* (Princeton: Princeton University Press, 1998), 73; Nancy E. Rose, *Workfare or Fair Work* (New Brunswick, NJ: Rutgers University Press, 1995), 38.

44. Amenta, *Bold Relief,* 75.

45. Michael B. Katz, *In the Shadow of the Poorhouse* (New York: Basic Books, 1986), 225–226.

46. Ibid., 228–229.

47. Rose, *Workfare or Fair Work,* 79–80.

48. Jill Quadagno, *The Color of Welfare: How Racism Undermined the War on Poverty* (New York: Oxford University Press, 1994), 66–67, 84–85; Rose, *Workfare or Fair Work,* 115.

49. Blau, *Illusions of Prosperity,* 128–130.

50. Lisa Plimpton and Demetra Smith Nightingale, "Welfare Employment Programs: Impacts and Cost-Effectiveness of Employment and Training Activities," in Barnow and King, *Improving the Odds,* 51–52.

Chapter 10

1. Joint Center for Housing Studies of Harvard University, *The State of the Nation's Housing 2000* (Cambridge, MA: Harvard University, Press, 2000), 9.
2. National Low Income Housing Coalition, *2002 Advocates' Guide to Housing and Community Development Policy* (Washington, DC: National Low Income Housing Coalition, 2002), 56; Joel Blau, *The Visible Poor: Homelessness in the United States* (New York: Oxford University Press, 1993), 61.
3. Lawrence Mishel, Jared Bernstein, and John Schmitt, *The State of Working America 2000–2001* (Ithaca, NY: Cornell University Press, 2001), 270–271; National Low Income Housing Coalition, *2000 Advocates' Guide to Housing and Community Development Policy* (Washington, DC, 2000), 8.
4. National Low Income Housing Coalition, *2002 Advocates' Guide*, 56.
5. Peter Dreier, "Why America's Workers Can't Pay the Rent," *Dissent* 47.3 (summer, 2000): 39; Matt Richtel, "Bay Area Real Estate Prices Too Hot for Some to Touch," *New York Times*, May 29, 2002.
6. A "working family" is defined as one that earns at least half of its income from employment, and whose total income falls between $10,700 a year (the minimum wage) and 120 percent of the local area median income. Among this group, 76 percent, or 2.4 million households, spend more than half of their income on housing. Michael A. Stegman, Robert G. Quercia, and George McCarthy, "Housing America's Working Families," in *New Century Housing* 1, 1 (June 2000): 1–2.
7. Dreier, "Why America's Workers Can't Pay the Rent," 38.
8. National Low Income Housing Coalition, *2000 Advocates' Guide*, 13; National Low Income Housing Coalition, *Out of Reach 2001: The Growing Wage-Rent Disparity* (Washington, DC, 2001).
9. Cited in Dreier, "Why America's Workers Can't Pay the Rent," 38.
10. National Low Income Coalition, *2000 Advocates' Guide*, 13; Center for Housing Policy, *Housing America's Working Families* (Washington, DC: National Low Income Housing Coalition, 2000), 2; E. Richard Bourdon, Congressional Research Service, *Housing Issues in the 106th Congress, August 7, 2000* (from HUD, *Rental Housing Assistance—The Worsening Crisis*, March 2000).
11. Center on Budget and Policy Priorities, *In Search of Shelter: The Growing Shortage of Affordable Rental Housing* (Washington, DC: Center on Budget and Policy Priorities, 1998).
12. See, for example, Richard White, *Rude Awakening: What the Homeless Crisis Tells Us* (San Francisco: Institute for Contemporary Society, 1992); Alice S. Baum and Donald W. Burnes, *A Nation in Denial: The Truth about Homelessness* (Boulder, CO: Westview Press, 1993).
13. The HUD study is entitled *Report to the Secretary on the Homeless and Emergency Housing* (Washington, DC: Government Printing Office, 1984); the 3 million figure comes from Mitch Snyder and Mary Ellen Hombs, *Homelessness in America: The Forced March to Nowhere* (Washington, DC: Community for Creative Nonviolence, 1984); the 500,000 to 600,000 estimate is contained in Martha R. Burt and Barbara E. Cohen, *America's Homeless: Numbers, Characteristics, and the Programs That Serve Them* (Washington, DC: Urban Institute, 1989). For the most recent census, see Martha Burt and Laudan Aron, *America's Homeless II*, http://www.urban.org/housing/homeless/numbers/index.htm, accessed July 10, 2000.
14. Urban Institute, *The National Survey of Homeless Assistance Providers and Clients* (Washington, DC: Urban Institute, 1999); Kristen Brown, "Outlawing Homelessness," *Shelterforce* 21, 4 (July–August 1999): 13–15, 29.
15. See Kenneth T. Jackson, *Crabgrass Frontier: The Suburbanization of the United States* (New York: Oxford University Press, 1985).

16. Joint Center for Housing Studies of Harvard University, *The State of the Nation's Housing 2000*, 19.

17. Thomas J. Sugrue, *The Origins of the Urban Crisis* (Princeton: Princeton University Press, 1996), 64.

18. Helene Slessarev, "Racial Tensions and Institutional Support: Social Programs During a Period of Retrenchment," in Margaret Weir, Ann Shola Orloff, and Theda Skocpol, eds., *The Politics of Social Policy in the United States* (Princeton: Princeton University Press, 1988), 370.

19. Theda Skocpol, "The Limits of the New Deal System and the Roots of Contemporary Welfare Dilemmas," in Weir et al., *The Politics of Social Policy in the United States*, 306.

20. John Yinger, "Housing Discrimination and Residential Segregation as Causes of Poverty," *Focus* 21, 2 (fall, 2000): 52.

21. Ibid.

22. George Glaster, "Housing Discrimination and Urban Poverty of African-Americans," *Journal of Housing Research* 2, 2 (1991): 87–122.

23. National Low Income Housing Coalition, *2000 Advocates' Guide*, 74–76.

24. National Housing Conference, *A History of Progress Since 1931: Building a Better Future* (Washington, DC: National Housing Conference, n.d.), 10.

25. Peter Marcuse, "Housing Policy and the Myth of the Benevolent State," in Rachel Bratt, Chester Hartman, and Ann Meyerson, eds., *Critical Perspectives on Housing* (Philadelphia: Temple University Press, 1986), 255.

26. Blau, *The Visible Poor*, 75.

27. Calculated from the Committee on Ways and Means, U.S. House of Representatives, *2000 Green Book*, (Washington, DC: Government Printing Office), 951, and the National Low Income Housing Coalition, *2002 Advocates' Guide*, 10.

28. National Low Income Housing Coalition, *2002 Advocates' Guide*, 20.

29. M. Ann Wolfe, "Housing Opportunities for People with AIDS (HOPWA)," *Congressional Research Reports*, October 12, 2000.

30. National Low Income Housing Coalition, *2000 Advocates' Guide*, 29–30.

31. Morton J. Schussheim, *Housing the Poor: Federal Programs for Low-Income Families* 43–44; National Low Income Housing Coalition, *2002 Advocates' Guide*, 25.

32. Schussheim, *Housing the Poor*, 50–51; National Low Income Housing Coalition, *2000 Advocates' Guide*, 47–49.

33. Schussheim, *Housing the Poor*, 33–34; National Low Income Housing Coalition, *2002 Advocates' Guide*, 10, 39.

34. National Low Income Housing Coalition, *2002 Advocates' Guide*, 12, 43–44.

35. Ibid., 47.

36. National Low Income Housing Coalition, *2000 Advocates' Guide*, 72–73.

37. National Low Income Housing Coalition, *2002 Advocates' Guide*, 54.

38. Schussheim, *Housing the Poor*, 27.

39. Ibid., 27–28.

40. Ibid., 32.

41. Winton Pitcoff, "New Hope for Public Housing?" *Shelterforce* 21, 2 (March–April 1999): 18–19.

42. National Low Income Housing Coalition, *2002 Advocates' Guide*, 61.

43. Ibid., 79; Schussheim, *Housing the Poor*, 24–26.

44. National Low Income Housing Coalition, *2002 Advocates' Guide*, 83; Schussheim, *Housing the Poor*, 38–39.

45. National Low Income Housing Coalition, *2000 Advocates' Guide*, 104, 122; Schussheim, *Housing the Poor*, 22; Committee on Ways and Means, *2000 Green Book*, 951.

46. Dennis Hevesi, "Cracks in a Pillar of Affordable Housing," *New York Times*, November 18, 2001.

47. National Low Income Housing Coalition, *2002 Advocates' Guide*, 10.

48. Committee on Ways and Means, *2000 Green Book*, 947; National Low Income Housing Coalition, *2002 Advocates' Guide*, 101.

49. National Low Income Housing Coalition, *2002 Advocates' Guide*, 91.

50. Schussheim, *Housing the Poor*, 39–43; National Low Income Housing Coalition, *2002 Advocates' Guide*, 91; Housing Assistance Council, "USDA Budget Proposal," *HAC News* 31. 3 (February 4, 2002): 1–4.

51. Schussheim, *Housing the Poor*, 9–19; Evelyn Nieves, "Drug Ruling Worries Some in Public Housing," *New York Times*, March 28, 2002.

52. Vee Burke, *Cash and Non-Cash Benefits for Persons with Limited Income: Eligibility Rules, Recipient and Expenditures Data, FY 1996–FY 1998* (Washington, DC: Congressional Research Service, December 1999).

53. National Low Income Housing Coalition, *2002 Advocates' Guide*, 56.

54. Peter Dreier, "The Truth about Federal Housing Subsidies: Socialism for the Rich, Capitalism for the Poor," in Chester Hartman, Rachel Bratt, and Michael Stone, eds., *Housing: Foundation of a New Social Agenda* (Philadelphia: Temple University Press, forthcoming), table 5.

55. "2000th Endorser Backs National Housing Trust Fund," *Safety Network: The Newsletter of the National Coalition for the Homeless* 21, 2 (spring 2002): 4. The National Housing Trust legislation suffered a setback in the summer of 2002, when the House Financial Services Committee voted 35–34 against the legislation. See "Down but Not Out," *Shelterforce* 24, 4 (July/August 2002): 4.

56. See Eleanor Novek, "You Wouldn't Fit in Here," *Shelterforce* 23, 2 (March–April 2001): 10–13.

57. National Housing Coalition, *A History of Progress Since 1931*, 1.

58. Ronald Lawson, *The Tenant Movement in New York City, 1904–1984* (New Brunswick, NJ: Rutgers University Press, 1986).

59. Karen Ceraso, "What Ever Happened to the Tenants' Movement?" *Shelterforce* 21, 3 (May–June 1999): 10–14.

60. Michael Katz, *In the Shadow of the Poorhouse* (New York: Basic Books, 1986), 171–175.

61. Cited in National Housing Coalition, *A History of Progress Since 1931*, 5.

62. Jill Quadagno, *The Color of Welfare* (New York: Oxford University Press, 1994), 105.

63. Rachel Bratt, "Public Housing: The Controversy and Contribution," in Bratt et al., *Critical Perspectives on Housing*, 341.

64. Schussheim, *Housing the Poor*, 31.

Chapter 11

1. Karen Davis, *The Quality of American Health Care: Can We Do Better?* (New York: Commonwealth Fund, 2000), 1–5.

2. The distinctions among different kinds of rationing are drawn from Candyce Berger, "Managed Care: Challenges to Survival and Opportunities for Change," *Smith College Studies in Social Work* 71, 1 (November 2000): 19–33.

3. Barbara Martinez, "With New Muscle, Hospitals Squeeze Insurers on Rates," *Wall Street Journal*, April 12, 2002; John Mullahy and Barbara L. Wolfe, "Health Policies for the Nonelderly Poor," *Focus* 21, 2 (2000): 32–37; Committee on Ways and Means, U.S. House of Representatives, *2000 Green Book* (Washington, DC: Government Printing Office, 2000), 794.

4. Leighton Ku, *The Number of Americans without Health Insurance Rose in 2001 and Appears to Be Continuing to Rise in 2002*, Washington, DC: Center on Budget and Policy Priorities, October 7, 2002.

5. Barbara Crossette, "Canada's Health Care Shows Strains," *New York Times*, October 11, 2001; Mullahy and Wolfe, "Health Policies for the Nonelderly Poor," 34.

6. Robert Pear, "Rise in Health Care Costs Rests Largely on Drug Prices," *New York*

Times, November 14, 2000; Milton Freudenheim, "Employees Are Shouldering More of the Health Care Tab," *New York Times*, December 10, 2001.

7. Marc Miringoff and Marque-Luisa Miringoff, *The Social Health of the Nation* (New York: Oxford University Press, 1999), 67, 52–53.

8. Crossette, "Canada's Health Care Shows Strains"; The OECD Observer, *The OECD in Figures—1997 Edition* (Paris: Organization for Economic Cooperation and Development, 1997), 49; Miringoff and Miringoff, *The Social Health of the Nation*, 53.

9. Catherine Jones, *Patterns of Social Policy: An Introduction to Comparative Analysis* (New York: Tavistock, 1985), 140–141.

10. Michael Katz, *In the Shadow of the Poorhouse* (New York: Basic Books, 1986), 141–145.

11. Karen Davis, "Universal Coverage in the United States: Lessons from Experience of the 20th Century," *Journal of Urban Health: Bulletin of the New York Academy of Medicine* 78, 1 (March 2001): 48–49; Michael B. Katz, *The Price of Citizenship: Redefining the American Welfare State* (New York: Owl Books, 2002), 261–266.

12. Gregory L. Weiss and Lynne E. Lonnquist, *The Sociology of Health, Healing, and Illness*, 2d ed. (Saddle River, NJ: Prentice-Hall, 1997), 305, 316–319.

13. Kip Sullivan, "On the 'Efficiency' of Managed Care Plans," *Health Affairs* 19, 4 (July/August 2000): 139–148.

14. Milton Freudenheim, "HMOs Are Pressed on Many Fronts to Reinvent Themselves," *New York Times*, December 18, 2000; Martinez, "With New Muscle, Hospitals Squeeze Insurers on Rates."

15. Milton Freudenheim, "A Changing World Is Forcing Changes on Managed Care," *New York Times*, July 2, 2001.

16. Robert Pear, "HMO's for 200,000 Pulling Out of Medicare" *New York Times*, September 10, 2002.

17. Cited in Freudenheim, "A ChangingWorld Is Forcing Changes on Managed Care."

18. Committee on Ways and Means, *2000 Green Book*, 889, 892; Mullahy and Wolfe, "Health Policies for the Nonelderly Poor," 32–37.

19. Committee on Ways and Means, *2000 Green Book*, 904, 927.

20. Raymond Hernandez, "States Calling for More Help with Medicaid," *New York Times*, December 10, 2001; Committee on Ways and Means, *2000 Green Book*, 902, 913–914.

21. Leighton Ku and Brian Bruen, *The Continuing Decline in Medicaid Coverage* (Washington, DC: Urban Institute, December 1999), 1–2; Leighton Ku and Shannon Blaney, *Health Coverage for Legal Immigrant Children: New Census Data Highlight Importance of Restoring Medicaid and SCHIP Coverage* (Washington, DC: Center on Budget and Policies Priorities, October 10, 2000), 3.

22. John Holahan, Joshua Wiener, and Susan Wallin, *Health Policy for the Low-Income Population: Major Finding from the "Assessing New Federalism" Case Studies* (Washington, DC: Urban Institute, 1998), 1.

23. Department of Health and Human Services, Centers for Medicare and Medicaid Services, *Medicaid Managed Care Enrollment: Summary Statistics as of June 30, 2001*, 1.

24. Janet D. Perloff, "Medicaid Managed Care and Urban Poor People," *Health and Social Work* 21, 3 (August 1996): 189–195; Bruce E. Landon and Arnold M. Epstein, "Quality Management Practices in Medicaid Managed Care," *Journal of the American Medical Association* 282, 18 (November 10, 1999): 1769–1775.

25. Robert Pear, "A Million Parents Lost Medicaid, Study Says," *New York Times*, June 20, 2000; Marilyn Ellwood, *The Medicaid Eligibility Maze: Coverage Expands, but Enrollment Problems Persist* (Washington, DC: Urban Institute, December 1999), 10; Hernandez, "States Calling for More Help with Medicaid."

26. "Nursing Home Costs Today," *Kiplinger's Retirement Report*, September 2000; Robert Pear, "9 Out of 10 Nursing Homes in U.S. Lack Adequate Staff, a Government Study Finds," *New York Times*, February 18, 2002.

27. Joshua M. Wiener and David G. Steveson, "State Policy on Long-Term Care for the Elderly," *Health Affairs* 17, 3 (May/June 1998): 81–100; Harriet L. Komisar, Judith Feder, and Daniel Gilden, *The Roles of Medicare and Medicaid in Financing Health and Long-Term Care for Low-Income Seniors* (New York: Commonwealth Fund, 2000), 3.

28. Komisar et al., *The Roles of Medicare and Medicaid in Financing Health and Long-Term Care for Low-Income Seniors*, vii, viii; Stephanie Maxwell, Marilyn Moon, and Mathew Storeygard, *Reforming Medicare's Benefit Package: Impact on Beneficiary Expenditures* (New York: Commonwealth Fund, May 2001), v.

29. Medicare, *Medicare Premium Amounts for 2002*, http://www.Medicare.gov/Basics/amounts2002.asp, accessed June 4, 2002.

30. Actual 2001 Medicare spending, from http://www/cbo.gov, accessed June 4, 2002, less projected 2001 premiums collected, from Committee on Ways and Means, *2000 Green Book*, 99.

31. Social Security Administration, *Status of the Social Security and Medicare Programs: A Summary of the 2002 Annual Reports by the Social Security and Medicare Board of Trustees*, http://www.ssa.gov.oact/TRSUM/trsummary.html, accessed April 19, 2002; Robert Pear, "Trustees Extend Solvency Estimates for Two Benefits," *New York Times*, March 20, 2001.

32. Marilyn Moon, "Medicare," *New England Journal of Medicine* 344, 12 (March 22, 2001): 928–931.

33. Marsha Gold, "Medicare+Choice: An Interim Report Card," *Health Affairs* 20, 4 (July/August 2001): 120–138; Robert Pear, "HMO's Flee Medicare Despite Rise in Payments," *New York Times*, December 4, 2001.

34. Davis, "Universal Coverage in the United States," 48; Frank Ullman, Brian Bruen, and John Holahan, *The State Children's Health Insurance Program: A Look at the Numbers* (Washington, DC: Urban Institute, 1998), 1.

35. Ullman et al., *The State Children's Health Insurance Program*, 2.

36. Robert Pear, "40 States Forfeit Health Care Funds for Poor Children," *New York Times*, September 24, 2000.

37. See Brian D. Smedley, Adrienne Y. Stith, and Alan R. Nelson, *Unequal Treatment: Confronting Racial and Ethnic Disparities in Health Care* (Washington, DC: National Academy Press, 2002).

38. See, for example, Ichiro Kawachi, Bruce P. Kennedy, Kimberly Lochner, and Deborah Prothrow-Stith, "Social Capital, Income Inequality, and Mortality," *American Journal of Public Health* 87, 9 (September 1997): 1491–1497; P. D. Sorlie, E. Backlund, and J. B. Keller, "U.S. Mortality by Economic, Demographic, and Social Characteristics: The National Mortality Study, *American Journal of Public Health* 85, 7 (July 1995): 949–956, on income inequality and health; and Paula M. Lantz, James S. House, James M. Lepkowski, David R. Williams, Richard P. Mero, and Jieming Chen, "Socioeconomic Factors, Health Behaviors, and Mortality," *Journal of the American Medical Association* 279. 21 (June 3, 1998): 1703–1708, on the significance of the correlation regardless of health behaviors.

39. Alejandro Reuss, "Cause of Death: Inequality," *Dollars & Sense*, no. 235 (May–June 2001): 10–12; Ichiro Kawachi, Bruce P. Kennedy, and Richard G. Wilkinson, eds., *The Society and Population Health Reader: Income Equality and Health* (New York: New Press, 1999).

40. Ku, *The Number of Americans without Health Insurance*.

41. Jennifer Steinhauer, "Another Terror Victim: Health Care," *New York Times*, November 18, 2001.

42. Kaiser Commission on Medicaid and the Uninsured, *Health Insurance Coverage in America: 1999 Data Update* (Washington, DC: Kaiser Foundation, 1999).

43. Davis, "Universal Coverage in the United States," 51–52.

44. Abby Scher, "Access Denied: Immigrants and Health Care," *Dollars & Sense*, no. 235 (May–June 2001): 8; Michael Perry and Susan Kanel, *Barriers to Health Coverage for*

Hispanic Workers: Focus Group Findings (New York: Commonwealth Fund, December 2000).

45. Jocelyn Guyer, Mathew Broaddus, and Annie Dude, *Millions of Mothers Lack Health Insurance Coverage* (Washington, DC: Center on Budget and Policies Priorities, May 10, 2001), 1.

46. Davis, "Universal Coverage in the United States," 46.

47. Robin Toner, "Why the Elderly Wait . . . and Wait," *New York Times*, June 23, 2002.

48. Robert Pear, " 'Budget Office's Estimates for Drug Spending Grow," *New York Times*, February 24, 2001; Sheryl Agy Stolberg, "No Simple Answers to Rising Costs of Drugs for the Elderly," *New York Times*, September 3, 2000; Robert Pear, "Rise in Health Care Costs Rests Largely on Drug Prices," *New York Times*, November 14, 2000; citing the *Families US* report, The Center for Responsive Politics, *Prescription Drugs*, December 28, 2001, http://www.open secrets.org/news/drug, accessed December 28, 2001.

49. Robin Toner, "Rising Drug Costs a Power Issue for National and State Politicians," *New York Times*, April 1, 2002; Robert Pear, "States Creating Plans to Reduce Costs for Drugs," *New York Times*, April 23, 2001.

50. Pharmaceutical Research and Manufacturers of America, "Do Pharmaceutical Companies Make Too Much in Profits?" 1, December 28, 2001, http:www.pharma.org/ publications/brochure/questions/toomuchprofits.phhtml, accessed December 28, 2001; Dean Baker, "Drug Prices in Crisis: The Case against Protectionism," *Dollars & Sense*, no. 235 (May/June 2001): 21–24.

51. For the data on comparative prices, see Congressman Bernard Sanders, "New Figures Prove Pharmaceutical Industry Continues to Fleece Americans," 2, December 28, 2001, *http://bernie.house.gov/prescriptions/profits.asp*, accessed December 28, 2001.

52. Sheryl Gay Stolberg and Jeff Gerth, "How Companies Stall Generics and Keep Themselves Healthy," *New York Times*, July 23, 2000.

53. Melody Petersen, "New Medicines Seldom Contain Anything New, Study Finds," *New York Times*, May 29, 2002. The National Institute for Health Care Management conducted the study.

54. Amy Goldstein, "Prescription Drug Plan Sent to Skeptical Congress," *Washington Post*, February 1, 2001.

55. Baker, "Drug Prices in Crisis," 21–24.

56. Robert Pear, "Furious Lobbying is Set Off by Bill on Mental Health," *New York Times*, November 6, 2001.

57. Phillip Fellin, *Mental Health and Mental Illness* (Itasca, IL: F.E. Peacock, 1996), 10.

58. Ibid., 11–13, 63.

59. P. H. DeLeon, G. R. VandenBos, and E. Q. Bulato, "Managed Mental Health Care: A History of the Federal Policy Initiative," in Rodney L. Lowman and Robert J. Resnick, eds., *The Mental Health Professional's Guide to Managed Care* (Washington, DC: American Psychological Association, 1994).

60. Robert Pear, "Drive for More Mental Coverage Fails in Congress," *New York Times*, December 19, 2001.

61. See Denis J. Prager and Lesslie J. Scallet, "Mental Health Should Be Part of General Health Policy," and Charles Kiesler, "Mental Health Should Be Independent of General Health Policy," in William Barbour, ed., *Mental Illness: Opposing Viewpoints* (San Diego: Greenhaven Press, 1995), 239–252.

62. For a philosophical justification of the need for such a system, see Milton Fisk, *Toward a Healthy Society* (Lawrence: University of Kansas Press, 2000).

63. Marc Champion, "Britain Feels Pressure as Public Services Continue to Decay," *Wall Street Journal*, March 9, 2001.

64. See, for example, Adam Clymer, "House Bill Asks 8.4% Payroll Tax for Canadian-Style Health Plan," *New York Times*, January 29, 1994.

65. Crossette, "Canada's Health Care Shows Strains"; Rod Mickleburgh, "Canadians Reject Radical Health-Care Changes: Most Blame Inefficiencies, Poll Finds," *Toronto*

Globe and Mail, January 26, 2002; U.S. General Accounting Office, *Canadian Health Insurance: Lessons for the United States* (Washington, DC: General Accounting Office, 1991).

66. Robin Toner, "Backers of Canada-Type Health Plan: Idealistic, Outmuscled but Scrapping," *New York Times*, May 4, 1993.

67. Karen Davis, Cathy Schoen, and Stephen C. Schoenbaum, "A 2020 Vision for American Health Care," *Archives of Internal Medicine* 160, 22 (December 11, 25, 2000): 3357–3364.

68. Robert Kuttner, *Everything for Sale* (New York: Knopf, 1997), 116.

69. Ellen Frank "Making Patients Pay," *Dollars & Sense*, no. 235 (May/June 2001): 34–37.

70. Public Citizen, "Rx Industry Goes for the KO," *Congress Watch*, November 2000, Washington, DC, http://www.citizen.org/congress/drugs/factshts/campaign$.htm, accessed November 3, 2000.

71. Families USA, "Consumer Groups Criticize Newsweek for Transgressing Ethical Boundaries by Working with the Pharmaceutical Drug Lobby," October 2, 2001, http://www.familiesusa.org.media/press/2001/newsweek/htm, accessed January 4, 2002.

72. Aetna, "Coalition Announces Progress on Improving the Health Care Experience," http:www.aetna.com/about/press/feb07_01.html, accessed January 16, 2002; Charles Noble, *Welfare as We Knew It* (New York: Oxford University Press, 1997), 133; Dan Morgan, "Lobbyists Get Aggressive on Health Care Issue," *Washington Post*, July 5, 1999; Annenberg Public Policy Center of the University of Pennsylvania, "Alliance for Quality Nursing Home Care/American Health Care Association," January 2001, http://www.appcpenn.org/issuads/Alliance%20for%20Quality%20Nursing%20Home%20Care.htm, accessed January 16, 2002; National Alliance for the Mentally Ill, *NAMI Mission and History*, http://www.nami.org/history.htm, accessed April 26, 2002.

73. Shankar Durwaiswamy, "Ballot Initiatives, Legislative Proposals Offered Universal Single-Payer Health Care Activity around the Country," *MassNurse News Article*, http://www.massnurse.org/News/000009/uvalhcworld.htm, accessed January 16, 2002.

74. Pam Belluck, "Small Vote for Universal Care Is Seen as Carrying a Lot of Weight," *New York Times*, November 16, 2001.

75. Vermont Health Care for All, "Recent History of Health Care Reform Efforts in Vermont, 1987–1999," http://www.vthca.org/history.htm, accessed April 26, 2002.

76. Durwaiswamy, "Ballot Initiatives."

77. I. M. Rubinow, "20,000 Miles over the Land: A Survey of the Spreading Health Insurance Movement," *Survey* 37, 22 (March 3, 1917), cited in Theda Skocpol, *Protecting Soldiers and Mothers: The Political Origins of Social Policy in the United States* (Cambridge, MA: Harvard University Press, 1992), 202.

78. For a succinct overview of this history, see Mary Ann Jimenez, "Concepts of Health and National Health Care Policy: A View from American History," *Social Service Review* 71, 1 (March 1997): 34–50.

79. Davis, "Universal Coverage in the United States," 47; Paul Starr, *The Social Transformation of American Medicine* (New York: Basic Books, 1982), 243–244; Walter Trattner, *From Poor Law to Welfare State* (New York: Free Press, 1999), 228–229.

80. Starr, *The Social Transformation of American Medicine*, 280–286.

81. Theodore R. Marmor, Jerry L. Mashaw, and Philip L. Harvey, *America's Misunderstood Welfare State* (New York: Basic Books, 1990), 182–184.

82. See Marie Gottschalk, *Labor, Business, and the Politics of Health Care in the United States* (Ithaca, NY: ILR Press, Cornell University, 2000).

Chapter 12

1. Peter K. Eisinger, *Toward an End to Hunger in America* (Washington, DC: Brookings Institution Press, 1998), 2.

2. Ibid., 3, 5.

3. Janet Poppendieck, *Sweet Charity: Emergency Food and the End of Entitlement* (New York: Viking Press, 1998), 5–6.

4. Eisinger, *Toward an End to Hunger in America*, 15–16.

5. U.S. Department of Agriculture, Office of Analysis, Nutrition, and Evaluation, *Guide to Measuring Household Food Security*, revised 2000, http://www.fns.usda.gov/oane/MENU/published/FoodSecurity/FSGuidesum.htm, accessed February 3, 2002.

6. Center on Hunger and Poverty, *Food Security Measurement: Concepts and Definitions*, http://www.centeronhunger.org/fsimeas.html, accessed February 3, 2002.

7. Victor Sidel, "The Public Health Impact of Hunger," *American Journal of Public Health* 87, 12 (December 1997): 1921–1922.

8. Sandra H. Venner, Ashley F. Sullivan, and Dorie Seavey, *Paradox of Our Times: Hunger in a Strong Economy* (Medford, MA: Center on Hunger and Poverty, 2000), 3.

9. Ibid., 5; Donald Rose, "Economic Determinants and Dietary Consequences of Food Insecurity in the United States," *Journal of Nutrition* 129, 2 (1999): 517–520.

10. Food Research and Action Center, *State-by-State Rates of Household Hunger and Food Insecurity, 1997–1999*, p. 4, January 2002, www.frac.org, accessed January 30, 2002; U.S. Conference of Mayors, *A Status Report on Hunger and Homelessness in American Cities* (Washington, DC: U.S. Conference of Mayors, 2001), 1.

11. M. Nord and F. J. Winicki, "Prevalence of Hunger in Rural Households," *Rural Conditions and Trends* 11, 2 (December 2000): 80–86.

12. Venner et al., *Paradox of Our Times*, 5.

13. K. Alaimi, R. R. Briefel, E. A. Frongillo, and C. M. Olson, "Food Insufficiency Exists in the United States: Results from the Third National Health and Nutrition Examination Survey (NHANES III)," *American Journal of Public Health* 88, 3 (1998): 419–426; Jennifer Kasper et al., "Hunger in Legal Immigrants in California, Texas, and Illinois," *American Journal of Public Health* 90, 10 (October 2000): 1629–1633.

14. Elizabeth Becker, "Shift from Food Stamps to Private Aid Widens," *New York Times*, November 14, 2001; Pamela Loprest, "How Are Families That Left Welfare Doing? A Comparison of Early and Recent Welfare Leavers," *Urban Institute* (April 2001): 1–8.

15. America's Second Harvest, *The Fact about Childhood Hunger*, http://www.secondharvest.org/childhunger/child_nutrition.html, accessed November 21, 2001; Katharine Alaimo, Christine M. Olson, Edward A. Frongillo Jr, and Ronette R. Briefel, "Food Insufficiency, Family Income, and Health in U.S. Preschool and School-Aged Children," *American Journal of Public Health* 91, 5 (May 2001): 784.

16. Katharine Alaimo, Christine M. Olson, and Edward A. Frongillo Jr., "Food Insufficiency and American School-Aged Children's Cognitive, Academic, and Psychosocial Development," *Pediatrics* 108, 1 (July 2001): 44–53; Sidel, "The Public Health Impact of Hunger," 1921.

17. D. Rose and V. Oliveira, "Nutrient Intakes of Individuals from Food-Insufficient Households in the United States," *American Journal of Public Health* 87, 12 (1997): 1956–1961.

18. Eisinger, *Toward an End to Hunger in America*, 12–14, 39, 68.

19. Kenneth Finegold, "Agriculture and the Politics of U.S. Social Provision: Social Insurance and Food Stamps," in Margaret Weir, Ann Shola Orloff, and Theda Skocpol, eds., *The Politics of Social Policy in the United States* (Princeton: Princeton University Press, 1988), 218–219; Ardith L. Maney, *Still Hungry after All These Years: Food Assistance Policy from Kennedy to Reagan* (Westport, CT: Greenwood Press, 1989), 9.

20. For the best statement of this argument, see Poppendieck, *Sweet Charity*.

21. Food Research and Action Center, "Food Stamp Participation Increases in July, 2002; Is 2.4 Million Persons Higher Than in July 2000," http://frac.org/html/news/fsp/02july.html, accessed October 23, 2002; Committee on Ways and Means, U.S. House of Representatives, *2000 Green Book* (Washington, DC: Government Printing Office,

2000), 865–869; Food Research and Action Center, *Food Stamp Program*, http://www.frac.org/html/federal_food/programs/fsp.html, accessed February 1, 2002.

22. Food Research and Action Center, *Food Stamp Program*, February 1, 2002, http://www.frac.org/html/federal_food/programs/fsp.limits2002.html, accessed February 1, 2002; Committee on Ways and Means, *2000 Green Book*, 869, 889.

23. Committee on Ways and Means, *2000 Green Book*, 876; Poppendieck, *Sweet Charity*, 71.

24. U.S. Department of Agriculture, Office of Analysis, Nutrition, and Assistance, *Characteristics of Food Stamp Households: Fiscal Year 2000*, 2001, xv–xvi.

25. U.S. Department of Agriculture, Office of Analysis, Nutrition, and Evaluation, *The Decline in Food Stamp Participation: A Report to Congress*, July 2001, 1–2, 14.

26. Eisinger, *Toward an End to Hunger in America*, 48–49; Food Research and Action Center, *State Government Reponses to the Food Assistance Gap* (Washington, DC: Food Research and Action Center, 2000), 8; Nina Bernstein, "Burial Plots, Bingo, and Blood in the Quest for Food Stamps," *New York Times*, August 12, 2000.

27. Food Research and Action Center, *Special Supplemental Nutrition Program for Women, Infants, and Children*, http://www.frac.org/html; shfederal_food/programs/programs/wic.html, accessed February 1, 2002; Grain.Net, "Bush Signs Bill That Boosts Funding for USDA Biosecurity Efforts," January 10, 2002.

28. Peter H. Rossi, *Feeding the Poor* (Washington, DC: American Enterprise Press, 1998), 44.

29. Food Research and Action Center, *Special Supplemental Nutrition Program for Women, Infants, and Children*.

30. U.S. Department of Agriculture, Office of Analysis, Nutrition, and Evaluation, *National Survey of WIC Participants*, October 2001, and Food Research and Action Center, "With Nearly One in Four Native American Households Hungry or on Edge of Hunger, WIC Is Making a Health Difference," http://www.frac.org/html/news/wic01.html, accessed February 1, 2002.

31. Rossi, *Feeding the Poor*, 6; Barbara Delaney, "Commentary," in Rossi, *Feeding the Poor*, 120; Eisinger, *Toward an End to Hunger in America*, 62; Center on Budget and Policy Priorities, *Low WIC Funding Levels Would Cut Nutrition Help for Women and Children* (Washington, DC: Center on Budget and Policy Priorities, October 15, 2001), 1.

32. Food Research and Action Center, *National School Lunch Program*, October 2001, http://frac.org/html/federal_food_programs/programs/nslp.html accessed February 1, 2002.

33. U.S. Department of Agriculture, *National School Lunch Program*, http://www.fns.usda.gov/cnd/Lunch/AboutLunch/faqs.htm, accessed February 2, 2002.

34. Ibid.

35. Eisinger, *Toward an End to Hunger in America*, 68.

36. U.S. Department of Agriculture, *The School Breakfast Program*, http://www.fns.usda.gov/cnd/Breakfast/aboutBFast/faqs.htm, accessed March 1, 2002.

37. Ibid.; Food Research and Action Center, *School Breakfast Program*, May 2001, http://frac.org/html/federal_food_programs/programs.sbp.html, accessed March 1, 2002.

38. U.S. Department of Agriculture, *Eating Breakfast: Effects of the School Breakfast Program*, http://www.fns.usda.gov/oane/MENU/Published/CNP/FILES/SBPEXSUM.htm, accessed February 2, 2002; Food Research and Action Center, *FRAC Scorecard Estimates Service Gap in States Leaves at Least 1.9 Million Low Income Children without Breakfast*, http://www.frac.org/html/news/112701/html, accessed November 27, 2001.

39. Food Research and Action Center, *Good Choices in Hard Times: Fifteen Ideas for States to Reduce Hunger and Stimulate the Economy* (Washington, DC: FRAC, February 2002), 18–19.

40. Food Research and Action Center, *FRAC Estimates Service Gap Leaves More Than 3.1 Million Children Unserved in Summer Food and Leaves $190 Million in Unspent Resources*, July 17, 2001, http://frac.org/html.news/071701.html, accessed February 1, 2002.

41. U.S. Department of Agriculture, *Summer Food Service Program*, http://www.fns

.usda.gov/cnd/Summer/About/faqs.html, accessed March 4, 2002; Food Research and Action Center, *Hunger Doesn't Take a Vacation: Summer Nutrition Report* (Washington, DC: Food Research and Action Center, 2001), 3, 5.

42. U.S. Department of Agriculture, *Summer Food Service Program*.

43. Eisinger, *Toward an End to Hunger in America*, 70–71.

44. Food Research and Action Center, *FRAC Estimates Service Gap Leaves More Than 3.1 Million Children Unserved in Summer Food and Leaves $190 Million in Unspent Resources*; Food Research and Action Center, *Hunger Doesn't Take a Vacation*, 4.

45. U.S. Department of Agriculture, *Why Is CACFP Important*, February 1, 2002, http://fns.usda.gov/cnd/Care/CACFP/aboutcacfp.htm, accessed March 5, 2002.

46. Ibid.

47. Food Research and Action Center, *Child and Adult Care Food Program*, May 2001, http://www.frac.org/html/federal_food_programs/programs/cacfp.html, accessed February 1, 2002.

48. Poppendieck, *Sweet Charity*, 88; Food Research and Action Center, *The Emergency Food Assistance Program*, http://www.frac.org/html/federal_food_programs/programs/tefap.html, accessed February 1, 2002.

49. U.S. Department of Agriculture, Food Nutrition Service Food Distribution Fact Sheet, *The Emergency Food Assistance Program*, April 2002, http://www.fns.usda.gov/fdd/programs/tefap/tefaphome.htm, accessed May 19, 2002; Institute for Research on Poverty, "The Private Assistance Food Network," *Focus* 21.3 (spring 2001): 12–16.

50. Institute for Research on Poverty, "The Private Assistance Food Network."

51. Mathematica Policy Research, *Hunger in America 2001 National Report* (Chicago: America's Second Harvest, 2001), 1.

52. Eisinger, *Toward an End to Hunger in America*, 110–119.

53. Poppendieck, *Sweet Charity*, 209–231.

54. Janet Poppendieck, personal communication, May 19, 2002.

55. Viviana A. Zelizer, *The Social Meaning of Money* (New York: Basic Books, 1994), 129.

56. Fred Magdoff, John Bellamy Foster, and Frederick H. Buttel, eds., *Hungry for Profit: The Agribusiness Threat to Farmers, Food, and the Environment* (New York: Monthly Review Press, 2000), 11.

57. Barbara Claffey and Thomas Stucker, "The Food Stamp Program," in Don Hadwiger and Ross Talbot, eds., *Food Policy and Farm Programs* (New York: Academy of Political Sciences, 1982), 41.

58. For a history of these interventions, see, for example, Maney, *Still Hungry After All These Years*.

59. Finegold, "Agriculture and Politics of U.S. Social Provision," 232–233.

60. Eisinger, *Toward an End to Hunger in America*, 45, 75–76.

61. Cited in David Wagner, *What's Love Got to Do with It: A Critical Look at American Charity* (New York: New Press, 2000), 1.

62. Ibid., 17–19.

63. Eisinger, *Toward an End to Hunger in America*, 92–96, 102.

64. Janet Poppendieck, "Want among Plenty: From Hunger to Inequality," in Magdoff et al., *Hungry for Profit*, 191–194.

65. Gordon Gunderson, *The National School Lunch Program* (Washington, DC: United States Department of Agriculture, Food and Nutrition Services, 1971), 5–7; Finegold, "Agriculture and the Politics of U.S. Social Provision," 218–219.

66. Eisinger, *Toward an End to Hunger in America*, 38–41, 66.

67. Joel Blau, *Illusions of Prosperity* (New York: Oxford University Press, 1999), 143.

Figure Credits

p. 5 Courtesy of Kirk Anderson.

p. 10 Photo courtesy of Ralph Mercer/Indexstock.

p. 23 Courtesy of Schlesinger Library, Radcliffe Institute, Harvard University.

p. 30 Photo courtesy of Library of Congress.

p. 39 Photo courtesy of Jacob Halaska/Indexstock.

p. 53 Photo courtesy of Lonnie Duka/Indexstock.

p. 68 Source: Economic Snapshot, Economic Policy Institute, January 2001.

p. 71 Source: U.S. Census Bureau/Deborah Blau.

p. 75 Courtesy of Kirk Anderson.

p. 76 Source: *Economic Snapshots*, Economic Policy Institute, April 2002.

p. 85 Source: *Economic Snapshots*, Economic Policy Institute, May 2002.

p. 91 Photo courtesy of Ellabelle Davis Photograph Collection, Photographs and Prints Division, Schomburg Center for Research in Black Culture, The New York Public Library, Astor, Lenox and Tilden Foundations.

p. 96 Photo courtesy of Ewing Galloway/Indexstock.

p. 104 Source: U.S. government/Deborah Blau.

p. 106 Photo courtesy of Michael Pawlyk/Indexstock.

p. 112 Source: International Institute for Democracy and Electoral Assistance.

p. 130 Courtesy of *Life*, 1913.

p. 138 Courtesy of Kirk Anderson.

p. 147 Courtesy of Horatio Alger Association.

p. 155 Publicity still from *Father Knows Best*.

p. 163 Courtesy of Kirk Anderson.

p. 175 Photo courtesy of Carol Werner/Indexstock.

p. 186 Photo courtesy of Jan Halaska/Indexstock.

p. 204 Source: *Harper's Weekly* (cover), February 10, 1912.

p. 216 Photo courtesy of Susan Ruggles/Indexstock.

p. 217 Photo courtesy of Ewing Galloway/Indexstock.

p. 229 Courtesy of the *New Yorker* Collection 1970, J. B. Handelsman from cartoon bank.com. All rights reserved.

p. 240 Source: *Harper's Weekly*, December 19, 1868.

p. 247 Source: *American Labor Legislation Review*, December 1918.

p. 250 Photo courtesy of Key Color/Indexstock.

p. 254 Photo courtesy of Stock Montage/Indexstock.

p. 258 Photo courtesy of Ewing Galloway/Indexstock.

p. 268 Photo courtesy of Mark Reinstein/Indexstock.

p. 280 Source: U.S. Census Bureau/Deborah Blau.

p. 293 Photo courtesy of Ewing Galloway/Indexstock.

p. 295 Source: National Center for Children in Poverty, www.nccp.org.

p. 295 Source: U.S. Department of Health and Human Services/Deborah Blau.

p. 297 Source: Pamela J. Loprest, "Who Returns to Welfare?" Urban Institute, 2002.

p. 303 Source: *Economic Snapshots*, Economic Policy Institute, July 2001.

p. 308 Photo courtesy of SW Production/Indexstock.

p. 315 Sources: U.S. Census Bureau; David Ellwood/*New York Times*.

p. 315 Source: Hirsh and Macpherson, *Union Membership and Earning Data Book: Compilations from the Current Population Survey*, 2002.

p. 327 Photo courtesy of Key Color/Indexstock.

p. 340 Source: National Low Income Housing Coalition.

p. 342 Photo courtesy of S. Debenport/Rebelartist.com.

p. 343 Source: U.S. Department of Housing and Urban Development/Deborah Blau.

p. 348 Photo courtesy of Frank Siteman/Indexstock.

p. 362 Courtesy of the *New Yorker* Collection 1993, Dana Fradon from cartoon bank.com. All rights reserved.

p. 374 Photo courtesy of Len Rubenstein/Indexstock.

p. 378 Photo courtesy of Matthew Borkoski/Indexstock.

p. 385 Photo courtesy of Howard Sokol/Indexstock.

p. 389 Reprinted with permission from "Probability of Persons under Age 65 Being Uninsured by State," *Health Insurance Is A Family Matter* (National Academies Press, 2002). Copyright by the National Academy of Sciences. Courtesy of the National Academies Press, Washington, D.C.

p. 390 Source: U.S. Census Bureau/Deborah Blau.

p. 400 Source: Labor Problems and Labor Legislation, 1922.

p. 404 Photo courtesy of SW Production/Indexstock.

p. 406 Source: *Economic Snapshots*, Economic Policy Institute, August 2001.

p. 413 Photo courtesy of Eliot Cohen/Indexstock.

p. 421 Courtesy of City Harvest, New York, New York.

p. 434 Photo courtesy of Piotr Powietrzynski/Indexstock.

Index

African Americans (*continued*)
  equal opportunity contradictions for, 182, 209
  feminism and, 152, 158, 161–62
  first national movement, 246–47
  health care inequity and, 386–87
  home ownership by, 339
  housewives leagues, 206
  housing discrimination and, 345–46, 355
  individual acts of resistance by, 177, 178
  Ku Klux Klan and, 239–40, 246
  as low-wage workers, 86, 161
  members of Congress, 104
  Montgomery (Ala.) bus boycott, 263
  mutual aid societies, 235
  New Deal and, 257
  "pan-toting" by, 177
  post-Civil War to Progressive Era, 238–39
  post-World War II to Great Society, 261–65
  prison population makeup and, 269
  public assistance racial myths and, 270
  racial inequality and, 162–65, 167–68. *See also*
    racism
  rural housing for, 359
  segregation and, 29–30, 162, 168, 208, 209, 259,
    263, 345–46, 370
  "separate but equal" doctrine and, 238–39
  single mothers, 154, 156, 161
  slavery and. *See* slavery
  Social Security and, 252, 285, 288
  social work professional organizations, 266
  stereotyping of, 156
  structural conflict and, 208–9
  as uninsured Americans, 388
  urban migration by, 345, 370
  voting rights and, 31, 98, 112, 221, 238, 240
  women's rights and, 206
  See also civil rights movement; desegregation;
    race; racism
African Female Union, 235
African Methodist Church, 235
afterschool programs, 158, 419
Agent Orange, 43
aggregate demand, 72
Agricultural Adjustment Act (1933), 409
Agricultural Adjustment Administration, 253, 427
Agricultural Research, Extension, and Education
    Act (1998), 413
agriculture. *See* farmers; farm workers
Agriculture Department, U.S., 333, 407
  Farm Service Agency, 47
  Food and Consumer Service, 45
  food and nutrition programs, 43, 46, 416–20,
    425, 428
  Food and Nutrition Service, 405, 412, 415, 417,
    418
  rural housing programs and, 359, 360

AIDS. *See* HIV/AIDS
Aid to Dependent Children, 32, 44, 252, 283, 310
Aid to Families with Dependent Children, 21, 44,
    45, 138, 270, 271, 294, 336, 380, 428. *See
    also* Temporary Aid to Needy Families
Aid to the Blind, 45, 252
Aid to the Permanently and Totally Disabled, 45
Aiken, George, 428
Alaska, 417
alcohol abuse. *See* substance abuse
alcohol consumption, 8
  movements against, 201, 235
alienation, worker, 149, 150
alimony, 143
Alinsky, Saul, 218–19
Alliance for Quality Nursing Home Care, 397
All-Indian Pueblo Council of New Mexico, 323
almshouses, 223–24, 225, 230, 231, 235
altruism, 124, 128
AMA. *See* American Medical Association
American Association of Retired Persons, 354,
    397
American Association of Social Workers, 249, 256
American Civil Liberties Union, 121
American Civil War. *See* Civil War, U.S.
American Creed, 188
American Enterprise Institute, 91, 309
American exceptionalism, 108, 116–17
American Federation of Labor, 203–4, 256
American Federation of Labor-Congress of
    Industrial Organizations, 84, 204
American Federation of State, Municipal and
    County Employees, 332
American Health Care Association, 397
American Hospital Association, 397
American Indians. *See* Native Americans
American Medical Association, 397, 401
American Protective Association, 192
American Revolution, 196, 230
Americans with Disabilities Act, 176
American Telephone and Telegraph Company, 84,
    236
anarchism, 213
anger, about social welfare programs, 306, 309
anomie, 187
Anthem Blue Cross/Blue Shield, 399
Anthony, Susan B., 234
antiabortion movement, 193
anti-authoritarianism, 213
antiblack movements, 192–93, 197–98
anti-Catholic movements, 192
anticommunism, 261, 271, 401
  McCarthyism, 197, 213, 261, 262, 265
antidiscrimination laws, 30, 176
antigay policies, 31–32. *See also* gay bashing
antiglobalization movement, 183, 213, 272, 273

antihunger organizations, 427. *See also specific groups*

anti-immigrant movements, 192

anti-Jewish movements, 192

antinuclear movement, 210

antipollution laws, 72

antipoverty programs, 67, 301. *See also specific programs*

antirape hot lines, 143, 176

antitobacco movement, 196

antitrust policy/legislation, 242–43, 244
  law suits, 71

antiviolence programs, 143

antiwar movements, 193–94, 200, 210, 213
  Iraq invasion, 183
  Vietnam War, 189, 191, 262–65

Arendt, Hannah, 187

Arizona, 114, 306

Arkansas, 418

armed forces. *See* military policy

Army-McCarthy hearings, 197, 261

Arthur Andersen, 58, 88

Aryan Supremacists, 192

Asia, postcolonial, 259

Association to Improve the Condition of the Poor, 234, 235

AT&T, 84, 236

atomic bomb, 258, 260

Attica (N.Y.) prison uprising (1970s), 190

Australia, 213, 339, 373

authoritarian personality, 186–87

authority, technical expertise and, 169, 170

automatic disentitlements, 280

automatic stabilizers, social welfare benefits as, 35

automobiles, 344

autonomy
  ideological perspectives on, 124, 127, 128, 129, 133, 158
  professionals and, 170

Bachrach, Peter, 28

Back of the Yards Neighborhood Council, 219

Bacon, Nathaniel, 227

bailouts, corporate, 138

Balanced Budget Act (1997), 380–81, 384, 385

balance of payments, 68

Baltimore and Ohio Railroad, 237

banks, 72–73, 370
  mortgages and, 168, 346, 347, 353–54, 364
  Native American housing and, 358
  New Deal and, 251, 332
  Panic of 1873 and, 237
  reserve requirements, 73
  See also Federal Reserve Banks; Federal Reserve Board

Baratz, Morton, 28

Barro, Robert J., 63–64

Basic Income Grant, 279, 301–2, 304–5

battered women. *See* domestic violence

Beard, Charles and Mary, 237

Beat movement, 262

Begala, Paul, 111, 112

belief systems. *See* ideological perspectives; religion

benefits, 51–54
  universal vs. selective programs, 51
  See also specific programs

Beveridge Plan, 131

bias, mobilization of, 28

BIG. *See* Basic Income Grant

big government, 107, 115, 398
  conservative view of, 135, 136, 155

Bill of Rights, 98

biological inferiority, 162–63

bisexuals, 176, 273

Black Masons, 235

Black Power movement, 197, 200, 209, 217, 264

blame
  for homelessness, 341, 342
  ideological issues, 330, 331
  unworthy poor and, 435

blindness
  Medicaid and, 380
  Supplemental Security Income and, 45, 252, 271, 281, 282, 291–92, 304, 309

block grants, 294, 295, 325–26, 391
  community development, 352–53, 356
  Indian housing, 358
  New Federalism and, 98

Blue Cross/Blue Shield, 398

boarding schools, 29

bonds, government, 69, 73, 285

Bonus March on Washington (1932), 283

Boston, Mass., 230, 261

Boston Medical Center, 417

boycotts, 178, 180, 206, 263

Boyte, Harry, 218

Brandeis Center on Hunger and Poverty, 427

Bread for the World, 427

breast cancer, 373

Breckenridge, Sophonsiba, 369

Britain, 196, 237, 259
  Beveridge Plan, 131
  colonial America and, 225–28
  common law, 105
  home ownership in, 339
  National Health Service, 394
  Poor Law Reform (1834), 224, 232
  Poor Laws (1601), 223, 310
  social welfare tradition, 222–24

Brown Power movement, 197

Brown v. Board of Education (1954), 105, 196, 247, 263, 265

Bruce, Blanche, 238
Bryan, William Jennings, 240–41
Buchanan, James, 93
Buchanan, Pat, 198
budget, federal, 41, 75
    Balanced Budget Act and, 380–81, 384, 385
    debt, 69
    deficits, 69, 74, 137, 260, 269
    surpluses, 27, 69
    See also deficit spending
Bull Moose Party, 400
bureaucracy, federal, 107–8, 114
Bush, George H. W., 266, 282, 410
Bush, George W., 102, 111, 266
    campaign contributions to, 88
    corporate scandals (2002) response by, 38, 89
    food policy, 410
    health care policy, 381, 384
    presidential election victory of, 97
    Social Security privatization proposal, 284, 288, 290
    TANF reauthorization, 295, 296
    tax cut proposals, 69, 74, 137–38, 267
business and industry, 58
    antitrust and, 71, 242–43, 244
    CEO pay and, 70, 88, 222
    conservative views of, 138
    economic function of social policy and, 35–37
    economic policymaking and, 71–72
    employment policy and, 312, 326–29, 332
    federal bureaucracy and, 108
    interlocking directorates, 242
    mass production, 231
    monopolies, 61, 71–72, 222, 236, 240, 242, 243–44
    muckrakers and, 245
    need definition and, 132
    New Deal and, 251–52, 256
    1990s economy and, 83–84, 272
    oligopolies, 61, 72, 243, 441n.10
    on-the-job death and injury, 281–82, 297–98
    political actors and, 91
    post-Civil War to Progressive Era, 236–37
    post-World War II to Great Society, 262, 265
    post-1969, 267–68, 272
    profit motive, 132–33, 182–83
    robber barons and, 61, 222, 237
    scandals (2002), 38, 58, 60, 82, 87–89, 268, 289
    social costs of, 82
    social function of social policy and, 34
    social need recognition by, 6
    social problem definition and, 7
    Social Security contributions by, 41
    social welfare spending as boost to, 26
    undocumented alien hiring laws and, 31

See also corporations; proprietary agencies; small businesses
business cycles, 69–70, 72
Business Roundtable, 397
busing, for school integration, 193, 211
BYNC. *See* Back of the Yards Neighborhood Council

Cabinet, U.S., 101, 102. *See also specific departments*
CACFP. *See* Child and Adult Care Food Program
California, 232, 300, 390, 419
    Enron scandal and, 88
    food stamp program, 414
    health care reform initiatives, 399
    Proposition 13 (1978), 270
Calvin, John, 222
Calvinism, 222–23
campaign financing, 37–38, 88, 113–14, 211, 396
Canada
    home ownership, 339
    life expectancy, 376
    national health insurance program, 375, 394
    North American Free Trade Agreement, 322
    political parties, 212
    prescription drug costs, 391
    voter participation, 111
capital gains taxes, 25, 74
capitalism, 59, 94, 95, 181
    feminist view of, 126, 129–30, 143, 144, 159, 160–61, 205
    ideology and, 124, 126–30, 140–41, 149–52, 211–12
    Marxist analysis of, 201, 202–3, 205
    New Left view of, 213
    post-World War II to Great Society perspectives, 259, 262
    profit motive and, 132–33, 135, 140, 141
    unregulated, 237, 251
    See also market economy
capital punishment, 221
care, need for, 133–34
caregiving, 133, 142, 160
caretaking, 36, 142, 245
Carnegie, Andrew, 61, 236, 239
Carter, Jimmy, 115, 266, 377, 392, 401
cash assistance programs, 35, 43. *See also* income supports; public assistance
cash benefits, 52
categorical programs, 40, 45, 330, 377, 392, 423. *See also specific programs*
Catholic Charities, 427
Cato Institute, 26
CBS-TV, 409, 441n.10
CCA. *See* Corrections Corporation of America

CCC. *See* Civilian Conservation Corps
CDBGs. *See* community development block grants
Census Bureau, U.S., 167
Center on Budget and Policy Priorities, 427
Centers for Medicare and Medicaid Services, 42, 46
Central High School (Little Rock, Ark.), 265
Central Intelligence Agency, 102
CEOs, 70, 88, 222, 272
CETA. *See* Comprehensive Employment Training Act
Chamber of Commerce, U.S, 329, 396, 397
character, poor people and, 307, 308, 315
charismatic leaders, 185–87
charities, private. *See* private charities
charity organization societies, 241, 242, 248, 249
Charleston, S.C., 229
checks and balances, 97, 100, 110, 114, 115
Cheney, Dick, 102
Chevron Oil Corporation, 244
Chicago, Ill., 231–32, 255, 261
    housing reform, 369
    Hull House, 241, 245
    riots, 246, 264
Chicago Conference of the Federation of the Unemployed, 332
chief executive officers, 70, 88, 222, 272
Child Abuse Prevention and Treatment Act (1974), 48
Child and Adult Care Food Program, 46, 410, 419, 422, 428
child care
    day care programs, 27, 257–58, 295–96, 315, 419, 422, 423
    as feminist issue, 142, 159
    for-profit centers, 24
    as government policy issue, 27–28, 158
    laissez-faire conservative view of, 136
    tax credits, 52
child custody, 206
child labor, 204
Child Nutrition Act (1966), 46
children
    adoption of, 48, 273
    community health services for, 48
    family ideological outlook and, 154, 156
    food and hunger and, 407, 408, 409, 414
    food and nutrition programs, 46, 410, 415–19, 422, 423, 427, 428
    in foster care, 48, 354
    health care and, 46–47, 377, 380, 381, 384–86
    mortality rates, 376
    in no-parent families, 296
    poverty and, 299
    public assistance programs for, 44. *See also specific programs*
    socialization of, 160–61

state health insurance plan for, 385–86
    Supplemental Security Income eligibility, 292
    as uninsured Americans, 388
    women's role in rearing of, 142
    See also child care
Children's Bureau, 48, 242
Children's Health Insurance Program of 1997 (CHIPs). *See* State Children's Health Insurance Plan
child support payments, 143, 299
child welfare legislation, 243
child welfare services, 48
China, 59, 196, 213, 271
Chinese Communist Revolution (1949), 196, 212
Chinese Exclusion Act (1882), 31
CHIPs (Children's Health Insurance Program of 1997). *See* State Children's Health Insurance Plan
choice, 215
cholera, 376
Christian Coalition, 211
Christian Right, 176
Church of England, 223
CIA, 102
cigarettes. *See* smoking
CIO, 203–4, 256, 261
Citigroup, 62
Citizens for Better Medicare, 396
citizenship
    constitutional guarantee of, 238
    rights of, 132, 140
    SSI eligibility and, 291
civic standards, 133
civil disobedience, 178
civil disorders. *See* riots
Civilian Conservation Corps, 257, 314, 316, 333
"civilizational restoration," 163
civil rights, 95, 97, 140, 221
    Fourteenth Amendment and, 98, 238
    legislation, 30, 176, 196, 221, 258, 262–65, 345, 354
Civil Rights Acts (1964, 1965), 196, 221, 263, 264, 265, 345, 354
civil rights movement, 30, 111, 115, 121, 201
    collective behavior theories and, 189, 192, 193–94, 196
    Communist Party and, 213
    incremental reform and, 210
    jobs and, 331–32
    master collective action frames and, 215–17
    as New Left movement, 213
    post-World War II to Great Society, 176, 262–65
    post-1969 perspectives, 272
    racial conflict and, 208–10
    social conservative view of, 135

welfare reform legislation, 44, 292

youth employment program legislation, 315

See also House of Representatives, U.S.; Senate, U.S.

Congress of Industrial Organizations, 203–4, 256, 261

Congress of Racial Equality, 217

Congress of Workers and Farmers, 332

Connecticut, 88, 228, 399

consciousness-raising, 212, 264

consensus building, 117

conservatism, 122, 123–24

    anticommunism and, 261, 271

    charity movement and, 241

    collective action frames, 214, 215

    economic functions of social policy and, 36–37

    family issues and, 134, 152–57

    federalism and, 99

    food and hunger issues and, 404, 420

    full-employment legislative initiatives and, 334, 335

    general welfare issues and, 126–27

    government's role and, 135–38, 139–40, 211

    homelessness and, 342, 344

    housing policy and, 347, 353–54, 369, 371

    human nature perspective of, 123–24

    Legal Service Corporation funding and, 49

    minimum wage increases and, 86

    need definition and, 131

    neoclassical, 124

    political functions of social policy and, 38

    political opportunity structures theory and, 197–98

    post-World War II to Great Society, 261, 265

    post-1969 perspectives, 266–75

    prescription drug benefits and, 136, 391

    public assistance and, 137, 156, 215, 309

    public choice theory and, 93–94

    racial inequality and, 162–65

    school voucher support and, 24, 138, 157

    social functions of social policy and, 33–34

    social movements and, 137, 176, 211

    social problem construction and, 7

    social reproduction needs and, 77

    Social Security program and, 41–42, 138, 288

    tax policy and, 74, 270

    women's role and, 141

    work and work ethic and, 145–48, 149

Constitution, U.S., 97

    amendment approval, 96

    Bill of Rights, 98

    on Congress's structure, 102

    divided government and, 114

    due process guarantee, 98, 238

    Equal Rights Amendment proposal, 265, 272

    federalism and, 98

    judicial interpretation of, 106–7

    post-Civil War amendments, 98, 238

    reserve clause, 98

    See also specific amendments

consumer demand, need definition and, 131

consumer groups, 396

consumerism, 132–33, 259

Consumer Price Index, 66–67

consumer protection, 211

Cooke, Jay, 237

Coolidge, Calvin, 249

cooperative federalism, 98, 99

corporate scandals (2002), 38, 58, 60, 82, 87–89, 268, 289

    Bush (George W.) response to, 38, 89

    social welfare implications, 87–89

corporate welfare, 25–26, 138

corporations, 61–62, 63

    antitrust and, 71, 242–43, 244

    bailouts of, 138

    CEOs of, 70, 88, 222, 272

    downsizing of, 83–84, 153

    multinational, 62, 267, 273

    New Deal economics and, 251

    post-Civil War to Progressive Era, 236–37

    post-1969, 267, 272

    1990s economy and, 83–84, 272

    taxes paid by, 74–75

    See also monopolies

corporatist social policy, 242–43

Corrections Corporation of America, 269

corruption, political, 211, 244–45

COSs. *See* charity organization societies

cost of production, socialization of, 35–36

cost-push inflation, 66

costs. *See* social costs

Council of Economic Advisors, 102, 295

CPI-U. *See* Consumer Price Index

CRA. *See* Community Reinvestment Act

crack cocaine, 8

crime, as housing policy change trigger, 347, 370, 371

criminal justice system

    civil rights concerns, 221

    domestic violence initiatives, 143

    drug felons, 44

    imprisonment rates, 66, 269

    prisons, 24, 66, 138, 269

    probation and parole, 49

Crisis of Democracy, The: Report on the Governability of Democracies to the Trilateral Commission (Huntington), 137

critical elections, U.S. politics and, 114–15, 116

cross-endorsements, 109

crowd theory, 184, 185, 186, 187, 200

Cuba, 213

Cuban Revolution (1959), 212
cultural feminism
 family perspective and, 158, 159–60
 general welfare concerns and, 129
 government's role and, 142–43
 human nature perspective of, 125–26
 identity politics and, 200
 incentive argument theory and, 194
 separatist women's movement and, 217
 work and work ethic and, 151
cultural inferiority, 163
culture, professional, 169, 170–71
culture of poverty, 163
CWA. *See* Civil Works Administration
cyclical theories of social change, 12
cyclical unemployment, 65

Darwin, Charles, 239
day care programs, 424
 for adults, 419
 for children, 27, 257–58, 295–96, 315, 419, 422, 423
Debs, Eugene, 246
debt, federal, 27, 69
decision making, political, 92–95
Declaration of Independence, 221
Declaration of Sentiments, 206
Defense Department, U.S., 107
defiance, mass, 178, 180
deficit, budget, 69, 74, 137, 260, 269
deficit, trade, 68–69
deficit spending, 250, 251, 259–60, 262
deindustrialization, 153, 198, 199, 204
demand. *See* supply and demand
demand-pull inflation, 66
democracy
 crowd theory view of, 185
 definitions of, 95–97
 equal opportunity as key tenet of, 182
 Jeffersonian conception of, 367
 majority rule and, 97
 in Marxist theory, 203
 participatory, 95–96, 213
 radical, 213
 return to, 217
 socialist perspective of, 212
Democratic Party, 91, 109, 111, 238
 African Americans and, 209–10, 261–62
 campaign contributions to, 88
 civil rights issues and, 196, 345
 critical elections and, 115
 food policy issues and, 425, 428
 gay rights movement and, 196
 ideological labeling of, 123
 New Deal and, 251, 257
 New Democrats and, 214

political machines and, 244, 261
 post-World War II to Great Society, 261
 post-1969, 266, 268
 as tenant group ally, 368
 voter mobilization by, 113
Democratic Socialists of America, 121
"democratic wish," 115
demonetization of services, 77
demonstrations. *See* social protest
Denmark, 61
dependence, humanistic liberalism on, 124, 128
depression (economic), 35, 69, 70, 206, 237
 jobs and job training programs and, 332
Depression of 1837, 203, 231
Depression of 1930s. *See* Great Depression
deregulation, 71, 72, 82, 83, 88, 267–68, 272
desegregation, 180
 of armed forces, 257
 of public transportation, 263
 of schools, 30, 105, 196, 247, 258, 263, 265
Detroit, Mich., 190, 261, 345
deviance, social movements as, 184–89
devolution, 138
diagnosis, as social work skill, 249
diagnostic-related groupings, 9, 274, 377
difference, politics of, 201
differently abled persons, 199
Dionne, E. J., 112
direct democracy, 95–96
direct primaries, 110
disability benefits
 general assistance programs, 300
 Social Security, 41, 262, 265, 279, 284, 290–91, 304, 310
 for veterans, 43
 See also workers' compensation
disabled people
 employment services for, 48
 equal opportunity contradictions for, 182
 food stamp program and, 413
 health care and, 377, 383, 384. *See also* Medicaid; Medicare
 housing discrimination and, 355
 low-cost housing for, 47
 nursing home care for, 46
 rights movement, 121, 176, 189, 210, 216
 Supplemental Security Income and, 45, 252, 271, 281, 282, 291–92, 304, 309
Disabled Veterans Outreach Program, 325
discount rate, 72–73
discouraged workers, 66
discretionary spending, 41, 75
discrimination, 216
 contradictions about equal opportunity and, 182, 209
 in housing, 261, 345–46, 354–55

powers of, 101–2
See also presidency; *specific agencies and departments*
Executive Order 11246, 197
expectations, need definition and, 132
experience rating, 42
exploitation, 150, 201, 202
externalities, economic, 72

factionalism, political, 100
factors of production, 60
factory system, 203
Fair Housing Act (1968, 1988), 354
Fair Labor Standards Act (1938), 204
fair market rent, 339, 358
fairness, as social welfare policy goal, 15–16
faith-based agencies, 23, 138
Falwell, Jerry, 156–57
family
  caregiving by, 133, 160
  definition of, 153
  homelessness and, 341
  ideological views of, 122, 135, 137, 139, 142, 152–62, 196, 211, 214
  ideology development role of, 120
  as resource distribution site, 134
  socialization role of, 33, 36
  social reproduction and, 36–37, 76–77, 206
  types of, 153–61, 186, 214
  See also children; motherhood; parents; single mothers
family allowances, 158
Family Assistance Plan (1969), 271
family ethic, 144, 229–30, 275, 307–8
  industrial, 233–34
family leave, 158, 159
family policy, 158
family preservation, 48
Family Support Act (1988), 335
family values, 156, 196, 211, 214
Fannie Mae, 346
farmers, 313
  food programs and, 409–10, 420, 423–24, 425
  New Deal and, 253
  populism and, 240, 241
  rural housing and, 359
farming out, 228
farm overproduction, 409
farm policy, impact of, 27
Farm Service Agency, 47
farm workers, 47, 216, 324, 359
fascism, 185, 186, 192
fatherhood, conservative view of, 154
Father Knows Best (television program), 154
FBI, 197

federal budget. *See* budget, federal
federal bureaucracy, 107–8, 114
federal debt, 27, 69
Federal Deposit Insurance Corporation, 353
Federal Economy Act, 257
Federal Emergency Relief Administration, 257, 333, 334
Federal Employee Loyalty Program, 261
Federal Employees Health Benefits Plan, 395
federal government. *See* government
Federal Home Loan Mortgage Corporation, 346
Federal Housing Administration, 355, 363
Federal Housing Authority, 168
Federal Insurance Contributions Act, 285
federalism, 98–108
  checks and balances, 97, 100, 110, 114, 115
  separation of powers, 100, 101–7, 110, 114, 115
federal matching rate, 380
Federal National Mortgage Association, 346
Federal Reserve Bank, 72–74, 97, 364
Federal Reserve Board, 27, 346, 353
Federal Surplus Commodities Corporation, 409, 427, 428
Federal Surplus Relief Corporation, 425
Federation of Unemployed Workers Leagues of America, 332
fee-for-service health care programs, 377
Feldstein, Martin, 80–81
"fellow servant" doctrine, 281
Feminine Mystique, The (Friedan), 264
feminism, 31, 122–23, 201
  African Americans and, 152, 158, 161–62
  family issues and, 152–53, 158–62
  gendered conflict view and, 205, 207
  general welfare concerns and, 129–30
  government's role and, 141–45
  human nature perspective of, 125–26
  identity politics and, 200
  incentive argument theory and, 194
  individual acts of resistance and, 178
  master collective action frames and, 217
  need definition and, 133–34
  post-1969 perspectives, 272
  social policy's social function and, 34
  social reproduction and, 36, 142, 143
  social work professionalism and, 173
  work and work ethic and, 150–52
  See also women's movement
feminists of color, 152, 158, 161–62
FERA. *See* Federal Emergency Relief Administration
feudalism, 59–60, 78, 145, 181, 224
Feuer, Lewis, 187, 190
FHA. *See* Federal Housing Administration; Federal Housing Authority

FICA. *See* Federal Insurance Contributions Act
Fifteenth Amendment, 98, 238
financial capital, 62–63
financial institutions. *See* banks; stock market
Financial Services Modernization Act (1999), 353
fiscal policy, 72, 74–76, 111
fiscal welfare, 24–26, 52
Fisher Body Plant, 256
Flacks, Richard, 191
Flexner, Abraham, 248
Florida, 306, 390
flour riots, 206
FNS. *See* Food and Nutrition Service
Foner, Eric, 233
Food and Consumer Service, 45
food and food policies, 14, 40, 296, 403–29, 435
  as basic human need, 78, 79
  economics of, 423–24
  emergency assistance programs, 404, 407, 410, 418, 419–23
  historical insights on, 427–29
  hunger definition and, 405–9
  ideology of, 425–26
  nutrient deficiencies and, 408–9. *See also* nutrition programs
  politics of, 424–25
  post-1969 perspectives, 274
  in poverty line determination, 67, 68
  program classification, 422–23
  program overview, 410–22
  program overview chart, 411–12
  school-based programs, 46, 410, 416–19, 422, 423, 427, 428
  social movement initiatives and, 409–10, 423–24, 427
  surpluses and, 409–10, 420, 422, 424, 425, 427–28
  voluntary programs, 274
  See also food stamps
Food and Nutrition Service, 405, 412, 415, 417, 418
food assistance network, private, 410, 420–22
food banks, 407, 418, 420
food insecurity, 406, 407
food pantries, 274, 404, 422, 424
Food Research and Action Center, 419, 427
food security, 405–6
Food Security Measurement Project, 405
food stamps, 24, 35, 79, 265, 424, 428
  eligibility criteria, 50–51, 280, 409, 413–14, 423, 425, 428
  as in-kind benefit, 52
  outreach programs, 410
  poverty line determination and, 68
  program overview, 45, 410–15, 422, 423

Reagan cuts, 271, 274
  as selective program, 43
Ford, Henry, 344
foreign policy, 20, 21, 101, 258, 259, 265
for-profit programs. *See* proprietary agencies
foster children, 48, 354
foundations, 7
  drug research by, 392
  political, 91
401(k) accounts, 301
Fourteenth Amendment, 98, 238
Fox Network, 441n.10
frames, collective action, 214–17
France, 196, 259, 339, 373
Frankfurter, Felix, 105
Fraser, Nancy, 162
Freddie Mac, 346
Freedman's Bureau, 30, 238
freedom. *See* liberty
Freedom Rides (1961), 263, 265
free laborers, 227, 230, 233
free social spaces, 218
free speech, 221
free trade, 267, 273
  North American Free Trade Agreement, 315–16, 322
French Revolution, 185, 196
Freud, Sigmund, 146, 148, 185–86
Frick, Ford, 236
frictional unemployment, 65
Friedan, Betty, 264
Fromm, Erich, 186–87
F scale personality inventory, 186–87
Fugitive Slave Law, 232
Full Employment Act (1946), 262, 265, 328, 332, 334
full-employment coalition, 215
full-employment programs, 326, 328–29, 332–35
fundamentalist religious organizations, 197

Galbraith, John Kenneth, 131
Gandhi, Mohandas, 263–64
GAO. *See* General Accounting Office
GA programs. *See* general assistance programs
Garrison, William Lloyd, 208, 234
Garvey, Amy Jacques, 208
Garvey, Marcus, 208
gasoline taxes, 344
gay bashing, 32, 193, 272–73. *See also* homophobia
Gay Liberation Front, 272
gay rights movement, 39, 121, 176, 189, 201
  Clinton presidency and, 196
  family definition issues and, 153
  identity politics and, 200
  incremental reform and, 210
  master collective action frames and, 216

human capital, lack of, 164
humanistic liberalism
    family issues and, 157–58
    general welfare perspectives, 128
    government's role and, 140
    human nature and, 124
    need definition, 132
    racial inequality concerns, 165–66
human nature, ideological views of, 122, 123–26
human needs. *See* needs, basic human
human rights, 165–66
Humphrey-Hawkins Act (1978), 328, 332, 333, 335
hunger, 274, 403–10, 423–24, 426–27
    nutrient deficiencies and, 408–9
    prevalence of, 407–8
    See also food and food policies; nutrition programs
Hunger in America (television documentary), 409
Hunger Prevention Act (1988), 420
Hunter, Robert, 245
Huntington, Samuel, 137
Hutton, Edward F., 256

IBM, 61, 84
Ickes, Harold, 369–70
IDAs. *See* Individual Development Accounts
identity, New Social Movement theory and, 199–201
identity politics, 199–200
ideological perspectives, 119–73, 435
    colonial America, 226–27
    independence through Civil War, 233–34
    post-Civil War to Progressive Era, 239
    Progressive Era to New Deal, 245–46
    New Deal through World War II, 253–54
    post-World War II to Great Society, 262–63
    post-1969, 271–72
    alternative outlooks, 121–22
    definition of ideology, 119–20
    employment policy and, 330–31
    family and, 122, 135, 137, 139, 142, 152–62
    food policy and, 425–26
    general welfare and, 126–30
    governmental role and, 122, 127–28, 131–32, 134–45
    health care policy and, 397–98
    housing policy and, 366–67
    on human nature, 123–26
    income support program and, 307–8
    individuals and, 120–21
    need definition and, 130–34
    professionalism and, 169–73
    racial inequality and, 122, 162–69
    social change and, 122–23
    social movements and, 210–19

    social policy change and, 13, 16, 122–23
    society and, 121
    work and work ethic and, 145–52
    See also specific ideologies
Illinois, 300
immigrants, 33
    anti-immigrant movements, 192
    detention centers, 24, 138
    exclusionary laws and policies, 31
    food and hunger and, 407
    food stamp program and, 413, 428
    market economy and, 78
    Medicaid program and, 380, 381, 388
    political machines and, 244
    public assistance restrictions for, 44, 295
    rent strike participants, 206
    Supplemental Security Income and, 45
    undocumented aliens, 31, 413
    as uninsured people, 388
Immigration and Control Act (1986), 31
impartiality, as social work norm, 170, 171
impersonality, as social work norm, 170
incentive argument theory, 193–94
inclusiveness, New Deal ideology and, 253–54
income
    food and hunger and, 407
    as health care inequity factor, 387
    housing and, 339–41, 344, 361, 371, 468n.6
    ideological perspectives, 127, 128, 134
    inequities, 70–71, 387
    national guaranteed, 271, 301–2, 305
income support programs and policies, 14, 40, 279–311, 435
    economic perspectives, 302–5
    economic policy impact on, 27
    generosity of, 304, 306
    historical insights on, 310–11
    ideological views of, 307–8
    indirect corporate benefits of, 26
    means-tested programs, 43, 292–93, 306
    politics and, 306–7
    program overview chart, 286–87
    social change triggers and, 281–84
    social movements and, 308–9
    See also public assistance; Social Security; unemployment insurance
income taxes, 43, 74, 242, 244. *See also* Earned Income Tax Credit
income test, 43
indentured servants, 225, 227, 230
Independent Party, 91, 109
India, 59, 88, 264
Indian Appropriation Act (1871), 29
Indian Housing Block Grant, 358
Indians, American. *See* Native Americans
Indian Trade and Intercourse Act (1802), 29

market economy (*continued*)
   gendered conflict and, 206
   historical perspectives on, 77–78, 224
   laissez-faire conservatism and, 127, 137
   liberalism and, 139, 140
   post-1969 perspectives, 267–69
   professionalism and, 169
   profit motive and, 132–33, 135, 140, 141
   racial discrimination and, 164
   social welfare spending and, 79–80
   women's household work and, 161
   See also capitalism
marketplace, 435
   faith in, 116
   health care and, 373–75, 376, 395–96, 398
   instability as social change trigger, 281–82
   need definition and, 131, 132–33
   as resource distribution site, 134–35
market populism, 271–72
marriage
   antigay policies and, 32
   conservative views on, 154
   feminist views on, 142, 152
   public assistance regulations, 32, 44, 296
   working wives and, 257
   See also divorce
marriage contracts, 159
Marx, Karl, 13, 125, 128, 149, 150, 201, 202, 204
Marxism, 94, 95, 151, 198
   class conflict tenet of, 201–5
   radicalism and, 124–25, 128–29, 140
Massachusetts, 228, 231, 399
mass production, 231
mass society theory, 184, 187
master collective action frames, 215–17
maternal leave, 142
maternal mortality, 376
Mazon, 427
McCarren-Walter Act (1952), 31
McCarthy, John, 194
McCarthy, Joseph, 197, 213, 261, 265
McCarthyism, 197, 213, 261, 262, 265
McCone Commission, 187
McCulloch v. Maryland (1819), 105
McKinley, William, 241
MDTA. *See* Manpower Development and Training
   Act
Mead, Lawrence, 147
means tests, 43–47, 50–51, 253, 292–93, 306, 314
Mechanics' Unions Trade Association, 203
media
   ideology development and, 120
   oligopolies in, 61, 441n.10
   presidential visibility and, 101
   social problem recognition and, 6, 7, 245

Medicaid, 265, 274, 375, 397, 398
   eligibility criteria, 280, 380, 395
   government spending on, 75–76
   immigrants and, 380, 381, 388
   as in-kind benefit, 52
   Medicare and, 382–83, 384
   nursing homes and, 46, 380, 381–82, 438n.12
   overview of, 46–47, 377, 380–83
   private agency reimbursement for, 24
   as selective program, 43
   State Children's Health Insurance Program and,
      385–86
   WIC program and, 415
medical leave, 158, 159
medical social work, 9
medical technology and research, 376–77
Medicare, 41, 79, 265, 274, 375, 377, 397
   age eligibility reduction, 395
   funding of, 285
   government spending on, 75–76
   health maintenance organizations and, 379
   as in-kind benefit, 52
   Medicaid recipients and, 382–83, 384
   overview of, 42, 383–84
   prescription drug benefit, 136, 211, 388, 390,
      391, 396
   private agency reimbursement for, 24
   social policy impact on, 9
Medicare+Choice program, 384
Medigap insurance policies, 384
men
   in colonial America, 227
   cultural feminist view of, 159–60
   family role of, 153, 154
   health care inequality and, 386
   industrial family ethic and, 233–34
   life expectancy, 376
   as low-wage workers, 86
   sexual violence and, 142–43
   voting rights and, 110, 112–13, 221
   women's economic dependence on, 143, 144,
      145, 152, 233
   See also division of labor; gender; patriarchy
mental asylums, 230–31, 236
mental health systems, 49
   for-profit, 24
   managed care, 24, 49, 393
   U.S. policy inadequacies, 392–93
Mental Health Systems Act (1980), 392
mental illness, 230–31, 236
   advocacy groups for, 397
   federal policies, 392–93
   homelessness and, 341
   Supplemental Security Income for, 291–92
   See also mental health systems

mental retardation, 291
Mental Retardation and Community Mental
    Health Center Construction Act (1963), 49
menu costs, 64
merchant class, 227, 228
Merck, 87
Merrill Lynch, 88
Merton, Robert, 191
Mexican Americans, 407
Mexico, 322
Michigan, 300, 390, 399
microeconomics, 59, 63–65, 71–72
Microsoft, 71
middle class, 222
    social movements and, 200–201
    women's activism and, 205, 206, 207
migrant workers, 324, 359, 418
Milford Conference, 249
military policy
    antigay, 31–32, 196
    armed forces desegregation, 257
    government spending and, 26–27, 75
    impact of, 26–27
    pensions, 280
    post-World War II to Great Society, 260
    Reagan administration, 271
    social conservative view of, 135
    See also veterans
militias, 197
Milk, Harvey, 273
Mills, Wilbur, 147
minimum wage, 339
    decline in, 85–86
minimum wage laws, 36–37, 204, 256
Minnesota, 282, 399, 414
minority leaders, in Congress, 104
Mississippi, 418
Missouri, 390, 399
Mobil Oil Corporation, 244
mob mentality, 186, 187. *See also* crowd theory
Model Cities, 265
monetary policy, 72–74, 96–97
    Populist "easy money," 241
monopolies, 71–72, 222, 236, 242
    agricultural, 240
    antitrust and, 71, 242–43, 244
    definition of, 61
    Standard Oil breakup, 72, 243–44
Montana, 399
Montgomery (Ala.) bus boycott, 263
moralism, 245
moral leadership, 156
Moral Majority, 176, 211
Morgan, J. P., 236
Morone, James, 115–16

Mortgage Bankers Association of America, 348
mortgages, 364
    federally guaranteed, 344, 347, 355, 364, 370
    interest as tax deductions, 25, 338, 362–63, 370
    redlining and, 168, 353–54
    secondary, 346
motherhood, 309
    child custody rights, 206
    community health services, 48
    conservative view of, 154
    cultural feminist view of, 129, 159
    health insurance and, 388
    maternal leave and, 142
    maternal mortality and, 376
    nutrition programs and, 415–16
    teenage, 6–7, 44
    See also single mothers
mothers' pensions, 32, 242, 244, 248
Motorola, 84
Motor Voter bill (1993), 113
Mott, Lucretia, 205–6
Moynihan, Daniel P., 154, 156
muckrakers, 245
multiculturalism, 201
multinational corporations, 62, 267, 273
Murdoch, Rupert, 441n.10
Murray, Charles, 147, 156, 309
mutual aid, 53
mutual aid societies, 235
mutual benefit societies, 229
mutual exchange, 93
Myrdal, Gunnar, 182

NAACP, 208, 247, 263, 272
NAFTA, 315–16, 322
NAFTA-Transitional Adjustment Assistance
    Program, 322
Nash, Gary, 230
NASW. *See* National Association of Social
    Workers
National Academy of Sciences, 68, 387
National Advisory Committee on Civil Disorders,
    182
National Affordable Housing Act (1990), 349,
    355, 356, 371
National AIDS Strategy (1996), 352
National Alliance for the Mentally Ill, 397
National Association for the Advancement of
    Colored People, 208, 247, 263, 272
National Association of Colored Women, 208
National Association of Manufacturers, 256, 329,
    397
National Association of Real Estate Boards, 348
National Association of Social Workers, 11, 174,
    266

"pan-toting," 177
parental leave, 31
parental rights, 32, 135
parents
    conservative views of, 135, 154
    public assistance restrictions and, 44
    single, 32, 44, 143, 154, 155, 156, 158, 161,
        304, 308
    teenage, 6–7, 44
    See also children; family; motherhood
Parks, Rosa, 263
parole, 49
Parsons, Talcott, 12, 153, 154, 157, 187
participation, right of, 132, 140, 166
participatory democracy, 95–96, 213
part-time workers
    increase in, 87
    involuntary, 66, 87
    women as, 152, 161
patents, drug, 391
paternalism, 142–43
patriarchy
    as family structure, 156–57, 159–61, 186
    feminist view of, 125–26, 129–30, 141–45, 151–
        52, 159–61, 205, 266
    gendered conflict issues and, 205, 207
    right-wing women's groups and, 143
    status strain theory and, 193
patronage, political, 108, 109, 110
pay equity, 142, 151, 158, 159, 252, 265
payroll taxes
    Medicare, 42, 285, 383
    Social Security, 41, 80, 256, 273, 283, 285, 305
    unemployment insurance, 42, 292–93
peace movement, 193–94, 200, 210, 213. See also
    antiwar movements
peer influence, 120
Pendleton Act (1883), 108
Pennsylvania, 390
pensions, 259
    civil service, 280
    401(k) accounts, 301
    mothers', 32, 242, 244, 248
    Townsend movement and, 255, 283
    for veterans, 43, 244
    See also retirement insurance
Pentagon, terrorist attack on (2001), 26–27, 270
Perkins, Frances, 255
permanency planning, 48
personal connections, use of, 167
Personal Responsibility and Work Opportunity
    Reconciliation Act (1996), 44, 336
pharmaceutical industry. See drug companies
Pharmaceutical Research and Manufacturers of
    America, 396
PHAs. See public housing authorities

Philadelphia, Penn., 230, 231, 261, 264, 427
philanthropy, 53
Physicians for a National Health Program, 399
picketing, 178
PICs. See Private Industry Councils
Pierce, Franklin, 236
Piven, Frances Fox, 110, 179, 180, 281
plain meaning of the text theory, 106
plantation economy, 225, 230, 232
Plessy v. Ferguson (1896), 239
pluralism, interest-group, 92–93, 94
Plymouth colony, 228
point-of-service plans, 378
Poland, 217
police departments, 143
policy, definition of, 20
policy analysis model of social policy change, 13–
    14, 18, 434–35
political action, collective behavior and, 194–95
political actors, 90–91
political control, as social change trigger, 281, 282
political equality, 97, 221
political foundations, 91
political functions, of social welfare policy, 32, 37–
    38, 117
political liberty, 97
political machines, 244, 261
political opportunity structures theory, 195–98
political parties, 91, 109–11, 217
    campaign contributions to, 88
    ideological labeling of, 123
    labor-based, 116, 202–3
    radical, 212–13
    voter mobilization by, 113
    See also specific parties
political power, 7, 28, 54
political rights, 140, 221
political science, 92–97
politics, 90–118
    colonial America, 225–26
    independence through Civil War, 232–33
    post-Civil War to Progressive Era, 238–39
    Progressive Era to New Deal, 244–45
    New Deal through World War II, 252–53
    post-World War II to Great Society, 260–62
    post-1969, 270–71
    decision-making theories and, 92–95
    democracy definitions, 95–97
    federalism and, 98–108
    of food policy, 424–25
    of health care policy, 396–97
    of housing policy, 365–66
    income support program and, 306–7
    of jobs policy, 329–30
    majority rule's importance in, 97
    social movements and, 176, 178

social need recognition and, 6
social policy change and, 13, 15–16, 122
social workers and, 117–18
term limits and, 37–38
See also government, U.S; political parties
politics of disruption, 179, 180
poorhouses. *See* almshouses
Poor Law Reform of 1824 (U.S), 32
Poor Law Reform of 1834 (Britain), 224, 232
poor laws
    Britain, 223, 224, 228, 232, 310
    United States, 32, 226, 228, 231
Poor Laws of 1601 (England), 223, 310
poor people
    food and hunger and, 407, 408, 414, 423–24, 426
    poverty line and, 44, 46, 67–68, 413, 415
    selective program eligibility criteria, 50–51
    social protest by, 179–80, 283
    stereotypes concerning, 275
    worthy vs. unworthy concept of, 32, 230, 275, 282, 292, 304–5, 307, 308, 309, 435
    See also poverty
poor people's movements, 39, 179–80, 195
Poppendieck, Janet, 404
popular culture, 120
popular sovereignty, 97
populism, 213, 222, 240–41
    market, 271–72
Populist movement, 239, 240–41
Port Huron Statement (1962), 461n.90
Portland, Oregon, 297
POS plans. *See* point-of-service plans
POS theory. *See* political opportunity structures theory
postindustrial society, collective action in, 198–99
potential hunger, 405
poverty, 57, 79, 222, 235, 276, 306–7
    absolute calculation method of, 67
    almshouses, 223–24, 225, 230, 231, 235
    Calvinist view of, 222–23
    charity organization societies and, 241, 242
    in colonial America, 228–30
    culture of, 163
    Earned Income Tax Credit and, 279, 310
    empirical analyses of, 245–46
    equal opportunity contradictions for, 182
    food and hunger issues, 403, 407, 408, 414, 423–24, 426
    health care issues, 376, 377, 380–383, 387, 388. *See also* Medicaid
    homelessness and, 341, 347–48
    housing issues, 339, 341, 342, 345, 346, 347, 357, 364–66, 369–72
    Individual Development Accounts and, 300–301
    jobs programs and, 314–15, 330

market populism and, 272
McCarthyism and, 261
older women and, 289
post-World War II to Great Society, 262–63
Reagan's view of, 271
relative calculation method of, 67–68
selective program eligibility criteria, 50–51
settlement houses and, 241–42
stereotyping of, 275
underclass theory and, 187
welfare-to-work issues, 296–97
women's rights and, 205, 206
work and work ethic, and, 145–48
See also poor people; War on Poverty
Poverty (Hunter), 245
poverty line, 44, 46, 67–68, 413, 415
poverty wage, 86
power
    feminist views of, 129, 151, 152, 205
    interest-group pluralism and, 92
    in Marxist theory, 202–3
    political, 7, 28, 54
    political action availability and, 179
    professionalism and, 170
    purchasing, 35, 134, 292, 305, 424
    redistribution of, 211, 217
    unequal distribution of, 198–210
PPOs. *See* preferred provider organizations
pragmatic liberalism
    family issues and, 157–58
    general welfare and, 127–28
    government's role and, 139–40
    human nature perspective of, 124
    need definition and, 131–32
    racial inequality and, 165
predetermination, 145
preferred provider organizations, 378
pregnancy
    health care programs, 46–47, 158
    income loss during, 142
    Medicaid program and, 380
    nutrition programs and, 46, 415–16
    teenage, 6–7
    See also abortion rights
prejudice, 165, 167, 168–69
prenatal care, 46–47, 158
Presbyterian Hunger Program, 427
prescription drugs, 136, 211, 388, 390–92, 396
presidency, U.S., 100, 101–2, 110
Presidential Commission on the Status of Women, 197
President's Committee on Urban Housing, 370
prices, 63–65, 267
primary elections, 91, 110
prime interest rate, 73, 346
priming the pump, 74

public housing authorities, 345, 360–61, 366

public job creation programs, 316, 325–26, 328, 329, 332

public policy, 20–21, 148, 160, 435

public schools. *See* education and schools

public services, 268

punishment, 184, 275

purchasing power, 35, 134, 292, 305, 424

pure milk law, 235

pure public goods, 64–65

Puritans, 146

Quality Housing and Work Responsibility Act (1998), 347, 361, 371

Quincy, Josiah, 231

quintiles inequality measurement, 70

race, 162, 234, 275
  health care inequity and, 386–87
  housing and, 338, 339, 344–46, 355, 365, 366
  low-wage workers and, 86, 161
  Marxist view of, 128, 205
  post-1969 politics of, 270
  single-parent households and, 143, 154, 156
  social construction of, 166–67
  social welfare program stratification and, 52
  status strain theory and, 192–93
  structural conflict theory and, 207–10

race-neutral/color-blind policy, 142, 152, 163–64, 167–68

racial discrimination, 162–69, 345

racial formation, 207–8

racial hierarchies, 165–66

racial inequality, ideological perspectives on, 122, 162–69

racialization, 207–8

racial profiling, 165

racism, 30, 165, 167, 200, 209
  feminism of color view of, 161–62
  institutional, 167–69
  McCarthyism and, 261
  right-wing organizations and, 197–98
  scientific, 211
  social conservative view pf, 164
  socialist feminist view of, 126, 130, 143
  women's work and, 152

radiation, 43

radical feminism. *See* cultural feminism

radicalism, 122–23
  collective action frames, 215
  economic function of social policy and, 35
  family issues and, 134, 152–53, 158
  feminist criticism of, 141
  general welfare and, 128–29
  government's role and, 140–41

  human nature perspective of, 124–25
  market economy and, 135
  need definition and, 132–33
  political function of social policy and, 37
  racial inequality and, 166–69
  social function of social policy and, 34
  social movements and, 211–13
  work and work ethic and, 149–50

radical left, Progressive Era and, 246

railroads, 237, 344

rallies, protest, 180

rape, 31, 142–43, 160, 176

rational choice theory, 193–94

rational crowd theory, 190

rationality, 124, 125, 127
  collective behavior theories, 189–94
  crowd theory and, 185
  racial discrimination and, 165

rationing of health care, 374–75, 379, 393, 395

RCA, 249

reactionary movements, 211

Reagan, Ronald, 138, 291, 410
  conservative agenda of, 115, 139, 266, 271
  family ideology of, 155–56
  food policy, 409, 418, 426, 428
  health care policies, 9, 377, 392–93
  homelessness and, 342
  housing policy, 358, 371
  jobs programs, 273–74, 325, 335
  politics of race and, 270
  presidential leadership by, 101
  tax policy, 74, 282
  women's issues and, 197

real estate industry, 344, 346, 347, 360–61, 365, 370

real estate speculation, 337

rebellions
  in colonial America, 227–28
  for gay rights, 273
  personal, 178
  by slaves, 228

recession, 35, 72, 259
  definition of, 69, 70
  income support programs and, 305
  jobs and job-training programs and, 332
  unemployment insurance and, 292, 294

Reconstruction era, 238

recreation centers, 419

Rector, Robert, 156

redlining, 168, 353–54

Red Power movement, 197

red scare, 261, 265

Reed, Ralph, 136

Reed, Stanley, 105

reference groups, 191

Wolff, Edward, 71
women
  affirmative action protections, 197
  breast cancer victims, 373
  caregiving and, 133, 142, 160. *See also* child
    care
  caretaking and, 142, 245
  in colonial America, 227
  community health services and, 48
  credit ratings for, 31
  divorce and, 41, 288, 289, 309
  economic dependence on men of, 143, 144,
    145, 152, 233
  empowerment of, 142, 143
  equal opportunity contradictions for, 182
  family ethic and, 144, 233–34, 275, 307–8
  family role of, 153, 154, 158–61
  food and hunger and, 407–8
  food and nutrition programs for, 46, 410, 415–
    16, 422, 423
  health care inequity and, 386
  household labor and, 144, 150–51, 152, 160–61,
    205, 215
  individual acts of resistance by, 178
  life expectancy, 376
  as low-wage workers, 85, 86, 151, 152, 161
  as members of Congress, 104
  mothers' pensions, 32, 242, 244, 248
  New Deal and, 257
  parental leave, 31
  paternalism toward, 142–43
  protective labor laws for, 143–44
  public assistance and, 295, 296–97, 305
  rape and, 31, 142–43, 160, 176
  reproductive rights. *See* abortion rights
  sexual objectification of, 129, 142
  social reformers, 241, 245
  social reproduction role of, 36, 143, 206
  Social Security and, 41, 142, 144, 252, 288–
    89
  as state legislators, 104
  unemployment insurance and, 142, 294
  as uninsured people, 388
  widows, 288–89, 309
  in work force, 27–28, 142, 144, 150–52, 158,
    257
  World War II and, 27, 257–58
  See also gender; motherhood; pregnancy
women's movement, 4, 16, 31, 37, 39, 121, 176
  collective behavior theories and, 189, 196,
    197
  family issues and, 153, 157
  incremental reform and, 210
  master collective action frames and, 216
  as New Left movement, 213

  nineteenth-century, 205–6, 234–35
  social conservative view of, 135
  structural conflict issues and, 205–6
  suffrage rights and, 31, 206, 216, 221, 234, 247–
    48
  transformative change goals, 211
  twentieth-century, 263, 264, 265, 272
  welfare state development and, 145
  See also feminism
Wood, James, 191
work
  Calvinist view of, 222–23
  household, 144, 150–51, 152, 160–61, 205,
    215
  ideological perspectives on, 122, 124–25, 126,
    145–52
  occupational safety rules, 58
  public assistance requirements, 44, 46, 48
  See also division of labor; jobs and job training;
    work ethic
Workers Alliance of America, 255, 332
workers' compensation, 279
  catalyst for, 281–82, 309
  generosity of, 304
  historical insights concerning, 310
  program overview, 297–98
  Progressive Era reforms and, 242, 243, 244, 400–
    401
work ethic, 36, 78, 145–52, 330, 367, 397
Work Experience Program, 48
workfare, 48, 274, 312, 314–15, 333, 335–36
Workforce Investment Act (1998), 48, 274, 313–
    26, 331, 332, 333, 336
Workforce Investment Boards, 319
workhouses, 223–24, 229–30, 235
Work in America (1971 report), 149
Work Incentive Program (1967), 48
Work Incentive Program (1972), 334
working class
  African American, 209
  women's rights and, 205, 206
  See also proletariat
working family, definition of, 468n.6
work norm enforcement, 35, 307
workplace. *See* jobs and job training
work-relief programs, 333
Works Progress (Projects) Administration, 257,
    314, 316, 332, 334
World Bank, 62, 82, 273
WorldCom, 58, 82, 87
World Hunger Year, 427
World Trade Center attack (2001), 26–27, 270
World War I, 196, 248, 401
World War II, 194, 196, 250, 397
  food and nutrition programs, 428